D0723056

DRUG ABUSE

This text provides a thorough understanding of the parameters of drug abuse, broadly defined. Conceptual issues regarding definitions of drug use, misuse, abuse, and dependence are discussed in full. In addition, this text serves as a comprehensive source of information on the etiology, prevention, and cessation of drug abuse. It organizes etiologic, prevention, and cessation information into neurobiological, cognitive, microsocial, and macrosocial/physical environmental units. For example, modification of neurobiological, cognitive, social, and larger socioenvironmental and physical environmental influences are addressed in separate chapters. This text addresses a variety of theoretical bases currently applied to the development of prevention and cessation programs, specific program content from empirically based model programs, and program processes and modalities. It is hoped that this text will facilitate advancement in the arena of research on drug problems.

Steve Sussman, Ph.D., FAAHB, received his doctorate in social-clinical psychology from the University of Illinois at Chicago in 1984. He is a professor of preventive medicine and psychology at the University of Southern California. He studies the utility of empirical program development methods and the addictions broadly defined, including tobacco and other drug abuse etiology, prevention, and cessation. He has authored more than 300 publications. His projects include Towards No Tobacco Use, Towards No Drug Abuse, and Project EX, which are considered model programs at numerous agencies (e.g., Centers for Disease Control and Prevention, National Institute on Drug Abuse, National Cancer Institute, the Office of Juvenile Justice and Delinquency Prevention, Substance Abuse and Mental Health Administration, Center for Substance Abuse Prevention, Colorado and Maryland Blueprints, Health Canada, U.S. Department of Education, and various state departments of education). He received the honor of Research Laureate for the American Academy of Health Behavior in 2005 and is currently president of the academy (2007–2008).

Susan L. Ames received her Ph.D. in preventive medicine with a focus on health behavior research from the University of Southern California in 2001. She completed her doctoral training with support from a National Cancer Institute Cancer Control and Epidemiology Research Training Grant. Dr. Ames is an assistant professor with the Transdisciplinary Drug Abuse Prevention Research Center at the Institute for Prevention Research, Department of Preventive Medicine, Keck School of Medicine, University of Southern California. She has been co-investigator on several substance abuse prevention projects funded by the National Institute on Drug Abuse. Her research emphasis is on the mediation of implicit processes and competing social, personality, and cultural constructs in the etiology and prevention of risk behaviors (e.g., drug use and HIV-risk behavior) among at-risk youth and adults. Her research focuses on new prevention and harm reduction strategies for addictive behaviors and new assessments and prediction models of substance use and risky sexual behavior. Other major interests include neurobiological processes and brain structures associated with implicit processes and addictive behaviors. Dr. Ames has published in a variety of American Psychological Association journals and journals that emphasize the addictive process and health behaviors. She worked in substance abuse treatment for nearly a decade.

Drug Abuse

Concepts, Prevention, and Cessation

STEVE SUSSMAN
University of Southern California

SUSAN L. AMES
University of Southern California

CAMBRIDGE
UNIVERSITY PRESS

CAMBRIDGE UNIVERSITY PRESS
Cambridge, New York, Melbourne, Madrid, Cape Town, Singapore, São Paulo, Delhi

Cambridge University Press
32 Avenue of the Americas, New York, NY 10013-2473, USA

www.cambridge.org
Information on this title: www.cambridge.org/9780521716154

© Steve Sussman and Susan L. Ames 2008

This publication is in copyright. Subject to statutory exception
and to the provisions of relevant collective licensing agreements,
no reproduction of any part may take place without
the written permission of Cambridge University Press.

First published 2008

Printed in the United States of America

A catalog record for this publication is available from the British Library.

Library of Congress Cataloging in Publication Data

Sussman, Steven Yale.
Drug abuse : concepts, prevention, and cessation / Steve Sussman, Susan L. Ames.
    p.   cm.
Includes bibliographical references and index.
ISBN   978-0-521-85892-2 (hardback)
ISBN   978-0-521-71615-4 (pbk.)
1. Drug abuse.   I. Ames, Susan L., 1956–   II. Title.
[DNLM: 1. Substance-Related Disorders – etiology.   2. Social Behavior.   3. Substance-Related Disorders –
psychology.   4. Substance-Related Disorders – therapy. WM 270 s9649d 2008]
RC564.s8384   2008
362.29–dc22   2007029964

ISBN   978-0-521-85892-2 hardback
ISBN   978-0-521-71615-4 paperback

Cambridge University Press has no responsibility for
the persistence or accuracy of URLS for external or
third-party Internet Web sites referred to in this publication
and does not guarantee that any content on such
Web sites is, or will remain, accurate or appropriate.

Contents

Preface   *page* vii

Acknowledgments   xi

SECTION ONE: CONCEPTS AND CLASSES OF DRUGS

1 Concepts of Drugs, Drug Use, Misuse, and Abuse   3
2 Further Classifications Relevant to Substance Abuse and Dependence   18
3 Types of Drugs, History of Drug Use and Misuse, and Costs of
   Drug Misuse   30

SECTION TWO: ETIOLOGY

4 Current Multivariable Models   57
5 Neurobiologically Relevant   69
6 Cognitive Processes   87
7 Social Interaction and Social Groups   98
8 The Large Social and Physical Environment   109
9 Assessment   123

SECTION THREE: PREVENTION

10 Concepts of Prevention   139
11 Neurobiologically Relevant   155
12 Cognitive Processes   168
13 Social Interaction and Social Groups   179
14 The Large Social and Physical Environment   193

SECTION FOUR: CESSATION

15 Concepts of Cessation   207
16 Neurobiologically Relevant   225
17 Cognitive Processes   237
18 Social Interaction and Social Groups   248
19 The Large Social and Physical Environment   262

SECTION FIVE: CONCLUSIONS AND THE FUTURE

20 Conclusions and Recent and Future Directions   277

References   295
Author Index   337
Subject Index   348

Preface

The topics of drug misuse and abuse are anchored by the terms used to define or describe them. Using current economic strain-type terminology, the annual economic cost of "drug abuse" has been estimated to be approximately $600 billion worldwide and $200 billion in the United States (Sussman & Ames, 2001). Approximately 70% of the costs are related to *decreased productivity* (illness, premature death, and incarceration), 10% are due to the *costs related to health care* (prevention, treatment, and hospitalization), and 20% of the costs are related to *property damage and enforcement efforts* (Office of National Drug Control Policy, 2001; Sussman & Ames, 2001).

Misuse of drugs by the general public incurs a notable percentage of these costs. For many people, drug misuse appears to be a voluntary, social behavior. There are people who feel reasonably comfortable with themselves and their lives but may misuse some drugs (particularly alcohol and tobacco but also other drugs, such as over-the-counter medications) on occasion as a part of celebratory rituals or to relieve disease symptoms. These people may have succumbed to social pressures to celebrate or may lack information on how to use a drug or drugs correctly, which could lead to negative consequences.

The misuse of drugs can lead to accidents and brief periods of nonproductivity. The probability of anyone suffering an accident that causes potential injury (usually minor) nears 100% over the course of many years. Many "normal" people consider "living life" and using a drug as increasing the likelihood of experiencing an accident. Of course, drug misuse may increase the odds of an accident occurring in the near future because of effects that may impair coordination and planning skills. Public campaigns that (1) attempt to make drug misuse a less acceptable behavior, (2) provide instruction on proper use of nonprescription and prescription drugs, or (3) provide means to reconcile the costs of prohibition with the costs to society morale and productivity are quite important to reduce drug use-related costs for a wide audience.

For many people, drug cessation also appears to be a voluntary, self-directed effort. Certainly, some of these people may die because they make unwise choices pertaining to their drug misuse. However, deaths among these people demonstrate a pattern of behavior in which drug use is a relatively minor part of their lives, more specifically that they hardly used drugs and/or used very little or that they often only used drugs on occasions socially deemed as appropriate. We doubt that everyone who is drunk on New Year's Eve or at a rock concert is somehow physiologically abnormal and prone to negative drug consequences.

There are also some drug users who experience a more dramatic and elongated fate. Some people continue to misuse drugs even though they routinely experience negative consequences. In other words, they experience recurrent, consequential behavior that bewilders the drug user as well as the observer. A continuum notion of drug misuse helps in the clarification of behavior (Sussman & Ames, 2001). One may place drug misuse on a continuum of drug involvement, consisting perhaps of (1) frequency or quantity of use, (2) subjective degree of lack of control over frequency or quantity of use, (3) preoccupation with use to the exclusion of other activities, or (4) public consequences of use. People at one end of the continuum may misuse drugs as a participant in an occasional social event (e.g., a holiday). They may have subjective control over the occasion and the amount consumed, although they occasionally may overuse drugs and suffer the adverse consequences as a "mistake." They may view each decision to use or overuse drugs as a conscious decision, not as an impulse over which they have no control.

Persons on the other end of the continuum use drugs frequently or use too much on most use occasions. They may report a subjective degree of lack of control over frequency or quantity of use, or perhaps they think they are in control; however, others observe their drug use as adversely and repetitively affecting their lives. They suffer numerous public consequences of use that hardly appear to be merely a rare mistake of judgment. They may try to limit their exposure to public settings to reduce the probability of public consequences. They may feel surprised, confused, or frustrated by the changes they experience in their behavior as a result of drug intake. If they try to reduce or discontinue their drug use, they may find, to their surprise, that they are unsuccessful.

Regarding recurrent and consequential drug misuse, researchers may have chosen the wrong outcome variable as the focus. In particular, drug abuse, drug misuse, or drug use may not be the right dependent (outcome) variable. "Drug abuse" generally refers to an official definition involving legal, social, safety, and role-based consequences stemming from recurrent drug use (American Psychiatric Association, 2000). This concept provides the rudiments for diagnosing a problem, but it does not provide three useful behavioral determinants of outcomes for more valid diagnoses: *etiology, process,* and *prognosis.* A variety of social and environmental variables predict diagnosable consequences of risky lifestyle behaviors that make identification of a consistent process for diagnosis difficult. For example, the behavior of getting drunk and using public transportation to get home likely has different consequences than the behavior of getting drunk and attempting to drive home. The likelihood of using public transportation is contingent in part on its availability. Of course, it might be difficult to defend an argument that adding a bus system can avert drug abuse. The point is that much of the variation in the behavior is unexplained when examining whether certain consequences occur, because very complex situational factors may affect the occurrence of consequences.

Another difficulty in establishing an etiology or process to a drug abuse diagnosis is that behavioral consequences are defined in part by the social context within which they occur. For example, drinking too much at a wedding may be considered appropriate in some groups, whereas it may be inappropriate in other groups. Further, a set of consequences describes or defines the result of a behavior but does not explain the reasons for the behavior that precedes the consequences (etiology). Many people in recovery from drug abuse will suggest that drug use was a solution "to the problem" at first. Unfortunately, even after drug use begins to cause more problems than it solves, physiological and psychological dependence mechanisms make cessation extremely difficult for some people. Drug use behavior may then become a more attractive option than experiencing withdrawal symptoms (Sussman & Unger, 2004) or the unmedicated realization of the years of devastation one may have caused to self or others. (In addition, drug use may still feel good.) Thus, the etiology of trying drugs, continuing to use them, or maintaining drug use after consequences set in may differ and may not easily confirm or disconfirm a particular etiological system.

Using "drug misuse" as an outcome variable, although not bounded by an official set of criteria, is fraught with value-laden biases. That is, drug misuse to one person or in one culture may not be considered drug misuse to another person or in another culture. Any recreational drug use may be considered drug misuse to some groups (e.g., Church of the Latter Day Saints and Scientology) but may be considered normative to other groups (e.g., Rastafarians and the Church of Spiritual Enlightenment). Drug misuse also may vary in meaning over time (see Chapter 2 of this text on the ancient history of drug use).

Using the term *drug use* as an outcome variable could imply that all drug use is dangerous or immoral. It is useful to remember that at some points and locations in history, the mere use of a range of available psychoactive substances was labeled as deviance, with users being called "sinners," which was then followed (e.g., in the United States in the 1920s) by a period of criminalization. The "medicalization" and "pathologization" of substance use (disorders) and users is a relatively recent process (e.g., Terry & Pellens, 1928). In summary, these three drug behavior terms do little to help explain the difficulties in living experienced by persons at the relatively "hopeless" end of the continuum.

Related work on problem behavior syndromes, process and substance addictions, and notions of substitute addictions suggests that people on that "problem" extreme of the continuum will engage in different behaviors that are problematic for very similar reasons (Sussman & Ames, 2001). These behaviors may include using various drugs, gambling, compulsive sex or shopping, or even out-of-control eating. What then should be the focus of our work if not drug abuse, drug misuse, or drug use per se?

This text intends to provide a better understanding of the parameters of drug abuse, broadly defined. Simply put for the moment, one may assert that substance abuse is a multifactorial biopsychosocial process that involves a variety of negative consequences to the individual or to the individual's social environment, involving not only environmental and social influences that may be amenable to change but also intraindividual differences in susceptibility resulting from a complex interplay of genetic influences on neurobiological processes that affect personality, affect, and cognition. We present one general systems model that illustrates a process that can lead to and maintain problematic drug use.

In addition, this text serves as a comprehensive source of information on the prevention and cessation of tobacco and other substance abuse. Many of the intraindividual influences (e.g., neurobiological) are more difficult to change or simply are not changeable with current methods and technology, but nevertheless, they play a significant role in substance abuse vulnerability and eventually may be amenable to modification. Modification of neurobiological, cognitive, social, and larger socioenvironmental and physical environmental influences are addressed. This text addresses a variety of theoretical bases currently applied to the development of prevention and cessation programs, specific program content from empirically based model programs, and program processes and modalities (settings of delivery). We have organized etiologic, prevention, and cessation information into neurobiological, cognitive, microsocial, and macrosocial units.

This text, although serving as a scholarly source for researchers, also intends to be of relevance to educated practitioners, drug dependency counselors, and students. The text provides a thorough, integrative perspective toward drug abuse and its prevention and cessation for different contexts and populations.

Acknowledgments

We thank the University of Southern California, the National Institute on Drug Abuse, and the California Tobacco-Related Disease Research Program for giving us the flexibility to write this text. We also thank Cambridge University Press, Philip Laughlin, and Eric Schwartz for their interest in working with us. We have tried to provide an international relevance to the book, and we thank all of our colleagues around the world who have helped us think globally. Also, we thank Beth Howard, Pallav Pokhrel, and Katie Greczylo for their editorial assistance and Alan Stacy for providing a flexible and supportive research environment. We also want to thank the people in our lives who taught us how to think outside the box (Alan Sussman, Harry Upshaw, Alexander Rosen, Robert Rychtarik, Brian Flay, and Michael Borens). Finally, we thank our families (Rotchana, Guang, Evan, Max, Mikey, Terry, Bill, Karen, Pam, Marc, and Ethel) for providing the balance in our lives that made it possible to go for the big picture.

This book is dedicated to the memory of Karen Anne Ames, a beloved sister, friend, and incredible scholar.

CONCEPTS AND CLASSES OF DRUGS

1   Concepts of Drugs, Drug Use, Misuse, and Abuse

First the man took a drink, then the drink took a drink, then the drink took the man.

– Recovery movement proverb

This first chapter provides a discussion and clarification of various concepts relevant to drug abuse. Although we attempt clarification of many terms and concepts, it is important to note that there are different substantive distinctions and "fuzzy" boundaries between the concepts. For example, distinctions between drug misuse and abuse, and terms such as *street drugs* or *hard* or *soft drugs* are somewhat ambiguous and perhaps dependent on sociocultural contexts. The chapter begins by providing an overview of a definition of a drug, drug use, and drug action and then distinguishes drug use from misuse and provides terms used to refer to drugs that might be misused.

What Is a Drug and Drug Use?

A drug is a substance that can be taken into the human body and, once taken, alters some processes within the body. Drugs can be used in the diagnosis, prevention, or treatment of a disease. Some drugs are used to kill bacteria and help the body recover from infections. Some drugs assist in terminating headaches. Some drugs cross the blood–brain barrier and affect neurotransmitter function. The varieties of drugs that produce a direct or indirect effect on neurotransmitter function in the brain are of primary interest in this book.

Drugs are processed by the body in four steps, and these drugs also may have various effects on each other when used together. First, "administration" refers to how the drug enters the body (e.g., ingestion [swallowing], inhalation [smoking or vaporous], injection [intravenous, intramuscular, subcutaneous], or absorption [through skin or mucous membranes]). Most classes of drugs are used through several alternative methods. For example, marijuana may be smoked or swallowed. Methamphetamine may be smoked, swallowed, sniffed, or injected. Heroin may be sniffed, smoked, or injected. Depending on the method of administration, drugs generally exert their effects within an hour of intake (e.g., through ingestion) or within minutes or seconds of use (e.g., through injection).

Second, *distribution* refers to how efficiently a drug moves throughout the body. Distribution is influenced by the size of the various drug molecules and their solubility – protein, water, fat bound – among other factors. As a general rule, the rate of entry of a drug into the brain is determined by the fat solubility of the drug (Julien, 2005). The rate of entry is faster if the fat solubility is greater. Conversely, highly ionized drugs, such as penicillin, penetrate the blood–brain barrier poorly.

Third, *metabolism* refers to the effects (action) of the drug. All drugs that might be misused or abused "feel good" in different ways; for example, the drug user may feel more alert, relaxed, or happy. Almost all drugs that are misused or abused affect mesolimbic reward pathways. However, each drug also may have specific target receptor sites in various brain structures and affect some different neurotransmitter pathways (see Chapter 4 for more detail on the brain). For example, there are concentrations of opioid receptors in the nucleus accumbens, whereas functionally important nicotinic receptors are found in the medial habenula, the superior colliculus, and the anteroventral thalamic and interpeduncular nuclei. Amphetamines mimic the effect of norepinephrine at its receptor sites and significantly impact dopaminergic activity in the mesolimbic reward circuitry. Benzodiazapines (e.g., Valium) are less likely to be a sole drug of abuse (though they are associated with withdrawal symptoms that may last 3 weeks), perhaps because they act primarily on the γ-aminobutyric acid (GABA) neurotransmitter system and not the dopaminergic system (Julien, 2005).

Drugs can have four different types of *interaction effects* when used together (Sussman & Ames, 2001). First, these effects may be additive (e.g., $1 + 1 = 2$; the effects of the drugs simply add together). Second, these effects may be synergic (e.g., $1 \times 1 = 5$; the effects become much, much stronger when the drugs are used together). Third, these effects may be potentiating (e.g., $0 + 1 = 2$; a drug may exert its effects only in conjunction with the use of another drug). Finally, these effects may be antagonistic (e.g., $1 - 1 = 0$; the effects of two or more drugs may cancel each other out).

Fourth, *elimination* refers to the breakdown and excretion of drugs from a body. Drugs are excreted in time primarily through sweating or urination, involving the skin and kidneys. Drugs have measurable and differential distribution and elimination half-lives (i.e., the amount of time it takes for half of the drug to reach sites of action and be eliminated from the body). For example, nicotine, when smoked in a cigarette, has a 9-minute distribution half-life (very fast) and a 2-hour elimination half-life. Marijuana, when smoked, has a similar distribution half-life, but it also has a 28- to 56-hour elimination half-life, which involves complex metabolic processes. Nicotine is metabolized mostly through the liver, whereas tetrahydrocannibinol (THC; the active ingredient of marijuana) may be stored and released slowly from various bodily organs. As a general rule, regular interval dosing can result in a relatively steady blood level concentration of the drug that is reached after approximately six elimination half-lives (see Julien, 2005).

Overdoses

Overdosing refers to taking enough of a drug such that functioning is grossly impaired and even survival may be jeopardized. Regarding drug use action, there are doses that produce the intended effect for a percentage of drug users (i.e., effective dose) and a dose that will kill the drug user (i.e., lethal dose). Different means of administration, time for distribution, time for action, time for elimination, and context factors may affect the effective-to-lethal dose relation. Overdosing often refers to reaching a near-fatal dose but not always; it may also mean loss of function such that special care is needed (Figure 1.1).

Overdosing tends to result in admissions to emergency rooms. About 31% of emergency room visits in the United States are due to the combined use of alcohol and other drugs.

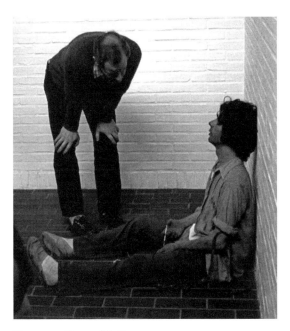

Figure 1.1. Drug addiction.

Of those individuals admitted for overdoses, approximately 30% are admitted because of cocaine use, 18% because of marijuana use, 17% because of use of benzodiazepines, 17% because of use of narcotic drugs (14% because of heroin use), 6% because of amphetamine or methamphetamine use, and the remainder are admitted because of use of drugs such as Tylenol or Advil, selective serotonin reuptake inhibitors (SSRIs), and sedatives (see discussion in Levinthal, 2005).

An overdose is less likely to occur if a drug is used in the same location (known as "behavioral tolerance"). Physiological tolerance for a drug involves adjustment in bodily organs to the presence of the drug (metabolic tolerance; e.g., faster metabolism of alcohol in the liver with repeated alcohol intake) and neural adaptations to a drug (cellular tolerance; postsynaptic receptors may become less sensitive to a drug and presynaptic sites may manufacture less of an endogenous ligand [naturally occurring neurotransmitter] to compensate for the introduction of the drug that mimics its effects; for a drug that blocks transmission, an increased number of receptor sites may be manufactured or an increased amount of the endogenous ligand may be supplied), which also may effect the lethal dose. Of course, regular use of drugs can lead to physical dependence (i.e., physical and/or psychological withdrawal symptoms occur when drug use is stopped abruptly). Craving the effects a drug produces can be referred to as "psychological dependence," which is affected by neurobiological processes (e.g., associative learning processes; for discussion, see Weiss, 2005; for review, see Franken, 2003).

What Are Drugs of Misuse?

Drug use really implies only that one has taken a drug into the body and that the drug will go through the four steps of processing. However, the whole idea of problematic drug use stems from the perception that drug use can lead to negative or undesired consequences. There are at least three terms that may be applied to use of a drug: use as appropriate, directed, or prescribed. Use as appropriate implies that there are no specific directions for frequency and quantity of use. However, one generally learns bounds of frequency and quantity of use that generally do not lead to undesirable consequences. For example, drinking one or two alcoholic drinks in a sitting over the course of several hours is unlikely to result in negative effects (e.g., obvious intoxication, depending on the context, or accidents). Use as directed connotes that there exists instruction on use frequency and quantity. Over-the-counter drugs provide such instructions. Finally, for drugs that require a physician's approval, a prescription is provided that also describes the active or safe frequency and quantity of use. If a drug is used inappropriately, not as directed, or not as prescribed, one might say that the drug is being misused. Of course, one might use too little of a drug for it to be effective. Arguably, that would be an example of drug misuse. However, most drugs that affect neurotransmitter function are said to be misused when they are used too often and/or at too high a quantity. Higher drug use may lead to danger (e.g., toxicity, intoxication), whereas lower than recommended use probably will not.

The U.S. Drug Enforcement Administration (DEA) was created in 1973 to enforce the provisions of the Controlled Substances Act of 1970 (http://www.usdoj.gov/dea/index.htm). The DEA shares concurrent jurisdiction with the U.S. Federal Bureau of Investigation regarding narcotics enforcement matters. The Controlled Substances Act provides the authority and administrative structure to establish scheduling of drugs to avoid hazards to public safety, monitoring of use of different drugs, including manufacture, distribution and labeling, and offences and penalties for violations of the rules the DEA establishes. Some rules also extend to drug paraphernalia. These drug schedules with examples are shown in Table 1.1.

The types of drugs of misuse that this text focuses on are those that are relatively likely to cause negative consequences if used too often or at too high a quantity, that generally tend to readily cross the blood–brain barrier and affect neurotransmitter function, and that in some way achieve a function desired by the drug user. Desired functions of these drugs tend to be described as alterations in arousal, affect, or sensory perception/cognitive experience. Drugs that alter arousal, affect, or sensory-cognitive experience often are referred to by one or more terms.

Terms Used to Refer to Drugs That Might Be Misused

Drugs that affect the central nervous system (CNS) can be classified by the substance from which they are derived, such as *opiates* or *opioids*, or by their effects on the human nervous system, such as *stimulants, hallucinogenic drugs*, or *psychotropic drugs* (Julien, 2005). Although there might be overlap in the drugs that each of these terms encompasses, these terms are relatively unbiased. (Certainly, for example, there are exceptions that might be defined across categories; ecstasy may be defined alternatively as a stimulant or a hallucinogen or both.) There are several typologies of classes of drugs that are not purely based on physical qualities of drugs. We briefly discuss five widely applied terms: *street drugs, hard or soft drugs, illicit drugs, designer drugs*, and *club drugs*. We discuss the meaning of these terms and consider the usefulness of such variable drug terminology (see Sussman & Huver, 2006).

Table 1.1. DEA drug use schedules

Schedule and definition	Examples of drugs
Schedule 1: drug has no current accepted medical use, high potential for abuse	2,5-dimethoxyamphetamine, cathinone (constituent of "Khat" plant), GHB, heroin, LSD, marijuana, ecstasy, mescaline, methaqualone, morphine methylbromide, peyote, psilocybin
Schedule 2: drug has current accepted medical use, high potential for abuse	Amobarbital, amphetamine, cocaine, codeine, Demerol, methadone, methamphetamine (speed), morphine, nembutal, opium, oxycodone, phencyclidine, preludin, Ritalin, Seconal
Schedule 3: drug has current accepted medical use, medium potential for abuse	Amobarbital/ephedrine capsules, anabolic steroids, ketamine, Marinol, Paragoric, Tylenol with codeine
Schedule 4: drug has current accepted medical use, low potential for abuse	Ativan, Dalmane, Darvon, Librium, Miltown, Placidyl, Redux, Rohypnol, Valium, Xanax
Schedule 5: drug has current accepted medical use, lowest potential for abuse	Lomotil, Kapectolin PG, Motofen, Robitussin AC (liquid suspensions)

Street Drugs

The term *street drugs* is contained within the Web site of the National Institute on Drug Abuse, has its own heading within the OVID Medline Search Engine, and is commonly displayed in print (e.g., Bartlett & Steele, 2004) and on Web sites (e.g., http://www.streetdrugs.org). With such widespread use, one might expect that this term is well understood and consensually used in one way. However, this is not the case. A literature search conducted by Sussman and Huver (2006) of the use of the term *street drugs* in the popular and scientific literatures resulted in a consensus on seven definitions. The seven different definitions of the term *street drug* based on these sources of information were as follows: (1) all drugs used recreationally, (2) a term implicating violence or other crime (sold illegally; involvement of "pushers"), (3) "street terms" (slang) for drugs that may reveal a subcultural language or indicate drug use combinations (e.g., http://www.whitehousedrugpolicy.gov/streetterms), (4) drugs manufactured unprofessionally (not in official labs), (5) impure drugs, (6) reflecting a street or poor lifestyle, or (7) physically dangerous drugs. These terms are not mutually exhaustive and exclusive.

Recreational drugs are those used for nonmedicinal purposes, in particular, for fun or leisure. This label provides a very wide umbrella as a definition. Several medication and drug guides tend to refer to all recreational drugs as being street drugs (e.g., www.allpsych.com/drugs.html). Many people do use drugs as a form of recreation. However, some people may use drugs, such as methamphetamine, to drive long distances or to lose weight rather than to achieve pleasure (a utilitarian motive; Sussman & Ames, 2001). Yet, many people might refer to methamphetamine as being a prototypical street drug (www.cbc.ca/news/background/drugs/crystalmeth.html) that is used for many purposes (Sussman, Dent, & Stacy, 1999). Thus, it is not clear to what extent this definition is useful.

Illicit drugs are obtained and sold illegally by dealers or sellers on the street (e.g., http://library.thinkquest.org/TQ0310171/street_drugs.htm; Reif, 1999; Smart, Adlaf, & Walsh, 1992). Drug companies, in particular, tend to refer to illicit drugs as being street drugs.

Figure 1.2. Methamphetamine laboratory.

However, there are many exceptions to this definition of the term. In Dutch legislation, possession of cannabis is tolerated (up to 30 g, equivalent to almost 1 oz). Yet cannabis is as likely to be referred to as a street drug in the Netherlands as it is in the United States, where federal laws do not permit its possession, growth, sale, or use (Sussman & Ames, 2001). Some may refer to nicotine and alcohol as street drugs, which is at odds with the current definition but could be consistent with the first (recreational) definition (http://allpsych.com/drugs.html). Glue is legal, but it may be used as a type of inhalant and is commonly referred to as a street drug (http://library.thinkquest.org/TQ0310171/street_drugs.htm).

Many drugs have *street terms* that are applied to them. For example, methamphetamine often is referred to as "speed" and cocaine has been referred to as "Charlie" (http://www.whitehousedrugpolicy.gov/streetterms). Interestingly, street drug terms may serve as valuable diagnostic cues to the mental state and drug history of the drug user (Johnson, Michels, & Davis, 1991). Although street terms often refer to street drugs, it is possible that some street drugs are not labeled with street terms. If so, this definition is flawed. Of course, if all drugs have slang terms, then arguably this definition could refer to any and all drugs.

Drugs manufactured in home laboratories or not by professional companies have been labeled street drugs (e.g., Marshall, 2003). For example, consistent with this definition, "moonshine" (a home-brewed alcoholic beverage) would be an alcohol street drug but Jack Daniels (http://www.jackdaniels.com/age.aspx) would not. However, the "professionalism" with which some drugs that are considered street drugs are produced may make one doubt the value of this definition. For instance, although ecstasy (3,4-methylenedioxymethamphetamine [MDMA]) is manufactured in clandestine laboratories, these laboratories are operated by highly trained staff and can hardly be called "unprofessional," and analyses of MDMA indicate purity of 80% to 90% (Parrott, 2004) (Figure 1.2).

Alternatively, one may mean "not licensed" when referring to "unprofessionally manufactured." Unlicensed manufacturing of a drug would seem to suggest an illicit type of street drug. Conversely, it is interesting to note that 100,000 deaths per year occur from adverse drug reactions to pharmaceutical (licensed) drugs, a number five times greater than the number of deaths caused by unlicensed street drugs, according to Bartlett and Steele (2004). Moreover, many pharmaceutical drugs are sold on the street. Some people might think of these drugs as street drugs as well (http://www.usdoj.gov/dea/pubs/abuse/4-narc.htm), and many street drugs are "cut" with pharmaceutical drugs.

Impure drugs indicates impurity, adulteration, or dilution in the manufacturing of the drug (e.g., http://www.drugscope.org.uk/resources/faqs/). *Impurities* are substances present in the drug as a natural result of how it was made rather than substances that are deliberately added. *Adulterants* are drugs that are added to mimic or enhance the effects of the drug being offered. For example, sometimes amphetamines have been cut with caffeine or ephedrine. *Diluents* are compounds such as sugars or baking soda that are used to "bulk out" the deal (make more money per assumed quantity of drug). Heroin may vary in purity from 30% to 80% and is often cut with other opium alkaloids, sugars, and sometimes diazepam. Although emergency room physicians treat many patients who have used illegal drugs, little is known about the relative toxicities of the abused drug versus the drug additives. Current thinking and research suggests that additives play only a minor role in the majority of emergencies (Shesser, Jotte, & Olshaker, 1991). This definition may overlap in meaning with the definitions of "unprofessional" or "illicit."

Street drugs sometimes are implicated as representative of a *street or lower class lifestyle* or as definitive of the drug user, such as street youth (e.g., Ginzler & Cochran, 2003) or homeless drug users (e.g., Deren et al., 2003). In this sense, drug use is integrated into "street life." When one lives "on the street," one may live in, for example, empty buildings ("squats"), on a friend's couch, in a car, or under a bridge (Sussman et al., 1999). Survival may include drug dealing as a means of income or as a means to cope with exposure to the elements (weather) and vulnerability to crime. Drugs used by "street people" vary but may include alcohol, heroin, methamphetamine, crack, cannabis, or glue sniffing. Drugs may be chosen based either on their use as a means of barter or income or because of their relatively low cost. However, many of these types of street drugs have been used at raves or other party or clublike venues composed of relatively wealthy individuals (www.clubdrugs.org). Thus, this definition may provide some descriptive (or literary) value but does not apply to many drug users (although some of these drugs, if abused consistently, may eventually lead individuals into a street life [e.g., see http://www.pbs.org/wgbh/pages/frontline/meth/]).

Sometimes street drugs directly imply *dangerous drugs* (e.g., Cheng, 1999). In this sense, many drugs may be referred to as street drugs because most are facilitative or predictive of accidents or psychotic symptoms and several are predictive of depressed mood, cardiovascular disease, or digestive/excretory difficulties (Sussman & Ames, 2001). Still, street drugs may vary in danger. For example, some people would refer to hallucinogens as street drugs, yet they are perhaps among the relative safe types (even though they are listed in Schedule 1 of the DEA scheme). As with the previous definition, this one has a potential descriptive function and applies to some street drugs but not to the full range of street drugs.

Some of these definitions are used to keep the public image of one entity (e.g., the pharmaceutical industry and the alcoholic beverage industry) apart and "cleaner" than drugs or drug distribution systems that do not fall under their domain of control. Some definitions are used to refer to relative danger. Yet, other definitions appear to imply the improper or nonlegitimized use of a drug. We might say that a street drug may be defined as any drug that is misused; that is, any drug that may have dangerous consequences and is considered improper to use either intrinsically or in the social context within which it is used.

Hard and Soft Drugs

A distinction is often made between hard and soft drugs. *Hard drugs*, such as heroin, methamphetamine, and crack/cocaine, generally are considered more dangerous and can lead to dependence. The most abused hard drug in the world today is methamphetamine. There are approximately 1.5 million methamphetamine addicts in the United States (see http://www.pbs.org/wgbh/pages/frontline/meth/). Purportedly, the use of hard drugs may result in more immediate negative consequences than that of soft drugs because of their high dependence potential, which may result in increased compulsive drug taking and the perpetration of income-generating crimes as a means of supporting drug use. Hallucinogens also would be considered hard drugs, in spite of the fact that they have no addiction potential. Thus, this supposed difference between hard and soft drugs is not universal across drug types.

The term *soft drugs* is often used to refer to drugs such as cannabis, alcohol, and nicotine, of which use allegedly does not result in as severe a degree of physical dependence and may appear less dangerous in connotation (Jonnes, 1996; Sussman, Rohrbach, Skara, & Dent, 2004). There are at least two problems with this distinction. First, soft drugs are not less dangerous than hard drugs per se. Long-term use of cannabis has deteriorating effects on the nervous system, causes damage to the lining of the lungs, and can cause dependence and addiction (Sussman & Ames, 2001; Sussman et al., 1996). Generally considered as soft drugs – perhaps mistakenly because of their wide availability – alcohol and nicotine are both highly addictive and dangerous. Alcohol is the most widely used drug in Western society (and the world). Approximately 14 million Americans meet the criteria for alcohol abuse or alcoholism and heavy drinking is related to a number of cancers and liver and heart damage. Alcohol is estimated to cause 2 million deaths per year worldwide (Sussman & Ames, 2001). Nicotine is highly addictive and tobacco use is the single largest preventable cause of death in the world (Sussman & Ames, 2001). Tobacco use is associated with approximately 30% of all cancer deaths annually in the United States.

Second, the distinction between hard and soft drugs and corresponding legislation are not internationally established. In the Netherlands, legislation for hard drugs (defined as drugs of an unacceptable risk) differs from that of soft drugs (e.g., hemp products). The Dutch employ a policy of tolerance with respect to soft drugs. In some municipalities, soft drugs may be sold in so-called coffee shops, with a maximum supply of 500 g. Strictly speaking, possession of either hard or soft drugs is illegal, but one will not be prosecuted for possessing half a gram of hard drugs or 30 g of soft drugs for personal use. Arguably, the terms *hard* and *soft drugs* are useful as a means of grouping specific drugs into categories, and the highest prevalence drugs are the ones that tend to get labeled as soft drugs, but this terminology is not well descriptive of the effects or consequences of the drugs.

Illicit Drugs

The term *illicit drugs* is typically used to set illegal drugs apart from legal drugs or pharmaceuticals. It is apparent from the above discussion on hard and soft drugs that the legality (or the quality of the illegality) of a specific set of drug categories is not universal. As another example, in political and medical arenas in the United States, there is debate about legalizing cannabis for medicinal purposes. Cannabis can relieve side effects of chemotherapy and help control seizures in patients suffering from epilepsy. Furthermore, it can be beneficial for patients with glaucoma, migraine headaches, acquired immunodeficiency syndrome (AIDS) wasting syndrome, multiple sclerosis, spinal cord injuries, arthritis, and chronic pain (Gurley, Aranow, & Katz, 1998; Smith, 1998). Currently, medical marijuana use is legal in some states (e.g., California), whereas it is illegal on a federal level (http://www.drugpolicy.org/statebystate/).

In addition to the debate about legalizing cannabis, in the light of the previously mentioned deteriorating and addictive effects of alcohol and nicotine, one can argue that it is regrettable that alcohol and nicotine are licit drugs. This term is appropriate and precise as a label for what legislation entails within a specific geopolitical and historical context.

Designer Drugs

Designer drugs are synthetic drugs that are equivalent to an existing drug in chemical structure but for a minor modification (Sussman & Ames, 2001). Scientists refer to designer drugs as *substance analogs*. The new drug (child) will have the same or very similar pharmacological effects as the original drug (parent). For example, ecstasy is one of the most widely used designer drugs, with a chemical structure similar to that of methamphetamine (Christophersen, 2000). It has been put forward that designer drugs were created to bypass legislation of the U.S. Drug Enforcement Administration (Jerrard, 1990). In the past, drugs were not illegal until they were classified as controlled substances by law. In 1986, the Controlled Substances Act was modified to ban all variations of controlled substances, hence banning all designer drugs. This term seems fairly precise, although because of the continuing production of designer drugs, it is impossible to comprehensively list drugs under this label.

Club Drugs

The term *club drugs* is a generic term for drugs used in clubs or bars or at trance parties or raves, mostly by adolescents or emerging adults. Often, youth will dance or gather together all night at these venues. Arguably, such dances permit youth to be involved in a social recreational activity, be involved in a shared youth ritual, and experience a symbolic transition to adulthood. However, drug use often is inextricably associated with these situations. Club drugs, also referred to as *party drugs*, are most commonly taken orally in tablet form and include ecstasy, Rohypnol (the "date rape" drug), γ-hydroxybutyric acid (GHB), ketamine, and lysergic acid diethylamide (LSD), among others (http://www.clubdrugs.org/). There is no comprehensive list of what drugs are considered club drugs, although their location of use is suggested as being in group clublike situations. Certainly, many club drugs are used outside of party situations, such as in youths' bedrooms (Sussman & Ames, 2001). This term appears to have the same difficulties in clarity as does the term *street drugs* (see Table 1.2).

Search for Clarification of Words Used to Describe Drugs That Can Be Misused

Terms described by Sussman and Huver (2006) included *street drugs* (and several variants), *hard* or *soft drugs*, *illicit drugs*, *designer drugs*, and *club drugs*. Although *illicit drugs* are defined

Table 1.2. Drug use terms and descriptions

Terms	General description	Example(s)
Drug	A substance that can be taken into the body that alters one or more processes within the body	Alcohol, nicotine, cocaine, marijuana, etc.
Street drug	Any drug that is misused; that is, any drug that may have dangerous consequences and is considered improper to use either intrinsically or within the social circumstances in which it is used	Alcohol (in underage drinking), heroin, methamphetamine, crack, cocaine, marijuana
Hard drug	A drug that is generally considered to be more dangerous, with a higher risk of dependence than soft drugs	Heroin, methamphetamine, crack/cocaine
Soft drug	A drug whose use supposedly does not result in as severe a degree of dependence as a hard drug and is often considered relatively less dangerous by society, although the negative consequences may be just as or more severe (e.g., lung cancer from tobacco use)	Marijuana, alcohol, nicotine
Illicit drug	An illegal drug; that is, the drug is not a legally prescribed drug/pharmaceutical	Marijuana, cocaine, heroin, LSD
Designer drug	A synthetic drug very similar in chemical makeup to an existing drug and thus exerting similar pharmacological effects as the existing drug	Ecstasy
Club drug	A drug whose use primarily occurs in clubs, bars, and trance parties, such as raves, and usually by adolescents or young adults	Ecstasy, Rohypnol ("roofies"), GHB, ketamine ("special K"), LSD

Note: The term descriptions above are not mutually exclusive and can change depending on the context in which or by whom they are used.

by presence of legislation, and *designer drugs* have a chemistry-oriented definition, *hard/soft drugs* and *club drugs* are terms that achieve their meaning, like *street drugs*, primarily by the contexts within which they are used. The kind of meaning of a term can be either denotative/operational or connotative/associative. Denotative meanings are objective and univocal, whereas connotative meanings are more ambiguous and implied. For example, the word *opiates* is pharmaceutically denotative and there is agreement on the meaning of this word (including finer delineations such as natural, semisynthetic, and synthetic opiatelike products; Julien, 2005). The meaning of *street drugs* is highly connotative and is multi-interpretable as such (as are *hard/soft drugs* and *club drugs*).

Sussman and Huver (2006) recommended caution in use of these multi-interpretable terms. Background information should be provided and an elaborated definition of the term is essential. This elaborated definition could be one that provides (1) the context of its meaning (e.g., street drugs as those drugs used by youth that live in abandoned buildings away from parents), (2) use of additional descriptors that provide synonymous information within that context (e.g., cheap drugs and easy to obtain), and (3) an acknowledgment that this term is intended to be defined for that context (i.e., is not invariant; e.g., by street drug in the present context is meant drugs popularly used by those who live in abandoned buildings away from parents). In cases in which a natural language term is imprecise, and is a proper subject for analysis from the perspective of fuzzy set theory (Turksen, 2006), use of an elaborated definition that provides explicit mention of context, use of synonyms or relevant descriptors, and use of explicit context-linking statements can help anchor such descriptors of drug types so that they serve a reasonably clear and useful function.

Formal Definitions of Drug Abuse

Drug use pertains simply to the use of a drug. A drug may be injected (e.g., heroin and speed), smoked (e.g., crack cocaine, marijuana, speed, heroin, and cigarettes), sniffed (e.g., inhalants and cocaine), huffed (inhalants), swallowed (e.g., pills), or sometimes absorbed through the skin (e.g., the nicotine patch). Drug misuse means not using a drug in the manner in which it was intended (as appropriate, as instructed, or as prescribed). Drug abuse may be defined as the accumulation of negative consequences resulting from drug misuse (American Psychiatric Association [APA], 2000; Newcomb & Bentler, 1989; Sussman, Dent, & Galaif, 1997).

A formal definition of *substance abuse disorder* is provided by the *Diagnostic and Statistical Manual of Mental Disorders* (DSM-IV-TR; APA, 2000). Drug abuse is a maladaptive pattern of drug use leading to clinically significant impairment or distress, as manifested by one or more of four symptoms or criteria in a 12-month period.

1. Recurrent drug use may result in a *failure to fulfill major role obligations* at work, school, or home. Repeated absences, tardiness, poor performance, suspensions, or neglect of duties in major life domains suggests that use has crossed over into abuse.
2. Recurrent drug use in situations in which it is *physically hazardous* is a sign of abuse. Operating machinery, driving a car, swimming, or walking in a dangerous area while under the influence indicates drug abuse.
3. Recurrent drug-related *legal problems*, such as arrests for disorderly conduct or for driving under the influence, are indicative of abuse.
4. Recurrent use despite having persistent or recurrent *social or interpersonal problems*, caused or exacerbated by the effects of the drug, is indicative of abuse. For example, getting into arguments or fights with others, passing out at others' houses, or acting inappropriately in front of others (which is disapproved of) is indicative of abuse.

In summary, drug use that leads to decrements in performance of major life roles, dangerous action, legal problems, or social problems indicates substance abuse disorder.

There are seven other criteria that, if met, constitute substance dependence. A diagnosis of substance dependence, a more severe disorder, would subsume a diagnosis of substance abuse. The criteria for substance dependence provided by the DSM-IV-TR (APA, 2000) include a maladaptive pattern of drug use leading to clinically significant impairment of distress, as manifested by three or more of the following seven symptoms occurring in the same 12-month period:

1. *Tolerance is experienced.* There is either a need for markedly increased amounts of the drug to achieve the desired drug effect or a markedly diminished effect with continued use of the same amount of the drug.
2. *Withdrawal is experienced.* Either a characteristic withdrawal syndrome occurs when one terminates using the drug or the same or a similar drug is taken to relieve or avoid the syndrome.

3. The drug often is taken in *larger amounts or over a longer period* than was intended. For example, an alcohol-dependent man may intend to drink only two drinks on a given evening but may end up having fifteen drinks. Alternatively, he may decide to "party" over the weekend; however, the party lasts for 2 weeks, until he runs out of money.

4. There is a *persistent desire or unsuccessful effort to cut down or control drug use.* For example, an alcohol-dependent man may decide to become a controlled drinker. He may intend to drink only two drinks every evening; however, he ends up having fifteen drinks on some evenings, two drinks on some evenings, and twenty drinks on other evenings.

5. *A great deal of time is spent on activities necessary to obtain the drug, use the drug, or recover from its effects.* For example, a person may travel long distances or search all day to "score" a drug, may use the drug throughout the night, and then may miss work the next day to recover and rest. In this scenario, two days were spent for one "high."

6. *Important social, occupational, or recreational activities are given up or reduced because of drug use.* For example, the drug abuser may be very high, passed out, or hung over much of the time and thus may not visit family and friends like he or she did before becoming a drug abuser.

7. *Drug use continues despite knowledge of having a persistent or recurrent physical or psychological problem* that is likely to have been caused or worsened by the drug. For example, someone who becomes very paranoid after continued methamphetamine use and is hospitalized but continues to use it after release from the hospital exhibits this last symptom.

The definitions of drug abuse and dependence provided above were developed primarily to identify adult drug abusers, individuals from the ages of 18 to 65 years. There are several ways in which the manifestations of consequential drug misuse (i.e., substance abuse) may differ between teens and adults (Table 1.3).

Differences between Adolescent and Adult Substance Abuse

The ways in which adolescents differ from adults in the development and expression of substance abuse raises important questions as to whether different diagnostic criteria should apply to youth than that which is currently applied to adults in the DSM-IV. Adolescent substance abuse may differ from adult substance abuse in at least seven ways.

First, regular use may or may not be considered abuse in adults, whereas it might be considered abuse in youth because of the potential of such use to interfere with brain developmental growth and adjustment tasks (Leccese & Waldron, 1994; Newcomb & Bentler, 1989; Tarter, 2002). Conversely, some researchers and practitioners have argued that some substance use represents normal development among teens as they begin to explore different life roles (Newcomb, 1995).

Second, the stochastic process of substance abuse to dependence is not clear-cut among teens (this may be true of adults, too, but to a less extent; Blum, 1995; Martin & Winters, 1998; Newcomb, 1995). For example, an early consequence of teen substance use is the development of tolerance to a drug, a substance dependence criterion. Another early consequence is excess

Table 1.3. Definitions of substance abuse and substance dependence based on the criteria of the *Diagnostic and Statistical Manual of Mental Disorders* of the American Psychiatric Association

Substance abuse disorder	A maladaptive pattern of drug use that meets one or more of the following four criteria within a 12-month period: 1. Failure to fulfill major life roles 2. Use occurs in or leads to physically hazardous situations 3. Drug-related legal problems 4. Persistent social/relationship problems
Substance dependence disorder	A maladaptive pattern of drug use that meets three or more of seven criteria within a 12-month period: 1. Tolerance is experienced 2. Withdrawal symptoms on attempted cessation 3. Drug is taken in larger amounts or over a longer period of time than intended 4. Persistent desire or unsuccessful effort to cut down or control drug use 5. The user spends excessive amounts of time obtaining the drug, using it, or recovering from its effects 6. Drug use leads to the abandonment or reduction of important life activities 7. Use continues despite knowledge of or the existence of persistent physical and/or psychological problems

time spent on getting the drug, using it, and recovering from its effects. Eventually, the young drug user develops social and role consequences and shows unsuccessful efforts to control use, legal consequences, and use in dangerous situations. Even later in the temporal order of consequences, the user exhibits withdrawal symptoms, uses larger amounts over a longer period, gives up important activities, and demonstrates continued use despite drug-related problems (e.g., paranoid reactions leading to hospitalization). This order of symptoms has led some researchers to suggest the withdrawal gating hypothesis; that is, that a greater weighting on substance abuse dependence given to withdrawal symptoms would preserve the stochastic perspective of abuse to dependence disorders (Chung, Martin, & Winters, 2005; Langenbucher et al., 2000).

Third, adolescents may tend to exhibit less overall physical dependence and fewer physical problems related to use (alcohol, in particular) and consume less overall. Rather, teens may exhibit more binging-type behavior – for example, drinking as much as adults when they do drink but drinking on fewer occasions and presumably being less prone to blackouts (Arria, Tarter, & Van Thiel, 1991; Bailey & Rachal, 1993; Deas et al., 2000; Leccese & Waldron, 1994). However, adolescents who begin to drink (or use other drugs) more heavily and regularly will tend to become dependent on alcohol (or other drugs) much more quickly than will adults (e.g., less than a year versus over several years; Deas et al., 2000).

Fourth, high-risk situations may differ between adolescents and adults. In particular, adolescents may be relatively likely to use drugs in situations in which they are not responsible for the caretaking of others. In addition, they are relatively likely to be experimenting with unfamiliar, new behaviors, which leads to a higher probability of accidents (e.g., drinking and driving).

Fifth, teens may have relatively higher rates of dual diagnosis; that is, comorbidity of substance use disorders and other mental health disorders (Brannigan, Schackman,

Falco, & Millman, 2004). More than half of the youth in treatment for substance use disorders have other psychopathology in addition to substance use problems (e.g., depressive and anxiety disorders, social phobia, posttraumatic stress disorder [PTSD], conduct disorders, or oppositional defiant disorder; see Abrantes, Brown, & Tomlinson, 2004; Tomlinson, Brown, & Abrantes, 2004).

Sixth, teens may be relatively less likely to seek treatment and relapse more quickly than adults do after treatment (Cornelius et al., 2003; O'Leary et al., 2002). Currently, only 10% of the estimated 1.4 million teens with an illicit drug problem are receiving treatment compared to 20% of adults (Substance Abuse and Mental Health Services Administration, 2002). In fact, the first systematic investigation of highly regarded treatment programs for teens in the United States has only very recently been conducted (Brannigan, Schackman, Falco, & Millman, 2004). The results of that evaluation indicate that there is much improvement needed in existing programs. Given potential differences in the nature of teen versus adult substance abuse disorder, it is also possible that teen-specific substance abuse is currently underestimated in prevalence. Thus, formalized treatment as currently developed may be less effective for teens than for adults.

Finally, adolescents may have a higher likelihood of suffering consequences specific to adolescence (e.g., problems at school, statutory difficulties, and truncated development; Blum, 1995; Newcomb & Bentler, 1988b). In fact, the effects of drug use on the individual and on society can be especially great during adolescence or in young adulthood (Newcomb & Bentler, 1988a; Sussman, Dent, & Galaif, 1997). A variety of negative consequences can occur. First, for example, adverse immediate consequences occur (e.g., overdoses and accidents; the incidence of older adolescent and young adult drinking and driving is double that of the general population; Bennett et al., 1993). Second, those teenagers who are heavy drug users also tend toward early involvement in family creation and divorce or unhappiness in these relationships. Third, crimes such as stealing, vandalism, and violence are associated with heavy drug use in adolescence and emerging adulthood. Fourth, drug-abusing youth are less likely to graduate from high school or take longer to graduate. Fifth, although these youth tend to earn more money than nonusing same-age peers, they also tend to seek less skilled employment sooner than their peers and job stability is lower. Sixth, drug-using youth are more likely to develop disorganized thinking and unusual beliefs that may interfere with problem-solving abilities and emotional functioning. Seventh, adaptive coping and achievement behavior are lessened. Eighth, heavy hard drug use predicts greater social isolation and depression among youth. Finally, drugs of abuse also may lead to health consequences, including cardiovascular complications, lung problems, and digestive or excretory problems, which begin to develop in adolescence (Sussman & Ames, 2001). More systematic research is needed to increase our understanding of specifics of adolescent substance abuse (Table 1.4).

Summary

This chapter addressed a variety of drug-relevant concepts and attempted to clarify terminology used, providing distinctions among ambiguous terms. For example, the term *street drugs* is used in a variety of ways to refer to drugs that may be misused. As another example, drug use simply refers to the act of using drugs. Using drugs for unwarranted

Table 1.4. Drug abuse as a function of developmental life period

Child	Adolescent/emerging adult	Mature adult	Senior citizen
Any drug use is considered drug abuse because a child's body and brain are rapidly developing. Medication given by a parent to a sick child is an exception.	Regular drug use can be considered abuse in many cases due to the high potential for drugs to interfere with brain development and growth.	Regular drug use without a DSM-IV substance abuse disorder diagnosis is typically not considered abuse. Meeting consequence criteria for DSM-IV substance abuse disorders is considered drug abuse.	Use of medications as prescribed by physicians is drug use. Drug abuse often occurs when legal prescription medications are mixed or misused and may involve DSM-IV criteria, especially physical hazard.

(not as appropriate, directed, or prescribed) reasons is drug misuse. Drug abuse may be defined as decrements in performance of major roles, dangerous action, legal problems, and social problems. When tolerance and withdrawal are experienced and one loses the ability to predict and control his or her drug use, drug dependence is being described. These differentiations in use behavior help quantify level of drug use and problems resulting from use.

2 Further Classifications Relevant to Substance Abuse and Dependence

This chapter provides additional classifications pertaining to drugs of misuse. First, the World Health Organization (WHO) Diagnostic Scheme is presented and compared to the DSM-IV scheme. Next, withdrawal symptoms for different types of drugs are described. The chapter then addresses the issue of whether drug abuse should be considered a disease and provides alternatives to the disease perspective of drug abuse. A behavioral perspective of drug abuse, as opposed to a disease perspective, has significant implications for treatment and service agencies. Finally, the chapter provides a discussion of other substance and process addictions and addresses coexisting substance misuse and mental health problems.

The WHO Diagnostic Scheme

The tenth revision of the *International Statistical Classification of Diseases and Related Health Problems* (ICD-10; WHO, 2003) provides eight classifications of consequences from the use of a substance in its section on mental and behavioral disorders due to psychoactive substance use (chapter 5; F10–F19):

1. "Acute intoxication" includes disturbances in brain function or behavior or complications (e.g., coma) related to the effects of a drug.
2. "Harmful use" refers to a pattern of use that is damaging one's physical or mental health.
3. A "dependence syndrome" is defined by a strong desire to take the drug, difficulties controlling use, persisting in use despite harmful consequences, a higher priority given to use than other activities, increased tolerance, and withdrawal.
4. "Withdrawal" refers to the time-limited effects of lowering dosage or stopping use of a drug (similar to as previously defined).
5. It may or may not include "delirium."
6. A "psychotic disorder" may occur during or following drug use and is characterized by hallucinations, delusions (e.g., paranoia), excitement or stupor, and extreme affect.
7. An "amnesic syndrome" is associated with chronic prominent impairment of recent and remote memory due to drug use.
8. "Residual or late-onset psychotic disorder" is one that was directly related to drug use but persists beyond the period in which a direct drug effect is occurring.

Thus, the ICD-10 definition is focused on mental or physical health complications and is not focused on social, legal, or environmentally hazardous consequences of use, as is the DSM-IV.

Withdrawal Symptoms

Withdrawal symptoms, also referred to as an "abstinence syndrome," consist of readjustments in physical functioning and behavior attributed to the overactivity of the nervous system. These symptoms are experienced when physically dependent individuals cease their drug use, particularly when cessation is abrupt (APA, 2000). Withdrawal symptoms vary from drug to drug. Alcohol, sedative, hypnotic, or anxiolytic withdrawal may involve autonomic reactivity, increased hand tremor, insomnia, nausea or vomiting, transient illusions or hallucinations, psychomotor agitation, anxiety, or grand mal seizures. Amphetamine or cocaine withdrawal includes fatigue or exhaustion, depression, unpleasant and vivid dreams, insomnia or hypersomnia, increased appetite, or psychomotor retardation or agitation. Opioid withdrawal includes dysphoric mood, anxiety, nausea or vomiting, muscle aches, abdominal cramping, tearing, rhinorrhea (i.e., runny nose), sweating, diarrhea, yawning, fever, and insomnia. Nicotine withdrawal includes depressed, anxious, or irritable mood; insomnia; difficulty concentrating; restlessness; decreased heart rate; constipation; sweating; and increased appetite. Phencyclidine (PCP) has no or few withdrawal symptoms, although its use is associated with anxiety, rage, seizures, and induction of psychotic disorder. Caffeine has few withdrawal symptoms, except perhaps for some fatigue, difficulty concentrating, and headache (see discussion of caffeine later in this chapter). Although not recognized until recently by researchers (APA, 2000), even to the dismay of generations of chronic users (Marijuana Anonymous, 1995), cannabis has a few withdrawal symptoms – fatigue, difficulty concentrating, stomach pains, some agitation, perhaps anger, and vivid dreams, especially among chronic users (Zickler, 2000). Hallucinogens are not known to have withdrawal symptoms, although there have been occasional reports of flashbacks (highlike states) in some people who have stopped using these drugs (Table 2.1).

Is Drug Abuse a Disease?

The disease concept of drug abuse and addiction is controversial, with arguments endorsing the disease model and arguments against the validity of the disease model. According to Timmreck (1998), disease is

an elusive and somewhat vague concept and is defined socially and culturally as well as scientifically. Any disruption in the function and structure of the body can be considered a disease. Disease is defined as a pattern of responses by a living organism to some form of invasion by a foreign substance or injury, which causes an alteration of the organism's normal functioning. Disease can be further defined as an abnormal state in which the body is not capable of responding to or carrying on its normally required functions. Disease is also a failure of the adaptive mechanisms of an organism to counteract adequately the invasion of the body by a foreign substance, resulting in a disturbance in the function or structure of some part of the organism. (p. 28)

Timmreck goes on to suggest that diseases may be acute or chronic and infectious or noninfectious. Heart disease, cancer, paralysis, diabetes, and alcoholism are included as

Table 2.1. Withdrawal symptoms for different types of drugs

Drug type	Typical withdrawal symptoms
Alcohol, sedative, hypnotic, or anxiolytic	Autonomic reactivity, hand tremor, insomnia, nausea/vomiting, brief delusions or hallucinations, psychomotor agitation, anxiety, and/or convulsive seizures
Amphetamine or cocaine	Fatigue, depression, vivid dreams or nightmares, insomnia or hypersomnia, increased appetite, and/or psychomotor retardation or agitation
Opioid	Depressed mood, anxiety, abdominal cramping, nausea/vomiting, diarrhea, muscle aches, tearing, runny nose, sweating, fever, yawning, and/or insomnia
Nicotine	Depressed, anxious or irritable mood, insomnia, difficulty concentrating, restlessness, decreased heart rate, constipation, sweating, and/or increased appetite
PCP	Little or no withdrawal symptoms
Caffeine	Few withdrawal symptoms; some fatigue, headache, and/or difficulty concentrating
Cannabis	Fatigue, difficulty concentrating, stomach pains, agitation, anger, and/or vivid dreams
Hallucinogens	None (rare reports of flashbacks, not withdrawal related)

Note: The drug types are based on the Sussman and Ames (2001) health behavior scheme.

chronic and noninfectious diseases. Genetic, behavioral, and environmental influences may cause these diseases (Figure 2.1).

The disease concept of drug abuse emerged with the intention of changing public attitudes about blame and punishment to concern and treatment (Cunningham, Sobell, & Sobell, 1996). Substance abuse once was used to describe or suggest acts of immoral individuals who disobeyed the law and used drugs at the expense of family and friends. Nevertheless, it was also understood that the substance abuse often went beyond an individual's self-control after sustained periods of use. In 1870, the American Association for the Cure of Inebriates was established and attempted to define substance abuse as a disease and place substance abuse within the charge of hospitals for scientific treatment. (Chapter 3 provides many more details.) Whether or not the disease concept of substance abuse has helped to decrease perceptions of immorality of drug abusers remains unclear. Presently, however, it appears that most laypeople perceive drug abuse or addiction as a disease. In addition, there is the perspective that drug abusers become more willing to take responsibility for self-care if they view their drug abuse as a disease (Vaillant, 1990).

A comprehensive concept of the disease model of alcoholism was attributed to E. M. Jellinek in 1960 (Jellnick, 1952, 1960). In 1965, the American Psychiatric Association began using the term *disease* to describe alcoholism, and in 1966, the American Medical Association subsequently followed. The disease concept of alcoholism has since been generalized to addiction to other drugs. Generally, there is an assumption that there exists baseline vulnerability in prone individuals long before drug use began. The "disease of addiction" is viewed as a primary disease and is not secondary to some other condition. This is in contrast to the concept of dual diagnosis (discussed later), whereby the addictive behavior may be secondary to or intermingled with some other psychological condition.

Figure 2.1. Early depiction of problem consequences from alcohol abuse.

Limitations of the Disease Concept of Drug Abuse

There are limitations of the disease concept of addiction. First, clinicians have no independent means of verifying the existence of the disease; that is, it is difficult to separate factors (e.g., a poison or a virus) from symptoms (e.g., high temperature) in these behavioral disorders (e.g., using drugs heavily might be used to indicate both symptoms and factors of the disease). Second, behavioral symptoms may be defined as more or less disordered depending on the socioenvironmental context. That is, drug abuse may fall along a continuum of disordered behavior, as opposed to the binary perspective often used to define a disease.

Third, variation in behavioral symptoms may or may not reflect the same underlying factors of drug abuse. For example, there are various patterns of drug abuse, from a single-use catastrophe to periodic problem use and to heavy or uncontrolled use. It is unclear whether these variations reflect the same underlying processes or etiology. Fourth, the etiologic factors for drug abuse as a behavioral disorder are still being investigated. It may be that both quantitative and qualitative differences in susceptibility exist. For example, with drug abuse defined as a distinct disease, the various addictive behaviors are considered qualitatively distinct (e.g., compulsive gambling, drug abuse, overeating); that is, common underlying processes across these problem behaviors often are not considered. Moreover, defined as a disease, the capacity for self-management and assuming responsibility for one's behavior may be undermined. Finally, defined as a disease, treatment options may be limited. Moderation goals may not be acceptable and this may prevent some individuals from seeking treatment (e.g., some may be willing to begin treatment to try to become controlled drinkers and, if that fails, become abstinent).

The Brain Disease Concept

An alternative concept of addiction as an acquired "brain disease" has evolved with advances in neuroscience and cognitive psychology. This perspective suggests that following voluntary repetitive drug use behavior, changes in the brain occur and these structural and chemical changes in the brain affect the addictive process. That is, continued drug use results in neuroadaptive changes in the brain and the formation and strengthening of memory associations. These neuroadaptations appear to be, at least in part, responsible for some of the cognitive and emotional disruptions that are characteristic of substance abusing individuals. Continued drug use may result in a "loss of inhibitory control" or compulsive drug craving, drug seeking, and use that interferes with normal functioning. Although researchers are still unraveling the relevant mechanisms that underlie the addictive process, new research methodologies (e.g., functional magnetic resonance imaging [fMRI] and structural MRI) have increased our understanding of the brain mechanisms through which drug use modifies perception, memory, and emotional states. Although acknowledging a potential vulnerability component, emphasis is placed on an acquired dysfunction.

Reconsideration of the Disease Concept

A drug abuse continuum perspective: With all the advances in the study of addiction, for many the question still remains: is the continuing use of drugs while incurring various negative consequences a disease or some other type of disorder? Some conceptualize a disease as an acute infectious type (e.g., the flu), whereas others may consider chronic, noninfectious types of diseases as "real" diseases (e.g., heart disease). One may ponder whether substance addiction is similar to cardiovascular disease, which involves negative consequences to vital cardiovascular organs. The individual with cardiovascular disease may suffer a variety of health consequences such as stroke or heart attack that restrict participation in normal activities. This disease can result from intake of fatty foods, lack of exercise, and cigarette smoking, among other factors. The operation of these factors on cardiovascular disease is mediated by some process involving preparedness to wear down the cardiovascular system (heredity) plus elicitation of plaque buildup and lack of mobility of its organs.

Perhaps substance abuse is an outcome condition similar to that of cardiovascular disease in that it involves negative consequences that result from intake of a substance and a *biological preparedness*. For example, substance abuse may be mediated by processes involving heredity, neurotransmitter homeostatic function, as well as other factors. Drug use may do something for abusers but it also does something *to* them. Normal functioning may be disrupted, adaptive mechanisms often fail, and numerous consequences occur over time. Sometimes drug use behavior may appear under control or in remission, and at other times it appears to progress with negative outcomes.

Substance abuse may be examined along a continuum. At one end of this continuum, individuals who misuse drugs are relatively "disease-free" but tend to engage in maladaptive behaviors over which they have choice and control. These individuals may repetitively use drugs (e.g., they experiment and "party"), and over time they may abuse drugs. These individuals, however, choose to live a certain lifestyle, resulting in maladaptive behavior that may or may not result in other disease states associated with use (e.g., cirrhosis of the liver). If these individuals are stopped or prevented from continuing use, they can then choose to engage in more prosocial activities and learn alternative coping mechanisms and self-efficacy.

However, individuals at the other end of the continuum may have no control over their use. Some individuals use for the first time and appear to lose control of their use. These individuals can be likened to a toggle switch that is either on or off; they must abstain because they have no control processes once the switch is in the "on" position. They may use until they die unless someone else can turn their switch off and keep it off. There is no choice or rational explanation for their behavior. These individuals may destroy their lives and the lives of those around them to use their drug of choice. Seemingly, as one moves toward a more "at risk" end of the continuum, choice and control processes diminish.

Researchers are currently working toward understanding the processes that cause the difference in loss of control among those at different points of the continuum. Various factors exacerbate drug abuse, including biologically based differences in metabolic processes (e.g., differences in activity of alcohol dehydrogenase or other enzymes), differential susceptibility to the rewarding effects of drugs (e.g., variation in neurochemistry), early traumas (e.g., sexual abuse), co-occurring conditions (e.g., personality disorders), and differences in behavioral regulation (e.g., tolerance for frustration or emotional discomfort). Some processes that affect drug abuse (e.g., choosing drug-using friends) are under individual control but many are not (e.g., biologically based susceptibility to pharmacological effects), and it does appear that the less control the individual has over these types of processes, the more likely the individual is to behave as if he or she is experiencing a "real" disease-notion of substance abuse. This perspective of substance abuse is conceptually similar to a continuous, normal distribution (i.e., the bell-shaped curve); that is, at one end of the curve a small percentage of the sample exhibits maladaptive lifestyles, and, at the other end of the curve, a small percentage of the sample exhibits a "disease state," but the majority of individuals are distributed in the middle along the continuum (Sussman & Ames, 2001).

Substance and Process Addictions

Schaef (1987) proposed a typology consisting of substance and process addictions in an attempt to differentially classify various addictive/compulsive behaviors. *Substance addictions* involve all mood-altering products, including drugs (e.g., caffeine, nicotine, alcohol, cocaine, and heroin) and food-related disorders (e.g., anorexia, bulimia, and overeating). *Process addictions* consist of a series of actions that expose one to "mood-altering events" on which one becomes dependent (e.g., gambling, excessive sex, workaholism, excessive exercise, excessive spending, and excessive television watching). The distinction between substance and process addictions could also reflect similar underlying causal mechanisms. Substance addictions involve direct manipulation of pleasure through use of products that are taken into the body. Intake of these products may have a direct effect on neurochemical systems (e.g., pleasure systems and dopamine). Alternatively, process addictions may involve a more indirect manipulation of pleasure though situational and physical activities.

However, the same neurochemical reactions that occur with substance addictions may also occur with process addictions.

Substance Addictions

Through ingestion of a substance, an individual may attempt to achieve a desired or expected state. Repeated use of a substance may lead to a variety of consequences. Similarly, the ingestion of substances other than drugs of abuse (i.e., food) might also change one's mood or be a means of "self-medicating" (i.e., using food to feel better). Food addiction is a disorder characterized by a preoccupation with food, the availability of food, and, for many, the anticipation of pleasure from the ingestion of food. Food addiction can involve the repetitive consumption of food contrary to an individual's wishes, resulting in loss of control and/or preoccupation with the restriction of food, body weight, and body image. Like drug addiction, some food addictions may, over time, lead to neuroadaptive changes in the brain and an acquired brain disease (e.g., anorexia nervosa). Eating disorders such as compulsive overeating, anorexia nervosa, and bulimia nervosa, as well as binge eating and dieting failure, affect millions of people worldwide. Binge eating (eating larger amounts of food in short periods of time, at least twice weekly) is the most prevalent food disorder in the United States. Once binging begins, binge eaters feel unable to stop; they feel out of control when overeating. Hudson, Hiripi, Pope, and Kessler (2007) found that among a national sample of 2,980 individuals in which eating disorders were assessed, 3.5% of women and 2% of men reported lifetime prevalence of binge eating (lasting an average of 8 years). Conversely, 0.9% of women and 0.3% of men reported lifetime prevalence of anorexia nervosa (lasting an average of 1.7 years) and 1.5% of women and 0.5% of men reported bulimia nervosa, lasting an average of 8.3 years (Hudson, Hiripi, Pope, & Kessler, 2007).

Many people suffer from cycles of dieting, binging, starving, persistent weight problems, and food and weight obsessions. Often consequences occur after failed attempts at weight regulation, which include rebound weight gain, cravings, feelings of failure, and damage to social, emotional, and physical well-being, as well as a variety of negative health outcomes, including death for some. For example, obesity can result in high blood pressure, cardiovascular disease, some cancers, and diabetes. In the United States, as assessed through use of the body mass index (BMI), approximately two-thirds of adults in the United States are overweight (BMI $\geq$ 25, which includes those who are obese). Nearly 30% of the adult population is obese (BMI $\geq$ 30; 28% of males, 33% of females) (http://win.niddk.nih.gov/statistics/index.htm#preval). Moreover, obesity is becoming a growing problem among youth. Individuals who suffer food disorders show a pattern of abuse not too dissimilar from drug abuse. Many individuals with food addictions/eating disorders also misuse alcohol and other drugs, as well as misusing slimming pills, laxatives, diuretics, diet pills, and ipecac (Mitchell, Specker, & Edmonson, 1997).

Process Addictions

Process addictions, such as gambling, compulsive sex, workaholism, compulsive exercise, and excessive spending, are problem behaviors that exhibit drug abuse–like behavior patterns and are associated with drug misuse/abuse. For example, *gamblers* whose repeated losses lead to serious financial and psychological problems are increasingly being labeled as "compulsive" or "pathological" (i.e., the individual has a disease). *Compulsive gambling* can disrupt personal, family, and/or vocational pursuits. Several similarities have been reported between compulsive gambling and drug abuse. For example, the states of arousal and euphoria sought by gamblers seem similar to the high derived from using drugs. Compulsive gamblers tend to increase the size of their bets or the odds against them to increase excitement, analogous to drug tolerance effects (Spunt et al., 1998). Researchers also have found the equivalence of drug withdrawal symptoms in compulsive gamblers (e.g., irritability, depressed mood, and obsessional thoughts). Roy et al. (1988) found biological differences between gamblers and controls in the noradrenergic neurotransmitter system; specifically, pathological gamblers show greater concentrations of by-products of norepinephrine that are associated with the facilitation of arousal, excitement, and thrills (sensation seeking).

Individuals commonly consume alcohol and other drugs when gambling. Drugs are often used to stay awake while gambling, free drinks are served in many casinos, and most racetracks have bars (Spunt, Lesieur, Hunt, & Cahill, 1995; Spunt et al., 1998). Pathological gamblers report higher rates of alcoholism and other drug misuse than that of the general population. Although males are more likely than females to be pathological gamblers, among women pathological gamblers participating in Gamblers Anonymous (a twelve-step self-help program for gamblers; http://www.gamblersanonymous.org/), the rate of alcohol and drug misuse is approximately two to three times higher than that of the general female population. Rates of pathological gambling are four to ten times higher for drug misusers than for the general population. Some heroin addicts are able to support their addiction through gambling or hustling at gambling games. In a study of 462 individuals in a methadone maintenance treatment program in New York City, 59% of the pathological gamblers reported using heroin, almost half reported using alcohol, and 23% reported using cocaine more than 50% of the time or always while gambling (Spunt et al., 1998). Researchers have also reported a relationship between pathological gambling and participation in criminal activity (mainly property crimes), as well as drug dealing, to obtain money to gamble and pay debts (Spunt, Lesieur, Hunt, & Cahill, 1995; Spunt et al., 1998).

The relationship between *risky sexual behavior* and drug use has been conceptualized as (1) a result of the disinhibiting effects of drugs consumed and subsequent diminished decision-making and judgment (e.g., Leigh & Schafer, 1993) and (2) as a behavioral manifestation of a more general problem behavior orientation (Donovan & Jessor, 1985; Sussman, 2005c). Drug abuse is associated with sexual abuse, prevalence of sexually transmitted diseases, prostitution, and sexual decision-making (i.e., frequency of safe sex).

The DSM-IV provides diagnoses for various sexual disorders and dysfunctions. However, there is continuing debate about the notion of sexual addiction as a drug abuse–like phenomenon (e.g., perhaps the suggestion of a brain disease; both facilitate dopaminergic turnover; Sussman, 2005c) versus a maladaptive coping, social learning-type phenomenon (i.e., people may not have learned the skills to act differently; Carnes, 1996; Sussman, 2005c). There may be commonalities between sex addiction and drug abuse thoughts and behaviors, including obsessions, loss of control, compulsive behavior, continuation despite adverse consequences, escalation of behaviors, and high relapse rates after treatment. Many drug abusers also report being addicted to sex (Schneider, 1994). Several competing twelve-step groups exist as a means of support for individuals who identify as sex addicts (e.g., Sex Addicts Anonymous [SAA; www.saa-recovery.org]; Sex and Love Addicts Anonymous [SLAA; www.slaafws.org]; Sexaholics Anonymous [SA; www.sa.org]; Sexual Compulsives Anonymous [SCA; www.sca-recovery.org]; and Sexual

Recovery Anonymous [SRA; www.sexualrecovery.org]), as well as cognitive behavioral-related approaches (e.g., Rational Recovery, http://www.rational.org/welcome.html; Positive Realism, www.sexualcontrol.com).

Workaholism is an addiction to working. It is not currently formally recognized as a mental disorder in the DSM-IV or ICD-10. However, work can be a compulsive behavior similar to other process addictions. Workaholism is characterized by feelings of being driven to keep working, as well as perfectionism, nondelegation of responsibility, and job stress. Workaholic behavior interferes with other life domains (Spence & Robbins, 1992).

Working long hours is a relatively prosocial activity and possibly a harm reduction strategy for individuals coping with other compulsive or addictive behaviors. For instance, pathological gamblers, when not gambling, may be workaholics (APA, 2000), or addicts in recovery may choose to work excessively as they change their lifestyles. If working behavior results in a lack of fulfillment of other life roles, such as effective interpersonal relationships, effective parenting, or performance of necessary life skills (e.g., purchasing a car), then consideration of strategies for engaging in a more balanced, healthy life is recommended. Workaholism may be associated with poorer emotional and physical well-being (Burke, 2000). Compulsive work is recognized as a problem behavior in the recovery movement (e.g., Workaholics Anonymous; http://www.workaholics-anonymous.org/).

Participation in *exercise or physical activity* often is negatively associated with addiction (Donovan, Jessor, & Costa, 1993). Exercise tends to exert many positive effects, including decreasing low-density lipoprotein (LDL) cholesterol and heart rate, and increasing high-density lipoprotein (HDL) cholesterol, oxygen utilization, and metabolism. It is often used in the treatment of drug abuse. However, even exercise can become a craving for some people when it is engaged in compulsively (e.g., going jogging three times per day), when other life roles are neglected, when not exercising leads to depressed mood, and when it leads to repeated injuries (Griffiths, 1997; Thaxton, 1982). Compulsive runners have been likened to anorexics in that "their behavior becomes pathological as a result of an extreme degree of constriction, inflexibility, repetitive thoughts, adherence to rituals and need to control themselves and their environment" (Peele & Brodsky, 1992, p. 42).

One could speculate that someone who exercises to maintain a sense of balance might experience "dis-balance" if he or she had to stop exercising suddenly (e.g., as a result of a sports accident). Then, this individual might resort to drug use while injured. Because exercising may stimulate endorphin turnover; other drugs that provide a similar function may be used once exercise is not a viable option. Currently, no widely publicized support groups exist for compulsive exercisers, although this is an issue that has been addressed by eating disorder support groups.

Participation in *excessive buying behavior* (e.g., compulsive shopping), which leads to unsecured debt, also is not recognized as an official mental disorder by the DSM-IV (APA, 2000). Yet, one of every twelve residents of the United States is overwhelmed by debt. This process addiction is associated with its own twelve-step program composed of at least 400 groups worldwide, Debtors Anonymous (Mundis, 1986; www.solvency.org). Debtors Anonymous was founded in 1976 by a man who had been sober in Alcoholics Anonymous for 27 years. Compulsive spenders repeatedly incur debt despite negative emotional, social, and financial consequences. These individuals tend to greatly value money as a solution to problems (Hanley & Wilhelm, 1992), and they are also relatively likely to suffer from drug

Table 2.2. *Substance and process addictions: a comparison*

	Description	Causal mechanism(s)	Examples
Substance addiction	Compulsive behavior that involves *ingestion* of mood-altering *substances*.	Direct manipulation of pleasure as a result of the intake of a substance; neurochemical changes usually occur (e.g., increase dopamine release).	Drug addictions (e.g., caffeine, nicotine, alcohol, and heroin). Food addictions (e.g., anorexia, bulimia, compulsive overeating, and binge eating).
Process addiction	Compulsive behavior that involves mood-altering *actions and events*.	Indirect manipulation of pleasure via situational and physical activities; neurochemical changes similar to those of substance addictions may also occur.	Compulsive gambling, workaholism, excessive spending, sex addictions.

abuse, eating disorders, and pathological gambling (e.g., Schlosser, Black, Repertinger, & Freet, 1994) (Table 2.2).

Dual Diagnosis

Dual diagnosis is the term used to refer to individuals with co-occurring drug- or alcohol-related problems and psychiatric disorders. A dual diagnosis is determined when each of the disorders is established independent of the other; that is, one disorder is not a cluster of symptoms resulting from the other disorder. In 2003, according to the Treatment Episode Data Set (TEDS), which provides data on annual admissions to substance abuse treatment, 21% of adolescents admitted had a psychiatric problem in addition to an alcohol or drug problem. In comparison, among adult admissions, 19% had co-occurring disorders. Female adolescents admitted to substance abuse treatment were more likely to have co-occurring disorders than males, and the majority of those with co-occurring disorders admitted to treatment were White (http://www.drugabusestatistics.samhsa.gov/dasis.htm; http://www.drugabusestatistics.samhsa.gov/mh.cfm; Treatment Episode Data Set (TEDS): 1992–2002 [Substance Abuse and Mental Health Services Administration, 2003]).

Findings from clinical samples diagnosed with both a substance use disorder and mental disorder have been found to be more treatment resistant than individuals with a primary disorder of either type (Brady & Sinha, 2005; Margolese et al. 2004). Of the various mental disorders considered in the DSM-IV, substance use disorders appear to be more strongly associated with externalizing disorders (e.g., conduct/antisocial personality disorders, oppositional-defiant disorder, attention-deficit/hyperactivity disorder) than with internalizing disorders (e.g., mood and anxiety disorders; Krueger et al., 2003). Further, Kessler reported in an epidemiological review of dual diagnosis that the majority of individuals with co-occurring disorders reported their "first mental disorder occurred at an earlier age than their first substance disorder. Prospective studies confirm this temporal order, although significant predictive associations are reciprocal. Analyses of active and remitted mental disorders suggest that some primary mental disorders are markers, while others are causal risk factors for secondary substance disorder" (Kessler, 2004, p. 730).

Although lifetime prevalence of substance use disorders is approximately 17% in the United States, the lifetime prevalence of substance use disorders among those with schizophrenia diagnoses are estimated to vary from 48% to 64% (Margolese et al., 2004). The most commonly used substances among patients with psychotic disorders are nicotine, alcohol, marijuana, and cocaine. The lifetime prevalence of substance use disorders among individuals suffering from any mood disorder is approximately 32% (56% bipolar, about 30% unipolar), those with an anxiety disorder is estimated to be 24% (36% if a panic disorder is involved), and those suffering from obsessive-compulsive disorder is 33%. Substance abuse among individuals with diagnoses of mental disorders is of some concern because co-occurrence of mental disorders may lead to an increased risk of relapse for either or both disorders. Some explanations for the co-occurrence or association among substance use disorders and mental disorders include common factors leading to both problems (e.g., common underlying susceptibility processes), secondary diagnosis of one condition from the other, and bidirectional functions in which each condition leads to the other (Mueser, Noordsy, Drake, & Fox, 2003).

Summary

Most formal criteria used in the diagnosis of substance abuse focus on the consequences of one's use. The WHO ICD-10 definition focuses on mental or physical health complications, whereas the American Psychiatric Association DSM-IV focuses on social, legal, or environmentally hazardous consequences of use. To some extent, whether or not one is determined to be a "drug abuser" is dependent on the bias of the observer despite formal criteria used by clinicians and researchers in making this determination. The observer may choose to minimize or exaggerate consequences, view them as being or not being recurrent enough, focus on a single dimension of functionality (e.g., work performance) to the exclusion of other life dimensions (e.g., involvement in social activities or social networks), or take a stance that veers from these formal diagnostic systems (e.g., will search for presence of "true" addictive thinking to know that someone is a "real" alcoholic or drug addict). Differential prevalence of drug abuse among different groups may reflect true differences in prevalence, access to different groups, or systematic biases in the tendency to diagnose different groups as suffering from a substance abuse disorder. Some subsequent chapters of this book will examine potential biases in prevalence.

This chapter also presented perspectives of drug abuse as a disease and alternatives to a binary conceptualization. One's perspectives on whether "drug abuse" is a disease has significant implications for treatment because individuals are labeled as "problem users" by a range of experts through various service or treatment agencies and through law enforcement agencies. Drug abuse appears to share characteristics that could define it as a disease. For example, drug abuse can result in the disruption of normal functioning and failed attempts to stop a dysfunctional pattern of behavior. Additionally, drug abuse shares some notions of causation with other chronic, lifestyle disorders, such as heart disease, and a need for treatment to arrest the problem. Alternatively, or additionally, drug abuse may be a "brain disease" resulting from drug-induced structural and chemical changes in the brain. Or, drug abuse may be viewed as a continuum of control in which individuals at one end of the continuum are relatively disease-free but engage in maladaptive behaviors over which they have some control. At the other end of the continuum, there are individuals who seem to have no choice or control over their use.

We conjecture that individuals at the "choice" end of the continuum may engage in only one compulsive problem behavior and when they gain control over that behavior, they may be fine. However, those individuals at the other end of the continuum may find that no matter what the activity they dabble in – gambling, working, sex, shopping, or drug use – they will do it excessively. That is, as one moves toward the "no-control" pole of the continuum, the breadth of problem behaviors may fan out.

Drug abuse is associated with a variety of other compulsive behaviors (substance and process addictions) and mental disorders that may or may not have underlying processes similar to drug abuse. Because drug abuse and other compulsive behaviors as well as various mental disorders co-occur, the study of their co-occurrence may aid in more targeted prevention and treatment efforts.

3 Types of Drugs, History of Drug Use and Misuse, and Costs of Drug Misuse

Various drug type classification systems have been compiled based on chemical structures, pharmacological action, and/or the observable behavioral effects of the drug action. Drugs of misuse enter the bloodstream and circulate through the system after being injected, inhaled, swallowed, or absorbed through the skin. Each drug has an "affinity" for specific receptor cell sites and may act as an antagonist or agonist. Antagonist drugs block or reduce cell response to natural agonists, usually one's own neurotransmitters ("endogenous ligands"). Conversely, agonist drugs stimulate specific receptors and may increase cellular activities. This chapter provides information on the various drug type classification schemes and an overview of the drugs within these classifications. These classifications help clinicians and researchers to understand observable effects and consequences of drug action and addiction potential. The chapter then addresses the case of caffeine and the case of tobacco. Next, the chapter addresses the history of drug use and abuse and concludes with current costs to society of drug abuse.

Types of Drugs

Around the world, approximately 15% of the population older than 18 years of age is considered to have serious drug use problems (other than nicotine addiction, which itself may involve up to 25% of the world's population), and this percentage has remained fairly constant since the early 1980s. Of these drug abusers, about two-thirds abuse alcohol and one-third abuse other drugs. Across the continents, the other major drugs of abuse are marijuana, amphetamines, cocaine, and heroin. Approximately 2.5% of the world's population abuse marijuana, 0.5% abuse stimulants, 0.3% abuse cocaine or opioids, and up to 1.7% abuse other drugs (e.g., inhalants, depressants, hallucinogens; Sussman & Ames, 2001; White, 1999). Many individuals who try illicit drugs do not go on to abuse them. As an example, approximately 33% of the populations of the United States and Australia, and 10% to 20% of the population of different European countries, report lifetime use of marijuana (U.S. Department of Health and Human Services [DHHS], 1998b). Yet, only 2.5% of the world's population use marijuana so regularly as to incur recognizable consequences.

Various drug classification systems (that overlap to some degree) have been compiled to help differentiate drugs of abuse; five of these systems are reviewed here (as reviewed in part in Sussman & Ames, 2001). These classifications are as follows: (1) the American Psychiatric Association's *Diagnostic and Statistical Manual of Mental Disorders* (DSM-IV-TR), (2) the

World Health Organization's *International Statistical Classification of Diseases and Related Health Problems* (e.g., tenth revision; WHO, 2003), (3) the U.S. Drug Enforcement Administration's (DEA) and Coast Guard scheme, (4) the Julien (2005) biomedical-type scheme, and (5) the Sussman and Ames (2001) health behavior scheme.

Diagnostic and Statistical Manual of the American Psychiatric Association

There was no agreed-on system of the diagnosis and classification of substance abuse in the United States until publication of the DSM series. Definitions of substance abuse/dependence have varied dramatically since the initial publication of the DSM-I in 1952 (Freedman, Kaplan, & Sadock, 1976). For example, in the DSM-I, there was a category of drug addiction; however, it was vague in scope. In addition, both alcoholism and other drug addiction were subsumed within a sociopathic personality disturbance category, suggesting that they stemmed from certain personality features.

In the DSM-II, published in 1968, a category of drug dependence was included that was composed of physiologic (addiction) and psychic (state) components to make the definition less vague. In the DSM-II, drug addiction or dependence referred to opium, synthetic analgesics, barbiturates, other hypnotics and sedatives, cocaine and other psychostimulants, cannabis, hallucinogens, and other drugs (e.g., volatile solvents). Tobacco and caffeine use were not included explicitly in any category, and alcoholism was placed in its own category.

In the DSM-I, alcoholism was not defined separately if it was symptomatic of another disorder. Alcoholism became defined as a category regardless of its relation to other disorders in the DSM-II. In addition, four categories of alcoholism were defined (episodic, habitual excessive, addiction, and other), and physiological and psychological tracks were delineated. Physiological dependency to alcohol included withdrawal symptoms of gross tremor, hallucinosis, seizures, delirium tremens, and tolerance. Evidence of tolerance included a blood alcohol level of more than 150 mg without evidence of intoxication, a fifth of whiskey for more than 1 day for a 180-pound person, and blackouts. Several alcohol-related diseases (e.g., alcoholic hepatitis) were considered clinical features. A behavioral, psychological, and attitudinal track included drinking in spite of medical and social contraindications or loss of control.

The DSM-III was first published in 1980 (with a DSM-III-R revision in 1987), and this volume distinguished between abuse and dependence. In the DSM-III-R, psychoactive substance abuse required a maladaptive pattern of use that is demonstrated by continued use despite persistent social, occupational, psychological, or physical problems that were caused or made worse by use, or by recurrent use in physically hazardous situations, for at least a 1-month duration or at least one symptom two or more times over the past year. Further, at least three of nine of the following were necessary for a classification of psychoactive substance use dependence (some of the symptoms of the disturbance must have persisted for at least 1 month or have occurred repeatedly over a longer period of time):

1. Substance often taken in larger amounts or over longer periods than intended;
2. Persistent desire or one or more unsuccessful efforts to cut down or control substance use;
3. A great deal of time spent in activities necessary to get the substance (e.g., theft), taking the substance (e.g., chain smoking), or recovering from its effects;

4. Important social, occupational, or recreational activities given up or reduced because of substance abuse;
5. Continued substance use despite knowledge of having a persistent or recurrent social, psychological, or physical problem that is caused or exacerbated by use of the substance;
6. Marked tolerance – need for markedly increased amounts of the substance to achieve intoxication or desired effect (e.g., doubling quantity from early use), or markedly diminished effect with continued use of the same amount;
7. Characteristic withdrawal symptoms;
8. Substance often taken to relieve or avoid withdrawal symptoms; and
9. Frequent intoxication or withdrawal symptoms when expected to fulfill major role obligations or when use is physically hazardous.

The DSM-III attempted to provide more empirical and within-person-based symptomatology, provided a multiaxis diagnosis (e.g., occupational impairment), and influenced greatly the DSM-IV (the diagnostic criteria for the DSM-IV were described in Chapter 2). Drugs classified in the DSM-III-R were the same ones as classified in the DSM-IV.

The DSM-IV, first published in 1994 (with text revision published in 2000), divides drug abuse disorders into 13 classes: (1) alcohol-related disorders, (2) sedative-, hypnotic- or anxiolytic-related disorders, (3) amphetamine- (or amphetamine-like) related disorders, (4) cocaine-related disorders, (5) caffeine-related disorders, (6) cannabis-related disorders, (7) hallucinogen-related disorders, (8) inhalant-related disorders, (9) nicotine-related disorders, (10) opioid-related disorders, (11) phencyclidine- (or phencyclidine-like) related disorders, (12) polysubstance-related disorders, and (13) other (unknown) substance–related disorders (APA, 2000). In other words, the number of drug categories changed from ten categories in the DSM-II (including alcohol) to thirteen in the DSM-III-R and DSM-IV. Alcohol was grouped along with the other drugs, caffeine and tobacco (nicotine) were now considered categories, and inhalants and phencyclidine (PCP) were in independent categories, whereas other categories were now grouped together (opium and synthetic analgesics and barbiturates with sedatives). With the publication of the DSM-III, drug dependence was no longer included under personality disorders, perhaps reflecting greater importance being placed on substance abuse as a separate entity.

WHO International Classification of Diseases

The ICD-10 (e.g., see WHO, 2003) divides drugs of abuse or dependence into ten categories: (1) alcohol, (2) opioids, (3) cannabinoids, (4) sedatives or hypnotics, (5) cocaine, (6) other stimulants, including caffeine, (7) hallucinogens, (8) tobacco, (9) volatile solvents, and (10) multiple drug use or other drug use (particularly when the drugs being taken are not known). These drugs are divided to discern abuse, dependence, and psychological (e.g., psychosis) and medical consequences, similar to the DSM-IV formulation.

U.S. DEA's and Coast Guard Scheme

The U.S. DEA and the National Guard categorize drugs by their effects into six categories: (1) narcotics (e.g., opium, heroin, and meperdine; twelve types listed),

(2) depressants (e.g., chloral hydrate and barbiturates; five types listed), (3) stimulants (e.g., cocaine, amphetamines, and Ritalin; six types listed), (4) hallucinogens (e.g., peyote and lysergic acid diethylamide [LSD]; six types listed), (5) cannabis, and (6) steroids. These categories are considered in terms of their abuse potential, safety or dependence liability, and degree of therapeutic benefit (U.S. DEA and National Guard, 1996).

Julien Biomedical-Type Scheme

Julien (2005), in his text *A Primer of Drug Action*, divides drugs of abuse by specific neuroanatomical effects and topical interest into nine types. These nine types are as follows: (1) depressants-type 1 (which includes barbiturates, sedative-hypnotics, and general anesthetics), (2) depressants-type 2 (alcohol and inhalants), (3) benzodiazepines and "second generation" anxiolytics (e.g., zolpidem and buspirone), (4) psychostimulants-type 1 (cocaine and amphetamines), (5) psychostimulants-type 2 (caffeine and nicotine), (6) opioids (analgesics), (7) cannabis, (8) hallucinogens (anticholinergic, catecholinergic, serotonin-like, and PCP types), and (9) steroids.

Sussman and Ames Health Promotion Subjective-Behavioral Scheme

Sussman and Ames (2001) divide drugs of abuse by subjective and behavioral effects into eight classes: (1) depressants (which include alcohol, sedatives for relaxation, hypnotics to induce sleep, anxiolytic to reduce anxiety, and anticonvulsants such as barbiturates), (2) PCP, (3) inhalants, (4) stimulants, (5) opiates, (6) hallucinogens, (7) cannabis, and (8) others. All depressants are classified together because they slow down, relax, or "knock out" an individual. PCP is placed in a separate category because its effects are both depressant and hallucinogen-like and may precipitate violence. Inhalants generally exert sedative effects, but their administration (sniffed or huffed) is quite different from other depressants. All stimulants tend to "speed up" the individual and make one nervous or more aware. All opiates relieve pain, and may relax or amotivate the user, whether or not they are derived from opium or are synthetic. All hallucinogens expand cognitive perceptions and may lead to perceptual distortions and easily agitated behavior. Marijuana may cause one to "mellow out" and/or "be paranoid" or alter one's perceptions (e.g., time may appear to slow down). Finally, there are "other" new drugs of abuse (e.g., steroids, ecstasy, γ-hydroxybutyrate [GHB], ketamine), which may or may not fit into one of the previous seven health behavior-related categories. These types of drugs are placed in the eighth category (other) because they have short abuse histories (fewer than 20 years' duration). Following is a brief review of drug categories based on the Sussman and Ames health behavior scheme (Sussman & Ames, 2001) (Figure 3.1).

Depressants

Depressants are generally taken orally and slow down the central nervous system. Intoxication may include slurred speech, deficient coordination, nystagmus (rapid eye movements), attention or memory impairment, sedation, anxiety reduction, and euphoria, and generally lasts 4 to 5 hours on a single dose. Alcohol is the most commonly used depressant. Approximately half of the U.S. population older than 12 years use alcohol each year. Beer is approximately 5% ethanol, wine is approximately 10% to 18% ethanol, and liquors range

Figure 3.1. Sussman and Ames Health Behavior Scheme. *Depressants:* (a) beer. *PCP:* (b) PCP, crystalline form and dissolved in water. *Inhalants:* (c) inhalant. *Stimulants:* (d) cocaine; (e) crack cocaine; (f) methamphetamine; (g) ecstasy. *Opiates:* (h) heroin; (i) Vicodin. *Hallucinogens:* (j) LSD; (k) peyote. *Marijuana:* (l) marijuana. *Others:* (m) steroids; (n) ketamine.

from about 21% to 50% ethanol (e.g., Scotch is approximately 40% ethanol). It takes about 1 hour to metabolize the alcohol in one 1-ounce scotch drink. Alcohol can become lethal when the blood alcohol content (BAC) reaches about 0.35%. Alcohol has multiple effects on neurotransmission. For example, it may inhibit a subtype of glutamate receptor (glutamate-N-methyl-D-aspartate or NMDA; i.e., alcohol inhibits excitation and can lead to ataxia [shaky and unsteady movements related to posture and coordination] and impair learning), activate γ-aminobutyric acid (GABA; leading to sedation, relaxation), induce endogenous opioid release (indirectly affecting dopamine release; leading to pleasure, reward), facilitate anandamide release (also indirectly affecting dopamine release), interfere with serotonin release (disrupting rapid eye movement [REM] sleep, perhaps), and augment adenosine (a neuromodulator; leading to sedation).

Other depressants include alcohol-like barbiturates (e.g., Seconal, Nembutal), methaqualone (dopers, Quaaludes), sedative-hypnotics (e.g., Placydil, Doriden), and minor tranquilizers (e.g., Valium, Librium, Tranxene, Rohypnol [the latter known as "roofies" sometimes used as a "date-rape" drug]). Effects vary but can last 8 to 12 hours. These drugs have complex mechanisms of action, but several do inhibit glutamate receptors and augment or are agonists of GABA neurotransmission (Julien, 2005).

There are also sedative-hypnotic look-alike drugs, which generally contain 25 to 50 mg of the antihistamine doxylamine succinate, which is found in Formula 44 and Nyquil and at high dosages may provide antiadrenergic, antimuscaric, and antiserotonergic effects (which can result in sedation and impaired learning and disrupt dream-type sleep). Also contained in these types of products are antitussives (cough suppressants), especially dextromethorphan HBr (DXM), which at high doses acts as a dissociative analgesic and central nervous system depressant. Several of these products also contain alcohol (10%). Thus, these over-the-counter drug cocktails may serve multiple functions and are abused by teens.

Among youth, DXM is one of the most abused ingredients in over-the-counter medications. DXM is found mostly in cough suppressants, especially those medications such as Robitussin, Coricidin Cough & Cold, and Contac. At the recommended dosage, DXM is relatively safe but in higher amounts, DXM acts like PCP and is dangerous. DXM is a semisynthetic narcotic, classified as a dissociative anesthetic (with sensations of floating), similar to PCP and ketamine. Recreational use of DXM is referred to as *robo-tripping* and *robo-dosing*, and users of DXM are sometimes referred to as *syrup heads*. DXM is also referred to as robo, tussin, skittles, triple C, vitamin D, or dex. The addiction potential of this drug is not yet known due to a lack of research, but there have been numerous reports from emergency rooms of DXM-related overdoses and crises.

PCP

PCP was originally developed in 1956 as a human surgical anesthetic, and then as an animal anesthetic and tranquilizer, but is no longer used as such (since 1979). PCP can be smoked or taken orally, and intoxication involves intense analgesia, delirium, stimulant and depressant actions, staggering gait, slurred speech, and vertical nystagmus, and it can produce catatonia and paranoia, flushing, coma, violent behavior, and memory loss effects. Some researchers label PCP as a hallucinogen rather than a depressant because of its mixed actions (Winger, Hofmann, & Woods, 1992). PCP, like ketamine (described later), is an antagonist of one type of glutamate receptor (NMDA).

Inhalants

There are four main groups of inhalants: solvents (e.g., glue, typewriter correction fluid, gasoline, and antifreeze), aerosols (e.g., spray paint and cooking spray), amyl and butyl nitrite (e.g., Rush, Locker Room; room deodorizers), and anesthetics (e.g., nitrous oxide, "laughing gas"; used as a propellant/food additive). Glass vials of amyl nitrite make a distinctive noise when crushed – hence the term "poppers." There are about twenty-three chemicals involved in inhalant abuse. Inhalants are well-known causes of kidney, brain, and liver damage. One of the most preferred inhalants is toluene, which is a solvent used in such adhesives as airplane glue, such aerosols as spray paint, and such commercial solvents as paint thinner. Its long-term use destroys functioning of the cerebellum. Toluene activates the mesolimbic dopaminergic system, as do some other inhalants, but the nitrites mainly act through muscle relaxant effects (Julien, 2005).

Inhalants are cheap, available, inconspicuous, fast acting, and tend to involve few legal hassles. Use is through huffing, fluting, or bagging (through mouth, nose, or nose and mouth). An inhalant high lasts 5 to 15 minutes. Inhalant intoxication includes euphoria, headaches, dizziness, nausea, and fainting.

Stimulants

Stimulants are taken orally, smoked, sniffed, or injected. They include cocaine (such as freebase and *crack*), amphetamines (e.g., Dexedrine and Benzedrine), methamphetamine (methedrine; *speed, crystal meth, ice, crank*), 3,4-methylenedioxymethamphetamine (MDMA; ecstasy), nicotine, caffeine, and amphetamine-like products (Preludin or Ritalin [methylphenidate]). Stimulants speed up the central nervous system for as long as 2 to 4 hours on a single dose. Intoxication generally includes euphoria, fatigue reduction, a "sense" of mental acuity, energy, emotional lability, restlessness, decreased appetite, and hypervigilance and can include irritability and paranoia. Cocaine, despite its different chemical structure, operates in the same way as other stimulants. Cocaine is still recognized as a legitimate local anesthetic, but for no other purpose. Cocaine is used recreationally in coca leaves, as a paste (mixed with tobacco; bazuco), as a powder (cocaine hydrochloride), or as free-base cocaine or crack (which removes the hydrochloride and renders cocaine smokeable).

Amphetamines remain in the blood longer than cocaine, and most have more peripheral sympathomimetic (increased heart rate and respiration, decreased appetite; "electric") effects than cocaine. Benzedrine was synthesized in 1932 as a nonprescription inhalant for asthma sufferers. It became a means to increase alertness, and restrictions on its supply increased as of 1965. The only current primary clinical uses for stimulants are for hyperactivity and narcolepsy and perhaps for a few people as a means of weight control. However, truck drivers, students, and various night workers have used a variety of stimulants to help them stay awake and alert. During World War II, stimulants were distributed to British, American, and Japanese troops to raise morale and improve fighting ability (Pickering & Stimson, 1994). This drug category is perhaps the fastest growing category of misuse internationally.

Stimulants often enter a country through its "club scene" and then become more widely used as a means of keeping people awake while working long hours. Stimulants tend to increase or augment dopaminergic (reward, anticipation) and serotoninergic (self-administration initiation "motive," maintenance of pleasure) neurotransmission

(Julien, 2005). Cocaine and methamphetamine directly increase dopamine brain levels by facilitating dopamine release and inhibiting its reuptake (Baler & Volkow, 2006; Koob & LeMoal, 2001). In fact, methamphetamine (an amphetamine derivative and the most abused stimulant worldwide) causes a huge release of dopamine in the nucleus accumbens, and this dopamine release is greater than almost all other drugs and natural rewards.

Continued use of some stimulants can result in changes in how the brain operates and an inability to experience pleasure naturally. For example, chronic use of amphetamines (and cocaine) may result in the temporary loss of approximately 20% of dopamine receptors in the nucleus accumbens, at least for 4 months since the last exposure (Volkow et al., 2001). There is also some evidence that chronic methamphetamine use may alter dopamine transporter density in other brain structures (e.g., the striatum) for as much as 3 years following cessation of use (McCann et al., 1998). In addition, chronic cocaine and amphetamine (e.g., methamphetamine) users may experience formification hallucinations (e.g., they experience bugs in their skin that need to be scratched out; Levinthal, 2005), repetitive behaviors ("tweaking"), and bizarre delusions (e.g., personalization of objects).

Methamphetamine abuse is a growing concern in the United States, accounting for many treatment admissions and individuals serving time in prison. Although past year use was reported by only 2.5% of high school seniors in the United States in 2006, according to the Monitoring the Future Survey (Johnston, O'Malley, Bachman, & Schulenberg, 2006), a concurrent national survey of 500 county law enforcement agencies revealed that methamphetamine was their number one drug problem (www.naco.org). Also, in 2002, methamphetamine was reported as the primary drug of treatment admissions, compared to heroin and cocaine, in ten of thirteen western states and in six states in other regions of the country (http://oas.samhsa.gov/dasis.htm).

Although amphetamines have been around for some time, this derivative (methamphetamine) appeared on the scene in the United States on the West Coast in the 1980s and has since been moving eastward. Because this drug is made from ingredients that were easily procured throughout the 1980s and 1990s, and are still found in cold medicines – ephedrine and pseudoephedrine – it has been relatively easy and quick to manufacture. The key ingredients for the production of methamphetamine were manufactured at only nine major factories in the world, but drug cartels were able to contract with these factories and access large-scale supplies of ephedrine and pseudoephedrine without the factories becoming aware of their use. Attempts to inhibit the manufacturing of methamphetamine by regulating access to these ingredients have resulted in new organized networks of production and distribution. For example, when large quantities of pseudoephedrine from Mexico were stopped from entering the United States, individuals involved in methamphetamine manufacturing engaged in "smurfing" or the buying of two or three packs of pseudoephedrine at a store and then moving to another store to buy two or three packs more, and so on, until they had the quantities needed to produce the drug. Currently, it appears that the majority of the production of methamphetamine in the United States still is centered on the West Coast and Mexico, but this may change as the East Coast becomes increasingly exposed to the drug. Drug cartels operating from Mexico presently dominate the wholesale trafficking of this drug into the United States. These organized groups still have access to wholesale ephedrine sources of supply and are producing unprecedented quantities of high-purity drugs with distribution networks throughout the western United States.

Ephedrine (also known as ephedra or *ma huang*, which has been used in China for 5,000 years) is an amphetamine-like stimulant found in dietary supplements and contained in Vicks Inhaler and Sudafed. It is five times weaker than amphetamine. In 2004, the Food and Drug Administration (FDA) banned the sale of dietary supplements that contain ephedrine. For many years, supplements containing ephedrine were found to cause unreasonable risk of illness or injury. Ephedrine was linked to heart attack, stroke, and death in the absence of any other causal factors in numerous cases before it was banned. Cough suppressants containing ephedrine are also now regulated. Chemically, it is L-methamphetamine, an isomeric form of the street drug, D-methamphetamine.

Phenylpropanolamine is an antihistamine or vasoconstrictor used to decongest nasal mucosa, and a diet aid, with ephedrine-like action. Propylhexedrine is found in decongestant inhalers and may have complications like those of ephedrine. It has amphetamine-like stimulant effects but is much less potent than amphetamine.

Ecstasy, which was referred to as "Methylsafrylamin" when it was synthesized in 1912 by Merck as a precursor to another drug that was a failed attempt as a blot clotting agent (see Freudenmann, Oxler, & Bernschneider-Reif, 2006), is also referred to as *E, XTC, Adam,* and *beans.* There are numerous names for specific concoctions. Ecstasy is a ring-substituted amphetamine congener of the methoxylated amphetamines; one structural congener is MDA (methylenedioxyamphetamine). The chemical structure of MDMA is similar to that of methamphetamine (and mescaline) with a substitution of a phenyl ring with a methlene-dioxy group. It exerts an amphetamine-like reaction: the heart rate accelerates; it suppresses appetite; there may be an occurrence of tremor, tight jaws, grinding of teeth, back pain, numbness of extremities, and feeling cold, and – for some people – nausea, nystagmus, heart attacks, seizures, and possibly death. Positive reactions include enhancement of com-munication or intimacy; it generally is not an aphrodisiac, as some folklore suggests. Some people might classify MDMA as a hallucinogen because it may produce perceptual changes such as increased sensitivity to light or tactile sensation (it acts primarily on serotonergic neurotransmission), but its effects primarily are stimulation (e.g., it increases heart rate and awareness), and its effects may last 3 to 6 hours. MDMA acts primarily on serotoninergic receptors, slightly on dopamine and norepinephrine transporters, and indirectly decreases GABA neurotransmission. Chronic abuse of MDMA may produce long-term damage to serotonin-containing neurons in the brain (U.S. DHHS, 1999a). Imaging studies of the brains of those who have never used ecstasy compared to those who have indicate that ecstasy harms neurons that release and transport serotonin. This suggests that MDMA produces deficits in serotoninergic functioning, and younger brains (those under age 18) appear to be more susceptible to the neurotoxic effects of MDMA.

Caffeine is a stimulant contained in coffee and is discussed in more detail later (see "The Case of Caffeine: Is This a Safe Drug?"). Nicotine is contained in tobacco products (cigarettes, cigars, pipes, and smokeless tobacco). It activates specific nicotinic acetylcholine receptors, which then activate dopaminergic, acetylcholinergic, and glutamate neurotransmission.

Ritalin (methylphenidate) and Adderall (dextroamphetamine and amphetamine combi-nation) are examples of types of pills that are prescribed for attention deficit and hyperactiv-ity disorder (ADHD). Since 1996, informal efforts to tighten the monitoring of prescriptions for these two drugs have occurred due to some misuse of them by high school and college students to stay awake or "get high" (e.g., by being crushed and snorted; Levinthal, 2005). Now the U.S. DEA classifies Ritalin as a schedule II drug, and it has various street names (*vitamin R, R ball*, and *cramming drug*). Approximately 2% of older teens and emerging adults have reported using Ritalin recreationally in the past 30 days, 4% report annual use, and 20% report lifetime recreational use (Sussman, Pentz, Spruijt-Metz, & Miller, 2006).

There are also two stimulant plants – betel nut and khat. There are five active alkaloids in betel nut; khat's main ingredient is cathinone, which is chemically similar to that of amphetamine.

Opiates

Opiates include some twenty alkaloids that act on opioid receptors and generally are taken orally, smoked, or injected, although they can also be sniffed or inhaled. Some are derived from the opium poppy, whereas others are synthetic. Opiates include morphine, codeine, and thebaine (all of natural origin); heroin, hydrocodone, hydromorphine, and oxycodone (all semisynthetic); and meperdine, fentanyl, and pentazocine (all synthetic). Intoxication generally includes slurred speech, analgesia, slowed respiration, drowsiness, euphoria, and possibly itching. The effects of one dose may last around 3 hours. There are approximately a half million opiate addicts in the United States. Opiates augment endogenous opioid (e.g., endorphins) neurotransmission; endogenous neurotransmitter receptors are located throughout the central nervous system (CNS). Mu-opioid receptors (with subtypes mu-1 and mu-2) appear to be present in all structures in the brain and spinal cord, including the nucleus accumbens. The mu-1 receptors are involved in morphine-induced analgesia and euphoria. The morphine antagonist naloxone has a much higher affinity for the mu-opioid receptors than other opioid receptors (e.g., kappa, delta, sigma, and epsilon). Exogenous opioids may also inhibit GABA neurons via mu-opioid receptors, thus disinhibiting dopaminergic neurons and increasing dopaminergic input in the nucleus accumbens (Julien, 2005).

Hallucinogens

Hallucinogens generally are taken orally and include indole (serotonin-like) alkylamines such as LSD, DMT (*N,N*-dimethyltryptamine), and psilocybin ("magic mushrooms"; 4-phosphoryloxy-*N,N*-dimethyltryptamine), which activate serotonin receptors in the medial prefrontal cortex and anterior cingulate cortex and may disrupt processing in the pontine (dorsal) raphe; catecholamine-like phenylalkylamines such as mescaline (peyote and trimethoxy-phenethlamine) and DOM (2,5-dimethoxy-4-methylamphetamine STP), which act on norepinephrine, dopamine, and serotonin receptors and hence exert stimulant as well as hallucinatory effects; and anticholingergic antagonist psychelics (e.g., scopolamine; by blurring vision, eliciting mental confusion, and otherwise clouding brain function). There are more than 100 natural or synthetic hallucinogens. Intoxication generally includes sensory changes experienced as visual illusions and hallucinations, alteration of experience of external stimuli and thoughts, and an intermingling of senses (synesthesia) and can involve paranoia and thoughts of losing one's mind. The effects of hallucinogens may last an average of 12 hours (for LSD, a dose of approximately 100 µg). The lethal to effective dose of LSD is 300–600:1. Street substitutions include amphetamines, PCP, strychnine (strong stimulant used in rat poison), and anticholinergic hallucinogens that are rarely sold directly on the "street" (scopolamine and stropine; e.g., belladonna or deadly nightshade, jimsonweed).

Nutmeg and mace are household spices sometimes abused for their hallucinogenic properties (one to two teaspoons; Julien, 2005). They contain myristin and elemicin, which are chemically similar to mescaline. They may lead to feelings of unreality, euphoria, and visual hallucinations, but nutmeg in particular may make one vomit.

Cannabis

Cannabis (Δ^9-tetrahydrocannabinol, Δ^9-THC) generally is smoked, though it can be taken orally, and it can produce a sense of well-being and relaxation, loss of temporal awareness, and impairment of short-term memory. Cannabis also can produce anxiety, paranoia, and a sense of derealization. Effects for a single dose may last around 5 hours. The lethal to effective dose is 1,000:1, although lung damage, accidents, and short-term memory problems are documented consequences of use. Marijuana occurs in leaf and resin (hash, hash oil) forms, and a synthetic form of Δ^9-THC, marinol, which is used as an oral pill clinical adjunct for glaucoma and cancer. Activation of cannabinoid receptors (involving the endogenous neurotransmitter, anandamide, or THC) inhibits release of GABA (blocks its inhibition effects) and partially facilitates release of glutamate (excitatory effects), involving the frontal cortex, hippocampus, cerebellum, and basal ganglia, among other structures. In addition, its neurotransmission interacts with dopaminergic and opioid neurotransmitters, facilitating their transmission (Julien, 2005). Cannabis is the most prevalent illegal drug used around the world. About 40% of the U.S. population age 12 or older has tried cannabis at least once, and about 10% has tried it within the last year.

Other Drugs

There are many drugs that could be considered as additional categories of use. One might call these "other" categories. Perhaps these categories will become "official" by the DEA or other organizations. The anabolic-androgenic steroids are one such "other" category. Steroids are a recognized and separate category in the DEA/Coast Guard and Julien schemes, though not in the APA, ICD-10, or Sussman and Ames schemes. Approximately 18 different steroid products exert their effects by overwhelming the hypothalamic-pituitary hormonal system, creating abnormally high testosterone hormone levels that lead to such peripheral effects as nonnatural building of muscle mass. Steroids also can cause mood swings, depression, irritability, and aggressiveness. These drugs generally are taken orally, but they also may be injected intramuscularly. These drugs may be useful in recovery from trauma. There are, however, numerous negative consequences of use, including high blood pressure, potential heart attacks, liver tumors, transient infertility, tendon degeneration, acne, and severe mood swings. Between 4% and 11% of teen males and 1% to 3% of teen females in the United States had tried steroids in the mid-1990s. In 2004, 1.8% of 19- to 30-year-olds reported trying steroids; the highest rate of annual use of steroids was among 19- to 20-year-olds at 0.8% (Johnston, O'Malley, Bachman, & Schulenburg, 2005).

Also among the "other" drug types, there are different types of drugs that have become popular in public circles, and are referred to as "designer drugs." Some of these drugs may have been newly synthesized, but probably most drugs referred to as designer drugs have been around for a while, have received renewed popularity, and may or may not have become associated with one of the previously presented established drug use classification categories. For example, GHB (γ-hydroxybutyrate; also called *liquid X, G*, or *Georgia home boy*) is a drug that was synthesized in 1960 for use as an anesthetic and at present is considered a treatment option for narcolepsy. GHB acts on the dopaminergic system by stimulating dopamine production and by preventing release at the synapse. It comes in a powder or liquid form, generally is taken orally (1.5 to 3 g powder), and it provides alcohol-like central nervous system depressant effects lasting up to 4 hours, including sedation, subjective relaxation, and possibly increased gregarious behavior. It also has growth hormone-releasing effects. It may produce psychotic symptoms, coma, and seizures, and is a recent nightclub "date rape" drug (www.clubdrugs.org). It can be lethal when mixed with other depressants, and "homemade" forms tend to be mixed with trace poisons (e.g., heavy metals, lye, and "industrial" solvents).

As another example, ketamine (special K) is an anesthetic that has been approved for human use since 1970. It is produced in liquid form or as a white powder that is injected, snorted, or smoked with marijuana or tobacco. At high doses it can produce dreamlike states, hallucinations, delirium, impaired motor function, depression, and potentially fatal respiratory problems (NIDA, 1999a). Effects last about 1 hour. The U.S. DEA currently anticipates future synthetic drugs of abuse (Cooper, 2000; http://designer-drug.com/synth/index.html), including derivatives of LSD, tryptamines, phenylakylamines (e.g., mescaline), PCP, stimulants, sedatives-depressants, and analgesics.

The Case of Caffeine: Is This a Safe Drug?

Caffeine is a drug that is loosely regulated. The general consensus has been that caffeine has only minor negative consequences on health, and therefore, there are no governmental restrictions on its use. The fatal dose for caffeine consumption is approximately 80 to 100 cups of coffee in rapid succession or an intake of about 100 NoDoz pills. This is a difficult dosage to swallow, and in general, there are fewer than ten caffeine fatalities per year in the United States. However, caffeine use can induce withdrawal symptoms for most caffeine users with as little intake as 100 mg of caffeine per day (i.e., about one cup of coffee). The DSM-IV-TR (APA, 2000) includes caffeine-induced disorders and caffeine withdrawal among its nomenclature.

The average daily intake of caffeine in the United States is approximately 200 mg (APA, 2000). This includes approximately 400 mg/day among coffee drinkers and approximately 100 mg/day among non-coffee drinkers (who intake caffeine through other products; Fredholm et al., 1999). Caffeine is consumed in a number of different substances. For example, a 5-oz cup of coffee contains 60–150 mg of caffeine (instant coffee contains less caffeine than brewed), the same quantity of tea contains 40–80 mg, and hot cocoa contains 5–8 mg. An 8.3-oz can of Red Bull contains 80 mg. Regarding pills, one Dexatrim contains 200 mg, one NoDoz contains 100 mg, one Excedrin contains 65 mg, and one Anacin contains 32 mg of caffeine. Caffeine is also found in several non-cola soft drinks (e.g., Mountain Dew contains 55 mg/12 oz). In addition, chocolate contains caffeine. For example, milk chocolate contains 1–15 mg/1 oz, dark chocolate contains 5–35 mg/1 oz, and a 225-ml container of chocolate milk contains 2–7 mg. A can of Jolt cola contains 71 mg, whereas a can of Coca-Cola contains 45 mg.

Caffeine is a mild stimulant and diuretic (i.e., it increases urine production). It also reduces fine motor coordination, constricts blood vessels, and relaxes air passages. Caffeine is an adenosine A1 and A2A receptor antagonist in that it blocks access of adenosine to its receptors. Adenosine is a neuromodulator that influences a slowing down of nerve cell activity and is important for deep sleep. By inhibiting adenosine, norepinephrine firing tends to increase (e.g., in the locus ceruleus, where most of its cell bodies are located, producing alertness). Caffeine also increases serotonin turnover. Caffeine does not markedly increase the release of dopamine, and it does not increase activation of D1 dopaminergic receptors in the nucleus accumbens, as do most other drugs of abuse. It enhances motor effects of D1 receptor agonists; its effect on the nucleus accumbens is in a decrease in receptor cell activity. It increases postsynaptic transmission of D2 receptors in the prefrontal cortex but may not markedly replace the functions of endogenous ligands or atrophy their production.

It is presently unclear what impact caffeine consumption has on health. Some sources suggest beneficial health effects, whereas others suggest negative health consequences of caffeine use. These are summarized briefly as follows.

1. Caffeine delays the onset of sleep for occasional users. However, there is no evidence that quitting caffeine use improves sleep, and it has a relatively minor effect on sleep onset among relatively heavier drinkers.

2. Caffeine at lower doses (20–200 mg) is associated with positive subjective effects, including alertness, energy, and enhanced concentration and motivation. At higher doses, subjective effects may also include nervousness, anxiety, restlessness, and tension.

3. High doses of caffeine can induce a state of anxiety, but most people adjust their dose to minimize experienced anxiety. For individuals who suffer from anxiety disorders, it is possible that higher doses of caffeine could make them feel worse (APA, 2000).

4. Moderate doses of caffeine may improve behavioral routine and speed, but could interfere with the ability to incorporate new information.

5. Caffeine might have analgesic properties that assist in alleviating headache pain, and its bronchial relaxation effects might assist in the relief of asthma.

6. Higher levels of caffeine use have been found to be linked to a lower incidence of Parkinson disease. However, as with studies on its negative effects (e.g., on bone loss in women), replication studies that control for numerous confounders may dampen the importance of this finding.

7. Caffeine may slightly reduce appetite.

8. Caffeine does not appear to affect the course of normal labor and delivery, though there have been a few studies showing that high intake (e.g., seven cups of coffee a day or more) is associated with slightly elevated risk of either stillbirth or infant deaths.

9. Irritable bowel syndrome, acid reflux, bladder irritation, and abdominal pain may be worsened by caffeine intake due to its acidity.

10. Children who consume caffeine at higher doses are at relatively high risk for other drug use when they reach adolescence (Collins, Graham, Rousculp, & Hansen, 1997). Possibly, children who use caffeine to moderate their alertness may begin to associate use of a drug with desired psychological changes, which may then lead to use of other drugs to induce other psychological changes.

11. The DSM-IV defines caffeine intoxication as being recent consumption of caffeine, usually in excess of 250 mg (two to three cups of brewed coffee) that results in five or more symptoms, including restlessness, nervousness, excitement, insomnia, flushed face, diuresis, gastrointestinal disturbance, muscle twitching, rambling flow of thought and speech, tachycardia or cardiac arrhythmia, periods of inexhaustibility, ringing in the ears, or psychomotor agitation. Caffeine intoxication, however, rarely occurs (Fredholm et al., 1999).

12. Caffeine can be addictive. Withdrawal symptoms generally begin 12 to 24 hours after sudden cessation of caffeine consumption and reach a peak after 20 to 48 hours, for

most people lasting only a couple of days but for others lasting as long as a week. These symptoms include a moderately unpleasant headache, weakness, drowsiness, anxiety, nausea, and increased muscle tension.

13. Caffeine causes tachycardia, palpitations, a rise in systolic and diastolic blood pressure that may or may not pose a health threat (1–8 mm Hg rise), and a small decrease in heart rate. Partial tolerance to the effects of caffeine on blood pressure and heart rate usually develops in a couple of days. Although caffeine consumption has been implicated as a possible risk factor for myocardial infarction, the data support is equivocal, especially after controlling for confounders such as cigarette smoking.

14. Two components of coffee – cafestol and kahweol – can raise plasma cholesterol. These components are removed when coffee is prepared by filtration, percolation, or prepared as an instant form. Boiled and Turkish coffee, and to some extent espresso and mocha coffee, do contain these substances and can raise cholesterol slightly (0.1 to 0.5 mmol/L) during prolonged use. Combining coffee drinking with cigarette smoking may raise plasma homocysteine, which also is predictive of cardiovascular disease.

15. Concerns that caffeine consumption may be carcinogenic have largely vanished.

Recent research generally does not support most claims that caffeine use is dangerous. However, researchers are continuing to evaluate the effects of caffeine on health, both positive and negative, and its effects will be better understood in the years to come (Fredholm et al., 1999). In the meantime, some physicians may request that their patients suffering from cardiovascular-related diseases reduce or stop caffeine use and request that pregnant women, patients with digestive system problems related to excess acidity, and individuals with anxiety disorder not use caffeine. Some clinicians treating addicts may suggest that their patients not use caffeine or other substances that may exert psychological effects or withdrawal symptoms. Children should avoid caffeine intake until they develop the ability to effectively understand and differentiate safe from dangerous substance use.

The Strange Case of Tobacco

Tobacco was grown for centuries in the Americas and was acquired by Europeans at the time of Columbus's voyages (Levinthal, 2005). Tobacco use became quite popular in Europe in the 1600s. It was alternatively touted for its medicinal qualities for preventing various illnesses and curing cancer (e.g., by Jean Nicot, the French ambassador to Lisbon, in 1556), and decried as a noxious drug that was dangerous to the heart and lungs (e.g., by Dr. William Vaughn in 1617 and by Dr. Tobias Venner of Bathe in 1650; see Sussman, 1999).

The invention of the cigarette-rolling machine occurred in Virginia in the 1880s, and during World War I these prerolled cigarettes became popular among soldiers. Tobacco use popularity steadily rose. Scientific research on the consequences of tobacco use started to accumulate in the 1950s (Sussman, 1999). Since the 1964 report to the Surgeon General on the health consequences of smoking, the public health community has played a key role in focusing efforts to reduce the continuing toll of tobacco use by discouraging smoking initiation and promoting smoking cessation.

Nearly one-quarter of adults throughout the world – an estimated 2 billion people – continue to smoke cigarettes. If current trends continue, 8.4 million smokers are estimated to die annually of smoking-related deaths by the year 2020. Tobacco use remains the most major preventable behavioral cause of death and disease in the United States. Despite the adverse health outcomes and enormous costs associated with smoking (e.g., lung cancer, heart disease, and chronic obstructive lung disease), approximately 3 million children and adolescents begin smoking each day. At least 70% of these young smokers want to quit smoking but only approximately 5% succeed. Even smoking as few as one to four cigarettes per day leads to approximately a 50% increase in overall prevalence of disease, including approximately a 400% and 275% increase in prevalence of lung cancer and ischemic heart disease, respectively (a pack a day or more leads to a 300% increase in overall prevalence of disease and 3,000% and 400% regarding lung cancer and ischemic heart disease; Bjartveit & Tverdal, 2005).

How is it that the most hazardous substance is legal while relatively less hazardous substances are not legal? It is possible that gross alterations in behavior, even under controlled contexts, are frightening to many people in Western cultures. Because cigarette smoking does not produce gross alterations in behavior, it may be considered socially "safe." Other substances that are associated with far fewer consequences such as LSD are illegal because they do produce gross alterations in behavior or behavioral restraint (Levinthal, 2005). However, alcohol use produces gross alterations in behavior and yet it is legal (at least since the end of prohibition). Powerful historically based forces have lobbied to keep cigarette smoking and alcohol use legal. Large social climate-based "movements" may influence perceived safety and availability of different drugs and, thereby, influence drug use prevalence (Johnston, O'Malley, Bachman, & Schulenberg, 2005). Worldwide changes in the perception and control of tobacco use is now occurring through signing and ratifying the Framework Convention on Tobacco Control (FCTC) treaty, as discussed in Chapter 10.

Drug Use in Ancient Times

The use of drugs for various reasons is documented in the archives of ancient history (Julien, 1998; Levinthal, 2005; Saah, 2005). Opium was known for its pain-relieving effects from the time of the Sumerians (4000 B.C.) and the Egyptians (2000 B.C.; Rehman, 2001). An opium pipe was excavated in Cyprus, for example, dating back to about 1200 B.C. (Levinthal, 2005). Opium was used in Roman medicine, and in the Middle Ages, opium, wine, and spices were mixed together to create laudanum (developed by a Swiss physician, Paracelsus, in 1520). Various forms of laudanum were used over the next 400 years. In 1680, the well-respected English physician Thomas Sydenham wrote about the efficacious pain-relieving qualities of opium (Jonnes, 1996). In the United States, opium was sold in drugstores without prescription throughout the nineteenth century (Brecher, 1972). In 1898, pharmacologist Heinrich Dreser, of the Bayer company, introduced heroin to the patent medication industry (heroin was first synthesized by C. R. Adler, in 1874, in London; Jonnes, 1996) (Figure 3.2).

The chewing of coca leaves (which is about 2% "cocaine") was known to occur at least since 5000 B.C. to curb appetite, permit long hours of labor, and for euphoric effects, particularly among Andean cultures, although use of the more pure cocaine form has been in existence for only a little over 100 years (isolated by Alfred Niemann, a German chemist, in 1859; Levinthal, 2005; Peterson & Stillman, 1977; Saah, 2005). In 1884 Sigmund Freud published *Uber Cocoa* in which he noted the exhilarating and lasting euphoria experienced

Figure 3.2. Old Bayer heroin bottle, originally containing approximately 5 grams of heroin.

with the use of cocaine and recommended medical conditions for which cocaine could be used as a treatment (e.g., wasting diseases, asthma, digestive disorders, and as an aphrodisiac; Jonnes, 1996).

Marijuana apparently was used as a pain medicine in the ancient Middle East, and the Chinese used cannabis medicinally as early as 2727 B.C. Cannabis was also noted in the *Atharvaveda* ("Science of Charms"), a Hindu sacred text, around 1200–800 B.C. as one of five sacred plants of India, and it was used medicinally and ritually as an offering to the Hindu god Shiva. Residue of the drug was found by Israeli scientists with the skeleton of a girl who died in childbirth 1,600 years ago (www.druglibrary.org/schaffer/History/1600BC.htm). Written references to marijuana use date back 3,000 years (Walton, 1938). The ancient Greeks tended to use alcohol rather than marijuana but they traded with, and commented on, the marijuana-eating and inhaling peoples (e.g., in the writings of Herodotus; Walton, 1938). An urn containing marijuana leaves and seeds, unearthed near Berlin, Germany, is believed to date from 500 B.C. (Walton, 1938). Thus, cannabis appears to have spread through European regions at least since that time. The Spanish introduced marijuana into Chile approximately 500 years ago (Bouquet, 1951). Between 1850 and 1937, marijuana was widely used in American medical practice for a wide range of conditions, particularly as extract of hemp (e.g., for pain relief and asthma by Parke-Davis and Squibb [now Bristol-Myers Squibb] pharmaceutical companies; Sussman et al., 1996).

The first alcoholic beverage is assumed by some researchers to be fermented honey (mead), dating from at least as far back as 8,000 B.C., and distillation of alcohol to liquor (wine into brandy) began in the Middle Ages (Levinthal, 2005). Alcohol use has continued to be legal throughout most of history in most locations around the world, in part because it is very easy to manufacture in the home. Ethyl alcohol remains the most widely preferred drug.

Around the same time that mead was introduced, inhabitants of Timor and the Thailand areas commonly used betel nut, Australian aborigines and indigenous Americans used nicotine from local plants, and Africans used khat. These plants often were thought of as food sources (reduced appetite; Saah, 2005).

There is evidence of the use of mushrooms with psychedelic properties (e.g., psilocybin) in Guatemalan ceremonies 3,500 years ago. Similarly, peyote, as well as mushrooms and morning glory seeds, were used for centuries by Aztec and other Mexican Indians (Schultes, 1969, 1995, 1998). According to Schultes, the Spanish, who conquered Mexico, viewed the peyote practices as diabolical. In the United States, European Americans attempted to outlaw peyote use in the later 1800s and early 1900s while Native Americans protected its use for religious purposes. LSD was developed relatively recently by Albert Hoffmann, a Swiss chemist, in 1943. LSD was distributed to psychiatrists and psychologists to evaluate its potential for aiding the psychotherapeutic process and for treating mental disorders. In the 1960s, LSD became a "street drug" promoted by Harvard professor Timothy Leary and others for use as a means for achieving personal insight. LSD became illegal in 1966 and its use has since declined.

Inhalants were used as part of Babylonian, Egyptian, and Greek religious ceremonies (perfumes, gums, vapors). However, synthesis of most inhalants misused in current times is of relatively recent origin (Levinthal, 2005). For example, nitrous oxide was first created in 1798 by Sir Humphrey Davy. Nitrous oxide became widely popular for recreational use during the 1800s and remains a readily available propellant (e.g., for whipped cream) and drug of misuse. Ether was also introduced in the 1700s. However, most solvents were synthesized as recently as the 1950s.

Sedative-hypnotics and antianxiety drugs have a very brief history. Chloral hydrate was synthesized in 1832. Barbituric acid was first synthesized in 1864 by Adolf von Baeyer, but barbiturates were first developed in the first 30 years of the twentieth century (Levinthal, 2005). Methaqualone was developed in 1965 (and made illegal in 1984). The first antianxiety drug was developed in 1955 (meprobamate or Miltown), and the benzodiazepines were introduced in the 1960s. The antianxiety drug buspirone (BuSpar) was developed in 1986.

As discussed next, widespread instances of drug misuse are relatively difficult to find in ancient history. Saah (2005) noted that there were often a limited amount of resources in ancestral environments. As such, there was little overactivity of salient (wanting) behavior. Neurotransmitter function (particularly the mesolimbic dopaminergic system) relied on cues from the environment rather than needing to establish a built-in regulatory system of salience. In other words, drugs tended to be used as available, but were not particularly associated with wanting behavior, as basic needs from the environment were wanted and worked hard for. Arguably, repetitive use of drugs was unlikely. As resources accumulated in developing civilizations, such environmental cues may have not been as omnipresent. The potential for drug abuse increased because there was no "built in" human regulatory system (Saah, 2005).

As a counterargument, we believe that alcohol, cannabis, and opium misuse probably occurred as long as they were used. They may not have been as major a problem as they are today because in the past the demands on behavior likely were very different. Regarding most other substances of abuse, we believe that many are the result of modern technology.

Drug Abuse in Ancient Times

Ancient use of several drugs served socially desired medicinal, ritualistic, and religious functions. These drugs also were used recreationally (Julien, 1998; Levinthal, 2005; Saah, 2005). Not surprisingly, discussions of the negative effects of some drugs appear anecdotally throughout history. In *Confessions of an English Opium Eater* (de Quincey, 1822; http://www.druglibrary.org/schaffer/index.htm), initial use of opium was described as "divine enjoyment," as happiness that might be bought for a penny and carried in the waistcoat pocket. Social embarrassment while using opium (e.g., talking nonsense about politics, necessitating friends to apologize for the person with the acknowledgement that the individual was using opium) and a tendency to walk among the poor in London at night (potentially dangerous behavior) were documented – with an overall favorable attitude toward opium. However, de Quincey did note that he would die if he continued using opium (Jonnes, 1996). In 1840, the Chinese government outlawed traffic in opium, recognizing the ascendancy of opium smoking in China. However, the British compelled the Chinese to allow the opium trade, and after these "Opium Wars, the opium trade was legalized and production in China increased.

In *An Opium-Eater in America* (Blair, 1842), Blair describes multiple negative experiences he attributed to opium intake, including getting into fights, using even while continuing to suffer negative life consequences, experiencing a great increase in tolerance, suffering bad withdrawal or other physical symptoms (e.g., headaches, stomach sickness, parched throat, restlessness, sleep difficulties, and skin peeling), experiencing psychotic reactions, losing friends, and feeling a sense of depression and hopelessness.

Conversely, evidence exists that some assertions about addiction to opium are myths. Of particular importance in the United States was the myth of the "soldier's disease," whereby there were as many as 400,000 opium addicts at the end of the Civil War in 1865. Jerry Mandel (2002; http://www.druglibrary.org/SCHAFFER/history/soldis.htm) provided an analysis of the writings about soldier-addicts and found little support for the assertion in literature appearing around the time of the Civil War, even though opium was plentiful (generally used to rub on wounds with a knife). According to Mandel (2002), the origins of the myth began in writings around 1915 with little basis in fact, particularly in the work of Terry and Pellens (1928).

Recognition of opium addiction led to development of patent medications to treat it (often these formulas contained opium). In addition, in 1880, Dr. Edward C. Huse wrote about the use of cocaine for the cure of an opium habit (Jonnes, 1996). Cocaine grew in popularity during this period. In "The Nightmare of Cocaine" (Anonymous, 1929), a man from the United States wrote about the development of his addiction to cocaine while fighting in France in World War I. He reportedly substituted cocaine for alcohol use and believed that he fought much better. Subsequently, he used cocaine regularly and experienced a sustained period of his life that included rushing thoughts and haphazard traveling, lack of sleep, weight loss, tolerance and withdrawal symptoms and cravings, loss of spouse, and social isolation. Dr. William Halsted, who later had been chair of the John Hopkins University Department of Surgery, began in 1884 a lifelong struggle with cocaine that left him remote and eccentric, with occasional absences from work, after being considered very outgoing earlier in his life (Jonnes, 1996).

Both opium and cocaine were contained in numerous products back in 1900 (e.g., Bayer heroin and Coca-Cola; Levinthal, 2005). By 1900, approximately 250,000 Americans (of 75 million) were opiate addicts and 200,000 were cocaine addicts. Controlling for overlap in drug use, approximately 1 in 200 Americans (0.5%) was an opium or cocaine addict (Jonnes, 1996). (Recall that in present times, 0.3% abuse these drug types, representing a slight decrease in percentage prevalence.) In 1905, Samuel Hopkins Adams, a famous muckraker at the time, exposed the patent medication industry's use of great amounts of opium and cocaine in their medicines (Jonnes, 1996).

In 1875, the city of San Francisco, responding to press against widespread opium use in the city, passed one of the first antidrug laws in the United States. This law attempted to rid the city of the opium-smoking dens of Chinatown. Later, the Pure Food and Drug Act (1906) mandated disclosure by manufacturers of the amount of a habit-forming drug (alcohol, opium, or cocaine) in products. This act provided a warning to those who might not use medicines containing these drugs if they were fully informed. In 1911, the first International Conference on Opium, held at The Hague, attempted to control the international opium trade. In 1914, the Harrison Narcotics Tax Act was passed, restricting the sale of habit-forming drugs such as cocaine and opium. All physicians and druggists who handled cocaine and opiates needed to register with the Internal Revenue Service, the agency monitoring their activities. This act essentially restricted use of these drugs to documented medical purposes. Enforcing the act necessitated developing a specialized police force and led many users to experience cravings and seek alternative means to acquire their drug of choice, including trying to obtain prescriptions by becoming inpatients at sanitariums.

In 1919, the U.S. Supreme Court ruled that physicians did not have the right to maintain addicts on drugs (the *U.S.* v. *Doremus* case; http://supreme.justia.com/us/249/86/), and in 1922, physicians were no longer allowed to prescribe for an addict even in diminishing amounts with the intention to cure (the *U.S.* v. *Behrman* case; http://supreme.justia.com/us/258/280/case.html). In 1923, Dorothy Davenport produced one of the first antinarcotics movies, *Human Wreckage*, in memory of her husband, who died due to causes related to long-term morphine use. Thus, media attempts began to inform the public of the damage incurred by opiates. In 1930, the Federal Bureau of Narcotics was established, as well as three narcotics "farms" for treatment, due to the passage of the Porter Bill in 1929. The international illegal opium trade began just after passage of the Porter Bill and has been credited to the New York gambler Arnold Rothstein (Jonnes, 1996). Increased enforcement efforts (e.g., the Bureau of Narcotics) ensued. In 1973 the Bureau of Narcotics and Dangerous Drugs was renamed the Drug Enforcement Administration.

In "The Tale of Two Hashish-Eaters" (*1001 Arabian Nights*; http://www.druglibrary.org/ schaffer/hemp/arab1.htm), marijuana was referred to as a "hilarious herb" that was purchased often (one person spent his daily wage, after a little food, to purchase marijuana). Engaging in socially embarrassing behaviors, such as dancing naked in public while under the influence of marijuana, were noted. In 1857, Ludlow described his experiences with marijuana use. According to Ludlow (1857), his experiences included battles with dependence on marijuana, particularly a preoccupation with marijuana use that replaced the persuit of all other types of excitement, continuous intoxication, attempts to quit and relapsing, craving, depression, abnormal dreaming (including dreaming like he was intoxicated), and seeking the care of a physician to try to quit marijuana use. The Marijuana Tax Act was passed in 1937 and served to tax growers, sellers, or buyers of marijuana products. However, severe penalties were installed for violations (e.g., 5 years in prison or a $2,000 fine). By 1937, marijuana was illegal in 46 states, and in the 1950s, federal penalties for its possession increased.

Alcohol misuse and abuse has been noted throughout written history; for example, in writings of Herodotus (450 B.C.); in records from Pompeii (70 A.D.); in the proclamations of Domitian (80 A.D.) against widespread drunkenness in Rome; in the works of

Figure 3.3. Federal agents destroying barrels of alcohol in the United States during the prohibition era.

Shakespeare, such as in his descriptions of Sir John Falstaff (1600); in the passage of the "Gin Act" in England in 1736; and in a description of the behavior of pirates in Robert Louis Stephenson's book *Treasure Island* (1882); among many, many others (Warner, 1992). On February 22, 1842, Abraham Lincoln gave a "Temperance Address" before the Springfield, Illinois, Washington Temperance Society (the "Washingtonians"). In this address, he discussed the negative effects of intemperance and becoming a "redeemed specimen of long lost humanity." He attributed much vice, misery, and crime to abuse of alcohol but also supported kind treatment of those who had fallen victim to alcohol addiction. In fact, he attributed a relatively high percentage of victims of alcoholism as having shown signs of brilliance and capacity for generosity.

The Woman's Christian Temperance Union (WCTU) was formed in 1874, and the Anti-Saloon League was formed in 1893, eventually leading to increasingly negative attitudes towards alcohol use (http://prohibition.osu.edu). Thwing (1888), in the *Quarterly Journal of Inebriety*, described the United States as a breeding ground for alcoholism, due to the feverish rush of life (e.g., intense competition in education and business lives, advanced technology, emphasis on urbanization) developed in the United States (Figure 3.3).

In 1918, the 18th Amendment of the U.S. Constitution was passed, which outlawed the manufacture, transportation, and sale of alcoholic beverages (other than as prescribed as a medication by a physician using specific forms). States ratified the amendment a year later, and alcohol marketing became illegal in the United States until 1935, when the 21st Amendment repealed the 18th Amendment. Interestingly, overall ethanol use decreased from an average of about 2 gallons of ethanol per year among persons of drinking age (1850–1919) to about 1 gallon (in 1934). In 1942, use was back up to 2 gallons and in 1969 and thereafter increased to an average of 2.5 gallons (Doernberg & Stinson, 1985).

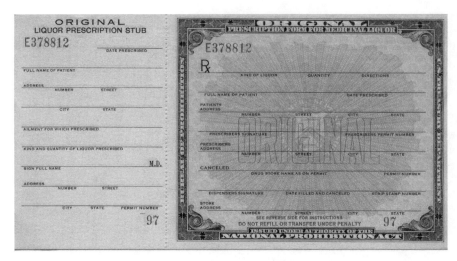

Figure 3.4. An alcohol prescription form from the 1920s used to acquire prescription alcohol, usually whiskey, for medicinal purposes.

Deaths from alcoholism decreased from an average of around 5 per 100,000 before prohibition to 3 per 100,000 during prohibition, although rates were increasing closer to preprohibition levels by the end of prohibition. Arrests for drunken behavior and crime increased dramatically during prohibition. For example, in 1919 and 1920 total arrests for intoxication-related behavior in Philadelphia decreased below preprohibition levels (from around 40,000 per year to around 20,000 per year) but by 1925 increased to almost 60,000 (www.druglibrary.org/prohibitionresults.htm) (Figure 3.4).

With the ending of Prohibition, the Federal Bureau of Narcotics (formed in 1930) turned its attention to marijuana. As mentioned, by 1937 most states banned the drug and then it was declared a narcotic by federal law (Marijuana Tax Act of 1937, the Boggs Act of 1951, and Narcotic Control Act of 1956; Sussman et al., 1996).

Opium dens, hashish houses, and alcohol saloons operated for a couple hundred years in Europe and the United States. (Alcohol saloons certainly operated in ancient Rome, as well.) Use of these drugs in private or public environments was associated with relatively high levels of use and sometimes with other illegal activity (e.g., gambling and prostitution). Public opinion toward environments dedicated to drug use tended to be particularly negative (Kane, 1883; Walton, 1938). To this day, bars and inns that serve alcohol are prevalent worldwide (Figure 3.5).

Current Costs of Drug Abuse

In the United States, the overall cost of drug abuse to society (i.e., of illegal drugs, not including tobacco, alcohol, or prescription drugs) was estimated to be $143.4 billion in 1998 (Office of National Drug Control Policy, 2001). The cost was estimated to have increased at 5.9% per year from 1992 to 1998. In 1998, 69% of the costs were estimated to be due to loss of productivity, 9% to loss of health, and 22% to "other" reasons. An analysis of these categories is revealing. A total of 55.6% of productivity costs are due to incarceration and crime careers. The remainder of the costs is related to premature death (11% of total

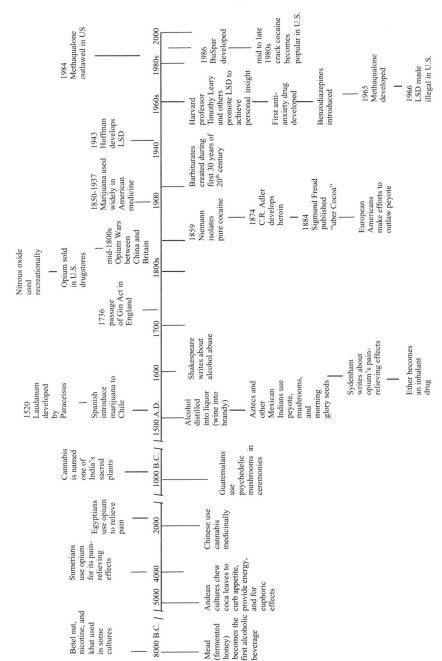

Figure 3-5. Historical timeline of various substances from use in ancient times to developments in the present.

costs), drug abuse-related illness, hospitalization, and productivity-employment loss. Loss of health subcategories include community-based treatment, federally provided specialty treatment ($21 million being provided in prisons), prevention and treatment research and training, and medical consequences treatment. "Other" costs are all crime-related costs and include police protection, legal adjudication, departments of correction services, supply reduction approaches (interdiction), legal defense, and property damage. In other words, 60% of drug abuse-related costs are due to law enforcement efforts and the illegal status of drugs.

A recent Surgeon General's report indicated that total costs of tobacco use (cigarette smoking) are approximately $157.7 billion per year. Direct treatment of tobacco use in the United States costs approximately $75.5 billion annually, the annual loss of productivity from smoking is approximately $81.9 billion, and neonatal costs are approximately 366 million (U.S. DHHS, 2004). Thus, the total costs from cigarette smoking are as much as the total costs of all illegal drugs combined. Likewise, a recent National Institute on Alcohol Abuse and Alcoholism (NIAAA) report (Harwood, 2000) indicated that the total costs of alcohol use were $184.6 billion in 1998, including $29 million in medical or treatment costs, $36.5 million in lost productivity due to premature death, $86 million of lost earnings due to alcohol-related illness, and $34 million due to alcohol-related crimes.

Another econometrics study conducted in Australia provided analyses of separate categories of drugs (e.g., tobacco, alcohol, and illegal drug costs) and the associated social costs, which were divided into tangible (e.g., crime, health, productivity, accidents, and fires) and intangible costs (loss of life and pain and suffering) (Collins & Lapsley, 2002). The total social costs of drug use in Australia from 1998 to 1999 were $34.4 thousand-million dollars. Of these costs, 53% were tangible and 47% were intangible. A total of 61% were tobacco related, 22% were alcohol related, and 17% were illegal drug related. Among the tangible costs, tobacco use accounted for none of the crime costs, 79% of the health costs, 46% of productivity costs (at the workplace or at home), no road accidents, and all of the drug-related fires. Alcohol use accounted for 29% of the crime costs, 16% of the health costs, 18% of productivity costs, 82% of drug-related road accidents, and no fires. Illegal drug use accounted for most of the crime costs (71%), 5% of the health costs, 36% of the productivity costs, 18% of road accidents, and no fires. In calculating costs this study attempted to estimate lives lost and lives saved as a result of different drug use. Some positive health effects of alcohol but not other drugs were discussed (94% of benefits was light drinking among persons 60 years old or older). A total of 23% of social costs in Australia were estimated as crime related. Of the tangible crime costs, all were related to enforcement efforts.

As a summary of these data in the United States, total costs of illegal drug abuse averaged $715 per person living in the United States in 1998. Excluding crime enforcement costs, these costs were $286 per person. Including tobacco and alcohol abuse, the total costs increased to approximately $2,429 per person in 1998, and excluding crime enforcement, costs would be $1,818 per person. In Australia, total costs of drug abuse (which also included tobacco and alcohol use) averaged $1,811 per person in 1998 and $1,378 excluding crime enforcement efforts. Costs due to crime enforcement are high in both countries ($500 to $600 per year per person). Some individuals have argued that legalization might reduce costs or perhaps reduce use of some legal drugs (e.g., Robins, 1985).

Controlling for enforcement efforts, there are many specific costs of drug abuse that add up to a total of $1,400 to $1,800 per person annually. For practically all recreational drugs, abuse of them is associated with the production of psychotic symptoms (e.g., paranoid ideation) and injury (accidents, violence, overdoses). Often, purchasing and time spent using drugs cause financial problems. Several drug categories cause cardiovascular, respiratory, digestive, or excretory dysfunction, or problems in cognitive function (Sussman & Ames, 2001). One recent study found that within 32 years of treatment, 49% of a large convenience sample of heroin addicts had died (on average, prior to 60 years of age) and that 28% had died within 20 years of treatment (Hser, Hoffman, Grella, & Anglin, 2001). Likewise, considered across studies with varying size samples of alcoholics, approximately 20% die by a 10-year follow-up (John & Hanke, 2002). Using national mortality data on alcohol risk drinking in Germany, the median age of death in alcohol attributable mortality was found to be 15 and 24 years below the median age of death among the general male and female population, respectively; age of death among alcoholics appears highest in the age range from 35 to 64 years (see John & Hanke, 2002).

Summary

It is useful to distinguish classes of drugs for clinical diagnostic utility; the classifications help clinicians in making medical and psychological treatment recommendations and plans. For example, the DSM-IV addresses differences in drugs' potential for dependence, abuse, intoxication, withdrawal, and psychotic and mood effects. Knowing the behavioral effects of the pharmacological action of classes of drugs helps in understanding cognitive and affective distortions and other observable behavioral consequences of abuse (Sussman & Ames, 2001). Some drugs are very likely to have lethal consequences, whereas others are not; some produce recognizable withdrawal symptoms, whereas others do not; some substances have greater addiction potential, whereas others do not seem to produce compulsive drug use behavior. But, despite distinctions in the classes of drugs, all of the substances addressed in this chapter can be abused and can lead to substance abuse-related disorders.

This chapter also provides a historical perspective of various drugs of abuse. In summary, drugs such as opium, cocaine, marijuana, alcohol, and some hallucinogens have been used for centuries, generally as medicines or for religious ceremonies. However, occasional reports of drug abuse or addiction appeared in the popular literature. The types of reported symptoms included dangerous behaviors while under the influence, illegal behaviors, social consequences, not being able to fulfill one's life roles, preoccupation with drug use, cravings and withdrawal symptoms, and exclusion of other activities. These symptoms are consistent with modern definitions of substance abuse and dependence disorders (APA, 2000). The actual prevalence of substance abuse and dependence in ancient times is not clear, although it would appear to be low, based on what has been written (other than writings about alcohol abuse that appeared to be prevalent throughout recorded history, e.g., in Pompeii). However, one could speculate that the percentage of drug abusers in ancient times was similar to the percentage of drug abusers today (Goode, 2005), but that drug abuse was just more tolerated by ancient societies than by modern ones.

Substance abuse and dependence disorders cross all ages, gender, ethnicities, and educational and socioeconomic status, leaving virtually no group unaffected. Substance use can result in a variety of negative physical, psychological, and social health effects to an individual, and its effects can be acute (resulting from a single dose or a series of doses) or chronic (resulting from long-term use; Sussman & Ames, 2001). Moreover, the high costs to society that result from substance abuse and dependence disorders are notable.

ETIOLOGY

4   Current Multivariable Models

Let us assume there is agreement on what the constituents of problem drug use are. The previous chapters suggest that although there is some variation in what might encompass problem drug use, there is some consensus that negative consequences to the individual or to society as a function of drug intake characterize problem drug use. Certainly, drug misuse is a multifactorial biopsychosocial problem; that is, the pathways to problem drug use are complex and cannot be explained by simple cause-and-effect models. Researchers have provided evidence for numerous predictors of drug use and misuse. Some predictors are within the individual (e.g., genetics, brain systems and structures, and cognitive processes), which one might label as biological or psychological in focus, and some predictors occur in the individual's environment. These latter social and physical environment-type processes may occur in small social groupings and interactions, or they might encompass a large social and physical environmental climate and entail such variables as drug distribution routes and defensible space. Increasingly, researchers have moved toward more "complex, dynamic, multidimensional, level/phase structured, nonlinear, and bounded (culture, time, place, age, gender, ethnicity etc)" underpinnings of substance use behavior (Lessov et al., 2004, p. 1519). Consequently, several different integrated substantive models of substance abuse have been developed.

This chapter presents examples of current multivariable etiologic models of drug abuse. Subsequent chapters explore more deeply the components of these models and, as a result, may help the reader discern for him- or herself the adequacy of the current multivariable models.

Risk and Protective Factors

One relatively simple means of integrating a variety of influences on drug abuse has been to add single concepts or predictors together. This is referred to as a "risk and protective factors" approach to the etiology of drug abuse. Risk factors for drug abuse are those diverse factors that contribute to the initiation and continuation of drug use. Biologically based susceptibility, impulsiveness, relatively young age at onset of drug use, perception of low risk of engaging in problem behaviors, chaotic home environments, ineffective parenting, lack of attachment to parents, failure in school, poor social and coping skills, aggression, negative peer influence, and poverty – among other predictors – all contribute to the later

The Two Paths

What Will The Boy Become?

AT 15
STUDY & CLEANLINESS

AT 15
CIGARETTES & SELF-ABUSE

AT 25
PURITY & ECONOMY

AT 25
IMPURITY & DISSIPATION

AT 36
HONORABLE SUCCESS

AT 36
VICE & DEGENERACY

AT 60
VENERABLE OLD AGE

AT 48
MORAL-PHYSICAL WRECK

Figure 4.1. Early illustration of two potential paths one could choose through the lifespan; that is, whether or not to engage in risky behaviors such as drug use.

development of drug abuse. Some risk factors are less amenable to change (e.g., genetics) than others (e.g., negative peer social influence and unstructured time) (Figure 4.1).

Alternatively, protective factors are those characteristics that reduce the risk of substance abuse and promote positive development. Cooperativeness, social competence, attachment to parents, family supervision, having conventional friends, placing an importance on high achievement in school, neighborhood cohesiveness, and lack of drug availability are among factors that have been found to be protective against drug use (Bry, McKeon, & Pandina, 1982; Hawkins, Catalano, & Miller, 1992; Johnson & Pandina, 2001; Smith, Lizotte, Thornberry, & Krohn, 1995; Sussman & Ames, 2001).

Risk and protective factors show cumulative effects on the prediction of drug use and abuse. One can combine these factors additively. The more risk factors individuals have, and the fewer protective factors individuals have, the more likely it is that they will use and abuse drugs in the future (Bry, McKeon, & Pandina, 1982). Different factors, however, may vary in importance for different groups or stages of use (Johnson & Pandina, 2001). Depending on the outcome of interest, these factors may differ in (1) the manner in which they affect outcomes (direct or indirect effects), (2) their strength of impact (low, medium, or high), and (3) their stability (relatively stable or dynamic condition). These factors also appear to form a rough qualitative continuum. They range from simple markers (i.e., surface indicators including gender and race) to moderators (e.g., augmenting influences, such as the presence of a co-occurring disease or disorder) to mediators (primary causal mechanisms, such as exposure to drug use) of dysfunctional outcomes (Johnson & Pandina, 2001).

Biopsychosocial Models

A second approach is to carefully delineate "nonoverlapping" factors and then combine factors together. This approach has been used in different "biopsychosocial" models (Sussman & Ames, 2001). These models demonstrate the attempt to group risk factors according to biological, psychological, and social categories. Indeed, the introduction to this chapter provided a biopsychosocial model-type presentation. Individuals are differentially vulnerable to drug abuse through certain genetic mechanisms (e.g., genes that influence metabolism and genes that influence neurobiological systems), psychological factors (e.g., cognitive processes), and social groupings (e.g., small groups and cultures). This general type of model suggests the need to consider radically different sources of predictors, and it highlights the need for individuals from different disciplines to work together to better understand drug abuse. This paradigm views dysfunctional behavior as a product of neurobiological, psycho/behavioral, and socio/environmental factor arrays, as well as a product of the complex and dynamic interactions of these factors (Johnson & Pandina, 2001). A biopsychosocial approach aids in placing different sets of predictors or influences into different categories and is a heuristic method (i.e., provides some order and suggests useful hypotheses).

Problem Behavior Theory

Problem Behavior Theory (PBT) is a comprehensive psychosocial framework developed by Jessor and Jessor (1977) to explain adolescent behaviors that violate social and legal norms of society. Jessor and Jessor suggest that among many teens there is a general propensity to behave in deviant ways. PBT proposes that problem (deviant) behaviors satisfy psychosocial functions for adolescents. These functions include the following: (1) a display of opposition to the norms and values of conventional society, (2) coping mechanisms for frustration, failure, and feelings of inadequacy; (3) demonstration of unity with one's peer group; (4) an affirmation of personal identity (e.g., being bad); (5) a symbol of transition to adult status; and (6) an assertion of holding nonconventional values (Jessor, 1984, 1987).

Involvement in problem behaviors is a function of "problem proneness," which is determined (for the most part) by an interaction of personality (e.g., alienation and rebelliousness), behavioral (e.g., going to parties or to church), and perceived environmental systems (e.g., social approval and social support regarding drug use or non-drug use). These systems are composed of elements that help to control (inhibit) or instigate (promote) risk behaviors (Jessor, 1987; Jessor & Jessor, 1977; Newcomb & Earleywine, 1996). Each system is intended to be predictive of a variety of problem behaviors.

Personality System

The personality system consists of three structures. First, there is a motivational/instigation structure that focuses on an individual's motivation toward goals (e.g., independence, health values, and academic achievement). Second, there is a personal belief structure that encompasses beliefs about oneself (e.g., self-esteem and depression) and society and reflects "rejection or repudiation of society or of a sense of isolation or separation from its normative hold over one's behavior" (Jessor & Jessor, 1977, p. 25). Third, there is a personal control structure that encompasses attitudinal acceptance of conventional or nonconventional activities (e.g., religiosity or intolerance for deviance).

Perceived Environmental System

This system consists of distal and proximal structures that affect an individual's perception of his or her sociopsychological environment. Perceived environment explains the extent to which an individual's social environment is perceived as family – versus peer oriented. *Distal structures* are believed to be indirectly related to problem proneness and include perceived family support and peer support for, and control against, involvement in problem behaviors. For instance, if one's perceived family orientation is associated with a stronger affiliation with conventional norms, there is a reduced likelihood of participating in problem behaviors. *Proximal structures* include perceptions of peer and family approval of problem behaviors and modeling of particular behaviors (e.g., perceived prevalence of problem behaviors among peers).

Behavioral System

The behavioral system is composed of conventional (prosocial) behaviors and problem (antisocial) behaviors. Jessor and Jessor (1977) consider problem behavior to be "behavior that is socially defined as a problem, a source of concern, or as undesirable by the norms of conventional society and the institutions of adult authority" (Jessor & Jessor, 1977, p. 33). This includes such behaviors as adolescent alcohol and drug use, sexual activities, driving under the influence, and delinquent crime (Hays, Stacy, & DiMatteo, 1987; Jessor, 1984, 1987; Orpinas, Basen-Engquist, Grunbaum, & Parcel, 1995; Sussman, 2005c). According to PBT, activities with the family, or involvement in church activities, are incompatible with drug use, gambling, and other problem behaviors. And, although there is support for a general syndrome of problem behaviors, there is at least some evidence that substance abuse may load separately from some other forms of delinquency (see discussion in Sussman, 2005c).

Triadic Influence Theory

Petraitis, Flay, and Miller (1995) reviewed 14 multivariate theories of adolescent experimental drug use to derive an integrated model. Theories were grouped into cognitive-affective (e.g., reasoned action and planned behavior), social learning (e.g., social learning and social cognitive/learning), commitment and social attachment (e.g., social control and social development), intrapersonal theories (e.g., social ecology, self-derogation, multi-stage social learning, and family interaction), and relatively comprehensive theories (e.g., problem behavior, peer cluster, vulnerability, and domain).

Cognitive-Affective Theories

The cognitive-affective theories examine attitude types and valences, perceived pressures to use drugs and motivation to comply with those perceived pressures, and perceptions of others' control over one's behavior versus one's own control. In addition, one's intention to use drugs was considered as an immediate outcome of these other variables.

Social Learning Theories

The social learning theories examine the role of observation of others, imitation of others' behavior, social reinforcement for engaging in drug use behavior, and the creation and maintenance of outcome and self-efficacy expectations. Outcome expectations are the beliefs that if one engages in certain behaviors certain outcomes are likely to occur, whereas self-efficacy expectations are the beliefs that one is able to successfully engage in certain behaviors. The social learning theories place a relatively greater emphasis on observational learning characteristics as opposed to attitudinal perceptions.

Commitment and Social Attachment Theories

Commitment and social attachment theories examine lack of economic or social opportunity, disorganized neighborhoods, inappropriate socialization, inadequate social skill development, and social conflict as precursors of drug use. Commitment to institutions, attachment with significant others, and social equality are key features that protect one from drug use.

Intrapersonal Theories

Intrapersonal theories examine the impact of perceived stress, low self-esteem, inadequate coping, and deviant socialization and neglect on drug use. Essentially, clinical psychological functioning is assessed.

Comprehensive Theories

The comprehensive theories examine personal (psychological and attitudinal), perceived social environment or socialization, and activity participation structures. In addition to these three conceptual structures identified by the comprehensive theories (e.g., which includes PBT), the vulnerability and domain theories represented among the comprehensive set of theories examine relatively more closely the biological contributions to drug abuse.

Triadic Influence Theory attempts to classify the elements of these fourteen theories to three substantive domains (*interpersonal, attitudinal/cultural,* and *intrapersonal*), with differing "distances" from performance of drug use behavior (*ultimate, distal,* and *proximal*). Within the interpersonal domain, ultimate variables include home stress, distal variables include drug use role models, and proximal variables include social-related drug beliefs (e.g., perceived social approval for drug use and estimates of prevalence of drug use). Within the attitudinal/cultural domain, ultimate variables include community disorganization (community stress), distal variables include development of hedonic values or alienation, and proximal variables include expectancies regarding drug use benefits minus costs. Finally, within the intrapersonal domain, ultimate variables include biological temperament (biological stress), distal variables include low self-esteem and poor coping, and proximal variables include refusal self-efficacy and intentions to use drugs. One may interpret this theory to reflect that within three domains of one's life, which involve significant others, one's (social and physical) environment, and within one's "own skin," an individual may suffer negative experiences or stressors. These stressors may become part of one's schemas about the nature of people, social organizations, and oneself. If an individual's beliefs, expectancies, and attitudes/intentions about drug use are favorable, drug use may be inevitable.

Stage Modeling

Although not addressed in several of the previously presented theories, such as the Triadic Influence Theory, it is generally agreed that social, situational, and environmental factors are likely to be more influential in low-level or early drug use, whereas intrapersonal factors tend to predict higher levels of use (U.S. Office of Technology Assessment [OTA], 1994). An individual generally is subject to many events over a period of time before experimentation progresses to abuse (Wills, Pierce, & Evans, 1996). Obviously, not all individuals choose to experiment with drugs, and not all individuals who experiment with drug use progress to problematic use or abuse. So what reinforces the continuance of a maladaptive behavior such as drug abuse? Some individuals are more susceptible to the addictive process than others as a result of numerous risk factors, and those who are susceptible vary in the *drug* or *drugs of choice* they abuse. The fact that different predictors may operate at different points in the history of an individual's drug use suggests the operation of stages. One *can* begin to delineate stages before the person has ever tried a drug (Flay et al., 1983; Levanthal & Cleary, 1980; Sussman et al., 1995). Flay et al. (1983) developed a theory of cigarette smoking development stages that also has been applied to the use of other substances.

First Stage

In the first stage, the nonuser undergoes a preparation phase, in which socioeconomic, personality, family, and peer factors operate. Risk-takers, those of low self-esteem, and those with family and peers that use drugs or hold attitudes of tolerance for deviance are most likely to begin drug use themselves. In addition, it is possible that neurobiological factors may play a role (e.g., perhaps related to the manufacture of dopamine in the ventral tegmental area or related to emotional processing in the extended amygdala; Franz & Koob, 2005). Conversely, youth who form close attachments with their parents, whose parents are relatively well educated and well attached to each other, and who form close attachments to teachers and place an importance on school performance are relatively unlikely to think about trying drugs.

Second Stage

Peer social influence factors primarily operate in the second stage, during which the individual may try the substance. Frequency of direct peer pressure influences the likelihood of coping successfully through use of refusal assertion or other skills. The more frequent the influence attempt, the less likely such coping will be used successfully. Certainly, though, perceptions of high prevalence of drug use and peer approval of drug use are important determinants of whether one tries a drug, regardless of any actual attempts to influence one to use. Low parental monitoring leads to increased likelihood of exposure to peers who are drug users. Peer drug use offers, and curiosity about drug effects, facilitated by social informational sources (e.g., advertisements), may lead someone to desire to try drugs. Perceptions of drug availability and safety also may be important (Johnston, O'Malley, Bachman, & Schulenberg, 2005). Youth who form conventional peer attachments, whose peers and parents interact positively with each other, who are involved in religious or service activities, or who take on caretaking activities and create a pleasant home environment for themselves are relatively unlikely to try drugs.

Third Stage

During the third stage, the individual enters into an experimental phase, in which outcome expectancies (e.g., to experience pleasure or decrease perceived stress or negative affect), use habits, and physiological reinforcement are shaped. Associative memories or implicit associations regarding drug effects are also being formed (Stacy & Ames, 2001). Those adolescents who do not enjoy initial drug use experiences are not subjectively encouraged to keep trying the drug. Also, those adolescents who become involved in conventional activities (e.g., school sports) are relatively less likely to experiment with continued drug use.

Fourth and Fifth Stages

In the fourth and fifth stages, the person eventually becomes a regular adolescent user (i.e., uses regularly at least once a week) and a regular adult user (i.e., uses regularly every day, or in binge periods), and physiological reinforcement, identity as a user, automatic cognitive processing (e.g., cue-behavior-outcome memory associations), and addiction factors dominate in affecting use. Adolescents who place some importance on health as a valued asset, who are socially assertive, who use drugs at lower frequencies, and who seek out conventional or prosocial coping channels are relatively likely to quit drug use earlier than those who do not possess those same values and traits.

Forming a Behavioral Relationship with Drugs: The PACE Stage Model

The PACE stage model proposed by Sussman and Unger (2004) suggests that the development of a firm behavioral relationship with drug use is a function of four variables: *pragmatics, attraction, communication,* and *expectation* (PACE; see Sussman & Unger, 2004).

Pragmatic Variables

Pragmatic variables operate to discern whether one can acquire a drug and use it regularly. Pragmatics involves four aspects. First, there must be a supply of drugs available in the environment. If not, no relationship can develop with the drug. If a drug is available, then other aspects must be considered. One needs to be aware that there is a supply of drugs available. Advertisement for the drug must reach the potential consumer by way of any number of channels (e.g., word of mouth, observation of sales, public venues such as clubs or bars, or even viewing an early evening news story). Next, an individual must have "acquisition skills"; that is, one needs to know how to obtain the drug from the source. An individual needs to know how to form relationships with people who have the drug, how to bring up the topic without being threatening, how to make the transaction a pleasant experience, how to negotiate a price (if necessary), and how to arrange an exchange. Also, one needs to be able to make the transaction without suffering unacceptable consequences to self. (Of course, as an individual continues to use a drug, self-defined unacceptable consequences may become fewer in kind and number.) Finally, an individual needs to have a means of exchange; that is, one needs to offer money or services in exchange for the drug.

If the pragmatic variables are favorable to trial of a drug, the drug may be used. Drugs that are easier to obtain are more likely to be used; however, different individuals are willing to go to varying extremes to locate and obtain different drugs. For example, relatively "dis-balanced" individuals may hope that a drug they had heard about will make them feel good, and they may be willing to expend a great deal of effort to try to experience that effect (Sussman & Unger, 2004). Many youth are curious about the effects of different drugs (Hahn et al., 1990; Sussman et al., 1995). If the drug is in the possession of an individual who feels dis-balanced, that person might be curious about the drug's effects, possibly as a means to seek a sense of balance, and, if the opportunity arises, the person will try the drug. Situational opportunity and curiosity predict that the drug will be used.

Some drugs may be initially experienced as both pleasant and unpleasant to some people. Youth may rely on the reports of more experienced drug users or on other information that suggests that continued use (practice) will increase the overall pleasantness of a drug's effect (Glynn, Levanthal, & Hirschman, 1985). Different drugs vary in their delivery of pleasant effects (which also is a function of the potency, manner of use, and context of use of the drug), and different individuals may enjoy the effects of different drugs. For example, individuals who feel chronically depressed may enjoy a drug with stimulant effects, whereas individuals who feel chronically anxious may enjoy a drug with more relaxant effects. The differential enjoyment of different drugs may be similar to notions about using drugs as self-medication (Khantzian, 1985), although the emphasis here is on overall subjective enjoyment of the effects of the drug rather than emotional relief per se.

Attraction

The attraction of a drug may be due to the anticipated balance it may temporarily restore to an individual's affective or arousal functioning. It is not surprising that drug misusers describe their early experiences with drug use as very pleasant, comforting, restoring, or warming. (For an initially affective/arousal "balanced" person, drug use may or may not throw them out of balance and could make them feel uncomfortable.) Someone who is dis-balanced may appreciate the drug effects that may alter subjective thinking, mood, sensory perceptions, or behavior. Attraction also involves the pleasantness ascribed to the drug stimuli and the drug use context, as well as drug effects. One may feel attracted to the sight of the drug, the way it smells or tastes, the sounds made when it is used, or the way it feels to the touch. One also may enjoy the way in which the drug is packaged, how it is used, paraphernalia associated with its use, when it is used, and with whom it is used in public and private settings. As one continues to use the drug, a relationship is developing that involves acquiring, using, and recovering from the effects of the drug, and a system of communication about the drug.

Communication

Communication involves comfort of interaction about the drug while under its influence and when not under its influence. Communication involves use of drug-specific words that associate drug use with life experiences and show an understanding of the language of drug use (e.g., "4:20" is jargon that refers to marijuana use in the United States by many experienced users: the time of day to use, Earth Day, and a penal code). Interaction with other drug users becomes embedded with a commonality of terms that refer to the drug, its paraphernalia, or subjective experience. The person may self-identify with drug use-related groups or activities. Communication about the drug, therefore, can be a way of forming or solidifying social relationships with other drug users. Drug use continues indefinitely to the extent that individual expectations from the drug are met, which may occur in the context of a social network or networks of other drug users (Sussman, Pokhrel, Ashmore, & Brown, 2007).

Expectations

In the PACE model, drug expectations are beliefs that the drug is providing solutions to experiential requests. Initially, expectations formed may be related to curiosity over whether the drug can reduce the dis-balance. Eventually, several new expectations may be formed as drug use continues. In particular, one may expect that drug use will help one live life more comfortably (or with more "adventure") in the immediate present. To the extent that drug use is not also interfering with personal comfort, drug use may continue. Interference with an individual's ability to carry out social, physical, or vocational roles or "outside" interference with an individual's drug use, or subjective feelings of guilt, compete against the expected functions that the drug fulfills. However, as an individual's social activities begin to increasingly involve the drug and other drug users, it may become possible to convince oneself that the drug use does not interfere with and may even actually facilitate one's daily activities.

Distal and Proximal Factors

The concept of distal and proximal factors was introduced earlier in the discussion of theoretical models (e.g., Problem Behavior Theory and Triadic Influence Theory). *Distal factors* provide the background for potential drug use. Distal factors include those variables that increase or reduce access to or interest in other (prosocial) activities, or increase access to, or vulnerability for, drug use. *Proximal factors* are those variables that tend to operate just prior to, or during, drug use experiences. A stage model notion seems to overlap with the distal–proximal perspective. Certainly, a preparatory stage is more distal to drug use than an initiation stage, for example. These perspectives, however, are still separable because both distal and proximal factors could be placed into the same stages. For example, poverty generally is considered a distal drug use variable, whereas peer dares to use drugs generally are considered a proximal variable. Both poverty and peer dares could influence drug use initiation. Likewise, the long-time experience of poverty and proximal variables such as physiological reinforcement from drug use could influence regular drug use. Certainly, more research is needed to better integrate stages of use with distal-proximal notions (Table 4.1).

Summary

Various integrative theories of drug use and abuse were presented in this chapter, including combinations of risk and protective factors, biopsychosocial models, deductive/theoretical

Table 4.1. *Comparison of multivariable etiological models of drug use*

Model/model type	General concepts	Examples
Risk and protective factors	Adds together a variety of single concepts or influences to predict drug use. Risk factors are those that may contribute to the initiation and continuation of drug abuse. Protective factors are those that reduce the risk of substance abuse and promote positive development.	Risk factors: some known correlates of drug use are impulsiveness, chaotic home environment, failure in school, aggressive behavior, low socioeconomic status. Protective factors: some known protective factors are social competence, attachment to parents, motivation for high academic achievement, neighborhood cohesiveness.
Biopsychosocial models	Biopsychosocial models delineate "non-overlapping" factors, and then combine them together according to biological, psychological, and social categories. These models view problem behavior as a sum of these three categories of causal factors, in addition to the complex interactions among them.	Biological factors: genes that control metabolism, genes that influence neurobiological systems, neurotransmission. Psychological factors: cognitive processes, affective states. Social factors: small groups (e.g., peers), cultures, communities or neighborhoods.
Problem Behavior Theory	Suggests that deviant behaviors satisfy psychosocial functions for adolescents. Involvement in problem behaviors is a function of problem proneness, resulting from an interaction of personality, behavioral, and perceived environmental systems, which may act to inhibit or instigate risk behaviors.	Problem behavior satisfies various psychosocial functions for adolescents; for example, as a display of opposition to conventional norms and values, as a means of coping with negative feelings and experiences, as a demonstration of group unity, as an affirmation of identity, as a symbol of transition to adult status, and as a means of asserting nonconventional values. Personality system: consists of three structures: motivational/instigation, personal beliefs, and personal control. Behavioral system: composed of prosocial/conventional and antisocial/problem activity participation (e.g., church versus party participation). Perceived environmental system: consists of distal and proximal factors that affect one's perception of his or her social-psychological environment (e.g., family conflict [distal] and family modeling of drug use [proximal]).
Triadic Influence Theory	Combines the elements of 14 theories of adolescent experimental drug use (i.e., elements from cognitive-affective theories, social learning theories, commitment and social	Interpersonal domain: ultimate variables include home stress, distal variables include drug use role models, and proximal variables include social-related drug beliefs. Attitudinal/cultural domain: ultimate variables include community disorganization, distal variables include

Table 4.1. (*continued*)

Model/model type	General concepts	Examples
	attachment theories, intrapersonal theories, and comprehensive theories) into three substantive domains with different "distances" from performance of drug use behavior. Substantive domains are interpersonal, attitudinal/cultural, and intrapersonal. Three "distances" from behavior are ultimate, distal, and proximal.	development of hedonic values or alienation, and proximal variables include expectancies regarding drug use benefits minus costs. Intrapersonal domain: ultimate variables include biological temperament, distal variables include low self-esteem and poor coping, and proximal variables include refusal self-efficacy and intentions to use drugs.
Stage modeling	Because different predictors may operate at different points in the history of an individual's drug use, stage modeling suggests the operation of stages. The development of a drug use/abuse problem can be divided into several stages, even before a person has ever tried a drug.	First stage: The nonuser is in a preparation phase in which socioeconomic, personality, family, and peer factors are highly influential. Neurobiological factors may also play a role. Second stage: An individual may try a drug. The primary operative factors in this stage are those of peer social influence. Perceptions of drug availability and safety may also be influential in this stage. Third stage: An individual enters into an experimental phase. Outcome expectancies, use habits, physiological reinforcement, and implicit associations are formed and shaped during this stage. Fourth and fifth stages: The person becomes a regular user of a drug. Physiological reinforcement, identity as a drug user, automatic cognitive processing, and addiction factors play a primary role in affecting use.
PACE stage model	Suggests that the development of a firm behavioral pattern of drug use is a function of four variables: pragmatics, attraction, communication, and expectation (PACE).	Pragmatic variables operate to discern whether or not one can acquire a drug and use it regularly. Attraction to a drug may be the result of one's anticipated restoration of balance of his/her emotional or arousal functioning. It also involves the pleasantness attributed to drug stimuli, drug use context, and drug effects. Communication involves one's comfort of interaction about the drug while both under and not under its influence. Expectations or beliefs regarding the drug's ability to provide solutions and help one live life more comfortably in the immediate present. Expectancies continue to form and develop as drug use persists.

(*continued*)

Table 4.1. (*continued*)

Model/model type	General concepts	Examples
Distal and proximal factors	The concept of distal and proximal factors is important in other theoretical models, such as Problem Behavior Theory and Triadic Influence Theory. Distal factors provide the background for potential drug use, while proximal factors tend to be influential just prior to or during drug use experiences.	Distal factors include those variables that increase or reduce access to or interest in prosocial activities, or increase the vulnerability for drug use (e.g., poverty). Proximal factors operate just prior to or during drug use, and include such factors as peer dares and peer pressure.

models, stage modeling, and distal-proximal notions. These multivariable etiologic models have increased our understanding of the complexity and interconnectedness of multiple influences contributing to drug abuse. An intricate interplay of physiological reward mechanisms, affective and cognitive individual difference variables, and social and physical environmental influences affect substance use susceptibility and sustainability. Although many of the variables discussed in this chapter may predispose an individual to use drugs, predisposition does not *cause* this complex behavior. Even if someone uses drugs, many individuals who are predisposed do not become drug abusers, whereas others do. That is, a variety of influences and events are likely to occur in the process or progression from drug initiation/experimentation to regular use and abuse. Drug abuse arises in part from repetitive experiences with drugs and learned associations between events that are meaningful to the individual.

Understanding the diversity and various levels of influence of correlates and predictors of drug abuse is a daunting task. Perhaps there are just too many different pathways to drug abuse or different subtypes of drug abusers, and all one can do is delay the onset of use or help a drug user discontinue use so abuse will not result. But, perhaps an integration of the integrative theories will emerge, providing an even clearer understanding of drug abuse etiology. Clearly, a need to continue exploring predictors of drug abuse and to identify at-risk individuals among diverse populations exists because of implications for the health and well-being of individuals and society. The following chapters examine domains of predictors more closely.

5   Neurobiologically Relevant

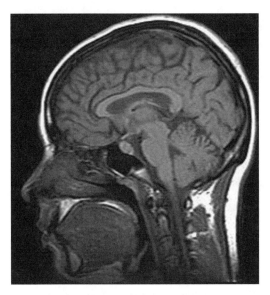

Figure 5.1. Neurobiological processes: How does brain function influence drug use behavior?

The neurobiology of addiction involves an array of biologically based determinants of motivation and behavior that affect individual differences in susceptibility to the addictive process. The extent to which an individual is responsive to reinforcing drug effects is partially genetically derived, involving metabolic and neurobiological variations that promote (or inhibit) drug use (or promote other behaviors such as gambling that, consequently, produce similar effects on one's neurobiology) and partially derive from drug use-related experiential learning, resulting in biological consequences of use. As an example of the latter, repetitive drug use can result in the formation and strengthening of drug-relevant memory associations and neuroadaptive changes in the brain. As one may surmise, it is possible that one's genetics primes one to tend toward engagement in drug-related behaviors that then result in the strengthening of drug-relevant memories that, in turn, may result in habitual drug use. These two aspects of "responsiveness" to drug use, genetics and the formation of drug-relevant memories, are likely intertwined, although not necessarily. This chapter addresses the neurobiological control over addictive behavior and provides an overview of the brain systems and structures involved in the process. In addition, we present a comprehensive model of drug misuse that relies heavily on the neurobiological control of behavior (Figure 5.1).

Preparedness to Abuse Drugs

Prior to any drug use, some individuals have a relatively nonoptimal pattern of neurotransmitter (e.g., dopamine and serotonin) and neuroendocrine (e.g., adrenocorticotropic hormone) activity. This inadequate neurotransmitter function may be related to a relatively low production of biologically desirable neurotransmitters, a low number of receptors for these neurotransmitters (Levinthal, 2005), irregular firing of neurons, or other unknown causes. One may speculate, for example, that there are neuro-anatomical or neurotransmitter wiring pathway differences between persons suffering from addictions and those who do not. Lyon and McClure (1994) made this suggestion regarding the origins of schizophrenia in his investigations with mice. He further suggested that some of these differences may occur through prenatal events. Recently, he suggested that the same types of differences may lead to the addictions (M. Lyon, personal communication, April 2006). Following from his logic, drugs or behavioral interventions can only alter flow in certain systems or manage behavior – however, the person suffering from addictions is qualitatively different from others and probably will remain so even while not abusing drugs or under the best of circumstances. Such differences would manifest themselves in brain function (e.g., differences in brain levels of various neurotransmitters) and behavior (e.g., restlessness, irritation, discontentedness; Alcoholics Anonymous, 1976).

Dopamine Receptor Hypothesis

Perhaps the most popular hypothesis regarding neurobiological bases for the addictions is one asserting insufficient dopamine reception. For example, Volkow et al. (2001) suggest that some individuals have relatively fewer D2 dopamine receptors, which might predispose them to fall victim to drug abuse and other addictive behaviors. This notion is consistent with physiological research on individual differences in neurotransmitter receptors. Although the precise physiological mechanisms are still being debated, it has been hypothesized that low levels of D2 receptors may result in a generalized *reward deficiency syndrome* among some individuals (Blum et al., 1990). That is, some individuals, because of their neurochemistry, have difficulty deriving feelings of reward or pleasure from ordinary activities and this predisposes them to seek alternative behaviors to compensate for the lower level of activation of the brain reward circuitry (Noble et al., 1991). In other words, these individuals may engage in behaviors that produce physiological feelings of reward, such as drug use, eating, gambling, or other sensation-seeking behaviors, at least under conditions in which such activities are readily accessible and prosocial alternatives are not accessible.

This syndrome appears to be a consequence of variations in reward pathways of the brain. Individuals exhibiting a reward deficiency syndrome appear more likely to have variations in genes that code for the production of dopamine receptors. One variant allele implicated in the reduction in the number of dopamine receptors is the DRD2 A1 allele (Blum et al., 1990). One could speculate that fewer dopamine receptors implies that an individual cannot biologically achieve a desired level or sense of well-being from stimuli that are generally experienced as rewarding by others; that this individual experiences as a *sense of dis-balance* (e.g., under- or overaroused, subjectively too elated or sad/anxious). Therefore, to reach a baseline "normalized" level of well-being (or an ideal state), these individuals may engage in more sensation-seeking or risk behaviors such as drug misuse (Figure 5.2).

The specific behavior chosen is likely to be influenced by a variety of other variables, including other biologically based dispositional traits, social group, sociocultural, and environmental factors. At this time, different drugs of abuse are known to increase or decrease (depending on the drug) levels of glutamate, γ-aminobutyric acid (GABA), serotonin, and acetylcholine or possibly other neurotransmitters (see Table 5.1). To date, however, there is no evidence that any drug of abuse serves to temporarily decrease levels of dopamine (a key player in substance misuse) turnover in the nucleus accumbens. Most drugs of abuse facilitate dopaminergic neurotransmission in the brain.

Individuals who feel relatively "out of balance" (i.e., they cannot biologically achieve a desired level or sense of well-being) may seek out activities or other individuals to help them achieve some sort of balance or a sense of wellness. Some individuals may find a means of adapting (at least temporarily) with the help of parents, guardians, or other significant others. Potentially, through learning processes, functional "rewiring" of the neural systems may occur; new neural connections form that provide a foundation for achieving some sense of well-being (Bukowski, 2003). These individuals are somehow able to achieve a "naturally" balanced physiological arousal/affective status. Similarly, when some dis-balanced youth reach school, they may be able to adapt with supportive teachers who reward them for good behavior, even though they may experience less than optimal neuroelectrochemical wiring. These youth may, however, still have a sense of being chronically "off keel" in affect or arousal, as opposed to feeling a sense of self-comfort much of the time. As an example, some youth grow up feeling a lack of well-being through a relative imbalance in affect (e.g., feeling hostile, sad, or experiencing rapid affect fluctuations) or arousal (e.g., feeling bored or overwhelmed or experiencing rapid arousal fluctuations). These youth may form certain cognitive perceptions (e.g., of being different, less than or greater than, or dissatisfied with their social world), perpetuating a sense of being chronically dis-balanced (Sussman & Unger, 2004).

Some individuals who experience a sense of dis-balance may achieve and maintain an affective or arousal balance by consistently engaging in prosocial behavior, which could include regular exercise (however, this can also be carried to extremes), intense involvement in homework and hobbies, highly structured time, or possibly caretaking activities. Free time may be perceived as dangerous to such individuals. For some individuals, a normalizing physiological rewiring has not taken place and is unlikely to take place. Rather, they have engineered their lives to increase rewarding stimuli. Possibly, a normalizing rewiring can occur only during certain phases in one's life but not others (e.g., critical periods in neural development), or perhaps some individuals are unable to normalize wiring due to a relatively greater degree of dis-balance. The lifelong ability of the brain to change with learning and reorganize neural pathways is referred to as brain plasticity or neuroplasticity (e.g., Vernadakis, 1996). Functional changes in the brain occur as a result of learning and new experiences. Many individuals, however, remain "at risk," in the sense that if they are unable to continue to engage in a specified adaptive behavioral routine due to diminished opportunity or injury, they may be prone to seek replacement activities to regain a sense of

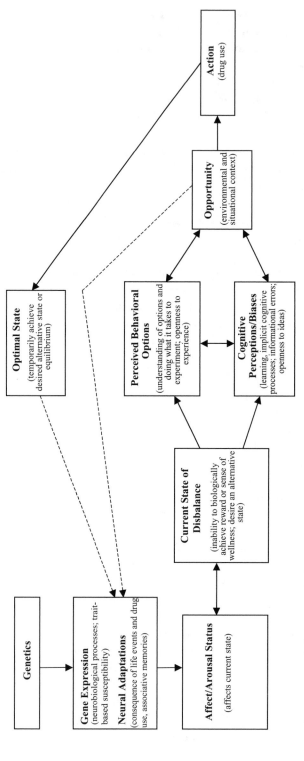

Figure 5.2. Dis-balance model of drug misuse and abuse. The individual experiences a state of dis-balance; that is, the person is unable biologically to achieve fairly consistent states of reward or sense of well-being and is motivated to change or desires an alternative state – a perceived ideal or optimal state. The current state is affected by neurobiological systems, which in turn, have an effect on affect/arousal status. Current state affects perceived behavioral options (i.e., knowledge of various alternatives and openness to experience) and cognitive perceptions and biases, which influence each other and are encouraged or inhibited by social/cultural and physical environments labeled in the diagram as "Opportunity." Opportunity consists of the number and relative frequency of available alternative behaviors and situational context such as individual past experiences. Opportunity also affects gene expression and neural adaptations (e.g., drug-related associative memories). Opportunity also tends to be proximal to goal-directed behavior. Given relatively few perceived behavioral options, implicit and explicit cognitive processes favorable toward drug use, and an opportunity to use being immediately available without obvious alternatives present, action occurs. That is, drug use experimentation may begin and then based on feedback about successfully achieving one's optimal state, use is sustained, and misuse, abuse, and dependence may occur.

Table 5.1. Pattern of neurotransmitter effects of different types of drugs

	DA	ST (5-ht)	NE	Ach	GABA	GLU	MuOp	Anan	Aden	Mus
Alcohol	Increase	Decrease			Increase	Decrease	Increase	Increase	Increase	
Minor tranquilizer					Increase					
PCP						Decrease				
Inhalant	Increase									
Stimulant	Increase	Increase								Increase
Nicotine	Increase			Increase		Decrease				
Caffeine	Increase	Increase	Increase						Decrease	
Opiate	Increase	Increase			Decrease		Increase			
LSD		Increase								
Mescaline	Increase	Increase	Increase							
Scopolamine				Decrease						Increase
Cannabis	Increase				Decrease	Increase	Increase	Increase		
MDMA	Increase	Increase			Decrease					
GHB	Increase									

Abbreviations: DA = dopamine; ST (5-ht) = serotonin; NE = norepinephrine; Ach = acetylcholine; GABA = γ-amino butyric acid; GLU = glutamate; MuOp = mu-opioid; Anan = anandamide; Aden = adenosine; Mus = muscarinic (muscarinic receptor antagonists [e.g., atropine and scopolamine] cause confusion, which is considered fun by some); a minus sign after increase or decrease notation indicates relatively little impact.

balance. Based on what is immediately available in their social or physical environments, these activities may or may not serve prosocial functions. Other persons may be able to live out their lives in subjective misery and may exert perpetual cognitive vigilance not to behave "poorly."

Various researchers promote neurobiological systems models as the key determinant of substance abuse (e.g., Koob & LeMoal, 2001; Sussman & Unger, 2004; Tarter et al., 2003). The next sections of this chapter provide an overview of contributing components to a systems perspective.

Genetic Variation

Genes are the basic unit of heredity, the particular segments of a DNA molecule on a chromosome that determines the nature of an inherited trait. The investigation of genotype variation (i.e., genetic polymorphisms and allele associations [locations along a gene or genes]) may provide information about individual differences in risk for substance misuse and abuse. Genes might contribute to susceptibility to risk behavior by influencing the structure or function of neural circuits during brain development and/or in adulthood. In turn, brain circuitry influences how individuals respond to drug intake, food intake, and engagement in social interactions, as examples of behaviors with reinforcing implications, whereas adaptations in brain circuitry as a consequence of drug exposures or other behaviors influence subsequent behavior (Nestler, 2000; Nestler & Landsman, 2001).

Genes also may affect individual differences in metabolic processes. Variation in genes that influence the biological processing of alcohol and other drugs may increase or decrease susceptibility to problem use. As an example, the operations of alcohol dehydrogenase metabolizing enzymes help to explain some observed ethnic differences in the susceptibility to alcohol abuse. Genetic variation in acetaldehyde degradation, alcohol-metabolizing enzymes, alcohol dehydrogenase (ADH), and aldehyde dehydrogenase (ALDH) is responsible for an alcohol-induced flushing reaction found in some Asian groups that make alcohol use less rewarding. This reactivity, in turn, reduces susceptibility to alcohol-related problems (Suzuki, Matsushita, & Ishii, 1997; Wall, Thomasson, Schuckit, & Ehlers, 1992). In addition, genetic variants of cytochrome P450 2A6 (CYP2A6) nicotine metabolizing enzymes and cytochrome P450 2E1 (CYP2E1) alcohol-metabolizing enzymes are associated with differences in metabolic processes. These variations in genotypes have been implicated in risk for substance abuse and dependence (Pianezza, Sellers, & Tyndale, 1998; Tyndale & Sellers, 2001).

In general, as discerned by twin studies of those for whom problem drug use has developed, genetic factors account for 30% to 60% of the variance in identification of abusers of various drugs (Goudriaan, Oosterlaan, de Beurs, & Van den Brink, 2004; Lessov et al., 2004). Genetic investigative approaches, which include detection of linkage peaks for complex phenotypes (linkage peaks describe where on the same chromosome genes tend to segregate together), require large sample sizes, the use of refined phenotypes (i.e., well described realized functional expression of the genetic constitution of a trait), and incorporation of covariates in statistical analyses. As a result, research findings have been inconclusive (Lerman, Patterson, & Shields, 2003; Lessov et al., 2004). Additionally, theory regarding which gene snips to analyze has been lacking. Further, although genes impact the environment, the phenotype expression of multiple gene alleles may be altered dramatically through differential environmental exposures, which complicates the knowledge base.

Moreover, although genetic factors contribute to drug misuse susceptibility, they probably do not cause observable complex drug behaviors in a deterministic manner. Increasingly, it is also evident that drug use itself alters gene expression (phenotype); that is, the function of genes responsible for receptors, enzyme function, and neurological processes may be changed by substance use (Lessov et al., 2004). Clearly, the role of genes, their interactions with each other and environmental factors, and participation in various activities that are accessible within environments are influential in promoting alcohol and other drug misuse susceptibility.

A number of linkage studies for alcohol intake using Collaborative Studies on Genetics of Alcoholism (COGA) data have reported linkages to chromosomes 1, 4, 6, 7, 15, and 19 for alcoholism. Possible candidate genes that map around the region of the chromosome 1 linkage include opioid binding, prostaglandin receptors, protein kinase activity (an enzyme that modifies other proteins through phosphorylation), and the adenosine A3 receptor. Association studies additionally implicate the DRD2 gene (dopamine D2 receptor; located on chromosome 11), GABA receptor complex genes (chromosomes 4, 5, and 15), the serotonin transporter gene (chromosome 17), and, most recently, the neuropeptide Y gene (chromosome 7) in alcohol-related phenotypes. In addition, interindividual variations in the D4 dopamine receptor gene (DRD4) have been shown to affect variation in smoking behavior (Hutchison et al., 2002). Research also has supported the occurrence of gene–gene interactions between the dopamine D2 and D4 receptor genes that in combination may affect smoking behavior, cessation, and relapse (Lessov et al., 2004).

For cocaine and methamphetamine, reports of failing to find significant associations between drug dependence and gene polymorphisms (e.g., the dopamine DRD2 receptor gene or the serotonin transporter gene) outnumber those showing positive associations. In some studies, the dopamine DRD2 receptor gene has been significantly associated with heroin, alcohol, and nicotine dependence (Lerman, Patterson, & Shields, 2003; Lessov et al., 2004). Additionally, polymorphism in the mu-opioid receptor gene has been shown to be associated with heroin dependence in some studies. Different phenotype measures (e.g., those related to drug experimentation versus established drug use) show different magnitudes of heritability, may show linkages to different chromosomal regions, may be associated with different candidate genes, and may have independent interactive effects between genetic and environmental risk factors (Lessov et al., 2004). To date, much of the genetics research has been directed to substance use behavior, but other types of compulsive behavior (e.g., food, sex, gambling, and exercise) may possibly involve similar genetic underpinnings (see Nestler & Landsman, 2001). Genetic-based work is ongoing and will help increase our understanding of the role of genes in substance misuse susceptibility (Table 5.2; Figure 5.3).

Brain Systems Involved in Drug Use

To begin to understand the essence of recurrent drug abuse-related consequences, some speculation about the "wiring" of brain systems helps. The human brain is made up of billions of nerve cells (neurons). These nerve cells constantly communicate with each other to process information. The connections among the neurons in the various parts of the brain

Table 5.2. Neurobiologically relevant etiological variables of drug abuse

The following may affect one's likelihood of becoming a drug misuser or abuser:

- Nonoptimal neurotransmitter and/or neuroendocrine activity (e.g., insufficient dopamine, serotonin, or norepinephrine reception); hypothetically, may be due to discordant innervations of the ventral tegmental area (VTA) by the amygdala and the hypothalamus, which may lead to a sense of imbalance; may be related to dis-balance of subjective affect or self-control (e.g., anger, depression, boredom, anxiety, guilt, apprehension)
- Variations in reward pathways of the brain (e.g., "reward deficiency syndrome"); may be related to feeling the need to "self-medicate"; may be related to variations in biologically based preferences for novelty or stimulation (i.e., sensation seeking, impulsivity)
- Exposure to early pre- or postbirth trauma (e.g., maternal drug or alcohol use during pregnancy) or repeated physical and/or emotional abuse in early childhood that leads to under-development of key brain structures; may be related to inability to bond, relate, or connect with institutions and/or significant others; may be related to dispositional attitudes such as unconventionality, rebelliousness, and tolerance of deviance
- Genetic variations (i.e., genetic polymorphisms and allele associations; differences in metabolic processes)
- Gene–gene interactions (e.g., between the dopamine D_2 and D_4 receptor genes in smoking behavior, cessation, and relapse)
- Variation in actions of certain neuropeptide transmitters (met-enkephalin, dynorphin, neuropeptide Y [NPY], corticotrophin-releasing factor [CRF], and others)
- Abnormalities in the structure and function of the orbitofrontal cortex
- Dysfunction of higher cognitive inhibitory and control processes that affect behavioral regulation (e.g., executive control processes)
- Neural adaptations (e.g., sensitization) to drugs and drug-related stimuli
- Dysregulation of the neurotransmission-hormonal (modulator) system that results from repetitive drug use

affect brain function. Neurotransmitters are synthesized in neurons and different neurons are home to different neurotransmitters. Neurotransmitters are the electrochemical message transport medium (Figure 5.4).

Substances of abuse can disrupt brain chemistry because they are similar in size and shape to natural brain chemicals and therefore affect behavior and thought processes. Drugs may occupy nerve cell receptors and start an "unnatural" chain reaction of electrical charges. These electrical charges may cause brain nerve cells to release their own brain chemicals or neurotransmitters. Some drugs "grab" onto a nerve cell and act like a pump, flooding the brain with excess neurotransmitters. Other drugs can prevent certain nerve cells from absorbing or reabsorbing chemicals, resulting in unnatural floods of chemicals in the brain. Some drugs of abuse can prevent neurotransmission by binding to receptors on receiving neurons, shutting down the production of certain neurotransmitters. Any of these changes in an individual's normal chemical balance result in unusual feelings (e.g., feeling "high"). Over time, continued drug use may result in neural adaptations in the brain; figuratively, the brain may "expect" a drug to occupy certain nerve cells to function normally (Koob & LeMoal, 2001).

Given that there are individual differences in neurochemistry and that all individuals do not have that "magical" chemical mix that allows them to feel good normally, some individuals get a "bigger bang" or experience drug effects as more intensely rewarding than

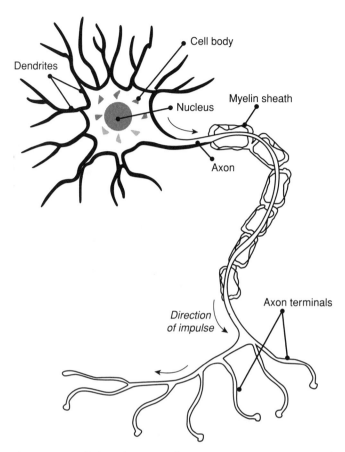

Figure 5.3. Depiction of a nerve cell or neuron. Nerve cells constantly communicate with each other to process information.

others. To illustrate how drugs can affect the mix of chemicals in one's brain, one could think about a favorite song and the manner in which the instruments are mixed to provide that "magical mix" or optimal output. Now, one might think about turning up the bass or remixing the song (this is similar to ingesting a drug and turning up the transmission of a particular neurochemical or various neurochemicals). In remixing the song, one has changed the relationship of the bass to each of the other instruments in the mix, which, in turn, may also change the relationship of the other instruments to each other and the output. The ingestion of drugs "remixes" one's brain chemistry and for those in a chronic state of dis-balance, drug use may temporarily provide that "magical neurochemical mix" or sense of well-being, resulting in the subsequent pursuit of the feelings (e.g., reward or pleasure) this remix provides.

Brain Reward Systems

Many naturally occurring rewards (e.g., sex, food, or video gaming), as well as the ingestion of drugs of abuse, activate similar brain reward systems involving mesolimbic dopamine pathways (Bardo, 1998; Berridge & Robinson, 2003; DiChiara, 2002; LeDoux, 2002; Wise,

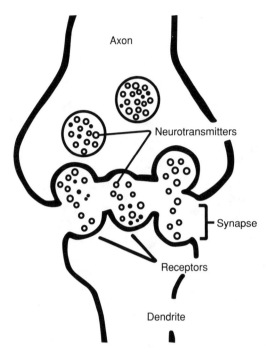

Figure 5.4. Diagram of a synapse. A chemical synapse is a junction between nerve cells that allows information to be conveyed (via neurochemicals) from one cell to another.

1996, 1999). Dopamine, through various neuronal systems, affects aspects of addictive behaviors, including arousal, reward, and motivation.

The mesolimbic dopamine system involves a dense projection of dopamine neurons from the midbrain's ventral tegmental area (VTA) to the nucleus accumbens (a collection of neurons located in the striatum [a subcortical part of the brain consisting of the caudate nucleus and the putamen]) and to the prefrontal cortex (the anterior part of the frontal lobes; see Schultz, 1998, 2001). Almost all drugs of abuse increase dopamine activity in the nucleus accumbens. Moreover, the influence of dopamine neurons in the nucleus accumbens (and some anatomically connected structures) extends to the encoding and processing of proximal stimuli that are associated with rewarding experiences, including the cognitive processing of drug-associated stimuli (Cardinal & Everitt, 2004; Robbins & Everitt, 1999; Setlow, 1997; Wise, 1999). As noted by Cardinal and Everitt (2004), "One important contribution made by the nucleus accumbens is to the process through which neutral stimuli, once paired with a reinforcer such as a drug, have the capacity to motivate behavior" (p. 156). Increased dopamine transmission in the nucleus accumbens reinforces the repetition of behaviors, influencing learning, attentional processes, and the strengthening of associations of reinforcing effects (DiChiara, 2002).

Dopamine is also associated with anticipatory behaviors as well as novel behaviors. Animal researchers have provided evidence that exposure to novel experiences taps into and activates some of the same reward systems in the brain as those activated by drugs of abuse (Bardo, Donohew, & Harrington, 1996). Animal researchers have also found that exposure to stimuli previously associated with reward can trigger a neurobiological anticipatory response (e.g., automatic associative effects of drug cues) that can occur rapidly at the synaptic level, several seconds before a behavioral event. For example, Phillips et al. (2003) detected 100-ms pulses of dopamine release in the nucleus accumbens of rats elicited by a cue that had been previously associated with cocaine. The cocaine-associated cues elicited approach behavior immediately following the subsecond pulses of dopamine release. Schultz (2004) has noted that dopamine neurons in the nucleus accumbens, amygdala, and orbitofrontal cortex "detect rewards and reward-predicting stimuli and are activated during the expectation of predictable rewards" (p. 139). Analogous to the animal research, repetitive drug use experiences with associated stimuli can lead to cue-triggered anticipation of rewards in humans (e.g., dopamine release). Early dopamine signals may convey information about the onset of reward before the behavior takes place and may influence learning (and behavior) by modifying neural transmission (see Schultz, 1998).

Variation in Response to Cues for Reward

Gray (1982) outlined two general motivational brain systems – the behavioral approach system (BAS) and the behavioral inhibition system (BIS) – that affect individual differences in behavioral responses to cues for reward. These interdependent systems influence whether an individual is likely to withdraw or avoid situations that involve novel or threatening cues or whether one is likely to engage in novel or risky behavior (e.g., drug use) in response to cues for reward. According to Gray, the BAS is mediated by dopamine pathways, involving the ventral tegmental area, ventral striatum, and nucleus accumbens. An active BAS is linked to more impulsive-type behaviors. Alternatively, the BIS is mediated by the septo-hippocampal system. An active BIS is linked to inhibiting behavior (Beauchaine, Katkin, Strassberg, & Snarr, 2001; Carver, 2004; Gray, 1987, 1990). There are now variations of interdependent motivational brain systems like the BAS/BIS framework that have been proposed to explain the influence of aversive and appetitive motivational processes affecting individual differences in behavioral response to varieties of reinforcers (e.g., Cacioppo, Gardner, & Berntson, 1999; Lang, 1995).

More on Neurotransmission Systems

In addition to dopamine systems, several other neurotransmitters are involved in the reinforcing and pleasurable effects of drugs of abuse. Other neurotransmitters implicated in drug abuse processes include serotonin (emotion maintenance and sleep processing), norepinephrine (emotion, sensory, awareness processing), acetylcholine (memory, sensory, motor, automatic nervous system [ANS] processing), GABA (major inhibitory neurotransmitter in the central nervous system [CNS]), and glutamate (memory, major excitatory function in the CNS and peripheral nervous system [PNS]).

Drugs of abuse also activate the release of opioid neuropeptides. Opioid receptors are widespread in the brain, overlapping a great deal with the dopamine system, and may be more relevant than dopamine regarding "liking" versus "wanting" a drug (Kelley & Berridge, 2002). Some researchers speculate that perhaps a distinct pleasure circuitry involving opioids exists (Peciña & Berridge, 2005). Some of the neuropeptide transmitters that have been implicated in drug misuse include met-enkephalin, dynorphin, neuropeptide Y (NPY), and corticotropin-releasing factor (CRF), as well as others (see Franz & Koob, 2005).

Brain Structures Involved in Drug Misuse

Various brain structures are involved in detecting sensory inputs, evaluating current state-ideal state discrepancies, searching for preferences and behavioral options information, entering into a behavioral sequence based on opportunity and planning, and reevaluating experience in terms of current state-ideal state feedback. Sensory information is processed for recognition and flows toward the lateral amygdala, which then may begin a process of affective evaluation of the sensory information. Outputs may then innervate the VTA of the brainstem, either directly from the amygdala or indirectly through structures such as the hypothalamus. Neurons that synthesize the neurotransmitter, dopamine, are located in the VTA and send their axons to the medial forebrain bundle throughout the forebrain. The midbrain relays sensory information via dopaminergic neurons that project to the striatum, nucleus accumbens, amygdala, and frontal cortex (Berridge & Robinson, 1995; Kandel, Schwartz, & Jessell, 2000; Schultz, 1998).

The hippocampus (which guides behavior on the basis of spatial and other relational environmental cues, processes episodic information, and regulates declarative long-term memory information) participates by way of its connections to the amygdala (the brain region involved in the processing, interpreting, and integrating of emotional functioning) and the nucleus accumbens. Likewise, the prefrontal cortex is connected to the nucleus accumbens, amygdala, and hippocampus and is involved with executive functions, including decision-making (e.g., future consequences of current activities), prediction of outcomes, and social "control" (the ability to suppress urges that, if not suppressed, could lead to socially unacceptable outcomes).

The anterior cingulate cortex receives inputs from dopamine cells in the VTA (behavioral arousal), as well as from the basal amygdala (conditioned incentives), ventral pallidum (motor control), and hippocampus (declarative processes), and it sends outputs to the nucleus accumbens and to the motor cortex (working memory, action initiation). It may be relatively important for the processing of cognitive information in making decisions and in resolving motivational conflict (executive processing).

The orbital cortex, an area of the ventral prefrontal cortex, located at the bottom of the frontal lobe, is implicated in emotional processing of incentives and in the temporary storage of incentive information. This area is associated with decision-making and good judgment in situations with fluctuating incentives and cues (e.g., Bechara, Damasio, & Damasio, 2000). This area is connected with the anterior cingulate cortex and also receives information from the amygdala and hippocampus.

There are numerous speculations about what constitutes the current state and the ideal state in one's brain. For example, one could speculate that regions in the amygdala (e.g., basal, medial, and posterior) may create the sense of one's current state, whereas regions such as the hypothalamus may provide or create the sense of one's ideal state. Discordant innervations of the VTA by the amygdala and the hypothalamus may create the sense of imbalance. In addition, involvement by reciprocal relations between the orbital frontal cortex and the nucleus accumbens may contribute to dis-balance once drug misuse begins (Volkow et al., 2001). Discordance may be genetically based or altered through experience.

Substance-Induced Neural Adaptations That Sustain Dis-Balance

Imaging studies of individuals with lesions in the orbitofrontal cortex (OFC) have shown this brain region to be active in the regulation of social behavior involving evaluative processes and response to social rewards (see, Bechara, Damasio, & Damasio, 2000; Beer et al., 2003; London et al., 2000), as well as stimulus-reward association learning and memory (Rolls, 1999). This brain region also has been implicated in the regulation of a variety of motivational behaviors (e.g. substance use, feeding and drinking; see Rolls, 1999). For example, in several studies using a gambling task to evaluate decision-making processes (i.e., choices about future consequences based on reward/punishment contingencies), Bechara and colleagues found that, when compared to nonsubstance dependent controls, a sample of substance-dependent individuals exhibited impaired decision-making. That is, the substance-dependent individuals were more likely to choose immediate rewards while incurring future negative consequences (see Bechara & Damasio, 2002; Bechara, Dolan, & Hindes, 2002). The choices they made were similar to the decisions made by individuals with lesions of the orbital frontal cortex.

Further, neuroimaging studies have implicated the orbitofrontal cortex in expectation of drug reward, drug craving, and judgments or decision-making influencing compulsive drug use (e.g., see Goldstein & Volkow, 2002; London et al., 2000). For example, the research of Volkow and colleagues suggests that neuroadaptations occur in the brain's orbitofrontal cortex following repetitive drug use and that these changes are key in understanding the maintenance of compulsive drug taking and the drive to use drugs despite consequences (for review, Goldstein & Volkow, 2002; Volkow & Fowler, 2000). They propose that the neural processes involved in compulsive drug taking (involving mesocortical pathways) appear to be distinct from the neural processes involved in subjective pleasure experienced from initial and early drug use (involving mesolimbic dopamine reward pathways; Volkow, Fowler, Wang, & Goldstein, 2002). The general implication of this work is that the maintenance of habit or compulsive drug taking appears to be more than a function of the effects of the dopamine reward circuitry; that is, compulsive drug taking involves dysfunction of higher cognitive inhibitory and control processes that affect behavioral regulation (Volkow, Fowler, Wang, & Goldstein, 2002).

Incentive-Sensitization Theory

Robinson and Berridge's (1993, 2000) incentive-sensitization theory focuses on the influence of neural adaptation (i.e., sensitization) to drugs and drug-conditioned stimuli as the underlying mechanism perpetuating drug use. They differentiate neural processes involved in motivational mechanisms or incentive salience to drug cues ("wanting") (i.e., mesocorticolimbic circuitry) and the neural substrates of pleasurable effects or "liking" (i.e., NAcc opioid neurotransmission) (Robinson & Berridge, 2003). They have proposed that the progressive dysregulation of neural substrates through repeated drug use is associated with an increase in behavioral sensitization contributing to addicts "wanting" (or craving) of drugs being disproportionate to the pleasure derived from drug use. Through drug use, drug-associated stimuli that acquire incentive salience through neural representation become "motivational magnets," able to "grab" the drug user's attention (see Berridge & Robinson, 2003; Robinson & Berridge, 2003). According to Robinson and Berridge, adaptations in the neural substrates of "wanting" are affected by the pharmacological effects of drugs as well as by processes of associative learning (Robinson & Berridge, 1993, 2003) and these processes influence behavior outside of conscious awareness or implicitly (see Robinson & Berridge, 2000).

Allostasis

Allostasis, a perspective coined by Koob and colleagues, is another explanation of drug misuse due to the dysregulation of the neurotransmission-hormonal (modulator) system that results from repetitive drug use (see Koob & LeMoal, 2001). According to the notion of allostasis, drug use may lead to opponent-process counteradaptation (e.g., dopamine transduction mechanisms: reduced output and activation of brain stress systems) that masks the effects of the drug. Pituitary-adrenal axis activation is triggered by the release of adrenocorticotropic hormone (ACTH) from the pituitary gland. ACTH release is in turn controlled by the release of hypothalamic CRF into the pituitary portal system. ACTH release leads to release of glucocorticoids, which increases CRF availability and its expression in the amygdala. Glucocorticoid receptors are in various brain regions, particularly the VTA. Arguably, glucocorticoid transmission may inhibit dopamine release, and heightened dopamine release could fire up stress systems. To increase dopamine availability and initially control feelings of anxiety or stress, the drug may be tried again and again. New set points of homeostasis may then be established. This adaptive response of the body and brain, or the ability to achieve stability through the change processes, is referred to as allostasis (see McEwen, 2002).

Developmental Influences on Affect Regulation and Cognitive-Behavioral Control

Early Trauma

Some individuals are exposed to early pre- or postbirth trauma. As an example, intrauterine feeding can lead to a variety of consequences for the fetus if the mother is using alcohol or other drugs. Fetal alcohol exposure can result in fetal alcohol syndrome (FAS), which is characterized by facial abnormalities, growth deficits, and central nervous system abnormality. In addition, fetal alcohol exposure may result in cognitive, executive function, and motor deficits, as well as attentional, hyperactivity, and sensory problems (Centers for Disease Control and Prevention, 2004; http://www.cdc.gov/ncbddd/fas/documents/FAS_guidelines_accessible.pdf). Although researchers have shown structural and neurobehavioral effects of fetal alcohol exposure (http://pubs.niaaa.nih.gov/publications/aa50.htm), it is unclear whether infant exposure to alcohol (and other drugs) causes a "dis-balance of wiring" in the brain, although it is feasible.

Arguably, repeated physical or emotional abuse in early childhood might negatively affect normal development and result in a dis-balance because the brain is rapidly developing during this time. Early stress and maltreatment produces a series of neurobiological events that may lead to enduring changes in brain development. Negative consequences may include reduced corpus callosum size (hence reduced communication between the cortical hemispheres); attenuated development of the left neocortex and anterior cingulate cortex, hippocampus, and amygdala (perhaps a deficit in overall synaptic density in these structures); enhanced electrical irritability in limbic structures; reduced functional activity of the cerebellar vermis (the primary region for multimodal sensory integration and mediating response to stress; Teicher et al., 2003); and possibly less hypothalamus-pituitary-adrenal (HPA) stress-related reactivity (Cicchetti & Rogosch, 2001), perhaps through an opponent-process mechanism (Fishbein, 2000), although findings on the relation of maltreatment with HPA reactivity are mixed at present.

For example, maltreated-internalizing/depressed children may exhibit relatively high cortisol levels (Cicchetti & Rogosch, 2001) and possibly lower serotonergic turnover as well (Fishbein, 2000). Maltreated children have difficulty selecting appropriate emotions when provided with contextual cues, and they have difficulty understanding that different people have different perspectives in situations (Pears & Fisher, 2005). Difficulty

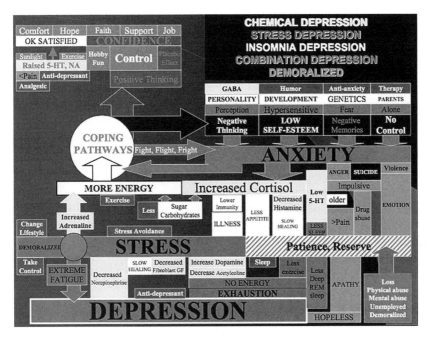

Figure 5.5. Hypothetical model relating depression to substance abuse: reveals the complexity of causation.

at a young age communicating emotions and perspectives in contexts may facilitate development of cognitive misperceptions that could, in turn, facilitate risk behaviors, including drug use.

Phenotype Expression of Neurobiological Processes Associated with Drug Misuse

The information presented previously on neurobiological processes suggests that there is an association between the behavioral expression of brain-based vulnerability and drug misuse. Prior to ever trying drugs or subsequent to trying drugs, a dis-balance of neurobiological processes may influence continued use. "Affect" and "self-control" are two examples of categories of complex neurobiological phenotypes that are commonly studied and that fit into a dis-balance perspective (Figure 5.5).

The *relief of a negative affective state* or the *expectancy of a desired affective state* may motivate an individual who had heard from others that drug use makes people happier, to try a drug, to continue use, or, for those in recovery, to lapse or relapse. Among at-risk youth, anger and depression have been found to be associated with substance abuse or dependence (Sussman, Dent, & Galaif, 1997). Among adults, several negative affective states have been found to influence relapse, including anger and depression, sadness, boredom, anxiety, guilt, apprehension, and anticipation of stressful events (Marlatt & Gordon, 1985; Miller, 1991). Although the co-occurrence of substance abuse and mood disorders is high (Kushner & Sher, 1993; Newcomb & Earleywine, 1996), the order of precedence in the "web of causation" between drug use and mood is not clear-cut. In other words, along with preexisting affective states that may lead to substance use, there is the likelihood that negative affective states result from substance misuse. Drug use could eventually make people feel more depressed or angry through drug effects on neurotransmitter systems, withdrawal symptom experiences, or psychological dependence (Johnson, 1980). If mood states precede drug use, this suggests a preexisting biological vulnerability to engage in drug use – that is, the existence of individuals who use drugs to "self-medicate."

The *self-medication hypothesis* of addictive disorders has been advanced by several researchers (e.g. Khantzian, 1985, 1997; Markou, Kostenn, & Koob, 1998; Uhlenhuth, Johanson, Kilgore, & Kosaba, 1981). This theoretical approach suggests that individuals use drugs as a means of controlling unpleasant feelings. Self-medication to relieve or escape these feelings or to obtain desired feelings may motivate an individual to engage in drug-taking behavior or to repeat the behavior (Khantzian, 1985, 1997; Markou, Kostenn, & Koob, 1998). There is empirical evidence supporting the contention that individuals seek out drugs as a means to self-medicate or avert negative affective states (e.g., Deykin, Levy, & Wells, 1987; Henry et al., 1993; Khantzian, 1985; Swanson et al., 1992; Teichman, Barnea, & Ravav, 1989). The notion of allostasis described under Allostasis suggests the neurobiological underpinnings of a self-medication notion (Koob & LeMoal, 2001).

Sensation Seeking/Novelty Seeking

Research in sensation seeking/novelty seeking suggests that there are variations in biologically based preferences for novelty or stimulation in individuals that affect susceptibility to reinforcing effects of pleasurable stimuli and the tendency to engage in risk behaviors such as substance use (see Zuckerman, 1994). This work has pointed to *sensation seeking* as an important trait, manifested in individuals likely to be susceptible to the reinforcing effects of pleasurable stimuli, including drug effects. Although the exact nature of implicated neurobiological systems in sensation-seeking individuals is not completely specified, dysregulation of the opioid system and lowered monoamine activity (affecting dopamine) appear to affect motivation to engage in risk behaviors (Zuckerman, 1994). Monoamine oxidase (MAO) degrades dopamine in the brain and is associated with behavioral regulation. The enzyme MAO is a biological correlate of impulsive sensation seeking that ties dopamine to sensation seeking, impulsivity, and drug use.

Zuckerman defined sensation seeking as "a trait defined by the seeking of varied, novel, complex and intense sensations and experiences, and the willingness to take physical, social, legal, and financial risks for the sake of such experience" (Zuckerman, 1994, p. 27). Sensation seeking has been associated with a variety of risk behaviors (e.g., driving under the influence [Ames, Zogg, & Stacy, 2002]; alcohol use [Stacy, Newcomb, & Bentler, 1993; Zuckerman, Ball, & Black, 1990]; and risky sexual behaviors [Donohew et al., 2000; McCoul & Haslam, 2001; Stacy et al., 2006]). Of course, a willingness to take such risks entails potential consequences, including that of drug abuse. Sensation seekers may be more eager to seek out and adopt new behaviors, even when those behaviors carry potential negative consequences, because of a biologically derived preference for stimulation. Early drug use experiences – whether they involve experimentation with drugs or mere exposure to drug use behaviors (e.g., in media messages, observations) – may be highly enticing for higher sensation-seeking individuals.

Animal researchers have also found higher novelty or sensation seeking to be associated with increased risk of substance use (e.g., Bardo, Donohew, & Harrington, 1996; Piazza, Deminiere, Le Moal, & Simon, 1989). For example, Piazza et al. (1989) observed the locomotor activity (or novelty seeking) of a random group of rats in a novel environment. Each rat was then categorized as either being a high responder or a low responder, based on the activity level in this novel environment. The rats were then tested for their tendency to self-administer amphetamine. Piazza et al. found that the high responders tended to self-administer more amphetamine than the low responders, suggesting that differences in response to novelty may affect susceptibility to the reinforcing effects of amphetamine (as well as other psychostimulants). Extrapolating these findings to humans, it is possible that higher sensation-seeking individuals have a tendency to use drugs more often than lower sensation seekers because they are more susceptible to pleasurable or reinforcing drug effects. Consistent with this perspective, a controlled laboratory study of humans demonstrated that higher sensation-seeking young adults were more sensitive to the subjective and physiological effects of both amphetamine and diazepam compared to lower sensation-seeking individuals (Kelly et al., 1999). However, it should be noted that sensation seeking has not always been linearly related to drug use (e.g., Simon, Stacy, Sussman, & Dent, 1994).

Impulsivity and Other Behavioral Regulation Traits

Another trait associated with drug use is *impulsivity or lack of behavioral inhibition* (Earley-wine & Finn, 1991; Jessor & Jessor, 1977). Impulsivity refers to the tendency to act immediately in response to stimuli without consideration of consequences or various behavioral options. Individuals may continually choose drug use as a behavioral choice to achieve initial positive effects, if they don't give delayed negative consequences much thought. Perry, German, Madden, and Carroll (2005) conducted a rat analog study. Rats were categorized as being either low or high impulsive based on their performance in a delayed reward-discounting task. On this task, impulsivity was defined as a preference for a small immediate reward over a larger delayed reward. When these rats were later tested to evaluate their tendency to self-administer drugs, the high impulsive rats were more likely to self-administer cocaine, and they did so at a significantly faster rate than the low impulsive rats. The researchers interpreted these findings as suggesting that impulsivity is a risk factor associated with substance use disorders in humans (e.g., de Wit & Richards, 2004; Fillmore, 2003).

Childhood and adolescent characteristics associated with drug use include not only sensation seeking and impulsivity but also other traits associated with behavioral regulation. One such trait is a *lack of regulation*, such as behavioral undercontrol (Sher, 1991). Some individuals, although able to think before acting, may seem unable to regulate the extent of their behavioral responses. They may overreact or underreact to circumstances, leading them to seek means to regulate their reactions (e.g., through drug use). Another trait associated with drug use is the *inability to bond*, relate, or connect with institutions and significant others (Newcomb & Earleywine, 1996). Although individuals may be able to think before acting, and may be able to regulate the extent of their reactions, they may still have difficulty obtaining a sense of belonging to institutions or groups of people for a variety of reasons. These reasons may include academic problems, a unique pattern of interests, or lack of access to resources. Additionally, the inability to bond may also reflect relatively high cortisol levels (Cicchetti & Rogosch, 2001) and lower serotonergic turnover (Fishbein, 2000), often associated with the experience of maltreated-internalizing/depressed children. Certainly, these individuals may lack a sense of coherence about their lives (see Antonovsky, 1984). Finally, dispositional attitudes such as *unconventionality, rebelliousness,* and *tolerance of deviance* are obvious correlates of counternormative behaviors such as drug use. These attitudes are likely to be related to sensation seeking and its neurobiological correlates.

Heritability of Phenotypes That Affect Dis-Balance

There is evidence from animal researchers that traits such as impulsivity or novelty seeking are heritable. Rodent strains that lack various genes (e.g., knock-out mice) have been bred to have different vulnerabilities to self-administer some drugs (Crabbe, 2002a, 2002b; Lessov et al., 2004) and to display behavioral variability in their responses to different drugs (Crabbe et al., 1999). For example, the selective breeding of low and high novelty responder rats has increased our understanding of the heritability of novelty seeking (Cools & Gingras, 1998). Different inbred strains of mice have demonstrated different rates of contact with novel objects (Peeler & Nowakowski, 1987) and varied levels of motor activity in a novel apparatus (Crusio, Schwegler, & van Abeelen, 1989). In addition, strain differences have been observed in some neurochemical markers; for example, the markers directly related to the functioning of brain dopamine systems (Vadasz, Laszlovszky, de Simone, & Fleischer, 1992). An operating hypothesis in animal research on sensation seeking has been that individual differences in sensation seeking associated with drug misuse susceptibility are mediated through biological differences in the mesolimbic dopamine reward pathway.

The genetic influence on the behavioral expression of sensation or novelty seeking also has been observed in humans. For example, Fulker, Eysenck, and Zuckerman (1980) examined 400 monozygotic and dizygotic adult twins to identify specific sources of variation in sensation seeking. They found sensation seeking to be primarily a function of genetic and within-family environmental factors. Genetic factors alone accounted for 58% of the variance in sensation seeking. In a recent study, Angleitmer, Riemann, and Spinath (2004) found twin similarity to be greater for a sample of German monozygotic than dizygotic twins on all of the Zuckerman Kuhlman Personality Questionnaire-III (ZKPQ-III) scales, except for the impulsivity subscale.

Summary

Many individuals are born with less than optimal neurochemistry; that is, some individuals are less likely to be able to biologically achieve reward, creating a sense of dis-balance. Individuals vary quantitatively on numerous physiological mechanisms and this variation contributes to a range of cognitive and behavioral consequences. Individual differences may increase or decrease one's susceptibility to drug misuse or abuse. Variation in genes and their expression influences neural and physical sensitivity to drugs, which, in turn, affects susceptibility to drug use motivation and reward and continued use (which may then alter phenotype expression of these genes). To date, researchers have not yet identified one gene or an inherited quality that single-handedly leads to drug abuse. However, significant strides have been made in understanding the actions of addictive drugs on neuronal circuitry and neurotransmitter systems. Continued research addressing heritability of individual variation in neurobiological processes of reinforcement, dependence, tolerance, and sensitization may help increase our understanding of drug abuse susceptibility.

6 Cognitive Processes

Figure 6.1. Information processing: How does it influence drug use behavior?

Addiction has been referred to as a "problem of perception" among those in the recovery movement, as well as by various researchers (Alcoholics Anonymous, 1976; Chuck, 1984; Ellis & Harper, 1975; Glynn, Levanthal, & Hirschman, 1985; Gorski, 1989; Johnson, 1980; Meichenbaum, 1977; Sussman, Earleywine, et al., 2004; Twerski, 1997). For example, Twerski (1997) considers drug abusers as exhibiting certain distortions of thought. According to Twerski, recognition of cognitive distortions and their remediation needs to come from outside the addict; the addict may block out certain information that must be provided by others. Although cognitive processing theories address how selective learning of information is likely to occur (e.g., attentional biases resulting from the strength of associations in memory), this literature is not able to provide a direct, logical explanation regarding how attentional biases might be created or how these biases lead to specific associational pathways. Moreover, it is not clear how it is that subsequent, more accurate, potentially corrective information is not adequately processed and incorporated as a part of one's cognitive structure. In this chapter, we present a general understanding of the formation and maintenance of cognitive misperceptions from several literatures – recovery movement, critical thinking (philosophy), social and cognitive psychology, health psychology, clinical psychology, health behavior research, and sociology (Figure 6.1).

In examining cognitive misperception-related phenomena across the various research arenas, Sussman (2005a) inferred four general types of cognitive variables that are relevant to an understanding of the processes underlying the formation and maintenance of addictions: (1) cognitive-information errors, (2) limits in rational cognitive processing, (3) belief–behavior congruence maintenance, and (4) situational/contextual distortions. First, cognitive misperceptions are formed that might make drug use appear to be an attractive option to a perceiver. "Cognition-information" errors may facilitate interest in trying and experimenting with drugs. These errors may serve to make drug use appear to be a statistically normative, acceptable, or subjectively desirable behavior. Once drug use begins, subjective drug effects and peripheral experiences may reinforce continued use. Both explicit and implicit cognitive processes may lead the user to develop automatic associations of use behavior to a variety of cues and outcomes that facilitate continued use (Stacy & Ames, 2001). Over time, negative consequences of drug use occur, but often corrective information is not deeply processed and drug misuse behavior does not change. Or perhaps, corrective information is simply overridden by an individual's earlier (and perhaps continued) response to the pharmacological effects of the drug and biological consequences of use. Corrective information needs to compete with preexisting drug-relevant associations or learned information (Stacy & Ames, 2001; Sussman & Unger, 2004; Wiers, de Jong, Havermans, & Jelicic, 2004). Cognitive processing limits (e.g., of executive functions, or related to time pressure) may impair successful competition with previously learned and reinforced information.

There may also be cognitive processes that actively deter learning new information. First, an individual may be driven to maintain belief–behavior congruence. That is, one may utilize cognitive processes that serve to either distance the perceiver from incongruence between beliefs and behavior, perhaps to keep incongruent information from consciousness. Alternately, one may utilize logical-appearing processes that more directly attempt to maintain congruence between the behavior (drug misuse) and one's beliefs. Second, one may distort the context of one's lifestyle to normalize one's behavior (situational/contextual distortions).

Cognition-Information Errors

Individuals' ascertainment of predictability and control in their lives is often based on previous experiences, and these experiences become their taken-for-granted world (Schutz & Luckman, 1973). The representativeness heuristic involves making judgments about the probability of an event based on an individual's experiential schema of how representative an event appears to be and the ease with which mental content comes to mind (i.e., accessibility) rather than relying on further evidence. Thus, errors of frequency or importance occur for *rare* or *vivid* stimuli (Kahneman, 2003), sometimes regardless of the distinctiveness of the stimuli within the encoding context (McConnell, Sherman, & Hamilton, 1994). These errors may be slanted as overestimates of frequency or importance of novel or vivid behaviors and underestimates of frequency or importance of negative consequences deriving from the behaviors.

Specific theories in health behavior research that provide explanations of these or similar phenomena include the *false consensus effect* (Sherman et al., 1983), *illusory correlation* (McConnell, Sherman, & Hamilton, 1994), *theories of implicit associative processes* or *implicit cognition* (e.g., for relevance to drug use, see Stacy, 1997; Stacy & Ames, 2001; Wiers & Stacy, 2006), and *unrealistic optimism* (Weinstein, 1982; Weinstein, 1987). The false consensus effect refers to a tendency to believe that one's own attitudes or behaviors are more prevalent than they actually are (e.g., the belief that everybody uses drugs just like oneself). Illusory correlation as applied to behavioral phenomena refers to a tendency to overestimate the co-occurrence of two infrequent events or objects, perhaps due to processing mechanisms related to the relative novelty of their co-occurrence (e.g., drug use behavior and very novel pleasurable events such as peak experiences). Theories of implicit associative processes or implicit cognition, in part, address behavioral and attentional biases based on automatic associative effects resulting from repetitive behavioral experiences. Unrealistic optimism is the tendency to perceive that the chance of one suffering an unexpected or undesired disease is less than is actually the case. Together, the cognitive experiences described by these theories may tend to sociologically "normalize" an individual's estimates of drug use frequency or appropriateness, lead one to infer greater pleasure of the outcomes of his or her behavior than is actually indicated in repeated experience, and lead one to discount the likelihood of negative consequences to self from drug use.

There are several specific examples of how cognitive-information errors occur among those at increased risk for participation in unhealthy lifestyles. Pertaining to errors in frequency estimation, relative overestimation of drug use prevalence, relative overestimation of peer approval of drug use, and relative underestimation of personal risk for negative drug use consequences may lead to (or stem from) problem drug use (MacKinnon et al., 1991; Sussman et al., 1988; Weinstein, 1982; Weinstein, 1987). Relative overestimation of the normative frequency of one's attitudes and behavior (false consensus) may differ by health area and may serve positive functions as well as negative functions for health (e.g., in depression it may serve a self-protective function; Tabachnik, Crocker, & Alloy, 1983). In the arena of drug abuse it serves a self-destructive function (e.g., Sherman et al., 1983; Sussman et al., 1988). These frequency errors tend to result from selective exposure to others that use drugs, a tendency to process vivid stimuli more deeply, and motivational distortions that conform to one's recent behavior (e.g., Sherman et al., 1983; Sussman et al., 1988).

Further, biased recall may result from the strength of associations in memory relevant to a behavior and its outcomes or other associates of the behavior (e.g., Stacy & Ames, 2001; Wiers & Stacy, 2006). In terms of cognitive information errors, familiarity with statements about drug effects, no matter whether they are provided as statements of myth or fact, may alter beliefs about drug effects, which may or may not be consistent with previously learned statements or behavior. Myths may become interpreted as facts (e.g., Krank & Swift, 1994) subsequently, reinforcing previously pleasurable subjective effects of drug use experiences. Unconscious (implicit cognitive) influences of past exposure to information can increase the probability of mistaking the source of a message and alter the impact of a message (see Jacoby, Kelley, Brown, & Jesechko, 1989).

Limits in Rational Cognitive Processing

Limits in rational cognitive processing are the second type of cognitive process that might facilitate the development and maintenance of drug misuse. Cognitive science and neuroscience have defined two general underlying cognitive processing systems: (1) explicit cognitive processes or declarative systems, including executive functions, and (2) implicit cognitive processes or nondeclarative systems. The general distinctions among the different cognitive systems are consistent with distinctions found in basic memory research (e.g., Nelson, Schreiber, & McEvoy, 1992) and social cognition (e.g., Bargh & Chartrand, 1999; Dovidio et al., 1997; Wilson, Lindsey, & Schooler, 2000). These systems operate simultaneously with direct behavior.

In this subsection on limits in rational cognitive processing, we discuss explicit cognitive processes relevant to drug abuse including executive functions and cognitive expectations. Next, we discuss expectations as components of memory and implicit cognitive processes. Finally, we discuss the potential interplay of explicit and implicit processes.

Executive Functions

Executive functions involve a variety of cognitive abilities that regulate and control other abilities and behaviors. Executive functions include mental operations involving planning or inhibiting behavior, cognitive flexibility and abstraction, judgment, self-monitoring or self-regulation of behavior, regulation of emotion, and working memory (e.g., Baddeley 1983, 1996; Baddeley & Wilson 2002). They are important for goal-directed behaviors (e.g., whether to engage in drug use). In addition to being affected by drug use, executive function processes detect changes in performance as a function of continued drug use. Decrements in performance may become recognized and logically attributed to drug use if deliberately processed (Sussman & Unger, 2004).

Corrective *executive operations are impaired* by time pressure, concurrent (multiple) task demands, mood fluctuation, or avoidance of having the desire or tendency to plan events (Kahneman, 2003; Matthys & Lochman, 2005). Any of these factors could lead to an increased chance of trying or continuing to use a drug. In addition, disruption of the frontal cortical area of the brain impairs some executive functions, including cognitive inhibitory and control processes that affect behavioral regulation (see Volkow, Fowler, Wang, & Goldstein, 2002). Repeated drug use may result in disruption of the brain's frontal cortical area, and these neuroadaptations may, in turn, affect the maintenance of compulsive drug taking or behavioral regulation (see Volkow & Fowler, 2000; Volkow, Fowler, Wang, & Goldstein, 2002). (Arguably, the direct impact of the aftereffects of a single drug use occasion, that is, a "hangover," also would seem to temporarily dull executive functioning.)

Corrective operations are also impaired by informational processing limits. Individuals act to the limits of their cognitive-behavioral repertoire, and their knowledge of behavioral choices. An individual may or may not be fully aware of living in a world of "free operants" (Epstein, 1992). In other words, one may not be aware that there are several choices they may make to obtain satisfactory life outcomes. This lack of awareness may come from different sources. First, one may be unable to comprehend subtle information or otherwise interact effectively enough with others so as to obtain needed information. Second, one may have difficulty keeping two or more options "in mind" in working memory (Stacy & Ames, 2001). Third, one may have difficulty generating and weighing alternatives (Matthys & Lochman,

2005). Finally, one may have difficulty with decisions related to initiating behavioral change. If someone does attempt to initiate change, he or she may have difficulty observing an impact on others (decision-making leading to information regarding matching of behavior to context).

Cognitive Expectancies and Drug Use

Variations of the formulation of expectancies have emerged since Tolman (1932) first proposed that animals are capable of anticipating behavioral consequences and then altering subsequent actions based on expectancies about connections between the behavior and environmental effects. Over recent decades, expectancies as a cognitive construct have been applied to research on alcohol and other drug use (for review, see Goldman, Brown, Christiansen, & Smith, 1991; Jones, Corbin, & Fromme, 2001; Leigh, 1989; Leigh & Stacy, 1991). In general, "expectancy" is conceptualized as the anticipated consequences of behavior or beliefs held about alcohol and other drug effects (e.g., Brown, Goldman, Inn, & Anderson, 1980; Fromme, Stroot, & Kaplan, 1993; Goldman, Brown, Christiansen, & Smith, 1991; Leigh & Stacy, 1991, 1993). Expectancies are subjective probabilities; therefore, distortions can occur and be a source of "irrational" behavior (e.g., continued drug use despite negative consequences). That is, individuals may over- or underestimate the likelihood of achieving an outcome (e.g., this drug makes me feel happy) from drug use. (Thus, expectancy errors serve as one source of cognitive-informational errors and indicate potential limitations of rational processing.)

Drug use expectancies are formed based on past experiences with drugs. As an example, the more often the behavior has led to reinforcement in the past, the more likely an individual will expect the behavior to result in a similar outcome. Among youth, information about alcohol (and other drug) effects and related contexts are learned based on individual differences in exposure to drug use-related situations, through observational learning, and through early personal experiences with use (Dunn & Goldman, 1996; 1998; Goldman, Brown, Christiansen, & Smith, 1991). Moreover, positive expectancies may be more proximal and more reliable predictors of substance use than negative expectancies. In other words, when individuals initially observe drug use or experiment with drugs, it is more likely that they will experience positive outcomes than negative outcomes, and initial positive outcomes may tend to drive subsequent use situations (Fromme, Katz, & Rivet, 1997; Stacy et al., 1990; Stacy, Widaman, & Marlatt, 1990). Of course, there is variation in the association of current alcohol use (and likely other drug use) and expectancies as a function of dose level (i.e., whether one consumes few, many, or too many drinks) and valence (e.g., whether one anticipates experiencing positive or negative effects from one's use) (see Wiers, Hoogeveen, Sergeant, & Gunning, 1997; Wiers, Sergeant, & Gunning, 2000).

Expectancies can consist of both cognitive (i.e., informational) and motivational components (affective incentive; see Goldman & Darkes, 2004; Goldman, Reich, & Darkes, 2006; Marlatt & Gordon, 1985). Expectancies have repeatedly been found to correlate with alcohol use and contribute to the initiation and maintenance of use (Earleywine, 1994; Goldman, Greenbaum, & Darkes, 1997; Leigh & Stacy, 1993), as well as predict subsequent alcohol use in adolescents and young adults (e.g., Christiansen, Smith, Roehling, & Goldman, 1989; Stacy, Newcomb, & Bentler, 1991). Moreover, expectancies as a cognitive mediator of behavior have been used to explain both volitional and nonvolitional behaviors (Stacy, Widaman, & Marlatt, 1990).

Expectancies as Components of Memory

Several researchers have conceptualized cognitions involving drug use expectancies as components of a memory process that influence decisions about alcohol and drug use (e.g., Dunn & Goldman, 2000; Goldman, Brown, Christiansen, & Smith, 1991; Rather & Goldman, 1994; Stacy, 1995; Stacy, Widaman, & Marlatt, 1990). In this perspective, the performance of a behavior at a given moment, in part, is a function of one's memory of the anticipated consequences of the behavior. As an example, expectancies may be construed as associations stored in long-term memory between the concept of alcohol or drug use and associated outcomes (e.g., Stacy, Leigh, & Weingardt, 1994; Weingardt, Stacy, & Leigh, 1996).

An expectancy framework advanced by Goldman and colleagues involves the application of a semantic network of associations in memory to explain alcohol use (e.g., Dunn & Goldman, 1996; Goldman, Brown, Christiansen, & Smith, 1991; Rather & Goldman, 1994; Roehrich & Goldman, 1995). Goldman and colleagues have studied the organizational structure of alcohol expectancies with the use of multidimensional scaling and modeled an expectancy memory network space consisting of units of information about specific anticipated consequences of alcohol use (e.g., Goldman & Darkes, 2004). They propose that activation of a portion of the expectancy network through exposure to alcohol stimuli may result in activation of a portion (proximal words) of the related network through links that bind the network (Rather, Goldman, Roehrich, & Brannick, 1992; Rather & Goldman, 1994). Various contexts lead to the activation of specific expectancies in one's expectancy network based on past alcohol use experiences which, in turn, affect the initiation of goal-directed behavior or alcohol use (see Goldman, Reich, & Darkes, 2006).

Implicit Cognitive Processes

Implicit cognitive processes involve relatively automatically activated cognitions that may at times be manifested in conscious stream of thought, as opposed to the deliberate processing of information. Research in social cognition suggests that the acquisition of automaticity (or unconscious influences on behavior) develops through the influence of frequent and consistent experiences with a specific social behavior, which, in turn, affects the likelihood of engaging in that behavior. Although initially conscious choice plays a large part in decisions about engaging in a specific behavior "to the extent the same expectations are generated, or the same behavior is enacted, or the same goal and plan are chosen in that situation, conscious choice drops out as it is not needed – it has become a superfluous step in the process" (Bargh & Chartrand, 1999, p. 468). William James (1890) frequently referred to the observed influence of prior experience on subsequent performance with diminished conscious awareness. According to James, "Any sequence of mental action which has been frequently repeated tends to perpetuate itself; so that we find ourselves automatically prompted to think, feel, or do what we have been before accustomed to think, feel, or do, under like circumstances, without any consciously formed purpose, or anticipation of results" (James, 1890, p. 24).

One hundred years later, Greenwald and Banaji (1995) wrote, "Implicit cognitive processes reflect traces of past experience (that) affect some performance, even though the influential earlier experience is not remembered in the usual sense – that is, it is unavailable to self-report or introspection" (p. 5). Implicit cognitions toward a specific behavior (e.g., drug use) result from a store of information that includes associations involving drug effects (e.g., pleasurable outcomes), drug-related situations or environmental contexts and drug-relevant stimuli. These associations in memory are strengthened through repetitive drug use experiences (see Stacy 1995, 1997) and affect behavior through a relatively spontaneous process (i.e., patterns of activation in memory) that circumvents rational decision-making processes (for more information, see Stacy, 1997; Wiers & Stacy, 2006). The relative accessibility and activation of memory traces of past drug use experiences are dependent on an individual's experiences with drugs (Stacy, 1995, 1997; Stacy, Leigh, & Weingardt, 1994; Wise, 1988). Individual differences in physiological reward systems are likely to differentially influence the strength of drug-relevant associations and memory traces of past drug use (e.g., a very positive physiological experience as the result of drug use is relatively likely to increase drug-relevant associations). Whether or not a drug-consistent cognitive state and propensity to use drugs are easily activated in a variety of situations is determined by the strength of associations in memory (Stacy, 1995, 1997; Stacy, Ames, Sussman, & Dent, 1996; Weingardt, Stacy, & Leigh, 1996). Moreover, it is improbable that healthy behavioral decisions or competing concepts are activated simultaneously when a drug-consistent activation pattern has been elicited. Several researchers now apply an implicit cognition approach to understanding substance use and addiction (for reviews, see Ames, Franken, & Coronges, 2006; Stacy, Ames, & Grenard, 2006; Wiers et al., 2006).

Interplay of Implicit and Explicit Cognitive Processes

The interplay between implicit and explicit cognitive processes is complex and to date is still being investigated. However, there is evidence that individuals are often unaware of influences on their behavior, yet they freely provide a rational explanation of their behavior (for review, see Nisbett & Wilson, 1977). Several researchers have proposed "dual process theories" to help understand implicit and explicit cognitive systems as determinants of behavior (e.g., Evans, 2003; Kahneman, 2003; Reber, 1993; Stanovich & West, 2000; for dual process approaches to addiction, see Wiers & Stacy, 2006). Stanovich and West (2000) provide a simple typology (i.e., System 1 and System 2) to help explain variations of these underlying cognitive systems. In characterizing the distinctions between Stanovich and West's two cognitive systems, Kahneman (2003) summarizes that

the operations of System 1 are typically fast, automatic, effortless, associative, implicit (not available to introspection), and often emotionally charged; they are also governed by habit and are therefore difficult to control or modify. The operations of System 2 are slower, serial, effortful, more likely to be consciously monitored and deliberately controlled; they are also relatively flexible and potentially rule governed. (p. 698)

According to Kahneman (2003), the implicit or automatic cognitive system (System 1) is the system governing the majority of human decision-making, whereas System 2 monitors the operations of System 1. This perspective of automatic processes being a sort of default mode guiding behavior, unless overridden by deliberate thought processes, has been expressed in social psychological theories for over a decade (e.g., automatic and controlled processes of prejudice, Devine [1989]; motivation and opportunity as determinants of attitude-behavior processes; Fazio [1990]).

Currently, there is a general view that multiple systems of cognition relevant to addictions exist (see Wiers & Stacy, 2006). Both explicit and implicit cognitive processes have been shown to independently predict substance use when included in the same statistical models (e.g., Ames et al., 2007; Stacy, 1997; Wiers, van Woerden, Smulders, & de Jong, 2002). Moreover, both cognitive systems likely play unique and independent roles in the development of addictive behaviors and likely interact and take on different "roles" regarding the performance of a behavior. For example, someone might observe himself/herself acting on impulse or relatively automatically and know that it is self-defeating (executive function) yet keep doing it anyway (irrational behavior driven by implicit processes). In this instance, one is acting on implicit processes, whereas one's executive control is serving as the "observer." Alternatively, it is possible for someone to resist drug use through the structuring of time (executive function), although thoughts of drug use and pleasure may spontaneously come to mind (implicit cognition). In this case, executive function is the actor and implicit processes are more or less inhibited (Sussman & Unger, 2004).

Contextual stimuli likely influence the relative operation of explicit or implicit cognitive processes. Patterns of neural activation, influenced by the strength of associations in memory, guide behavior implicitly by affecting thought processes and interpretation of situations, contexts, and other stimuli, as well as the accessibility and inhibition in memory of behavioral options (Stacy, 1995, 1997). Stimuli that evoke pleasurable drug-related memory associations can affect patterns of activation consistent with drug use, whereas stimuli that evoke negative or non-drug-using-related memory associations can affect more prosocial behavior.

Belief–Behavior Congruence

Most individuals prefer to live with their beliefs consistent (or harmonious) with their behavior, at least those that are brought to their awareness. Twerski (1997) has asserted that drug-addicted individuals tend to engage in *perceptual distancing*. According to Twerski, the tendency to distort, discount, or not deliberately process time and daily experiences insulates a person engaging in self-destructive behaviors from consequences of the behavior on self and others. This type of perceptual distancing would be a strong barrier against behavioral change.

Twerski proposes that drug-addicted individuals think in terms of brief chunks of time and therefore believe that changes should happen rather quickly. For example, stopping drug use for a period of 1 month may feel like a very long time to an addict, even though life course changes actually occur much more slowly. A second characteristic of drug-addicted individuals, according to Twerski, is that potential addicts may view their experiences as not being genuine. The characteristics described by Twersky also may be reconceptualized as categories of *logical fallacies* (Ellis & Harper, 1975; Kahane, 1990; Sussman, 2005a; Sussman, Dent, & Stacy, 1996; Twersky, 1997).

Three types of logical fallacies are particularly relevant: (1) fallacies of distraction, (2) causal fallacies, and (3) fallacies of ambiguity. *Fallacies of distraction* occur when the processing of insufficient information results in poor decision-making. For example, one might misuse terms such as *or*, *not*, *if–then*, or *and* operators. Thinking that you are either an alcoholic *or* you are not and *if* you are an alcoholic, *then* you will tend to be homeless is a concrete example of the fallacy of distraction. One is distracted away from logical evaluation of the quality of one's life. *Causal fallacies* occur when the identification of the cause of a behavior or event is misconstrued. For example, stress causes smoking versus smoking causes one to feel stress; others complain so that one has to drink versus one drinks and this leads others to complain. *Fallacies of ambiguity* occur when phrases are used unclearly or inconsistently. For example, statements such as "you are sober today, so you are not alcoholic" versus "you are sober today, but you usually are drunk" may result in the cognitive-perceptual distancing of the perceiver from his or her self-destructive behavior.

Aside from distancing from an awareness of discrepancies between one's beliefs and one's behavior, someone may more actively attempt to maintain belief–behavior congruence. Awareness of equivocation or discrepancies between one's beliefs or desires and their behavior leads to a tendency to want to change the discrepancies (motivation; Miller & Rollnick, 1991). Two classic social psychological theories that are relevant to this belief–behavior discrepancy are Balance Theory (Heider, 1958) and Cognitive Dissonance Theory (Festinger, 1957).

Balance Theory argues that one seeks to achieve consistency regarding the polarity (+ or −) of relations with others, one's self, and one's own beliefs (Heider, 1958). If one's beliefs are inconsistent with one's sense of self or others with whom one forms a relationship with or attitude about, one will be motivated to change the belief, one's sense of self, or the relationship. Of course, although balanced situations might be relatively easy to remember, they will not necessarily be pleasant unless the polarities created are all positive (West & Wicklund, 1980). Drug users may perceptually distance so as to ignore a cognitive imbalance, or they may change their beliefs to become more favorable toward drug use so as to maintain a relationship with another drug user.

Cognitive Dissonance Theory argues that people are motivated to perceive a consistency between their decisions/behaviors and cognitions/beliefs. To make cognitions more consistent with behavioral decisions, one might discount their importance, change them, or add new consonant cognitions/beliefs (Festinger, 1957). It is possible that discounting one's cognitions is similar to perceptual distancing, and new consonant cognitions may be formed to support drug use behavior.

Contextual/Situational Distortions

Most individuals prefer to perceive their lifestyle as appropriate, normal, and of value. Thus, individuals may misinterpret or distort their life experiences to make them appear as relatively appropriate or normal. Two examples of theories that apply to situational distortions are Mystification Theory (Lennard, Epstein, Bernstein, & Ransom, 1971) and Perceived Effects Theory (Smith, 1980).

Mystification Theory suggests that meanings of behavior may become confounded or distorted due to subjective effects of experiences interpreted within contexts (Lennard, Epstein, Bernstein, & Ransom, 1971). The process of mystification involves the definition of issues and situations in such a way as to obscure their most basic and important features. In one's social world, behaviors previously defined as normal behavior may become defined as not normal (e.g., mild social anxiety), and drugs may be promoted to fix this behavior. Drugs may achieve their experiential effects by bypassing meaning and means such that the experiential outcome is not the "real" outcome (e.g., drug induced relaxation is not the same as learning to become more at ease in social situations by learning social skills). Also, the effects of drugs are derived not only by the pharmacological qualities of the drug but also by beliefs about the drugs and the social context within which drug use occurs. Thus,

Table 6.1. Cognitive etiological variables of drug abuse

The following may affect one's likelihood of becoming a drug abuser:

Cognitive-information errors
  • Errors of frequency or importance
  • False consensus effect
  • Illusory correlation
  • Implicit associative processes/implicit cognition
  • Unrealistic optimism
Limits in rational cognitive processing
  • Explicit cognitive processes
    – Having impaired corrective executive operations (due to time pressure, concurrent task demands, mood fluctuation, or avoidance of planning)
    – Variation in cognitive inhibitory and control processes (due to impulsivity, or incomplete development of frontal brain structures)
    – Cognitive or motivational drug use expectancies
  • Implicit cognitive processes
    – Memory associations (often the result of repetitive drug use behavior)
Belief-behavior congruence maintenance
  • Perceptual distancing
  • Logical fallacies
    – Fallacies of distraction
    – Causal fallacies
    – Fallacies of ambiguity
  • Active maintenance of belief-behavior congruence (*Balance Theory, Cognitive Dissonance Theory*)
Situational/contextual distortions
  • Mystification (*Mystification Theory*)
  • Perception of effects (*Perceived Effects Theory*)

it is understandable that a variety of myths regarding drug use and its effects can occur. For example, someone might view himself or herself as having formed meaningful friendships just because they use drugs together (Ames, Sussman, & Dent, 1999; Sussman, Dent, & Stacy, 1996). Another example of the mystification process is when someone begins to "get use to a drug." For example, with some drugs, such as cigarettes, an individual may become sick when he or she first uses them but may be taught by others that through continued use one becomes use to the drug and learns how to use it correctly; at that point, he or she will stop getting sick and enjoy use (bypassing the "real outcome" that "warning signals" are no longer operational and that the beginnings of addiction, tolerance, is in operation).

Perceived Effects Theory (Smith, 1980) suggests that most acts are intended to benefit the actor so that some consequences of drug use are grossly misperceived, but they may explain initiation of drug use because they appear to benefit the actor. For example, one may reinterpret a negative consequence of drug use (e.g., losing one's car in a parking lot) as being positive (e.g., funny). Also, one may interpret a positive consequence of drug use (e.g., spending time with another person while using drugs) as being more positive than it really is (e.g., true love and meaningful friendship). As escalation of use progresses, greater distortions of reality may justify continued use and abuse.

Summary

A combination of a variety of cognitive processes may lead to distortions of thought and compose an "addictive thinking" process (Table 6.1). Information distortions may lead to retention of "facts" that are not accurate. Limitations in cognitive processing permit the solidification of cognitive-information errors. Inaccurate facts may lead to the perception of belief–behavior congruence. Situational distortions may operate to maintain a sense of certainty regarding one's information–belief–behavioral processing of one's world.

Individuals may develop steadfast positive beliefs about drug use through social learning processes (Bandura, 1986), based on subjective experiences (Stacy & Ames, 2001), or due to peculiarities of learned behavior–outcome associations (Sussman, Dent, & Stacy, 1996). An illustration of this potential sequence of the four cognitive processes discussed in this chapter pertains to how marijuana use might be justified to regularly co-occur with driving a car. In this example, someone might link marijuana use to slowing down and link safe driving to slowing down. As a result of these associations, he or she may develop the cognitive-information error that marijuana use leads to safe driving; that is, if marijuana use is linked to slowing down and safe driving is linked to slowing down, then marijuana use is associated with safe driving. Cognitive processing of a favorable relationship between marijuana use, driving, and perceived safety may solidify to the extent that no car accidents initially occur while driving under the influence of marijuana intake. Cognitive processing limits may interfere with being able to process that although marijuana use might lead one to drive slower, one might also feel drowsy or experience a dangerously slower reaction time (Sussman et al., 1996). One may also believe that one should drive safely, so marijuana use is a good drug to use to be able to drive more safely – an example of belief–behavior congruence. Finally, one may view people who deter marijuana users from driving as uninformed villains – an example of contextual/situational distortion.

7   Social Interaction and Social Groups

This chapter examines small group-level effects on individuals that may facilitate drug use. Small group interactions involve verbal (word content and intonation) and nonverbal (body language) behavioral exchanges. Each member of the group interprets the meaning of the interactions that transpire, and these perceptions of interactions that occur may differ across group members. Therefore, a distinction between perceived or egocentric social phenomena and observed, group-level social phenomena is generally recognized (e.g., as in smoking; Hoffman, Sussman, Unger, & Valente, 2006). The topics presented in this chapter include possible egocentric and group-level effects on drug use. The topics presented include the family unit and parenting, peer social influence, social learning, social support, social networks, deviant subcultures, and group identification.

The Family Unit and Parenting

Youth begin or do not begin to have drug-related experiences through parental and older sibling discussions of use and modeling of use (Flay et al., 1994). In addition, family interactions may serve to facilitate later drug use or protect against later use. Youth from single-parent homes, or those who spend relatively less time with parents or guardians (latch-key children), are relatively likely to use drugs later on (Dwyer et al., 1990; Griffin et al., 2000; Richardson et al., 1989). These findings are remarkable and require careful consideration, given the increasing number of single-parent homes in the United States (and several other countries), as well as households where it is necessary for all adults in the home to work.

In general, "parenting styles" have been a focus of evaluation in understanding the relationship of parental treatment of children to childhood problem behaviors. For instance, one parenting style involves the degree of closeness or warmth the parent and child experience with each other. Close bonds, enabled through nurturing and accepting communications by the parent, tend to be associated with more prosocial childhood behavior. Possibly, the amount of time the parent spends with the child is particularly relevant to this aspect of parenting because the less time spent with the child, the less time warm communications occur. Both the quality of time (e.g., low on family conflict) and the quantity of time may be meaningful determinants of more positive behavioral outcomes (Dwyer et al., 1990; Richardson et al., 1989).

In addition to warm (good-quality) parenting and spending time with the child, parental monitoring of the child's activities and limit setting also are predictive of later drug use.

Baumrind (1978) provided a two-by-two matrix of parenting based on consideration of parental warmth and parental limit setting. Authoritative parents who are high on warmth and high limit setters appear to raise children who are better adjusted. These parents encourage achievement among their children and bring their children in on decision-making. Children reared with this method of parenting tend to identify with low-risk peer groups and are relatively unlikely to use drugs (Brown, Mounts, Lamborn, & Steinberg, 1993). Authoritarian parents who are low on warmth but high limit setters, permissive parents who are high on warmth but low limit setters, and neglectful parents who are low on warmth and low limit setters, have been found to raise children who are less well adjusted and more likely to use drugs (Sussman, Pokhrel, Ashmore, & Brown, 2007). In addition, parents who use punitive discipline methods or argue with their spouses about discipline are more likely to report that their children are aggressive or have behavioral control problems (Kandel, 1990). This is particularly true of the primary caretaker. Also, parents who may react to their children's interest in smoking by trying to reward their children for not smoking may unintentionally lead to an increased likelihood that their children will smoke (Huver, Engels, & de Vries, 2006).

Substance abusers, to the extent that they are dysfunctional as parents, may tend to exhibit many poor parenting characteristics associated with later drug use by their children (Kandel, 1990; Loxley et al., 2004), as well as modeling drug use behavior (Loxley et al., 2004; Sher, 1991). Children of substance users may incur physical injury as a function of prenatal exposure to parental drug use on a variety of drug types (Loxley et al., 2004). In summary, children of family members who use drugs themselves, who experience a great deal of conflict within the family system, or who are not in close and constant monitored contact with parents tend to become involved in drug use. Parenting that is not firm, consistent, and kind or that is tolerant of deviant behavior tends to lead to drug use among offspring. As youth grow older, parents and other family members still exert a strong influence through friendship selection and continued role modeling (Flay et al., 1994).

Peer Social Influences on Drug Use

Researchers have repeatedly demonstrated that one of the strongest predictors of drug use among teens is friend and peer use of drugs (e.g., Barnes & Welte, 1986; Flay et al., 1994; Hoffman et al., 2006; Kandel & Andrews, 1987; Unger & Chen, 1999; Urberg, Degirmenci-olglu, & Pilgrim, 1997). For example, deviant peer groups tend to use drugs, offer drugs to each other within groups, and role model drug use. Association with such peer groups influences the likelihood that one will experiment with drugs. Social influence is an especially important predictor of drug use and abuse among teens (Figure 7.1).

Researchers in applied social psychology report two main types of pressure to use drugs that the peer group exerts on its members: (1) normative social influence and (2) informational social influence (see Deutsch & Gerard, 1955; Eiser, 1985; Sussman et al., 1995). *Normative social influence* is described as wanting members of the group to act consistently with the group to gain or maintain acceptance of other group members. For instance, if most group members "smoke weed" (marijuana) and drink alcohol, they may want other members of the group to behave similarly and conform to the behaviors of the group. Individuals may seek out groups with behaviors similar to their own (group "selection") or they may change their own behavior to conform (group "influence") to

Figure 7.1. Image of an all-night rave where alcohol and other drugs such as ecstasy are often used.

the group (Bauman & Fisher, 1986). The normative behaviors for youths' closest reference group may be inconsistent with behaviors among an individual's general cohort (e.g., more frequent or less frequent drug use behavior) and with societal norms.

Informational social influence can be construed as a form of teaching members of the group to share similar attitudes about various behaviors and their social meanings. That is, individuals may observe the behaviors of others who are also in the same situation to see how they behave, follow their example, and learn about the behavior and what to expect. The group acts as an information source for how to behave. For example, let's say someone is "hanging out" (Wills, 1986) with a group of relatively deviant kids and some of the others start drinking and passing a water pipe. This individual, however, has never smoked weed before and does not really know how to use a pipe or what to expect from the drug, but he or she wants to be a part of this group of kids. So, this individual watches the others and how they react and learns what to do and what to expect (e.g., does it feel good or not and is it okay to act silly or not). Basically, an individual seeks information from social situations, which, in turn, influences his or her behavior and perception of acceptable or prevalent behaviors. In return for yielding to normative or informational social influence, the group provides social reinforcers to its members. These reinforcers consist of various types of social support, as described later.

Parental social influence dominates over peer social influence until early adolescence, at which point parents exert more of an indirect influence on behavior through friendship selection (Flay et al., 1994). Generally, direct peer social influence effects on drug use are relatively likely to be exhibited most strongly among younger teens (Sussman, Earleywine, et al., 2004) prior to internalization of individual standards of behavior.

Social Cognitive/Learning Theory

One theory that is perhaps a specification of informational social influence is social cognitive/learning theory. According to social cognitive/learning theory (Bandura, 1986), drug use can develop through vicarious learning, modeling, and/or reinforcing pharmacological drug effects. In other words, role models act as teachers of where and when, how much, and how a drug is used. For example, an individual might learn that it is acceptable or prevalent to drink alcohol on weekends or during celebratory events. Role models also teach the probable outcomes of drug use (e.g., that moderate alcohol use enhances social interaction) and how to use certain drugs (e.g., to drink wine from a glass or beer from the bottle). According to this theory, an individual's behavior is for the most part regulated by cognitive processes, even though response consequences may mediate the behavior. For example, drug use effects, whether observed or experienced, are processed by the individual to form expectations of behavioral outcomes that may encourage or inhibit drug use.

Processes of social/cognitive learning are intertwined with culture; that is, observing drug use within a (different) culture with (different) outcomes can influence one's perception of and attitudes toward drug use behaviors. For instance, recreational marijuana use is tolerated in the Netherlands, whereas in the United States even the medical use of marijuana is highly controversial. If one is raised in the Netherlands, one may not consider marijuana use as being a deviant behavior (Sussman & Huver, 2006).

Social Support

"Social support" pertains to the assistance that people in social networks provide to each other. Social support is provided through a network of family, friends, and other acquaintances, and sometimes community agencies. The support provided by the network can increase one's sense of belonging, self-identity, purpose, and sense of well-being. There are various types of social support individuals can offer each other; for example, companionship, instrumental, conformity, and informational supports (Cohen, 1988).

Companionship refers to offers of spending time engaging in shared activities and providing emotional support through sharing life experiences. Individuals may decide to use drugs as a means of having others to spend time and share life experiences with; a "companion" type of support. *Instrumental* support includes provision of material goods or services, such as money or car rides. Friends, siblings, or other family members may purchase drugs for the individual – an example of an "instrumental" type of support.

Conformity refers to social pressure that may operate to encourage a person to engage in positive or negative behavior. In fact, lower expectations of friends and lower control by friends, along with unstructured time, may contribute to drug use (Hoffman et al., 2006). How and to what extent deviant group low expectations and "high control" may operate together as separate or as overlapping constructs remains to be determined (e.g., Akers, Krohn, Lanza-Kaduce, & Radosevich, 1979).

Informational social support implies provision of knowledge about the world that can help one surmount barriers in personal development. For instance, observing friends who seem to be enjoying drug use may make one more curious about drug use; friends may provide an "informational" type of support. This type of social support, social cognitive/learning theoretical notions, and informational social influence may overlap conceptually.

Social support provides a "boost" for the individual receiving the support. However, processes of social support (or influence) also may operate to result in a boomerang effect under certain conditions. For example, Gruenfeld and Wyer (1992) found that individuals who were exposed to a written argument against a belief consistent with what they believed (i.e., they already did not believe in the belief), and were not asked to consider the pragmatic implications of the assertions made, could change their perception of the validity of the belief. Thus, if youth are exposed to the belief within their peer group that "drug use is not fun" (an argument that may or may not be true) and they already believed that "drug use is not fun," they may begin to wonder if drug use indeed *might* be fun. Peer group effects thus are, in part, mediated by one's social cognition. Much still needs to be learned about the interaction of cognitive levels of etiology with social levels of etiology. Generally, the behavioral directions that peer group support provides depend on the composition of the social network.

Social Network Theory

The underlying assumption of social network theory is that an individual is influenced by others with whom he or she has contact and that an individual's position within larger social groups or structures can determine behavior, either through constraint to inhibit action or influences to act (Valente, Gallaher, & Mouttapa, 2004). Social network analysis maps many relatively "invisible" relationships between people, providing an organizational structure of social relationships. The methods of social network analysis consist of established proce-dures for measuring characteristics and dimensions of these relationships and use specific mathematical algorithms to calculate network constructs (see Scott, 2004; Wasserman & Faust, 1994). Social network methods generally are used in smaller organizations where the boundary of the network can be defined.

Sociometric social network measures are generated primarily at two ecological levels – the individual (e.g., one's positioning in the social network) and the group level (e.g., network density). There are numerous individual measures that can be generated from a single network question. For example, asking students for the names of their friends at school (e.g., one may be asked to list his or her ten best friends) can generate many indicators measuring, for each student, their relative centrality in a friendship network, their membership in groups, and reciprocity of ties. The same data can be used to generate network level indicators such as the degree to which the network is dense (tightly knit) or sparse, its centralization among a number of other groups, the number of cliques, and their overlap.

One unique aspect of social network analysis is its ability to categorize people in terms of their *position* within a network. By nature of their social relations, some people are more central or popular in a group (e.g., in a school classroom) than others. This determination might be made through an indication of the number of members of the group that indicate that this person is among their best friends. The most frequent and possibly useful position identified by social network analysis is *centrality*, the degree to which a person occupies a central position in the network. Those individuals occupying a central position within the network may be more influential in dissemination of information and regulation of behavioral norms. Because they are "linked" to relatively more members of the group, they are able to exert a greater control over information flow. Centrality can be measured in a variety of ways within the same network (see Valente, Gallaher, & Mouttapa, 2004).

Another position identified by social network analysis is the *liaison*. A liaison is a person who connects otherwise disconnected or weakly connected groups. Liaisons are paradoxical in that they are weakly connected to groups, yet these weak connections give them strength.

Granovetter (1973) referred to this phenomenon as the "strength of weak ties," because the ties were to people and groups the person does not often see or is not connected to through multiple channels. Yet the liaison has access to information and resources that the rest of the group does not have.

Isolates are individuals who seemingly have no connections to others in the network and can be identified by network analysis. In diffusion of innovations research, isolates have been shown to be later adopters of innovations because their position puts them outside the flow of information about new ideas (Rogers, 2003; Valente, 2002). Similarly, in a high-risk setting (e.g., where substance use is of high prevalence), being an isolate may offer protection because the individual is quarantined from negative influences in the group. However, isolates are often strongly connected to another group outside the social contexts of the networks often being examined in current research (e.g., school groups) and this other group may put them at risk. For example, a middle school student reporting no in-school friends may have friends outside the school (e.g., neighborhood friends) and these ties may influence the student to misuse substances (Valente, Gallaher, & Mouttapa, 2004).

In addition to measures of network position, network analysis can be used to create network measures that characterize a person's interpersonal environment. For example, *reciprocity* is the degree to which the people a person names as friends also name him or her as a friend. A high degree of reciprocity in a social network indicates a shared understanding of who likes whom. Low levels of reciprocity or an asymmetric network could possibly indicate a hierarchical structure, whereas higher levels of reciprocity may indicate more equality among network members.

A second measure of one's interpersonal environment is *personal network density*, the degree to which a person's ties are connected to one another. A dense personal network indicates that a person's friends know and like one another. Dense personal networks can reinforce behavioral norms consistently once a behavior is accepted or endorsed by a majority of the group.

Homophily, a third interpersonal environment measure, is the degree of similarity between two people; homophily can be studied within the context of social network analysis. For instance, in terms of a behavior (e.g., adolescent smoking), homophily refers to someone selecting friends who engage in shared behaviors (e.g., smoking). Researchers have found evidence for homophily by smoking status in adolescent friendships. For example, the variance in cigarette smoking between cliques has been found to be greater than the variance within cliques, suggesting that adolescents in the same cliques share the same smoking status (Ennett, Bauman, & Koch, 1994). Adolescents who have experimented with smoking are more likely to have friends who have either tried smoking or are current smokers than adolescents who have never tried smoking (Urberg, Degirmencioglu, & Pilgrim, 1997). Dense networks or multiple networks connected through liaisons provide a network-level examination of predictors and/or diffusion of drug use within a small groups system.

One could speculate that in terms of drug use, small tightly knit (denser) networks may be more behaviorally constraining and, as a result, limit members' exposure to alternative behaviors. For example, belonging to a tightly knit non-drug-using network may protect one from experimenting with drugs, whereas belonging to a tightly knit drug using network may greatly encourage drug use. A small, relatively dense drug-using network also may be the consequence of selecting drug use buddies from a more open expansive network, which might occur in some treatment settings (Dishion, Poulin, & Burraston, 2001). Identification with dense drug-using networks is a likely barrier to effective drug abuse treatment-seeking and outcomes. For instance, creation of new "using buddies" can occur as persons are exposed to each other in drug abuse treatment. Also, returning after treatment to a social environment that includes a dense network of drug using buddies could easily jeopardize one's sobriety.

Alternatively, more "open" or expansive social networks, with more social connections and many ties (although perhaps weaker), are more likely to expose individuals to a wider range of information and opportunity than smaller, relatively dense networks. Consequently, individuals in larger networks may be more likely to be exposed to both anti-drug use and pro-drug use information and behaviors. Regarding pro-drug information, the large-sized network may provide the information and means necessary to procure drugs and drug paraphenalia, provide drug using friends to "run with," and provide a systemic means of distribution. Therefore, individuals in more expansive networks require the necessary skills to be able to resist pressures from other individuals within the network or seek out prosocial members within the network.

Youth may be members of a variety of networks at school, at home (including the neighborhood), at other public places (church, religious institutions, clubs, the park), and while engaging in formalized activities (e.g., sports and recreational activities). An individual's network connections may be different in different contexts and may possibly influence drug use as well as nonuse differentially. Much more research is needed on the interface of youths' multiple social networks in their daily lives. However, one may tentatively conclude that the more interested a youth is in using drugs, the more social contacts one makes during the day who are also interested in using drugs, and the more approval one receives from multiple social networks for being interested in using drugs, the more likely one is to use and continue using drugs. One may become entrenched in deviant subcultures.

Deviant Subcultures

The process of socialization is a means of transmitting cultural or subcultural norms (e.g., the appropriateness of the frequencies of different social behaviors, such as personal space, establishing eye contact, voice volume, and speech content and frequency) and obtaining a social identity. Group socialization is a form of learning appropriate behaviors of certain groups and differs across different groups of people. *Differential socialization* refers to the group-specific channeling of the development of beliefs, intentions, expectations, norms, perceptions, and modeling of social behaviors. Differential socialization processes may lead one to hold beliefs and perceptions that drug use is tolerable by others in one's social environment (Akers, Krohn, Lanza-Kaduce, & Radosevich, 1979). This may affect an individual's intention to initiate use. Family conflict, poor supervision, or drug use tolerance by parents, family modeling of drug-using behavior, and deviant peer group association are processes of differential socialization that have been found to be quite influential in facilitating experimental drug use (for review, see Hawkins, Catalano, & Miller, 1992).

Prosocial bonding or *constraint* refers to ties to conventional society that might prevent deviant behavior. Without prosocial bonds available and actively restraining maladaptive behavior, it is relatively easy to form delinquent subcultures (Hirschi, 1969). The basic notion of delinquent subcultures is that differential socialization may lead to group norms that serve to rationalize problem behavior (Akers, Krohn, Lanza-Kaduce, & Radosevich,

1979; Cohen, 1955). These rationalizations may reflect group norms that exist in opposition to dominant social values and occur in subcultural groups. Cohen, and some sociologists since (e.g., Bordua, 1962), argued that certain youth subcultures engage in problem behaviors due to a gross reaction against middle-class society, as an expression of a general negativism, and because they find such activities to be a great deal of fun in the short run. There are, of course, other youth who strongly react against middle-class norms and values but find alternative acceptable means of expressing their discontent (e.g., involvement in community activism).

There are several variants of the deviant subcultures notion. One such variant is *neutralization theory* (Sykes & Matza, 1957). Neutralization theory suggests that those individuals who exhibit problem behavior actually do internalize dominant social norms. Norms, however, are viewed as qualified guides for action, limited by situational variables (e.g., killing during war is okay; Agnew & Peters, 1986; Dodder & Hughes, 1993; Shields & Whitehall, 1994; Sykes & Matza, 1957). Techniques of neutralization include denial of responsibility for one's behavior (e.g., one's drug use was beyond his or her control), denial of injury (e.g., believing one's drug use behavior is not harming anyone), denial of the victim (e.g., "ripping someone off" to obtain money for drugs and believing they deserved it), condemnation of the condemners (e.g., being busted for drug use and feeling the police are hypocrites), and appealing to higher authorities (e.g., loyalty to one's drug using network and their "causes").

Recent work on "deviant talk" provides exploration into the development of deviant interactions that underlie such subcultural groups. Deviant or rule-break talk is defined as utterances that contain antisocial or norm-breaking elements. Talk about stealing, lying, aggression, illegal acts, favorable depictions about drug use (i.e., talk about "being bad"), as well as swearing and rude or offensive gestures, removing clothes ("being bad"), and positive reactions to rule-break behavior (e.g., laughing, reinforcing reactions to bad behavior) are exemplars of rule-break topics and deviancy training. Although many youth engage in deviant talk and rule-break behavior, those youth who become absorbed more and more in such talk are at increased risk for future problem behavior (Granic & Dishion, 2003). Time spent with deviant peers, positive reactions among deviant peers for rule-break behavior, and processes where deviant youth attempt to and succeed in attracting attention among lower risk peers are all aspects of deviancy training, which can lead to subsequent exposure to and increases in drug use (Dishion, 2000; Dishion, Poulin, & Burraston, 2001; Poulin, Dishion, & Burraston, 2001). Although youth may fall into various social networks, and may differentially socialize into deviant peer groups, they also tend to identify with these or other peer groups about which they provide names and lifestyle descriptors.

Group Identification

Social scientists have long noted the tendency for people to place themselves and others into consensually recognized and labeled social types. Adolescents tend to segregate themselves into different peer group types and give names to these peer group types. This has been illustrated in movies such as *The Breakfast Club* (1985) and *Clueless* (1995). Peer group names that adolescents give themselves or each other suggest the groups' lifestyle characteristics, such as shared beliefs, interests in clothes and music, and preferences for specific activities. As discussed by Brown and Lohr (1987), adolescents may identify with groups to develop a sense of identity and a positive self-concept and an increased sense of personal autonomy from parents. In addition, these group categories may reinforce cultural norms by indicating successful and unsuccessful ways of participating in the culture.

Teens may "place" themselves into peer group types in at least two ways. First, they may simply identify themselves with a certain peer social type regardless of any direct interaction with other peers. In this sense, they are making a statement about the type of teen they are within the culture (i.e., they are stating the name of the reputation-based collective in which they feel they take part). Second, these adolescents may actually participate in peer groups that reflect the larger collective. The peer groups provide a check on whether they view youth as "really" a member of the peer group type or only someone who tries to be part of the group (a "wannabe"). Adolescence is a period when individuals begin to make independent choices about life. At this time, adolescents are in the process of moving toward a social world where they are among peers and away from the closed environment of the parental home where the immediate family largely influences them. Due to a lack of experience adolescents are often not sure about the lifestyle decisions they should make (e.g., balancing their social and school lives, vocational orientation). In need of support and direction they are likely to search for a place to belong among a group of peers by conforming to the norms of the group. Peer groups thus either vicariously or directly facilitate adolescents' transition into the larger social environmental world.

The peer group identification literature began at least four decades ago. In some of the earliest work, Clark (1962) suggested the existence of three teen peer groups that he named "Funs" (the elite group), "Academics" (involved in school courses), and "Delinquents" (the deviant group). Subsequent peer group identification studies provided data-based support for a similar pattern of general types of peer groups, ranging generally from three to six in number and similar lifestyle features of these groups.

Several studies have found that peer group identification is related to problem prone behaviors such as substance use and risk-taking. Sussman, Pokhrel, Ashmore, and Brown (2007) provide an exhaustive review of forty-four peer-reviewed quantitative or qualitative studies completed on adolescent peer group identification. Adolescent peer group identification as defined in this literature is one's self-perceived or other-person-perceived membership (i.e., how other people, adults or peers, view one) in discrete teenage peer groups. The studies reviewed suggest that adolescent peer groups consist of five general categories differentiable by lifestyle characteristics: Elites, Athletes, Academics, Deviants, and Others. Sussman and colleagues found that the Deviant adolescent group category consistently reported relatively greater participation in drug use and other problem behaviors across studies, whereas Academics and Athletes exhibited the least participation in these problem behaviors. Additional research is needed in this arena to better understand the operation of adolescent group labels (Table 7.1).

Summary

This chapter provided an overview of the effects people in one's intimate support systems might have on whether an individual initiates drug use. The values and behaviors of parents, siblings, friends, and other role models affect the learning experiences of an individual and interactions between the individual, support systems, and society. Social support comes from one's social networks or single connections to others (i.e., relationships with friends,

Table 7.1. Social interaction and social group etiological variables influencing drug use

Social group influences on behavior	
Family unit and parenting	Family interactions may serve as protective or risk factors for subsequent drug use (e.g., conflict-ridden versus warm interactions). Parenting styles affect problem behaviors. Quality and quantity of family time a child experiences and parental monitoring of a child's activities are examples of factors predictive of later drug use.
Peer social influence	Friends and peer affiliation can inhibit or promote drug use behaviors. For example, affiliation with drug using groups influences the likelihood that one will experiment with drugs. Friend and peer use of drugs is considered to be one of the strongest predictors of drug use among teens.
Social/cognitive theory	Suggests that drug use can develop through vicarious learning, modeling, and/or through reinforcing pharmacological drug effects. Role models act as teachers of the time and place, quantity, and methods of drug use. According to this theory, cognitive processes primarily regulate behavior; however, response consequences play a role in mediating behavior, as do cultural components that influence perceptions and attitudes towards drug use.
Social support	Social support refers to the assistance that people in social networks provide to each other. Social support may be provided through a network of family, friends, and other acquaintances, and sometimes through community agencies. The various types of social support that individuals can offer each other include companionship, instrumental, conformity, and informational supports.
Social networks	Social networks influence an individual's choices about those with whom he/she has contact and with whom he/she interacts, which can determine behavior, either through constraint to inhibit action or influences promoting action. Social network analysis categorizes individuals in terms of their position within a network, as well as the composition of the network. For example, individuals occupying central positions within a network tend to be more influential in dissemination of information and regulation of behavioral norms.
Deviant subcultures	Differential socialization may lead to group norms that serve to rationalize problem behavior or deviant subcultures. Differential socialization involves the group specific channeling of the development of beliefs, intentions, expectations, norms, perceptions, and modeling of social behaviors.
Group identification	Refers to the tendency for people to identify or place themselves and others into a consensually recognized and labeled group, which may promote or inhibit drug use behavior. Group categories may reinforce cultural norms by indicating successful and unsuccessful ways of participating in a particular culture.

parents) and comes in different forms (e.g., companionship and instrumental). Social support may directly influence an individual's behavior (e.g., peer pressure to use drugs and drugs purchased by friends or family) and/or social support may interact with other influences (e.g., stress, physiological vulnerability, and social cognition) in the development or nondevelopment of substance use and abuse. Social support tends to help assist one with coping with negative life events, but types of coping depend on differential socialization processes that often are controlled through selective social networks.

Social network analysis provides a means of understanding the organizational structure of social relationships through the mapping of relationships among individuals within and across groups and the diffusion of behaviors. Belonging to a small tightly knit non-drug-using network might be protective against drug use experimentation by limiting members' exposure to informational drug use influence. The alternative – belonging to a small tightly knit drug using network – might encourage drug use and select out anti-drug use information. Self-identification with a deviant subgroup, engaging in deviant talk, and associating with deviant subgroups perpetuate deviant behaviors. Individuals are strongly influenced by their most intimate social groups but also through the larger social and physical environment, which is the topic of the next chapter.

8   The Large Social and Physical Environment

This chapter addresses the larger physical and social environmental influences on drug misuse development (e.g., drug availability and neighborhood organization), including geographic and cultural information that characterizes one's environment. Several theoretical models have been used to examine this etiologic arena. For example, Szapocznik and Coatsworth's (1999) Ecodevelopmental Model – based in part on Bronfenbrenner's (1979) Ecological Systems Theory – examines the child within and across ecological systems that may be involved in risk and protective processes that influence drug use. These processes represent interactions of youths with their families, community units, and larger scale physical and cultural influences. The present chapter focuses on molar levels of analysis or influences of these larger scale complex systems.

Physical environmental influences on drug misuse vulnerability can be categorized as the size, density, and configuration of geographical areas that could either constrain or facilitate drug misuse. Such influences include large-scale constraints, such as the presence of prosocial physical environmental resources like museums and fitness clubs or views of nature that have calming effects. Aspects of an environment reflective of community disorganization that could lead to psychological stress and maladaptive coping include exposures to dilapidated or unprotected structures that provide places for drug distribution, high alcohol outlet density, or crowding, crime presence, and noise. We place community disorganization as a "physical" environmental influence though it could also be conceptualized as a large social environmental influence. Because both of these large-scale influences are inextricably intertwined, we have chosen to define large social environmental influences more narrowly for the purposes of this chapter.

Large social environmental influences on drug misuse include culturally expressed communications within the large physical environment (e.g., the mass media such as newspapers, billboards, and movies, in various languages, with various role models being depicted) that also could constrain or facilitate drug misuse. Constraints include availability and communication of equitable arrangements for multiple cultural groups and anti-drug or prosocial communications. Risk factors may include racism or other forms of ethnic tension, nonproductive acculturative processes, and mass media advertisements and movies or works in print favorable to drug use. Adolescents (and adults) are routinely exposed to a variety of cultural norms and contexts through experiences with peers, family members, and through their neighborhood, as well as through exposures to the media and the World Wide Web. Understanding the effect of these varying cultural/large social environmental contexts on drug use and misuse is important for etiologic purposes as well as for prevention and treatment programming (e.g., consideration of cultural sensitivity and biases).

This chapter first focuses on physical environmental antecedents, including the physical surroundings, socioeconomic status, drug distribution routes, and relevant measurement models (e.g., Geographical Information Systems). Next, social environmental antecedents are described. Cultural constructs are described, including consideration of gender and ethnicity-as-culture and acculturation processes. Finally, the influence of the mass media is described.

Physical-Environmental Antecedents of Drug Use

Physical-environmental antecedents of drug use include the influence of an individual's physical surroundings, such as geographical location, dwelling contexts, and changes occurring in these contexts (e.g., disorganization and modernization). Environmental influences that are associated with, and perhaps motivate, experimentation with drugs include neighborhood disorganization, economic deprivation, and the availability of drugs (American Psychological Association [APA], 2006; Hawkins, Catalano, & Miller, 1992).

Neighborhood disorganization refers to a lack of centralized authority or the rapid changeovers of authority, which may result in insufficient methods or degree of monitoring and regulating behaviors within the community. Because of this lack of behavioral regulation, individuals residing in more chaotic neighborhoods are relatively likely to be exposed to unsanctioned instances of social disobedience (especially in densely inhabited metropolitan regions), such as public drunkenness, drug dealing, and gang-related activities (APA, 2006; Skogan & Lurigio, 1992). In addition, abandoned buildings, and other building structures that provide many enclosed public areas or the lack of defensible space, lend themselves to a greater incidence of crime perpetration and drug use. These types of buildings tend to be more prevalent in dense, urban, disorganized neighborhoods.

Socioeconomics, Locations, and Drug Use

Adverse socioeconomic conditions (often manifested in dilapidated physical building structures and densely populated living spaces) may limit one's access to more prosocial recreational opportunities (e.g., nearby presence of movie theatres and money for movie tickets). The influence of adverse economic conditions in early and later life might also expose one to relatively greater drug-related criminal activity, such as observation of drug sales as an alternative means of generating income (Mason, Cheung, & Walker, 2004). Relatively low socioeconomic status tends to be associated with greater drug use among adults (Wills, Pierce, & Evans, 1996). For example, the use of crack cocaine is prevalent among economically deprived groups and ethnic minorities who reside in large metropolitan areas. There exists, however, the perennial question: Does drug abuse lead to a downward drift into adverse socioeconomic conditions, or does lower socioeconomic status lead to drug abuse? For instance, do individuals living in adverse conditions tend to self-medicate more than individuals in relatively better economic situations? In addition, other confounding factors affect the relationship between adverse socioeconomic conditions and self-medication (e.g., mental health status) (Figure 8.1).

Figure 8.1. Abandoned buildings and urban decay provide conditions that lend to a greater incidence of crime perpetration and drug use.

Among adolescents, a variety of influences, such as family dynamics and peer-group association, affect the relative importance of socioeconomic influences on drug use. One could speculate that familial and other social influences can protect children from prodrug influences. As youth grow older, however, these protective influences can fade. As adults, lower socioeconomic conditions can be associated with a myriad of challenges to self-worth and security (if one has not yet become upwardly mobile through positive peer influences; e.g., from school). Some young adults may seek out means of self-medication under these disadvantaged circumstances. In addition, those youth whose parents suffer economic losses may be relatively likely to use drugs. For example, a recent study found that parental loss of a job, which is indicative of a decrease in a family's socioeconomic status, was associated with subsequent experimentation with cigarettes by youths (Unger, Hamilton, & Sussman, 2004). Conversely, young adults who are successful economically may be able to afford to purchase large quantities of expensive drugs, may become addicted, and then may suffer a rapid descent in socioeconomic status. Probably, both self-medication and downward drift operate as explanations of the association between socioeconomic status and drug abuse.

Environmental Availability of Drugs

The *availability* of drugs in an individual's environment can influence drug use. Availability includes ease of distribution, access, and acquisition of drugs. Ease of distribution refers to the establishment of a "business" structure, with relatively little resistance to transporting drugs in and out of a location. Access refers to one's knowledge about where to tap drug supplies along a distribution route. Interestingly, among teens, access to illegal sales by store owners (of tobacco, alcohol, or over-the-counter drugs) has only a small effect on purchases.

Most teens obtain their purchases through provision by friends (older or younger than 18 years old), parents, or siblings, regardless of store enforcement of no sales to a minor policy (Dent & Biglan, 2004; McCabe, Teter, & Boyd, 2004).

Finally, ease of acquisition refers to one's ability to obtain the drug. Near proximity of drugs in an individual's environment can result in more frequent exposures to drug use activities and may provide more opportunities to acquire the drugs. Indeed, acquisition of various drugs is easier in poorer, urban areas. However, although the visibility of illicit drugs is 600% greater in poorer neighborhoods, illicit drug use is only approximately 30% more likely to occur than in wealthier neighborhoods – perhaps because these poorer neighborhoods also serve as places for those from wealthier neighborhoods to purchase drugs (APA, 2006; Saxe et al., 2001).

Points of Distribution and Drug Use

It is possible that differences in use frequency are related to distance from major points of drug distribution (e.g., New York City and Los Angeles, large port cities). Indeed, observed regional variation in drug use prevalence has been found within the United States. In particular, residents of communities in the Northeast or West are more likely to use drugs than residents of the Midwest or South (Adams, Gfoerer, & Rouse, 1989; Almog, Anglin, & Fisher, 1993; Warner et al., 1995).

Points of drug production (e.g., opium fields), manufacturing (e.g., heroin creation), and distribution routes tend to identify regions at high risk for abuse (U.S. DEA, 1996; U.S. DEA, 1997; U.S. DHHS, 1998b; White, 1999). Currently, a majority of cocaine is produced and manufactured in Colombia. For distribution, it travels through Mexico and the Caribbean to different markets; generally, cocaine travels first throughout the Americas and then to Europe. Cocaine-type drugs dominate in North and South America. Cocaine-type drugs (cocaine, crack-cocaine, and basuco or coca paste) are predominant in all nineteen countries in the Americas and are responsible for close to 60% of all treatment cases in the Americas. Among the larger countries in the Americas (United States, Mexico, and Brazil), approximately 30% of treatment demand is related to cocaine abuse. In Europe, 3% of treatment admissions are for cocaine abuse. Traffickers based in South American countries, Japan, the United States, and Nigeria bring cocaine to Asia. Thus, abuse of cocaine is spreading throughout the world, though highest abuse is around the main production centers and along distribution routes.

Ninety-five percent of opium is currently grown in Myanmar (Burma) and Afghanistan (85% of the total is grown in Afghanistan). Much of the opium travels from Afghanistan into Iran, Tajikistan, and northern Pakistan. It then travels through Turkey, other Eastern European republics, and Russia, where it eventually travels into Western Europe or the United States. A great deal of opium also travels out from Myanmar into China and into Canada and the United States. It also travels from Myanmar through Malaysia and into Western Europe. The majority of treatment admissions in South Asia and East Asia are for heroin abuse. In most parts of Europe, the main problem drugs are opiates (mostly heroin abuse). Approximately 70% of treatment demand in Europe is linked to opiates (Figures 8.2 and 8.3).

Cannabis is grown all over the world. However, major hotspots of production and distribution are California (in the United States), Mexico, Jamaica, Amsterdam, Cambodia (which makes its way to Europe through Malaysia), and the Philippines. In America and Europe, cannabis is the second largest drug creating treatment demand (9% of treatment admissions in Europe are for cannabis abuse). In Asia, cannabis is the third

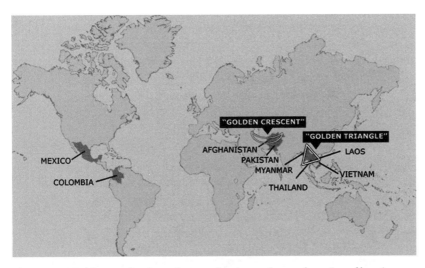

Figure 8.2. World map of major opium production and manufacturing of heroin.

largest problem drug. Treatment for cannabis abuse is quite diffusely spread out around the world.

Physical Environment Network-Type Models of Substance Use

A general network approach involves creating a quantitative, systems-level model of the impact of substance use and misuse on the community (Gorman et al., 2004). This entails creating a network model that can describe spatial and temporal interactions between key components of the community system. Such a model is essentially self-contained; the components and interactions between components of the model stand independent of other aspects of community systems. However, the parameters of the model depend on a set of specified inputs, some of which are community-level control variables (e.g., transportation systems, location of stores that sell alcohol, and traffic flow) and some of which are inputs beyond community control. The latter would include, for example, state-level taxation in the case of alcohol or federal laws pertaining to deterrence or punishment for possession in the case of illicit drugs. From the model, one can measure outputs that are of direct interest to the good of the community (such as violent acts or drug use hangouts in a specified public space). The ultimate goal of developing these types of models is to create a tool to explore and predict how changes in the control variables can influence positive changes in the outputs.

Such network models can best be understood in terms of a set of fundamental components (Brantingham & Brantingham, 1993; Chowell, Hyman, Eubank, & Castillo-Chavez, 2002; Strogatz, 2001). In their simplest form, network models consist of a set of nodes and a collection of directed edges between nodes. In the case of drug-related outputs, the nodes will by and large correspond to geographic locations in the community where drug-relevant events take place. Examples include locations of alcohol outlets, parks, pedestrian interaction zones, homes, and freeway on-ramps. Associated with each node is a collection of discrete and continuous functions, termed *attributes*, that measure activities at the nodes. These attributes are time dependent. For example, if the node represents a liquor store, then two attributes that might be assigned are the expected number of underage youth who visit

Figure 8.3. Opium poppy harvest in north Manchuria, Manchukuo.

the store each hour multiplied by the probability that an underage visitor to the store makes a purchase. Physical environment network-type models might hold promise as a means to map out drug manufacture, transportation, and distribution systems through diverse geographical contexts (see Gorman et al., 2004, for more details).

Another related type of measurement of drug-relevant features in the physical environment makes use of Geographic Information Systems (GIS). GIS is a set of tools that captures, manages, analyzes, and visualizes spatial data. GIS also examines the processes that may shape spatial patterns. Most data by default have a spatial component, such as the location where data are gathered. Spatial data can be captured in a GIS by digitizing, a process that transforms paper maps into a digital format, allowing users to readily manipulate these data. Large, relational geospatial databases can be developed by integrating geographic information with other information, such as social, economic, cultural, and environmental information. Because this information can be tied to specific geographical features, such as counties, census tract areas, or even addresses, GIS affords researchers the opportunity to overlay multiple layers of information with a unified geographical referencing system. GIS can be viewed as a special kind of information system in which information is related by its shared spatial identity (Burrough, 1986; Clarke, 2002; Mason, Cheung, & Walker, 2004; Star & Estes, 1990). GIS utilizes "spatial relationship" concepts such as adjacency (e.g., "Does Census Tract A share a boundary with Census Tract B, hence promoting interaction between the two?") and connectivity (e.g., "Is Street A connected to Street B, allowing a continuous flow of movement?"), in interpreting the social network an individual establishes in his/her neighborhood.

The terms *geo-coding* and *geo-referencing* are used to describe a process by which a specific location is given a label identifying its location with respect to some common reference point. Geo-coding is applied by employing GIS that uses street addresses as well as the

Typologically Integrated, Geographically Encoded Reference (TIGER)/Line files provided by the United States Census Bureau. TIGER files represent the features of the Earth as points, lines, or polygons referenced to specific geographic locations by such conventional means as longitude and latitude and state plane coordinate systems or *x-y* coordinates from a specific frame of reference (see Mason, Cheung, & Walker, 2004).

Mason, Cheung, and Walker (2004) used GIS to first extract environmental information (in terms of posited protection and risk) of a subject's residential zip code area. For example, the locations of alcohol outlets, libraries, boys and girls clubs, crime incidences, and parks were geo-coded. This process allowed Mason and colleagues to transform street addresses of an inner city Washington, D.C., location into pairs of coordinates. Mason, Cheung, and Walker (2004) were able to compute the linear distances between the homes of substance users and the reported "risky" and "safe" places. For example, they found that, on average, the distance between the homes and the safe places for substance users was three times farther than the distance between the homes and the risky places for these individuals. More exciting research is on the horizon in the study of environmental influences on drug misuse.

Cultural Influences on Drug Use

Cultural precursors of behavior include the intergenerational, geographically derived group differences that impact large groups of individuals. Some examples of cultural antecedents that might affect drug use include life habits and rituals that are important and meaningful to the group, normative structures and expectations ("cultural morality"), and beliefs and attitudes about reasons for drug use and drug effects. The cultural context may aid in determining which drugs are available, preferable, and valued at a given time (e.g., use of certain types of tobacco in a narghile by some Arab cultures; Shihadeh, 2003), whether experimentation is acceptable, and what one's expectations about the effects of a drug might be (Heath, 1999).

An example of a "life habit" and "normative structure" is the regular use of wine with meals in France. Some children in France learn that wine is a food rather than merely an alcoholic beverage; they learn to drink wine with meals and are able to buy wine in stores. However, in the United States, it is illegal to buy alcohol before the age of 21, and children are not supposed to drink any alcohol. Another example of a normative structure pertains to the acceptance, availability, and recreational use of marijuana and hashish in the Netherlands (a "harm reduction" approach), whereas in the United States even the medical use of marijuana remains controversial. In the Netherlands, "coffee shops" are allowed to sell marijuana to individuals in the amount allowed "for personal use only" or possession of 5 g of marijuana or hashish per person. Many of these "coffee shops" even provide menus with varieties of marijuana from which to choose.

An example of a unique cultural "ritual" that involves "beliefs pertaining to drug use" is the use of the hallucinogen peyote by certain groups of Native Americans in the Church for Spiritual Enlightenment (in the United States; Julien, 2005). Cross-culturally, looking across several countries, a defining characteristic of whether people suffer from drug abuse appears to be their ability to perform their culturally specific roles. If they are viewed as unable to carry out their life roles because of drug use, they are considered to be drug abusers (Quintero & Nichter, 1996). These culturally specific roles may vary by gender or ethnicity.

Gender

Cultural-based gender differences often exist in research examining prevalence and consumption of alcohol, marijuana, and other drugs, as well as engagement in other health
behaviors (e.g., Lex, 1991, 1994; Szalay, Inn, & Doherty, 1996). Drug use has been found
to be more prevalent among males than females (e.g., Barbor, 1994; Johnstone, 1994). For
example, in most surveys and studies of problematic opiate use, males outnumber females
by ratios varying from 2:1 to 4:1 (Grant, 1994).

Gender per se is a description of group differences and not an explanation of why these
group differences exist. Gender differences in drug use might be explained by a consideration
of sex-role expectations and differential stigma associated with drug use. For example,
males are often taught to deal with problems by engaging in goal attainment (instrumental
orientation), rather than by talking about difficulties (expressive, nurturing, or nurture-
seeking orientation). Using drugs might be one means by which males cope with stress or
a sense of dis-balance. Alternatively, females might be more likely to seek social support
(Sussman & Ames, 2001). The magnitude of gender differences currently observed, however,
is likely to be changing among younger cohorts in more recent decades, given changing sex-
role expectations. As females pursue more instrumental goals and perhaps decrease in
expressiveness (e.g., seeking social support), drug use and abuse may increase in prevalence
as a maladaptive coping option. However, females who have multiple roles, such as being a
wife and mother and working outside the home, tend to have lower rates of alcohol-related
problems than those who do not engage in multiple life roles (Wilsnack, Wilsnack, &
Klassen, 1986). Possibly, taking on both instrumental and expressive sex roles (androgyny)
may serve a more protective function among women (and men).

There also may be a worldwide expectation that females do not misuse drugs and that
drug misuse among females is more stigmatizing than drug misuse among males. Related,
females tend to be underrepresented in traditional alcohol and drug treatment programs
worldwide (U.S. DHHS, 1998b). Some possible reasons for the discrepancy between males
and females seeking treatment may be due to more than prevalence of drug abuse. It is
possible that female drug abusers do not seek treatment as often as males because they fear
the loss of custody of their children or access to childcare. Additionally, they may lack health
insurance or other means of economic support, or they may fear reprisal from authorities,
spouses, boyfriends, or other persons in society (Chasnoff, 1991). Females may be more
likely to try to hide their drug use problems.

Female substance abusers are different from male substance abusers in at least three other
ways. First, female drug abusers often report being victims of traumatic life events, such
as child abuse, sexual abuse, rape, and domestic violence (Teets, 1990, 1997; Woodhouse,
1992). To illustrate, in a national sample of 1,099 females older than the age of 20, Wilsnack,
Vogeltanz, Klassen, and Harris (1997) found that females with histories of child sexual abuse
were significantly more likely to report alcohol use and dependence than females without
histories of child sexual abuse. In addition, females that reported child sexual abuse histories were more likely to report illicit drug use and lifetime use of prescribed psychoactive
drugs. In general, females are more likely to report histories of childhood abuse than males
(Briere, 1992), and those exposed to childhood sexual or physical abuse are four to twelve
times more likely to use alcohol or other drugs (Felitti et al., 1998). However, sexual or physical abuse appears to be a risk factor that affects drug use initiation as well as maintenance
of drug use among both genders (by a factor of 2; Kilpatrick et al., 2000). Kilpatrick et al.

(2000) found in this national-level study that gender failed to interact with child abuse as a predictor of teen substance abuse or dependence. More work is needed on the direction of causality of potential gender effects on physical abuse and drug abuse. For example, female drug users are more likely to be subject to physical victimization than their male counterparts (Brooner, King, Kidorf, & Bigelow, 1997). However, it is not totally clear to what extent physical or sexual abuse of females precedes or follows drug abuse.

Second, although males have more alcohol-related problems and dependence symptoms than females (Malin, Coakley, & Kaelber, 1982; Wilsnack, Wilsnack, & Klassen, 1984), *among heavy drinkers*, females are equal to or surpass males in problems resulting from alcohol use. Consequences of alcohol consumption appear to be accelerated in females, and chronic alcohol abuse exacts greater physiological impairment (e.g., alcohol-related organ damage) earlier in females, despite consuming less alcohol than males (Hill, 1984; Tuyns & Pequignot, 1984). Female alcoholics (and abusers of other drugs) have death rates 50% to 100% higher than those of male alcoholics, and a greater percentage of female alcoholics die from suicides, alcohol-related accidents, circulatory disorders, and cirrhosis of the liver (Hill, 1982). One could also conjecture that women who are heavier users of other drugs also may present relatively greater problems from their drug use. The cultural underpinnings of this difference are only speculative but could reflect greater self-medication due to reactions from others for violating a norm that females should not drink or use drugs.

Third, females have to deal with fetal health risks related to drug use during pregnancy. Several fetal health risks associated with drug use have been identified. For example, cigarette smoking has been associated with low-birth-weight infants and slowed growth. Fetal alcohol syndrome (FAS) is a syndrome associated with high levels of alcohol exposure and is characterized by facial anomalies, growth retardation, and central nervous system deficits. Maternal alcohol use results in more serious neurological and behavioral abnormalities in the fetus than maternal use of cocaine, heroin, and marijuana (see Kyskan & Moore, 2005). Additionally, female drug users who are HIV seropositive risk transmitting the virus to their fetuses. Among the total cases of pediatric AIDS in the United States, approximately 54% are related to either maternal injection drug use or maternal sex with an injecting drug user (Quinn, Ruff, & Modlin, 1992). Pregnant female drug users are also at increased risk for miscarriage, stillbirth, low weight gain, anemia, thrombocytopeia, and hypertension (Hershow et al., 1997). Certainly, part of the stigma against female drug use may derive from potential harm that could come to the child.

Ethnicity as Culture?

In the United States, several researchers have found White ethnicity to be associated with relatively greater drug use among adolescents and adults (Galaif, Chou, Sussman, & Dent, 1998; Johnston, O'Malley, & Bachman, 1999; Newcomb & Earleywine, 1996). It is possible that White ethnicity is also associated with less extended familial support, leading to greater substance use as a means of coping. However, among individuals with a lifetime history of dependence, Blacks are significantly more likely than Whites to report 12-month duration of substance dependence. Possibly, once dependent on drugs, some ethnic groups have less access to health care and other community resources, leading to a more sustained period of drug dependence. Some ethnic groups may also experience a greater allostatic load (racial discrimination, controlling for other factors), particularly in adulthood, that may make recovery more difficult.

Ethnicity, however, interacts with other demographic variables such as gender, age, and type of drug in predicting prevalence of drug use. For example, the prevalence of use of alcohol, marijuana, hallucinogens, and cocaine among adolescents in the United States tends to be highest among Latino and White males, followed by Latino and White females, then Black males, and then Black females. Alcohol use disorders tend to decline with age among males in White and Black ethnic groups but increase among Blacks females as they reach 30 to 44 years of age. Also, examined across gender among adults, rates of current use of cocaine is approximately 1.4% for Blacks, 0.8% for Latinos, and 0.6% for Whites (Sussman & Ames, 2001). Perhaps taking on, or giving up, key adult responsibilities (jobs, parenthood) may be associated with such apparently complex patterns of drug use.

Typically, Asian groups have reported lower rates of alcohol abuse and dependence than other ethnic groups in the United States. Researchers attribute some of the observed ethnic differences in the incidence of alcoholism to variation in alcohol-metabolizing enzymes (Luczak et al., 2002; Wall, Thomasson, Schuckit, & Ehlers, 1992; see Chapter 5). For example, among some Asian groups, individuals experience what is called a *flushing response* after consuming alcohol. This alcohol sensitivity reaction resulting from variation of alcohol-metabolizing enzymes is believed to contribute to lower alcohol consumption and dependence (i.e., individuals who experience a fast flushing response are likely to drink less alcohol to achieve intense effects). Researchers examining the relationship between the flushing response and drinking behavior found that those experiencing a flushing response reported drinking significantly less than "nonflushers" with respect to both frequency and amount consumed (Suzuki, Matsushita, & Ishii, 1997). However, Native Americans in the United States, many of whom also exhibit a flushing response, have relatively worse alcohol and drug problems than other groups. Thus, a socially disadvantageous position within a culture may contribute to differences in problem use as a function of ethnicity, controlling for the contribution of other factors, such as genetic variations in metabolic processes.

Another important cultural construct is *acculturation* (Diaz-Guerrero, 1984). This construct pertains to *changes* that transpire in cultural rituals, norms or social consensus, or beliefs. New cultural influences may interface with a person's native culture, or the person may move to a location that provides a new host culture. Generally, acculturation is defined as the degree to which individuals adopt or prefer a culture to which they are more recently exposed. The degree to which a group or individual distances themselves from their native culture increases as more time is spent in the environment of a different culture (i.e., acculturation can be construed as a social learning process; Szalay, Canino, & Vilov, 1993). Level of acculturation in the new environment can affect drug use through exposure to cultural attitudes favorable toward use or positive expectations of drug effects. Drug use or abuse might also occur when individuals are separated from traditional cultural groups that discourage drug use (lack of restraining influences of the native culture). Alternatively, the stress resulting from failure to bond successfully to a new culture may increase the probability of drug use.

Ethnic pride may be an important predictor (protective factor) of drinking in many ethnic groups. A recent study by Scheier and colleagues found that, although poor social skills led to greater alcohol use, ethnic identity (e.g., having a lot of pride in one's ethnic group and its accomplishments) moderated the effects of social skills on alcohol use among a sample of Black (60%) and Latino (40%) adolescents (Scheier, Botvin, Diaz, & Ifill-Williams,

1997). In that same study, in a statistical model, including both perceived competence (self-management and persistence) and ethnic identity as predictors of alcohol use, ethnic identity directly and inversely predicted alcohol use among the adolescents. Thus, ethnic identity (pride) may be a strong direct protective factor among disadvantaged groups.

Mass Media

An important macro-level sociocultural influence affecting drug use initiation and experimentation is the increasing role of the media and worldwide access to information. The World Wide Web provides incredible access to information about drugs of abuse and means of producing these drugs. Different cultures may influence each other's beliefs regarding drug use to the extent that they use a shared language on the Web (e.g., www.legalize.org/global/). Also, television and movies may inadvertently promote drug use by conveying images of role models or idols, such as rock stars romancing heroin addiction, models who are chain smokers, movie stars addicted to alcohol, or rappers who sing about marijuana (Sussman et al., 1996). Movie images, in particular, are likely to be viewed internationally and influence the host culture within which they are viewed. Even if an individual does not attend to images portrayed by the media, the *mere exposure* to these images has been shown to affect preferences for objects (for more about the mere exposure effect and preference literature, see Kunst-Wilson & Zajonc, 1980; Zajonc, 1980). But, do these preferences influence choice behavior? Should the media be required to reduce the glamorization of drug use in the movies and on television? Should the media be required to provide more realistic portrayals of consequences of use, abuse or dependence? Or should the media be required to limit viewing patterns (e.g., use of an R rating)?

Clearly, the media are an important relay of information and, as such, influence behavioral options. Researchers have shown that repeated exposure to images affects reactions and preferences (Theus, 1994). For example, advertisements that associate smoking with excitement-seeking cues and social popularity have been shown to be important influences in the onset of smoking (see Wills, Pierce, & Evans, 1996). In a study among 2,998 7th graders in southern California, increased exposure to televised alcohol advertisements was found to be associated with increased beer consumption in the eighth grade (Stacy, Zogg, Unger, & Dent, 2004). Media coverage of health risks or benefits associated with alcohol and other drug use may influence use patterns among large groups of individuals. For instance, media coverage of beneficial health effects of wine drinking may rouse changes in beliefs among the population, and change or increase patterns of drinking. The media has the ability to diffuse information very rapidly, affecting large groups of individuals. The potential international cultural impact of the media cannot be overstated.

Media exposure makes available information that may have been formerly unavailable. For example, repeated exposure to alcohol advertising may render drinking or other drug use behavior more accessible in memory. Repeated exposure to advertising coupled with images of idols or role models who use drugs can be a toxic combination. Those predisposed or at risk to use or abuse drugs, and those already using, may selectively attend to or expose themselves to advertisements, images, and media programs that reinforce their beliefs and behaviors. Consequently, awareness of the range of drug use or drinking options and associated stimuli (e.g., perceived reinforcing social images) may increase. Conversely, these individuals may tend to ignore or not attend to anti-drug use information that is portrayed through the same or other channels, given a developing tendency to screen out antidrug input from one's selective attention.

Cigarette Smoking in the Movies

Smoking prevalence in the movies tends to be higher among male actors, antagonistic characters that are depicted, persons depicted as low in socioeconomic status, in independent movie productions, and in R-rated movies (Omidvari et al., 2005). Interestingly, a systematic review of the top ten movies on the weekly box office charts revealed that cigarette smoking prevalence is approximately the same in contemporary American movies and in the general U.S. population (23% vs. 25%; Omidvari et al., 2005). However, smoking in movies rarely depicts negative health outcomes; conversely, the smokers in movies often appear to be in very good shape (Charlesworth & Glantz, 2005).

Sargent et al. (2004) examined the effect of parental R-rated movie restrictions on smoking initiation (i.e., ever tried smoking) among 10- to 14-year-olds. Statistically controlling for confounders, including maternal support and control, they examined baseline "never smokers" onset an average of 17 months later. Only 19% of the sample reported that parents would never let them go to R-rated movies, whereas 29% were allowed to see them once in awhile, and 52% could view them some or all of the time. Sargent and colleagues found that 10% of the sample tried smoking during the follow-up period; 2.9% of those whose parents forbade R-rated movies smoked, 7.0% of those allowed to watch R-rated movies once in awhile smoked, and 14.3% of those whose parents allowed them to watch R-rated movies some or all of the time smoked.

These findings differed as a function of parental smoking (if no parental smoking: 1%, 4%, and 12%, respectively, tried; if there was parental smoking: 12%, 14%, and 18%, respectively, tried). That is, if the parents were smokers, the impact of the media was much less. Also, only 4.9% of those youth with "strict" parents had high exposure to R-rated movies, whereas 20% of youth with "somewhat strict" parents and 54% of youth with "very lenient" parents had such exposure to R-rated movies. One percent of the sample with strict parents began smoking, 2% with somewhat lenient parents began smoking, and 7% with much more lenient parents began smoking. The biggest difference in smoking initiation was between the very lenient parents and the somewhat lenient parents, suggesting that the overall amount of exposure to R-rated movies is a key variable. That is, 5% versus 20% high exposure is not that important, whereas 20% versus 54% high exposure is quite relevant. This would suggest that there is a threshold of exposure under which relatively less effect would be obtained.

Sargent et al. (2005) noted that limitations of the study included having evaluated only "ever tried smoking" and the sample, which consisted of students from New Hampshire and Vermont. Sargent and colleagues (2005) subsequently conducted a national survey and were able to replicate their findings in the national sample. A recent caveat is that in recent years the balance of exposure to smoking incidents has now shifted from R-rated films (in the New England study) to PG-13 films (Charlesworth & Glantz, 2005; Polansky & Glantz, 2005).

In evaluating 12- to 17-year-olds between 1988 and 2003, Polansky and Glantz estimated that youth received half their exposure to smoking from R-rated films and half from youth-rated films. It is possible, as a risk reduction approach, that if smoking depicted in any movie results in the movie being rated R, then perhaps this would decrease the prevalence

Table 8.1. Larger social and physical environmental etiological influences on drug use

Factors affecting drug use	
Neighborhood disorganization	A lack of centralized authority or rapid changeovers of authority can result in a lack of behavioral monitoring. Individuals residing in more chaotic areas may be more heavily exposed to social disobedience. Abandoned buildings and enclosed public spaces may result in greater incidence of drug exposures and crime perpetuation.
Socioeconomics	Adverse socioeconomic conditions may prevent the promotion or availability of prosocial activities. Adverse socioeconomic conditions may increase exposures to drug-related criminal activity. A decrease in protective factors (familial or social support) may affect some to self-medicate with drugs under disadvantaged circumstances. Conversely, individuals of high socioeconomic status (SES) may be able to afford large quantities of drugs, causing a descent in SES due to addiction.
Environmental availability	Ease of distribution, access, and acquisition of drugs in an individual's environment may influence drug use.
Cultural influences	Life habits or rituals, normative structures and expectations, and beliefs about drug use and its effects may affect drug use.
Gender differences	Sex-role expectations within one's environment and differential stigma associated with use may affect drug use prevalence or self-disclosure.
Ethnicity	Ethnicity may interact with demographics such as gender, age, and type of drug in predicting drug use. Ethnic pride may play a role as a predictor (protective factor) in many ethnic groups.
Acculturation	Exposure to changes in cultural rituals, drug use norms, or beliefs about drugs may affect drug use. That is, the degree to which individuals adopt a culture to which they are recently exposed may inhibit or promote drug use depending on the culture they are from and the new one they are exposed to.
Media and worldwide access to information	Varieties of mass media including advertisements intended to repeatedly expose individuals to certain types of drug-related behaviors are suspect of promoting drug use. Certain forms of media have been shown to affect an individual's preferences and behavioral options towards drug use. For example, movies glamorize various drug-related behaviors and may promote cigarette smoking and alcohol use. Mass media can disseminate large amounts of information quickly and to various sources. For example, information about drugs, their effects, and ways to manufacture and obtain them can be found on the World Wide Web.

of depiction of smoking in movies and youth exposure to depictions of smoking. R ratings are about 50% efficient in keeping youth from viewing those films (Table 8.1).

Summary

This chapter addressed macro-level physical and social environmental influences on the development of substance use. Of course, these physical and sociocultural environmental influences alone may not determine behavior, but they help define the communities within which social learning is shared. Macro-level physical and sociocultural environments help determine the diffusion of knowledge, which is affected by social interactions among individuals within a common culture. Physical structures tend to identify the types of communications that occur within them (e.g., consider conversations occurring in a library, at a church, at a bar, or in an adult Internet chat room). Culture, including shared language, norms, contexts, and beliefs often direct the daily behaviors of individuals, including communication contents within different locations. Cultural contexts, as well as drug use patterns, have spatial and temporal aspects, which can be evaluated with newer methods of network analyses that will increase our understanding of drug use patterns across communities.

Adolescents and adults are routinely exposed to a variety of environmental contexts meshed with cultural norms communicated in a range of experiences with others, as well as through exposures to the media and the World Wide Web. These contextual influences direct whether, where, and how one will use drugs. In terms of drug abuse, however, multiple experiences or active participation in a drug use subculture ultimately may eclipse the influences of a more general cultural background.

9   Assessment

An examination of etiology of drug misuse would not be complete without consideration of assessment of the outcome variables: drug use, drug misuse, drug abuse, or drug dependence. In general, by later adulthood there is likely to be a history of many years of drug misuse or abuse among drug users. Alternatively, the history of abuse is relatively brief among youth. There are also many methods to assess drug use, misuse, and abuse among adults. The assessment of drug abuse in youth has been less often studied, yet the highest prevalence of drug abuse is during the teen and emerging adulthood years. Life circumstances during these developmental periods are different from those experienced later in adulthood. Because drug misuse among teens and emerging adults is of the highest prevalence worldwide, and because etiology, prevention, and cessation most closely interface during the teen and emerging adulthood years, this chapter focuses on assessment during these periods (12–25 years old) (Figure 9.1).

Due to relatively less assessment research specific to adolescents and emerging adults, many methods available for use with these populations are adaptations of adult interviews and questionnaires. Methods available to aid in the assessment of drug use and diagnosis of substance abuse among adolescents and emerging adults include examinations of an individual's behavioral and family characteristics, physical findings and complaints, and laboratory tests. Clinically, as with adults, assessments to determine diagnosis and treatment planning typically rely on an in-depth drug use history and psychiatric and physical examinations. This chapter reviews various assessments frequently used to diagnose parameters of a person's drug abuse or dependence, beginning with examples of unstructured examinations and interviews and followed by examples from the large inventory of structured assessments. Given that substance abuse is a biopsychosocial process, many of these assessments tap into a variety of drug use *motivations* that are neurobiologically based (e.g., drinking or using drugs to feel good, feeling very good in early drug use experiences), cognitively based (e.g., perceptions about drug use, outcome expectancies), socially based (e.g., wanting to fit in), and perhaps large physically or social environmentally based (visibility of drug use and access to drugs in one's community or culture). Additionally, these assessments tap into various *consequences* of use that are neurobiologically based (e.g., withdrawal symptoms, difficulty experiencing pleasure when sober), cognitively based (e.g., disordered thoughts or misperceptions about one's use), socially based (e.g., interpersonal problems), and large physically or social environmentally based problems (e.g., police presence or monitoring and being arrested for disorderly conduct or driving under the influence, causing extensive

Figure 9.1. College students completing a self-report questionnaire in a classroom setting.

fires particularly through cigarette smoking, cost of health insurance and need for treatment, decreased work productivity, involvement with the jail system, feeling stigmatized within the culture).

Reasons for and Goals of Assessment

There are several circumstances in which adolescents and emerging adults might be assessed for potential drug misuse (Sussman & Ames, 2001). These include situations that involve employment, particularly positions in which public safety is paramount (e.g., lifeguards, delivery personnel, vehicle drivers, and babysitters), obtaining a driver's license, and participating in student athletics. Adolescents and emerging adults might also be assessed when they experience sudden and significant drops in school performance, avoid social situations, or display sudden changes in mood and emotional lability. Or they may be assessed at the discretion of the parents when there are social problems suspected to be related to drug use or when the adolescents or emerging adults already have a history of drug use.

The initial goal in assessment is to determine the nature of an individual's involvement with drugs of misuse and to assess psychological and medical status, psychosocial functioning, social support networks, attitudes toward drug use, and motivation for initial abstinence. Detailed information is obtained regarding one's drug use history and related consequences and comorbidity. Neurobiologically relevant questions that might be asked include the following: Have you taken or tried any drugs? What do you use? How much (quantity)? How old were you when you first used? What were your first experiences with drug use like? What are your experiences with drug use like now? How much control do you think you have over your drug use? How long do your using episodes last? What happens? What do the drugs do for you? How do they make you feel?

Table 9.1. Four etiologic targets of assessment

Type of domain	Examples of relevant questions
Neurobiologically based	How old were you when you first tried drugs? How did they make you feel? What do drugs do for you?
Cognitively based	What are your beliefs about drug use and abuse? How often do you think about drugs? How often do thoughts about drug use just pop to mind?
Socially based	Do your parents or friends use drugs? Have you experienced any sexual or physical abuse?
Physical or social environmentally based	How many liquor stores are near your home? What were you taught about your culture's attitudes toward drug use?

Cognitively relevant questions that might be asked include the following: What are your beliefs about drug use and abuse? How did you get into using drugs? Do you ever plan how you will use drugs in the future or plan on how you might avoid them? In what situations do thoughts about using drugs just "pop" to mind? Do you seem to lose control over any other areas of your life? How about gambling? Sex? Spending? Eating? Exercising a lot? Are you studying or working very long hours? Do you experience any suicidal or homicidal ideation?

Socially relevant questions that might be asked include the following: Do your peers use any drugs? Does your best friend use drugs? Do your parents use drugs? Have you experienced any legal or social problems from drug use? Have you ever gone to a psychiatrist or other professional for mental health concerns? Have you experienced any sexual or physical abuse? (Any disclosure of intended physical harm to self or others would need to be reported by the interviewer to the appropriate agency.)

Large physical or social environmentally relevant questions that might be asked include: Do you live in an area in which a lot of drugs are available? How many liquor stores are near your home? Are the names of the drug dealers well known in your neighborhood? Have you ever caused or suffered any property damage while using drugs? What were you taught about your culture's attitudes toward drug use?

Because of response demand problems, it is helpful to use corroborative methods of assessment. These might include family members' reports, nonusing friends' reports, or biochemical methods. Of course, some differences in judgment as to whether one is a drug abuser should be based on such variables as the age of the drug user. For example, any use of an illicit drug, or drugs such as inhalants, by a child or young teen indicates potential immediate danger (Table 9.1).

Mental Status Examination

A mental status examination generally is conducted as a systematic means of gathering psychological and behavioral data. The purpose is to provide an initial screening of an individual's mental health status and to help suggest other means of assessment to determine whether a diagnosis of a formal psychiatric disease should be made. The mental status examination includes the assessment of appearance, attitude and behavior, speech, affect, thought and language, and perceptions and cognitive functioning, such as insight and judgment (Schottenfeld, 1994).

When performing a mental status examination, the following questions are examples of those that might help to provide a guideline to determine whether an adolescent or emerging adult is suspected of drug abuse or other psychopathology. Does the individual appear to be withdrawn, socially isolated, undernourished, agitated or depressed, tired, unable to concentrate, indifferent to pleasurable activities, or unkempt in physical appearance? Is the individual hostile or uncooperative, evasive, or defensive and are there any discrepancies in reports of autobiographical events (i.e., lies, missing information)? Have any delusions or visual or auditory hallucinations been reported? If so, what were the circumstances? Was the individual under the influence of mood-altering drugs at the time? After answering these questions, the individual might be assessed through a more specific interview assessment.

Drug Treatment History

The use of interviews or self-reports that elicit information regarding an individual's prior involvement in drug treatment programs, psychiatric facilities, self-help support groups (e.g., twelve-step programs), or public sanctions (e.g., court, juvenile hall, camps, or community schools) can be quite useful. These data can assist in understanding an individual's level of drug dependence (i.e., where he or she falls on the drug abuse continuum), occurrence of other compulsive behaviors and psychiatric difficulties, and motivation to stop using. Also useful is information regarding the longest period of abstinence endured with the help of a structured environment and without the help of a structured environment. Many individuals will disclose that while in juvenile hall or prison ("locked up"), or while in treatment as inpatients, they can remain abstinent, but when in the community, without some structure, they are unable to remain abstinent.

Frequency, Quantity, and Method of Drug Use, and Family Drug Use

Although questioning individuals about the frequency and quantity of drug use may not be essential in making a diagnosis of substance abuse, it is nonetheless associated with drug abuse-related dysfunction (Rychtarik, Koutsky, & Miller, 1998, 1999). Of course, there are some individuals who experience severe consequences while using relatively low levels of drugs (e.g., flushing and palpitations that some Asian groups experience with alcohol use), and there are some individuals who appear to experience few consequences on relatively high levels of regular use. However, high quantities of intake are highly correlated with occupational, educational, social, and medical impairment. Frequency of use indicates how often individuals are using a drug. Frequency of drug use can be measured through self-reports of lifetime estimates of use, yearly estimates of use, monthly use, and/or daily estimates of use. Unfortunately, this type of assessment lacks precision because of memory biases, social desirability, denial, and other response demands.

Recent use does not indicate the length of time or the extent of the addiction, but it does help to disclose the most current and reliable autobiographical events. Quantity of use is more predictive of problems or disruptive drug use than frequency (e.g. binge drinking vs.

small amounts of daily use; see Annis, 1984; Newcomb & Felix-Ortiz, 1992). According to the National Household Survey on Drug Abuse, binge drinking is defined as consuming five or more drinks on one occasion for at least 1 day in the past 30 days. Alternatively, heavy drinking is defined as drinking five or more drinks on the same occasion on 5 or more of the past 30 days. The use of a drinking diary can help improve the quality of self-reported data regarding binge or heavy drinking (e.g., Dennis et al., 2004); however, compliance with keeping careful records of intake can be problematic (e.g., social desirability confounder, trying to write records while drunk).

The assessment of the method of drug intake also may help one to understand the level of misuse or addiction for those drugs that vary in means of use (e.g., cocaine and heroin). For instance, many individuals with crack cocaine addiction may have originally started their use by snorting powdered cocaine. Eventually, they may have switched to a different form of the drug – smoking crack – that is cheaper and readily available in small quantities and that immediately potentiates dopamine transmission in the brain. Assessment of family history of drug use may further help to assess the level of addiction, perceived problems and consequences, attitudes toward drug use, and probability of relapse. Current use among significant others, and perceptions that drug use is simply a part of normal behavior, could lead one to expect future struggles with drug use. In all of these assessments, if the interviewer desires, he or she may conceptually organize the questions into neurological/biological, cognitive, microsocial, and macroenvironmental categories.

The Structured Clinical Interview for the Diagnostic Statistical Manual IV

The *Diagnostic and Statistical Manual of Mental Disorders of the American Psychiatric Association* (DSM-IV-TR) is widely used in establishing whether an individual has a drug abuse disorder (APA, 2000). This manual contains specific criteria sets for substance abuse, dependence, intoxication, and withdrawal applicable across different classes of drugs. The Structured Clinical Interview for the Diagnostic Statistical Manual IV (SCID) is a broad-spectrum instrument that adheres to the DSM-IV decision trees for psychiatric diagnosis and encourages multiple paths of exploration, clarification, and clinical decision-making. It can be tailored to a variety of populations (First, Spitzer, & Gibbon, 1996, for DSM-IV Axis I Disorders). This interview is a primary measure of substance abuse and substance dependence disorders, with specific clarification regarding efforts to decrease or control use, continued use despite problems, specific withdrawal symptoms of a drug, and assessment of comorbidity.

Structured Assessments of Alcoholism That Could Be Used with Adolescents or Emerging Adults

The CAGE questionnaire (Ewing, 1984) is a self-report screening instrument that uses the mnemonic CAGE to assess problems with alcohol. It is a relatively sensitive four-item instrument that assesses attempts to *Cut down* on drinking, *Annoyance* with criticisms of drinking, *Guilt* feelings about drinking and use of alcohol as a morning *Eye-opener*. When someone responds "yes" to two or more questions, that individual is suspected of having alcohol problems. These questions can be adapted for other drug use, as well, by replacing the word *drinking* with *drug use*, and *a morning eye-opener* with *the drug to get you started in the morning*. The focus of this questionnaire is on consequences of use related to an individual's response to others' perceptions of his or her use, resultant feelings, and attempts to quit. Attempts to change behavior may or may not come from outside sources (e.g. one's small social group) that, in turn, may cause guilt feelings or cognitively based conflict.

The RAFFT test (relax, alone, friends, family, trouble) was developed similarly to the CAGE but as a brief screen specifically for teens. (It applies well to emerging adults, too.) The RAFFT consists of five items (e.g., "Do you drink to relax, to feel better about yourself, or to fit in?" (Riggs & Alario, 1989). Relatively recently, Knight and colleagues (1999) adapted the RAFFT along with several other measures to create a brief screening of alcohol and other drug abuse. The six-item CRAFFT test resulted (Car, Relax, Alone, Forget, Family or Friends complain, Trouble). Items address riding in a car driven by someone under the influence, drinking or using to relax, drinking or using alone, forgetting things while drinking or using, family or friends telling one to cut down, and getting into trouble while under the influence. The CRAFFT shows good convergent validity and internal consistency. The items on this assessment represent neurobiologically based (drinking to relax), cognitively based (poor decision-making, as in riding in a car driven by someone under the influence, forgetting things while drinking or using), and socially based (drinking alone) drug use motivations, as well as socially based consequences of use (family or friends telling one to cut down) and environmentally related consequences (getting into trouble while under the influence).

The Adolescent Alcohol Involvement Scale (AAIS) consists of fourteen items and examines type and frequency of drinking, last drinking episode, reasons for drinking, drinking situations, effects of drinking, and cognitive perceptions about drinking (Mayer & Filstead, 1979). This measure shows a moderate internal consistency and convergent validity with a substance use disorder diagnosis.

The Adolescent Alcohol Expectancy Questionnaire (A-AEQ; Brown, Christiansen, & Goldman, 1987) was developed to evaluate anticipated effects of alcohol consumption among adolescents. This 100-item inventory assesses expected effects in several domains including global positive changes, changes in social behavior, improved cognitive and motor abilities, sexual enhancement, cognitive and motor impairment, increased arousal and relaxation, and tension reduction.

The Comprehensive Effects of Alcohol (CEOA) questionnaire (Fromme, Stroot, & Kaplan, 1993; Stroot & Fromme, 1989) was developed to assess positive and negative alcohol effects and the subjective evaluation of those effects. This seventy-six-item measure consists of several expected positive effects, including factors that address sociability, tension reduction, courage, and sexuality, and several negative effects, including factors addressing cognitive and behavioral impairment, risk and aggression, and self-perception. The CEOA was developed among college students (emerging adults) but has been found to be comparable to the Adolescent Alcohol Expectancy Questionnaire (see D'Amico & Fromme, 1997).

The Alcohol Abstinence Self-Efficacy Scale (AASE; DiClemente, Carbonari, Montgomery, & Hughes, 1994) consists of temptation and self-efficacy items that are self-rated to assess an individual's confidence to resist use in several drinking situations. This instrument is composed of twenty efficacy and twenty temptation items (with four subscales). Key outcome variables include cues related to negative affect; social, physical, and other concerns; and withdrawal and urges (Table 9.2).

Table 9.2. Structured assessments of alcoholism that could be used with adolescents or emerging adults

Scale name	Type and number of items	Purpose of assessment	Examples of content and domains assessed
CAGE	4-item self-report questionnaire	The focus is on consequences of use related to one's response to others' perceptions of his or her use, resultant feelings, and attempts to quit.	*Cut* down on drinking; *Annoyance* with criticisms of drinking; *Guilt* feelings about drinking; and use of alcohol as a morning *Eye* opener.
RAFFT test (relax, alone, friends, family, trouble)	5-item self-report questionnaire	Designed as a brief screening tool specifically for teens.	Do you drink to relax, to feel better about yourself, or to fit in?
CRAFFT test (car, relax, alone, forget, family or friends complain, trouble), derived from RAFFT	6-item self-report questionnaire	Evaluates the neurobiologically based, cognitively based, and socially based motivations to drink, as well as socially and environmentally based consequences of use.	Riding in a car driven by someone under the influence; drinking or using to relax; drinking or using alone; forgetting things while drinking or using; family or friends telling one to cut down; getting in trouble while under the influence.
Adolescent Alcohol Involvement Scale (AAIS)	14-item self-report questionnaire	Designed to assess type of alcohol use and how often it occurs.	Last drinking episode; reasons for initial drinking behavior; situation in which drinking occurs, etc.
Adolescent Alcohol Expectancy Questionnaire (A-AEQ)	100-item self-report questionnaire	Designed to evaluate the anticipated effects of alcohol use by adolescents.	Global positive changes; changes in social behavior; improved/impaired cognitive and motor abilities; sexual enhancement.
Comprehensive Effects of Alcohol (CEOA)	76-item self-report questionnaire	Designed to assess positive and negative alcohol effects and the subjective evaluation of those effects.	Expected positive effects: sociability, tension reduction, liquid courage. Expected negative effects: cognitive and behavioral impairment, risk and aggression, self-perception.
Alcohol Abstinence Self-Efficacy Scale (AASE)	40-item self-report questionnaire (20 self-efficacy, 20 temptation)	Designed to evaluate an individual's self-confidence to resist temptation in several drinking situations.	Cues related to negative affect, social, physical, and other concerns; withdrawal and urges.

Structured Assessments of Other Drugs of Abuse That Could Be Used with Adolescents and Emerging Adults

The Substance Dependence Severity Scale (SDSS; Miele et al., 2000) is a clinician-administered structured interview (composed of thirteen items) that was developed to assess severity and frequency of dependence across a range of drugs, based on the DSM-IV. The test/retest, joint rating, and internal consistency reliabilities across alcohol, cocaine, heroin, marijuana, and sedative users is good.

The Chemical Dependency Assessment Profile (CDAP) is a 235-item multiple-choice and true/false self-report instrument used to assess substance use, dependence problems and treatment needs among adolescents and adults. Domains addressed include quantity/frequency of use, physiological symptoms, situational stressors, antisocial behaviors, interpersonal problems, affective dysfunction, treatment attitudes, impact of use on life functioning, and expectancies (Harrell, Honaker, & Davis, 1991). This assessment taps into neurobiologically based, cognitively based, and socially based drug use motivations and consequences.

The Problem Oriented Screening Instrument for Teenagers (POSIT) is a 139-item self-administered yes/no questionnaire that was developed by the National Institute on Drug Abuse as part of their Adolescent Assessment/Referral System (Rahdert, 1991). The POSIT contains ten scales: substance use/abuse, physical health status, mental health status, peer relations, family relations, educational status, vocational status, social skills, leisure and recreation, and aggressive behavior/delinquency. This measure has good convergent validity, internal consistency, and test/retest reliability and it takes 20 minutes to complete. This measure takes into account all four etiologic domains presented in this text.

The Drug and Alcohol Problem (DAP) Quickscreen consists of thirty yes/no items and discriminates well between high-risk and low-risk users (Klitzner, Schwartz, Gruenwald, & Blasinsky, 1987). This assessment was developed for use in primary care offices and includes the prototypical item: "Has anyone (friend, parent, teacher, or counselor) ever told you that they believe that you may have a drinking or drug problem?"

The Rutgers Alcohol Problem Index (RAPI) (White & Labouvie, 1989) consists of twenty-three items that address consequences of alcohol and other drug use related to psychological functioning, delinquency, social relations, family, physical problems, and neuropsychological functioning. This measure has been found to correlate highly with DSM-III-R criteria for substance use disorders (.75-.95; White & Labouvie, 1989).

The Inventory of Drinking Situations (IDS; Annis, 1982) or the Inventory of Drug Use Situations (Annis & Graham, 1992) assesses the contextual aspects of alcohol or other drug use and provides information about relapse situations. This inventory consists of either 42 or 100 items (with eight subscales) to evaluate drinking/drug use situations, including unpleasant emotions, physical discomfort, pleasant emotions, testing personal control, urges and temptations, conflict with others, social pressures, and pleasant times with others.

The Adolescent Diagnostic Interview (ADI; Winters & Henly, 1993) is a 15-minute evaluation used to assess the need for treatment of drug misuse among adolescents. This interview includes the evaluation of various cognitive, interpersonal, and school functioning factors that may contribute to alcohol or drug misuse. The instrument consists of twenty-four items.

The Personal Experience Inventory (PEI; Winters, Stinchfield, & Henly, 1993) is a comprehensive questionnaire used for detection of problem consequences and potential risk factors believed to predispose youth to misuse or maintain drug misuse. This 276-item questionnaire helps to quantify level of involvement with a variety of drugs and the severity of problems in personal, family, and psychosocial domains. Cognitive, social, and nearby environmental impacts are addressed. A variation of this inventory also exists for adults (Winters, 1999).

The Adolescent Drug Abuse Diagnosis (ADAD) is a comprehensive structured interview consisting of 150 items used to assess substance abuse and other problem areas. The format is adapted from the well-known adult tool, the Addiction Severity Index (ASI; McLellan, Luborsky, Woody, & O'Brien, 1980). This interview addresses nine life areas, including medical, school, work, social relations, family relationships, legal, psychological, and alcohol and drug use (Friedman & Utada, 1989).

Comprehensive Addiction Severity Index for Adolescents (CASI-A) is an instrument designed to provide an in-depth, comprehensive assessment of the severity of adolescents' addiction and problem consequences. This structured interview also is adapted from the Addiction Severity Index (ASI; McLellan Luborsky, Woody, & O'Brien, 1980). Ten domains are assessed and include the following: psychological, peer relationships, family history, sexual relationships, physical abuse, significant life changes, use of free time, substance use effects and treatment experiences, leisure activities, educational experiences and plans, legal history, and psychiatric status, including prior treatment experiences (Meyers, McLellan, Jaeger, & Pettinati, 1995).

The Substance Abuse Subtle Screening Inventory (SASSI-A) consists of eighty-one items and ten scales (face valid alcohol, face valid other drugs, family-friends risk, attitudes, symptoms, obvious attributes, subtle attitudes, defensiveness, supplemental addiction measures, and correctional). It is not clear, however, that the different scales measure empirically separable phenomena. The face valid content measures show the best convergence with interview-based measures on substance use impairment (Nishimura et al., 2001; Rogers, Cashel, Johansen, & Sewell, 1997).

Other promising measures of alcohol or other drug abuse among teens and emerging adults includes the Global Appraisal of Individual Needs (GAIN; Dennis et al., 2004), Form 90 Timeline Followback (TLFB; Dennis et al., 2004), Perceived Benefits of Drinking and Reasons for Drug Use Scale (Petchers & Singer, 1987; Petchers, Singer, Angelotta, & Chow, 1988), Adolescent Drug Involvement Scale (adapted from the AAIS; Moberg & Hahn, 1991), Adolescent Problem Severity Index (APSI; Metzger, Kushner, & McLellan, 1991), the Juvenile Automated Substance Abuse Evaluation (JASAE; see ADE Inc., 1987), and the Minnesota Multiphasic Personality Inventory-Adolescent (MMPI; Weinberg, Rahdert, Colliver, & Glantz, 1998) (Table 9.3).

Examples of Popular Structured Assessments Used with Older Adults

A few popular adult alcohol or drug abuse assessment inventories should be mentioned. These may or may not be appropriate for some teens or emerging adults. The Alcohol Use Inventory (AUI; Horn, Wanberg, & Foster, 1990; Littrell, 1991; Rychtarik, Koutsky, & Miller, 1998) is a 228-item multiple-choice self-report inventory. It was systematically developed to measure alcohol problems. There are twenty-four subscales with seventeen

Table 9.3. Structured assessments of "other drugs of abuse" that could be used with adolescents or emerging adults

Scale name	Type and number of items	Purpose of assessment	Examples of content and domains assessed
Substance Dependence Severity Scale (SDSS)	20-item clinician-administered structured interview (7–10 alcohol and drug screening items; 13-symptoms)	Designed to assess the severity and frequency of dependence across a range of drugs based on the DSM-IV criteria.	Recent severity of harmful drug use and dependence, consequences of use.
Chemical Dependency Assessment Profile (CDAP)	235-item (true/false) self-report questionnaire	Designed to assess substance use, dependence problems, and treatment needs among adolescents and adults.	Quantity/frequency of use, physiological symptoms, situational stressors, antisocial behaviors, interpersonal problems, affective dysfunction.
Problem Oriented Screening Instrument for Teenagers (POSIT)	139-item (yes/no) self-report questionnaire	Developed by National Institute on Drug Abuse to measure four etiological domains.	Substance use/abuse, physical health status, mental health status, peer relations, family relations, social skills, etc.
Drug and Alcohol Problem (DAP) Quickscreen	30-item (yes/no) self-report questionnaire	Designed to be used in primary care offices to differentiate the high- and low-risk users.	Assesses whether anyone (friend, parent, teacher, or counselor) ever told the individual they believe they may have a drinking or drug problem.
Rutgers Alcohol Problem Index (RAPI)	23-item self-report questionnaire	Designed to assess the consequences of substance use in a variety of areas; found to correlate highly with the DSM-IV criteria for substance abuse.	Consequences relating to: psychological functioning, delinquency, social relations, family, physical problems and neuropsychological functioning.
Inventory of Drinking Situations (IDS) or Inventory of Drug Use Situations	42 to 100-item self-report questionnaire	Designed to evaluate drinking/drug use situations for information on relapse situations.	Unpleasant emotions, physical discomfort, pleasant emotions, testing personal control, urges and temptations, conflict with others, social pressures, and pleasant time with others.
Adolescent Diagnostic Interview (ADI)	24-item 15-minute, structured interview	Designed to assess the need for treatment of drug misuse among adolescents.	Evaluation of various cognitive, interpersonal, and school functioning factors that contribute to misuse.

Table 9.3. (*continued*)

Scale name	Type and number of items	Purpose of assessment	Examples of content and domains assessed
Personal Experience Inventory	276-item self-report questionnaire	Designed to detect problem consequences and potential risk factors believed to predispose youth to substance use.	Level of involvement with a variety of drugs; severity of problems in personal, family and psychosocial domains.
Adolescent Drug Abuse Diagnosis (ADAD)	150-item structured-interview	Adapted from the Addiction Severity Index (ASI) to assess substance abuse and other problem areas.	Nine life areas addressed: medical, school, work, social relations, family relationships, legal, psychological, and alcohol and drug use.
Comprehensive Addiction Severity Index for Adolescents (CASI-A)	150-item 45- to 90-minute semistructured interview, derived from Addiction Severity Index for Adults	Designed to assess the severity of adolescents' addiction and problem consequences.	Assesses peer relationships, family history, sexual relationships, physical abuse, significant life changes, use of free time, substance use effects and treatment experiences, leisure activities, educational experiences and plans, legal history, and psychological and psychiatric status.
Substance Abuse Subtle Screening Inventory (SASSI-A)	81-item self-report questionnaire	Designed to assess face valid content measures in relation to substance-use.	Assesses face valid alcohol, face valid other drugs, family-friends risk, attitudes, symptoms, obvious attributes, subtle attitudes, defensiveness, and supplemental addiction measures.

primary scales characterizing individuals along various dimensions. The dimensions are grouped according to benefits from drinking, drinking styles, drinking consequences, and concerns about and recognition of a drinking problem. The primary scale factors include the following: (1) drinking to improve sociability; (2) drinking to improve mental functioning; (3) drinking to manage or change mood; (4) drinking to cope with marital problems; (5) gregarious versus solitary drinking; (6) obsessive-compulsive drinking or constantly thinking about drinking; (7) continuous, sustained drinking; (8) loss of behavior control when drinking; (9) social-role maladaptation; (10) perceptual withdrawal symptoms (alcohol hallucinosis, delirium tremors); (11) somatic or physical withdrawal (shakes, hangovers, convulsions); (12) drinking provokes marital problems; (13) quantity of alcohol used; (14) post-drinking worry, fear, and guilt; (15) external support to stop drinking; (16) ready to quit; and (17) recognition of drinking problems.

The AUI primary scales often identify three general profiles of problem drinkers (Rychtarik, Koutsky, & Miller, 1998, 1999). First, there are low impairment problem drinkers. They are likely to show a later onset of problem drinking and seek treatment as outpatients. They also are likely to be relatively successful in their social and vocational lives. Second, there are medium impairment drinkers. They are similar to the first type of drinker in that they show relatively good social adjustment. However, they are more likely to report a history of physical, emotional, or sexual abuse and depression. Finally, there are high impairment drinkers. They show the greatest social and vocational impairments, high levels of previous physical, emotional, or sexual abuse, highest levels of sustained drinking, and highest levels psychopathology (depression, anger, or sociopathy).

The Comprehensive Drinker Profile (Miller & Marlatt, 1984) is a structured interview. Detailed information is obtained on an individual's alcohol consumption history, motivation, behavior, and self-efficacy. This interview was developed to determine treatment modality.

The Michigan Alcohol Screening Test (MAST) is a twenty-five-item questionnaire used to screen for consequences of problem alcohol use and perceptions of alcohol-related problems. This questionnaire was established to identify abnormal drinking by addressing social and behavioral consequences (Selzer, 1971). This measure can be used to place drinkers into early (mild impairment), middle (moderate impairment), and late (severe impairments) stages (or levels of impairment) of alcoholism. The Brief MAST is a shortened ten-item version that is relatively effective in discriminating alcoholics from nonalcoholics. The items are designed to describe extreme drinking behaviors and to establish the presence of negative consequences of excessive alcohol consumption. Examples of discriminating items are as follows: Have you ever attended a meeting of Alcoholics Anonymous? Have you ever gone to anyone for help about your drinking? Have you ever been in a hospital because of drinking?

The MacAndrew Alcoholism Scale/Revised (MAC/MAC-R; MacAndrew, 1965, 1989) is a subscale of the MMPI, a standardized questionnaire developed by Hathaway and McKinley (1943). This inventory can be used to help rule out possible psychopathology. Some profiles characterize alcohol and/or drug abuse as a form of self-medication for depression (e.g., the 24/42 scale). The MAC/MAC-R consists of forty-nine items that differentiate between alcoholic patients and nonalcoholic psychiatric patients (Clopton, 1978; Clopton, Weiner, & Davis, 1980; Svanum, Levitt, & McAdoo, 1982). The scale also has been found to help identify individuals who are at risk for developing alcohol-related problems (McCourt, Williams, & Schneider, 1971). One limitation of the scale is that it does not effectively differentiate alcohol abusers from other drug abusers (Burke & Markus, 1977). Additionally, female alcoholics consistently obtain higher scores than males with similar difficulties (Butcher & Owen, 1978). Higher scores suggest potential drug abuse but are also suggestive of extraversion, assertiveness, risk-taking, and the possibility of having experienced blackouts and difficulty concentrating. Low scores are suggestive of introversion, conformity, and low self-confidence, as well as being contraindicative of drug abuse.

The Addiction Severity Index (ASI) is a structured clinical research interview designed to provide information about various areas of an individual's life in which there often exists dysfunction associated with drug abuse. Problem areas assessed include medical, legal, drug abuse, alcohol abuse, employment, family, and psychiatric problems. Reliability and validity data for the ASI have been extensively reported (McLellan et al., 1980, 1985;

Rounsville, Kosten, Weissman, & Kleber, 1986). McLellan and colleagues developed a strategy for obtaining a composite score based on the sum of several individual questions within each problem area.

The Drug Use Screening Inventory (DUSI) (Tarter, 1990) is a self-report inventory and is used to quantify problems in several areas, including drug use, psychiatric disorders, behavior, family, peer, work, school, social skills, leisure and recreational time, and health. Both adult and adolescent versions exist.

Biochemical Assessment of Drug Use among Teens and Emerging Adults

Urine toxicology screening can play an important role in assessment and treatment of adolescents and adults with substance use problems. These tests provide validation of the accuracy of self-reported substance use when properly conducted and when the results are properly interpreted to minimize errors (e.g., false-positive or false-negative test results). Biochemical assessment of drug use also might be used among adolescents and emerging adults to initiate early treatment, to rule out other possible illness or potential health problems when individuals are brought into the emergency room, to facilitate fair play in sports and scholarship, and to provide legal reasons to prove one's innocence (see Sussman & Ames, 2001). Positive test results for any substance are generally confirmed by a second test on the same urine sample, using a different analytic method. Alternative, but more expensive, methods to urine analyses are hair, saliva, and blood analyses.

For initial drug use screening, the most commonly used tests are immunoassays (e.g., radioimmunoassay, enzyme immunoassay, and fluorescence polarization immunoassay). Immunoassays involve the measurement of labeled and unlabeled antigen (drug or metabolite) and antibody interactions (Goldberger & Jenkins, 1999). In drug testing, the antigen is a drug or metabolite and its corresponding labeled analog, and the antibody is a protein grown in an animal and directed toward a specific drug, metabolite, or group of similar compounds. More selective screening assays used for confirmation include gas chromatography/mass spectrometry (GC/MS), gas chromatography (GC), and high-performance liquid chromatography (HPLC). Chromatography consists of a variety of techniques used to separate mixtures of drugs, their metabolites, and other chemicals into individual components based on differences in relative affinity for a mobile phase and a stationary phase.

The length of time a drug or its metabolites can be detected in urine is referred to as the *retention time*. Detection of drug metabolites is dependent on the sensitivity of the assay used. Drug concentrations are highest several hours after drug use and decrease to undetectable levels over time. Retention times differ according to (1) the type and amount of drug consumed, (2) whether use is occasional or chronic, (3) the method of drug use, (4) individual metabolic rates and excretion, (5) diet, (6) acidity of the urine, (7) fluid intake, and (8) the time of day.

Generally, the length of time drugs stay in the body varies across drug types. For example, cocaine and some hallucinogens (e.g., lysergic acid diethylamide [LSD]) are present in the body 12 to 48 hours. Drugs that are present in the body 1 to 3 days include methadone, opiates (heroin, morphine, codeine), proposyphene (Darvon), methaqualone (Quaalude), barbiturates (e.g., Phenobarbital), and amphetamines (crystal, ice, crank, methamphetamines; 1 to 2 days). Phencyclidine (PCP) used occasionally remains present in the body for 1 to 8 days, whereas when chronic use is present, PCP remains in the body up to 30 days. Finally, cannabinoids (marijuana) used occasionally are present in the body for 1 to 7 days, whereas daily chronic use causes cannabinoids to remain present in the body for 1 to 6 weeks.

Regarding tobacco use, expired carbon monoxide (CO) air samples can be analyzed immediately on collection, with a relatively short half-life (3 to 5 hours). Thiocyanates (SCN) are found in body fluids, partly as a result of detoxification of hydrogen cyanide in cigarette smoke (Luepker et al., 1981), and have a half-life of 10 to 14 days. However, SCN levels can be inflated by cyanogenic foods, such as cabbage, and can be influenced by factors that change intercellular fluid volume. The measurement of cotinine, a major metabolite of nicotine, is a more precise measure of nicotine intake and has a half-life of 30 hours (2- to 4-day detection period). A positive test with CO paired with a negative cotinine test could indicate marijuana use.

Summary

The assessment of substance misuse is essential in evaluating an individual's treatment needs and in ruling out other potential reasons for behavioral changes. Judgment, however, may vary among clinicians when deciding whether drug users are abusing drugs, despite the use of standardized diagnostic criteria. Structured interviews may be helpful in minimizing variability in judgments, but different opinions based on varying perspectives of drug abuse are still likely to occur. For example, some clinicians may err on the side of caution for the individual; that is, they may want to protect an individual's privacy. Other clinicians may err on the side of caution for society; that is, they may want to protect the rest of society from any potential harm (e.g., driving under the influence) an individual might cause. We speculate that most clinicians err on the side of protecting society. Moreover, some consequences of drug use are taken more seriously, perhaps more likely resulting in the diagnoses of drug abuse and precipitating the ushering of people into treatment. For example, being arrested for an income-generating crime, such as armed robbery as a result of a heroin addiction, is obviously a societal, legal problem – one that is placed on the public record, and one in which the perpetrator is likely to be restrained by agents of the public. However, if individuals have experienced no legal consequences related to their use, and no obvious interpersonal problems, they are less likely to become diagnosed as drug abusers.

To date, many interview and self-report assessment methods have been developed and implemented to help quantify drug use behavior and the severity of consequences associated with drug use. Still, the main determinant of whether an individual is diagnosed as being a drug abuser, or whether drug abusers are deemed able to maintain relative control over their use, or whether they are experiencing other co-occurring compulsive problem behaviors or psychiatric diagnoses relies heavily on clinical judgment – guided by public demand. In this sense, the larger physical and social environmental context plays a relatively important "backdrop" role in diagnosis.

PREVENTION

10 Concepts of Prevention

This chapter defines and discusses key concepts and program methods that have evolved with increased understanding of the complexity of substance use behavior and its prevention. In an effort to improve program effectiveness, and as a result of findings from evidence-based prevention programs, prevention interventions are now often designed for use in a particular setting or settings and tailored to address the needs of specific groups. Moreover, different prevention programs target persons across the life span (young children, elementary school youth, teens, emerging adults, adults). The use of interactive techniques (e.g., role-play, peer discussions) has been found to increase involvement in the learning process while reinforcing skills training and may be a *sin quo non* for prevention efficacy (see Botvin et al. 1995; Sussman et al., 1995; Sussman, Rohrbach, Patel, & Holiday, 2003; Tobler et al., 2000). This chapter also provides a discussion of the importance of reinforcing prevention goals with repeated interventions or booster programs, long-term follow-up, and worldwide reach of prevention efforts.

Prevention Definitions and Classifications

Historically, public health researchers and practitioners have divided the field of prevention programming into three levels. These levels are primary prevention (before the problem behavior starts), secondary prevention (before the disease starts), and tertiary prevention (before death is likely). However, new terms are now being used to further differentiate various levels of prevention programming. Prevention may be considered "universal" (designed to affect the general population), "selective" (designed to affect subgroups at elevated risk for developing a problem, based on social, psychological, or other factors), or "indicated" (designed to affect high-risk subgroups already identified as having some detectable signs or symptoms of a developing problem; Gordon, 1987). The key difference in meaning of these prevention vocabularies pertains to whether the focus is on the *chronology* of the problem or on the *target population*. Although there is, perhaps, an implication of chronology in the second definition, the direct focus is on fitting programming to a target group. Arguably, a universal prevention program could have a secondary prevention goal. For example, a program designed for the general population could hope to affect those across the spectrum of risk for drug abuse. Thus, there is a possibility of some overlap and nonoverlap among terms (Table 10.1).

Table 10.1. Definitions/classifications of prevention

Types of prevention	Definitions and programming
Chronology definition	
Primary prevention	Implemented on a population before the problem behavior starts
Secondary prevention	Targeting the population after the problem behavior starts but before the disease sets in
Tertiary prevention	Aimed to improve conditions for diseased individuals before death is likely
Target population definition	
Universal prevention	Designed to affect the general population
Selective prevention	Designed to affect subgroups at elevated risk for developing a problem, based on social, psychological, or other factors (e.g., children of alcoholics)
Indicated prevention	Designed to affect high-risk subgroups already identified as having some signs or symptoms of a developing problem (e.g., experimental drug users)

Note: All prevention programming focuses on preventing future behaviors or consequences from occurring, as opposed to recovering from consequences (cessation).

Deciding When to Use Prevention versus Cessation Programming

Another set of terms used to describe levels of an intervention is *prevention* versus *cessation*. Both prevention (at all levels) and cessation approaches encourage adoption of alternative, healthy behaviors and prevention of premature death. However, the central focus of impact of prevention work is on antecedents of behavior. Program participants are taught how to anticipate the impacts of antecedents (e.g., such as desiring to feel good, cognitive exposure to drug-related cues, social influence, or cultural norms) and counteract potential impacts with instruction of protective cognitions, behaviors, or access to protective social units (e.g., drug-free communities), as examples.

Cessation efforts address healing the "wreckage" of one's drug use. Cessation programs instruct how to cope with psychological dependence (emotional reliance) on a drug and physiological withdrawal from a drug (e.g., what types of withdrawal symptoms to expect, how long one will experience these symptoms, and how to cope with these symptoms without relapsing). Cessation work focuses on stopping a current behavior from continuing to arrest ongoing consequences and permit recovery of health. The goal also may involve teaching one how to live with permanent changes (e.g., drug-related injury).

One of the main justifications offered to pursue prevention considers that there are high relapse rates in adult cessation programs (approximately 75% at 1-year post-treatment; Sussman & Ames, 2001). Arguably, prevention programming among teens or emerging adults might inhibit, delay, or halt the addiction process that makes cessation so difficult. One might speculate that exposure to early prevention programming could potentially provide a type of proactive interference against later drug-facilitative-type information resulting in protection against any drug use or sustained drug use. Even for individuals caught up in cycles of drug misuse or abuse, indicated prevention programming could help minimize the time spent in a using cycle. Thus, there exists the expression "an ounce of prevention is worth a pound of cure" (Hirsch, Kett, & Trefil,

2002). A little precaution before a crisis occurs is preferable to doing a lot of fixing up afterward.

Unfortunately, the choice between implementing prevention or cessation approaches is not always evident. Youth at highest risk may not benefit from prevention programming. That is, an initial sense of arousal or affective dis-balance and beliefs about the potential promise of drug use as restorative of a sense of balance itself may override any protective program effects. Enjoyable, novel pharmacological effects from initial and early use may greatly interfere with recall and utilization of early protective information. Some youth may only benefit when they perceive negative consequences of use occurring to them on a consistent basis, making them appropriate candidates for early cessation efforts.

While at-risk persons are still quite young, a variety of prevention approaches might be attempted (Sussman, Earleywine, et al., 2004). Targeted prevention attempts to keep individuals from crossing an "invisible line" (Alcoholics Anonymous, 1976), where they "funnel" into a cycle of addiction and accumulation of negative consequences. It is not clear exactly where indicated prevention ends, however, and where cessation begins. Perhaps, "loss of control" over one's use is a cumulative process, so that at some point either prevention or cessation perspectives might be applied. At some later point, however, a greater emphasis on cessation is necessary.

Integrating Prevention and Cessation

Sometimes youth may already be strongly addicted to one substance (e.g., cigarette smoking) but may not be dependent physically on another substance (e.g., alcohol). Possibly, cessation programming would be needed to address the one substance, whereas prevention programming would be needed to address the other. For example, an early version of an evidence-based drug abuse prevention program (Project Towards No Drug Abuse) did not achieve effects on cigarette smoking, possibly because 46% of the sample already smoked cigarettes daily while not often engaging in some other drug use. In the revised curriculum, a smoking cessation component was added to the program, and then an effect on cigarette smoking was achieved (see Sussman, Dent, & Stacy, 2002; Sussman, Sun, McCuller, & Dent, 2003). Thus, cessation activities can appear with prevention activities in the same program to maximize program effectiveness.

It is also well known that prevention activities can be fruitfully added to cessation programs. This is the major concept behind relapse prevention research and practice (Marlatt & Gordon, 1985). Anticipating and counteracting cues and responses in "high risk" situations are essential in this approach, but the general concepts of relapse prevention may be extended. Programming is needed to link acquired knowledge and skills to potential "high risk" situations so that program contents are easily accessible from memory to effectively counteract pressures to use tobacco and other drugs fostered by these settings (see Stacy & Ames, 2001).

As a specific example, Sussman et al. (2005) developed and piloted a recurrence prevention education program among primarily indigent alcoholic liver disease inpatients, an example of tertiary prevention that also included relapse prevention features. This program instructed patients in alcoholic liver disease concepts and consequences, alcohol and tobacco cessation and relapse prevention coping skills, nutrition, good sanitation, medication compliance, resource advocacy, and decision-making/commitment to motivate improvement in lifestyle. Of those thirteen patients who completed the program, lifestyle improvement (with prevention of alcohol relapse) was observed at a 3-month follow-up, compared to twelve standard treatment patients. Programming is needed to link acquired knowledge and skills to potential "high risk" situations, so that program contents are easily accessible from memory to effectively counteract pressures to use tobacco and other drugs fostered by these settings (see Stacy & Ames, 2001).

The following subsections examine message content, modality of delivery, and implementer type overlap and nonoverlap of prevention and cessation programming. Message content refers to the types of strategies that are offered to prevent or stop drug abuse. Modality of delivery refers to the settings in which prevention or cessation programming might be offered. Implementer type refers to the training and orientation of persons that tend to deliver prevention or cessation programming.

Message Content

Across both prevention and cessation programs, similar message content themes have emerged (e.g., Hansen, 1992; Sussman, 2002a, 2002b). Listed below are five types of substantive contents that exist in both prevention and cessation programs:

1. The social influence-oriented approach focuses on counteracting social influences that serve to promote or maintain teen drug use. Program information includes refusal assertion skill instruction, instruction in awareness of sales promotions, media and peer social influences, and correction of social informational inaccuracies. Recent programs also address means of counteracting social influences in one's social networks (e.g., Valente et al., 2003).

2. Instruction in cognitive-behavioral techniques focuses on uncovering the topography of one's at-risk situations or drug use through self-monitoring, and learning how to cope effectively with stressful situations. For example, monitoring what smoking situations one comes across during the day may help one to avoid them. Monitoring one's smoking situations may help one to anticipate and cope with smoking urges. Stress coping strategies include how to seek out social support, utilizing relaxation strategies, "sitting with feelings" (e.g., waiting out curiosity to first try a drug or waiting through "urges" to delay continued use), engaging in role play to enhance social competency or general assertiveness, self-management and behavioral regulation, and learning and utilizing effective problem solving strategies.

3. Motivational enhancement focuses on techniques to clarify desire for change and reduce ambivalence toward change. This may include, but is not restricted to, a specific strategy such as motivational interviewing. This approach dedicates a significant amount of programming to attempt to increase a youth's motivation to not start (change a youth's intentions, for those curious about starting drug use), not escalate drug use, or to quit drug use. Motivational enhancement approaches assist individuals in clarifying their direction of change and increase their willingness to change. Motivational enhancement may include such strategies as giving advice, removing cognitive impediments to change, providing choices, and reconciling discrepancies between current behavior and desired goals.

4. Response-contingent reinforcement approaches focus on reducing problem behaviors, such as drug use or precursors of drug use with extrinsic rewards such as money,

prizes, or vouchers. Additionally, this approach can include differential reinforcement contingencies designed to strengthen more prosocial alternative behaviors. In attempting to reduce a problem behavior, the goal is to evaluate whether an offer of an extrinsic reinforcement or the possibility of reinforcement to an individual will induce behavior change or decrease the prevalence or frequency of drug use (e.g., Quit-and-Win Contest concept or contingency-based management where an individual is rewarded for desired behavioral changes). This approach has been used with young children in targeted prevention programming to decrease negative behaviors and increase cooperative behaviors, as well as with older youth and adults in cessation programming (Sussman, 2002a; Sussman & Ames, 2001; Sussman, Earleywine, et al., 2004).

5. Supply reduction approaches focus on arranging the social environment so that drugs are more difficult to obtain or use (e.g., price increases or access is restricted). By making drugs harder to obtain or use, it is theorized that costs (financial, time, or social) of drug use will increase for potential users or recent users, giving the individuals reason to think about behaviors other than using. In addition, supply reduction approaches diffuse the larger social environmental disapproval of tobacco or other drug use (Pentz, Bonnie, & Shopland, 1996).

Modality of Delivery

Modality of delivery refers to the channels or contexts within which the programming is offered. Prevention or cessation programming has appeared in numerous settings, including schools, medical clinics, prisons, community-based settings, family-based home or agency settings, and computer-based and systemwide efforts. It should be mentioned that the division of programming by contents and modality is sound logically; however, some program contents tend to be associated with certain modalities of delivery. For example, social influence programming tends to be delivered in a classroom setting while supply-reduction approaches tend to be delivered through enforcement agencies. One could conceive of a complete cross of substantive contents by modality for both prevention and cessation. The use of multiple prevention or cessation modalities is likely to maximize prevention or cessation effects in the long run (e.g., as a means of institutionalizing programming). Still, much research remains to determine which modalities, administered for how long, are needed to increase prevention or cessation programming effectiveness.

Program Implementers

Perhaps the most important variable in maintaining good quality of implementation for prevention or cessation is implementer selection. For example, teacher adoption and high-fidelity implementation of tobacco and other drug abuse prevention programs is positively associated with favorable attitudes toward the program, comfort with program content and approach, perceived self-efficacy to implement the program, independence, innovativeness, a confident and nonauthoritarian teaching style, good overall teaching skills, and characteristics such as being outgoing, adventurous, and well-organized (e.g., see Rohrbach, D'Onofrio, Backer, & Montgomery, 1996; Sobol et al., 1989). The same types of qualities are important in successful cessation work (Jennings & Skovholt, 1999; Miller & Rollnick, 2002). However, in general, individuals who engage in cessation work are expected to have more training in counseling techniques and are often trained to be more nondirective (to learn more about the problems involved) than in prevention work (Lichtenberg, 1997) and frequently come from different educational backgrounds (e.g., psychology or counseling programs versus education programs; Jennings & Skovholt, 1999). The importance of similarity between client and counselor has been emphasized in cessation programming but less so in prevention programming (e.g., Atkinson, Poston, Furlong, & Mercado, 1989). Different training backgrounds do divide prevention from cessation work and may be one explanation why these two approaches to behavior change are not more fully integrated.

Training of implementers is necessary for the efficacy of prevention or cessation programs. Self-preparation and workshop types of teacher training have been found to be equally efficacious in the prevention of cigarette smoking (Cameron et al., 1999). However, video-taped training, as compared to live workshop training, has been found to lead to a lower likelihood of program implementation and, when the program was implemented, led to fewer interactive approaches being used in the classroom (e.g., role-playing; Basen-Engquist et al., 1994). To maintain a reasonable quality of implementer delivery, it is wise to provide some initial monitoring of delivery by program staff. In another project that involved teacher training, those teachers who had been trained and then gathered relatively more experience in teaching violence prevention lessons achieved better effects than those who had been trained but had taught the prevention curriculum lessons fewer times (Aber et al., 1998). Thus, experience also is an important implementer variable. Use of person-to-person workshops and ongoing coaching from an experienced counselor or therapist are two central means of training people to deliver cessation programming. On occasion, use of one-way mirrors and tape recordings of sessions are used to monitor therapist quality (Lichtenberg, 1997; Miller & Rollnick, 2002) (Table 10.2).

Summary

Although prevention and cessation implementers tend to come from different training backgrounds, training and implementation evaluation techniques do overlap. In fact, there is a great deal of overlap in prevention and cessation program contents, modalities of delivery, and implementer skills. The rest of this chapter again focuses on prevention concepts, as do the subsequent four chapters. Then, parallel chapters focuses on cessation. In this way, the reader will be able to continue to consider the overlap and nonoverlap of these two perspectives toward drug abuse interventions.

Ancient History of Drug Abuse Prevention

There is a dearth of information prior to the late 1800s on types of prevention education for youth. One could speculate, however, that for untold years such education was provided by religious authorities in sermons delivered at services and through one-to-one moral or spiritual instruction. Informally, one could conjecture that parents may have warned their children about unsafe diets, which would likely include excess drinking or drug intake. It is likely that drinking and drug use were ritualized and were used primarily by adults only on certain occasions. By 1901, however, every state and territory in the United States had passed legislation mandating some form of temperance instruction to be taught in the public schools (Beck, 1998), because of the efforts of Mary H. Hunt and the Woman's Christian Temperance Union (WCTU).

Table 10.2. *Potential types of overlap between prevention and cessation programming*

Content of program message

Social influence-oriented	Focuses on counteracting social influences that serve to promote, initiate, or maintain drug use
Cognitive-behavioral techniques	Focuses on thoughts that affect feelings and behaviors; identifies at-risk situations, and enhances social competency, assertiveness, self-management and behavioral regulation, and learning and utilization of effective problem solving coping strategies
Motivational enhancement	Focuses on techniques to clarify desire for change and reduce ambivalence toward change; use of strategies to increase one's motivation to not start drug use, not escalate drug use, or to quit drug use
Response-contingent reinforcement	Focuses on reducing problem behaviors, such as drug use or precursors of drug use (e.g., poor classroom behavior) with extrinsic rewards such as money, prizes, or vouchers
Supply reduction approach	Focuses on arranging the social environment so that drugs are more difficult to obtain or use (e.g., price increases or restricted access)

Modality of delivery

Settings	Refers to the channels or contexts within which the programming is offered – both prevention and cessation programming may be delivered in varieties of settings (e.g., schools, medical clinics, prisons, community agencies, family home, computer-based, or systemwide)

Program implementation

Implementer characteristics	Good program implementer characteristics, such as favorable attitudes toward the program, perceived self-efficacy to implement the program, and good overall teaching skills are common to both prevention and cessation works
Implementer training	Training of implementers is necessary for the efficacy of prevention or cessation programs
Implementer experience	Previous program implementation experience is a desirable quality in both prevention and cessation program implementers

The WCTU believed that alcohol, tobacco, opium, and other drugs were the primary cause of social ills in the United States. Temperance education focused on the moral evils of using these drugs. Scare tactics were developed, including the use of graphic descriptions of physical consequences and moral degradation associated with drug use. For example, the use of alcohol was publicized as dulling moral centers of the brain, which, in turn, would lead to criminal behavior (Beck, 1998). In addition, small quantities of alcohol were thought to create an abnormal desire for more, which might become uncontrollable and destructive. Also asserted were the views that tobacco use stunts one's growth, poisons the heart, and impairs mental powers. In France, at this same time, drug prevention education emphasized avoiding the use of hard liquor while the moderate use of beer or wine was acceptable. This perspective was more in keeping with the views of the research community at the time.

When Prohibition was repealed in 1933, temperance education began to lose its foothold in prevention education. At that time, some locations in the United States continued to provide temperance education, some locations provided little instruction on drug effects, and in some locations a growth in responsible use programs began. Responsible use programs emphasized no use of restricted drugs but responsible use of alcohol and the concept of waiting until one is grown up (18 years of age) so that one can make a responsible, mature choice. Responsible choice education likely created a "forbidden fruit" contingency in which youth envied what adults were allowed to do (e.g., drink and smoke). It is unlikely that this type of education could have shown any effectiveness (Beck, 1998; Sussman, 2002b). Concurrently, scare tactics remained popular in mass media campaigns (e.g., the movie *Reefer Madness* [1936]), and additional laws went into effect restricting marijuana use (e.g., the Marijuana Tax Act of 1937).

Fear, Information, Values, and Drug Abuse Prevention

Prevention of drug abuse in school education began to be addressed seriously again in the United States after The President's Advisory Commission on Narcotic and Drug Abuse report was published in 1963 (Beck, 1998). At that time, fear-arousal, information, and values or affect clarification programs began to be implemented in schools. Many drug education programs were developed and implemented haphazardly by private companies, individual educators, and through an influx of federal support (Beck, 1998). Most of these prevention programs were based on the premise that if children knew why drug use was bad for them, they would choose to not start using (Edmundson et al., 1991; Evans, 1998; Sussman et al., 1995). The *fear-based* model assumed that if youth were frightened about the potential negative effects of drugs, then they would not want to experiment with drugs. Unfortunately, the arousal of fear and its impact tend to "wear away" over time, or fear-based messages are poorly manipulated (i.e., persons do not become fearful when exposed to those messages) such that effects of physical consequences programming have been equivocal (Evans, 1998; Sussman et al., 1995).

The *information-based* model assumed that providing adolescents with factual information about drug use would prevent them from engaging in the behavior (Evans, 1998). This approach, which is essentially a form of fear arousal according to Evans (1998), was found to be largely ineffective (Goodstadt 1978; Thompson, 1978). The *affective* or *values-based* model of drug abuse prevention addresses more global attitudinal changes directed at such factors as enhanced self-esteem, improved decision-making and goal setting, and clarification of one's life values. This model often does not include specific information about self-destructive behaviors, such as smoking or drug use (Durell & Bukoski, 1984; Evans, 1998). There is little evidence that this type of model is an effective means of drug use prevention (Hansen et al. 1988; Tobler 1986).

In the 1970s, a parent-power movement also gained widespread support, which led to the use of testimonials by former drug addicts, drug-free school weeks, removal of drug paraphernalia shops ("head shops"), and eventually use of a simplified version of social influence programming (e.g., "Just Say No" campaign). The effects of these programs generally are not known and are questionable. A renewed interest in a parent-power movement is evidenced by the establishment of and research on Parent Corps (see http://www.parentcorps.org/), which is being appropriately evaluated.

Social Influence-Based Programs

In 1976, Richard Evans and colleagues at the University of Houston developed the earliest *social influence-based* programs. The basic assumption was that "inoculation" to resist social pressures that serve as precipitants of use would prevent initial trial and experimentation. The idea was to expose young people to social pressures involving tobacco or other drug use in a safe environment and to teach them skills that could then be transferred to the real world. Subsequent generations of researchers were influenced to varying degrees by the work of the Houston group. Additional theoretical influences in these generations of research included McGuire's social inoculation and attitude change (e.g., persuasive communications) theories, Bandura's social learning theory, Jones and colleagues' attribution theory, Kiesler's commitment theory, Jessor's problem behavior theory, Levanthal's and Flay's tobacco use development models, wellness notions, and Meichenbaum's cognitive-behavior therapy (see Flay, 1985; Skara & Sussman, 2003; Sussman et al., 1995).

Modern comprehensive social influence programs can be differentiated from more narrowly focused social influence programs in that they tend to consider additional theories. Although earlier programs focused on instruction of refusal assertion training and combating direct social influences (e.g., advertisements, mass media depictions, and peer use), comprehensive social influence programs often contain other skills training (e.g., communication skills and assertiveness), provide instruction in decision-making, and include activism and public commitment components. Although social influenced-based, these additional components help adolescents to actively change aspects of their environment that may negatively affect their behavior, choose lower risk friends, or otherwise enter lower risk contexts. As a result, these programs tend to exert a stronger preventive effect on drug use than more narrowly based social influence programs (Tobler et al., 2000; Skara & Sussman, 2003).

Hansen (1992) reviewed the effects of drug education programming on a variety of outcome variables from forty-five published and unpublished studies and found the following: 31% of the outcome variables evaluated from *information-based* programs were positive, 19% of the outcome variables from *affective-based* education programs were positive, 51% of the outcome variables from *social influence* programs were positive, and 50% of the outcome variables from *multiple component* programs were positive. In contrast, 25% of the outcome variables evaluated from *information-based* programs were negative, 19% of the outcome variables evaluated from *affective-based* education programs were negative, 11% of the outcome variables evaluated from *social influence* education programs were negative, and none of the outcome variables evaluated from *multiple component* programs were negative. Nonsignificant outcomes include the following: *information* programs (44%), *multiple component* programs (50%), *affective* programs (62%), and *social influence* programs (38%). There were relatively fewer nonsignificant social influence programs compared to other types (Figure 10.1).

Other research by Hansen and colleagues (e.g., Hansen 1996; Hansen & McNeal, 1997) has provided additional information about etiology that aids in understanding the potential of different programmatic approaches to prevent the onset of drug use (Table 10.3). Their research uncovered twelve mediating variables that have been hypothesized (most which have shown some evidence) to act as change agents in substance use prevention programs, as follows (Hansen 1992):

1. *Normative beliefs* or the perceptions about the prevalence of drug use among close friends and same-age peers at school, and the acceptability of substance use among friends (these perceptions are often exaggerated; that is, teens often think that drug use is more prevalent and more acceptable than it actually is);

Table 10.3. *Twelve mediating variables hypothesized to act as change agents in substance use prevention programs*

Mediating variables	
Normative beliefs	Perceptions about the prevalence of drug use among close friends and same-age peers at school, and the acceptability of substance use among friends
Lifestyle/behavior incongruence	The degree to which an individual views substance use as incongruent with personally held current lifestyle and future aspirations
Commitment	Commitment regarding cessation of substance use, such as public statements of intentionality
Beliefs about social, psychological, and health consequences	Individual's beliefs about, for example, what it means to be a part of a group, what it means to have fun, and one's conception of health risk behaviors
Resistance skills	The perceived ability to identify and resist pressure to use drugs
Goal-setting skills	The degree to which one is able to engage in goal-setting behaviors
Decision skills	The degree to which teens understand and apply a rational strategy for making decisions
Prosocial alternatives	Awareness of and participation in enjoyable activities that do not involve substance use
Self-esteem	The degree to which one feels personal worth and perceives he or she possesses characteristics contributing to a positive self-evaluation
Stress management skills	Perceived skills for coping with stress, including skills for relaxing as well as for confronting challenging situations
Social skills	The ability to establish friendships, be assertive with friends, and get along with others
Assistance skills	The degree to which an individual believes in one's ability to give assistance to others who have personal problems

Source: From Hanson (1992).

2. *Lifestyle/behavior incongruence* or the degree to which an individual views substance use as incongruent with personally held current lifestyle and future aspirations (it is hypothesized that adolescents who perceive their desired lifestyle to not fit with drug use are protected);

3. *Commitment* regarding substance use, such as public statements of intentionality (e.g., statements such as "I have signed my name somewhere to show that I have promised not to use drugs"); also, items that assess a youth's private intentions (e.g., placing a personal statement on a wallet-sized card such as: "I have made a personal commitment to never smoke cigarettes");

4. *Beliefs about social, psychological, and health consequences* (e.g., an individual's beliefs about what it means to be a part of a group, to be less shy or do embarrassing things in a group, beliefs about having fun, having bad breath, experiencing health problems, dealing with personal problems, and the perceived probability and severity of getting into trouble can affect the effectiveness of substance use prevention programming);

5. *Resistance skills* or the perceived ability to identify and resist pressure to use alcohol, tobacco, marijuana, and other drugs (this refers to an individual's ability to say no [refusal assertion] and one's comfort or self-efficacy in saying no in a variety of contexts);

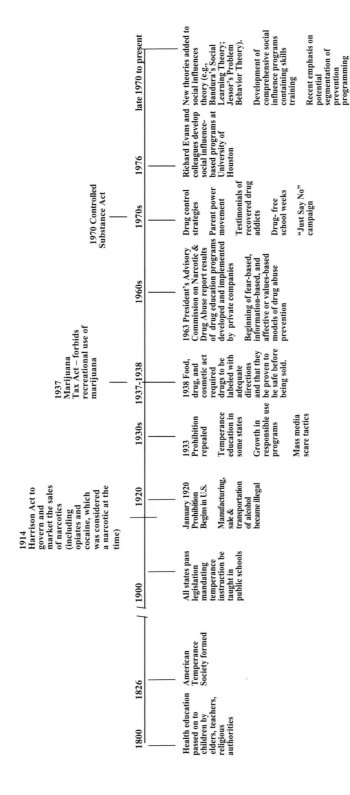

Figure 10.1. Historical timeline of developments in health education and prevention programs.

149

6. *Goal-setting skills* or the degree to which teens are able to engage in goal-setting behaviors (this includes being able to frequently establish goals, develop strategies for achieving goals, and persistence in achieving goals);

7. *Decision skills* or the degree to which teens understand and apply a rational strategy for making decisions;

8. *Alternatives* or awareness of and participation in enjoyable activities that do not involve substance use;

9. *Self-esteem* or the degree to which teens feel personal worth and perceive that they possess characteristics that contributes to a positive self-evaluation;

10. *Stress management skills* or perceived skills for coping with stress (this includes skills for relaxing as well as for confronting challenging situations);

11. *Social skills* or the ability to establish friendships, be assertive with friends, and get along with others; and

12. *Assistance skills* or the degree to which an individual believes they are able to give assistance to others who have personal problems (this includes being able to find help for oneself when experiencing personal difficulties).

Long-Term Follow-Up

Several modern drug abuse prevention program evaluations have included long-term follow-up. Skara and Sussman (2003) provided the first known literature review of twenty-five tobacco and other drug use prevention studies that had at least a 2-year follow-up and included at least a quasi-experimental design. The mean length of follow-up for the twenty-five studies was approximately 69 months, with a range of 24 to 180 months. Fifteen of twenty-five evaluation studies reported at least one (hypothesized) significant positive main effect for long-term smoking outcomes for experimental conditions relative to control conditions on such variables as ever, monthly, weekly, or daily smoking among baseline nonsmokers. The long-term mean reduction in the percentage of baseline nonusers who initiated smoking in experimental conditions compared to control conditions was 11.4% with a range of 9% to 14.2%.

Of the nine studies that provided long-term assessments of other drug use, such as alcohol and marijuana incidence and prevalence, six of the studies reported positive program effects. Long-term percent reductions from baseline to follow-up for experimental conditions relative to control conditions reductions ranged from 6.9% to 11.7% for weekly alcohol use, and a reduction of 5.7% was reported for 30-day marijuana use. Furthermore, of the seven studies that assessed alcohol or marijuana use and specified or suggested that their programs were designed to provide booster sessions, five had maintained long-term reductions in alcohol or marijuana use at the end of the long-term study period. The program contents of all twenty-five studies included prevention strategies that addressed social influences to smoke or use drugs and the development of skills to resist such pressures, and it was conjectured that more comprehensive (multifaceted) social influence programs were relatively effective measured initially and at follow-up.

Globalization of Prevention Efforts

Recently, the European Smoking Prevention Framework Approach (EFSA) was applied to six countries in the European Community (see de Vries et al., 2003, in a series of three articles, plus commentaries). The countries were the United Kingdom, Finland, Denmark, the Netherlands, Portugal, and Spain. In Spain, both Madrid and Barcelona took part as separate sites. Individual, school, parental, and out-of-school "levels" of prevention programming were targeted, with involvement of a national advisory board. Most countries focused on delivery of basic social influence-oriented school-based programming with very little out-of-school programming. Of the six countries, only Spain and Finland showed positive program effects. Eventually, prevention of multiple substances will be targeted in these ongoing studies. Possibly, a more broad-based approach in terms of contents and modalities will be taken.

Part of the need for globalization of prevention efforts stems from transnational drug trade efforts of tobacco and alcohol (Chaloupka & Nair, 2000) and illegal drugs. Distribution of illegal drugs involves international cooperation, often among many smaller groups of persons (White, 1999). Drugs need to be transported across borders, often hidden from view and enforcement efforts, and sold at prices that the consumer is willing to spend. Means to counteract these apparently well-coordinated efforts are needed. Interdiction is one means, but creating an international obligation to stop or not engage in drug trafficking is a major undertaking that needs consideration. In other words, not only are legal enforcement efforts needed but also social and moral obligations need to be addressed. One key obstacle, however, is that for a few countries, drug production and trafficking may be a primary source of income, sustaining these countries' economies.

An Example of the Necessity of Globalization

Framework Convention on Tobacco Control (FCTC): There are over one billion smokers worldwide. If current trends continue, 8.4 million smokers are estimated to die annually of smoking-related deaths by the year 2020 (Kaufman & Yach, 2000). Through recent international research and activism efforts, tobacco control is gaining momentum against a much longer international presence of tobacco promotion. These efforts include increasing the price of cigarettes, wide establishment and enforcement of no-smoking policies, restrictions on any media depiction of tobacco, and implementation of prevention and cessation programs for those at risk to begin or continue tobacco use (Yach & Bettcher, 2000).

Unfortunately, due to changes in international trade agreements, tobacco companies now exert a globalization of influence. Over the past 30 years, a series of international trade agreements greatly reduced tariff and nontariff barriers to trade goods, including tobacco (Chaloupka & Nair, 2000). Partly in response to the expansion of the World Trade Organization's Global Agreement on Tariffs and Trade to agricultural products in 1994, which opened up international trade as a nondiscriminatory enterprise (even though this was not intended to include products that injure human health), the tobacco industries now operate as transnational organizations that are able to provide tobacco products at relatively lower prices, team up with local growers, provide incentives to local storeowners, and market themes of sophistication, wealth, or attractiveness that compose a global cosmopolitan cultural demand for tobacco products (Yach & Bettcher, 2000). From 1993 to 1996, exports of tobacco products increased 42%, coupled with a 5% increase in international consumption (Chaloupka & Nair, 2000). Indeed, trade liberalization has been associated with increased cigarette smoking, particularly in low- to middle-income countries (Taylor, Chalouka, Guindon, & Corbett, 2000).

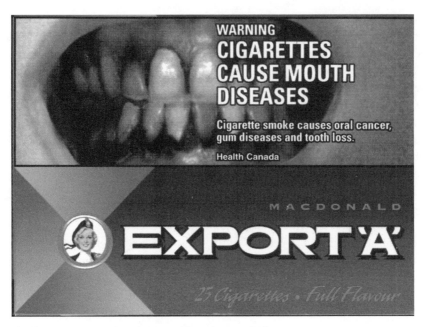

Figure 10.2. Warning found on Canadian cigarette packs.

In response, anti-tobacco forces created or expanded the domains of global anti-tobacco Web sites (e.g., GlobaLink), organizations (e.g., World Health Organization [WHO], World Bank, International Union Against Cancer [UICC], Centers for Disease Control and Prevention, Essential Action, and Health Canada), and global tobacco-free frameworks that emphasize information management, global regulation, and strong partnerships (e.g., FCTC and World No Tobacco Days; Chaloupka & Nair, 2000; Yach & Bettcher, 2000) (Figure 10.2).

In 2005, the WHO Framework Convention on Tobacco Control, an international agreement that commits countries to adopt strong tobacco control policies, entered into force. Approximately 168 countries have signed the treaty, and about 115 have become parties in the treaty. Framework conventions and protocols are legally binding for the countries that ratify them. Key provisions in the treaty encourage countries to (1) enact comprehensive bans on tobacco advertising, promotion, and sponsorship; (2) obligate the placement of rotating health warnings on tobacco packaging that cover at least 30% (but ideally 50% or more) of the principal display areas and can include pictures or pictograms; (3) ban the use of misleading and deceptive terms such as *light* and *mild* cigarettes; (4) protect citizens from exposure to tobacco smoke in workplaces, public transport and indoor public places; (5) combat smuggling, including the placing of final destination markings on packs; and (6) increase tobacco taxes (see www.FCTC.org). The FCTC also contains measures designed to promote and protect public health, such as mandating the disclosure of ingredients in tobacco products, providing treatment for tobacco addiction, encouraging legal action against the tobacco industry, and promoting research and the exchange of information among countries. How effective the FCTC will be in reversing the tobacco epidemic will be determined by how fully governments implement the obligations contained in the FCTC.

In a review of tobacco control efforts in several world regions, Sussman et al. (in press) present case studies that reflect the recent history of coping with the globalization of tobacco promotion in developing countries. These case studies highlight several points in the development of tobacco control worldwide. At first, tobacco control efforts involve some assessment of tobacco use prevalence and consequences; that is, an awareness of the problem is established (e.g., Tanzania). Then, there is the recognition that some action needs to be taken that might be policy/environment related, behavior related, or both. Feedback on policy or other programmatic success is assessed and preparations for additional programming are made (e.g., China and Nepal). Finally, a mature fighting stance against the tobacco industry is developed, which can serve as a role model for other countries, and there is maintenance of programming (e.g., Thailand). Instead of changes occurring across a linear time continuum, changes flare out in feedback loops over time across environmental and behavioral domains. New programming may result not just from static reactions to previous programming, but also from changes in the larger environmental context; for example, they may result from the need to counteract alternative routes the transnational tobacco industry takes to attract new customers.

When Should Programming Be Delivered in Human Development

Drug use prevention researchers found intriguing the critical period of young adolescence, in which tobacco and alcohol experimentation increases dramatically. Many researchers have felt that prevention programming should be delivered at this point in child development, during the trial phase of use (Flay, 1985; Sussman et al., 1995). Thus, most programming has focused on combating social influences, relatively strong antecedents of drug use during young adolescence.

Others now argue that prevention should focus on the very young, whereby those at high risk for drug abuse can be recognized at a young age and need assistance while they are rapidly developing (Tarter, Kirisci, & Mezzich, 1996). For example, findings from animal and human research indicate that those who initiate substance use at younger ages are more likely to become dependent on drugs, suggesting that substance exposure may disrupt normal processes of neurobiological development (De Bellis et al., 2000; Levin et al., 2003). These findings support the perspective that prevention programming should target very young at-risk youth. Researchers have found early intervention beneficial in directing individuals away from problem behaviors and to prosocial activities (see Ialongo, Poduska, Werthamer, & Kellam, 2001).

Others suggest that drug abuse prevention programming would be relatively effective if it was implemented when drug use is truly beginning to become problematic, among older teens for most people (Sussman, 1996). Still others could suggest that programming continue throughout childhood, adolescence, and emerging adulthood.

In a meta-analysis of ninety-four studies of school-based prevention programs, Gottfredson and Wilson (2003) "found that programs targeting middle school aged youth are slightly more effective than those targeting elementary school aged or senior high school aged youths, but the difference is not statistically significant. . . . Only for middle school programs does the evidence clearly imply effectiveness for reducing AOD [alcohol and other drug use]" (p. 36). The final chapter of this book (Chapter 20) further considers the importance of human development in implementation of prevention and cessation programming.

Summary

This chapter provided an overview of key concepts and contents of prevention programs, which may be delivered at institutions, at home, in the community, and at different points throughout the lifespan. In general, the goal of prevention programs is to keep drug use and abuse from occurring, although there are different levels of prevention intervention (primary, secondary, and tertiary). Further, prevention may be designated for different population foci (as universal, selective, or indicated). Drug misuse prevention programs focus on the antecedents (e.g., neurobiological, cognitive, social, or large physical and social environmental variables) of the problem behavior (i.e., drug abuse) and on anticipating and preventing future negative consequences, whereas cessation programming focuses on stopping the accumulation of damage incurred through drug abuse, learning to live with some experienced consequences, and permitting recovery of functioning.

There is some consensus that some types of prevention activities or programming are effective in reducing substance misuse (for a review, see Gottfredson & Wilson, 2003) and that these programs are most beneficial when an individual is developmentally able to learn the material, when the content of the materials are meaningful and relevant to the individual, when the materials are provided in contexts that permit exposure to most of the material, and when implemented by highly seasoned facilitators (Sussman, 2001). Whether programming might most fruitfully be provided over the entire life span is still not clear; however, teaching youth how to bond with institutions and family members is an important early preventive function. Also, affect management seems to be an important skill to instruct across the life span. During adolescence, social influence counteraction is important. If the person continues to use drugs, then motivation, skills, and decision-making appear to be important for successful prevention. Although not previously discussed in this chapter, prevention might also be useful for adults and elderly individuals who may begin to develop drug abuse problems as they move away from their extended families in adulthood or retire in later adulthood.

Integrating prevention with cessation information could be helpful for many individuals at all levels of drug use. This integration would maintain the relevance of programming for those whom prevention or cessation programming alone is not relevant (e.g., many nonusers or "triers" who participate along with regular users in the same settings).

Finally, program materials need to link acquired knowledge and skills to potential "high risk" situations, so that program contents are easily accessible from memory to effectively counteract pressures to use fostered by these settings (see Stacy & Ames, 2001). To maximize the effectiveness of prevention programs, program development testing is needed to create prevention activities and to integrate prevention and cessation activities. In addition, long-term follow-up is needed to further understand mediators of program effects at various stages of substance use and at various age-related developmental stages (Sussman & Wills, 2001).

11   Neurobiologically Relevant

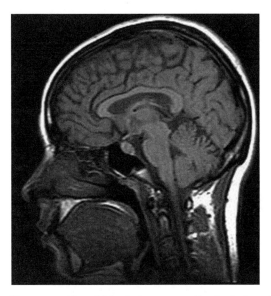

Figure 11.1. Neurobiological processes: Can brain function prevent one from becoming a drug abuser?

Variation in trait correlates (phenotypes) of neurobiological systems affects the degree and manner to which one may be vulnerable to reinforcing drug effects and may therefore require different, specific prevention approaches. In particular, some individuals are more susceptible to the reinforcing effects of drugs and therefore prevention and treatment efforts may need to be tailored to these at-risk people. In addition, different at-risk groups may exist. For example, sensation-seeking individuals may require a different type of programming than that required by anxiety-sensitive individuals (see Conrod et al., 2000), both groups being vulnerable to drug misuse. For example, sensation-seeking individuals may require fast-paced programming and healthy sensation-seeking alternative behaviors, whereas anxiety-sensitive individuals may require emotional learning or mood management programming including behavioral, contextual, or medication options (Figure 11.1).

In the future, the propensity for drug abuse by individuals or populations may be detected during screening through genetic testing. Pharmacotherapy as an adjunct to current

Table 11.1. *Types of neurobiologically relevant prevention programming*

Focus of programming	
Genetics	Future potential prevention programming based on genetic information might include individual screening and assignment to tailored programs; prophylactic medications to attempt gene function manipulation; and inserting or knocking out genes associated with drug use.
Neurotransmission	Correctly prescribed medications that counteract dysfunctional neurotransmission may reduce arousal or affective dis-balance that may promote drug use or result from drug use and aid in functionally rehabilitating neuronal connections.
Delay	Delaying exposure to drugs – *harm delay* – through direct instruction and close parental monitoring may aid in healthy neurobiological development, which in turn may reduce the likelihood of developing subsequent drug problems.
Emotional learning	Developing the ability to competently express oneself emotionally and socially through education programs involving, for example, emotional regulation may help individuals minimize a sense of dis-balance that might otherwise promote drug use.
Sensation seeking	Sensation-seeking individuals may have a neurobiologically based need for stimulation; therefore, they may need drug abuse prevention messages that are novel and exciting to grab their attention and pique their curiosity. Directing relatively higher sensation-seekers to alternative sensation-seeking prosocial activities could steer them away from drug use.
Self-control	Brain-based neurocognitive functions implicated in behavior regulation and decision-making may affect prevention program outcomes. Individuals with poorer self-control can be instructed on assertiveness, impulse control skills, and anger management to better develop self-control skills. These individuals may also be instructed to learn to think ahead and anticipate problem situations, as well as avoid high-risk situations. They may role-play high-risk social situations.

prevention approaches may be of assistance for some genotypes (e.g., use of dopamine agonists). The term *neurorehabilitation* is sometimes used to imply the ability to structurally or functionally rehabilitate, "rewire," or normalize the function of an individual's neurobiological circuitry. This chapter addresses rather novel areas: genetic-based, neurotransmission-based, delay, emotional learning, sensation seeking-based, and self-control programming as drug abuse prevention strategies. This chapter ends with a review of targeted drug abuse prevention programs. All of these approaches assume a neurobiological etiology (Table 11.1).

Genetics

It is becoming increasingly evident that drug use can alter gene expression; drug use can affect the function of genes responsible for enzyme function, receptor capabilities, neuropeptide manufacture, and other neural processes (Lessov et al., 2004). Lessov et al. (2004) wrote that as many as 103 genes may have altered expression following exposure to various drugs of abuse. Repeated drug use exposure may alter the rate of gene expression through "signal transduction mechanisms."

Signal transduction refers to the intercellular or intracellular transfer of biological activation/inhibition information through a signal pathway. In each signal transduction system, an activation/inhibition signal from a biologically active molecule (hormone, neurotransmitter) is mediated via the coupling of a receptor/enzyme to a second messenger system or to an ion channel. Signal transduction plays an important role in activating (or altering) cellular functions, cell differentiation, and cell proliferation. Quick progress is being made in the characterization of mechanisms that underlie the generation and processing of inter- and intracellular signals among work completed by biochemists, molecular biologists, cell biologists, immunologists, pharmacologists, and clinical researchers. Drugs that alter unhealthy signaling mechanisms that are precursors to drug experimentation (e.g., that decrease sensation-seeking tendencies) may exert drug abuse prevention effects. Likewise, just as drugs of abuse may alter cellular functions through effects on signal pathways, other drugs may counteract the effects of drugs of abuse and help restore optimal signaling mechanisms. Such drugs are being developed, though with many of them their characterization is not yet well known (e.g., varenicline tartrate [Chantix] for the treatment of nicotine addiction, acts to ease withdrawal symptoms and dampen effects of nicotine should one smoke again).

Most complex human behaviors (including drug use) appear to be multigenic. Indeed, to date, no single gene has been identified that can alone explain the complex traits that lead to drug misuse. It is therefore likely that the genomic substrates of drug use and misuse are infinitely more complex than what research has revealed to date. Given this caveat, it is possible that in the future a set of genetic markers could be identified and used to predict an individual's "risk" for developing drug dependence. Vigilance programs could then be developed to target youth at high genetic risk for drug experimentation. For example, it is known that children of alcoholics are at increased risk for drug abuse themselves (e.g., see www.nacoa.org). Current selective prevention programs for children of drug abusers may be the precursors of what eventually may be genetically based vigilance programs.

The biological knowledge of the potential for progressive involuntary drug use-to-abuse behavior may help in deterring high-risk youth from experimentation. Based on the presence of a set of known genes, individuals could be stratified on the basis of differential magnitude of genetic risk vulnerability for drug experimentation, continued drug use, and drug dependence. This type of risk assessment, which might involve establishing a typology of at-risk signal transduction processes emanating from a configuration of multiple gene alleles, could then aid in tailoring prevention strategies and potentially lead to the efficient use of resources and programming. For example, it may be possible to develop individualized interventions as adjuncts to existing programs that provide feedback about genetic risk and the behavioral expression of this risk and provide behavioral or pharmacogenetic techniques that work toward countering these influences.

Strategies that could be used include not only (1) screening and (2) assigning youth to receive tailored prevention programming but also (3) use of prophylactic medications to attempt gene function manipulation. Potential future treatment could also include (4) inserting or knocking out specific genes associated with risk for drug dependence (Plomin & Rutter, 1998). For example, by inserting new gene snips, or knocking out extra maladaptive gene snips, it is possible to directly alter the genetic impact on drug use effects.

Along similar lines, in the model presented earlier in this text (see Chapter 5), one may be able to change the inbred map that constitutes the basis for a sense of dis-balance. One could speculate that through gene function manipulation, an individual might not feel uncomfortable generally and might, in fact, find the effects of drugs uncomfortable. This type of genetic engineering is unlikely to occur in the near future, but technology subsequent to the mapping of the human genome is rapidly developing.

The use of genetic information for determining liability to drug misuse will require comprehensive genetic profiles for a wide array of genes implicated in drug dependence, and gathering this information in the general population may prove to be cost prohibitive. At some point, technology may be advanced enough where needed techniques become affordable.

A major area that will require intense scrutiny in the coming years concerns the ethical and societal issues associated with the use of such information. Health care providers and social workers will need to be trained to use appropriately individual genetic information in devising prevention and treatment plans. Informed consent and protection of individuals' privacy requires the utmost consideration, especially in minors. Despite these limitations, continued advances in the genetics of drug use are likely to significantly impact drug abuse prevention and treatment efforts, facilitating the development of both effective new behavior or gene manipulation interventions and pharmacology treatment strategies.

Genetic studies (e.g., allelic association studies) could inform efforts at each stage of prevention (i.e., primary, secondary, and tertiary) or with each type of population target (i.e., universal, selective, and indicated), provided that enough attention is focused on (1) the stage at which various study samples are in the substance use developmental process and (2) the close attention to phenotypic clarity at each stage. More research is needed to understand genetic risk in youth using longitudinal study designs. For example, behavioral data could be collected in childhood and adolescence, and then DNA samples could be obtained in the same individuals when they become adults to increase our understanding of complex traits associated with drug use to abuse behavior.

In addition, in exploring the role of genes, their interactions with each other and the interplay of genes and environmental factors, it is important that researchers and clinicians be aware of possible undesirable or unintended effects on individuals at risk to develop drug-related problems, those suffering from drug dependence, and families of those at risk or those suffering from drug dependence. In particular, those at risk should not be deprived of educational or employment opportunities, nor should access to health care and insurance benefits be compromised, just because they were assessed on their risk for drug abuse and were found to be at risk (Annas, Glantz, & Roche, 1995).

Finally, it is important to not lose sight of the numerous other behavioral, interpersonal, and sociocultural factors that may enhance the influence of and interact with genetic factors in contributing to drug misuse risk susceptibility. This is fundamental when developing new prevention and treatment protocols. Genetic vulnerability to drug abuse should avoid becoming teleological in impact, as these other factors need careful consideration.

Neurotransmission/Pharmacologically Based

Inbred genotypes may be expressed as dysfunctional neurotransmission phenotypes. These phenotypes may be manifested as difficulties in arousal or affect. Experienced dis-balance may, in turn, lead one to be curious about drugs or other activities that might functionally reduce the dis-balance. From a prevention perspective, one might suggest that correctly pre-scribed medications could be used to reduce the dis-balance instead of recreational, more dangerous, or functionally limiting drugs. Thus, for example, youth suffering from atten-tion deficit disorder, with or without hyperactivity, could be prescribed extended release formulas of Ritalin, Adderal, or other stimulant-like drugs (e.g., noradrenergic turnover enhancers) to achieve maximal arousal; possibly they would be less likely to seek and abuse illicit drugs later in life (Sussman, Pentz, Spruijt-Metz, & Miller, 2006). Similarly, depressed or anxious youth might use a selective serotonin reuptake inhibitor (SSRI; e.g., Prozac, Lexipro, or Zoloft), a selective dopamine reuptake inhibitor (SDRI; e.g., Wellbutrin), or a serotonin-norepinephrine reuptake inhibitor (SNRI; e.g., Serzone or Effexor) to restore affective balance, being cautious to monitor for serious negative side effects, such as suicidal ideation. Because neural development is affected by a variety of exposures (e.g., therapeu-tic drugs) and insults (e.g., illicit drug use) that influence cellular learning and memory, and may also affect subsequent susceptibility to substance misuse, pharmacotherapy as an adjunct to prevention approaches may be key for some individuals, as well as prophylactic. Alternatively, or in conjunction with pharmaceuticals, interventions may focus on chang-ing the influence of mediators of these neurobiologically based vulnerabilities to improve program efficacy.

Delay

Youth who are delayed from trying or experimenting with drugs (Jessor, 1984) might be better able to mature neurobiologically without interference of drug use effects. In fact, findings from animal and human research indicate that those who initiate substance use at younger ages are more likely to become dependent, suggesting that substance exposure may disrupt normal processes of neurobiological development (De Bellis et al., 2000; Levin et al., 2003). Simply finding ways to keep youth from drug use until they are at least age 20 or older, when the brain is more mature, might help to reduce the neurobiological consequences of drug use on teens (as well as other consequences). In addition, with the time available to learn drug-free coping skills, youth may be relatively less likely to develop a drug problem later on.

Childhood and adolescence are critical developmental periods in which dynamic devel-opmental transitions in brain structures and neural systems occur. For example, prefrontal brain regions are not yet fully developed by adolescence, and connections with limbic system structures are not fully formed, and these brain regions and connections have been impli-cated in executive cognitive control functions, including behavioral regulation or impulse control and decision-making processes (De Bellis et al., 2000; Gogtay et al., 2004; Laviola, Adriani, Terranova, & Gerra, 1999; Laviola, Macri, Morley-Fletcher, & Adriani, 2003). One may speculate that these developmental brain changes may render youth relatively highly susceptible to social influence and less able to cognitively control, self-monitor, or regulate behavioral tendencies. The neural development associated with these brain regions during youth may also affect sensitivity to the pharmacological effects of drugs. In fact, age-related variation in reward sensitivity has been observed in comparison imaging (magnetic res-onance imaging) of adolescent and adult human brains (Ernst et al., 2005). Brain images of activation of adolescent brains have revealed "a more active reward-related system (i.e.,

NAcc), and a less active harm avoidance-related system (i.e., amygdala)" relative to adults (Ernst et al., 2005, p. 1288). These findings suggest that the adolescence developmental period may be one in which persons are particularly susceptible to engaging in rewarding behaviors and, hence, a critical time for preventing or significantly delaying the onset of such activities as drug use.

Delay may be achieved in a number of ways. Direct instruction in brain development may be sufficient to assist many youth to wait to experiment with drugs until they are 20 (an average age in which cortical structures and connections may fully mature; Giedd et al., 1999). Close monitoring by prosocial adults may assist. Strong deterrents established for individuals who provide drugs to minors may also be helpful for younger teens. Parent education may help. In addition, it is possible that keeping adolescents' lives highly structured and very busy through 20 years of age may help. This may be accomplished through multioption schooling, availability of palatable jobs for teens, creation of extended communities, and other venues. Some current drug abuse prevention programming may assist in delaying drug use for several years (Skara & Sussman, 2003). There has not been much deliberate research in "delaying" drug use per se, so more work in this area is needed to ascertain its benefit. There is, however, a risk of the "forbidden fruit" phenomenon when youth are asked to wait before they do something that adults might or are permitted to do (Sussman, 2002b). More types of delay programming are worth pursuing. One might refer to this type of programming not as harm reduction programming but as "harm delay" programming, which could involve unique pathways of prevention research.

Social and Emotional Learning

Some aspects of social and emotional learning may be considered neurobiologically derived, particularly as applied to young children. Healthy social and emotional learning involves developing the ability to competently express oneself emotionally and socially to effectively manage one's daily life. This includes being able to form relationships, problem solve, and adapt to developmental and environmental demands (see Elias, 2006). The importance of social and emotional competence in successful development is becoming increasingly more evident. Some feel that prevention programming ought to be applied to very young children to enhance social and emotional learning, while the brain is still rapidly developing (Fishbein, 2000). An example of a program for young children that focuses on social and emotional learning is the I Can Problem Solve (ICPS) program. This program was implemented with 4-year-olds to teach these children how to think in ways that would help them successfully resolve interpersonal problems with peers and adults. The program consisted of daily 20-minute small group activities in the classroom for a 3-month period (using words, pictures, puppets, and role playing). Words that are precursors to understanding consequences and problem solving are instructed. Some research indicates that through the ICPS, young children learn alternative ways to solve interpersonal problems (http://www.researchpress.com/product/item/4628/).

Education programs might also include instruction on emotional regulation as an adjunct to an early intervention. For example, an intervention could focus on being able to recognize feelings in one self and others (e.g., facial expressions), being respectful of others' feelings, understanding meanings of emotions, and learning self-control (see Fishbein, 2000). In addition, instruction in how to communicate effectively with others, how to seek support, how to build relationships with others, and how to negotiate fairly might be reasonable prevention components (see Elias, 2006). Early intervention in instruction in these areas may improve social and emotional competence, which could, in turn, minimize a sense of relative imbalance for some youth and possibly help in normalizing one's wiring if exposure to these lessons occurs during critical periods in neural development.

Sensation Seeking-Based Programming

As noted by Bardo, Donohew, and Harrington, "exposure to novelty activates, at least in part, the same neural substrates that mediate the rewarding effects of drugs of abuse" (for review, Bardo, Donohew, & Harrington, 1996, p. 23). The reinforcing effects of drugs play a key role in promoting continued drug use behavior, especially in those more susceptible to drug effects (e.g., sensation-seeking or novelty-seeking individuals). Initial positive or neutral physical reactions to drugs may promote subsequent use, whereas initial aversive physical responses may inhibit subsequent use behavior. One suggestion for prevention is to consider that at-risk youth (e.g., sensation-seeking youth) may process information differently than lower-risk youth, and therefore prevention materials should be tailored accordingly.

Given evidence that individuals higher in sensation seeking have a neurobiologically based need for stimulation, it seems reasonable to assume that they need drug abuse prevention messages that are novel and exciting enough to grab their attention and pique their curiosity (e.g., see Pentz et al., 2006). In fact, Palmgreen et al. (2001) have found that public service announcements high in sensation-seeking value may have influenced higher sensation seekers' drug intake for several months following a media campaign. Novel, stimulating, and fast-paced media messages that are able to grab or increase adolescents' attention and affect learning may be more effective in influencing sensation-seeking individuals with lower baseline dopamine turnover (e.g., Palmgreen et al., 2001).

Directing higher sensation-seeking individuals to novel/sensation-seeking activities that may be more prosocial alternatives to drug use may be a useful prevention strategy. However, it can be difficult to find replacement activities that provide as much stimulation as drug use does yet are harmless and age appropriate. This is a challenge for interventionists, but with new technologies, it is possible that in the future various video games and immersive virtual realities/simulations may provide potential replacement alternatives (e.g., virtual sky diving).

In considering that youth may attend to and process information differently as a result of neurally based trait variation, Conrod and colleagues developed a set of personality-matched drug abuse prevention interventions for individuals classified as being sensation-seeking, anxiety sensitive, or hopeless. The prevention program materials focus on motivation enhancement and coping skills training and are designed specifically for targeted personality-specific groups at risk for substance misuse (see Conrod et al., 2000; Stewart et al., 2005). Conrod and colleagues have used the intervention materials for both cessation and prevention purposes. Among a sample of female drug abusers, ranging in age from 30 to 50, Conrod et al. (2000) found the personality-matched interventions to be effective in reducing alcohol- and drug-related problems over a 6-month period. In addition, among a sample of more than 5,000 Canadian youth, ranging in age from 14 to 17, who reported alcohol use within the past four months, significant reductions in binge drinking, drinking quantity, and problem drinking were found in the personality-specific intervention groups as compared to the control groups at 4-month follow-up (Stewart et al., 2005). These findings provide support for targeted interventions based on trait-based behaviors. However, a caveat to classifying individuals based on traits is that some individuals may overlap in dispositional traits (e.g., are depressed and sensation-seeking). Although the extent of overlap in traits has not been determined to date, this type of risk classification-prevention program protocol requires careful consideration of use of integrative components from the various interventions that might tap overlapping use motives.

Self-Control Programming

Brain-based neurocognitive skills may moderate teen prevention program outcomes. For example, social competency skills (as discussed earlier in this chapter), which are sometimes a mediator of drug use and misuse, are predicted by executive cognitive function and emotional perception (Fishbein et al., 2006). Executive cognitive functions are mediated by prefrontal brain regions implicated in behavioral regulation (e.g., inhibition) and decision-making processes (e.g., see Bechara, 2002; Gogtay et al., 2004; Laviola, Adriani, Terranova, & Gerra, 1999, 2003). Lower scores on tests of aspects of executive cognitive functioning have been found to be associated with current drug and alcohol use as well as with relatively lower social competence (Fishbein et al., 2006) and predict the onset of drug use disorders among adolescents (Tarter et al., 2003). Additionally, deficits in executive function have been associated with other risk factors for substance misuse, including conduct problems and antisocial behaviors (Bauer & Hesselbrock, 1999; Giancola et al., 1996; Giancola & Tarter, 1999).

Children with a family history of substance abuse disorders have been found to have lower executive functioning abilities and to be at increased risk of becoming drug abusers when compared to offspring of non-drug-abusing parents (see Giancola & Tarter, 1999). In one study, lower executive function scores in participants with a positive family history of alcoholism were predictive of their alcohol consumption 3 years after the initial evaluation, when controlling for previous use (Deckel, 1999). Children of alcoholic parents also have been found to display other problem behaviors that may be regulated by aspects of executive function, such as impulsivity, violence, and attention deficit/hyperactivity (Giancola et al., 1996).

Poor self-control involves behavioral, affective, and cognitive deficits. Poor behavioral self-control is associated with a need to regulate and stabilize mood, possibly preceding uncontrolled behavior or stemming from the consequences of uncontrolled behavior. Poor self-control behavior, along with difficulties in mood stabilization, increases risk for substance use and rapid escalation to high levels of use, which then can lead to physiological dependence (Wills & Stoolmiller, 2002). Self-control strategies cross physiological and personality boundaries because self-control also relates to coping motives for substance use, a strong predictor of substance use problems (Sussman, Earleywine, et al., 2004).

Developing self-control is an underpinning of personality organization, which includes not only behavioral and affective control but also cognitive control. Types of cognitions amenable to self-control interventions include attitudes, beliefs or expectancies, and values that promote (or inhibit) substance use, views of the world as hostile (or accepting), and social perceptions about substance use as being attractive (or unattractive). For example, some studies (see Sussman, Earleywine, et al., 2004; Wills & Dishion, 2004) among adolescents have found that poor self-control correlates with attitudinal tolerance for deviance and more favorable perceptions of tobacco and alcohol use, whereas good self-control is related to more favorable perceptions of teens that abstain from drug use. Self-control approaches can be useful for prevention programs with a focus on improving self and other perceptions, academic performance, and goals that are salient to teenagers and their parents, while minimizing the impact of negative life events.

With regard to prevention interventions, the program materials implemented need to be adequately individualized to address neurocognitive skills; individuals must be able to effectively understand and process information to be able to subsequently utilize program information when confronted with high-risk situations. As mentioned, the work by Bardo and colleagues attempts to permit maximum processing of information by sensation-seeking recipients, with neurocognitive processing that prefers presentations of rapidly changing stimuli (Pentz et al., 2006).

Training in elements of self-control skills may be essential. In self-control programming, youth learn to assess their self-control, particularly in social contexts. They learn the importance of thinking ahead and anticipating problem situations so that they are prepared beforehand to deal with problems that may arise, including situational avoidance. They also learn the importance of context (e.g., not laughing at a funeral). They may role-play high-risk social situations in which self-control may be threatened. Also, they may be instructed in assertiveness and anger management, and relaxation skills, to help them better control and manage their reactions in social settings. Finally, in these programs youth may be taught cognitive components (e.g., counting to ten, "not sweating the small stuff"; see Sussman, Earleywine, et al., 2004).

Summary of Evidence-Based Targeted Drug Abuse Prevention

Most targeted drug abuse prevention program developers assume that neurobiological risk directly or indirectly leads to drug misuse and that programming can be "targeted" for high-risk groups. That is, many problem behaviors, such as drug misuse appear to be, in part, the behavioral manifestation of neurobiological processes. One could even speculate that drug use and other problem behaviors are initiated to satisfy a sense of dis-balance that results from some common neurobiological underpinnings (along with environmental influences). Prevention programming may alter the course of one's neural development (toward more protective neuronal connections) associated with learning and memories (or specific neuronal connections) that can be reinforced and strengthened over time through participation in more prosocial activities.

Sussman, Earleywine, et al. (2004) evaluated twenty-nine evidence-based, targeted drug abuse prevention programs for their effects on drug use or other problem behavior among high-risk populations. The programs were identified through four primary sources: Blueprints for Violence Prevention, the Substance Abuse and Mental Health Service Administration's science-based prevention programs guide, and PsycINFO and MEDLINE searches of drug abuse prevention studies since 1970. Nine definitions of high risk were used across the various programs. Eleven programs focused on economic deprivation as the definition of high risk. Six programs focused on delinquent behavior as the identifying characteristic to target. Two programs each identified single-parent homes, drug use or exposure to drug use, family problems, alternative high-school attendance, or being at risk for dropout at a regular high school as characteristics to target high-risk individuals. Finally, one program each identified new immigrant status or residential facility placement as the defining characteristic of being at high-risk for drug abuse.

Among the programs reviewed, eight focused on preteens. For example, the Early Risers program defined its high-risk youth as those 6- to 10-year-olds who suffered economic deprivation and exhibited aggressive or oppositional behavior. Another five programs focused on a young teen age group. For example, Preventive Intervention defined its high-risk youth as those 7th to 8th graders who exhibited poor school and academic discipline and reported family problems. Another seven programs focused on an older teen age group. For example, Project Towards No Drug Abuse defined its high-risk youth as those attending alternative high schools. Finally, nine programs encompassed wide age ranges. For instance, Big Brothers and Big Sisters of America defined its high-risk youth as 6- to 18-year-olds living in single-parent homes.

Ten of these programs involved multiple, often flexible, settings of implementation. Another 13 programs focused on the school setting. Four programs focused on the home setting. Finally, two programs focused on a community agency setting. In general, these programs involved implementation by highly trained personnel.

Eighteen of these programs involved some motivational aspect, generally motivational enhancement, but sometimes they included extrinsic reinforcement strategies (i.e., reinforcement by manipulating environmental consequences of behavior such as by being paid contingent on performance). Twenty-six of these programs provided skills training. Finally, eighteen programs provided instruction in decision-making. Taken together, these programs appear to define a type of programming referred to as the motivation/skills/decision-making model (MSD; Sussman, Earleywine, et al., 2004). According to this model, targeted programming needs to (1) motivate the at-risk recipients to not desire to misuse drugs, (2) teach skills to bond to more conventional venues, and (3) train at-risk recipients in decision-making to tie motivation material to skills material and take right action. The MSD model tends to appear in a majority of these programs; however, all three components were included together in only nine of these programs.

Twenty of these programs involved at least one replication of the program, and fourteen involved three or more replications. Further, fourteen of these programs were tested through use of experimental designs, and nine involved use of only quasi-experimental designs. Effects on drug use were assessed and found in twenty-two of these programs. For example, the Reconnecting Youth program was implemented to youth at risk for dropout (Eggert et al., 1994). This program involved ninety sessions within a comprehensive high school class, delivered generally over a semester, with small student groups and highly trained teachers. Instruction included use of group support and providing life skills training (norm setting, self-esteem enhancement, mood management, communication skills, self-monitoring, monitoring goals, school bonding, and social activities), with feedback to parents. Program goals were achieved through use of a quasi-experimental design, showing effects for school performance (18% improvement in grades), drug use (54% decrease in hard drug use), and suicide risk (32% decline in perceived stress). This program involved all three components of the MSD model, except that motivation was provided through peer group support, not through provision in motivational enhancement strategies. These targeted programs present an optimistic picture for drug abuse prevention that is focused on at-risk youth. Targeted programs for high-risk populations could be interpreted as modifying phenotypical expressions of neurobiological underpinnings. However, future integrative research will be needed to examine the reality of this speculation.

Not all targeted prevention programs have been found to be effective. One published program that failed to find positive effects was Project PALS (Palinkas, Atkins, Miller, & Ferreira, 1996). This project was developed for teen girls who were pregnant or at risk for pregnancy and drug use. The program consisted of school-based delivery of sixteen sessions, once a week, in a classroom, with the goal of decreasing drug use. The PALS Skills Training Program involved instruction in assertiveness, providing and receiving feedback, social conversation, handling requests and asking for help, and mood management. This program was tested against a normative education program (called Facts of Life [FOL]), which instructed values and decision-making, sexuality issues and contraception, sexually transmitted diseases (STDs), drug use risks, sexual assault, prevalence, and norms material. Experimental evaluation (7-month postbaseline) indicated that the PALS program participants reported 2.9 times greater marijuana use than FOL among baseline nonusers. No other differences were found. It is possible that the program was not targeted to the right population, the mix of skills instructed was not appropriate, or that skill training alone (without appropriate motivation material) may not be effective in drug abuse prevention. In this population, perhaps sexuality information also is necessary to induce change. Researchers should examine these possibilities, and others, to further understand program failures as well as program successes (Table 11.2).

Potential Limitation of Targeted Prevention: Deviancy Training

Dishion and colleagues (Dishion, French, & Patterson, 1995) suggest from various findings that grouping high-risk youth may lead to increased drug use. That is, youth could actually learn deviant behaviors from each other in a program if they have unstructured or unsupervised time together. An essential feature of several targeted programs (e.g., Reconnecting Youth [RY] and Towards No Drug Abuse [TND] programs) is to build a positive peer culture with group norms that decrease drug involvement and drug use control problems among high-risk youth. Findings from the RY program suggest that a positive peer group component carefully fostered by a well-trained and competent group leader can direct the group toward lower risk behaviors. Similarly, classroom management in Project TND involves development of positive norms of classroom behavior. Further, interaction between youth is encouraged but is primarily teacher directed and highly structured (Sussman, Rohrbach, Patel, & Holiday, 2003). In both RY and Project TND, the teacher's role is to actively develop and maintain peer group support in the class by modeling support, positively reinforcing it among group members and negatively reinforcing deviant peer bonds and activities. The teacher creates and structures interactions among youth in prosocial directions. This structured interactional style may mitigate effects of deviancy training. From a neurobiological perspective, highly structured programs may impose an external executive process on at-risk youth who otherwise would not be able to maintain a focus that permits effective learning of material.

Potential Limitation of Targeted Prevention: Multiple Problem Behaviors

Acknowledging the relationship of drug abuse to other common adolescent problems may facilitate identification of effective methods of reducing drug abuse. Research addressing tobacco, alcohol, and other drug use, antisocial behavior, high-risk sexual behavior, and

Table 11.2. Elements of review of twenty-nine evidence-based,
targeted drug abuse prevention programs

Definitions of high risk	Number of studies
Economic deprivation	11
Delinquent behavior	6
Single parent homes	2
Drug use or exposure to drug use	2
Family problems	2
Alternative high school attendance	2
Being at "high-risk" for drug abuse	2
Immigrant status	1
Residential family placement	1

Study participants	Number of studies
Preteens	8
Young teens	5
Older teens	7
Wide age ranges	9

Study settings	Number of studies
Multiple community settings	7
School settings (or school plus family)	11
Community agency (can include school/ family)	11

Program contents	Number of studies
Motivational components	18
Skills training	26
Decision-making instruction	18

Note: Derived from Sussman, Earleywine, et al.'s (2004) review of twenty-nine
evidence-based, targeted drug abuse prevention programs.

depression increasingly recognize that these problem behaviors are interrelated and stem, to a large extent, from the same environmental and biologically based influences (e.g, Biglan et al., 2004; McGee & Newcomb, 1992; Sussman, Earleywine, et al., 2004).

Clearly, it is necessary to develop strategies that address the entire range of problems and the context that influence these problems. Indeed, further reductions in many problems require that we comprehensively target youth with multiple problem behaviors. It is clear that many of the same youth are prone to developing a larger (if not entire) range of problem behaviors. These youth are often identified early in life (e.g., Fishbein, 2000). These findings point to the importance of early intervention, before youth develop serious problems (Table 11.3).

Summary

A focus on implementing interventions that address neurobiologically based trait variations could enhance program effectiveness for those individuals highly vulnerable to reinforcing drug effects (Fishbein et al., 2006). Given that some individuals are simply more susceptible

Table 11.3. Possible limitations of targeted programming

Deviancy training	Grouping high-risk youth together may lead to increased drug use as the situation becomes conducive for these youth to learn deviant behaviors from each other.
Multiple problem behaviors	Programs targeted to high-risk youth may need to provide integrative components that tap into related or overlapping problem behaviors such as violence, drug use, and unsafe sex.

to the reinforcing effects of drugs for a variety of reasons (e.g., sensation seeking and anxiety sensitivity), prevention and treatment efforts may need to be tailored to address specific population needs. In fact, many prevention program developers have and continue to modify programs with increasing knowledge of known neurobiological risk (e.g., implementing training in social self-control). Perhaps, for some individuals, the earlier interventions are implemented the better to improve social and emotional competency and delay the onset of use. Moreover, in the future, some individuals who are highly susceptible to drug abuse based on various biologically based risk factors may elect to undergo genetic testing and choose pharmacological adjuncts to interventions to modify these influences on behavior. To minimize harm from drug abuse, the goal for some individuals, in part, might be to alter or normalize the course of their neural functioning or functionally rehabilitate neuronal connections reinforced and strengthened over time through involvement in more prosocial behaviors.

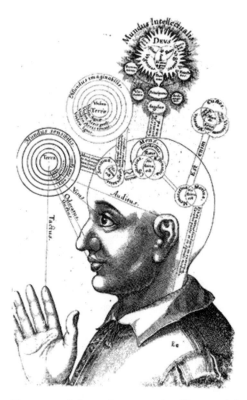

Figure 12.1. Information processing: How can it be changed to prevent drug abuse?

In preventing problem behaviors or affecting behavior change, one needs to address the importance of cognitive processes, in conjunction with emotion/arousal processes. As addressed in previous chapters, the influence of cognitive processes on behavior involves both rational and nonrational processes and motivations. Drug abuse or addiction is a prototypical example of nonrational behavior that is unlikely to be motivated by only rational decision-making. This chapter highlights several prevention strategies that focus on redirecting cognitive processes to prevent drug abuse. Although most cognitive-based prevention strategies focus on making use of explicit cognitive processes, such as rational decision-making, some strategies may tap into both rational and nonreflective (more automatic) cognitive processes. This chapter addresses prevention strategies that have been and are being developed to counteract (1) cognitive-information errors, (2) cognitive processing limits, (3) associative memory or drug-related implicit cognitive processes, (4) nonoptimal decision-making, (5) belief-behavior congruence errors, and (6) contextual/situational distortions (Figure 12.1).

Cognitive-Information Errors

There are several examples of prevention programming that have counteracted cognitive-information errors. As one example, drug use prevalence overestimates may be counteracted through an "overestimates reduction" prevention activity. In this activity adolescents (1) self-report whether they have used a particular drug in the last week and (2) engage in taking a poll on their perceptions of the numbers of their peers (e.g., within their classroom) that used the same drug over the same time period. Next, they are presented with a comparison of the actual percentage of use among their peers derived from their own self-reports of use (aggregated across all youth in the classroom), with the mean perceived estimate of the percentage of users. For example, youth self-reports have indicated that only 12% of youth at regular high schools report marijuana use in the last week and only 1% report use of lysergic acid diethylamide (LSD) in the last week. Yet, when asked about their peers (e.g., either estimates about peers in their classroom or estimates of use of 100 peers their age), youth estimate that 74% of their peers have used marijuana in the last week and 46% have used LSD in the last week (Sussman et al., 1995; Sussman, Craig, & Moss, 2002). Because of this cognitive-information error, some youth may have thought that they are among the few of their peers who do not use these drugs. By becoming aware that they tend to overestimate their perceptions of others (e.g., their peers' use), they realize that not everyone is using drugs "out there." In fact, they learn that relatively few are using and that they don't need to use drugs to fit in with peers. In other words, if they reduce their prevalence estimates, they may also reduce their expectations that they should use drugs in the future. In summary, relatively low prevalence estimates is predictive of lower drug use in the future (e.g., Sussman et al., 1988), and producing a conservative shift in cognitive information is a valuable preventive effort.

Cognitive-information error-related myth formation can also be counteracted through use of elaborative processing (Stacy & Ames, 2001). For example, as operationalized in a curriculum by Sussman and colleagues (Project Towards No Drug Abuse [TND]; Sussman, Craig, & Moss, 2002), a program could initially provide a discussion about the "kernel of truth" in any given myth and then discuss why the myth is, in fact, a myth. To illustrate, a prevention program might discuss the myth that individuals use drugs as a means of being emotionally protected from life stresses. The *kernel of truth* in this myth is that one might initially feel that their drug use is protective, at least temporarily, from negative life stressors; that is, they experience some temporary relief or pleasure from drug use that distracts them from real life events. The *myth*, however, is a myth because an individual thinks less clearly under the influence; that is, one's thinking may be distorted, and the individual may be more likely to become increasingly overreactive or underreactive (i.e., dis-balanced) or become victimized (e.g., get robbed or mugged) and, hence, incur greater stress. In terms of prevention programming, it may be important to elaborate on the difference between more immediate gratification and the impact of longer term negative consequences of use so that meaningful memories are constructed.

One caveat important to discuss is that a presentation of myths and truths could result in backfire effects (cf. Jacoby, Kelley, Brown, & Jasechko, 1989; Krank & Swift, 1994). That is, misattributions of the source of messages could have a negative impact on prevention programming if memory processes are not considered; myths could be retained as facts after the program is completed. For example, Krank and Swift (1994) demonstrated that myths about alcohol use could be retained as facts after only 24 hours had lapsed. They found strong main effects for prior exposure to myth messages and fact messages on an immediate posttest, but the likelihood of generating myth statements as true outcomes of alcohol use increased on a delayed test. In essence, individuals did not accurately attribute the source of the outcomes (myth or fact) they accessed from memory. Whether or not this type of misattribution influences program effects is currently being investigated; we speculate that through the use of elaborative processing strategies, myths are more likely to be retained in memory over time as being myths.

Cognitive Processing Limits

Cognitive processing limits could affect prevention programming effects; it may be important to tailor program components to train some types of executive functions (cf. Klingberg, Forssberg, & Westerberg, 2002; Olesen, Westerberg, & Klingberg, 2004). Executive functions are higher order cognitive constructs that are involved in the planning, initiation, and regulation of goal-directed behavior. Specific cognitive processing elements include attentional control, cognitive flexibility, judgment, and working memory (see Baddeley 1983, 1996; Baddeley & Wilson, 2002; Kane & Engle, 2002).

Executive functions are relevant to inhibitory control over behavior and counteracting the influence of more spontaneous cognitions and implicit processes. There is evidence that executive functions (e.g., working memory capacity) affect behavior by moderating the availability of resources an individual has access to during decision-making in complex social situations (e.g., Finn & Hall, 2004; Grenard et al., 2007; Payne, 2005). Complex social situations are likely to tax aspects of executive functioning for many youth. For example, situational interference (e.g., drug use cues or ambiguous contexts) could overload working memory resources, reducing one's ability to attend to and maintain information (e.g., intentions to resist drug use). The association between addictive behaviors and cognitive deficits (e.g., Bechara, Dolan, & Hindes, 2002; Bechara & Martin, 2004) suggests that the prevention of addiction and its treatment should encompass cognitive rehabilitation – that youth should be trained in enhancing executive functioning, such as attention focus, planning, abstract reasoning, rational judgment, learning from experience, and cognitive self-monitoring of behavior during goal-directed activities. For some vulnerable individuals with functional deficits in prefrontal cognitive structures reflected by hyperactivity or hyperreactivity and verbal learning problems, prevention programs may need to be supplemented with pharmacological adjuncts (as mentioned in Chapter 11).

Executive functioning capacity enhancement prevention efforts might attempt to make content or skills that are learned in programs more automatically accessible from memory in high-risk situations. That is, to counteract deficits in executive functioning capacity, drug abuse prevention materials could be tied to risky social situations so that this information is stored in long-term memory as new associates of drug use experiences. Then executive functioning or cognitive control becomes less of an issue because program materials may be more likely to be automatically activated in situations along with other associates of drug use when youth are immersed in situations with strong drug use cues (see Stacy, Ames, & Knowlton, 2004). The more automatically program information is accessed, the less is required of various aspects of executive functions (e.g., working memory, judgment, or decision-making). Overall, given the evidence supporting the influence of implicit cognitive processes on complex behavior (see Wiers & Stacy, 2006), interfering with or inhibiting the influence of drug-directed associative memories appears to be an important potential strategy for behavior modification.

Another potential direction for prevention programs involves designing interventions that more forthrightly help adolescents cope with cognitive challenges faced in high-risk situations. For example, one may be instructed in the use of guided learning strategies that help promote critical thinking and enhance self-monitoring and reasoned judgments to counteract more automatic tendencies when confronted with uncertain or risky situations with strong drug use cues. In addition, one may be instructed on categorization or processing of elements of situations so that they become less taxing on executive functioning resources. For example, practice in decision-making-related activities appears to be a key element of drug use prevention and cessation programs (e.g., Fiori et al., 2000; Sussman, Barovich, et al., 2004; Sussman, Earleywine, et al., 2004). In general, practice tends to facilitate performance. Steps of decision-making and practice in decision-making using hypothetical scenarios assist in being able to remediate difficulties in sorting out options and planning self-constructive action. As one continues to utilize steps of decision-making, cognitive processes involved will begin to become more automatic and solidify in memory.

Prevention programs have employed several decision-making strategies. For example, the protocol from Project Reconnecting Youth (Project RY) is S.T.E.P.S. The acronym stands for: *Stop, Think* of options, *Evaluate* options, *Perform* or take action on the chosen option, and then *Self-praise* for using steps for making healthy choices. The lesson *S.T.E.P.S. to Drug Use Control* follows skills training sessions that covered understanding S.T.E.P.S. as a decision-making model.

Project TND's decision-making component involves four steps. These steps are as follows: (1) *brainstorming* or making a list of ideas without judging them, (2) *weighing the pros and cons* or the benefits and costs of each idea, (3) *selecting the best option*, and (4) *following through* or trying that option and *reevaluating* the decision. These decision-making strategies are similar across different programs except that they have some different emphasis. For example, S.T.E.P.S. includes a self-instruction to begin decision-making and self-praise, whereas the TND sequence includes more of an emphasis on following through with the decision. Each program requires generating options, evaluating them, choosing the best option, and evaluating the outcome in an effort to make the next decision.

Teens tend to enjoy practicing decision-making in bogus problem situations. Youth soon learn to engage in the various steps with considerable skill. Training in decision-making operates on variables that are intermediate in the causal process and thereby strengthen individual profiles of self-control abilities so that they are more resilient in the face of proximal risk factors for drug use such as life stresses and peer pressures (Sussman, Earleywine, et al., 2004).

Implicit Cognition Strategies

Although explicit cognitive components are clearly important aspects of prevention programming, these approaches do not directly address relatively automatic patterns of activation in memory that govern behavior (i.e., implicit cognitive processes). Integrating strategies that address drug-relevant explicit cognitive processes and implicit associations are very likely to be important foci for future generations of prevention programs.

Many individuals approach initiation and experimentation of risk behaviors with pre-existing memory associations about the behavior (e.g., sexual risk taking, violence, or drug use exposure through the media or World Wide Web, or vicarious learning through parental or peer experiences) that can be activated in response to situational cues. One could make the case that any "exposure" translates to "experience" (cf. mere exposure effect; Zajonc, 1968) and that some initial association between drug use and outcomes is thus established. Consider the numerous television programs, movies, news items, advertisements, refuse, and observation of use that one is likely to experience long before one considers trying a drug. Memory associations or implicit cognitive processes thus formed can influence attentional, attitudinal, and behavioral directions. Moreover, implicit cognitive processes may override explicit processes, resulting in a loss of inhibitory control and perpetuating unintended behavior, which, in turn, may strengthen associations between the behavior and anything processed during a drug use event (Stacy, 1997; Stacy & Ames, 2001). Individual differences in accessibility to information as a function of exposure to different situations can help to explain why some cognition about consequences of use may predict drug use and others may not or why information presented in a prevention program may be learned but not necessarily applied to a drug use situation (see Stacy et al., 1990; Stacy, Widaman, & Marlatt, 1990).

To enhance the effects of prevention interventions, newly learned program information must compete with existing memory associations. This means that programs need to establish highly accessible new associations. To effectively enhance accessibility of newly learned program material, competing preexisting learned associations that promote a risk behavior must be eclipsed. Interventions may include memory enhancement components such as *elaborative processing of new associations* to help minimize the influence of these preexisting associations. For example, an intervention could focus on tying non-drug use coping program information (e.g., seek social support) and high-risk situations together in memory (see Stacy & Ames, 2001). With sufficient semantic relatedness to the preexisting memories through repetition, or simply through the novelty of the new memory created, program information may become accessible enough to spontaneously "pop to mind" when an individual is in a risky situation. *Elaborative processing* is one process that may be easily integrated into school-based programs and already may be a mechanism that can account for, in part, some program effects.

Elaborative processing has been described metaphorically as the "glue" that forms new associations in memory (Schacter & Graf, 1989). Elaboration involves processing two initially discrete pieces of information as a single, coherent unit (i.e., unitization; Graf & Schacter, 1999; Micco & Masson, 1991; Schacter & Graf, 1989). For example, increasing memory associations between program information and cues that characterize high-risk situations is a primary means of increasing accessibility during drug use decisions (Stacy & Ames, 2001). Cues may differ with age groups and with susceptibility or risk of drug abuse and can take on various features of situations, such as aspects of physical and social environments, feelings, and so forth, but they should be meaningful to the target population (Stacy & Ames, 2001).

The process of unitization requires that individuals conceptually elaborate two pieces of information to decrease the arbitrariness of these pieces of information and increase the significance of their relationship. Through conceptual elaboration, pieces of information become more strongly associated in memory. When pieces of information become unitized, the presentation of one aspect of that information activates the larger unit as a whole (Horowitz & Prytulak, 1969). Elaborative processing has been shown to affect performance on cued tests of implicit memory for new associations (e.g., Howard, Fry, & Brune, 1991; Micco & Masson, 1991; Schacter & Graf, 1989) and cued tests of explicit memory for new associations (e.g., Micco & Masson, 1991).

Both *conceptual elaboration* of two pieces of information (e.g., adolescents engaged in "pharming" with friends coupled with adverse consequences of this behavior) and *extensive study of newly learned concepts* (e.g., antidrug beliefs or consequences), possibly followed by repetitive priming and testing of newly learned associates, may enhance memory for the new content and increase the strength of the new association. Repetitive testing with performance feedback and restudy has shown large effects on explicit and implicit memory for new associations (Howard, Fry, & Brune, 1991). In this manner, explicit cognition components (e.g., changing beliefs about consequences of use, correcting misperceptions about peer norms, decision-making skills) addressed in a program can become more accessible when needed most (see Stacy & Ames, 2001).

Unitization through elaborative processing may be easier for individuals who have not already initiated regular drug use than for those who have already experienced reinforcing drug effects and have preexisting positive drug use-related memory associations that may compete with newly learned associations. For those at-risk youth, more intensive memory enhancement components using a different set of high-risk cues may be necessary. In other words, for these youth, prevention programs will need "to compete with implicitly activated memories for drug effects or experiences that are likely to be tied to neurobiologically based reward and habit systems" (Stacy, Ames, & Knowlton, 2004, p. 1604). The solution in this case would be to limit relatively automatic tendencies to engage in risky behaviors, which may require more intensive processing of information.

Implementation intentions may be another means of linking specific intentions to perform a behavior with situational cues such that a behavior becomes relatively spontaneously initiated. Implementation intentions specify a plan of action; that is, "When situation X occurs, I will perform behavior Y" (see Gollwitzer, 1999). This type of intervention requires the individual to identify aspects of an intention, such as specifying when, where, and how responses will be carried out (i.e., forming a mental representation of the situation), which delegates the initiation of goal-directed behavior to situational cues. When an individual is then confronted with a particular situation, the initiation of the specified goal-directed behavior has a greater chance of being automatically initiated by the situational cues (an established cue–response association), requiring little or no conscious intent. Implementation intentions focus on more spontaneous processes and have shown strong effects across a variety of health behaviors (see Gollwitzer & Sheeran, 2004; Orbell & Sheeran, 2002; for review, Prestwich, Conner, & Lawton, 2006). For example, some health behaviors in which implementation intentions have been found to be effective include breast self-exams (Orbell, Hodgkins, & Sheeran, 1997), exercise compliance (Milne, Orbell, & Sheeran, 2002), healthy eating (Armitage, 2004; Verplanken & Faes, 1999), vitamin C compliance

(Sheeran & Orbell, 1999), cervical cancer screening (Sheeran & Orbell, 2000), and binge drinking (Murgraff, White, & Phillips, 1996).

According to Gollwitzer (1999), implementation intention effects are more likely when "the strength of commitment to the formed implementation intention matters" and when "the strength of commitment to the goal intention for which implementation intentions are formed should also matter" (p. 499). But, how do these simple action plans or implementation intentions become relatively automatic? One could speculate that implementation intention effects might partially result from the elaboration of information and the unitization of cue–response associations, which ultimately increase accessibility of situational cues. Perhaps self-generation of information is a form of elaborative processing. That is, perhaps generating the when, where, and how a response may be executed creates strong new associative links between situational cues and the behavior.

The question remains, though: how do such simple plans compete with consistently performed "implementation intentions" to use drugs? Implementation intentions may work better for primary prevention rather than after drug use has been repetitively performed. Prestwich, Conner, and Lawton (2006) suggest that "implementation intentions can be used to automatically elicit behavior that deals with precipitating risk factors or inhibit addictive cognitions (e.g. 'When I feel stressed [tired, bored], I will perform yoga in my office'; 'If I feel stressed, I won't think about drinking')" (p. 461). It remains to be evaluated, however, whether implementation intentions can regulate habitlike behaviors or inhibit unwanted behaviors (such as drug abuse) that are already relatively automatic or spontaneous processes over the long term.

Attentional retraining is yet another potential intervention for future prevention and treatment programs. Because activation and accessibility of concepts in memory affects what stimuli an individual selectively attends to, attentional retraining components that work toward redirecting an automatic attentional bias for drug use cues may be a reasonable program component. It is not yet clear whether attentional biases can be sufficiently modified by therapeutic interventions; however, some programs are being developed that show promise (cf. Alcohol Attention-Control Training Programme [AACTP]; see Cox & Fadardi, 2006; Field & Eastwood, 2005). The Alcohol Attention-Control Training Programme developed by Cox and Fadari is a computer-based program being used to train problem drinkers to be less distracted by alcohol-related stimuli, which automatically activate drinking-related thought processes. The AACTP has been found to be effective in retraining some alcoholics to reduce attentional focus on alcohol cues, which, in turn, translates into lower alcohol use. The effects of the AACTP were found to persist at 3-month follow-up. Possibly, the AACTP protocol may show primary prevention effects as well, by redirecting at-risk (highly drug exposed) youths' attention away from drug cues.

Belief–Behavior Congruence

Individuals may engage in self-destructive behaviors that might even be contrary to their basic beliefs about themselves because they often do not think about how their beliefs relate to different behaviors. Belief–behavior discrepancies can be brought to awareness to help individuals not engage in self-destructive behavior. For example, there are at least four education-format examples that have attempted to make teens aware of their own discrepancies and be induced to reduce them through potentially healthful action. One application is in the arena of stereotyping. As studied in cognitive social psychology, among teens and adults, people tend to engage in "in-group/out-group" stereotyping (Fishkin et al., 1993). In-group members may perceive out-group members as more extreme and homogenous than they actually are. For example, high school and college youth are well aware that they are perceived as more uniformly extreme/deviant ("wild") than they actually are by younger peers or older adults. The stereotyping can lead to a self-fulfilling prophecy if individuals conform to such stereotypes. Alternatively, awareness of the stereotype can lead to counteracting it by engaging in prosocial action and informing others of their healthful pursuits.

The logic of stereotyping remediation for older teens

- Older teens take note that young peers or adults consider older teens to be deviants or stoners (using a provided list of twenty adjectives about older teens, such as being a loser, stoner, lazy, druggie, etc.; the older teens fill out the list based on what they perceive others think of them).
- Next, older teens rate themselves (e.g., using the same adjectives list) and they appreciate that older teens are somewhat deviant but not as bad as they believe others had stereotyped them.
- Then, older teens conclude that they should either give in to a self-fulfilling prophecy or rebel against it.

The tendency is to rebel against the stereotype when the discrepancy is brought to awareness (Sussman, Craig, & Moss, 2002).

A second example of making participants aware of a belief–behavior discrepancy is derived from Attitudinal Perspective Theory (Upshaw & Ostrom, 1984), another concept from cognitive social psychology. This theory posits that there are two different aspects of one's attitudes about behaviors or events. First, an individual has a general attitudinal perspective (e.g., as being a moderate). In fact, most youth and adults prefer to consider themselves as being "moderate" people (Sussman, Craig, & Moss, 2002). Separately, the individual has specific attitudes about specific behaviors or events (e.g., beliefs about gun control laws, no-smoking policy, or appropriate patterns of drug use). It is possible that someone's general attitude about him- or herself as a moderate person may appear contradictory with some specific attitude. If confronted with this discrepancy, an individual will tend to try to reduce it, which, in the present context, could lead to specific anti-drug use statements.

The logic of attitudinal perspectives remediation

- Individuals recognize a general self-attitude that they are a moderate type of person.
- The individuals also recognize a specific attitude that risky behavior, such as regular recreational drug use, is a behavior that they and other youth view as radical.
- The individuals (older teens) conclude that one should view him- or herself as a radical type of person, or one should not engage in the specific behavior (abuse drugs).

Individuals tend to change their behaviors rather than change their self-perception as a moderate person (Sussman, Craig, & Moss, 2002).

A third example is derived from a "health as a value" notion (Lau, Hartman, & Ware, 1986; Ritt-Olson et al., 2004; Sussman et al., 1993; Sussman, Earleywine, et al., 2004). This notion is that the more a person values health, the more likely the person is to refrain from health compromising behaviors. This construct may moderate the effects of one's perceived control over health and serve as a motive for engaging in healthy behavior (Lau, Hartman, & Ware, 1986; Ritt-Olson et al., 2004; Sussman, Craig, & Moss, 2002). For example, if someone places importance on good health to be better able to achieve life goals, that person may be motivated to not abuse drugs. More specifically, one may desire to attain certain goals (e.g., good grades), know that good health is needed to achieve these goals, be instructed to recognize that drug use may interfere with goal attainment, and therefore need to change either goals or drug use.

The logic of instilling health as a value

- Individuals consider what they want to accomplish in the future.
- They consider whether their health is important to accomplish these goals. (They are likely to agree.)
- Individuals then consider whether self-destructive behaviors (e.g., drug abuse) can interfere with their health. (They are likely to agree.)
- Individuals conclude that they should either give up their goals or they should not engage or continue to engage in the self-destructive behavior (e.g., misusing or abusing drugs).

Individuals tend not to want to give up their goals – *health as a value* becomes more important, and they think more seriously about their drug misuse (Sussman, Craig, & Moss, 2002).

Contextual/Situational Distortions

Mystification (or distorted meanings of behavior; see Chapter 6) may be counteracted by direct confrontation of the mystification process. For example, with cigarette smoking, one may be taught that getting sick when first smoking is the body's way of communicating warning signals that one is inhaling toxins. When one no longer feels sick when smoking, it does not mean that one is becoming used to using cigarettes. Rather, no longer feeling sick indicates a failing of warning signals, the beginning of tolerance. To impart this message to adolescents, prevention programs can integrate a component in which individuals read cards and role play different stages of use from trial, experiment, and regular use to dependence to death (e.g., see Glynn, Levanthal, & Hirschman, 1985; Sussman, Barovich, et al., 2004; Sussman et al., 1995).

A strategy that can be used in prevention programs to counteract drug-related experiences discussed by Perceived Effects Theory includes the use of humorous cartoons that can be discussed in a group situation (Sussman, Moss, & Craig, 2002). To illustrate one such cartoon, the actor comments on how funny it was when she was arrested, took a drug test, was handcuffed and booked, and asked for a retake of the mug shot. The reinterpretation of a very negative social and legal situation is made clear, and a realization of the cognitive misperception is made explicit (the arrest for drug misuse is not funny).

Table 12.1. *Types of cognitive processes-related prevention programming*

Focus of programming	Examples of programming
Cognitive-informational errors	Drug prevalence overestimates – point out discrepancies between perceived and actual prevalence of drug use among peers or engage in "overestimates reduction" activities. Error-related myth formation – use of elaborative processing strategies to clarify facts from myths.
Cognitive processing limits	Attention control, cognitive flexibility, judgment, and working memory – enhance through attention focus, planning, abstract reasoning, critical thinking/reasoned judgment, experiential learning, and cognitive self-monitoring activities.
Associative memory or drug-relevant implicit cognitive processes	Implicit cognitive processes (or spontaneous patterns of activation in memory that govern behavior) – memory enhancement strategies such as elaborative processing of new associations (to help minimize the influence of preexisting associations), formulate implementation intentions, and attentional retraining.
Belief–behavior congruence errors	Belief–behavior discrepancies – bring to awareness age-group or peer-group stereotypes, bridge discrepancies between self-perception and behavior, and enhance health as a value.
Contextual-situational distortions	Mystification (distorted meanings of behavior in situations) – direct confrontation of the mystification process. For example, use of psychodramas or "talk shows" can assist in eliciting responsibility and consequences information.

Appeals to personal responsibility and clarification of negative consequences perpetrated are essential to combating neutralization techniques. Use of psychodramas or "talk shows" can assist in eliciting responsibility and consequences information and achieving healthy changes. For example, in a "marijuana panel" talk show in Project Towards No Drug Abuse (Sussman, Craig, & Moss, 2002), various panelists report their experiences. Scripts are provided to all participants in the group who volunteer to take on various roles, and they can work off the scripts. Participants in this activity either serve as other panelists or as audience members. An ex-marijuana abuser reports that he or she "use to smoke weed everyday. It became a problem." The abuser says,

I felt like I couldn't make it through the day without at least one joint. I depended on marijuana to make me feel better. All I wanted to do was to be high and not think about anything. I told myself, and everyone else, that I did it because I was stressed. A lot of the jobs are asking for drug tests. I don't want to miss out on a job that I really want because of using weed. It's not worth it. Since I quit, I feel better. I have more energy and I'm finally taking care of the things in my life.

In this script, the marijuana abuser mentions that he or she used to blame continual marijuana use on stress, the neutralization technique of denial of responsibility. Then the person makes an appeal to personal responsibility and clarifies personal consequences suffered because of marijuana use. This may reduce tendencies toward use of techniques of neutralization among all participants in this activity. Having youth take on corrective roles in this talk show (psychodrama) type format may lead them to identify with the roles, which may provide a corrective effect on their behavior (Table 12.1).

Summary

Prevention programs may need to incorporate components that address cognitive mediators and moderators of drug misuse to enhance the effectiveness of preventive program information. A variety of prevention strategies have been developed and implemented in prevention programming, such as strategies to counteract cognitive-informational errors, cognitive processing limits, belief–behavior congruence, and contextual-situational distortions. However, the development of new components (e.g., components to counteract implicit cognitions favorable toward drug misuse) and modifications of strategies shown to be effective are necessary to advance prevention efforts and increase our understanding of mediators of program effects. Explicit cognition components are clearly important aspects of prevention programming; however, these approaches are unlikely to fully address such mediators as implicit memory activation or memory retrieval processes. Changing relatively automatic associative effects could be an important adjunct to interventions. As noted by DiChiara (2002), "Both cognitive, conscious (explicit/declarative), as well as associative, unconscious (implicit/procedural) mechanisms contribute to purposeful behavior" (p. 76). Assuming that both implicit as well as more deliberate or explicit cognitive processes affect behavior, learned program information needs to become spontaneously activated in memory (to compete with preexisting, drug-relevant associations) when behavioral decisions are being made (Stacy & Ames, 2001; Stacy, Ames, & Knowlton, 2004).

13   Social Interaction and Social Groups

Prevention programming administered in social settings is beneficial and perhaps funda-mentally central to inducing and maintaining change. Making use of the group can help correct adolescents' cognitive misperceptions, as well as provide a venue for practicing newly learned behavioral skills in social settings, with corrective input from educators, and peer feedback that may mimic real-world social situations. This form of programming often makes use of simulations of real-world settings. For example, learning how to avoid, escape, refuse, or otherwise correct social pressures facilitative of drug use, particularly among young teens, can be practiced in group settings. Practice facilitates performance if and when such pressures occur naturally in one's social environment.

There are several microsocial-level strategies that can help prevent one from drug misuse. For example, youth who take on responsibility for the care of others, who adaptively emo-tionally distance themselves from problem others, and who take on more prosocial pursuits (where they can find them) appear to be more resilient against drug misuse (Sussman & Ames, 2001). Thus, programming that facilitates such behavior (e.g., involvement in com-munity service) may provide a protective effect. Also, individuals who maintain a more hopeful outlook, develop good communication skills, and seek out prosocial support when needed tend to be more resilient against drug abuse (Hawkins, Catalano, & Miller, 1992; U.S. OTA, 1994). Instruction in communication skills and how to seek out social support might provide a protective impact. This chapter provides several examples of prevention program-ming that involve social interaction and the group, including the elements of comprehensive social influence/life skills programming, use of the peer social network, conscientiousness instruction, community unit-based involvement, and family-based involvement.

Elements of Comprehensive Social Influence Prevention Programs

As with other types of education programming, prevention programs that are highly inter-active (i.e., interaction among teacher with students and students with each other) tend to be the most successful (Sussman, Rohrbach, Patel, & Holiday, 2003). The *Socratic (interac-tive) method* of teaching is one in which questioning by the teacher is used to elicit from participants the pertinent prevention information. This process is preferable to a more didactic approach, reducing resistance to the message and encouraging discussion and consensus among group members. Also, group members are relatively more likely to value self-generated information. Thorough teacher training is necessary to effectively implement

Figure 13.1. School-based settings are a central means of delivery of substance use prevention program-ming because youth are a captive audience.

substance use prevention programs, particularly to make these programs highly interactive (Figure 13.1).

Tobacco and other substance use microsocial-level-type prevention programs with as few as five contacts or sessions (generally, school-based delivery) have been successful in delaying tobacco and other drug use onset (Skara & Sussman, 2003; Sussman et al., 1995). Additionally, it appears that *delivery* of a daily program is superior to a more spaced deliv-ery, although it is more important to provide all sessions of a program, even if presented over many weeks, then to deliver only a part of the program. *Homework* assignments are frequently used in prevention programs to encourage (1) review and personalization of material taught, (2) generalization of training from one setting to another (e.g., school to home), (3) discussion of material with others, and (4) expansion of the targets of the inter-vention (e.g., to siblings and parents). Not all prevention programs include homework tasks, and this process element of programming has not been well evaluated for its incremental contribution to program effects. The use of *booster material* to supplement substance use prevention core programming also may significantly enhance program effects, especially when repeated over a number of years (Skara & Sussman, 2003; Sussman et al., 1995).

Effective drug abuse prevention programs are generally divided into eleven substantive components (Sussman, 2002b). These eleven components are found in comprehensive social influences/life skills single component or systemwide programs (Tobler et al., 2000). These key components are presented next.

Listening and Communication Skills
The objective of *social skills training* is to teach different skills (e.g., listening and commu-nication skills), using a well-researched sequential process, including (1) demonstration of

appropriate behavior, (2) modeling of appropriate behavior, (3) behavioral rehearsal, and (4) feedback components. A repetition of this sequence might occur. Of course, with group school-based type programs, there is little time for any one-on-one training, so an abridged version of this sequential process is used with some success (Sussman et al., 1995).

One can improve both listening and communication skills by learning how to ask open-ended questions, establishing eye contact appropriately, nodding, and orienting one's body toward the other speaker. One can also ask questions of the speaker or listener to check for a mutual understanding of the communication sequence. One also can make sure that one's nonverbal behavior matches one's verbal behavior to exchange a consistent message. These skills are useful in social group situations.

Nevertheless, social skills training can create problems for some high-risk teens. Among high-risk youth, enhancing communication or assertiveness skills may increase the scope of social entertainment options and inadvertently improve a teen's ability to acquire drugs from new sources (Wills, Baker, & Botvin, 1989). Utilizing motivational enhancement methods prior to instructing specific skills may help provide non-drug use directions to increase flexibility of an individual's range of behaviors (Sussman, Earleywine, et al., 2004).

Also, there are cultural variations on what constitutes good social skills. For example, different norms exist regarding degree of personal space, acceptability of establishing eye contact, degree of smiling considered appropriate, and appropriateness of stating opinions that may diverge from the group (see Unger, Hamilton, & Sussman, 2004). Thus, one needs to make sure that the skills being instructed accurately reflect ethnic group norms of the participants. Overall, increasing social competence will have protective effects for teens.

Refusal Assertion Emphasis

Refusal assertion skill is one type of assertiveness skill, a social skill that involves how one might best refuse an offer or request of someone else. Generally, an assertive refusal is a simple, direct response that is not too passive (weak statement, such as "ask me tomorrow") or too aggressive (e.g., yelling at the requester). With an assertive refusal strategy one may acknowledge positive intent of the requester ("I know you are trying to be nice by offering me a cigarette"), state one's own position ("but I don't smoke"), and possibly offer an alternative ("I'll see you later in class"). Assertion refusal, although emphasized as being very important in earlier consensus statements, is not considered to be as central a feature of tobacco and other drug use prevention programming as it was in the past. Rather, manipulation of social normative perceptions appears to mediate program effects among young teens, perhaps not refusal assertion skills training per se. For example, MacKinnon and colleagues found that peer disapproval, negative outcome expectancies for drug effects, and relatively low prevalence estimates mediated effects obtained in the Midwestern Prevention Project. Refusal assertion skills instruction did not (Donaldson et al., 1996; MacKinnon et al., 1991). Similar findings have been uncovered in the arenas of alcohol use prevention (Project Alcohol Abuse Prevention Training) and tobacco use prevention (Project Towards No Tobacco Use [TNT]) (see Donaldson et al., 1996). Refusal assertion training can be useful to those who need such skill only if closely linked to normative material. Provided alone, one may come to believe that everyone "out there" uses tobacco or other drugs and that drug use offers are ubiquitous. As a consequence, one's refusal self-efficacy may decrease, and one may increase intention to conform to such perceived pressures by using tobacco and/or other drugs. In addition, training in drug refusal assertion may create reactance in some older adolescents who do not want to engage in such an exercise or otherwise have already taken a stance toward drug use. These older teens may feel that such an activity is demeaning or irrelevant (Sussman et al., 1995)

Short- and Long-Term Physical Consequences of Substance Use

These preventive activities do not address social influences but are included in some form in most comprehensive social influence programming. Certainly, a discussion of physical consequences is necessary to justify why one should learn to resist different types of influences to use drugs. One activity used in Project TNT includes discussion of a chain of consequences that begin with smoking and other drug use initiation, progresses to addiction, to disease, and through death. By uncovering a chain of consequences that conforms to use development transitions, youth can see how consequences accumulate as they continue to use drugs (Sussman et al., 1995). In addition, some myths about tobacco and other drug use can be corrected. For example, many youth believe that when coughing stops in early smoking experimentation, they are "getting use to" smoking. If youth are taught that what is really happening is that their bodily defense systems are giving up, that they are beginning to become addicted to nicotine, this information is likely to exert a preventive effect (Glynn, Leventhal, & Hirschman, 1985). Although this type of reasoning is a cognitive misperception type of correction, types of group activities might be used to instruct effectively the physical consequences of tobacco or other drug use. For example, this material might be instructed by lining up students and having them take on different "roles" in the different phases of tobacco use-to-consequences, as in Project TNT. Also, this information might be instructed through a group "game" or group dramatizations (e.g., role playing a funeral of someone that died from a drug overdose; Sussman et al., 1995).

Peer Group Unacceptability of Drug Misuse

Group activities involve participation of a whole set of youth (e.g., a classroom or youth group) and can affect conservative shifts in attitudes of its members by taking *group polls*. For example, instructors might take a class poll regarding whether *peers approve* of getting drunk on alcohol, using tobacco, or getting high on marijuana. Young individuals tend to believe that they, but not their peers, are the only ones who view tobacco and other drug use as unacceptable behavior. By taking a group poll youth learn that most of their peers also disapprove of drug use.

Effective programs have used 20-minute activities to decrease perceived approval of use. To illustrate, in a well-planned normative restructuring activity youth are instructed to stand under approve-disapprove signs regarding acceptability of tobacco and other drug use. A conservative shift in attitudes results as youth visibly understand that they and the majority (if not all) of their peers disapprove of use (see Sussman, 2002b; Sussman et al., 1995).

Correction of Use Prevalence Overestimates

A similar type of activity is used to reduce *prevalence of use overestimates*. Instructors may attempt to modify overestimates of the prevalence of drug use by taking a poll of self-reported drug use in the class along with youths' estimate of the number of their peers in the class that use drugs. The instructor then provides a comparison of the actual frequency of use to student estimates of that frequency among peers, the latter of which are generally markedly higher. The instructor explains, through group discussion, that youth may tend to overestimate the number of users among their peers, that relatively few youth use drugs, and that there is little actual pressure "out there" to use by peers.

Awareness of Adult Influences

Adult influences refer to modeling influences of significant others or other adult role models, particularly among youth that aspire to appear older to others. Youth are made aware of these influences through group discussions about adults, including celebrities in the news and significant others. In addition, one homework assignment that is sometimes used is to have young teens observe or interview an adult that is a cigarette smoker or has had a drug problem. By doing so, adolescents may appreciate that innocent curiosity as to why people use tobacco or other drugs can lead to problematic use, which, in turn, makes adults very unhappy.

Media Influences

Advertising influences also may model tobacco and other drug use and influence those individuals who aspire to express social images portrayed in advertising (e.g., "having fun" and "risk taking"). In prevention education, youth are made aware of adult advertising influences (referred to as instruction in media literacy) so that they are less likely to yield to these, often subtle, informational social influences. They may learn to correct false advertisements or act on various media influences through activism activities. For example, in Project TNT youth correct tobacco magazine advertisements by creating new ads that provide the opposite message (e.g., unattractive, boring) of that portrayed in the tobacco advertisement (e.g., beauty, fun). Tobacco counteradvertising activities also may include coloring smoker's teeth in ads yellow.

Activism

Activism activities also assist in the prevention of drug use. For example, youth may write letters to significant others, celebrities, the tobacco or alcohol industry, or the media to provide a correct portrayal of tobacco advertising or to encourage others not to use tobacco or engage in heavy alcohol use. Engaging youth in writing exercises may help them to personalize knowledge, become active learners, and encourage belief change through activism.

Self-Confidence Building and Decision-Making

Information on self-confidence building involves the use of cognitive techniques, such as making positive affirmations to self or others. The individual may engage in a series of steps that involve consideration of their assets and liabilities to assist them in making decisions that could increase self-confidence. Decision-making involves steps of learning how to rationally combine information to make self-fulfilling decisions in different problem areas. A range of possible options that include considering the benefits and costs of each option and then making a decision based on carefully considered information aid in leading to a logical decision. Self-confidence building and decision-making are distinguishable from ethical/moral decision-making (e.g., "maturity" and "responsible" adult behavior) and values clarification materials, which have not been shown to aid in the prevention of drug use.

Table 13.1. Types of social interaction and social group-related prevention programming

Name	Description
Comprehensive social influence programming	This type of programming involves a variety of education strategies to create awareness of social influences on behavior and to counteract these influences by enhancing social skills (e.g., listening and communication skills training, assertiveness training, social decision-making, and activism skills) and correcting social misperceptions (e.g., correction of use prevalence overestimates, normative restructuring, and media literacy).
Social network analysis	Social network data can be used to structure classroom-based workgroups and improve prevention program implementation. For example, peer leaders may be used to assist in program delivery, which may improve implementation.
Conscientiousness instruction	Conscientiousness instruction may enhance conscientiousness through use of group interaction, and instruction on the importance of cooperation, industriousness, social responsibility, and delay of gratification. This type of instruction might best take place in a group setting where group norms for cooperation and mutual support can develop.
Family-based programming	Family-based programming provides prevention materials to the family unit. The focus is on strengthening family dynamics including, for example, instruction in skills training and resource acquisition instruction, family therapy, contingency management, stimulus control, and social support training to prevent drug use.
Community units inclusive prevention	Multifaceted approaches to prevention utilize multiple (coordinated) delivery modalities, whereby youth receive a consistent message across community contexts and over time. For example, use of access reduction, family programming, mass media programming, involvement of community organizations, and school-based programming may combine to maximize prevention efforts.

Making a Commitment Not to Use Tobacco and Other Drugs

Obtaining a *public commitment* is another activity that involves writing and group action. Here, the participant engages in a writing activity (i.e., stating the commitment) that is then stated publicly to the group. Often, a decision-making sequence about drug use is completed first (e.g., to not misuse, not abuse). Next, a contract *not to use* drugs is provided. The signed contract is shared among the other youth in the group.

Smoking and Other Drug Use Cessation Materials for Teens or Adults

This type of material is most appropriate for older teens and for adults. It may be offered to children to give to their parents. It is useful material for regular smokers and drug users, who need information on how to cope with withdrawal symptoms (Table 13.1).

An Example of an Evidence-Based Comprehensive Social Influence Prevention Program

Teens ranging in age from 12 to 15 years (5th through 9th grades) are ideal candidates for the provision of comprehensive social influence programming, because trial of drugs accelerates in prevalence during this time and peer social influences to use drugs are relatively important to this age group. Project TNT is a model comprehensive social influence/life skills-type tobacco use prevention program that targets young teens (Sussman et al., 1995). Project TNT was designed to target the primary causes of cigarette smoking, smokeless tobacco use, and cigar and pipe smoking among teens. The theoretical basis of Project TNT is that youth will be best able to resist using tobacco products through being taught three general components. First, they are made aware of misleading social information that facilitates tobacco use (e.g., advertising, inflated prevalence estimates). Youth counteract "informational social influence." Second, they are taught skills that counteract social pressures to achieve approval by using tobacco (counteraction of "normative social influence"; e.g., normative restructuring, refusal assertion). Third, they are taught to appreciate the physical consequences that tobacco use may have on their lives (e.g., the beginnings of addiction; personally relevant physical consequences; Sussman et al., 1995). Project TNT counteracts different causes of tobacco use simultaneously given that the behavior is determined by multiple causes. This comprehensive approach is well suited to general populations of youth that may vary in risk factors that influence their tobacco use.

The Project TNT, 10-day, classroom-based curriculum provides detailed information about the health consequences of tobacco and addresses topics, including building self-esteem, active listening, communicating effectively, refusal assertion learning/practice, noncompliance coping (ingratiation and cognitive restructuring) to enhance self-confidence and decrease perceived social influence to use tobacco, counteracting advertising images and social activism to change norms, and decision-making/public commitment. Student involvement is maintained through the use of five homework assignments, classroom group competition, and a two-lesson booster program provided the next year.

Project TNT was first delivered to 7th-grade students, of whom 60% were non-Latino White, 27% Latino, 7% Black, and 6% Asian American (Sussman et al., 1995) in a large randomized controlled trial. Five conditions (four programs and a "usual school health education" or control) were contrasted using a randomized experiment involving 6,716 7th-grade students from forty-eight junior high schools in southern California. Four curricula were developed. Three were designed to counteract the effects of separate (single) program components (normative social influence, informational social influence, and physical consequences), whereas a fourth, comprehensive curriculum was designed to counteract all three effects. To determine outcomes, 1- and 2-year follow-ups were conducted after the core 7th-grade intervention was delivered.

The comprehensive (social influences plus physical consequences) curriculum showed the largest effects on behavior. This is the version that now is being disseminated throughout the United States and it is referred to as the Project TNT curriculum. Compared to the control condition ("usual school health education"), this program obtained significant effects on initiation and weekly use of smokeless tobacco and cigarettes. The program reduced initiation of cigarettes by approximately 26% over the control group, when 1-year and 2-year follow-up outcomes were averaged together. It also reduced initiation of smokeless tobacco use by approximately 30%; weekly or more frequent cigarette smoking was reduced by approximately 60%; and weekly or more frequent smokeless tobacco use was eliminated. These data indicate that the same tobacco use prevention program can be delivered to males and females, diverse ethnicities, diverse socioeconomic levels, across rural, suburban, and urban regions, and can be effective over the transition period from junior to senior high school (Sussman et al., 1995).

More recently, Project TNT (the comprehensive/combined program version) was found to be effective over a 1-year period when delivered among cohorts of 6th and 7th graders in various schools in fourteen East Texas counties (Meshack et al., 2004), and its cost effectiveness was established (Tengs, Osgood, & Chen, 2001; Wang et al., 2001). Project TNT is now considered a model program by numerous federal, state, local, and private agencies, including the U.S. Department of Education (as an exemplary program), Center for Substance Abuse Prevention/Substance Abuse and Mental Health Administration, National Institute on Drug Abuse, National Cancer Institute, Centers for Disease Control and Prevention (Program that Works from 1997 to 2002), and Sociometrics.

The Effects of Good Health Education and Interactive Programming

A good health educator is very important in motivating a preventive effort, regardless of curriculum content. Good health educators tend to be adaptive to different group situations and are enthusiastic, socially skilled, high self-monitors, and considerate of participant personalities. They believe in the material they are teaching, are well prepared to teach the material, and know how to facilitate interaction of participants with each other. They are good time managers, teach material quickly, but in small steps, tailor materials to different groups, and permit positive and extensive interactions with students while maintaining a professional demeanor (Rohrbach, Graham, & Hansen, 1993). The relative importance of health education performance compared to material contents is yet to be well assessed.

Social Network Analysis Approach to Prevention

Popular students are sometimes selected as peer educators in prevention programs, regardless of whether popularity in the classroom is related to tobacco or alcohol use. Alexander, Piazza, Mekos, and Valente (2001) showed that popular students, those receiving the most nominations as friends, were more likely to smoke in schools with high smoking prevalence and less likely to smoke in schools with low smoking prevalence. More recently, a peer-led interactive version of an evidence-based prevention substance use program, Project TND, found the networked method to reduce substance use among those students involved in a network of other students reporting low levels of substance use and an increase in substance use among those students with existing networks of substance using peers (Valente et al., in press). These findings suggest that peer leaders exemplify the norms for their communities and are likely to be earlier and perhaps heavier users of substances in communities where substance use is accepted. Because leaders are often seen as influential and harbingers of behavior, they are likely a reasonable choice to implement programs. However, their own behavior must be addressed, or they should only be involved in implementing programs in relatively low drug use contexts.

One example of the use of social network analysis in the drug misuse prevention area includes studies of peer leaders. In school-based studies, there has been a tradition of using peer leaders to assist in program delivery (e.g., Flay, 1985; Valente, Gallaher, & Mouttapa, 2004). Peer leaders are usually chosen by asking students to write the names of other students who they consider to be good leaders. The teacher collects the data and selects as peer leaders those students who received the most nominations. Valente and others have expanded this methodology to allow students to be assigned to a leader they nominated or were closest to sociometrically. In one study, Valente showed that use of a sociometric method of selection was more effective on program implementation measures than leaders popularly chosen but placed in groups defined randomly (Valente, Gallaher, & Mouttapa, 2004). This work suggests that network data can be used to help determine whether prevention programs can be more effective, using social network data to structure classroom-based workgroups and improve program implementation.

There are also other network applications. For example, network data can be used to define subsets, cliques, or groups within a network that can be targeted for intervention. Modification of certain elements of a network may lead to more expedient change than modification of other elements.

Often getting a group to change behavior can be easier than trying to change people individually. The group can reinforce program messages to its constituents and provide social support for maintaining the new behavior (e.g., more conscientious behavior).

Instruction in Conscientiousness

Conscientiousness refers to a propensity to follow socially prescribed norms of behavior (e.g., to be socially responsible, virtuous), to be goal-directed (e.g., industrious), and to delay gratification (e.g., practicing constraint, order, or self-control). In a review of a database of studies resulting from an article search consisting of consciousness-related terms and health-related behavior, Bogg and Roberts (2004) located 194 studies that were quantitatively examined. Conscientiousness-related traits were negatively related to all risky health-related behaviors uncovered (e.g., drug use, unhealthy eating, risky driving, risky sex, and violence) and positively related to all beneficial health-related behaviors (e.g., job attainment, exercise, and healthy eating). Although Bogg and Roberts did not provide an overall theoretical explanation of why these relations might exist, it appears that social responsibility beliefs, desire to contribute to the workforce and to others, and willingness to sacrifice immediate pleasure are consistently related to health and healthy behavior. Also, although Bogg and Roberts addressed a trait perspective in their discussion of conscientiousness, this construct is central in the recovery movement as well as many public works strategies (community service; Alcoholics Anonymous, 1976; Swisher & Hu, 1983). Perhaps, a willingness to be restrained enough in space or time to learn the best ways to live out situations is what helps people to be maximally healthy (see explanations of mindfulness approaches, e.g., Marlatt, 2006). Also, while in service to a group, an individual may bypass one's own "mis-wiring." In fact, this type of approach is reflected in healthy development-type programs (Roth & Brooks-Gunn, 2003).

Instruction in conscientiousness might best take place in a group setting where youth could discuss the importance of cooperation and group norms for cooperation could develop. Youth could discuss caretaking (e.g., babysitting, bathing, and academic instruction) they have been involved in for younger peers. In addition, talk shows or role playing could be utilized to instruct the importance of being industrious and socially responsible (Sussman, 2005a, 2005b; Sussman, Earleywine, et al., 2004) (Table 13.2).

Table 13.2. *Elements of comprehensive social influence programming*

Program content

- Listening and communication skills. Social skills training that enhances listening and communication skills is provided with the use of demonstration of appropriate behavior, modeling of appropriate behavior, behavioral rehearsal, and feedback components.
- Refusal assertion emphasis. Training on refusal assertion – a social skill – addresses how one might best refuse a drug offer or request of someone else; trains adolescents to refuse drug offers assertively but not aggressively or passively.
- Short- and long-term physical consequences information. Although not a strategy based on the concepts of social influences, discussing short and long term physical consequences of substance use are often incorporated in social influence programming to explain why it is important to not misuse drugs.
- Peer group unacceptability of drug misuse. Group activities, such as taking group polls on acceptability of drug misuse among peers, are used to make it known among members of the group that drug misuse is not as widely accepted by their peers as they may perceive.
- Correction of use prevalence overestimates. Activities similar to that used to clarify the true acceptability of drugs among peers are used to correct the overestimates of drug use prevalence among peers. (This also was mentioned as an example of a cognitive-informational error [see Table 12.1].)
- Awareness of adult influences. Adolescents often attempt to copy adult role-models when they use drugs; hence, discussions among youth are held with the focus on adult drug use as a problem behavior with grave consequences.
- Media literacy. Youth are made aware of adult advertising influences so that they are less likely to yield to pro-drug use images portrayed in the media.
- Activism. Youth are encouraged to participate in anti-drug use activism (e.g., writing letters to tobacco and alcohol industry) in order to personalize knowledge, become active learners, and encourage belief change in society.
- Self-confidence building and decision-making. Self-confidence building and decision-making help youth learn how to rationally combine information to make positive decisions in different problem areas.
- Making a commitment to not use drugs. Youth are encouraged to make public commitments (e.g., before a group of peers) not to use tobacco and other drugs with the assumption that such commitments put their self-respect at stake in order to discourage them from drug use.
- Smoking and other use cessation materials for older teens or adults. These materials are provided to older teens or adults who are regular smokers or drug users, who need information on how to cope with withdrawal symptoms.

Community Units

Most social influence-based programming occurs in the school classroom setting. School-based programming is a central means of delivery because youth are a captive audience to this type of programming, and there is evidence that indicates that school-based programming can be successful (Skara & Sussman, 2003). However, a multifaceted approach to prevention may improve school-based program effectiveness. By utilizing multiple (coordinated) delivery modalities, whereby youth receive a consistent message across community contexts and over time, program effects are most likely to be maintained. Systemwide approaches achieve the largest effects (although methodological designs often are less strong than studies of single units, e.g., schools only). Tobacco and other substance use access reduction, family programming, mass media programming, involvement of community organizations, and school-based programming may combine to maximize prevention efforts (Tobler et al., 2000).

Parent- or family-targeted prevention programs, as discussed below, include offering early childhood education, social support for parents, managing crises, parenting skills training, parent–child communication skills, and resource acquisition instruction or networking. Mass media-targeted programs, as discussed in Chapter 14, involve programs or public service announcements with novel, fast, and unconventional messages (e.g., the American Legacy Foundation TRUTH campaign), use of the Internet, and interactive CDs (e.g., video games and videos on sites such as YouTube). Additionally, alternative means to attract youth in prosocial "adventurous" activity include involvement in hiking clubs, drug-free dances, or other after-school events with prosocial adult mentors. These means to involve youth outside of school encourage entry into different environments (e.g., Congressional Youth Leadership Conference and Outward Bound). In addition, policy implementation and enforcement may contribute to other prevention programs. The simultaneous use of programs within and outside of schools over long periods may help maintain the positive effects that sometimes dissipate when school programs appear alone (Sun et al., 2006).

Involvement of *community agents* such as dentists, pediatricians, youth club leaders, local health service personnel, or even city leaders may help with prevention efforts, as well. Although their time to assist in this endeavor may be limited and the effects they exert consequently may be small (perhaps a 2% relative effect), they come into contact with many youth, are generally respected by youth, and are role models for youth. Simple advice to not use tobacco and other drugs and provision of self-help social influence-oriented material could be useful.

Family-Based Prevention

Family involvement is a relevant means of providing prevention material outside school and can lead to a 15% relative effect in compliant families (Sussman, 2005d). Families differ from individuals and other groups because of the often close and historical patterns of interaction within the unit. Therefore, it is important to recognize the influence of the family unit while providing assistance to the target individual or individuals (e.g., the drug misusers). According to Kumpfer's (1999) *transactional framework of resilience* the "transactional processes involved in the relationship between parents and their children are extremely important in moderating posited biological risk characteristics and promoting resilience" (Kumpfer & Bluth, 2004, p. 673) or vulnerability to problem behaviors. Therefore, it is necessary to strengthen and promote positive transactional processes within the family. Strategies that have been utilized to strengthen family dynamics include family skills training, brief family therapy (including structural, functional, and behavioral therapy), cognitive/behavioral parent training, and family support and education (for review, see Kumpfer, Alvarado, & Whiteside, 2003).

Other relevant family-based interventions include contingency management, positive reinforcement, stimulus control, social support training, affect clarification, expressed emotion modification, and the use of paradox procedures (the "Milan school"). One caveat, however, is that youth at highest risk for drug use are relatively unlikely to have parents who will take on the responsibility of teaching prevention material to them or serve as support persons.

Examples of evidence-based *family programming* include Strengthening Families and Family Matters. Kumpfer and colleagues developed the original Strengthening Families Program in 1983 (http://www.strengtheningfamiliesprogram.org/). It is a family skills-training program designed to increase resilience and reduce risk factors for problem behaviors in high-risk children, ages 6–12 years, defined as behavioral, emotional, academic, and/or social problems (see Kumpfer & DeMarsh, 1985). The program emphasizes improving family relationships, parenting skills, and youths' social and life skills. The program generally includes three 14-week courses: Parent Training, Children's Skills Training, and Family Life Skills Training. Parents learn to increase desired behaviors in children by using attention and rewards, clear communication, effective discipline, substance use education, problem solving, and limit setting. Children learn effective communication, understanding feelings, social skills, problem solving, resisting peer pressure, consequences of substance use, and compliance with parental rules. Families engage in structured family activities, practice therapeutic child play, conduct family meetings, learn communication skills as a family, practice effective discipline, reinforce positive behaviors in each other, and plan family activities together. Effects have been found on antisocial behavior, such as tobacco and other substance use, conduct problems, and improvement in social and life skills.

The Strengthening Families Program for youth ages 10–14 consists of seven sessions and four boosters. In 2-hour sessions, parents and youth spend the first hour apart and the second hour together in supervised family activities. Emphasis on creating a positive future orientation, age-appropriate expectations and roles, mutual empathy, making house rules, and listening to each other are central to the program. Effects have been found on drug use in several trials (e.g., a 33% relative reduction in ever trial of alcohol use at a 4-year follow-up, 10th-grade final wave of data collection; Kumpfer, Molgaard, & Spoth, 1996; Spoth, Reyes, Redmond, & Shin, 1999).

Karl Bauman and colleagues developed Family Matters in the late 1980s (http://www.sph.unc.edu/familymatters/). Family Matters is a home-based program designed to prevent tobacco and alcohol use in children 12–14 years old. The program is delivered through four booklets mailed to the home and follow-up telephone calls to parents by health educators. The booklets contain readings and activities designed to get families to consider general family characteristics and tobacco and alcohol use attitudes. Topics discussed include adult supervision and support, rule setting and monitoring, family communication, attachment and time together, education encouragement, family/adult substance use, substance availability, and peer attitudes and media orientation toward substance use. This program was delivered to 1,300 treatment and control parent–child pairs and showed effects on both tobacco and alcohol use at 3- and 12-months follow-up (83% of the families in the program completed one or more of the units, and 62% completed all four units; Bauman et al., 2000, 2001, 2002).

At least three other family-based multiple-problem targeted prevention programs, discussed later, have had an important impact in the drug abuse prevention field (see Sussman, Earleywine, et al., 2004). These programs have been designed to prevent even more severe problems in the future, although they are used with families of youth that already show problems in living.

Functional Family Therapy (FFT) is an indicated intervention involving family treatment designed for delinquent teenagers (http://www.fftinc.com/). Developed in the early 1970s by Alexander and colleagues, FFT focuses on family communication, and the establishment of rules and consequences. Several studies provide encouraging reports of the program's effectiveness. In a study by Waldron et al. (2001), researchers used FFT and an intervention with cognitive behavioral therapy on teens referred for marijuana use. Each of the interventions alone produced significant results on marijuana use at 4 months, but only the two interventions combined maintained these results at 7 months. In two earlier studies that utilized FFT, Alexander and colleagues (Alexander, Barton, Schiaro, & Parsons, 1976; Alexander & Parsons, 1973) found that improvement in family communication posttreatment led to a reduction in delinquency among the teens in the study. Note that all of the teens in these studies had histories of serious antisocial or delinquent behavior. Thus, achieving positive outcomes, even if only short-term, should encourage further research into the efficacy of FFT.

Multisystemic Therapy (MST), as its name suggests, targets individual, family, peer, school, and community influences of youth offenders with serious problems that may include violence, substance abuse, and severe emotional problems (http://www.mstservices.com/text/treatment.html). MST was developed in the 1970s and numerous researchers have since published the results of randomized trials of MST with the most consistent findings across studies being decreased (1) drug use, (2) rearrest, (3) self-reported criminal offense, and (4) days in out-of-home placements. Other consistent findings are improved family relations, school attendance, and psychiatric functioning. The effectiveness of this program, however, is considerably lower when not implemented with fidelity (Henggeler, Pickrel, & Brondino, 1999). In other words, all or key lessons need to be delivered as written by educators who are well-trained in using the strategies employed, and youth need to be able to receive all material in an atmosphere conducive to learning the material. The program developers have instituted training strategies that address these fidelity issues, thus shaping MST to be a very promising program for at-risk youth. For example, in one randomized control trial, in which 118 juvenile offenders received either MST or community services, alcohol, marijuana, and other drug use was significantly reduced (by 50%) at immediate posttest (Hengeler, Pickrel, & Brondino, 1999).

Multidimensional Treatment Foster Care (MTFC) is an evidence-based program that targets community, family, and peer factors that influence adolescents with a pattern of repeat criminal offending (http://www.mtfc.com/). The program is based on social learning principles and emerged from ongoing research at the Oregon Social Learning Center in Eugene, Oregon. Chamberlain and colleagues developed the first program in 1983, which targeted juvenile offenders. It has since been adapted to target various age groups with a variety of problem behaviors, including substance use and misuse. This intervention includes placement of youth in a foster home with a foster parent trained in behavior management who receives support from intervention staff. After the adolescent has begun to respond to the intervention in the foster home, and after the parents have received the same training and support as the foster parents received, the adolescent returns home. Chamberlain and Reid (1998) tested the intervention with eighty-five boys with felony and other criminal histories and found substantial benefits of the program. That is, following treatment the boys assigned to MTFC, when compared to those receiving community-based group care, served fewer days in detention or lock-up, had twice as much time living with parents, and had fewer misdemeanor and felony arrests and fewer self-reported index crimes and general delinquency. MTFC is a cost-effective alternative to incarceration; however, staff requirements are extensive, which may influence the ability of some groups to apply the program with fidelity, and effects on drug use need future evaluation. Nevertheless, as with each of the programs described above, results of the randomized trials are encouraging.

Summary

There are a variety of programs that make use of micro-level social groups that can help prevent one from drug misuse and aid in prevention programming. This chapter provided several strategies of prevention programs that involve social interaction and the group, including school-based prevention programming that involves social influence instruction, instruction in conscientiousness, community unit-based involvement, and family-based involvement. One could speculate that the closer one approximates real-world social situations in prevention interventions, including addressing family and peer group dynamics, the more likely program information will translate to high-risk situations in real-life settings that include pressures from family members, peers, and the community. Clearly, the micro-level social group impacts an individual's behavior and choices, and the group is a key point of intervention. Multifaceted prevention approaches that target the individual within peer groups (e.g., school-based programming), family members, and the community (e.g., physicians and legislators) may be most effective in preventing the onset of drug use and misuse, assuming sufficient implementation fidelity.

14   The Large Social and Physical Environment

Drug misuse prevention programming at the larger socioenvironmental level can have wide-ranging effects because large-scale influences are inextricably intertwined with multiple levels of experience. That is, if large socioenvironmental programming is virulent, it can affect micro-group and individual perceptions, attitudes, and behavior. Large social environmental influences on drug misuse prevention include culturally expressed communications through numerous community channels that may monopolize messages being provided to youth. For example, antidrug communications may be diffused through mass media messages such as newspapers, billboards, and movies, in various languages, with various role models depicted. Appropriately placed anti-drug misuse messages that are repeated several times might produce a preventive effect.

Large physical environmental influences on drug misuse include presence or level of drug manufacturing and distribution channels (e.g., presence of poppy fields) or, conversely, presence of prosocial physical resources (e.g., presence of well-supplied schools, libraries, and sports facilities). Prosocial resources availability (e.g., teen centers and libraries) might lead youth to seek out options other than drug use. Supply reduction approaches (e.g., policy enactment and enforcement) may decrease or redirect drug distribution, perhaps lowering drug use. This chapter focuses on larger social and physical environmental prevention approaches.

Large Social Environmental Change

Large social environmental prevention approaches (e.g., community interventions) often involve the systemization of a large social system within which prevention programming may be diffused. Community interventions may involve a range of program channels (e.g., school, family groups, media, community agencies, local government, church, and health groups), coalitions or partnerships, levels of community resources (e.g., face-to-face assistance and physical structures), depth of programming (e.g., intensity, number of contacts), and gatekeeper follow-through to facilitate program implementation (see Pentz, 1986).

Coalition building is important in addressing community concerns and affecting policy and social change and involves formation of partnerships among key organizations and individuals, regular meetings among partners, and action planning to bring about change. Coalitions bring together individuals and organizations within a community to build a power base network that can mobilize public awareness of social problems, influence social and political change processes, and provide innovative solutions to social problems. The creation of community action groups to lobby for anti-drug misuse legislation or facilitate dissemination of drug abuse prevention materials has shown promise. Social movements that decrease demand for a substance (e.g., the temperance movement) can result in a power base that subsequently leads to the enactment of legislation to decrease supply (e.g., prohibition). However, although social movements and concomitant legislation may decrease demand, these movements also can backfire and increase violations of the law, increase costs of enforcement or result in null or negative outcomes (Hallfors, Cho, Livert, & Kadushin, 2002).

Hallfors and colleagues (2002) examined twelve coalition sites that were involved in the Fighting Back program, a large-scale federal demonstration program to reduce the demand for drugs and alcohol in fifteen communities in the United States. They found that strategies aimed at youth or community outcomes failed to have significant effects, whereas strategies aimed at adults appeared to make drug use outcomes worse. In addition, many coalitions did not last very long. For coalitions to be most effective, they should be well organized, focused on specific goals, manageable, select evidence-based prevention programs and obtain assistance when implementing these programs. In addition, coalitions should consider their role as being primarily to coordinate units, restrict environmental access, and maintain good communication with researchers, health educators and evaluators to make sure that appropriate actions are taking place at each step of coalition building and action.

The oldest coalition, which began in 1992 and is itself an umbrella for more than 5,000 antidrug coalitions, is the Community Anti-Drug Coalitions of America (CADCA) organization (http://cadca.org/; retrieved May 16, 2006). As stated by CADCA on their Vision Statement:

Community coalitions – more than any other entity – are poised to connect multiple sectors of the community, including businesses, parents, media, law enforcement, schools, faith organizations, health providers, social service agencies, and the government. By acting in concert through the coalition, all of the partners gain a more complete understanding of the community's problems. Together, the partners organize and develop plans and programs to coordinate their anti-drug efforts. The result is a comprehensive, community-wide approach to substance abuse and its related problems.

CADCA holds numerous media events, antidrug gatherings, engages in information dissemination through newsletters and other literature, engages in lobbying efforts, and coordinates partnerships with coalitions and many antidrug organizations. Still, an evaluation of its impact on drug misuse is not known.

Media-Based Prevention Programming

Media-based programming may elicit preventive effects contingent on the adequacy of the reach of programming, the opportunity facilitated for interaction about the media program, and supplementation with other types of programming (Flay, 1981). The mass media can be a useful adjunct to a variety of interventions. Six stochastic steps that have been identified as needed for media-based programming to impart effects on individuals are as follows: (1) exposure to the communication, (2) awareness of the key messages, (3) knowledge change, (4) beliefs change, (5) behavior change, and (6) maintenance of belief and behavior change (see Flay, 1981). In other words, utilizing multiple media channels at prime viewing times, repetition, arousing personal involvement, being entertaining, involving discussion, and providing opportunities to act are important for a media message to exert influence on people. The mass media can affect very large social regions because of the potentially unlimited reach of the media.

According to DeJong (2002) and DeJong and Wallack (1999), for mass media campaigns to be successful, several criteria need to be met. First, a media campaign has to prompt reevaluation of individual risk and consideration of action. Second, the campaign must bring about a change in beliefs about the behavior being addressed. Third, the campaign should model or instruct new behavioral skills. Fourth, the campaign needs to facilitate the conviction that one can carry out the new behaviors, and in so doing health will improve. Finally, the mass media programming needs to instruct the importance of monitoring changed behavior and continued self-management. The contents of mass media campaigns that appear to have exerted the strongest effects on drug misuse have been those that depict a dramatic true consequence of drug use, take an activism stance, assert for greater autonomy experienced by non-drug use lifestyles, make appeals to sensation-seeking youth through fast-paced material with exciting activities being depicted, or attempt to correct misperceptions of drug use norms (DeJong, 2002; Emery et al., 2005; Hafstad et al., 1997; Palmgreen et al., 2001; Slater et al., 2005).

Flynn, Worden, and colleagues conducted some of the more rigorous assessments of the use of the mass media in studies of cigarette smoking prevention. With the use of a matched pairs design of school versus school plus media conditions in two metropolitan areas in Vermont and New York, these researchers found that the media component provided an incremental effect after 4 years of programming (2.6% versus 4.4% [at least one cigarette per week smoking prevalence] for school plus media versus school only; Flynn et al., 1992) and 2 years after that, when students were in 10th to 12th grades (about 17% versus 25%, respectively; Flynn et al., 1994). The findings from this study also were moderated by risk. Those at higher risk for continued smoking (they or their family member smoked at baseline) were impacted more strongly by the program (showed a relatively greater decrease in prevalence) than those at lower risk (Flynn et al., 1997).

The media program involved airing about fifteen television spots and eight different radio spots during each of the 4 years of the intervention. The media program consisted of themes of positive nonsmoker images, negative smoker images, improved refusal assertion, and attempts to lower prevalence estimates. Classroom teachers delivered the school-based program 4 days per year in grades 5 through 8, and 3 days per year in grades 9 and 10.

Palmgreen et al. (2001) utilized sensation seeking as a risk factor for drug misuse in the development of a prevention mass media campaign. In the sensation-seeking mass media campaign, program elements were integrated through use of advertisement storyboards and were evaluated by additional focus groups (Palmgreen et al., 2001). Revisions based on these evaluations were incorporated into five professionally produced 30-second television spots that involved material likely to appeal to youth high in sensation seeking (e.g., fast-paced and novel). After program development was completed, the campaign was implemented and evaluated using a controlled interrupted time-series design in two matched communities. The campaign reversed upward developmental trends in 30-day marijuana use among high sensation-seeking individuals (i.e., about a 10% decrease in use was observed the year following the campaign).

Slater and colleagues (2005) tested the effect of a within-school media campaign in combination with a community-based media effort. Eight media treatment and eight control communities were randomly assigned to conditions. The communities completed readiness workshops, training in use of media materials, and "self-empowered" media campaigns. Within the program condition, eight schools received within-school media plus a comprehensive social influence-oriented school-based program (i.e., the All Stars program consisting of a total of twenty sessions over 2 years), and eight schools received only the within-school media materials consisting of print materials and promotional materials with a Be Under Your Own Influence theme, promoting greater independence and autonomy. The program was developed to appeal to at-risk youth (e.g., rock climbing and four-wheeling were depicted) and was personalized to the schools in each of 2 years. Within the control condition, eight schools (12- to 14-year-old youth) received the school-based program only and eight schools received no treatment of any kind. Within-condition (i.e., media or no media conditions) schools were not randomly assigned. Two years postbaseline schools with no programming showed the highest cigarette, alcohol, and marijuana use. Schools with both components showed the least use, with levels of use about one-third to one-half that found in the no-treatment control condition. The schools with only one component showed about equivalent effects, a reduction of about one-sixth that of the no-treatment control. This study suggests that the use of media campaigns and school programs alone had about the same effects on drug use, with the use of both media campaigns and school programs having greater effects on drug use.

Interestingly, a study recently completed by Longshore, Ghosh-Dastidar, & Ellickson (2006) found that marijuana use in the last month was reported as being lower by youth who had been exposed to both the U.S. National Youth Anti-Drug Media Campaign and Project ALERT PLUS (a comprehensive social influence school-based drug abuse prevention program), but not to the ALERT program that did not include some revised features for high school youth, nor the campaign itself. This study provides further suggestion of the incremental effectiveness of including both school-based and media components.

Snyder and colleagues (2004) conducted a meta-analysis on the effect of mediated health communication campaigns on behavior change, all of which had involved use of at least one form of community-wide mass media. They examined average correlations between exposure to a campaign and behavior change across different arenas (a total of forty-eight campaigns, most targeting youth). Effect sizes varied from .15 for seat belt use, .13 for oral health, .09 for alcohol use reduction (access or education programs, targeted prevention; .07 for youth targeted programs), .05 for heart disease prevention (diet and exercise), .05 for smoking cessation (four of seventeen campaigns involved youth), .04 for mammography and cervical cancer screening, and .04 for sexual behaviors. In other work cited by Snyder and colleagues, youth drug abuse prevention campaigns showed an effect size of .06 to .08, and youth tobacco prevention campaigns showed an effect size of .05 to .06. Campaigns that target youth smoking or drug abuse prevention or cessation have failed to include an enforcement component and showed relatively low effect sizes.

Based on these studies, one may conclude that it is most wise to consider use of mass media to supplement other programming rather than relying only on the mass media to induce program effects. Nevertheless, as stand-alone interventions, mass media campaigns are an important medium for the dissemination of prevention messages in that they can

Figure 14.1. Internet-based programming provides a pragmatic means of surveying and intervening with various populations.

reach difficult-to-reach individuals, such as school dropouts, who otherwise may not receive school-based or other community programming.

Internet-based programming provides a very pragmatic means of surveying and intervening with various populations. Its use is inexpensive and convenient, and information is processed quickly (i.e., data can be analyzed instantaneously). However, the target population needs to know how to use the Internet, and the person-to-person direct contact that might be available through other means, such as the telephone or through face-to-face interactions, is missing (Pealer & Weiler, 2000). Newer technologies are now being examined that do involve direct person-to-person contact such as use of chat rooms with group and one-to-one written interaction features. Further, other newer high technology interventions are being considered, including virtual reality simulations, interactive computer and other communication devices (use of computer-based telephone conference calls and written interaction chat rooms [e.g., Skype)]), and portable computer devises (Keefe, Buffington, Studts, & Rumble, 2002), including use of cell phones (see Rodgers et al., 2005, regarding teen smoking cessation) (Figure 14.1).

A recent review of the literature on Internet-based teen smoking prevention and cessation programming uncovered a total of nineteen studies, four of which pertained to teen prevention (Walters, Wright, & Shegog, 2006). Of those studies, the two that were completed regarding the same project that involved mailed computer-generated feedback reports, smoking incidence was cut by more than one-third among program recipients when compared to controls in randomized designs at 6-month and 1-year follow-ups. Effects of programming failed to be found in the other two studies. Another recent study, which utilized group randomized trials to test the effectiveness of Internet-based programs to reduce smoking prevalence and positive smoking-related outcome expectancies, found a decrease in 30-day smoking prevalence and lower expectations for smoking in the future among its Australian and American adolescent subjects, respectively (Buller et al., 2006). The Internet remains a promising modality, but will become more valuable as it becomes more likely to be used on a daily basis by most teens (Sun et al., 2005).

Obtaining Social and Physical Environmental Resources

Several conceptual models relevant to emerging adulthood have been advanced that provide a language to organize the interaction between developing individuals and their environment. Among these are psychosocial process models focusing on the role of social integration and perceived availability of support, and "ecologically relevant approaches" that seek to understand functional changes of individuals as they are exposed to particular settings and contexts.

Relatively little research exists documenting the influences on drug use of provision of information on access to nearby resources, as indicated in a review by Sussman et al. (2004). Still, availability of environmental/community resources has been proposed as a potential elaboration of the *Diagnostic and Statistical Manual of Mental Disorders* (DSM) axes (APA, 2000), and the importance of providing access to socioenvironmental resources is part of the fundamental justification within fields such as social work and urban planning. For example, there is some suggestion of effectiveness on drug use in single-group studies by attendance of high-risk preteens and teens at community-based programs. These community programs involve bringing in an intensive and costly in-house network of social service resources to teens under one roof and appear to facilitate surmounting of hurdles in development these youth face (Sussman, Skara, & Pumpuang, in press).

Also, perception of availability of environmental resources, such as access to jobs, education, recreation, transportation, or drug and other counseling services in one's community could be enhanced among emerging adults by receiving such information through any number of modalities (e.g., as a telephone education program, through mass media communications). If provided as booster programming following receipt of drug prevention educational programming in school, this strategy could enhance hope for lifestyle stability with satisfactory self-fulfillment in a time and location efficient way.

There have been some evaluations of alternative programs for teens. Alternative programs attempt to provide resources to teens, enhance their perception of the availability of resources, or enhance their self-efficacy to find and utilize these resources. Kumpfer provided a thorough review of this literature (www.nida.nih.gov/about/organization/DESPR/HSR/dapre/KumpferLitReviewPartB.htlm; also see Swisher & Hu, 1983; Tobler, 1986). Generally, use of alternative programming has been considered relatively important among at-risk teens that arguably may not have access to or know how to seek out alternative resources for living. Kumpfer noted that a meta-analysis of the Center for Substance Abuse Prevention high-risk youth and family programs suggests that alternative programs are effective (www.drugabuse.gov/about/organization/despr/hsr/dapre/KumpferLitReviewPartC.html). However, some iatrogenic (increase in drug use) effects have resulted from involvement in certain alternative recreational activities. These activities include such venues as rock band concerts (e.g., "Battle of the Bands"), drug-free parties, or sports that involve peer or adult drug user involvement. In addition, some iatrogenic effects have resulted from youth involvement in some vocational or community service involvement (e.g., housing instruction and house painting, where adult drug users might be involved with youth). Conversely, academic achievement and aspirations-related activities, religious activities, antidrug activism-related involvement, and active personal hobbies are inversely related to drug use (Kumpfer, Williams, & Baxley, 1997). These latter activities tend to promote attachment to social institutions and adults in such a way that drug use is relatively less likely to be modeled.

Adults often assume that teens can access community services with little effort. In fact, few teens understand the availability of health services or other assistance. Simple information, including provision of telephone numbers and locations, can assist teens immensely. Coaching teens on techniques for achieving assistance can prove productive. Public assistance for life problems can help tremendously, but negotiating the bureaucratic difficulties inherent in many of the systems involved can require considerable skill. Direct instruction, modeling, and structured practice in resource acquisition skills may help youth to increase their knowledge and self-efficacy on how to acquire resources and to readily access resources when needed (e.g., use of the bus and other public transportation systems). These skills may generalize to acquisition of other resources later in life.

Supply Reduction

Legal regulation of substances can be accomplished by use of a prohibitory scheme (of production or distribution), a regulatory scheme (setting conditions of use, information about use, sanctions), and large social climate influence (drug use is good or bad because it is legal or illegal; Pentz, Bonnie, & Shopland, 1996). Until recently, the primary supply reduction tactic was interdiction (i.e., forbid use by actions of authorities). Interdiction has been expensive and not very successful (other than some street-level tactics to reduce availability) (Figure 14.2).

Consider, for example, supply reduction programming that focuses on changes in the alcohol use environment. There are many types of specific strategies that have shown effects on when, where, and how much alcohol is being used. Environmental prevention strategies include prohibitory policy mechanisms (e.g., raising the minimum drinking age, zoning [limiting use locations]) and regulatory policy mechanisms (e.g., alcohol taxation, setting blood alcohol level limits, and enforcement). Additional environmental prevention strategies include traffic safety education, server training and monitoring, and community involvement (e.g., coalitions of businesses and government leaders, point-of-sales stings, and media and family involvement; Hansen, 1994; Komro & Toomey, 2002; Williams & Perry, 1998), which can alter demand for alcohol and provide a means of regulation. Interestingly, for example, a point-of-sales sting event can reduce sales drastically to minors for approximately 3 months (Wagenaar, 2006).

Some other environmental manipulations, such as use of warning labels and provision of alternative youth activities outside of school, also may serve to reduce demand for alcohol or tobacco and potentially to limit exposure to these and other drugs. Results of these types of programs have decreased heavy drinking among youth and decreased the number of fatal car crashes (see review in Komro & Toomey, 2002; Wagenaar, Lenk, & Toomey, 2005). These various environmental-community-based prevention program components attempt to make alcohol use less accessible and less socially desirable and to make one's social environment more supportive to nonuse (Hansen, 1994; Komro & Toomey, 2002; Williams

Figure 14.2. No-smoking sign found in a European train station. Some environmental street-level tactics, such as signs banning the use of tobacco in public spaces, reduce exposure to and availability of some drugs.

& Perry, 1998). These programs are likely to be of relative importance in the prevention of youth alcohol use because alcohol is so widely available to youth, both outside and inside the home (Komro, Stigler, & Perry, 2005; Wagenaar, Lenk, & Toomey, 2005). Some means of regulating exposure to use, as well as education about social pressures to use alcohol, are warranted (Komro, Stigler, & Perry, 2005).

Tobacco Policies

Tax increases on cigarettes can curb youths' intention to begin smoking, though perhaps only large increases will decrease prevalence noticeably once people begin smoking (e.g., a 20% increase in price may lead to a reduction in use of 6%–10% among youth). Large warning labels placed on tobacco products using clear language in ways that might cue behavior may also be helpful (e.g., 33% to 50% of the pack or more; maybe a 2% reduction). Also, enforcement of access laws for tobacco and passive smoking laws among youth are important. For example, a full ban on smoking (no-smoking policy) in all public locations may lead to up to a 10% reduction, full bans on ads for tobacco may lead to a 5% reduction, and strict enforcement of youth access may lead to a 2% reduction in youth smoking prevalence (Sussman, 2005d). The two policy interventions that appear to have the greatest impact are tax increases and enactment and enforcement of restrictions of smoking (e.g., no-smoking policies) in public places.

Interdiction

Enforcement efforts have not been particularly successful as a means of supply reduction. Domestic enforcement costs four times as much as treatment for a given amount of user reduction, seven times as much for consumption reduction, and fifteen times as much for societal cost reduction (Rydell & Everingham, 1994). Yet, in 2002, U.S. federal funding for drug treatment totaled 19.1% of the U.S. "drug war" budget. On the demand side, the combined federal funding for prevention and treatment totaled about one-third of the "drug war" budget. On the supply side, law enforcement and interdiction used the remaining two-thirds of federal "drug war" funds. Yet treatment has a very large impact on subsequent crime, whereas interdiction does not. As noted in the earlier chapter on drug use history, in 1900, prior to any enforcement efforts, approximately 0.5% of the U.S. population abused cocaine or opiates, of 75 million people (Jonnes, 1996). Currently, approximately 0.3% of the U.S. population abuses these drug types (see Sussman & Ames, 2001). Although there has been some decrease in use, the effects are not enormous considering that these drugs were legal and widely disseminated by many companies in the early 1900s and are now illegal. Interdiction does show some effects but may only be useful in the context of demand reduction strategies (Pentz, Bonnie, & Shopland, 1996) and treatment (Rydell & Everingham, 1994).

Geographic Changes and Prevention

Perhaps by altering aspects of the geospatial environment, drug use incidence may decrease. Certainly, as suggested earlier, provision of alternatives in the environment is one means that may decrease drug misuse. Also, building structure upkeep may decrease drug use. Individuals who live in more peaceful and colorful environments may be less likely to resort to drug use. One may speculate that use of garden landscaping in urban environments actually may provide an effect on drug misuse, though this assertion needs future testing.

In addition, creation of defensible space (decreasing availability of hiding places for drug sales and use) and decreases in legitimized sales of drugs (e.g., number of alcohol outlets; Weitzman, Folkman, Folkman, & Wechsler, 2003) may decrease availability. In theory, planned communities may be created with the idea of maximizing the constructive support of the environment. Planned communities may be particularly important for groups of individuals who are in transition and have limited resources (e.g., students, immigrants, those released from prisons at risk for drug abuse), so that positive social learning is enabled.

Community Multicomponent Programs

The Midwest Prevention Project (MPP) is among the best known community-based interventions, referred to locally as Project STAR or I-STAR (Indiana Students Taught Awareness and Resistance). This program targeted avoidance and reduction of drug use, with special emphasis on prevention of cigarette, alcohol, and marijuana use in middle/junior high school. Five program components were implemented: (1) mass media coverage, promotional videotapes, and commercials about each program component; (2) an eleven- to thirteen-session social influence-based school program consisting of six homework sessions with parents followed by a five-session booster school program with three homework sessions; (3) a parent organization program involving parent–principal meetings and parent–child communications training; (4) a community organization program to organize and train community leaders to develop action groups; and (5) drug use policy change (see Pentz, 1995; Pentz et al., 1989). The MPP showed a 20% to 40% net program effect for the 3 years associated with program participation by students. Beyond the 3-year mark, the

Table 14.1. *Types of large social and physical environmental prevention programming*

Focus of programming	Description
Large social environment programming	Community interventions or action combine a wide range of program channels (e.g., schools, family groups, media, law makers, and community agencies), professional coalitions or partnerships, and levels of community resources. Perhaps by "flooding the field" with consistent drug misuse prevention messages, wide range, strong, and long-lasting effects are seen.
Media-based prevention programming	Media-based programming has the ability to reach a large audience and hard-to-find individuals, it can provide opportunities for interaction about the media program, and it provides supplementation for other types of programming.
Social and physical environmental resources	Establishing facilities that provide youth and emerging adults opportunities to obtain access to prosocial (e.g., drug-free recreation alternatives, jobs) and physical environmental resources (e.g., libraries, gymnasiums) serves as a community level intervention.
Supply reduction	Supply reduction involves legal regulation of substances and can be accomplished by use of a prohibitory scheme (of production or distribution), regulatory scheme (setting conditions of use, information about use, sanctions), and large social climate influence (e.g., that drug use is good or bad because it is legal or illegal).

MPP showed greater and more sustained effects on heavier use rates than those reported by school or other single-channel programs (Pentz, 1995). Although the program utilized a quasi-experimental design, it stands as a promising model of drug abuse prevention.

According to Pentz (1995), multicomponent community-based programs should involve substantial school programming to initiate behavior change in conjunction with a community organization structure and process that promotes mass media programming and coverage, parent and adult education, and informal or formal policy change (Pentz 1995; Pentz et al., 1989). It is possible that instead of a 15% average relative reduction in drug use obtained through single component programming, at least a doubling of the reduction of drug use could be obtained and, more importantly, maintained for a longer period of time (Pentz, 1995; St. Pierre, Kaltreider, Mark, & Aiken, 1992). Pentz acknowledges, however, that the relative cost-effectiveness of multicomponent community-based programs compared to single-channel programs, and effect contrasts of such programs to lengthy school-based programs, is yet to be determined (Table 14.1).

Summary

The larger social and physical environment appears to have a significant impact on constraining drug use prevalence and drug availability through anti-drug use policies and resources allotted for communicating prevention messages. Involvement of schools, the home, businesses, mass media, and local government, working together to plan more favorable social and physical environments appear to be key to a molar impact on prevention of drug abuse. Not only constraining youth from engaging in drug use but also providing the availability of and access to environmental resources that encourage more prosocial activities and self-efficacy in positive life management is a means to facilitate entry into new directions. Access to jobs, education, recreation, transportation, and other health and community services may assist in directing youth to seek out other means to spend their time or improve their options. In conjunction with other social and environmental preventive strategies, supply reduction strategies such as raising the age of legal use, limiting access, and limiting use locations are ways in which tobacco and alcohol use have been controlled. The larger socioenvironmental climate "sets the stage" for culturally expressed group and individual perceptions and attitudes that impact licit and illicit drug use policy change and the resources available for the prevention and treatment of drug misuse.

SECTION FOUR

CESSATION

15   Concepts of Cessation

Cessation of substance abuse is commonly linked to *consequences of use*. For example, an individual may experience legal consequences, such as being arrested, resulting in court mandated treatment. An individual may experience social consequences, such as interpersonal conflict related to use, and may be persuaded to enter a treatment program as a result. An individual may suffer an accident such as a car crash or near-drowning while under the influence (consequences related to use in dangerous situations). An individual may acknowledge the need for treatment after losing his/her job, home, car, friends, and family (job and personal role and social consequences). Alternatively, an individual may merely feel socially isolated, alienated, and fraught with physical reactions (e.g., shakes) that are unpleasant. There are many possible scenarios that bring individuals into treatment, but most are linked to negative consequences of use.

Although withdrawal symptoms from drug use will differ in length and severity of withdrawal reactions, depending on the drug or drugs used, treatment of substance abuse usually begins with withdrawal from whatever drug or drugs an individual has been abusing. Some individuals may be serving prison time for substance-related problems and are forced to withdraw in an unforgiving environment, whereas others may be medically supervised or able to withdraw from substances in more supportive environments. Even getting through this initial period of withdrawal continues to challenge practitioners, researchers, and the substance-abusing individual (Weil & Rosen, 1993).

In addition, program attrition or compliance to program protocols continues to challenge treatment program providers. Further, approximately 75% of individuals who attempt cessation and complete treatment for the first time relapse. One reason that relapse rates continue to be very high is because of the phenomenon of solidly "learned" relationships abusers have with drugs of abuse. Another key problem is the reappearance of the "dis-balance" of arousal or affect that may occur a few days, weeks, months, or even many years after terminating drug use. This dis-balance may be accentuated by the experience of emergent traumatic experiences, memories, and feelings of guilt and shame or entrance into socioenvironmental contexts strongly associated with previous drug use.

In addition, it is possible that neural changes that occur to compensate for the drug-induced overload further accentuate a sense of dis-balance for months following cessation. Specifically, the number of postsynaptic receptor sites for drug(s) of choice may have decreased or increased. In either case, the individual may now be even more dis-balanced than before ever experimenting with drugs. Therefore, quitting drug use and remaining drug-free is fraught with problems.

Other behavioral relationship factors also operate to maintain drug use as a lifestyle behavior. First, one may have mastered the pragmatics of drug use by structuring one's lifestyle to be able to successfully acquire and use the drug under numerous life circumstances. To give up drug use may conflict with the skills one has nurtured to acquire the drug, as well as primary daily activities that are structured around drug use, causing an experiential void. In other words, one has become an expert in drug-related behavior and now is faced with giving up much of the lifestyle built around this acquired knowledge. Second, one may remain highly attracted to the drug, the familiarity of its use, its sensory characteristics, and its effects (the effects are likely to still "work," at least within moments or hours immediately after use). Third, one may have become an "expert" in communications regarding the drug. Also, it may be a "relationship" of choice for those who suffer difficulties in achievement of successful interpersonal relationships. Drug abusers may need to learn new topics of conversation (e.g., prosocial recreation, popular lifestyle topics), while thoughts of pleasurable drug use continually pop to mind. One may need to make new friends, which may demand development of new areas of social interest, changes in public appearance, and behavior – essentially a new identity and tolerance of others that share non-drug interests. It may not be easy to switch social networks without leaving a physical environment for a new location.

Finally, one may still hope for expectations to be fulfilled in the future through drug use. Just as an individual might continue to pursue a relationship that is not working well, one might continue to engage in a relationship with a drug or try another drug. Even after quitting drug use, an individual may find that he/she has fond memories of when previous expectations of drug use were fulfilled, and one may act on that euphoric recall. A sense of dis-balance experienced within an unsatisfying social context, along with implicit positive memories of drug misuse, may become triangulated factors that overdetermine a return to problematic use. The solution is not just quitting drug use but learning how to achieve an ongoing sense of well-being or coping effectively throughout the "ups and downs" in one's life course without resorting to drug use or other risky patterns of behavior. This is not an easy outcome to achieve; most people do experience a variety of undesired events in life, including conflicts with loved ones, the deaths of loved ones, thwarted career hopes, and injuries of property and person.

As will be discussed in the next set of chapters, medications (e.g., selective serotonin reuptake inhibitors or selective dopamine reuptake inhibitor and bromocriptine), behavioral techniques (e.g., volunteer work and meditation), and seeking or embedding oneself in a milieu of social support might help someone who has stopped using drugs to maintain a day-to-day feeling of balance and avoid relapse. It may, however, take many annual cycles of a person's life before one can adjust to not using drugs each day. These annual cycles may be needed to create relatively automatic associative effects that diminish the accessibility of thoughts about drug use in certain situations and on certain occasions. For example, an individual may need to live through "February 2nd" three or four years in a row before the person no longer spontaneously associates February 2nd as a day when drugs are used. In addition, several annual cycles may be needed to achieve friendship networks within geographical contexts that are not centered on drug use and approach a sense of balance of arousal or affect by engaging in more prosocial activities. This chapter provides an overview of the history of drug abuse cessation treatment, general concepts of cessation, and targeted issues regarding current treatment of substance abuse. Current substance abuse treatment in this chapter will focus on the age groups at greatest risk: adolescence and emerging adulthood.

Ancient History of Drug Abuse Treatment

Very few references to treatment are mentioned in historical sources prior to the 1800s. Generally, early on, individuals with drug use problems sought assistance from religious authorities, or they were detained and "dried out" by legal authorities or sometimes sought the assistance of physicians or faith healers (Sussman & Ames, 2001). According to some sources, addicts were, to the extent possible, tolerated within society and would continue to work or go to school if not disruptive to others (Levinthal, 2005; White, 2005).

In 1774, as in various earlier points in history, a prominent figure, in this case Anthony Benezet, a physician and Quaker clergyman, wrote strong statements against the effects of alcohol use. He wrote the famous essay of its time, "Mighty Destroyer Displayed" (see White, 2005). Benezet's essay placed a relatively greater emphasis on depicting the drinker as being a slave to alcohol – in need of help by others. (Around this time, the *per capita* consumption of alcohol was up to seven gallons per year.) One prominent treatment used in the late 1700s and 1800s was to replace the "drug of choice" with another, less "destructive" drug. An example was to use laudanum ("wine of opium") in place of alcohol. Drug replacement therapy is still used today for detoxification purposes or as a harm-reduction strategy.

Baumohl and Room (1987) discuss the history of the treatment of alcoholism beginning with the Washingtonians (founded around 1840). The Washingtonians initially were a society composed of alcoholics trying to help other alcoholics. Over time, they allowed politicians and nonalcoholic reformers (i.e., persons who identified as sympathetic to alcoholics but who did not identify as being alcoholics themselves) to participate in the society. The Washingtonian Temperance Society was more broadly composed of "temperance crusaders" and often was thought to be the forerunner of Alcoholics Anonymous (A.A.; see Edwards, Marshall, & Cook, 2003). The development of this group was influenced by the writings of Benezet and his contemporary, Dr. Benjamin Rush (White, 2001), in which the problem drinker was said to have a medical (disease) problem rather than simply a moral problem (Figure 15.1).

Thirty years later, around 1870, the movement began to establish the inebriate asylum as a treatment regimen. The asylum provided an isolated environment in which the person with alcohol problems could abstain from alcohol abuse and be isolated from bad influences. Often legally coerced, the alcohol abuser would stay for several years (White, 2005). And, although institutionalization of alcoholics was medically led, moral regeneration was fundamental to the treatment plan. Abuse of other drugs, when addressed, generally followed the same course of treatment.

From 1820 to 1940, treatment approaches included beginning to perceive inebriates as "sick" rather than as simply immoral, pairing off reformed drunkards with those still having problems, engaging reformed drunkards as lecturers on their former degradation and current redemption, use of lodging houses and inebriate asylums, providing rewards for improvement, emphasizing use of relaxation and rest, and developing fulfilling roles for reformed drunkards in a life of service and spirituality (see McCarthy, 1984, on the

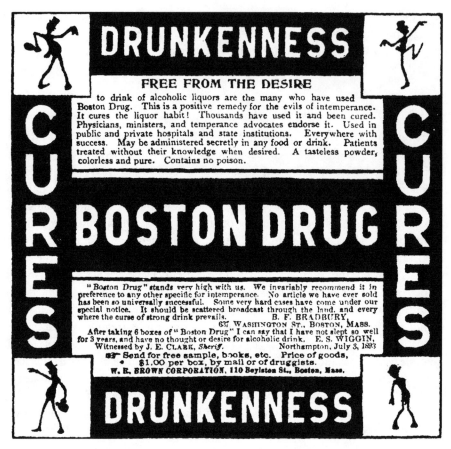

Figure 15.1. An example of an early advertisement for a cure for drunkenness.

Emmanuel Movement). The "moral treatment" approach involved community support to help direct the individual away from alcohol or other drug use. Inebriate homes were established to provide for short-term stays, followed by affiliation with local recovery support groups (White, 2005). In addition, religiously oriented urban rescue missions and rural colonies formed (e.g., Water Street Mission opened in 1872). There also was competition among private addiction cure institutes (e.g., the Keeley Institute; White, 2005). In addition, drug substitutes continued to be used. For example, a dilute form of morphine was recommended for opiate addictions (Nurses Research Publication, 1999). The first treatment provider society was formed in 1870, the American Association for the Study and Cure of Inebriety, which published its own journal (*Quarterly Journal of Inebriety*, from 1876 to 1914; White, 2005).

Many treatment institutions closed between 1900 and 1920 because of publicity on ethical abuses of these institutions, pessimism about their effectiveness, and lack of leadership, among other reasons (White, 2005). As a result, many chronic substance abusers wound up in rural inebriate penal colonies or on the back wards of insane asylums or local hospitals. Various treatment abuses, such as mandatory sterilization, electroconvulsive therapies, and bromide therapy, with high mortality rates, occurred during this period. Relatively better treatment was still provided by private hospitals and programs, religious-based organizations (e.g., Emmanuel Church), and mutual support groups. Many advances in the treatment of substance abusers have occurred since the 1930s.

Trends in Drug Abuse Treatment Since the 1930s

It is within this context of an apparently widespread sense of hopelessness about treatment, treatment abuses, and more promising and kind treatment through religious organizations that A.A. began in 1935, as an extension of the Oxford Groups (they referred to their subgroup as the "Alcoholic Squadron"). Bill Wilson, an alcoholic stockbroker, had been able to maintain 4 months of sobriety through a friend who belonged to the Oxford Groups. At a point when Bill was near relapse after a business meeting failure in Akron, Ohio, he met Dr. Bob Smith, an alcoholic surgeon who was still drinking, and the two created what eventually became known as Alcoholics Anonymous. The first 100 members of this group wrote the "Big Book," the main text for sobriety that was published in 1939. A.A. and related twelve-step groups emphasize twelve steps of a spiritual path of recovery and twelve traditions that emphasize mutual support and minimal leadership of the organization. A.A. has grown to at least 2.2 million members, in 175 countries, with more than 100,000 groups (White, 2005). Narcotics Anonymous (NA) began in 1947, Cocaine Anonymous began in 1982, and various secular-based organizations began in the 1980s and 1990s (e.g., Secular Organization for Sobriety [1985], Rational Recovery [1986], Moderation Management [1993], Self-Management and Recovery Training [SMART Recovery; 1994]).

Starting in the mid-1900s, many communities adopted public detoxification facilities. These types of facilities were popular in Europe, but trends toward criminalization led to a relatively low number of these facilities in the United States. In the 1940s and 1950s, several developments led to the "modern alcoholism movement" (White, 2005). A.A. reinstilled hope about the prospects of long-term recovery. The Research Council on Problems of Alcohol and the Yale Center of Studies on Alcohol were created. The "Minnesota Model" of treatment of substance abuse was developed, evolving from the combined program ideas and philosophies of the Wilmar State Hospital treatment program, Hazelden (a private treatment facility), and the Minneapolis Veterans Administration Hospital Program (Nurses Research Publication, 1999; White, 2005). This model emphasized (1) inpatient or residential care for a few weeks or months; (2) a focus on psychoactive substance use disorder with little or no attention to associated psychiatric conditions or individual psychosocial factors; (3) use of A.A. concepts, resources, and precepts including the "twelve steps" being central to recovery; (4) referral to self-help groups such as A.A. on discharge from residential or inpatient care, with limited or no ongoing professional treatment; (5) provision of limited family therapy, although the family may be oriented to A.A. principles and Al-Anon (a twelve-step group for the family members of alcoholics who, in general, meet separately from the alcoholic family member); and (6) nonacceptance of psychotherapy and pharmacotherapy for either substance abuse or psychiatric disorders. In addition, in 1958, the Synanon drug treatment program was established, marking the beginning of the therapeutic community, in which the treatment agents include a community of staff and other patients.

In 1956, the American Medical Association passed a resolution calling on general hospitals to admit an alcoholic individual as a "sick individual." In 1963, the American Public Health Association declared alcoholism a treatable illness. In 1966, passage of the Narcotics

Addicts Rehabilitation Act (NARA) permitted treatment as an alternative to incarceration for narcotics addicts. This act reflected the beginning of the renewal of a large social climate of medical treatment orientation toward the addictions and coincided with the development of methadone maintenance treatment.

From the 1960s to the present, the workplace became a center of prevention education, early detection, and referral for treatment and rehabilitation through company-sponsored employee assistance programs (EAPs). Many large companies today have prevention and treatment programs available to employees. These programs may take the form of an actual on-site counselor/health professional (e.g., nurse) or a program that employees are referred to through employee health insurance.

In 1970, the Comprehensive Alcoholism Prevention and Treatment Act was passed, which created, among other organizations and services, the National Institute on Alcohol Abuse and Alcoholism (NIAAA). The Drug Abuse Treatment Act was passed in 1972, which led to the creation of a national network of addiction treatment programs and the National Institute on Drug Abuse (NIDA).

Treatment Programs Today

The treatment of substance abuse in America and several other countries today is progressing toward a multidisciplinary approach to the problem. As new knowledge about drug dependency is revealed, this new information is being translated into additional treatment methods. Treatment increasingly focuses on identifying the dependent individual and on prevention of the progression of the dependence. Further, substance abuse treatment seems to be heading toward specialization of treatment methods (e.g., dual diagnosis, family dynamics, high profile clients, counseling disabled clients; see Nurses Research Publication, 1999) and ascertainment of addictions counseling competency and accountability (White, 2005).

Treatment programs are now being tailored to a variety of populations (e.g., children, adults, individuals, and groups) and utilize a variety of treatment agents (e.g. medical doctors, psychologists, social workers, nurses, or recovering addicts). Programs are provided in a variety of settings (e.g., hospitals, outpatient clinics, prisons, and inpatient or residential programs) and utilize a variety of treatment models (e.g., A.A., NA, milieu, cognitive-behavioral, and behavioral). Additionally, treatment programs frequently include strategies for family systems (including parenting classes), AIDS education and awareness, nutritional and physical activity education, and strategies to improve retention and compliance with treatment (Figure 15.2).

Stages of Recovery

When individuals enter a treatment setting, they may or may not be under the influence of drugs. If they are under the influence, they are initially relieved of symptoms of distress and discomfort related to withdrawal. Once a drug-free state is established, the "real" recovery work begins. Comprehensive drug abuse treatment programs tend to incorporate various formalized phases to guide substance abusers through changes in their behavior, including stabilization, early recovery, and middle-to-late recovery (e.g., Mueller & Ketcham, 1987). During stabilization, goals include initial detoxification or withdrawal from substances,

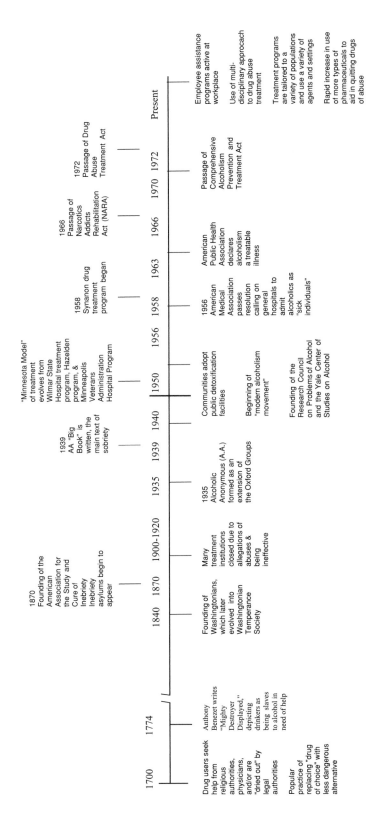

Figure 15.2. Historical timeline of the advances made in substance misuse treatment.

assessment of any comorbid psychological problems, medical care for health-related problems, and nutritional status assessment. Early recovery typically includes treatment planning for the change of long-term behavior, involving use of cognitive-behavioral therapies, skills training, counseling, and rehabilitative therapies. Middle-to-late recovery typically includes instruction in relapse prevention and provision of aftercare programs.

Several formal models of stages of recovery have been developed in addition to the stabilization, early, middle, and late recovery conceptualizations, described by Mueller and Ketcham (1987). Based on a disease model of alcoholism, Johnson (1980) proposed that individuals progress through the following stages of recovery: *admission, compliance, acceptance,* and *surrender*.

The first stage of *admission* occurs when individuals enter treatment settings and accept or admit that they have a substance abuse problem. This stage reinforces the disease concept of addiction. A disease perspective recognizes that individuals presenting for treatment are not responsible for their disease, but they are responsible for the process of recovery (Marlatt & Gordon, 1985; Zweben, 1993).

The second phase of recovery is *compliance*. Compliance involves a change in an individual's attitude from resisting to complying with treatment. *Resistance* is an individual's unwillingness to change or participate in his or her treatment and can be problematic. Without compliance, it is unlikely that cognitive and behavioral changes will occur.

The third stage of recovery, *acceptance*, involves personal responsibility for recovery. This occurs when an individual gains some insight into the severity of his or her problem. Gratitude may replace feelings of alienation from others. During this stage, there exists an increase of self-awareness and self-acceptance, and congruency in an individual's verbalizations, affect, and body language.

The fourth stage of recovery, *surrender*, is signaled by an "appropriate display of caution about the future" and the realization that aftercare is necessary for the continued maintenance of change. At this time, individuals may need the support of groups, such as A.A. and NA, to help them cope with future difficulties. At this stage of recovery, individuals are ready for outpatient programs and sober-living homes.

Gorski and Miller (1984, 1986) developed another formal model of the stages of recovery involving a series of developmental periods that affect physiological changes, including neurobiological changes and various goals for each developmental period. These developmental periods are as follows: (1) the *pretreatment period* or recognition of the addiction; (2) the *stabilization period*, which involves crisis management or recovery from acute withdrawal and severe symptoms of postacute withdrawal; (3) the *early recovery period*, or acceptance and nonchemical coping; (4) the *middle recovery*, at which time balanced living becomes a goal; (5) the *late recovery*, which involves personality changes; and (6) *maintenance*, which entails a significant period of growth and development. Certainly, the models reviewed earlier overlap. For example, all of the models concur that recovery is a developmental process that varies from individual to individual, progressing in stages, and that relapse is always a possibility (Figure 15.3).

Treatment Goals

Typically, the main goal of treatment programs is to help substance abusers abstain from any drug use, with the exception of caffeine and cigarettes (see later discussion on tobacco). In some programs, or for a small number of cases, the goal might be to provide

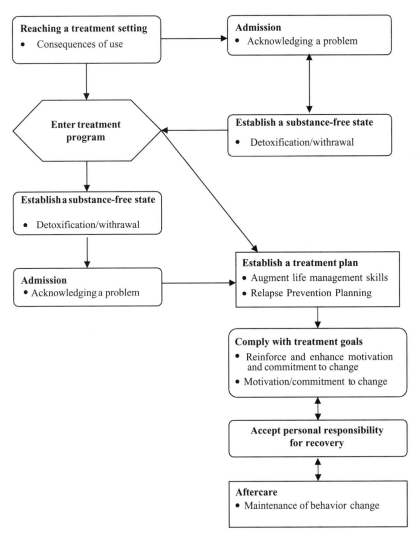

Figure 15.3. A treatment process model adapted from Sussman and Ames (2001). Some individuals suffer negative consequences and enter treatment without going through withdrawal and without acknowledging they have a problem. This is depicted by the path from reaching a treatment setting to entering treatment to establishing a substance-free state to admission. Others suffer negative consequences and acknowledge they have a substance abuse problem and go through withdrawal (or go through withdrawal and then admit they have a problem) and then enter treatment. This is depicted in the various paths from admission, withdrawal, and entering a treatment program.

regulatory controls over the drug use (e.g., to facilitate moderate or controlled use over alcohol). Some drug abusers may desire to control their use rather than quit. Other drug abusers may desire to quit, but have trouble quitting and desire at least to minimize consequences of their behavior (harm reduction).

Among treatment programs that are based on twelve-step models (a disease model of addiction), total abstinence is deemed necessary to recover from an addiction (at least for the "types" of alcoholics or addicts these programs intend to apply to). Total abstinence is defined as no use of alcohol or any other mood-altering drugs, with the exception of cigarettes or caffeine, which is the practice in many treatment programs. Alcohol use is not viewed as a safe alternative among drug addicts. Many substance abusers misuse alcohol in addition to other drugs, but some do not have a history of alcohol abuse. In general, though, abusers of drugs other than alcohol ("drug addicts") believe that use of alcohol quickly disinhibits control processes and may trigger associative memories compatible with drug use, reducing the probability of effective coping in high-risk situations. A drug lapse may then be inevitable if the individual values immediate gratification and loses perspective of long-term goals (Zweben, 1993).

For many individuals total abstinence is necessary; any use at all results in out-of-control use and negative consequences. The disease model produces a dichotomous restriction on the possible range of treatment outcomes; one is either "abstinent (exerting control) or in relapse (losing control)" (Marlatt & Gordon, 1985, p. 7). For those who accept the concept that addictive behaviors are overlearned habits that are modifiable, controlled use is a feasible treatment outcome. Strategies aimed at moderation of consumption (i.e., controlled drinking) may benefit some individuals. Of course, the ability to maintain controlled use of alcohol varies among individuals and may not be a viable or reliable option for most individuals abusing alcohol or other drugs. However, controlled drinking or use as a goal may at least bring individuals into treatment sooner. Those who fail at controlled use may then be willing to consider abstinence as a goal. In fact, the abstinence rate among those who choose controlled drinking as a treatment goal is about the same as those who choose abstinence as a goal (Galaif & Sussman, 1995).

Those few who become controlled drinkers tend previously to have been lighter drinkers. In addition, they have suffered fewer legal and social consequences, may report having been less likely to experience gross behavioral changes when drinking, and have been abstinent a few years before drinking again. They tend to drink one to four drinks on social occasions and/or only occasionally (Sussman & Ames, 2001). Interestingly, it appears that, at 1 year later, problem drinkers who receive treatment are twice as likely to become abstinent, but are half as likely to become controlled drinkers, than those who do not receive treatment (Peele, 1998). Possibly, this could reflect a social bias in which problem drinkers in recovery come to believe in an abstinence violation effect (Marlatt & Gordon, 1985). In other words, if they ever drink alcohol, they may feel that they "lost the game" and that they might as well give up and drink regularly again. For information on current popular moderation-allowable programs, please see Addiction Alternatives (www.addictionalternatives.com), DrinkWise (http://www.drinkwise.com/), or moderation management (www.moderation.org).

The secondary goal of most treatment programs is to reinforce the maintenance of behavior change through continued support, such as aftercare counseling, attendance in twelve-step programs, or involvement in skills programming such as relapse prevention programming. Treatment of addictive behaviors often involves relapse prevention. Relapse refers to the use of a drug after a period of abstinence. Recurrence of use can vary from a single event (slip or lapse) to a time-limited episode or a binge to a full-blown return to the frequency and pattern of use prior to abstinence (relapse; Marlatt & Gordon, 1985). The concept of a relapse also can refer to a chain of events preceding the recurrence of the drug use behavior (the relapse situation). Relapse appears to be linked to factors such as *failure to avoid drug use settings* (e.g., inappropriate social support networks, social pressure, and opportunity); *failure to maintain effective coping mechanisms* in high-risk situations (i.e., a loss of perceived self-efficacy when exposed to drugs); *interpersonal problems* (e.g., conflict), *negative affective states* such as anger, sadness, boredom, anxiety, depression, guilt, apprehension, and loneliness; and *drug cravings or intrusive thoughts about using drugs* (Daley & Salloum, 1999; Marlatt & Gordon, 1985).

Motivation

Motivation is an essential component of drug use cessation and the maintenance of behavior change. Motivation varies between individuals and may fluctuate within an individual at any given time during an effort to stop using drugs and during the maintenance of change. The willingness and ability to overcome unpleasant affect to achieve subsequent improved physical and emotional well-being is an important milestone. Several definitions of the concept of motivation for change have been proposed. Motivation may be a function of goals (*direction*) or tendencies to act (*energy*) (Bindra & Stewart, 1966). Additionally, the motivational source may be extrapersonal or intrapersonal. Conversely, others view motivation as an intrapersonal *state of readiness* to change (e.g., DiClemente et al., 1991; Miller & Rollnick, 1991; Prochaska & DiClemente, 1982). Conceptually, definitions of motivation all describe awareness of discrepancies between possible desired goals and current states (also see Nezami, Sussman, & Pentz, 2003). We describe four models of motivation.

The *Direction-Energy Model* addresses the need to consider two components of motivation – a *goal* and the *energy* to reach that goal (Bindra & Stewart, 1966; Emmons et al. 1995; Miller & Rollnick, 1991; Sussman, 1996; Young, 1936). A desire for self-image change, curiosity, and a desire for mood enhancement guide the goal component of motivation. The amount of energy invested in behavior change is guided by perceiving a match between one's behavioral responses with the demands of reaching the goal. In addition, the amount of energy invested in change is guided by one's embeddedness in a lifestyle about which a comfortable end state is perceived to be reachable and social or intrapersonal pressure to change (e.g., fear; Sutton & Eiser, 1984).

The *Transtheoretical Model* (DiClemente et al., 1991; Prochaska & DiClemente, 1982; Prochaska et al., 1985, 1990) consists of a series of stages of change with early stages involving establishing a commitment to a goal and later stages providing the energy to complete the goal. According to this model, an individual's *state of readiness* for change is conceptualized as his or her motivation for change. This model includes five stages.

The first is *precontemplation*, which is marked by a lack of interest in change. The second is *contemplation*: the realization of a problem, the evaluation of the consequences of one's present behavior, and consideration of behavior change. The third stage is *preparation*, when individuals are motivated to make behavioral changes; individuals focus on actions that will bring about behavior change. The fourth stage is *action*, the actual quit attempt and willingness to stay abstinent through withdrawal symptoms. The final stage is *maintenance*, which reflects an individual's efforts to avoid relapse and solidify changes made.

The *Intrinsic-Extrinsic Model of Motivation* proposes that goals are more likely to be obtained if the individual identifies with the desirability of obtaining that goal, as opposed to reaching the goal for some other reward (Curry, Wagner, & Grothaus, 1990). Different strategies, including motivational interviewing and proximal goal setting, have been shown to enhance intrinsic motivation (Manderlink & Harackiewicz, 1984). Several theories of behavior change emphasize intrinsic motivation (e.g., Health Behavior Model; Becker, 1974; Protection Motivation Theory; Rogers, 1975). Other theories focus on socioenvironmental elements (extrinsic rewards) that facilitate or motivate change (e.g., Social Learning Theory;

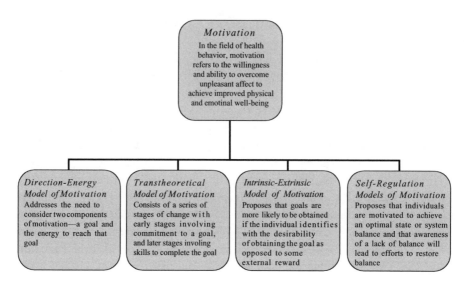

Figure 15.4. Various motivational models relevant to the treatment of addictive behaviors.

Rotter, 1954), whereas others combine personal (intrinsic) and social (extrinsic) aspects as influencing motivation for behavior change (e.g., Theory of Reasoned Action; Fishbein & Ajzen, 1975). There is an indication that extrinsic motivation will work as well as intrinsic motivation as long as behavior is performance dependent (see Nezami, Sussman, & Pentz, 2003).

Self-Regulation Models of Motivation propose that individuals are motivated to achieve an optimal state or system balance and that awareness of a lack of balance will lead to efforts to restore balance. Physiological mechanisms and self-initiated behavior are pursued to reach homeostasis or an ideal state (Sommers, 1972). In other words, individuals seek to reach a desirable subjective state (e.g., level of arousal; O'Connor, 1989), level of coping or store of psychosocial assets (Ho, 1992; Leventhal, Diefenbach, & Leventhal, 1992; Ockene et al., 1981), or physiological homeostasis (Sommers, 1972). The dis-balance model presented in this text is, in part, an example of a self-regulation model of motivation (see Figure 5.2 in Chapter 5; Figure 15.4).

Tolerance of Tobacco Use in Treatment Settings

Cigarette smoking in treatment programs is often accepted, is used as a shared activity among persons in recovery, and is cited with some fond reminiscing in recovery literature (e.g., A.A., 1976). Interestingly, nicotine dependence has been viewed as different from other dependencies because the consequences are less immediately severe and do not affect one's overt behavior as profoundly as does use of other psychoactive drugs. Frequently, addicts in treatment programs are encouraged to quit another drug first before attempting to quit smoking to avoid relapse (Hurt, Eberman, Slade, & Karan, 1993). However, 30% to 40% of chemical dependency patients desire to quit tobacco concurrently with their drug of choice (main drug or drugs abused). Cessation of tobacco use may actually reduce exposure to relapse cues, help cessation, and prevent relapse from others drugs (Hurt, Eberman, Slade, & Karan, 1993; Sussman, Patten, & Order-Connors, 2005). For example, nicotine affects similar neural pathways in the brain as other drugs of abuse (i.e., reward pathways), which could conceivably result in a chain of behavioral responses associated in memory and relapse to other drug use (cf. Stacy, Ames, & Knowlton, 2004). The recovery movement more recently has been promoting the aspiration that drug abusers in recovery quit smoking while quitting other drugs. With the advent of a no-smoking policy in recovery facilities and other public and private buildings, smoking cessation for people in recovery eventually will become quite prevalent.

Treatment of Adolescent and Emerging Adult Substance Abuse and Dependence Disorders

Beginning in the 1980s there was a dramatic increase in the number of specialized substance abuse treatment programs for adolescents and emerging adults. This advance was promising because these groups are at the highest age-developmental risk for substance abuse. However, most of the available adolescent and emerging adult substance abuse treatment programs are based on adult treatment models. They typically include modifications to address the special needs of adolescents and emerging adults. Currently, there are four primary treatment models used with adolescents and emerging adults: (1) the Minnesota Model, which is based on the twelve steps of A.A., (2) the therapeutic community (TC) model, (3) family therapy, and (4) cognitive behavioral therapy (Blum, 1995). Given the heterogeneous nature of substance use, and the relative lack of adolescent and emerging adult treatment research to date, it is not possible to recommend one specific treatment modality that is likely to be effective for all adolescent and emerging adult patients (Godley & White, 2005). Instead, researchers and clinicians generally recommend the inclusion of specific treatment elements and a continuum of care in all treatment modalities (e.g., the *Quick Guide for Clinicians*; Substance Abuse and Mental Health Services Administration, 2001).

Effective Elements of Treatment for Adolescents and Emerging Adults

To date, there have been relatively few treatment effectiveness studies conducted (Blum et al., 1997). Of note, Brannigan, Schackman, Falco, & Millman (2004), with the assistance of a twenty-two-member advisory panel, created a checklist of nine key elements of effective substance abuse treatment for adolescents. First, the panel agreed that programs should *conduct comprehensive assessments* that cover psychological and medical problems, learning disabilities, family functioning, and other aspects of youths' lives. Second, program services should *address all aspects of the youths' lives* (e.g., school, home, and public activities). Third, *parents should be involved* in the youths' drug treatment. Fourth, the *programming should reflect developmental differences* between teens and adults. Fifth, treatment programs should *build a climate of trust*, which might maximally engage and retain teens in treatment. Sixth, the treatment *staff should be well trained* in adolescent development, comorbidity issues, and substance abuse. Seventh, programs should *address the distinct needs of youth* as a function of their gender and ethnicity (i.e., gender and cultural competence). Eighth, programs should include *information on continuing care* (e.g., relapse prevention, aftercare plans, and follow-up). Finally, programs should *include rigorous evaluations* to measure success and improve treatment services.

Next, the researchers conducted in-depth telephone surveys of 144 broadly distributed (throughout the United States) highly regarded adolescent substance abuse treatment programs to determine the extent to which available programs met the criteria. Results indicated that the best programs were not more likely to be accredited but were more likely to be 20 years old or older and involve family therapy and a therapeutic community approach. Only

Table 15.1. *Effective elements of treatment for adolescents and emerging adults*

Conduct comprehensive assessments
  Assessments should cover psychological and medical problems, learning disabilities, and family functioning.

Address all aspects of the youths' lives
  Program services should address all aspects of youths such as school, work, home, and public activities.

Involve parents
  Parental involvement in youths' drug treatment is important. In emerging adulthood, involvement of other significant others (e.g., a mate) may be important.

Reflect developmental differences
  Developmental differences between adolescents, emerging adults and older adults should be reflected in treatment program protocol.

Build a climate of trust
  Treatment programs should build a climate of trust, which might maximally engage and retain teens and emerging adults in treatment.

Train treatment staff well
  Treatment staff should be well trained in adolescent development, emerging adulthood transitions, comorbidity issues, and substance abuse.

Address the distinct needs of youth
  Programs should address the distinct needs of youth as a function of their gender and ethnicity.

Information on continuing care
  Programs should include information on continuing care such as relapse prevention, aftercare plans, and follow-up.

Include rigorous evaluations
  Programs should include rigorous evaluations to measure success and improve treatment services.

---

approximately 19% of the treatment programs provided adequate comprehensive assessment, 33% provided adequate comprehensive treatment, 34% emphasized adequate family involvement, 44% adequately considered developmental appropriateness, 25% adequately established means that could encourage good retention, 54% reported adequately qualified staff, 10% adequately considered gender and cultural sensitivity, 39% adequately considered continuing care, and 6% adequately addressed process and outcomes evaluation (Brannigan, Schackman, Falco, & Millman, 2004). One could infer from these findings that most drug abuse treatment provided to adolescents at present is far from ideal. A similar statement may be made about emerging adults (18–25 years old), who might be considered too old for some adolescent programming (e.g., contracting with parents) but too young for programming generally used with adults (e.g., willingness to consider oneself as "powerless" over alcohol or a drug) (Table 15.1).

Not only are many treatment programs far from ideal but adolescents and emerging adults may not be motivated to enter or remain in treatment regardless of the type of treatment facility (O'Leary et al., 2002). For example, among 600 teens entering outpatient treatment, primarily for marijuana abuse and dependence, at facilities located in four urban U.S. locations, only 20% stated that they needed help for their problems associated with alcohol or drug abuse (Tims et al., 2002). Motivating youth to obtain assistance and stay in treatment is a difficult task because most of them may not feel they need any formalized treatment.

In one study, Weiner, Sussman, McCuller, and Lichtman (1999) used both open-ended and multiple-choice methods, as well as health educator-led focus groups, to assess issues related to marijuana use and cessation among a population of high-risk youth (adolescents and young emerging adults). A total of 806 students participated, assessed as two separate samples from twenty-one continuation high schools in southern California. Approximately 70% of the students were current marijuana users. More than half of the marijuana users surveyed had tried to quit and failed. Still, social images associated with marijuana smokers were predominantly positive and subjects expressed a lack of confidence in the efficacy of marijuana cessation clinic programs. "Quit in private, on your own, without any policies" received the highest mean rating for effectiveness on a list of ten possible cessation strategies. Other methods of achieving marijuana cessation that received relatively high ratings for effectiveness were either restrictive or punitive. "Inpatient stay" received the second highest mean effectiveness rating, "jail time" the third highest effectiveness rating, and "fines" and "driver's license suspension" received the fourth and fifth highest effectiveness ratings, respectively. Overall, participants reported that self-help and restrictive or punitive methods are the most effective types of marijuana cessation activities.

In another study, Sussman (2002a) conducted a review of sixty-six teen or emerging adult tobacco use cessation studies published between 1975 and January 2001, with a mean length of follow-up (for fifty-two studies) of 8.6 months. Control group cessation rates at follow-up ranged from 0% to 31% in the twenty-three program studies that reported it (mean = 7.2%). A total of forty-eight studies reported program quit rates at follow-up. Of the forty-eight studies that did provide data, an overall quit rate at time of follow-up was a mean of 11.5% (range = 0%–41%). Arguably, maintenance of program effects was achieved in teen cessation studies (12% versus 7%), with a near doubling of cessation relative to controls. Programs that involved manipulation of intrinsic or extrinsic motivation and provided cognitive behavioral strategies did the best at changing behavior over a 3- to 12-month follow-up period. The number of program sessions was positively related to program success for teen cessation. One conclusion that can be drawn from this review and a subsequent formal meta-analysis (Sussman, Sun, & Dent, 2006) is that motivation enhancement methods that take youth into extended treatment are keys to successful youth cessation programs.

Minors can consent to their own treatment in most states without parental notification, and perhaps providing awareness of and emphasizing confidentiality of treatment could help motivate more youth to seek help (Weddle & Kokotailo, 2002). It does appear that treatment of some kind for substance abuse is superior to no treatment and that aftercare services are important (Blum, 1995).

Predictors of Adolescent and Emerging Adult Substance Abuse Treatment Outcomes

Treatment outcomes among teens and emerging adults (e.g., 6 to 12 months posttreatment), which generally have consisted of use of measures of drug use and abuse and sometimes also quality of family relations, school behavior, or well-being, are affected by *pretreatment factors*. These pretreatment factors include pretreatment levels of parental substance use (in some studies but not all; cf. Marshall, Marshall, & Heer, 1994), sibling substance use, deviant attitudes, deviant behavior, impulsivity (Hsieh, Hoffmann, & Hollister, 1998; Latimer, Newcomb, Winters, & Stinchfield, 2000; Latimer, Winters, Stinchfield, & Traver,

2000), low self-esteem (Blood & Cornwall, 1994), young age of first use, and polydrug use (Blood & Cornwall, 1994; Marshall, Marshall, & Heer, 1994) but not pretreatment severity of drug abuse.

Treatment outcomes also are predicted by comorbidity of substance use disorders and other mental health disorders. Studies on adolescents and emerging adults with both substance use disorders and other mental health disorders have found greater severity of posttreatment drug involvement as well as higher relapse rates (see Brown, 1999; Tomlinson, Brown, & Abrantes, 2004).

Conversely, having abstinent friends, being socially and academically connected, and being goal oriented are protective (Latimer, Newcomb, Winters, & Stinchfield, 2000; Latimer, Winters, Stinchfield, & Traver, 2000). These are very similar to the protective factors that might inhibit the development of substance abuse or dependence, which include relatively high intelligence, problem-solving ability, social skills, high self-esteem, good family relationships, positive role models, and good affect regulation (Weinberg, Rahdert, Colliver, & Glantz, 1998).

Treatment outcomes also are predicted by certain *treatment factors*. These include length of stay (a longer stay predicts better outcomes), degree of parental involvement (more involvement predicts better outcomes among teens), aftercare participation (attendance predicts better outcomes; Hsieh, Hoffmann, & Hollister, 1998), having a realistic attitude and being able to achieve social support (Myers, Brown, & Mott, 1993), and ease of posttreatment contact with professionals (Stinchfield, Niforopulos, & Feder, 1994). Relapse rates appear similar to those of adults (Brown, Vik, & Creamer, 1989).

Quitting without Formalized Treatment?

There is some evidence that individuals recover from substance abuse problems spontaneously, without the help of formal treatment programs. However, there is a dearth of evaluation research on factors contributing to spontaneous recovery. According to a recent large-scale general population study of Canadians, only one in three people with alcohol abuse or dependence diagnoses ever seek treatment (Cunningham & Breslin, 2004). Of the 1,000 respondents in the study that sought some type of treatment in the past, 30% reported talking with a doctor, 12% reported attending self-help groups, 8% reported seeing other professionals (e.g., psychologist, social worker), and 7% sought inpatient or outpatient services. In another study, Cunningham (1999) found that between 54% and 88% of problem drinkers quit without formalized treatment, depending on the number of reported consequences (one to six reported). One may conjecture that the numbers of teens or emerging adults exposed to formal drug treatment programs are less than the numbers of adults.

It is not clear how many people quit using drugs on their own as a function of duration of use, but the longer and heavier a person uses a drug, the less likely the person will be to quit drug use without formalized treatment (e.g., Sussman & Dent, 2004), and social contextual factors may be of particular importance (e.g., Lynskey et al., 2003). These factors may include relative ease of access and early numerous pleasurable experiences associated with use. Although many people "mature" out of drug use, approximately 25% of them do not. Also, perhaps only 50% mature out of marijuana use, 20% mature out of heavy drinking, and very few quit tobacco use (Rohrbach, Sussman, Dent, & Sun, 2005).

Harm Reduction Strategies

Because relapse rates are disconcerting and many individuals have a history of reinforcing behavior that requires commitment to long-term change goals, which cannot be established overnight, the concept of harm reduction as a treatment strategy is important. Harm reduction, as a prevention or treatment strategy, is more respectful of responsible decision-making, emphasizing the need to understand an individual's ability to control his or her behavior (Erickson, 1995). Harm or risk reduction has been used to protect drug abusers from many life-threatening consequences and to help them quit use in small steps.

A principle feature of harm reduction is the acceptance that some drug users cannot be expected to presently cease their substance use. The general idea of harm reduction is to ameliorate adverse consequences of substance use and reduce one's risk of harm to self and others (Duncan et. al., 1994; Marlatt, Somers, & Tapert, 1993; Pentz, Sussman, & Newman, 1997). Harm reduction focuses on short-term goals that are accessible and achievable (Single, 1995). For example, a harm reduction approach goal might be to gradually guide an individual away from engaging in problem behaviors as well as to reduce the risks associated with involvement in target behaviors (Marlatt, Somers, & Tapert, 1993). Alternative behaviors may be seen as less immediately harmful and a step in the direction of decreased risk. For example, tobacco use might be considered a substitute behavior for another problem behavior, such as heroin addiction. Although tobacco use is associated with numerous negative health outcomes, the consequences may be perceived as less immediately severe than consequences of the use of other substances. (One may question the wisdom of this strategy, however, because addiction to nicotine-containing tobacco leads eventually to dire health consequences.)

Harm reduction programs began in the United Kingdom with drug abusers being prescribed heroin and cocaine for maintenance of their habits. The Netherlands subsequently adopted a policy in which drug addicts and users were viewed as normal citizens and not as criminals or dependent persons (Marlatt, 1998). Currently, many harm reduction strategies for substance abuse have been implemented in various countries, including needle exchange programs (to decrease the risk of contracting HIV, hepatitis C, and other blood diseases transmitted by shared needles), legal needle sales, methadone maintenance and detoxification programs, designated driver programs for drunk drivers, detoxification programs for drug addicts where they can legally obtain a daily dose under the care of a physician to help minimize physical withdrawals, and pharmacological adjuncts to substance use. Other beneficial harm reduction tactics used in various private community settings such as clinics or "street settings" include the instruction in safe methods of inhalant huffing, instruction in methods of safer sex and the distribution of condoms, AIDS awareness, the use of marijuana as a maintenance drug for other drugs, and tolerance of tobacco use (see Pentz, Sussman, & Newman, 1997).

Summary

Treatment programs can be effective in reducing the incidence of future negative consequences of drug abuse. However, a key prerequisite for effective treatment is that individuals who want to solve their drug abuse problems are willing to work hard and will comply with a treatment plan. To date, it is unclear if one form of treatment is superior to any other over substantial periods of time (Peele & Brodsky, 1992; Valliant, 1983). Perhaps individuals should be able to select treatments from a menu based on their willingness to comply with the treatment they will receive. In general, the literature provides evidence that some type of *long-term treatment*, formal or informal, is necessary to effectively treat problem drug use. Indeed, it appears that organizations providing long-term supportive treatment can minimize relapse while increasing sobriety maintenance (e.g., Fletcher, Tims, & Brown, 1997; Sussman et al., 1986).

Also, to minimize relapse and disrupt the course of addictive behaviors, continuous exposure to alternative reinforcing behaviors (i.e., rewarding health behaviors) is recommended and implemented in conjunction with traditional treatment and relapse prevention programs. Involvement in healthy hobbies, engaging in regular exercise, and development of healthy relationships are very helpful to the development of a balanced lifestyle.

Finally, we note that some individuals recover from substance abuse problems spontaneously without formal treatment programs. The evaluation of factors that contribute to spontaneous recovery may help provide insight into the interplay of factors affecting formal interventions, real-life events, and lifestyle changes.

16   Neurobiologically Relevant

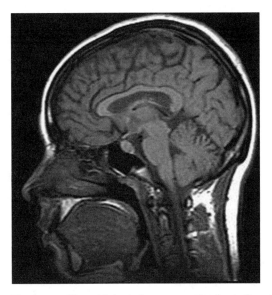

Figure 16.1. Neurobiological processes: Can brain function be modified to stop drug abuse?

We conjecture that most neurobiologically based treatment ideas are very similar to that indicated for prevention (e.g., genetic engineering and neurotransmitter manipulation). As with prevention work, these are topics of research for the future that may soon apply to treatment. Current models that most closely align to a neurobiological perspective tend to take a "disease model" stance; they postulate that drug misuse is a chronic, noninfectious disease suffered by those who are vulnerable (Sussman & Ames, 2001; Sussman & Unger, 2004). However, the range of those who are vulnerable or the place where people fall on a dimension of vulnerability to substance abuse or dependence is not well known. This current knowledge gap makes it difficult to tailor treatment approaches and maximize response to treatment efforts based on this model of treatment. Nevertheless, neurobiologically based treatment efforts are essential in the long run to counteract neurobiologically based characteristics of abuse or dependence; current efforts clearly benefit some individuals, and treatment protocols are evolving rapidly (Figure 16.1).

This chapter addresses recovery along the lines of concepts that we believe are consistent with a neurobiologically based perspective of substance abuse. First, pharmacotherapy for the treatment of withdrawal and as a harm reduction strategy among adults (emerging adults being grouped with other adults) and teens is discussed. Next, treatment of postacute withdrawal symptoms is discussed. Relapse warning signs are described that appear to arise, in part, from residual consequences of drug abuse as well preexisting neurobiological imbalances that may serve as reasons for self-medication. Finally, we speculate on the potential future of treatment interventions that take a neurobiological perspective (e.g., brain cell ablation or stimulation).

Treatment of Withdrawal Symptoms

Detoxification or managed withdrawal from drugs involves removing the toxic materials from an individual's body. Many people "detox" from a drug or drugs in private, without going into formalized treatment. They may suffer a range of symptoms. Sometimes a friend stands by to assist, perhaps providing less and less of a drug to gradually wean (taper) the drug abuser off of the drug or drugs. Many others go into formalized treatment to better reduce medical risks of withdrawal or to be monitored so as to successfully complete the withdrawal process instead of opting for continued use of a drug or drugs. As an institutionalized process, detoxification generally involves a 3- to 5-day inpatient stay at a detoxification facility with 24-hour intensive medical management. As a main part of detoxification, the individual is likely to suffer withdrawal symptoms that need to be managed to reduce potential for medical complications (e.g., seizures) and perhaps to reduce discomfort. Evaluation is very important because medical aspects of detoxification are contingent on the type of drug abused. We briefly discuss use of drugs to aid in withdrawal from different drugs of abuse categories.

Various drugs are used to help in the withdrawal from *alcohol* abuse; the list of these drugs is provided by Julien (2005, p. 120). Librium and other minor tranquilizers are used to ease withdrawal symptoms. Other medications include disulfiram and calcium carbimide (which allow aldehyde accumulation, resulting in noxious effects if any alcohol intake occurs; these drugs are also used for relapse prevention), naltrexone (reduces opioid receptor-related effects, reduces consumption), acamprosate (γ-aminobutyric acid [GABA] modulator, reduces craving), selective serotonin reuptake inhibitors (SSRIs) and buspirone (reduce depression or anxiety-related symptoms), ondansetron and ritanserin (serotonin antagonist; may reduce craving), carbamazepine (mood stabilizer; may reduce withdrawal), γ-hydroxybutyrate (GHB; may reduce withdrawal), and bromocriptine (dopamine agonist; may reduce craving).

For treatment of *benzodiazepines*, detoxification treatment includes gradually reducing the amount of drug taken, substitution of a longer-acting benzodiazepine, if appropriate, or substitution with use of phenobarbitol (Smith & Seymour, 2001). Often, detoxification of *sedative-hypnotics* includes initial use of phenobarbital substitution with tapering.

Treatment of *opioid* withdrawal may involve a variety of pharmacologic approaches. One may use symptomatic medication (agonists such as methadone and/or L-α-acetylmethadol [LAAM]), clonidine (which is used to treat high blood pressure and may relieve craving), use of ultrarapid detoxification (heavy sedation and use of the antagonist naltrexone), or use of buprenorphine (which has both agonist and antagonist properties). In addition, to ease opiate withdrawal, Darvon (propoxyphene), methadone, or a combination of naloxone with clonidine, while the patient is under sedation, have been used.

Stimulant withdrawal may be treated with dopamine agonists, bromocriptine, and amantadine. Generally, low stimulation, rest, and nutrition are emphasized. For *marijuana*, acute withdrawal is relatively brief (perhaps 3 days). For severe insomnia during marijuana withdrawal, trazodone (which has antidepressant and sedative properties) might be used. A tetrahydrocannibinol (THC) antagonist has been developed, rimonabant (SR141716), which may be used soon to help individuals quit marijuana use. *Hallucinogens* may be treated with temporary use of stimulants, but counseling is most relevant.

Detoxification is only a physically stabilizing aspect of treatment, perhaps the easiest, first step in cessation. Often it is tied to other programming, or referrals to other programming, to help the substance abuser remain drug free after the end of acute physical withdrawal. It helps reduce the neurobiological reactions of quitting "cold turkey" (i.e., abruptly and often with no assisting therapeutic drug), but initial stopping of drug use is perhaps the easiest step in recovery.

Pharmacotherapy as a Harm Reduction Approach

Agonist and antagonist maintenance treatment programs have been used to aid in managing abstinent lifestyles and preventing relapse, as harm reduction approaches. The idea here is to replace the drug or drugs of choice with a safer alternative or to manage abstinence so that if the drug or drugs of choice are used again in the future, the effects will be attenuated or will be unpleasant. Certainly, drugs used for treatment of withdrawal symptoms may be considered harm reduction agents as well, because they help the drug abuser taper off the drug with fewer consequences than might be experienced if no other drug agent was used.

Opioid Agonist Treatment

To minimize the disruptive and compulsive drug-seeking behavior associated with heroin addiction, various opioid replacement therapies or agonist maintenance treatment programs have been initiated. *Methadone*, a synthetic opiate, has been used for detoxification as well as abstinence maintenance for more than 30 years. It was originally synthesized in 1937 by German scientists affiliated with pharmaceutical companies for use as a surgical painkiller. Methadone is considered a full opioid agonist at mu-receptor sites; it binds to and activates mu-receptors to elicit an effect. It has a relatively short therapeutic action (half-life), suppressing withdrawal from other narcotics for 24 to 36 hours. As a result, individuals taking methadone generally make daily visits to methadone clinics, although some individuals may earn take-home bottle privileges as they become stabilized over time. Methadone maintenance therapy does result in physical dependency (with abuse potential), and withdrawal is relatively long and as difficult as (or more difficult than) withdrawal from heroin. However, methadone does reduce drug cravings and inhibits the "high feeling" produced by heroin. Some addicts may sell their methadone to get money to buy heroin, whereas others might use heroin on top of the methadone to feel euphoria.

Randomized controlled trials comparing methadone maintenance to placebo and other types of control conditions have shown methadone maintenance therapy, across cultural contexts, to effectively reduce illicit opiate use, crime rates, and lead to lower rates of human immunodeficiency virus (HIV) infection and mortality (for review, Farrell et al.,

1994; Kreek & Vocci, 2002). In a recent 6-year evaluation study of the prescribing practices for methadone maintenance therapy (MMT), Dickinson et al. (2006) found that the length of stay (retention in therapy) for individuals in MMT was longer when prescribed higher doses of methadone but that other treatment components were also important for successful treatment outcomes. Among adolescents, Kellogg et al. (2006) evaluated the effectiveness of MMT and retention of opiate-dependent adolescents involved in MMT over a 6-year period. The one-year retention rate was 48%, and a significant reduction in heroin use was found for those adolescents still in treatment at 1 year. Those youth who continued using heroin while on MMT were more likely to leave treatment within the first year. As a rule of thumb, it appears that MMT is effective for around 60% of opiate users.

Newer treatment alternatives to methadone include longer acting opioid agonists such as Orlaam (LAAM) and buprenorphine (Subutex). *LAAM* is a synthetic variant of methadone that was approved as an opioid replacement therapy in the U.S. marketplace in 1993, but its widespread usage has been slow. The duration of the therapeutic action of LAAM is approximately 48 to 72 hours or longer than methadone and therefore it can be administered three times weekly, requiring fewer clinic visits than methadone maintenance therapy. As of 2001, LAAM could be dispensed as a take-home medication. LAAM is also a mu-opioid agonist, decreasing opiate cravings and reducing withdrawal symptoms, and it does not produce a subjective high. Tolerance to LAAM will develop with prolonged use, resulting in withdrawal similar to withdrawal from morphine and other opiates. In more than 27 clinical trials LAAM has been shown to be comparable to methadone maintenance in reducing the use of opiates (see Rawson et al., 1998; also for review, see Kreek & Vocci, 2002). In a recent comparison study of LAAM and methadone maintenance among 315 patients, LAAM was found to be as effective as methadone in retaining individuals in treatment, and individuals taking LAAM were less likely to have positive urine tests for opiate use than those on methadone maintenance (Longshore, Annon, Anglin, & Rawson, 2005).

Buprenorphine is a partial opioid agonist that primarily affects activation of mu-opioid receptors. Buprenorphine is more costly than methadone, but it is less sedating and produces milder euphoric effects than heroin or methadone. In addition, withdrawal symptoms from buprenorphine are less severe than those of methadone, buprenorphine has less abuse potential than methadone, higher doses appear to have lower toxicity, and it has a longer half-life than methadone (Donaher & Welsh, 2006). In a study by Schottenfeld et al. (1997), both buprenorphine and methadone maintenance treatment were found to reduce drug use; however, abstinence rates from opiate use were higher for treatment with higher doses of methadone, followed by higher doses of buprenorphine and by lower doses of methadone, followed by lower doses of buprenorphine. In another comparison study of methadone and buprenorphine maintenance, methadone maintenance treatment retention rates were higher for individuals with co-occurring cocaine and opioid dependence, and individuals on methadone maintenance reported significantly longer periods of abstinence than those on buprenorphine maintenance (Schottenfeld et al., 2005).

Mattick, Kimber, Breen, and Davoli (2004) conducted a review of thirteen randomized clinical trials of buprenorphine compared with placebo or methadone maintenance for the treatment of opiate dependence. They found buprenorphine to be less effective than methadone in retaining individuals in treatment and high-dose buprenorphine to be inferior to methadone in inhibiting heroin use. Nevertheless, they found use of buprenorphine to be more effective than placebos.

Opioid Antagonist Treatment

Naloxone (Narcan) is an opiate antagonist, which blocks receptor activation regardless of "dosing." The mean plasma elimination half-life is 37 hours. Naloxone has been used as a rescue drug for opiate overdoses because of its high affinity for receptors; naloxone binds with opiate receptors and is able to block or replace the opiate at the receptor sites. Within a few minutes of a sufficient naloxone injection, an individual who has overdosed on an opiate generally will wake up. Recently, to reduce the abuse potential of buprenorphine, naloxone has been combined with buprenorphine in tablet form. In multicenter, randomized double-blind comparison trials of sublinqual tablets of buprenorphine, buprenorphine plus naloxone, and placebo treatment, both buprenorphine therapies were found to be effective in reducing opiate craving and use. Buprenorphine and buprenorphine/naloxone sublingual tablets were approved for the treatment of opiate dependence in 2002 (Fudala et al., 2003) and may be prescribed by eligible physicians (Vocci, Acri, & Elkashef, 2005).

Other opiate antagonists, naltrexone (ReVia) and nalmefene (Revex), both relatively new, have been used in the treatment of heroin addiction and alcohol dependence. *Naltrexone* blocks opioid receptors, attenuates the effects of opiates, and reduces cravings for alcohol and opiates. It has no known abuse potential. As an opioid-receptor antagonist, it is likely to modulate the mesolimbic dopamine pathways that are affected by alcohol use. Naltrexone does not result in dependence and can be terminated without any abstinence syndrome; however, it is associated with dose-dependent hepatocellular injury (for more information, see http://pubs.niaaa.nih.gov/publications/combine/FAQs.htm). Naltrexone is also occasionally used during and following rapid detoxification of opiates as a means of blocking opioid receptors and has recently been evaluated in the prevention of cocaine use relapse. In a randomized clinical trial to evaluate the efficacy of naltrexone in preventing relapse among cocaine-dependent individuals during 12-week outpatient therapy, Schmitz, Stotts, Rhoades, and Grabowski (2001) found that the use of naltrexone plus relapse prevention therapy was superior to relapse prevention alone, or drug counseling in conjunction with naltrexone, in preventing relapse (as measured by urinalysis at various points in time).

Nalmefene is similar to naltrexone but has a longer antagonist action and is more competitive in binding with subtypes of opioid receptors, reducing craving and the reinforcing effects of alcohol, and is less liver-toxic. In one randomized study of alcohol abuse cessation comparing the use of nalmefene with cognitive behavioral therapy to a placebo group with cognitive behavioral therapy over a 12-week period, nalmefene was found to significantly reduce relapse rates. However, there were no significant differences in groups on self-reported craving, mean number of consumed drinks on a drinking day, or the percentage of days abstinent from alcohol (Mason et al., 1999). The effectiveness of nalmefene in the treatment of alcohol dependence is still being investigated, and it is not Food and Drug Administration (FDA)-approved for treating alcohol-dependent individuals, although it is used for treating opiate-related overdoses.

Other Medications for the Treatment of Alcohol Dependence

The FDA has approved medications for the maintenance of the abstinence from alcohol dependence, including acamprosate (calcium acetylhomotaurine; Campral) and disulfiram (Antabuse) (Williams, 2005). *Acamprosate* is a synthetic substance that affects glutaminergic neurons and is thought to restore the balance of neurotransmitter systems compromised by chronic alcohol use. Acamprosate resembles a naturally occurring amino acid, homotaurine. In a review of fifteen randomized clinical trials of acamprosate in European countries, Mason (2001) concluded that it was safe and efficacious in prolonging abstinence and reducing relapse among alcohol-dependent individuals. In a review of various classes of pharmacological treatments for alcohol dependence, Garbutt et al. (1999) also found acamprosate, as well as naltrexone, to be more effective than placebo in treating alcohol-dependent individuals.

Disulfiram is a drug that produces an acute negative reaction to alcohol (e.g., flushing, throbbing headache, respiratory difficulty, and nausea) by inhibiting aldehyde dehydrogenase-metabolizing enzymes, resulting in elevated levels of acetaldehyde in the system. Disulfiram has been used for more than 50 years in the treatment of alcoholism; however, in a review of eleven controlled clinical trials on disulfiram in the treatment of alcohol dependence, research findings did not clearly established its efficacy (Garbutt et al., 1999). More recently, Disulfiram has been studied as a treatment for cocaine-dependent individuals and found to be promising in reducing use, especially in combination with cognitive behavioral therapy (e.g., Carroll et al., 2004). In a recent randomized trial, the use of disulfiram prior to cocaine administration increased plasma cocaine in the system, decreased clearance, and decreased subjective ratings of the cocaine "high" and "rush" (Baker, Jatlow, & McCance-Katz, 2007).

Nicotine Addiction

Pharmacotherapies for nicotine are listed in Fiori et al. (2000). First-line medications (found to be safe and effective, and approved by the FDA) include buproprion SR (sustained release) and nicotine replacement therapies (NRTs) such as nicotine gum, inhaler, nasal spray, or patch. Second-line medications (not FDA-approved for a specific treatment or having notable side effects) include clonidine and nortriptyline. Buproprion SR blocks the reuptake of dopamine and/or norepinephrine. It can be used with NRT, but not with (other) antidepressant medications. NRTs provide lower dosages of nicotine and hence provide a partial relief of withdrawal symptoms (without the carcinogenic ingredients). Clonidine is approved for use as an antihypertensive medication. Nortriptyline is a tricyclic antidepressant, and it has effects on dopaminergic, serotinergic, or noradrenergic neurotransmission. Buproprion and even NRT might be used for a long time after quitting smoking to make life more manageable and to reduce chances of relapse.

Pharmacotherapy with Teens

Kaminer (1995) discusses the option of using pharmacotherapy with teens, just as it has been used with adults. Possibly, medication might help ease potential withdrawal symptoms and might help in mood stabilization after quitting alcohol or other drugs. There has been very little research on the safety of using pharmacotherapy among teens (Kaminer, 1995). Studies on use of pharmacologic adjuncts to assist with tobacco-use cessation have not been promising thus far as applied to teens (Sussman, 2002a; Sussman, Sun, & Dent, 2006). Desipramine (a tricyclic antidepressant) has been used to treat cocaine dependence in a few case studies, with mixed results (Kaminer, 1995). Additionally, little evidence exists for the efficacy of drug-related medications for teens – such as use of methadone and naltrexone during detoxification (Weinberg, Rahdert, Colliver, & Glantz, 1998). However, although there is some debate, use of SSRIs or selective norepinephrine reuptake inhibitors

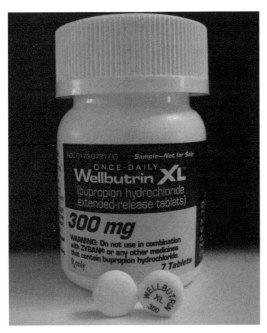

Figure 16.2. A bottle of the (possibly) selective dopamine reuptake inhibitor Wellbutrin.

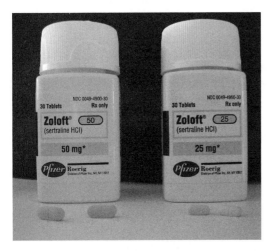

Figure 16.3. Bottles of the selective serotonin reuptake inhibitor Zoloft.

(SNRIs) is recommended for those young patients who are highly depressed or anxious. Medications for attention deficit and hyperactivity disorder (ADHD), including Ritalin (methylphenidate), could be abused but generally are not by the persons who are prescribed them (although some do provide these medications to their friends). Medications for ADHD with less potential for abuse are being developed (Sussman, Pentz, Spruijt-Metz, & Miller, 2006) (Figures 16.2 and 16.3).

The future of the use of medications with teens is not clear. Ethical concerns exist with this special population, including consideration of the rights of both parent and child, as well as potential interference with the rapidly developing brain of the young person. It

Table 16.1. Medications according to uses

Drugs of misuse	Medications to assist with drug cessation	Functions of medications
Nicotine	Buproprion SR, nicotine replacement therapy (NRT), Clonidine, Nortriptyline	Ease withdrawal symptoms, perhaps reduce depressive symptoms
Alcohol	Librium	Ease withdrawal symptoms
	Disulfiram, calcium carbimide	Ease withdrawal symptoms and help prevent relapse
	Naltrexone	Reduce consumption
	Acamprosate	Reduce craving
	Selective serotonergic reuptake inhibitors (SSRIs), Buspirone	Reduce depressive or anxiety-related symptoms
	Ondansetron, Ritanserin	May reduce craving
	Carbamazepine	Stabilize mood, may reduce craving
	GHB	May reduce withdrawal symptoms
	Bromocriptine	May reduce craving
Benzodiazepine	Phenobarbitol	Detoxify
Sedative-hypnotic	Phenobarbitol	Detoxify
Opioid	Methadone, LAAM	Ease withdrawal symptoms
	Clonidine	May relieve craving
	Naltrexone, Nalmefene	Detoxify
	Buprenorhine	Ease withdrawal symptoms
	Darvon (propoxyphene)	Ease withdrawal symptoms
Stimulant	Bromocriptine, Amantadine	Ease withdrawal symptoms
Marijuana	Trazodone	Ease withdrawal symptoms
	Rimonabant	May reduce craving
Hallucinogen	Stimulants	Temporary relief

is also suggested that young people have too little life experience to have the knowledge necessary to be fully informed and provide consent regarding use of a medication. These and other considerations limit research experimentation in this arena (e.g., Kaminer, 1995) (Table 16.1).

Treatment of Postacute Withdrawal

The phenomenon of postacute withdrawal (PAW; Gorski & Miller, 1984, 1986) refers to the period of up to approximately 18 months following acute withdrawal from drug use. Just as drug abuse is a biopsychosocial process, PAW is a biopsychosocial syndrome involving the occurrence of a variety of symptoms as a result of abstinence from drugs (e.g., related to restoration of neurobiological balance or dis-balance and the psychosocial stress of coping with life drug free). Postacute withdrawal may be affected by chronic stress, personality factors (e.g. depression, sensation seeking, and obsessive-compulsive disorders) and triggering events. Symptoms of PAW include the following: (1) the inability to think clearly; (2) emotional overreactivity, numbness, or artificial affect; (3) memory impairment or problems; (4) stress sensitivity; (5) sleep disturbances; and (6) physical coordination problems. The danger of PAW is that experiences of dis-balance

Table 16.2. *Types of neurobiologically relevant cessation treatments*

Treatments for withdrawal symptoms	Withdrawal from a drug may result in various unpleasant symptoms that can be alleviated through pharmacotherapy.
Harm reduction treatments	Harm reduction treatments involve agonist and antagonist maintenance strategies that aid in managing abstinent lifestyles and prevent relapse by replacing the drug of choice with a safer alternative.
Treatments for postacute withdrawal symptoms	Postacute withdrawal is a biopsychosocial syndrome involving the occurrence of a variety of symptoms as a result of abstinence from drugs. These symptoms may be alleviated through various pharmacotherapeutical treatments, as well as through social support and cognitive coping strategies.

may lead to early relapse. Two means to cope with PAW symptoms are to (a) become aware of and responsive to relapse cues and (b) mood management (Table 16.2).

Relapse Warning Signs

Gorski and Miller (1984, 1986) developed a list of relapse phases and warning signs based on analyses of histories of relapse-prone individuals committed to maintaining sobriety but who were unable to stay sober and returned to compulsive use. The relapse process entails several sequential phases.

First, individuals may experience *internal changes* in thinking, feelings, and behavior. They may not feel as though they are balanced. Next, they may engage in *denial* – individuals may stop being honest with others about their thoughts and feelings. Next, these individuals may engage in *avoidance* and *defensiveness*. Individuals might begin avoiding others or any situation that might force them to be honest about changes in thoughts, feelings, and behaviors. Soon individuals may experience *crisis building* – problems in sobriety that they do not understand. Soon these individuals may feel a sense of *immobilization*, being trapped while problems seem unmanageable. Soon individuals may begin to experience *confusion and overreaction*. That is, the individuals have difficulty thinking clearly and regulating their feelings and emotions. Next, they may experience *depression*. In other words, they may come to believe that life is not worth living and lack the desire to take action. At this point, *behavioral loss of control* begins. These individuals can no longer control their thoughts, feelings, and behaviors and they may experience feelings of helplessness. Next, *recognition of loss of control* occurs. That is, individuals realize that their life has become unmanageable. After that, these individuals may experience a sense of *option reduction*. They may feel trapped and unable to manage their lives; they may believe self-medication with drugs or alcohol is their only or best way out. At this point comes the final phase of *alcohol and drug use*. Individuals return to using; they try to control their use and they lose control.

Some externally controlled interventions might expedite the return to abstinence following a relapse, including urine testing, the use of antagonist drugs (such as naltrexone), regulatory controls of finances (e.g., turning monies over to family members), and structuring an individuals' time (Zweben, 1993). However, ultimately individuals need to establish control and self-regulatory mechanisms to maintain abstinence. One could speculate that with enhanced cognitive controls, a return of endogenous function of dopamine and serotonin, and changes in the neural substrates of memory (resulting from treatment and periods

Table 16.3. Gorski and Miller (1984, 1986) relapse warning signs

- Internal changes: Individuals experience internal changes in thinking, feelings, and behavior.
- Denial: Individuals are no longer honest with others about thoughts and feelings.
- Avoidance and defensiveness: Individuals begin to avoid others and situations that might force them to be honest about thoughts, feelings, and behaviors.
- Crisis building: Individuals begin to encounter problems in sobriety that they do not understand.
- Immobilization: Individuals begin to feel trapped, as problems seem increasingly unmanageable.
- Confusion and overreaction: Individuals have difficulty thinking clearly and managing feelings and emotions.
- Depression: Individuals become depressed.
- Behavioral loss of control: Individuals begin to lose control over their behavior.
- Recognition of loss of control: Individuals realize that their life has become unmanageable.
- Option reduction: Individuals begin to believe that self-medication with drugs or alcohol is their only or best way out.
- Alcohol and drug use: Individuals return to using drugs.

of abstinence) that non-drug behavioral options may become increasingly more accessible when an individual is confronted with threats to sobriety (i.e., enhanced control may allow the individual to put the "brake" on tendencies that result from previous experiences or habit) (Table 16.3).

Mood and Affect Management

There are a variety of medications for the management of mood and affective states that may aid in reducing the use of substances to self-medicate, prevent relapse, or serve as useful adjuncts for treating individuals with comorbid affective disorders and substance use disorders. Some of these medications include SSRIs, selective dopamine reuptake inhibitors (e.g., Wellbutrin), selective norepinephrine reuptake inhibitors (SNRIs) for depression and/or anxiety, a variety of benzodiazepines for the treatment of anxiety disorders, medications for obsessive compulsive tendencies (e.g., Anafranil and some SSRIs), and maintenance medications for bipolar disorder (e.g., lithium, Depakote). As alternatives to medications for mood and affect management, there are several techniques used in treatment that can be instructed to help individuals cope with negative affect or even learn to change affect.

One means of coping with negative affect is through engagement in contrary action that may subsequently lead to positive affect. Instruction in identifying one's own feelings and recognizing feelings in others may be important (Scott, Kern, & Coombs, 2001). Teaching self-forgiveness may help one improve his or her affect after the termination of a drug abuse episode. Setting aside free time every week to do a different type of activity may help balance out one's emotional states. Exercise and a good diet, as well as the use of medication, as needed, can also help in affect and mood regulation. Finally, simply waiting out negative emotional states may have an effect given that the experience is transient and not a sustained state.

Speculation about Future Treatments

There are future treatment possibilities on the horizon for individuals suffering from addictions. New means of providing an indirect impact on brain function may be developed, including manipulations of physical and social environments. One may conjecture about the various environments that might help each individual feel more at ease with his or her life, including manipulation of contingencies (e.g., simplification of lifestyle). Direct manipulations of brain function also are likely to develop. First, pharmacologic treatments may become more precise and better able to help individuals quit using their drugs of choice and maintain a comfortable lifestyle. For example, development of new centrally acting acetylcholine inhibitors may lead to higher mesolimbic dopaminergic neurotransmission, perhaps balancing the brain functioning of some addicts (Hikida, Kitabatake, Pastan, & Nakanishi, 2003). Second, stimulation or ablation of brain tissue may lead to better function among some addicts. For example, cholinergic cell ablation in circuits leading to the nucleus accumbens provides one means of altering brain function. Because acetylcholine may inhibit mesolimbic dopaminergic function, precise ablation may result in an increased turnover of dopamine leading perhaps to a balancing out in brain function (Hikida, Kitabatake, Pastan, & Nakanishi, 2003).

Hall (2005) mentioned that during the past 5 years, Russian and Chinese surgeons have used neurosurgical procedures to treat heroin addiction (involving a total of approximately 1,000 addicts), involving ablation of the nucleus accumbens (in China) or the cingulate gyrus (in Russia), to try to reduce self-reward or obsessive-related behavior, respectively. These procedures have been stopped since 2005. Hall (2005) questioned the safety, efficacy, and ethics of these procedures, preferring the use of opioid agonists (e.g., methadone), mixed agonist-antagonists (e.g., buprenorphine), or antagonists (e.g., naltrexone), until the advent of more precise surgical procedures, given uncertainties about the effects of ablation of structures implicated in a variety of life functions (e.g., food intake and sexual behavior), and because available evidence for its efficacy is minimal (i.e., based on uncontrolled case studies).

Third, some researchers speculate that vagus nerve stimulation (VNS) may reduce relatively maladaptive addictive behavior among some addicts. George et al. (2002) discussed the rapid expansion of VNS-related preclinical research, as well as clinical studies, that might address a variety of medical areas, including the addictions. They also mention that research advances in understanding VNS are occurring in the midst of growth of other forms of therapeutic brain stimulation, such as electroconvulsive therapy, transcranial magnetic stimulation, and deep brain stimulation. The vagus nerve runs between the brain and the abdomen. VNS is a surgical procedure in which a small generator is placed under the skin on the left side of the chest. A surgeon makes a second incision in the neck and connects a wire from the generator to the vagus nerve. A doctor programs the generator to send mild electrical pulses at regular intervals. These pulses stimulate the vagus nerve. It is possible that nerve stimulation protocols may be helpful; however, like any biomedical treatment, patients can always choose to discontinue treatment and resort to drug use or supplement such treatments with their drugs of choice. These possibilities, seen with the use of disulfiram and methadone maintenance therapy, may reflect a need to do more than biomedical modifications of addicted individuals. Motivating individuals with drug dependencies to continue to comply with treatment may take additional modifications, as described in the subsequent chapters of this text.

Finally, the future of gene therapy (the insertion of normal genes into cells or tissues that contain nonfunctional or mutant copies to restore normal functioning) as a treatment tool is uncertain. Although gene therapy may be able to treat some global disorders by replacing populations of cells, it may never prove effective in addressing diseases involving solid tissues, organs, and functions dependent on structures such as, for example, the brain (Rifkin, 2005).

Summary

This chapter provided an overview of some neurobiologically based treatment ideas. Unfortunately, to date, even with the many prophylactic pharmacotherapies and agonist and antagonist maintenance therapies shown to be effective, the problem of substance abuse/dependence, once established, for most individuals, continues. Drug abuse and dependence are chronic relapsing conditions that must be vigilantly managed by the individual. Medications in conjunction with a variety of other therapies, such as cognitive behavioral therapies and relapse prevention, may improve treatment outcomes for some individuals. Strategies to enhance compliance to and retention in treatment ought to be seriously considered when developing treatment protocol because they affect treatment outcomes.

The benefits of maintaining abstinence for longer periods of time, both to the individual and to society, have been established. New generations of medications, as well as alternative approaches, such as socioenvironmental manipulations, with continued focus on prevention strategies, are necessary to help minimize the harm of substance addiction. Advances in neuroscience, genetics, and social psychological research continue. These will lead to an increased understanding of the neural substrates, genetic markers, and psychosocial and environmental determinants that affect drug craving, tolerance, abstinence maintenance, and relapse. Neurobiological knowledge, integrated with psychosocial knowledge, ought to help refine available therapies.

17 Cognitive Processes

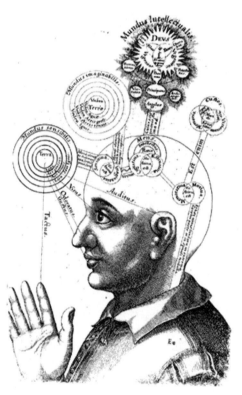

Figure 17.1. Information processing: How can it be changed to stop drug abuse?

An individual who has been abusing or is dependent on alcohol or other drugs may spend a great deal of time thinking about the drugs, drug rituals, and drug-related life circumstances. To give up drug use may then conflict or be inconsistent with the many thoughts nurtured that associate drug use with primary daily activities, which may cause a subjective experiential void. Experiencing life over long periods of time without drug use would help in creating new associative cognitive structures and memories that might be protective against future drug abuse (Figure 17.1).

Behavior modification interventions historically address observable antecedents and consequences of a behavior without acknowledging cognitive mediation of behavior. Even so, behavior modification techniques consist of a variety of behavior-rewarding modeling, reinforcement, and guiding (shaping) experiences to change drug use behavior that may indirectly change cognitive processes. Cognitive interventions include strategies to directly modify thinking to enhance executive control or other cognitive processes (e.g., classically conditioned, implicit processes, and so on) so as to permit drug use behavior cessation effects. This chapter discusses several cognitive treatment approaches, including specific cognitive-behavioral techniques, cognitive-behavioral inpatient programs, cue exposure therapy, cognitive-oriented self-help recovery programs, relapse prevention, and consideration of changing implicit and explicit cognition components in cessation.

Cognitive-Behavioral Interventions

Changing behavior patterns or frequency is instructed through use of any number of techniques. These techniques alter stimuli confronting the person ("stimulus control"), the way the person interprets these stimuli ("organism control"), responses the person emits ("response control"), or contingencies of reinforcement ("reinforcement control"; Goldfried & Davison, 1994; Gottman & Leiblum, 1974). This chapter focuses on organism control techniques for cessation.

One major organism control technique is *problem solving*. Problem solving (introduced in the chapter on prevention) involves a series of steps in cessation programming, including generating as many behavioral options as possible, examining the benefits and costs of each behavioral option (e.g., continued drug use, switching drugs, stopping drug use, and beginning meditation to be more mindful), and then trying to make the best decision based on the available options with the most benefits and least costs. After this examination, one might make a commitment to that decision and act, knowing that he or she can always reevaluate the decision after trying things out.

Directly modifying one's inner speech can be accomplished through use of such cognitive strategies as *cognitive restructuring* or self-instructional training. For example, when there is a self-defeating or irrational element to one's inner voice, cognitive restructuring helps in replacing or changing these cognitions. Cognitive restructuring involves recognizing and examining self-defeating cognitions and replacing them with self-fulfilling thoughts that may lead to a better, more rational direction of thought and behavior. When elements of one's inner voice are missing (e.g., one is impulsive), *self-instructional training* may help in guiding the individual to regulate his or her behavior. Self-instructional training involves examining and recognizing missing cognitions and adding cognitions through practice (out loud, then subvocally, and then thinking about it) so that one is led to a better direction of thought and behavior (Meichenbaum, 1977).

Cognitive-Behavioral Chemical Dependency Inpatient Programs

Cognitive-behavioral community-based residential programs for substance abuse consist of 24-hour supervised treatment. These residential treatment programs are frequently based on the principles of Narcotics or Alcoholics Anonymous, but they use a variety of methods to eliminate chemical dependency through continuous exposure to structured cognitive-behavioral programming. These programs include both behavioral tasks to modify habits, as well as cognitive restructuring. The objectives of these programs include (1) the elimination of dependency on all drugs (except nicotine and caffeine), (2) the development of self-awareness and self-worth, (3) the practice of self-discipline, (4) identification and clarification of problems that may threaten sobriety, (5) problem solving or effective decision-making strategies, (6) the enhancement of physical and psychological well-being, (7) the enhancement of coping mechanisms or coping skills training (e.g., cognitive coping such as cognitive restructuring), and (8) alternative solutions to self-destructive behaviors. These programs also assist in establishing or enhancing social support and healthy familial and interpersonal relationships through counseling and educational classes and milieu therapy. In addition, many of these programs provide relapse-prevention programming (described later in this chapter), assist in determining vocational aptitude and educational needs through skills development, assist in establishing realistic personal goals, and enhance access to and the utilization of community resources. They may also provide nutritional training and parenting skills training.

Treatment contracts in these programs tend to vary in length of stay (i.e., some are 30 days, some 90, some 4–6 months, and so on; also see Etheridge et al., 1997; U.S. DHHS, 1999b). People with high alcohol and drug involvement and individuals with cognitive impairments tend to benefit more by inpatient stays, with any type of treatment orientation, than those who are low in alcohol or drug involvement or are not cognitively impaired (Rychtarik et al., 2000). For those individuals who are highly dysfunctional but are able to return to loved ones in the evening, partial hospitalization is a potential choice. Thus, these programs provide direct manipulations of one's cognitive experience and indirect manipulations of cognitive experience through introduction of new, corrective behavioral experiences. They may also assist those who need improvement in general cognitive functioning.

Overall, the efficacy of cognitive behavioral therapy for the treatment of substance abuse, despite its prevalence in inpatient settings, remains to be determined. Nevertheless, components of cognitive-behavioral therapy have been correlated with positive treatment outcomes. For example, research findings suggest that individuals who are able to utilize a variety of coping skills, such as problem solving, when confronted with stressful or high-risk situations (e.g., Brown, Vik, Patterson & Grant, 1995; Donovan, 1996), and those whose self-efficacy is enhanced tend to be better functioning after substance abuse treatment (e.g., Maisto, Connors, & Zywiak, 2000; McKay, Maisto, & O'Farrell, 1993).

Cue Exposure/Cue Reactivity Approaches

Cue exposure and cue reactivity approaches are based on conditioning/learning models that underlie associative learning processes (Yin & Knowlton, 2006). For example, a preexisting association between an unconditioned stimulus (a drug) and an unconditioned response (the drug effect) results in the learned association of a variety of conditioned stimuli, such as other aspects of the drug use situation. To illustrate, repetition of the pairing of a negative mood state and drug use to achieve a desired outcome may result in the negative mood state becoming a conditioned stimulus capable of eliciting a conditioned response, such as drug-outcome cognitions and/or physiological reactivity. Classically conditioned responses have been produced in studies with animals and humans through the repeated administration of drugs (e.g., O'Brien, Childress, McLellan, & Ehrman, 1990). These conditioned responses (e.g., physiological reactivity) have been shown to persist after conventional substance abuse treatment and can predispose one to relapse (Chiauzzi & Liljegren, 1993; Childress, McLellan, Ehrman, & O'Brien, 1988; Niaura et al., 1988). These autonomic subjective responses also have been confirmed among individuals presenting for treatment for substance dependence when exposed to drug-related stimuli (O'Brien, Childress, McLellan, & Ehrman, 1990).

Cue exposure treatment protocols involve extinguishing conditioned responses through unreinforced exposure to conditioned stimuli. For example, someone who abuses cocaine might be exposed to cocaine-related stimuli such as white powder while simultaneously working toward reducing craving or a desire to use. Cue exposure protocols can reduce the desire to use that may be attributed to particular cues and prepare individuals to manage these cues outside of treatment in real-life situations. In addition, cue exposure paradigms provide an opportunity to practice coping responses (e.g., relaxation) that may, in turn, increase one's self-efficacy when reexposed to cues in the natural environment (Monti, Abrams, Kadden & Cooney, 1989).

Additionally, cue reactivity often is interpreted as a conditioned response to drug cues learned from repeated drug use (Drummond, 2000; Monti, Rohsenow, & Hutchison, 2000; Niaura et al., 1988; Rohsenow et al., 1990–1991; Rohsenow, Monti, Rubonis, & Sirota, 1994). Thus, cue reactivity paradigms involve the monitoring of a variety of physiological responses (e.g., salivation, heart rate, sweat gland activity, and neuroimaging) and obtaining self-reports of craving (or urges, as in Monti, Rohsenow, & Hutchison, 2000) during exposure to drug-related cues (e.g., paraphernalia and drug use situations). Significant increases in self-reports of craving have been found when individuals are exposed to drug-related versus drug-neutral stimuli (Carter & Tiffany, 1999). However, research has shown that the ability of urge (craving) to predict drinking after treatment is inconsistent (Monti, Rohsenow, & Hutchison, 2000), and cue-elicited craving appears to be less predictive of relapse than physiological cue reactivity (Carter & Tifffany, 1999; Drummond & Glautier, 1994; Rohsenow, Monti, Rubonis, & Sirota, 1994).

The goal of cue exposure and cue reactivity paradigms is to minimize responses to drug-related stimuli to minimize continued use. Although promising, there are several limitations to these approaches, including the possibility of spontaneous recovery over the passage of time (i.e., reintroduction of drugs may facilitate reoccurrence of conditioned stimuli and responses), availability of the drug in one's natural environment, the unreliability of some conditioned responses as predictors of drug use, the possibility that cue exposure treatment interacts with or is mediated by various cognitive processes (e.g., expectancies or implicit cognitive processes), and the possibility that treatment does not generalize to the natural environment (Conklin & Tiffany, 2001). In fact, it is possible that repeated exposures to cues could result in enhanced self-reporting of drug-related cognitions through exposure (Sussman, Horn, & Gilewski, 1990). Then, differential exposure to non-drug-related cues would be needed to reduce the retrieval strength of drug-related cues.

Cognitive Coping Programs as Alternatives to a Disease Model

Many drug abusers (alcoholics and addicts) may best regain control of their lives through a program that does not require moral betterment or belief in a higher power to gain sobriety as promoted by most twelve-step programs. Some individuals do not want to feel powerless or dependent on others or to attend meetings for the rest of their lives. Other self-help treatment alternatives to twelve-step programs place a major emphasis on individual-level cognitive coping, for example, Rational Recovery, SMART Recovery, and Secular Organizations for Sobriety.

Rational Recovery (RR), established in 1985 by Jack Trimpey, a "recovered" alcoholic, was originally based on the principles of Rational Emotive Therapy (RET). RET involves direct confrontation of one's irrational, self-defeating cognitive structures (Meichenbaum, 1977). For example, an individual may be confronted with the irrational belief that "one must be liked by everyone," which may have been associated with problem drinking. The individual learns that it is nearly impossible for one to be liked by everyone, which may then decrease self-perceptions associated with drinking or using. Rational Recovery is considered to be a nontraditional cognitive-oriented program of self-empowered recovery from substance dependency. Although Rational Recovery makes no demands on the participant, the individual should have the internal motivation and desire to maintain sobriety (abstinence from alcohol or other drugs). Rational Recovery advocates that individuals learn to abstain from drugs through many means, such as adhering to rational thought (Trimpey, 1989, 1996). Individuals learn that their use of a drug is an irrational decision or willful misconduct. Rational Recovery is a program in which the individual comes to terms with the issues of addiction and recovery and problem solves that there is no place for alcohol or other drugs in his or her life. The Addictive Voice Recognition Technique (AVRT) is used to overcome addiction; one learns to recognize and attend to the "voices in one's head" to overcome the perpetuation of the addictive behavior. That is, the rational voice, which inhibits continued use, competes with the addictive voice, which promotes continued substance use. The main goal is to strengthen the rational voice and weaken the irrational voice (the "beast") through logical self-dialogue.

Unlike Alcoholics Anonymous (A.A.), this program separates spirituality from sobriety. Meeting attendance is recommended to be between 6 months to 1 year, not lifelong; in recent times meetings are even discouraged because of the side effects of group experience. (Anecdotally, it appears that affiliation of Rational Recovery members with each other and the organization is much longer.) Moreover, the focus is on self-affirmation through taking responsibility for one's actions.

This approach identifies several specific irrational beliefs that perpetuate the addictive behavior and then offers a means to change one's emotions and behaviors. A key component of Rational Recovery is "The Big Plan," a commitment to never drink or use drugs again versus the twelve-step plan of managing "one day at a time." Rational Recovery focuses on the here-and-now and attempts to prevent relapses and to enhance self-esteem and personal empowerment. Individuals gain insight into how self-defeating beliefs encourage drinking or drug use behavior, as directed by one's "beast" or more primitive brain operations. Individuals learn to replace these thoughts with rational thoughts opposed to drinking or using (Trimpey, 1989, 1996). They feel empowered when they rationally choose not to drink or use again (their "rational" brain defeats their "irrational," "primitive" brain). Relapse prevention here involves the use of problem-solving strategies that could be used in "high-risk" situations – those in which the individual might be tempted to drink or use. In summary, Rational Recovery is a learning process based on rational self-empowerment, whereby the person "licks" the addiction and gains self-esteem in the process (also see www.rational.org).

Self-Management and Recovery Training (SMART Recovery) sponsors about 250 weekly support groups in North America for individuals who desire to abstain from any type of addictive behavior. Support groups are run by individuals who have had difficulties with drugs and by individuals who have had no personal struggles with drugs but who have received sufficient training. SMART Recovery argues that addictive behavior is problematic because it interferes with other activities and causes harm. The founders of SMART Recovery view addictive behaviors as learned habits that have become extreme and believe that the same learning contingencies apply to both substance and process addictions. Habit change is viewed as a psychological problem. The SMART program is cognitive-behavioral in orientation (Hovarth, 1999). Its Four Point Program involves enhancing and maintaining motivation (e.g., considering the costs and benefits of using and quitting and then increasing self-awareness), coping with urges (not acting on temptation, developing alternative cognitions and behaviors), solving other problems (e.g., identifying and resolving conflict), and balancing momentary and enduring satisfaction (see www.smartrecovery.org).

Secular Organizations for Sobriety/Save Our Selves (SOS) was formed in 1986 as a non-spiritual program specifically for those alcoholics or addicts who were uncomfortable with the spiritual nature of twelve-step programs (see http://www.sossobriety.org/). As a secular approach to recovery, abstinence and sobriety are both prioritized as separate issues from all other issues in one's life, including religion and spirituality. This nonreligious program encourages self-empowerment, self-determination, self-affirmation, and free thought. It is believed that sobriety can be successfully achieved through personal responsibility and self-reliance (Christopher, 1988). There are even self-help books for individuals to quit drinking and drug use that reflect a general philosophy of self-reliance (e.g., Dorsman, 1991).

SOS is a nonprofit national organization of autonomous, nonprofessional groups dedicated solely to helping individuals achieve and maintain abstinence. The only demand of SOS is that participants are sincere about wanting sobriety, the major goal of this program. Like twelve-step programs, this organization does not endorse any unrelated matters or become involved in any outside controversy. However, SOS does directly encourage the scientific study of drug abuse and it does not limit its beliefs to one theory of addiction. Members share experiences, information, strength, and encouragement in a friendly, honest, supportive, and anonymous atmosphere. Each group is self-supported, using only members' contributions. SOS also publishes a quarterly newsletter offering items of interest to recovering persons, professionals, and families of alcoholics and addicts. Many cessation strategies address cognitions as a focus and overlap with those suggested by Rational Recovery and SMART Recovery.

Relapse Prevention

The treatment of substance abuse and dependence often involves some type of relapse-prevention therapy. As noted in Chapter 15, relapse refers to events preceding the recurrence of drug use behavior and the subsequent use of a drug after a period of abstinence. A recurrence can vary from a single event (slip or lapse) to a time-limited episode or a binge to a full-blown return to the frequency and pattern of use prior to abstinence (relapse; Marlatt & Gordon, 1985). Although it is feasible that behavioral interventions with external controls during early recovery help individuals achieve abstinence following a lapse or relapse, establishing cognitive self-regulatory mechanisms are necessary for the maintenance of an abstinent state. Maintaining perceived self-control or self-efficacy and being able to exert effective coping skills when confronted with high-risk situations is essential to preventing relapse. If individuals do not effectively cope in response to high-risk stimuli, then self-efficacy (i.e., the perceived ability to cope when confronted with obstacles) may decrease and threaten one's ability to resist relapse. Regardless of measurement of coping skill level, individuals who experience greater changes in self-efficacy while in treatment have been shown to exhibit higher abstinence rates at follow-up (Miller, 1991).

Marlatt's Cognitive-Behavioral Relapse Prevention Therapy

Marlatt and Gordon (1985) conceptualize relapse prevention as a "self-management program designed to enhance the maintenance stage of the habit-change process" (p. 3). Relapse-prevention interventions assist in the acquisition and practice of effective coping strategies (i.e., cognitive and behavioral skills) for managing high-risk situations to enhance self-efficacy when faced with those situations (Larimer, Palmer, & Marlatt, 1999; Marlatt & Gordon, 1985). Relapse prevention is a *self-control program that combines behavioral-skills training, cognitive interventions, and lifestyle-change procedures, and is based on the principles of social learning theory*. The goals of the program for relapse prevention are (1) to anticipate and prevent the occurrence of a relapse after the initiation of a habit change attempt and (2) to help someone recover from a "slip" or lapse before it escalates into a full-blown relapse. Relapse prevention can be applied toward the effective maintenance of abstinence regardless of the methods used to initiate abstinence (e.g., attending A.A. meetings and aversion therapy).

Marlatt's relapse-prevention model proposes that individuals are not considered responsible for the development of their problem lifestyles but they are able to compensate for their difficulties in treatment by assuming responsibility for *changing their behavior*. As individuals undergo a process of reconditioning, cognitive restructuring, and the acquisition of various skills, they begin to accept greater responsibility for behavior change (Marlatt & Gordon, 1985). Individuals acquire new skills and learn new coping strategies through involvement in *self-management* of relapse prevention. Additionally, individuals are actively involved in the learning of mental processes including *awareness* of high-risk stimuli (vigilance) and *responsible decision-making*.

Individualized assessment of high-risk situations is an important element of Marlatt's relapse-prevention model. In general, assessment of high-risk situations is carried out either through therapist/patient interviews and descriptions about past relapse experiences, through various self-report instruments that assess likely drinking or drug use situations, or through self-monitoring of behavior (Larimer, Palmer, & Marlatt, 1999). Cognitive processes operate to recognize and monitor high-risk situations and relapse warning signs and to prepare an individual to avoid, escape, or cope with the situation when encountered.

The ability of an individual to adequately cope when in high-risk situations is a key for maintaining abstinence and enhancing self-efficacy. Enhancing one's *self-efficacy* or the expectation that one is able to effectively cope with high-risk situations without reverting to prior addictive coping responses is central to relapse-prevention therapy (Larimer, Palmer, & Marlatt, 1999; Marlatt & Gordon, 1985). Nevertheless, should a lapse or relapse occur, relapse-prevention therapy involves implementing strategies to address a type of cognitive distortion, referred to as an *abstinence violation effect* (AVE), or the feeling of loss of control over one's drug use and the perceived inability to engage in healthy behaviors. Cognitive restructuring strategies may help in challenging this type of distortion (e.g., challenging one's belief that he or she is a failure and unable to live an abstinent lifestyle) and help one to recover from temporary setbacks.

In Marlatt's relapse-prevention model, craving and urge management are also important treatment techniques to help individuals avoid relapse. For example, self-monitoring techniques can be used to evaluate urges (Marlatt & Gordon, 1985) and stimulus control techniques (e.g., removing drug use paraphernalia) can help in managing cravings and urges. Although there are several conceptualizations of cravings and urges, in Marlatt's model, cravings and urges are considered to be mediated by (1) conditioning elicited by stimuli associated with past gratification, and (2) cognitive processes associated with anticipated gratification (i.e., the expectancies for the immediate pleasurable effects of alcohol or a drug; Larimer, Palmer, & Marlatt, 1999, p. 155).

Outcome expectancies also are important cognitive determinants of relapse emphasized in relapse-prevention therapy – that is, when an individual encounters a high-risk situation, he or she may ignore or discount possible negative outcomes resulting from unhealthy behavior while anticipating only positive outcomes or the desire for immediate gratification. Relapse-prevention therapy assists in identifying high-risk situations, challenging expectancies affecting decision-making in those situations, challenging denial and rationalizations in those situations, and encouraging the generation of available alternative behavioral choices (see Larimer, Palmer, & Marlatt, 1999; Marlatt & Gordon, 1985).

The efficacy of relapse-prevention interventions relative to no-treatment controls has support in the literature (for reviews, Carroll & Comer, 1996 Irvin, Bowers, Dunn, & Wang, 1999). Relapse-prevention interventions have been found to be as effective as other treatment approaches and beneficial in reducing the intensity of relapse episodes (Carroll & Comer, 1996; Irvin, Bowers, Dunn, & Wang, 1999) and improving psychosocial functioning (Irvin, Bowers, Dunn, & Wang, 1999).

Implicit and Explicit Cognition in Cessation

A discussion of cessation and cognition would be incomplete without examining potential cessation approaches derived from the interplay between implicit (i.e., relatively automatic, effortless, associative, and difficult to control) and explicit (i.e., more effortful, consciously monitored, and deliberately controlled) cognitive processes (for definitions, see Kahneman, 2003). When an individual quits using a drug, it is likely that drug-related cues, behaviors, or outcomes will pop to mind across a wide variety of locations, situations, and times of day, particularly early in recovery. Presently, new strategies for changing implicit cognitive processes are on the horizon and may be a future focus for new generations of prevention and treatment programs (see Stacy & Ames, 2001; Wiers & Stacy, 2006; also Wiers, de Jong, Havermans, & Jelicic, 2004). Several prevention strategies for changing implicit cognitions toward drug use were addressed in Chapter 12, and similar components may be adapted for use in the treatment of substance abuse.

To date, some of the strategies noted later have been tested in laboratory settings but have not yet been implemented or evaluated in cessation programs, whereas others are still being developed or have been shown to work for other health behaviors. Nevertheless, one could speculate that various implicit cognition components may be integrated with current cognitive-behavioral approaches that assess and/or indirectly effect deliberately controlled cognitive processes to elicit behavior change such as drug abuse cessation. For example, an implicit cognition approach may be useful in assessing treatment progress or the relative accessibility of newly learned and practiced coping strategies for high-risk situations (i.e., what is spontaneously activated when high-risk cues are presented; Stacy & Ames, 2001). It may be that cognitive-behavioral approaches to behavior change already affect both implicit and explicit cognitive processes by directly challenging beliefs and/or irrational thinking and by building self-efficacy around alternative coping behaviors. Assessing not only explicit but also implicit cognitive processes may provide valuable information about one's treatment progress.

New intervention approaches to address the influence of implicit processes on addictive behaviors are now being evaluated in laboratory settings. One approach currently being evaluated uses varieties of *"attentional retraining."* The general idea is that an attentional bias for drug-related cues is an important determinant of cue approach behavior, drug craving, and drug-seeking behavior (see Franken, 2003) so retraining drug-dependent individuals to focus attention away from drug-related cues may, in turn, reduce craving and drug-seeking behavior. An attentional-retraining approach may prevent dysfunctional attentional bias from increasing in strength and promoting continued drug use. In this approach, measures used to assess an attentional bias are adapted to train attention away from drug-related cues. For example, in a visual probe task, a target replaces a drug-related picture in a number of cases, whereas, in retraining sessions, the target replaces a neutral picture in most cases. In this way, substance-dependent individuals implicitly learn to not attend to cues for their drug of choice. Initial findings from different labs have shown some promising findings using attentional-retraining paradigms (e.g., Field & Eastwood, 2005; Wiers et al., under review).

A second approach includes implementing techniques or interventions grounded in basic memory research that focus on the strengthening of new associations in memory (Stacy & Ames, 2001). For example, implementation of memory enhancement components such as *elaborative processing of new associations* may help minimize the influence of preexisting associations and promote the influence of more protective associative cognitive structures in long-term memory between certain drug abuse cessation materials and contexts associated with drug use. Then program materials may be more likely to be spontaneously activated in memory when an individual is confronted with strong drug-use cues (for discussion, see Stacy, Ames, & Knowlton, 2004). For example, an intervention could focus on tying non-drug use coping program information (e.g., seeking social support) and high-risk situations (e.g., finding beer on a kitchen counter) together in memory (Stacy & Ames, 2001). With sufficient semantic relatedness to the preexisting memories, through repetition, or simply through the novelty of the new memory created, program information may become accessible enough to spontaneously "pop to mind" when an individual is in a risky situation.

In addition, interventions could include components that focus on changing outcome expectancies or enhancing such executive functions as working memory or other more controlled inhibition mechanisms to potentially put the "brake" on behavioral tendencies resulting from more spontaneous or automatic processes. For example, an intervention might make negative alcohol outcome expectancies more salient or debunk positive expectancies that promote behavior through an "expectancy challenge" intervention. With an expectancy challenge intervention, some individuals consume alcohol and others consume placebos while engaging in various enjoyable interactions. Following the social

Table 17.1. *Types of cognitive processes-related cessation treatments*

Cognitive-behavioral interventions	Interventions focus on changing behavior patterns or frequency of behavior through the use of various techniques such as stimulus control, organism control, response control, and reinforcement control. Decision-making, self-instructional training, and cognitive restructuring are examples of organism/cognitive approaches.
Cognitive-behavioral chemical dependency inpatient treatment	These 24-hour supervised community-based residential treatments are frequently based on the principles of Narcotics or Alcoholics Anonymous. In addition, these programs utilize a variety of methods to eliminate chemical dependency through continuous exposure to structured cognitive-behavioral programming. Direct confrontation of thinking, belief change techniques, meditation, and self-talk techniques are typically used.
Cue exposure/cue reactivity treatment paradigms	Paradigms are based on conditioning/learning models that underlie associative learning processes. Cue exposure treatment protocols involve extinguishing conditioned responses through unreinforced exposure to conditioned stimuli.
Cognitive-coping programs	Cognitive-oriented self-help treatments involve self-help alternatives to twelve-step programs and place a major emphasis on individual-level cognitive coping. Examples of cognitive coping programs include Rational Recovery, SMART Recovery, and Secular Organizations for Sobriety. Rational emotive techniques and cognitive coping strategies (e.g., waiting out urges, distraction, self-talk), as well as decision-making, cognitive restructuring, and self-instructional training, typically are employed.
Relapse prevention	Cognitive-focused relapse prevention involves maintaining perceived self-control or self-efficacy and being able to exert effective coping skills when confronted with high-risk situations.
Explicit cognitive strategies	Potential explicit cognitive components include directly challenging beliefs and irrational thinking (e.g., with an alcohol expectancy challenge), building self-efficacy around alternative coping behaviors, and enhancing working memory and other executive functions.
Implicit cognitive strategies	Potential implicit cognitive components include attentional retaining, elaborative processing of new associations, and formulating implementation intentions.

activities, individuals attempt to determine who in the group actually consumed the alcohol (including themselves) and who did not. Errors made by individuals in identifying those individuals who consumed alcohol are pointed out to challenge one's expectancies about alcohol effects versus the actual pharmacological effects (e.g., Darkes & Goldman, 1993, 1998; Dunn, Lau, & Cruz, 2000; Wiers, Van de Luitgaarden, & Van den Wildenberg, 2005). Of course, this type of intervention is unlikely to be used for substances other than alcohol (although it is possible) and is not appropriate for youth, but it can be considered for young adults who are not suffering from substance use problems.

Alternatively, an approach that enhances executive functions (and could be used for all populations and all substances) might be to repeatedly role-play some complex social situations that might tax working memory to make coping responses more spontaneous. Aspects of working memory involved in making use of treatment information in demanding situations (e.g., high-risk situations) may be important determinants of effective behavioral control. Reduced attentional resources, whether based on individual deficits in one's executive functions or working memory load inherent in a given situation can reduce the chance of behavioral control. Also, it may be helpful to tailor treatment components to train working memory (cf. Olesen, Westerberg, & Klingberg, 2004) for individuals with lower working memory capacity that may need improved attentional resources.

Finally, another approach is to try to automatize action plans that lead to alternative behaviors instead of drug use. For example, *implementation intentions* or simple if-then action plans may lead to action without controlled processes. That is, establishing a cue–response association may give a specified goal-directed behavior a greater chance of being automatically initiated by situational cues. For example: "If I go to a party, then I will drink only cola." Because drugs negatively affect controlled processes, this type of strategy may help individuals to automatically regulate or control their use of alcohol and drugs (Prestwich, Conner, & Lawton, 2006). Implementation intentions have shown strong effects with several health behaviors (Gollwitzer & Sheeran, 2004; Orbell & Sheeran, 2002; for review, Prestwich, Conner, & Lawton, 2006) (Table 17.1).

Summary

This chapter focused on the importance of addressing cognitive components in the treatment of addictive behaviors. Cognitions, which mediate behavioral tendencies in addictive behaviors, are likely to be key determinants of treatment outcome success. Changing these mediators of behavior is not an easy process because for many people drug use has been reinforced through repetition of the behavior to satisfy individual motives of use (e.g., coping or to enhance positive affect). Learning and maintaining self-control over the addictive behavior is a constant struggle that is frequently lost and therefore treatment protocols must train relapse-prevention strategies. Changing addictive behaviors requires tapping into or somehow "hijacking" the cognitive mediators that control the drug use behavior to enhance the automatic self-regulation of one's behavior in high-risk situations. With increased understanding of the interplay between cognitive inhibitory control processes and associative cognitive processes and their influence on behavior, the advancement of current cognitive-behavior treatment protocols for drug abuse may be assured, with the goal of benefiting treatment outcomes.

This chapter presents drug misuse treatment from the perspective of social interaction processes and social group structure. There are many cessation strategies that make use of social processes. For example, sometimes a "motivational intervention" is implemented to confront the drug misuser with his or her detrimental effects on others. Once recognition of the problem behavior is understood or perhaps debated among the drug misuser and others, formal or informal treatment providers (e.g., a therapist, twelve-step sponsor or group) may be selected either by the drug misuser or by external agents.

Next, therapeutic relationships are attempted. If a solid therapeutic alliance is created (i.e., a trusting and mutually respectful relationship is developed), progress toward solutions to problematic substance use will be achieved. The person in recovery may attempt to learn alternative social behaviors. Social skills training, such as assertiveness training and anger or other mood management, may be needed for some individuals to attempt reintegration into a drug-free social world. Additional social-level therapeutic modalities may need to be provided as well, including involvement in a recovery community.

In this chapter, we include a brief discussion of the use of the Johnson Institute's motivational intervention. Next, we discuss the twelve-step group recovery model, selection of therapeutic agents, and establishing the therapeutic relationship. Use of motivational interviewing is mentioned as one tool for solidifying the therapeutic relationship. We then discuss social skills training, the therapeutic community model, sober-living homes, family therapy, group therapy, outpatient treatment, use of telephone hotlines, and use of behavioral contracting. Finally, naturally occurring social networks in cessation and a social perspective on relapse prevention are discussed.

Johnson Institute and Motivational Intervention

The Johnson Institute-style motivational intervention is a confrontational method used to encourage the substance abuser to acknowledge the negative impact of his or her problem on self and others and to be motivated to change through confrontation with family and significant others. This intervention involves the following five steps: (1) inquiry, (2) assessment, (3) preparation, (4) intervention, and (5) follow-up/case management (Storti, 2001). During an *inquiry*, individuals gather contact information and screen whether a particular individual requires an intervention. The *assessment* process generally involves family members or significant others that will participate in the intervention. *Preparation* involves rehearsal of what significant others will say when confronting the substance abuser. During the actual confrontation (the *intervention*), significant others express their feelings, their specific current concerns, and their worries about the future. During the *follow-up/case management* phase, the substance-abusing individual enters treatment. There is the potential for the intervention to backfire – that is, the substance abuser may oppose individuals confronting him or her. The substance abuser may not be willing to enter treatment or admit to having a drug problem. Family members and significant others are prepared for this outcome, although if conducted properly, it is likely that at least some acceptance of a problem will be acknowledged by the substance abuser.

There is some empirical evidence that the Johnson Institute approach is helpful in getting substance abusers into treatment and perhaps retaining them in treatment (Liepman, Nirenberg, & Begin, 1989; Miller, Meyers, & Tonigan, 1999). This approach, however, may not be as effective as less confrontive approaches. For example, in a randomized clinical trial, Miller, Meyers, and Tonigan (1999) randomly assigned 130 concerned significant others (CSOs) to one of three different counseling approaches: (1) an Al-Anon facilitation therapy designed to encourage involvement in the twelve-step program, (2) a Johnson Institute intervention to prepare for a confrontational family meeting, or (3) a community reinforcement and family training (CRAFT) approach teaching behavior change skills to use at home. All approaches were manual guided, with 12 hours of contact. Follow-up interviews continued for the subsequent 12 months. Miller and colleagues found that the CRAFT approach was more effective in engaging initially unmotivated problem drinkers in treatment (64%) as compared with Al-Anon (13%) and Johnson interventions (about 30%). This was in part because most CSOs decided not to go through with the family confrontation (about 70%) but among those who did, most (75%) succeeded in getting the drinker into treatment. All approaches were associated with similar improvement in CSO functioning and relationship quality.

Twelve-Step Recovery Group Model

We believe that twelve-step programming involves all four levels of cessation. However, we view the small group social level as most fundamental to these organizations. Twelve-step programs such as Alcoholics Anonymous (A.A.) and Narcotics Anonymous (NA) provide the basic philosophy of change for many inpatient and outpatient alcohol and drug abuse treatment facilities in the United States in particular but also worldwide. More importantly, these programs probably are the main sources of peer social support for the maintenance of habit change. A.A. and NA are abstinence-oriented, multidimensional, nonprofit, humanistic, voluntary, socially supportive, self-help fellowships for individuals for whom drug use has become problematic. Bill Wilson and Dr. Robert Smith, both self-proclaimed alcoholics, founded A.A. in 1935 (Figure 18.1). A.A. has become one of the most widely disseminated self-help treatment groups, and membership is estimated at more than 2 million. A.A. begat more than 100 other twelve-step programs based on the structure and principles of A.A. (e.g., NA, Marijuana Anonymous [MA], Cocaine Anonymous [C.A.], etc.). All of the twelve-step sobriety-based programs are based on a *disease model of addiction* and require complete abstinence from all drugs except coffee and cigarettes (although a Nicotine Anonymous fellowship also does exist; www.nicotine-anonymous.org). The only requirement for membership in twelve-step programs is the desire to stop using. The

Figure 18.1. Dr. Robert Smith and Bill Wilson, both self-proclaimed alcoholics, founded Alcoholics Anonymous in 1935.

twelve-step program model is self-supporting, does not accept outside contributions, and has no opinion on outside issues.

Arguably, the disease model of addiction proposed in the writings of twelve-step groups is consistent with neurobiological and cognitive models (discussed in the previous two chapters). Drug addiction and alcoholism are thought to be "allergies" that are manifested by a baseline subjective sense of restlessness, irritability, and discontent ("r.i.d."; A.A., 1976; MA, 1995; NA, 1988), in conjunction with (implicit) processes that perpetuate alcohol or drug use in high-risk situations. The alcoholic or drug addict, when sober, may feel quite uncomfortable within his or her skin and can fall victim to his or her alcoholic/addict "voice." Self-statements such as "I won't use cocaine as long as this terrible event doesn't happen, but it happened," "I could smoke marijuana safely under a certain condition; this is it," or automatic thoughts of "It would be nice to have a drink" may suddenly pop to mind as individuals pass by a club or experience emotional turmoil. When alcohol is imbibed or another drug used, often without much forethought, there may be a great calming effect, perhaps subjective alterations in sensory perceptions, and perhaps a greater subjective sense that one's role in the world is quite different than it was before drinking or using. At the same time, there may be a loss of control over the amount used, generally after using for a brief period of hours or days and loss of behavioral control exhibited while drunk or high.

However, the solution to addiction in twelve-step programs is very much group-based. The Twelve Traditions outline A.A.'s basic premises about the organization, such as ensuring members' anonymity and protecting the privacy and integrity of the organization, its leadership, and the sobriety of its members (Yoder, 1990). The Twelve Steps, which involve use of the first-person plural throughout ("we"), provide an internal process of change

Table 18.1. Twelve Steps program of recovery

1. We admitted that we were powerless over our addiction, that our lives had become unmanageable.
2. We came to believe that a power greater than ourselves could restore us to sanity.
3. We made a decision to turn our will and our lives over to the care of God, as we understood Him.
4. We made a searching and fearless moral inventory of ourselves.
5. We admitted to God, to ourselves, and to another human being the exact nature of our wrongs.
6. We were entirely ready to have God remove all these defects of character.
7. We humbly asked Him to remove our shortcomings.
8. We made a list of all persons we had harmed and became willing to make amends to them all.
9. We made direct amends to such people wherever possible, except when to do so would injure them or others.
10. We continued to take personal inventory and when we were wrong promptly admitted it.
11. We sought through prayer and meditation to improve our conscious contact with God, as we understood Him, praying only for knowledge of His will for us and the power to carry that out.
12. Having had a spiritual awakening as a result of these steps, we tried to carry this message to addicts (alcoholics), and to practice these principles in all our affairs.

Note: Also see www.alcoholics-anonymous.org or www.na.org.

through which members break through the "denial" that may accompany the addiction, admit to being powerless over alcohol or other drugs, and learn to make lifelong changes in daily living that include helping others (Spiegel & Mulder, 1986). By following the twelve steps, members learn to trust a "higher power," which could be their "home group" as well as a deity or another form as a means to obtain a daily reprieve from urges or thoughts of using drugs (e.g., Chappel, 1992). Individuals "work the steps" along with other members of the organization, including a sponsor.

Anonymity is an essential component of twelve-step programs, affirming the concept of *principles before personalities.* The anonymity of membership creates an atmosphere of intimacy, trust, and support. Members maintain personal anonymity at the level of the press, radio, and films. The twelve-step program is not connected with political, religious, or law enforcement groups. Individuals of all ages, races, sexual identity, and religion, or lack of religion, may join the program. However, an attitude of indifference or intolerance toward spiritual principles may defeat one's recovery. Honesty, open-mindedness, and willingness (H.O.W.) are essential components of the recovery process.

The group ("we") focus of twelve-step programming is evident in the Twelve Steps as a program of recovery (Table 18.1).

More on Peer Support in Twelve-Step Programming
The fellowship facilitated within these organizations provides extensive group support. For example, this includes twelve-step groups for young people: 250 links for young people in A.A. were found on the Internet (June 7, 2005, search), even though relatively few young people are interested in twelve-step programs. An essential component of twelve-step programs is that drug abusers help one another to stay clean and sober. These programs are built on the principle that a recovering alcoholic or addict can altruistically and effectively help a fellow addict to gain or maintain sobriety. Members openly talk about their struggles and successes and develop problem-solving skills, as well as friendships with others, comforted in the knowledge that they are not alone in their plight.

An important adjunct to the program is self-selecting a sponsor who provides support and helps to guide the individual in the program (Sussman & Ames, 2001). Twelve-step programs provide a means of social support through meetings, fellowship, and sponsorship as well as through clubs (particularly the A.A. Alano Clubs) that provide a gathering place for fellowship. A.A. weddings, funerals, and other events often are held within specific groups, meeting many of twelve-step program members' social needs in sobriety.

Support for and Criticisms of Twelve-Step Programs

There has been much anecdotal support of A.A., in particular, but relatively little controlled research. Often empirical support for the efficacy of A.A. is based solely on the number of individuals who participate in A.A. or on the testimony of individual members. However, some empirical outcome research does exist. For example, some correlational studies have shown a favorable relationship between A.A. participation and sobriety. Alternatively, studies of attrition in A.A. and experimental studies generally fail to support A.A.'s efficacy over other treatments (see Galaif & Sussman, 1995). Some work suggests that A.A., cognitive behavioral treatment, and motivational interviewing approaches are about equal in effectiveness for the treatment of alcoholism (Project MATCH; Connors, 1998).

Unfortunately, at present, only approximately 8% of the members of A.A. are 21–30 years old and only 2% are under 21 years old. Admitting to a sense of powerlessness, a key principle of twelve-step programs, may conflict with teens' search for autonomy, as may perceiving themselves as having to remain abstinent (perceiving themselves as having "hit bottom"; Rivers, Greenbaum, & Goldberg, 2001), both of which present potential barriers to effective twelve-step program participation. Treatment among teens needs to grapple with the tendency to engage in a relatively great deal of limit testing (Kaminer, 2001). Attendance at twelve-step meetings among teens (teens with teens) has been found to predict better outcomes. These outcomes are mediated by motivation but not coping (Kelly, Myers, & Brown, 2000). Social support (e.g., companionship) also may be important.

One major criticism of twelve-step programs is that some researchers and practitioners may think of the organization as having cultlike characteristics (Bufe, 1991). Some critics believe that twelve-step programs encourage dependence on the program itself, openly discourage skepticism, and may lead to a lack of involvement in other social organizations and resentment toward those not involved in the programs. Also, twelve-step programs have been criticized as becoming a substitute of one addiction for another. Furthermore, some members actively promote the idea that twelve-step programs are the only "road" to recovery. Those who do not readily embrace twelve-step concepts may be made to feel unwelcome at meetings (Bufe, 1991). In addition, those who do not remain in twelve-step programs may be accused of having "character defects" or lacking the desire to stop drinking or using instead of being sympathized with or being viewed as individuals pursuing other avenues of gaining sobriety (Trimpey, 1989, 1996).

However, there is no named leader and no hierarchical, authoritarian structure within the organization, and all groups are autonomous. Twelve-step programs do not exploit members financially, nor do they become actively involved in the political arena, exemplary of cults. They go to no lengths to retain members, nor are they supposed to actively recruit newcomers or provide closed, all-encompassing environments exclusively for members; rather, twelve-step programs provide an open environment for anyone who wants to stop drinking or using. Thus, twelve-step programs are not cults, although they appear to have some cultlike qualities, as do many fellowships. Twelve-step programs provide a *sense of belonging* to a group for many individuals who essentially have become outsiders from mainstream communities. This sense of belonging to a group that has insight into the drug abusers' experiences, and is willing to provide social support without judgment, is an important aspect that many other treatment protocols may not provide.

The Cure for the "Disease": On Spirituality

Twelve-step programs strongly espouse the notion that spiritual experiences are the means to arrest the diseases of alcoholism and drug addiction. Program literature asserts that these diseases are not only physical, mental, and emotional diseases but also diseases of the spirit (e.g., A.A., 1976). The topic of spirituality as applied to human affairs has a very long history. Perhaps the main influence in the twentieth century has been the work of William James. In 1902, James argued that the basis of personal religious experience is derived from two considerations: (1) that there is something wrong with the human condition as it "naturally stands" and (2) that people are remedied through connection with higher powers (see James, 1958). James's work influenced the thinking of the pioneers of A.A., which suggested that belief in a higher power, and attempts to conform one's behavior to that of the higher power, would lead to recovery from alcoholism. Wellness advocates, in turn, were strongly influenced by A.A. and espoused theories such as salutogenesis (belief in and comfort from holding a personal construct of life; Antonovsky, 1984). Wellness research and recovery movements are inextricably related. Arguably, conscientiousness (thinking of others) and experiential peace (or lack of negative affectivity) may be the two main components of spirituality that are attained through a change in beliefs and engagement in spiritual-related activities (Sussman, Nezami, & Mishra, 1997). Spiritual-related activities often appear to involve "good" actions within small groups.

Who Do Twelve-Step Programs Help?

These programs tend to help those who actively participate in the programs and become stable members. These programs seem to attract certain types of individuals. Stable members tend to be middle-class, male, gregarious (comfortable in social contexts), comfortable with high self-disclosure, and single or estranged from one's family. Also, stable members tend to have familial problems, feel anxious and lonely, are older and less educated, embrace a disease model, report more drug-related symptoms prior to treatment, and are more religious than nonmembers or those who drop out of these programs (Galaif & Sussman, 1995).

Who Should Be the Treatment Agent (Former Drug Abusers or Professionals)?

Twelve-step programs accept the therapeutic value of one drug abuser helping another – that one "alcoholic" or "addict" can best understand and help another alcoholic or addict. An integral aspect of many inpatient treatment programs based on the principles of NA or A.A. is the employment of certified chemical dependency counselors with personal histories of drug abuse and familiarity with the standards and values of drug-using groups. These individuals function as role models that, by example, demonstrate the contrasting drug lifestyle with more prosocial lifestyle changes. The belief is that the sooner drug abusers face their problems within society and in everyday living, the faster they become acceptable, responsible, and productive members of society. Ex-abusers treating current abusers lend credibility to treatment programs and insight into drug-using groups. Also, many professional non-drug-abusing ("normies") treatment agents often are provided with minimal training in chemical dependency while in professional school.

There are, however, aspects of treatment that ex-drug abuser counselors may not be able to thoroughly address or acknowledge as attributable to causes other than the "addiction disease." Therefore, treatment programs often employ professional personnel who might be better equipped to deal with issues of comorbidity (e.g., clinical depression, post-traumatic stress disorder, eating disorders, and bipolar disorder) and are able to teach social skills training and provide other therapeutic services (e.g., see Hovarth, 1999, or www.smartrecovery.org).

The Therapeutic Relationship and Motivational Interviewing

In any treatment, establishing a positive relationship with the substance abuser is a sin quo non of treatment success. The capacity for experiencing vicariously the substance abuser's experience (empathy); the ability to be oneself (genuineness); the ability to focus on the most immediate concerns first; the ability to express warmth, be consistent, be kind, and be culturally sensitive; and the ability to be patient are essential counselor characteristics (Lewis, 2005). Making direct use of the therapeutic relationship to induce behavioral change is what motivational interviewing is all about.

Motivational interviewing (Miller & Rollnick, 1991) is based on principles of cognitive therapy, Carl Rogers' client-centered approach, and the Transtheoretical Model. Motivational interviewing involves a series of procedures for therapists to help clients clarify goals and follow through with their efforts to change behavior. Motivation is conceptualized as the probability that a person will enter into, continue, and adhere to a specific change strategy (Council for Philosophical Studies, 1981). Motivation for change can fluctuate over time, especially for some highly ambivalent individuals unsure of change. *Addressing this ambivalence* is considered a key for facilitating behavioral change.

Motivational interviewing involves eight strategies to motivate behavior change (see Table 18.2). Motivational interviewing may prove a valuable brief treatment option for teens, although current data suggest its advantage over no treatment or other modalities in only approximately 30% of the studies within which it has been examined (see Grenard, Ames, Pentz, & Sussman, 2006). Adaptations of motivational interviewing, however, have been shown to be effective strategies among some groups, especially among alcohol abusing adult populations (for review, Burke, Arkowitz, & Dunn, 2002; Burke, Arkowitz, & Menchola, 2003; Dunn, Deroo, & Rivara, 2001; Noonan & Moyers, 1997).

Social Skills Training

An integral component of cognitive-behavioral programs implemented throughout treatment is social skills training. Social skills training also might be instructed as an adjunct

Table 18.2. *Motivational interviewing strategies to affect behavior change*

Giving advice	Involves problem identification, clarification of the need for change, and encouraging specific change; eliciting and reinforcing change goals is essential.
Removing impediments to change	Involves removing impediments to change through impediment identification, effective problem solving, and cognitive restructuring.
Providing choices	Involves providing a range of positive behavioral choices from which to choose; motivation to change is elicited from the client (the client "owns" change goals).
Decreasing desirability of not changing	Involves promoting benefits of behavior change; readiness to change is considered a fluctuating product of interpersonal interaction.
Empathy	Involves showing warmth, respect, caring, and understanding towards an individual; client autonomy and therapeutic partnership is emphasized.
Providing accurate feedback	Involves providing accurate feedback of an individual's behavior and outcomes to aid in altering or modifying risky behaviors.
Clarifying goals	Involves clarifying goals by confronting the individual about discrepancies between future goals and the present situation; identifying and removing equivocation is a key to change.
Development of self-efficacy	Involves supporting the development of self-efficacy through active helping.

to motivational interviewing (Grenard, Ames, Pentz, & Sussman, 2006). Social skills training may include the teaching or reinforcing of self-control skills (showing restraint under simulated high-risk conditions in social interactions; urge control), shaping of good listening or conversational skills (e.g., through direction instruction, role-play instruction, or by example), instruction of anger or other feeling management (e.g., learning how to cope with feelings in an appropriate manner in interpersonal situations through role-playing), and learning stimulus control approaches (learning how to remove oneself from drug cues such as escape from drug using groups).

Because a lack of social skills may influence drug use (e.g., the inability to refuse drug offers and involvement in drug-related activities), social skills training often involves assertiveness training. Methods of assertiveness training vary, but in general, assertiveness training focuses on enhancing appropriate expression of feelings and personal rights, and skills training in refusal of unreasonable requests of others. Role-playing is a primary vehicle for social skills training. Often modeling of assertive behavior, behavioral rehearsal, practice through role-playing, performance, and immediate feedback, and reinforcement components are included in the development of role-playing skills (Sussman et al., 1995).

One example of social skills training is instruction in drug refusal. Individuals brainstorm situations in which they have to refuse drugs, as well as ways in which individuals offer or pressure one to use. For example, drinkers might ask, "How come you're not drinking? What's the matter – you're too good to drink with us?" Recognition of risk situations helps the individual learn to resist social pressures. Individual goals may be established, such as feeling comfortable with refusal assertion and reinforcing a personal commitment to abstain, and a list of refusal techniques may be generated (Marlatt & Gordon, 1985). Role-playing is a technique used to provide opportunities to practice refusal methods in a nonthreatening, simulation environment in which mistakes do not lead to relapse.

Therapeutic Community Model

In this model, the community serves as the primary therapist. Although the client may have a primary counselor, everyone in the community (often in residential settings) has the responsibility to serve as therapists and teachers. Nearly all activities are part of the therapeutic process. Peers often lead peer-group meetings. Individuals involved in the therapeutic process are mainly responsible for their change process and also assume partial responsibility for the recovery of their peers. Clients are provided with increased responsibilities and privileges as they pass through structured phases of treatment within the community. For example, individuals who have relatively longer sober time may organize a residential setting social or lead a meeting on clean-up duties. One-on-one counseling, remedial education, and occupational training also are provided (Blum, 1995). Modification of the therapeutic community model for teens includes use of shorter stays, family member participation, limited use of peer pressure, and less reliance on use of life experiences to foster self-understanding (Jainchill, Bhattacharya, & Yagelka, 1995).

Sober-Living Homes

Community-based residential or sober-living homes are safe environments for those who have completed residential treatment or inpatient care or for those who need a structured living situation to maintain sobriety. These types of group homes are alcohol and drug-free environments where residents are expected to pay their own rent and buy their own food but live communally. Sober-living homes provide peer group support for those in recovery. Residents are expected to work or attend school or attend treatment sessions outside of the home. Generally, there are different treatment levels and staff supervision for different clients. For example, some clients may be under house arrest and need to be monitored more closely. Often twelve-step meetings are held in the group home, or residents may be required to attend a certain number of meetings outside the group home each week. Individuals are generally required to undergo random drug testing and there is zero tolerance for alcohol and other drug use or violence. Often, therapeutic community model features are included (e.g., those with more sober time take on more responsibility; peers helping each other recover).

Family Therapy

Family therapy tends to view alcohol and drug abuse as a family (systems) problem. In other words, focusing on changing part of the system (e.g., the substance abuser's behavior) may effectively change other parts of the system (e.g., other family members' behavior toward the drug abuser). Family relationships are viewed as problematic and boundaries within the family are viewed as distorted (e.g., enmeshed or disengaged). Family therapy is conducted with professional staff (Blum, 1995). In family therapy for drug abuse, the family's strengths and resources are utilized to assist in developing means for family members and the substance abuser to live effectively without drugs and to minimize the negative impact or consequences of the substance abuser's behavior on the family system or, in other words, to help the system integrate and heal. Family therapy (mediated by a professional) provides neutral turf for family members to express their feelings and concerns and a means of working toward improved communication among family members.

Family therapy may be particularly important for teen substance abusers. Some family-based treatments that have been relatively prevalent in the teen substance abuse disorder treatment literature include Structural/Strategic Family Therapy, Multidimensional Family Therapy (MDFT), and Multisystemic Family Therapy (MST). In general, these treatments attempt to involve all family members, improve parent–child communication, and provide skills training for parents (child management practices such as limit setting and appropriate parent behavior) and youths (appropriate role as a teen; Liddle & Dakof, 1995; Weinberg et al., 1998).

Liddle et al. (2004) contrasted outpatient peer group therapy with family-based treatment (MDFT) among eighty low-income, urban youth and found family therapy to be superior over the course of treatment. In several other recent studies, family-based teen substance abuse treatment has been found to lead to relatively greater recruitment and retention than other modalities (Kaminer & Slesnick, 2005). It is less clear, however, if family-based treatment is superior in behavioral outcomes to other treatment approaches. An outpatient combined cognitive-behavioral group therapy and family therapy program (Family and Coping Skills, FACS; 3-month duration) for treatment of substance abuse and depression was found to be feasible and was associated with improvement in mood and substance abuse-related behavior (for marijuana, not alcohol) the week following treatment among a sample of 13 teens (Curry et al., 2003). A similar pattern of results was found in a randomized clinical trial involving 114 teens (Kaminer & Slesnick, 2005). At 4 months' follow-up, a significant reduction in marijuana use was found in the combined treatment and functional family therapy condition. At 7 months' follow-up, the combined treatment and psycho-educational group therapy were relatively effective, compared to family treatment only. Thus, a combined/comprehensive approach in treatment appears to work better than family or group approaches alone. The latter two approaches show equivocal relative effects on behavior.

Group Therapy

Group therapy provides a means for drug abusers trying to recover to provide corrective feedback to each other and is relatively less expensive than individual therapy. However, individual attention and the potential for deviancy training could result by group participation (O'Leary et al., 2002). Group therapy, with other clients, provides peer support, feedback, and confrontation, guided by a trained leader. In-depth attention on psychological issues that might occur in group therapy is relatively unlikely to occur in use of self-help groups. In early recovery, the therapist serves as a coach and a monitor. As recovery progresses, the therapist helps group members resolve issues of trauma and learn intimacy with others, as well as learn how to express feelings appropriately.

Social Resources and Outpatient Treatment

Outpatient services are appropriate for individuals who have a diagnosis of substance abuse but do not require treatment in residential facilities, partial hospitalization (e.g., day treatment), or inpatient settings. Outpatient services may be most appropriate when an individual's environmental support systems (e.g., family and those with whom the individual lives) and clinical indicators do not impact negatively on the treatment process or reduce the likelihood of success. Outpatient treatment is counterindicated if the individual is suicidal, is violent, or demonstrates any thought disorder or other concomitant emotional, psychological, or behavioral crises that require more intensive supervision, and when the individual reports difficulties maintaining sobriety without 24-hour supervised treatment. For example, Funk, McDermeit, Godley, & Adams (2003) found that teens with a history of victimization showed better outcomes in residential care than as outpatients.

Outpatient services often provide weekly group therapy, personal counseling sessions, random drug testing, and case management, designed to assist those who are abstinent and adjusting to the community. In addition, effective problem solving may be instructed and reality therapy, as well as several cognitive-behavioral approaches, may be utilized (Etheridge et al., 1997). Outpatient treatment may range from 2 to 20 hours a week of treatment, depending on the psychiatric and social concerns of the individual. For example, Rivers, Greenbaum, and Goldberg (2001) found that weekly or twice-a-week individual outpatient treatment, which included psycho-education and instruction in use of decision-making, was associated with improvement of depression and anxiety-related symptoms at 8 weeks' follow-up among 129 teen substance abusers. In a study among 194 youth who attended a structured, outpatient, group-based treatment program, Battjes et al. (2004) found decreased levels of self-reported marijuana use (but not alcohol use) up to 12 months post-entry into treatment. In general, outcome evaluation research of intensive outpatient treatment suggests that mutual-help group participation treatment paradigms are associated with better outcomes (Kelly, Stout, Zywiak, & Schneider, 2006; Mathias, 1999).

Use of Hotlines

Hotlines provide a means for a person to reach out for assistance either when contemplating quitting drug use, to search for treatment, or for support to prevent relapse. Various toll-free hotlines have been set up to provide 24-hour service for emergency and other treatment information. For example, these include 1-800-COCAINE, 1–888-4-AL-ANON, and the National Institute on Drug Abuse referral helpline, 800-662-4357 or 800-662-HELP. Many twelve-step programs also have people on phone lines 24 hours a day to provide assistance to a phone caller, as well as pathfinders, who provide information on local meetings over the telephone.

Contracting with Another Person

Contracting is a method of formalizing or reinforcing an individual's commitment to change and is helpful when individuals express ambivalence about change or have been unable to maintain abstinence or control their behaviors. Contracting usually involves a written agreement, signed and agreed on by involved parties, that includes behavioral constraints on observable behaviors through the use of reinforcers. Contracting can include contingencies describing penalties for violation of the contract (such as paying a fine in the event of a lapse or relapse) and positive reinforcers (i.e., tangible goods such as food or money) for conforming to the contract. This approach may work while the contract is in operation. For example, contracting between members of a couple in which one member is alcoholic has shown some promise (e.g., Behavioral Couples Therapy; O'Farrell & Fals-Stewart, 2000). Contracts with chemically dependent patients are the core of primary treatment and

Table 18.3. Types of social interaction and social group cessation treatments

Therapeutic community model	The community serves as the primary therapist. While the client may have a primary counselor, everyone in the community (often in residential settings) has the responsibility to serve as therapists and teachers. Peers often lead peer group meetings. Individuals involved in the therapeutic process are mainly responsible for their change process and also assume partial responsibility for the recovery of their peers.
Sober-living homes	Community-based residential homes that are safe environments for those who have completed residential treatment or inpatient care, or for those who need a structured living situation to maintain sobriety.
Family therapy	Provides neutral turf for the drug abuser and other family members to express their feelings and concerns and a means of working toward improved communication among family members.
Group therapy	Provides a means for drug abusers working toward recovery to provide corrective feedback to each other and is relatively less expensive than individual therapy.
Outpatient treatment	May provide weekly group therapy, personal counseling sessions, random drug testing, and case management. In addition, effective problem solving may be instructed and reality therapy, as well as several cognitive-behavioral approaches, may be utilized. Outpatient services are most appropriate when one's environmental support systems and clinical indicators do not impact negatively on the treatment process or reduce the likelihood of success.
Hotlines	Toll-free telephone lines that provide 24-hour service for emergency and other treatment information. They provide a means for a person to reach out for assistance either when contemplating quitting drug use, to search for treatment, or for support to prevent relapse.
Contracting with another person	A method of formalizing or reinforcing one's commitment to change. Can involve a written agreement, signed and agreed upon by involved parties, that includes behavioral constraints on observable behaviors through the use of reinforcers. Contracting can include contingencies describing penalties for violation of the contract and positive reinforcers for conforming to the contract.

continuing care, according to Talbott and Crosby (2001), who described a study in which a contract for chemical dependence treatment and healthy lifestyles may decrease relapse by 20%. Likewise, behavioral contracting between youth and their parents may involve the use of reinforcements contingent on activities that are incompatible with drug use behavior and adhere to appropriate family roles.

The use of external restraints or penalties, however, can backfire. For example, when a relapse contract expires or the contingencies lose their incentive appeal, an individual may drink or use other drugs again (Marlatt & Gordon, 1985). Contracting is not a method shown to be effective in the cigarette smoking cessation literature (Fiori et al., 2000). The timing of the contract needs to be calculated well, there needs to be a means to monitor the contract closely, and the contract needs to be set up as an enforced understanding rather than as some type of legally binding document (Talbott & Crosby, 2001). Even though a contract may be working well, eventually the contract ends and natural social environmental contingencies need to be set up following its termination. Fading contingencies to reflect the natural social environment is a key to successful use of contracting, but it is not an easy task to accomplish (Table 18.3).

Social Network Analysis Approach to Cessation

One example of the use of social network analysis in the drug cessation arena includes studies of drug injectors. For example, Latkin (1998) recruited street opinion leaders to communicate safe injecting practices and showed that these opinion leaders adopted the safe injecting messages themselves and effectively communicated it to others. In other words, an effective way to provide harm reduction treatment in street settings is by having the naturally occurring leaders serve as role models to others in their social network. One may conjecture that use of sociometric techniques to identify naturally occurring drug using group peer leaders could lead to some knowledge on how to mobilize the group to quit abusing drugs. Much research is needed in this arena.

Relapse: A Social Perspective

Recovery from substance abuse is difficult, even with exceptional treatment resources. For example, although relapse rates are difficult to accurately obtain, it has been reported that, among adults, 70% of alcohol dependent users experience at least one relapse within a year after treatment. Similar relapse rates for heroin, nicotine, and marijuana users have been documented (Sussman & Ames, 2001). Often, recovery is a long-term process and frequently requires multiple episodes of treatment. As with other chronic illnesses, relapses to drug use can (and more often than not do) occur during or after initially successful treatment outcomes. Recovering individuals may require prolonged treatment and multiple episodes of treatment to achieve long-term abstinence.

Relapses are most likely to occur within the first 12 months of the discontinuance of substance use. Relapses may be triggered by a number of life stressors (e.g., divorce, break-ups, the death of a loved one, loss of job or income, periods of illness or poverty) or to a seemingly ordinary exposure to a person or place associated with previous substance use. It is believed that two primary factors may play a key role in protecting against relapse – the development of adaptive life skills and ongoing drug-free social support, such as that found in twelve-step programs. In fact, a meta-analysis study of adults that investigated the relationship between long-term sobriety and A.A. attendance and involvement found positive outcome effects (Tonigan, Toscova, & Miller, 1996). Ongoing therapy and social support assistance for family members is also recommended because substance dependence has a serious impact on family functioning and because family members may inadvertently maintain behaviors (e.g., facilitate relapse) that initially tolerated or supported the substance use behavior.

Summary

A variety of treatment strategies involving social interaction, peer groups, and peer support were presented in this chapter. Because drug abuse does not affect only the drug abuser but also significant others and communities (e.g., dramatic driving-under-the-influence events on the freeways), it makes sense for treatment agents to engage significant others, including sober peers, in an individual's recovery process. Inpatient programs that require social interaction (e.g., through communal living, family and group therapy, and peer participation) as well as social skills training may effectively help build and reinforce one's self-efficacy to change one's behavior. Even though there is a need for continued improvement in treatment outcomes, it appears that the mutual-help group participation treatment paradigms (e.g., twelve-step programs) are an important component of treatment, providing peer support, aftercare support, and reinforcing positive aspects of sober living. Alternatively, for some (especially those individuals new to recovery), this form of peer support can result in failure to complete a treatment program or relapse, because interaction with peers with similar experiences may result in inappropriate decision-making and companionship. Nevertheless, continuous exposure to reinforcing drug-free behavior through social interaction and peer support may effectively minimize relapse for many individuals.

This chapter describes larger social and physical environments that provide access channels to substance misuse treatment and may minimize negative consequences to the individual and others in the systems with whom he or she interacts. Macro-level systems (e.g., work environments, schools, and community housing, with their physical and social character-istics) suffer from or address the problems and costs associated with substance misuse. For example, drug misuse may result in a variety of urban environmental stressors, including violence, vandalism, and deteriorating housing, and vice versa, urban stressors may perpet-uate the use of drugs as a means of coping with these environmental stressors (e.g., Galea, Ahern, & Vlahov, 2003). Modification of urban environments and introduction of social services attempt to ameliorate substance abuse problems.

As a second example, substance misuse impedes productivity of workers and can result in absenteeism, drug-related illnesses and injuries, increased health care expenditures, low employee morale, theft, and premature death (Sussman & Ames, 2001). In addition, costs of drug abuse are associated with various drug-related crimes, incarceration, and lost pro-duction due to drug-related crime careers and correctional services. Worksite and penal systems have implemented means to assist in the cessation of substance abuse.

Drug abuse is a public health problem that needs to be addressed by larger systems. The drug abuser may reach treatment systems through a variety of channels – for example, as a comatose or psychotic patient at a hospital, an employee who is having work relationship problems, or the perpetrator of a crime to obtain money for drugs. This chapter discusses available treatment options enacted or provided by larger systems for drug abusing indi-viduals.

Reaching a Treatment Setting

Presently, there is a shortage of treatment providers and programs in the United States and elsewhere in the world. Most of the inpatient residential treatment programs, as well as outpatient settings, methadone and other specialty clinics, and other agonist maintenance treatment programs in the United States, have long waiting lists. These waiting lists can be especially long for those individuals who have no resources with which to pay and are in dire need of treatment (e.g., they are living in the streets and have no money for food or drugs on which they may be physically dependent). Many chronic drug abusers use up their monetary resources on drugs, are often underemployed or unemployed and have no insurance, and are unable to pay for formalized treatment. For those drug-abusing individuals who still have health insurance, the inpatient stay coverage provided is often very limited. In general, the longer one remains in treatment, the better the treatment outcome (Hubbard et al., 1989; Simpson, Joe, & Brown, 1997), and with limited insurance stay coverage (e.g., 30 days or less), treatment outcomes are relatively unlikely to improve.

Still, approximately 15% of drug abusers manage to reach formal treatment settings (Nurses Research Publication, 1999). How do individuals actually reach treatment settings and enter treatment programs? As noted in Chapter 15, entering treatment and ceasing drug use appears to be linked to *negative consequences of use*. For example, some individuals experience negative social consequences or are behind on credits at school, are in trouble at work, or have lost their jobs, homes, cars, and friends and can no longer ignore the need for treatment. Many individuals experience legal consequences, such as being arrested, resulting in court-mandated treatment. Being arrested and court ordered to treatment may not be such a bad event for many individuals, because it may actually disrupt negative behaviors earlier than otherwise expected (minimizing more severe future problems) and keep individuals in treatment longer (without insurance) with potentially better outcomes (Fletcher, Tims, & Brown, 1997). In fact, some studies investigating treatment outcomes have found no difference between those coerced into treatment and those who voluntarily enter treatment. In fact, in several studies, those individuals coerced into treatment had better outcomes. However, still other studies have found that those coerced into treatment do not do as well as those volunteering (see Farabee, Prendergast, & Anglin, 1998). Clearly, not all treatment is the same and treatment characteristics may affect some of these findings. As negative consequences accumulate, though, the drug abuser may independently seek assistance or be asked or coerced to seek assistance.

Settings Where Individuals May Be Reached by Programming

Reaching substance abusers in multiple settings has been suggested as being potentially very important to strengthen treatment effectiveness. There are many examples of means of reaching youth and adults needing treatment in community settings. Two examples relevant to youths are student assistance programs in schools and physician assistance. In addition, treatment programs for adult drug abusers are provided in a variety of additional settings, including hospitals, prisons, and residential facilities.

School Environments

In the school setting, youth who abuse drugs are likely to fall behind in class work or fail to show up for class (truancy). Substance abusing youth might have verbal or physical altercations with other students, be caught stealing other students' property, have visible mood swings or react inappropriately, appear in class smelling of alcohol or marijuana, or appear unkempt, tired, or withdrawn. Student assistance programs are generally available for these youth. These youth may initially reach a student assistance treatment setting through a contact with someone at the school, perhaps a teacher, the security guard, other students, or the school nurse. For example, a teacher may observe that a student's behavior is symptomatic of drug misuse and refer the student for monitoring by other teachers or school counselors and perhaps arrange a meeting with family members.

Student assistance programs vary in the degree of comprehensiveness, but they typically include training in drug education, including signs and symptoms of drug misuse and training in intervention techniques and referral skills to address the needs of the substance abuser. Typically, there may be around 5 hours of in-service training for staff (school personnel or community members) and peer counselors regarding conceptions of addiction, how to recognize drug problems, and referral services. Peer counselors may lead education groups, which instruct coping skills and values development. Peer support groups may also be available for those youth who struggle to get and stay clean and sober. Usually these groups also provide referral information and take a twelve-step group support model approach. Finally, sometimes a resource library and peer advising are available (Bosworth, 1996), or a student may be referred to a youth program specializing in working with substance-abusing youth not affiliated with the school.

Community Health Care

Primary care physicians may screen for problems and refer youth to drug and mental health counseling (Levy, Vaughan, & Knight, 2002). Primary care physicians can be trained as agents of outpatient treatment (Kaye, 2004), particularly if minimal programming can be used. To date, there is little research on using the physician as a treatment agent for teen drug abuse; however, research in this arena has now begun. (There is a great deal of information regarding physician-practice smoking cessation treatment; Fiori, Prendergast, & Anglin, 2000.)

When dealing with extreme populations, such as runaway youth, screening them for drug abuse is very difficult because they are relatively unlikely to have contact with traditional systems of care. Other means of disseminating cessation treatment and referral information to extreme populations may include programs offered in conjunction with harm reduction outreach approaches, such as needle exchange programs and dissemination of condoms that may occur at locations where use is prevalent. In addition, public health care facilities often screen for drug abuse as part of all standard care. Stabilization of living situations for homeless youth is very important (e.g., easy access to housing shelters and outreach) to be able to draw these youth into the community and into treatment (Farrow, 1995).

Work Environments

Approximately 40% of drug abusers have a problem with absenteeism on the job, and 40% show up to work late on a regular basis. At least 30% make mistakes on the job. In addition, 25% have problems with the boss, 25% have problems completing work, and 10% suffer on-the-job injuries. Those employees most likely to work while using drugs are males under 30 years old who are unhappy with their jobs and who frequently socialize after hours with coworkers, away from the place of employment (Hollinger, 1988). Co-workers who do not abuse drugs are affected by their peers' drug abuse, reporting relatively low work identity when they experience high use among co-workers (Bennett & Lehman, 1996).

Since the mid-1950s, businesses and government agencies have developed various policies to deal with employee drug abuse. Employee assistance programs (EAPs) were developed with the intent of motivating employees to improve their performance rather than risk losing their jobs; using these programs, companies also could attempt to contain rising health care costs and reduce corporate losses. Most of these policies support a treatment orientation, dealing with the drug problem when it has gotten out of hand. Such programs tend to be offered in organizations that include relatively older workers.

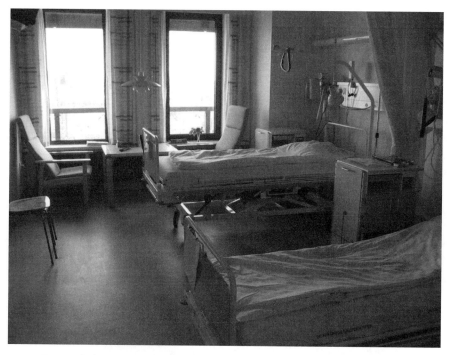

Figure 19.1. Image of a hospital room. Drug abusers may find that if they require medical care and are placed in a hospital setting, they may experience both physical and psychological withdrawal symptoms. They should fully disclose their drug abuse history to the attending physician.

Involvement in an EAP generally is intended to be separate from personnel records, and participation doesn't typically affect job ratings. EAP components may include (1) educational and counseling programs, including crisis counseling; (2) supervisory training in confronting troubled employees; (3) drug testing and other diagnostic screening services; as well as (4) referral services (Bennett & Lehman, 1996). In addition, (5) informal networks of recovering professionals and skilled labor groups have developed and formed self-help and activism groups. Future programming ought to consider carefully the organizational culture of the workplace and the local community that interacts with the workplace. Increasing cooperation within the organizational hierarchy and networking with local resources could improve the efficacy of EAP programs. A popularly used EAP interview guide has been developed and is available for downloading (Bray & Zarkin, 1999, http://www.drugfreeworkplace.gov/ResourceCenter/r108.pdf).

Hospital Settings
Several drug-related disorders involve placement in a hospital. An individual also may be hospitalized for other medical reasons likely or unlikely to be related to drug misuse at the time when the need for drug-related treatment is identified. The medical patient needs to be treated, of course, for his or her medical condition; however, disclosing drug use behaviors may be critical for optimal care. For example, if a patient needs to undergo surgery and is physically dependent on alcohol or another drug, such as heroin, the patient may need to be medically detoxed before undergoing surgery. Of course, this may not be possible in the case of some emergency situations (Figure 19.1).

While the patient is at the hospital, he or she will be discouraged from drinking any alcohol or using any drugs other than those prescribed for the medical condition. This is a situation in which the patient may experience both physical and psychological withdrawal symptoms, including becoming irritable and depressed. It is possible that the patient may sneak some drug use while in the hospital, complain of pain to obtain drugs, or simply brave it out. A physician may ask the patient if he or she has been drinking, smoking, or using other drugs as part of a health status assessment in reaction to the qualities of the disorder reported, the sight of apparent withdrawal symptoms, or evidence obtained through biological data collection. The patient may deny having a problem. Alternatively, because the patient is away from drug-related cues, the illness may provide a teachable moment during which the patient may seek to stop abusing drugs. For some, brief hospital-based inpatient treatment, followed by extended outpatient therapy and participation in self-help groups may be recommended. Health assistance may include warnings about consequences of drug use and encouragement to quit using, group self-help meetings on the unit, bedside counseling, and administration of self-help materials (e.g., Stevens, Glasgow, Hollis, & Mount, 2000, regarding cigarette smoking cessation).

Prison Settings

In 2000, the Arrestee Drug Abuse Monitoring Program (ADAM) found that 64% of male arrestees and 63% of female arrestees tested positive for at least one drug at the time of arrest at 29 sites. In 2002, about 68% of jailed inmates met substance abuse or dependence criteria during the year before their admission to jail; 63% of those inmates who met criteria for substance abuse or dependence had participated in substance abuse treatment programs previously, and about 25% reportedly committed crimes to get money for drugs (U.S. Department of Justice, 2002). Approximately 60% of prisoners in federal institutions are serving time for drug-related offenses (http://www.ojp.usdoj.gov/bjs/drugs.htm). About 25% of federal inmates and one-third of California state prison inmates report participating in prison treatment programs (http://www.ojp.usdoj.gov/bjs/drugs.htm). In the United States, the majority (70% to 98%) of individuals who served time for drug-related crimes relapsed in the year following release if they did not participate in treatment programs while in prison (see United Nations, 2003).

Among juveniles arrested at nine correctional sites scattered throughout the United States, more than half (males and females) tested positive for at least one drug (National Institute of Justice, 2003). Presently, substance abuse treatment for incarcerated youth is offered in fewer than half of juvenile detention facilities, yet about 40% of incarcerated youth meet criterion for alcohol or other drug abuse and dependence (Stein et al., 2006).

In 1989, the Federal Bureau of Prisons initiated substance abuse treatment strategies for inmates with drug use histories. Inmates participate in drug education treatment programs if they violate either parole or supervised release because of drug-related activities, a presentencing investigation reports that alcohol or drug use contributed to the offense, or a sentencing judge recommends that they participate in drug treatment while incarcerated. Any inmates who volunteer for and meet the criteria of having a drug use disorder based on the criteria of the *Diagnostic and Statistical Manual of Mental Disorders* (DSM) are eligible. The federal bureau programs involve drug education classes and nonresidential treatment at every bureau institution. Residential drug abuse treatment programs exist at approximately half of the bureau's institutions, transitional drug abuse treatment is found at all institutions, and community transitional drug treatment exists for inmates at community corrections centers.

Inmates participating in residential drug abuse treatment programs are housed together in separate units of prisons that are reserved for drug abuse treatment. Prison programs may include intensive half-day treatment programming (5 days a week), with the rest of the day focused on vocational and educational training. In addition, aftercare treatment services are provided for inmates who have completed residential treatment and have returned to the general prison population (http://www.bop.gov/inmate_programs/substance.jsp).

In the United States, individual states may also have designated substance abuse treatment facilities that are specifically for rehabilitating and treating substance-abusing offenders. Substance abuse treatment for those serving time may include detoxification-stabilization, counseling or residential treatment, pharmacological maintenance, participation in twelve-step programs or other self-help groups, and drug and alcohol education programs. In addition, a number of community-based alternatives to incarceration are now being used for drug offenders.

Some states have programs for first- and second-time offenders that do not require incarceration. For example, the state of California has drug diversion programs for first- and second-time, nonviolent drug offenders. These programs require the drug offender to attend drug education classes for a total of 50 hours or 5 months, once weekly, and participate in twenty twelve-step program meetings for a total of 30 hours. Drug courts are an alternative to drug diversion; the courts arrange for substance abuse treatment (mostly outpatient treatment) and other services and monitor progress in treatment. In 2000, California passed Proposition 36, the Substance Abuse and Crime Prevention Act for multioffenders court referred to treatment programs in lieu of going to jail or prison for nonviolent crimes. Individuals referred to Proposition 36 treatment programs receive up to a year of drug abuse treatment and 6 months of aftercare. Evaluation of the Proposition 36 programs has shown that these programs are saving taxpayers money, effectively reducing incarceration costs, and that treatment outcomes are best for those who complete the program (for more information, see Longshore, Hawken, Urada, & Anglin, 2006). The criminal justice system is responsible for approximately 50% of referrals to drug treatment programs within the community (Anglin, Prendergast, & Farabee, 1998; Maxwell, 1996).

Treatment modalities for individuals on parole or probation include therapeutic communities for adults and adolescents; pharmacological maintenance programs, such as methadone, naltrexone, and buprenorphine; various outpatient drug treatment programs, including counseling services (individual, group and family, peer group support); and aftercare (generally twelve-step meetings), relapse prevention, and vocational counseling. Multimodality programs include a variety of resources, such as inpatient care, education enhancement, drug education, vocational training, medical care, and therapeutic communities.

Treatment options may include helping to increase inmate motivation for change, providing education regarding awareness of effects of substance abuse, and teaching skills such as self-control, as well as general social skills, to help inmates learn how to avoid setting themselves up for relapse. In addition, skills relevant to employment and leisure situations may be taught and may include prerelease planning. Finally, relapse management is taught. Overall, training for inmates requires relatively intense, long periods (up to 1 year) to elicit an effect, because many in this population are removed from mainstream society (Lightfoot, 1993). Unfortunately, on discharge from prison, ex-inmates are generally not prepared to reenter mainstream society; they have no job or money, weakened family ties, and little social support. Without sufficient support and monitoring, many individuals violate parole or probation and revolve back into prison on the heels of drug use.

Aftercare of some kind may be the most important element in the maintenance of cessation (e.g., Sussman et al., 1986). One inexpensive and accessible aftercare treatment component is twelve-step program participation as well as other self-help programs (e.g., Secular Organizations for Sobriety/Save Our Selves [SOS]). Twelve-step aftercare participation has been shown to be effective in maintaining abstinence from alcohol and other drugs among those individuals who attend meetings more than once weekly (Florentine, 1999). These programs may provide an invaluable means of support for those persons newly released from prison and may provide them with a means to be useful to others and keep busy. However, such aftercare programs do not necessarily provide all needed resources to all of its members. For individuals in recovery, making use of environmental resources is very important to maintain a clean and sober lifestyle. Most of these resources may be found in local telephone books, through calling directory assistance, through looking through social service directories (e.g., Rainbow Resource Directory), as well as by contacting the local Council on Alcohol and Drug Dependence Office. Use of drug courts and drug education for prisoners may reduce recidivism (to the criminal justice system) from approximately 80% to 20% among those who select to participate (which is the minority); that is, down 60% for all those referred to drug court (San Bernardino drug court, personal communication, December 1, 2006).

Family Home

Traditional schools of thought tend to view family members of drug abusers as functioning in a dysfunctional system (e.g., Johnson, 1980). The empirical data indicate that families of alcohol/drug abusers show lower levels of cohesion, expressiveness, independence, intellectual orientation (including problem-solving skills), and active-recreational orientation and higher levels of conflict (e.g., hostile communication) than do non-drug-abusing families. However, these conditions simply relate to a dysfunctional family system, across a variety of disorders, not necessarily to use of drugs per se (Sher, 1993).

The empirical literature also suggests that spouses of drug abusers have more psychological problems than do spouses of nonabusers. They tend to either be depressed and anxious or psychopathic, and they may dominate the relationship if their drug-abusing spouse is relatively socially incompetent. They are relatively likely to have been raised in or come from families with other drug-abusing family members. In addition, children of drug abusers tend to exhibit lower achievement behavior, more behavioral problems, and lower self-esteem. There is some tendency to grow up to become drug abusers themselves, although some children of drug abusers are more likely to avoid drug use than other people (they may be afraid to use drugs because of what they experienced; Sher, 1993). There is little support for the concept of different family roles (e.g., the "hero" or "scapegoat"), although responsibilities for home tasks do tend to shift to non-drug-abusing family members.

Interestingly, families of binge users tend to function more poorly than families of steady, functional users. Cohesive and affectionate families have better effects on the drug-abusing member's behavior than disengaged and hostile families. Family members do not tend to decompensate (get worse) when the drug abuser quits using (Gordon & Barrett, 1993). Thus, families with drug abusers that function better tend to function better regardless of use; however, they may function even better if the user stops using.

Traditional treatment for the family, aside from confronting the abusers (the intervention approach), would be to avoid enabling the drug abuse (i.e., acting in ways that support continued drug use, such as cleaning up the consequences produced by the drug abusers). Family members would do better if they let the drug abuser hit bottom (i.e., reach a low-point in one's using career so that one is honestly receptive to assistance), seek treatment or support separately from the drug abuser, and do so with emotional detachment. In addition, though, empirical research suggests that treatment is likely to be more successful in keeping the family together when both the drug abusers and other family members are seen together rather than when they are seen separately. Thus, therapy, both apart from and with the drug abuser, is recommended as part of a treatment program. Also, for the drug use to stop, the drug use behavior should be a focus of the treatment (Littrell, 1991).

Family Assistance Programs may instruct the family regarding the parameters of addiction. All family members might do well to receive some sort of counseling. They may need to be separated from the drug abuser if the drug abuser needs to go through a detoxification program or desires an inpatient stay. After a month or so, regular family treatment sessions are recommended. Key treatment characteristics include instruction in family skills training, potentially through in-home support, and family therapy to improve family communication, decrease conflict, and improve parenting (O'Farrell & Fals-Stewart, 2000).

Residential Facilities

Residential facilities involve a myriad of placements for the disabled, homeless, and elderly. Unfortunately, there is a lack of substance abuse programming within these facilities. Although there is variation across residential facilities, the statistics that apply to individuals in some facilities are frightening. For example, in nursing homes, 20% to 50% of elderly residents have alcohol-related problems. Moreover, there is a tendency for medication to be used as a means of chemical restraint, particularly in nursing homes (Mansdorf et al., 1999). Many individuals who might otherwise be homeless reside in public residential facilities, such as homeless shelters and psychiatric hospitals. Perhaps 50% are considered dually diagnosed; that is, they are drug abusers and they have some psychiatric impairment.

Residential facilities could benefit from training staff to be aware of substance abuse signs and symptoms. Physicians affiliated with these facilities ought to scrutinize medications being administered to residents and provide education to staff regarding the potential for drug abuse among the tenants. The nursing staff ought to be involved in inpatient education regarding drug abuse and drug screening and help coordinate care that might counteract drug use as a means of spending one's time. More of a reliance on behavioral interventions (e.g., contingency management) should be considered in addition to medication as means of curtailing disruptive behavior. Residents also could be assessed for potential independent living. If possible, self-help participation and relapse prevention and job or leisure training skills should be offered. Certainly, keeping residents busy in a structured context is preferable as a means to bypass reliance on maladaptive coping.

Mass Media Programming

One form of cessation programming that has extensive reach is the mass media public service announcement (PSA). In general, drug use cessation public health messages include any media announcement, for which there is no charge, which educates and increases awareness about the consequences of drug use. Although the effectiveness of PSAs is yet to be fully determined, some anti-drug use public health messages have been found to be effective. For example, Palmgreen et al. (2001) found that when targeting sensation seekers with fast-paced, novel, and stimulating televised campaigns, adolescent marijuana use was reduced in high-sensation seekers (Palmgreen et al., 2001). In addition, Sussman et al. (1994) found that a televised tobacco cessation program could reach a range of diverse individuals but that those who intended to quit smoking in the next 3 months and who had a tendency to use self-help materials were also those who tended to view programming and read the campaign messages. Perhaps, for those who are ready to stop using, and who tend to search their environment for assistance of their own accord, media campaigns may attract their attention and reinforce their intentions to quit using drugs.

If designed for and targeted to appeal to specific individuals (e.g., sensation seekers), it appears that some PSAs may be effective, and certainly have the ability to reach large groups of individuals. For example, this may be one of the few types of drug use cessation strategies that most hard-to-reach high-risk youth may be exposed to. One caveat, however, is that many public service campaigns assume that individuals behave rationally and want to change drug use behaviors and that information regarding consequences can affect behavioral change. As the evidence accumulates implicating implicit and dual processes in addictive behavior, it is becoming increasingly clear that drug use (and other addictive behaviors) is not simply a rational choice behavior. Mass media campaigns may reinforce individuals who are already motivated to change but may have little or no effect on those who appear unwilling to change. Unfortunately, it may be the case that nothing can affect some individuals and that they may need to hit bottom (if there is one) before change will ensue. Nevertheless, a new generation of targeted antitobacco and other drug use public health campaign developers may want to consider the impact of more automatic influences on behavior and means of tapping into these influences, in addition to the use of more rational approaches.

Finally, for some individuals, the extent to which particular drug use behavior is considered "normal" within a subculture may impede change. Environmental, cultural, and large-scale social influences may contribute to and reinforce continued drug use (for example, some street youth cultures). With increasing availability to Internet access (e.g., Internet cafes, Internet availability in shelters), Web-based media campaigns and interventions that provide anonymous access to treatment information and care may be one approach to reaching extreme, hard-to-reach populations (e.g., see http://alcoholicsanonymous.9f.com/AASoberChatOnline.htm).

Geographic Applications as an Adjunct to Treatment

Geographic Information Systems (GIS) may be helpful in determining spatial components that may be protective or increase the risk of drug abuse and interfere with cessation efforts.

(Although not formerly presented, GIS also may be relevant to prevention effort.) GIS provides digital formats of larger physical areas that may be used to clarify spatial patterns or relationships among neighborhoods. For example, GIS may help in identifying building structures that provide easy access to drug dealing or places to gather to use drugs and the connectivity of streets that might allow for free flow of drug trafficking and affiliation with drug networks or interactions among social networks that inhibit or promote drug use. In addition, GIS can provide information about the density of liquor stores or drop-in centers, adjacent parks, and other recreational facilities that may interfere with or encourage cessation efforts.

By integrating geographic information with sociocultural and other environmental information in cessation efforts, individuals working toward being clean and sober may be able to avoid entering locations flooded with relapse cues (both social and physical) that may threaten cessation. Geographic applications may also effectively enhance cessation efforts and decrease relapse rates by manipulating the availability of supportive physical structures (A.A. and NA club houses, 24-hour drop-in centers) and removing drug-facilitating structures (e.g., buildings with lack of defensible space and alcohol outlets) within a given geographical radius (Mason, Cheung, & Walker, 2004).

Large-Scale Policy for Substance Abuse Treatment

The U.S. drug policy is divided into three major priorities, (1) stopping drug use before it starts (prevention), (2) intervening and healing drug users (treatment), and (3) disrupting the drug market. Presently, the largest amount of money, by far, is allocated to disrupting the drug market. This, of course, may change as the government changes and views of substance abuse change. In terms of prevention, for example, the Department of Education is allocated monies for student drug testing and grant assistance to local educational agencies to encourage drug-free schools. In addition, the Office of National Drug Control Policy (ONDCP) is allocated money for media campaigns that specifically encourage antidrug attitudes and strategies. In terms of treatment, for example, monies are allocated to the National Institute on Drug Abuse for research in understanding etiology, risk and protective factors, physical and behavioral effects, and prevention and treatment efforts; monies are also allocated to the Substance Abuse and Mental Health Services Administration (SAMHSA) to help in developing innovative substance treatment options for those in recovery. In addition, the Office of Justice Programs receives funds for Drug Court Programs to provide treatment and aftercare programs as well as mandatory drug testing as alternatives to incarceration. Finally, in terms of disrupting the market, for example, the ONDCP is provided money for eliminating opium poppy production in Afghanistan and to secure the borders from drug trafficking, as well as community-oriented policing (e.g., cleaning up methamphetamine labs; see http://www.whitehousedrugpolicy.gov/publications/policy/o7budget/parti_exec_ summ.pdf).

Similarly, the World Health Organization (WHO) drug policies focus on prevention and reduction of the incidence and prevalence of substance use as well as demand reduction. In addition, the WHO provides information to countries based on the best evidence on managing drug problems to reduce health and social drug-related problems. The WHO is also involved in recommendations regarding the regulatory control of substances (Table 19.1).

Table 19.1. *Types of larger social and physical environmental cessation treatments*

Types of programs	Settings	Description
Student assistance programs	School	Typically include training in drug education (e.g., signs and symptoms of drug misuse) and training in intervention techniques and referral skills to address the needs of the substance abuser.
Outpatient training programs	Community health care	Primary care physicians may be trained as agents of outpatient treatment; they screen for substance abuse problems, provide brief advice, and refer youth or adults to drug and mental health counseling.
Employee assistance programs	Workplace	Work-centered treatment may include educational and counseling programs, including crisis counseling, supervisory training in confronting troubled employees, drug testing and other diagnostic screening services, referral services, as well as providing help through informal networking of recovering professionals.
Family assistance programs	Family home	Treatment for the family may include instruction in parameters of addiction, instruction in family skills training – potentially through in-home support as a supplement to clinic meetings; and therapy to improve family communication, decrease conflict, and improve parenting and strengthen the family system. Therapy both apart from and with the drug abuser is recommended as part of a treatment program.
Inpatient programs	Hospitals, clinics	These programs target individuals admitted into hospitals for drug-related or unrelated health reasons and may involve strategies such as warning drug abusers of the consequences of drug use, encouraging them to quit, arranging self-help meetings on the unit, providing counseling, administrating self-help materials, and referrals to treatment.
Prison treatment programs	Prisons	Prison programs may include detoxification-stabilization, counseling, pharmacological maintenance, participation in twelve-step programs or other self-help groups, and drug and alcohol education programs, vocational training, and provision for aftercare.
Residential treatment programs	Recovery homes, sober living homes	Recovery and sober living residences may include involvement in twelve-step programs, cognitive-behavioral therapy, drug and alcohol education, monitoring by legal authorities (e.g., home arrest), and vocational and educational counseling.

Table 19.1. (*continued*)

Types of programs	Settings	Description
Residential treatment for special populations	Residential facilities for the elderly, homeless, and disabled individuals	There is a lack of substance abuse programming within these types of facilities. However, physicians ought to scrutinize medications being administered to residents, and provide education to staff regarding the potential for drug abuse among the tenants. Reliance on behavioral interventions (e.g., contingency management) in addition to medication monitoring as means of curtailing disruptive behavior could be considered.
Mass media programs	All settings can be reached through print, radio, and visual media	Through high-tech public service announcements, mass-media programming is able to disseminate drug abuse cessation messages, which educate and increase awareness about the consequences of drug abuse, and may supplement other programming in the large social environment.
Policies for substance abuse treatment	All settings can be reached through enforcement of policies applicable to them	National and international-level policies may assist drug abuse treatment directly or indirectly by investing resources into the problem. For example, policy makers may direct monies into research that fosters the understanding of etiology, risk and protective factors, physical and behavioral effects associated with drug abuse. Other policies may lead to channeling drug abusers arrested for illegal action into treatment. Policies may be enacted that advocate treatment or treatment referrals across many life settings. These types of policies have led to many of the approaches used in the settings listed in this table.

Note: Each of the specific settings above, through referrals, vocational, educational, or residential needs, are likely to contact other of these settings in a network of interacting units. It is this network, guided by policy enactment and enforcement, and communicated through the media, that provides the true picture of large social and physical environmental change.

Summary

This chapter provided an overview of a variety of larger social and physical settings where individuals may be reached by programming or provided access to cessation programs. To date, there is still a shortage of programs available for many in need of treatment; for example, those individuals who have no insurance, those "serving time" in prison without treatment options, and those who simply cannot or do not want to be reached by programming. Nevertheless, access to substance abuse treatment programs is increasing (e.g., in the prison and juvenile justice systems). In terms of cost, public and self-help settings are generally less expensive than private settings, and in terms of convenience, self-help and some public settings (e.g., the work site and school settings) generally are more convenient than many private settings.

Mass media campaigns should not be ruled out as effective wide-reaching cessation programs or as having the potential to reinforce sobriety messages for those in recovery.

Early detection through drug education and awareness in a variety of larger social settings, access to a variety of treatment options – including community-based residential treatment – for those in need, continued refinement of program components, and increasing insurance treatment stay limits may all contribute to better treatment outcomes. Finally, being aware of the geographic context of drug abuse may assist in designing environments in which drug abuse is relatively less likely.

CONCLUSIONS AND THE FUTURE

20   Conclusions and Recent and Future Directions

Figure 20.1. The future is today.

The previous chapters of this text considered the etiology, prevention, and cessation of drug use problems from the perspectives of neurobiology, cognition, small groups, and the large social and physical environment. These four levels of explication of drug problems were presented in separate chapters; how they fit together with each other was not discussed in great detail. We, of course, do not know the precise underlying mechanisms that explain how these components fit together; however, several perspectives can be applied in understanding how their influence might be integrated.

First, there is the notion that these different perspectives represent distinct conceptual entities that measure different types of variables. For example, for some people, their neurobiological makeup may lead to drug problems for them (but not others). For others, being thrust into an environment in which everyone is a drug abuser may lead to becoming a drug abuser. Perhaps, multiple components exert an addictive effect in other people. In examining variables across large groups of individuals, it is possible that neurobiological, cognitive, group, and environmental factors exert independent, addictive main effects on behavior.

Second, there is the notion that these variables cluster together into meaningful aggregates. People who experience neurobiological "dis-balance" may tend to think in certain ways that bind them into drug-using groups that tend to cluster in certain social and physical environments. The history of opium dens in poor areas visited by persons of ill repute may be consistent with this perspective.

Third, there is the notion that these variables are nested such that the large social and physical environment provides a setting within which only certain groups may congregate. These groups may provide an information flow within which certain types of cognitive processing of information may occur. The types of cognitive processing that occur may set a course of neurobiological processing. It is interesting that the lowest levels of cigarette smoking in the United States occur in the Virgin Islands and in Utah, where smoking historically is discouraged by the religion, culture, and structural relations among the persons living in these areas. This molar background provides a sociogeographical framework within which groups identify and intrapersonal functions operate.

Fourth, there is the possibility of a transactional model of relations among these four variables; they all may affect each other. One's neurobiological dis-balance may lead one to search out sensations in novel environments, and novel environments may alter one's neurobiological functions. These variables may impinge on the groups with which one tends to associate, which may also result in altering the environment, and so on.

All of these models may apply to some extent (i.e., additive, clustered, nested, and transactional). Possibly, these different models are suggestive of different types of prevention and cessation programming. For example, the nested model may suggest one focus much effort on altering the larger environment. An aggregate model may suggest a focus on high-risk groups or situations. Main effects models may suggest separate prevention components for each type of variable. A transactional model may suggest that there be a focus on how a prevention strategy affects each type of variable and relations among variables.

There is much work to be done in the future on the causal and statistical modeling of the relations among these variables. In addition to these models, one needs to model in time as a variable. Changes can occur over time in one's neurobiology as one grows older. Thought processes change through cumulative experience. Groups with which one associates may change dramatically in a lifetime, and the larger world changes greatly as technology advances and as governments come and go. A universal answer to the etiology of drug problems may never be realized. As presented earlier in this text, even what constitutes drug consequences may vary over time and in different locations. In addition, controlling for physical dangers of use, different drugs obtain different levels of social acceptability. For example, although smoking any marijuana may be considered inappropriate, drinking large amounts of alcohol might be considered acceptable.

And so it is with this framework regarding the lack of certainty about the etiology of drug problems and the lack of certainty regarding constituents of drug abuse, or how constituents combine, that this last chapter presents suggestions on current prevention and cessation research needs. First, we consider the need for taxonomy of etiology and prevention and cessation strategies as a function of risk and age group. A consideration of breadth of programming also is included. Next, we discuss the difficulty of prevention and cessation of alcohol use in general and among special populations. Heavy alcohol use has tended to be tolerated through the ages. Only at the point where obvious physical or social injury are incurred is one intervened. Why alcohol use has a special status, and how to deal with this, is noted. Next, we examine the current emphases on transdisciplinary and translation work. The importance of program development and dissemination in such work is mentioned. Finally, we propose a list of issues we feel are most important to grapple with for the next generation of drug abuse researchers.

Etiology, Prevention, and Cessation: Need for Taxonomy

Arguably, in chemistry and biology, we began learning about the nature of things through development of classification systems (e.g., Mendelov's table). Subsequent to seeing patterns among chemical "elements" or different "species," we began to formulate hypotheses about tendencies to give off electrons or on evolution, respectively. Thus, developing good descriptive systems is very important in science. They serve as the "launching pad" of theory creation. We may have the beginning of an explicit taxonomy of drug abuse etiology, composed of four classes or variables that are related to each other in several plausible ways, that soon will lead to new insight about etiology of drug problems. We do not yet have an established taxonomy of drug abuse prevention or cessation strategies, though there are the beginnings of one suggested by such research organizations as Communities That Care (CTC).

The CTC process is an operating system that provides research-based tools to help communities mobilize to promote the positive development of children and youth and to prevent adolescent problem behaviors that impede positive development, including substance abuse, delinquency, teen pregnancy, school dropout, and violence. The CTC process was developed by David Hawkins and Richard Catalano to help communities plan, implement, and evaluate proven-effective prevention programs to meet their particular needs. Among the five phases of the CTC process is the attempt to develop a community profile (prioritize community risk and protective factors) and address community priorities, matching proven-effective programs that address a variety of community units to specific community needs. Such taxonomy may vary by a variety of risk, contextual, or developmental factors (as examples). The CTC process offers matrices that indicate developmental period, appropriate strategy for that period, risk factor assessed for that period, and protective factors being provided through use of the strategy (http://www.channing-bete.com/prevention-programs/communities-that-care/).

The only other such matrix that divides programming by strategy and level of prevention (universal, selective, indicated) was provided by Sussman and Ames (2001). This matrix considers both prevention and cessation. Just as with Mendelov's table in chemistry, integrative descriptive work is a reasonable starting point for prevention or cessation program-based theoretical development (Sussman & Sussman, 2001). Certainly, across any type of programming, there are some common features that are likely to apply, including trust building among facilitator and participants, facts about the health behavior and consequences information, knowledge of high-risk situations, general social communication skills enhancement, decision-making, and interactive learning (Sussman & Ames, 2001). These types of skills bring people together with each other and help one understand what one is getting into when one participates in risky or healthy behaviors. These strategies are relevant for prevention and cessation programming.

Also, there appears to be some programming that might be intrinsically universal, including making a public commitment (as opposed to a private commitment) and normative restructuring or prevalence overestimates reduction (in which most of the population demonstrates healthy lifestyles). These universal programming techniques apply to a general population, the assumption being that most exhibit moderate behavior. These strategies would seem relevant to prevention or health promotion programming but might not apply to those trying to quit using a drug.

Targeted programming appears to involve strategies that address individuals already invested in lifestyles favorable to drug abuse. These strategies include making explicit and resolving equivocation, motivating change, instructing cognitive and behavioral coping, instructing mood management, and providing information on recovering from damage already experienced because of unhealthy courses of behavior (e.g., Sussman & Ames, 2001). These strategies seem relevant to selective or indicated prevention and cessation programming, but hardly seem relevant to the general population. Thus, as a start of the development of an explicit taxonomy, one could detail program strategies as a function of type of programming (e.g., universal, selective, and indicated) or other factors, such as stage of development.

Consideration of Age of Population

It is most plausible that different types of programming are relevant for youth in different age groups. Obviously, youth in different age groups demonstrate different reading levels, perceptual-motor development, and level of abstraction (Hansen & Altman, 2001). Just as school topics, the media, parenting, and friendship products vary across age groups, so would drug education-type programming. In addition, one rarely observes a young child using drugs, though there are exceptions (e.g., young inhalant or cigarette smokers who sometimes use to decrease appetite, particularly where there is a scarcity of food). Other variables tend to differentiate those youngsters at risk for later drug use and abuse.

Young children who tend to blame others in conflict situations appear hypersensitive about fulfillment of immediate needs (e.g., food and comfort), and those who are not grounded in ongoing supportive and educative interactions with significant other adults are relatively likely to resort to "acting out" as a means to express their dissatisfaction (Kellam et al., 1989; Shedler & Block, 1990). These youth may tend to perceive that their acting out behavior is appropriate. By blaming others, they may show belief–behavior congruence, and their alignment with other such youth may indicate creation of a contextual distortion (Matthys & Lochman, 2005). Prevention or cessation programming to be well matched for young children not only should address developmental limitations but also should correct for behavioral irregularities that might signify a long pathway to drug abuse. For the time being, it appears that parental education about consistent, firm, and kind parenting, as well as teaching the child self-control and helping the child to perceive a closeness with parent or guardian and first school teachers through meetings that provide appropriate feedback (complement the child, but not the behavior; teach conversation skills, decision-making through use of dolls; proper use of time-out), may help in appropriately regulating behaviors. In addition, perhaps some work on resource acquisition and early academic preparation skills may assist.

As presented earlier in this book, some effective programs have been created, though there is much more to learn. Programming may be limited or need alteration when applied to children or parents with special needs (traumatized, intellectually challenged).

Older children are more influenced by family than friends until early adolescence. Elementary school-age youth may have only recently heard about some drugs but probably exhibit little curiosity to try them at the present time. The same types of strategies used for young children may apply to children 6–11 years old, provided in a more verbal-based manner (social skills, self-control, parenting being provided, academic skills). Some facts about short-term and long-term consequences of drug use may be provided. A greater emphasis on having the child meet with adults at institutions other than the home may be important at this age (e.g., teachers, counselors, and church leaders). Parents may need to focus on who the child's friends are and take an active role in friendship selection and monitoring. Parents should be good role models, as well as agents of socialization.

Young teens who are curious about solutions to their sense of dysregulation, and who are approached by other teens who share a similar curiosity, may seek out or yield to offers to try drugs or engage in other risky behaviors (Sussman et al., 1995). Drug prevalence overestimates reduction, improvement in difficulties in decision-making, and confrontation of alienation beliefs may be strategies that can assist with prevention (initial trial or early use) efforts (Sussman, Dent, & McCuller, 2000; Sussman, Earleywine, et al., 2004). As discussed previously, young teens (12 to 15 years old) are ideal candidates for the provision of comprehensive social influence program material. Work with family relations still is important although parents are relatively unlikely to serve as a mechanism of friendship selection (they might be trained to do some monitoring). Academic remediation may be important. For some young teens, drug abuse cessation treatment will be relevant; treatment could include inpatient stay, intense family therapy, and work on sexual issues as well as drug issues.

Dynamic social changes occur between early adolescence (junior high school) and later adolescence (high school). As *older teens*, youth solidify a sense of self and become more resistant to direct influence. They also tend to live in contexts of heterosexual crowds, less mutually dependent on peers. Intrapersonal motivations become more important (Sussman, Earleywine, et al., 2004). Intrapersonal motivations tend to dominate as a precipitant of risky or health behaviors throughout adulthood. Tobacco and other drug use may come to serve more as a stress-coping, intrapersonal function as the substance use acquisition process enters a more advanced phase. High school-based prevention material should be provided so that youth will recall and put into practice relevant prevention strategies that are relatively likely to involve stress-coping skills (motivation, skills, and decision-making) as opposed to social influence material. A motivation/skills/decision-making model is relevant for both prevention and cessation efforts with older teens. Mentoring-type programs that involve older, prosocial adults outside the home may be relevant for elementary age, young teen, and older teen youth. Assistance with employment skills and resource acquisition may become quite relevant for older teens. For some older teens, education in parenting skills may be needed.

The period of *emerging adulthood* (18–25) is one in which youth grapple with the prospects of new opportunities and need to select among opportunities, thereby bypassing other opportunities by selecting a subset. Young people leaving high school are expected to seek out and select from among new opportunities. These include the following: (1) assuming career avenues and financial independence, (2) learning skills of independent living (buying or renting a place to live), (3) growing in self-care skills (cooking, cleaning, grooming, buying goods, traveling), and (4) participating in social adventures (e.g., love and young adult groups). Social adventures may eventually lead to commitment in relationships (e.g., marriage and children). Youth may also transition from a relatively high level of family conflict in adolescence to the reduction of such conflict in emerging adulthood as they achieve emotional distance from parental demands and regulations and begin to associate more with peers. Successful transitioning through emerging adulthood involves being able to view exploration of life options as positive, hold positive general attitudes about life, become increasingly other-oriented (nurturing), and not feel subjectively caught inbetween adolescence and adulthood. For emerging adults, fear or lack of hope that one will be able to satisfactorily settle down into adult roles is a driving source of pressure that might lead one to resort to drug use or other self-destructive behavior.

Youth that transition poorly through emerging adulthood exhibit unconventional behavior (e.g., drinking alcohol in public and having a child out of wedlock), unconventional attitudes (e.g., tolerance of deviance), and poor self-control; they may use anger coping and may show interpersonal difficulty. These youth tend to enter adult roles early ("precocious development") prior to being prepared to take on such roles. They tend to drop out of high school or attend part-time education, get married and quickly divorced, become parents while relatively young, and take on undesired full-time employment. They also are relatively likely to exhibit unrestrained drug misuse and abuse. The same motivation skills/decision-making model used with older teens, along with motivational interview strategies, and assistance with helping emerging adults find comfortable means to "settle down" into adulthood is essential.

Among *adults* between the ages of 25 and 50, there may be many movements in personal and work life. Sometimes positive events occur and at other times negative events transpire. Prevention and cessation strategies that emphasize coping skills and decision-making, and provision of legal, medical, and other resources, are likely to be relatively important. In addition, group support to help these persons cope with the grief of losing a parent or other older relatives is likely to be important in preventing drug abuse or relapse.

Among the *elderly*, prescription medication misuse (especially of benzodiazapines, barbiturates, and anti-inflammatory drugs) is the most common form of drug abuse. Many elderly persons frequently ingest two or more prescription medications and may obtain medication from more than one physician. In fact, individuals older than age 65 average thirteen prescriptions each year. Physicians are not always aware of medications prescribed by others or alcohol use patterns among their patients. The rate of elderly drug misuse and abuse of prescription medications is approximately twice as high as that for other adult age groups, but drug problems may be underestimated or not detected because the elderly are stereotyped as nonusers. Drug abuse estimates among individuals older than age 55 in the United States range from 500,000 to 2.5 million. This relatively low prevalence may reflect a cohort effect (lack of involvement in drug use for a generation), the reduced survivorship of drug abusers, or a maturing-out phenomenon. However, drug abuse in the elderly may increase threefold over the first quarter of the current millennium as those who began use in the 1960s and thereafter continue to remain users into old age.

Relatively lower quantities of drug use among the elderly may qualify as abuse because of the potential for drugs of abuse to exert life-threatening consequences. Drug effects on the elderly may be more long lasting because of relatively slower metabolic rates. Slowing metabolic rates, coupled with ingestion of many medications, may result in an increase in the likelihood of harmful drug interactions. Older adults are subject to many significant life changes that put them at risk for drug dependency. These stressful life changes include retirement, excessive leisure time, and loss of significant others (i.e., loss of social networks and social support). Other life adjustments that place the elderly at risk for drug abuse include potential functional loss and deterioration of physical and mental well-being, resulting in increased rates of use of prescription medications.

For older adults, one's purview of life as one in which to achieve a subjective sense of wisdom versus a subjective sense of despair (Erickson, 1968), as shaped by socioenvironmental experiences, such as amount of free time, lack of structure, and number of significant others remaining in one's social circles, may drive an individual to resort to constructive or destructive behavior. Programming that assists in continuing to help the elderly perceive a sense of social usefulness (e.g., by caretaking for other people or pets, volunteer work, and involvement in the Gray Panthers [activism]), means of enjoyment at a reasonable cost (e.g., which can be obtained through information provided by the American Association for Retired Persons and attendance at elder hostiles), and sense of independence (e.g., good medical care and supportive caretaking others obtained through reputable agencies) are essential. Also, close medical supervision of medicines being used by the elderly person is essential to prevent unwanted addiction and other consequences. In each of the developmental periods noted earlier, individuals may seek out available resources, logically consider options, and make decisions that are life-fulfilling to self and others (Table 20.1).

In summary, we need a taxonomy that integrates risk status, human development, theoretically based etiologic factors (a weakness of a CTC approach, which is more descriptive and eclectic), and processes of change with prevention and cessation strategies and modalities. A good "forest-eye" view of the addictions is needed to be able to do this. This larger view also may need to go way beyond drug addiction. Other addictions (both substance and process addictions), such as gambling, overeating, or uncontrolled sexual behavior or danger-seeking, may share similar underlying functions (Sussman, 2005c), and may need to be addressed through comparable means.

Breadth of Programming

One area that has not received much research attention is breadth of programming. Drug abuse prevention or cessation could involve addressing use of a single drug, use of any of several drugs, or behavior that pertains to drugs and healthy lifestyles. Programming that encompasses more than drug abuse could subsume substance and process addictions or even health promotion more broadly considered, such as instruction in good diet and exercise. Arguments that favor focusing on a single drug or on drug abuse include being able to provide a sufficient amount of drug-focused information, the possibility that different drugs might be used for different reasons, and the need to keep programming to a reasonable

Table 20.1. Potential prevention and treatment components by age group

Age group	Possible components
Young children (< 6 years)	Parent counseling (e.g., content involving increasing consistent, firm, and kind parenting skills)
	Education of parent in caretaking skills; what is expected and how to implement what is expected
	Elicit supportive and educative interactions of caretakers with child
	Teach self-control for caretaker and child
	Help child perceive closeness with parent (or guardian) and first school teachers (e.g., kindergarten and 1st grade); use of props may be involved (e.g., puppets)
	Resource acquisition assistance and skills instruction for caretakers
	Academic preparation skills for child and caretakers (e.g., preschool, adult school)
Older children (6–11 years)	Many of the same types of strategies as those used for young children, but using more verbal-based methods; instruction in emotion and needs recognition and communication may be very important
	Have children interact with adults outside the home (e.g., teachers)
	Parental proactive role in friendship selection and monitoring of children's friendships
	Parents should be good role models
	Knowledge of short-term and long-term consequences of drug use
Young teens (12–15 years)	Comprehensive social influence prevention programming
	Parent monitoring of friends (e.g., meet friend's parents)
	Academic remediation
	For some, drug abuse cessation treatment may be needed
Older teens (16–19 years)	Training in stress-coping skills (motivation/skills/decision-making) specific to drug abuse prevention
	Mentoring programs with prosocial adults outside the home
	Assistance with employment skills and resource acquisition
	For some older teens, education in parenting skills
	For some, drug abuse cessation treatment may be needed
Emerging adulthood (20–24 years)	Similar motivation/skills/decision-making model as that used with older teens for prevention
	Motivational interviewing strategies
	Assistance with transitioning and "settling down" into adulthood
	Drug abuse cessation treatment may be needed
Adults (25–50 years)	Enhance coping and decision-making skills, as prevention
	Provision of legal, medical, and other resources
	Remedial education or vocational training, if indicated
	Drug abuse cessation treatment may be needed
	Group support, including membership in self-help groups to maintain cessation
Elderly	Help enhance a sense of social usefulness to others and enjoyment
	Help develop a sense of independence
	Close medical supervision of medications
	For some, drug abuse cessation treatment may be needed

length. In addition, funding often comes from agencies that address specific drugs, although times are changing with funding often coming from multiple agencies. One main argument that favors the concurrent prevention or treatment of multiple drugs is that different drugs serve similar underlying functions (e.g., mesolimbic dopamine activity, associative learning processes, problem proneness, peer group solidarity, physical environmental disruption). Information can be efficiently provided that counteracts use of any one of several drugs by focusing on common underlying functions.

Even more inclusive, one may argue that unhealthy lifestyles in general reflect common underlying functions. Sedentary living, fatty diets, and drug use might best be counteracted together as a joint expression of a lack of wellness or problem proneness (Sussman & Ames, 2001). One review study suggests that prevention programs with a wide breadth are nearly as effective as narrowly focused programs (Johnson, MacKinnon, & Pentz, 1996). Although only a handful of studies were included in that review, the results suggest common underlying mechanisms at work that bridge levels of exploration (molecular to molar factors; Sussman & Unger, 2004) and provide a behaviorally healthful effect. Conscientiousness (industriousness and thinking of others, having a positive attitude), for example, appears to be one such underlying remedial factor in human living (see Sussman, 2005a, 2005b).

Not All Drugs Are Alike: The Unique Status of Alcohol and Alcohol Abuse

Alcohol kills more people than all other drugs except nicotine. Yet the use of alcohol has permeated almost all societies throughout most of recorded history. There have been a few unsuccessful periods of prohibition and there are some subcultures in which alcohol is used relatively little (e.g., some Islamic societies and the Latter Day Saints). Indeed, the abuse of alcohol has led to establishment of its own institute at the National Institutes of Health (National Institute of Alcoholism and Alcohol Abuse, NIAAA). Overall, however, this is one drug that has been largely accepted across different societies alongside a widespread denial that alcohol use is dangerous (Hansen, 1994). Prevention of alcohol abuse, and cessation of heavy drinking among large general populations, has been relatively difficult to affect among substances of abuse (Komro & Toomey, 2002). Because of the special status of this drug of abuse and dependence, we earmark it as a major direction for future research.

At least four major reasons exist for this quandary – that being the fact that alcohol causes great negative consequences yet remains widely accepted. First, ambiguity surrounds information about the dangers of alcohol use. Small doses of alcohol are purportedly healthy, at least among an adult population (Dufour, 1999). Generally, available guidelines suggest that no more than one drink a day for women and two drinks a day for men (i.e., 12 oz of beer, 5 oz of wine, or 1.5 oz of 80-proof spirits) are considered a ceiling of healthy drinking (Dufour, 1999). Many adults do get drunk, particularly during certain holidays (e.g., New Year's Eve), perhaps suggesting that some drunkenness is not perceived as causing irreversible consequences. Arguably any drinking is dangerous for a young teen because it could set up a pattern for heavy drinking as a young adult. Among youth, it is not clear that small doses are injurious, although they are illegal. Certainly, larger doses of alcohol may be dangerous, particularly while the nervous system is still developing (Williams & Perry, 1998). Unfortunately, relatively few treatment agents will warn youth about the dangers of alcohol use. For example, at present only about 50% of primary care physicians warn their young patients about the risks of alcohol abuse (Millstein & Marcell, 2003).

Second, that alcohol use is illegal among youth but not among adults may present alcohol as "forbidden fruit" among teens. Many cultures, through use of rituals, special events, specialty shops, or in their mass media, promote use of alcohol as a means of social lubrication, sophistication, or as rites of passage to adulthood. Because adults can legally drink, youth may be more tempted to drink than if drinking were not appropriate for anyone. Alcohol use among adults is widely promoted through the media, in advertisements, in movies, and on television. Countless movies depict teens "growing up" and drinking to excess and experiencing almost transcendent pleasure. Advent of warning labels on alcohol products is a new phenomenon and, arguably, these warning labels carry little power in the content of their messages. Not surprisingly, the major causes of death among older teens and emerging adults are alcohol related.

Third, alcohol generally is easy to obtain by teens as well as by adults. It can even be manufactured at home with readily available products. Simply purchasing brewer's yeast or yeast used to make bread and adding water and sugar and time can result in an intoxicating beverage. It would seem difficult to demand that yeast be sold behind the counter at grocery stores, for example. Unlike other drugs, if an individual wants to drink and is inventive, there simply is no means of deterrence. Deterrence can be focused only on sales of commercially produced alcohol products. Demand for proof of age is enforced in some countries but not in many others. Also, there are many venues, such as weddings, in which youth are permitted or encouraged to drink. Supply reduction regarding alcohol is a difficult task.

Finally, many researchers popularly assert that different youth or adults are differentially susceptible to incurring chronic problems with alcohol. "Alcoholism" is influenced by a complex interaction of multiple genes and environmental factors. Possibly, up to 50% of alcoholism has a genetic basis (Gordis, 2000), which may be related to variation in genes that influence metabolic processes, neurobiological systems, and dispositions. These genetic influences may result in relatively early onset and sensation-seeking tendencies. Some people may assume that a progression of alcohol use among vulnerable individuals is intractable based on genetic research and, consequently, prevention would not be successful. Genetic research, however, runs parallel to and separate from other research findings, suggesting that social and environmental variables are largely responsible for delayed initiation of alcohol use (Williams & Perry, 1998). Even though a blanket of skepticism clouds the progress of alcohol prevention, this work continues to prevent negative consequences that adolescents who drink alcohol may experience.

For the future, either safe levels or frequencies of "getting drunk" need to be established or else great discouragement of getting drunk ever should be promoted by researchers and practitioners. Until a more detailed understanding of the parameters of safe drinking is understood, arguably, it will be difficult to make progress in alcohol control. Certainly, statements about the safety of one or two drinks per day are simplistic and don't take into account parameters of intensity of drinking on drinking occasions and heavy drinking days interspersed among nondrinking days. Prevention and cessation programmers need more clear parameters on which to construct their programming.

Special Populations

One arena where relatively little prevention or treatment work on alcohol or other drug abuse and dependence have been completed is with special populations. Demographics, most often, delineate special populations. There is a recent impetus for studying special population issues based on health disparities. Special populations include minority groups, females, those in rural regions, those who are relatively poor, those individuals about whom relatively less is known (etiology), those for whom less programming has been developed, and those for whom less programming has been delivered (reduced access or reach). In America today, youth as well as adults from special populations are underresearched, underserved, and poorly represented in prevention studies. However, as discussed below, special populations may be well represented or even overrepresented in treatment inpatient populations. Within the National Institutes of Health, special population research is becoming a focal point, as illustrated by the significant investment by the National Institute on Alcohol Abuse and Alcoholism in the prevention of teenage alcohol-related problems in special populations (U.S. DHHS, 1998a).

Social influence programming or comprehensive life skills training is considered the most effective programming currently available and may be relatively effective for minority youth as compared to White youth (Tobler et al., 2000). However, the effectiveness of this programming on alcohol use is relatively weak when compared to other drugs (Komro & Toomey, 2002). In addition, it is important to note that most drug abuse prevention research has been conducted with White majority populations. For example, in Tobler and colleagues' (2000) review of 207 drug abuse prevention program studies, only 42 studies involved greater than a 50% non-White majority (20% of the studies).

Recently, Sussman (2005e) completed an exhaustive review of alcohol prevention programs among special populations. Among Hispanics, twelve of fourteen programs reported behavioral outcomes data. Of the twelve programs, 58% found preventive effects. Among Blacks, twelve of fifteen programs reported behavioral outcomes data. Of these twelve programs, 58% found preventive effects. Among Asian Americans, all five programs reported behavioral outcomes data and 60% of the programs found preventive effects. Among Native Americans, five of seven programs reported behavioral outcomes, and all five found preventive effects. Finally, 58% of the programs conducted at least in part in rural regions showed preventive effects (twelve of thirteen programs reported behavioral data). The pattern of these findings suggests that approximately 60% of currently developed alcohol prevention programming show effects on the alcohol use behaviors of different special populations.

Programs that include provision of bicultural education along with life skills material appear to be particularly promising. Most of these prevention studies were conducted with schools although about 50% included a family involvement component, 12% involved a media component, and 10% also emphasized environmental strategies. Both nondiscriminatory policies and empowerment motives may be important mediators of the effects of these types of programs. In addition, it is not clear why culturally focused components added to effective demand reduction programs increase their efficacy. Potential mediators (e.g., increased receptivity versus increased ethnic pride) should be examined. Clearly, much more research is needed among minority populations both in mixed-ethnic group settings and in monoethnic settings.

The evidence for involvement of special population participants involved in cessation treatment work appears to differ from prevention work. As reported by Rounds-Bryant, Kristiansen, and Hubbard (1999) in a survey conducted from 1993 through 1995 of 3,382 participants from six nationally dispersed urban areas, residential patients tended to be male and Black or Hispanic and had often been referred by the juvenile or criminal justice system. The current support indicated for inpatient substance abuse programs likely includes majority and minority populations. However, much work regarding this speculation is needed.

Very little quantitative empirical work on cultural sensitivity has been completed in the teen substance abuse treatment arena. However, research has shown that cultural factors should be considered, for example, regarding treatment placement decisions. A study conducted by Dinges and Duong-Tran (1993) found that Native American adolescents showed intense emotional strain, which can be counterproductive to treatment, when removed from their family for inpatient setting treatment. Thus, for some youth, it may be advantageous to ensure that family bonds are not disrupted by out of home placements. Instead, such youth may be better served through a more intensive outpatient setting; however, if inpatient treatment is more appropriate, it should be accompanied by frequent family contact and support.

At this point in time, it is not clear what might be the most effective composition of ethnic group-oriented programming. One possibility is that deep structure culturally appropriate programming (Kumpfer, Alvarado, Smith, & Bellamy, 2002), which considers critical values and traditions of a culture in specific social sectors, might be most effective. However, almost none of this type of programming has provided an evaluation of behavioral effects. A second possibility is that surface structure culturally appropriate programming, which considers and adapts graphic material and names, as examples, is sufficient to make ethnic-oriented programming maximally effective (Kumpfer, Alvarado, Smith, & Bellamy, 2002). Current evaluations of such programming are promising (e.g., Botvin, Griffin, Diaz, & Ifill-Williams, 2001a, 2001b). One caveat is that there may be a tendency for implementers to add ethnic-specific elements of programming, while reducing the dosage provided of the evidence-based program material. This change in the programmatic soup's ingredients could reduce the program's overall effectiveness (Kumper, Alvarado, Smith, & Bellamy, 2002).

A third possibility is that generic programming is relatively effective in the prevention of alcohol use and that interactive contents permit incorporation of ethnic-specific features (Dent et al., 1996). Indeed, in any given community, diversity exists among members of ethnic groups and between ethnic groups, and sensitivity to each other's differences may be imperative to mobilize unifying action that prevents alcohol use. If a program can't address all groups involved in the programming, then perhaps a more generic form is needed. It would appear that generic programming is effective across gender, socioeconomic status, and region. Regarding any special population, a direct test of these three program formulations (deep structure, surface structure, or generic) has not yet been completed.

Youth is one type of special population that often is not considered. Youth are relatively unlikely to receive substance abuse cessation treatment. Of the few studies completed on youth, noted methodological flaws in studies include small sample sizes, lack of placebo-type control groups, lack of random assignment to conditions, insufficient descriptions of treatments or facilitators, inadequate follow-up of dropouts, and lack of biochemical validation (Deas & Thomas, 2001; Kaminer, Burleson, & Goldberger, 2002; Liddle & Dakof, 1995). The first randomized trial to provide follow-up data beyond 12 months was completed by Henggeller and colleagues (2002), in their evaluation of Multisystemic Therapy (MST) at a 4-year follow-up among juvenile offenders (80 of 118 youth had been randomly assigned to MST or usual community services). Effects were maintained for aggressive criminal activity but not for property crimes, and an effect was apparent for marijuana abstinence (see Sussman, Skara, & Ames, 2006). Thus, much more work is needed on youth in recovery and should be considered as a notable special population.

Transdisciplinary Work

It has become a truism that drug abuse is a multifaceted, complex public health problem that requires the efforts of multiple disciplines to address the biological, psychological, and social aspects that contribute to the prevention of the onset and progression of the disorder (APA, 2000). However, merely acknowledging the need for involvement of multiple disciplines is not sufficient. In fact, increasingly it is becoming the case that merely including measures of convenience from multiple disciplines to capture different perspectives, to explain more variance in behavior, or to present a comprehensive program package is both theoretically and practically inadequate.

Theories and findings from discrete disciplinary and research foci can be used in integrative ways to build "new prevention science." The transdisciplinary approach creates a synergy through combining diverse theories and findings with the potential for evolving into new entities important in their own right. A transdisciplinary focus may help to "open up the box" to explain for whom specific prevention or cessation approaches work best and under what conditions. A transdisciplinary approach to understanding or controlling for cohort and contextual differences, and statistically controlling for varying influences at different levels of analysis, would help set expectations for future prevention and cessation research.

Rosenfield (1992) provided one of the early reviews of transdisciplinary research, proposing that such an approach could yield qualitatively different results than those discovered by multidisciplinary or interdisciplinary teams. She defined transdisciplinarity as a problem-focused approach that blurs the boundaries between disciplines with the assumption that investigators using the approach must have sufficient knowledge of each other's disciplines to enable effective communication. The result is a new assimilation of ideas and methods. Rosenfield provided an informative history of effective but relatively rare transdisciplinary integrations across social and medical sciences beginning in the 1940s. In her view, transdisciplinary research can be differentiated from both multidisciplinary research and interdisciplinary research (which involves investigators from different arenas working on similar research problems, separately or together), with transdisciplinary research having the greatest potential for innovation. In transdisciplinary research, a new integrative vocabulary is forged across disciplines and creates new syntheses (e.g., neurobehavioral science). Of course, one may argue that different types of team approaches may be used to answer different questions and that the transdisciplinary approach may not be needed or desirable to address all research questions. Still, at the very minimum, the transdisciplinary perspective has not been used often and is an exciting perspective to pursue (see Fuqua et al., 2004).

Translation

Translation research refers to an extended process that links basic work to application and application to dissemination. As an example, in the drug abuse prevention arena, examination of associations of D4 dopamine receptor genes with mesolimbic dopamine pathway operations and the trait of sensation seeking has led to an active model of information exposure that develops fast-paced dramatic portrayals in televised PSAs designed to reduce marijuana use among high sensation-seeking adolescents. Campaigns so developed have been found to reverse upward trends in 30-day marijuana use among high sensation-seeking youth, and institutionalizing this type of campaign is ongoing (Palmgreen et al., 2001; Pentz et al., 2006; Slater et al., 2005).

Of course, a reciprocal and iterative process of using basic science discoveries to develop innovative prevention and treatment strategies is one keystone of translation. Using basic science to inform prevention and treatment research and using discoveries from prevention and treatment research to develop new questions for basic science are important feedback loops of translation. Translation research requires not only different phases (e.g., from basic research to application and back) but also different programmatic and scientific roles within and across phases. These roles may involve persons from rather different academic backgrounds that develop a consensual model of inquiry (i.e., transdisciplinary research) to be able to engage in effective translation. First, there are basic etiologic researchers (e.g., cognitive science, neuroscience, and social inequities) who engage in research that may or may not include suggestion of an application. Second, there are applied etiologic researchers who take basic research in a general area and apply it to a topic (e.g., drug abuse etiology). Third, there are strategist-type researchers who take applied etiology and develop strategies that have an ultimate aim to affect behavior (prevention or cessation), perhaps with a more proximal effect on a community or on neurotransmitter firing. Fourth, there are context adapters who take strategies and place them in a context (e.g., schools and homes). Finally, there are "institutionalizers" who "hard-wire" a program into a context (e.g., policymakers). This list of roles does not exhaust the types of roles that exist or are possible but summarizes some typical roles. Also, although a researcher might focus primarily on one role, he or she might take on additional roles in any category. For example, a basic researcher might suggest an intervention that no other researcher in the chain of translation considers. Nevertheless, the characterization of roles from basic researcher to institutionalizer seems to map well into what many researchers do.

Interestingly, although treated as two different topics, transdisciplinary work and translation work are part of a matrix that may represent a new "revolution" of drug abuse prevention and cessation research. We are asked to bridge across disciplines and consider solutions that might have an enduring behavioral impact from the onset of our work (Sussman, 2006). This text provides one example of an effort to accomplish just that purpose, to represent a bridge to a new transdisciplinary research culture that pertains at the same time to translation work. Two extremes of translation work warrant mention here. These topics were not discussed much elsewhere in this text but they are essential to develop programming that might have an impact and implement effective programming that could be utilized by the public. These two areas are of program development and diffusion research.

Importance of Empirical Program Development
A program is only as strong as its weakest link. Health behavior program development involves two central ideas. The first concept is that programs are developed beginning with certain theoretical notions of participants' crucial needs and relevant mechanisms of change. The second concept is that the movement from theory to the completed program involves a series of steps or stages. What these stages are may vary widely across projects. However, the idea is to evaluate a program while developing it to make a program as strong as possible from the outset. Sussman (2001) proposed a six-step "program development chain" model. The program development steps are (1) theory and assessment, (2) pooling

and warehousing, (3) concept evaluation, (4) immediate impact evaluation, (5) program construction and piloting, and (6) immediate outcomes/mediation assessment.

First, concurrent with the assessment of a target population's needs, a theory of program mediation should be developed to address the identified needs. Program activities that plausibly might address these health needs should come to mind, but health behavior program development begins with use of theory, an organized set of concepts that suggest the causal mechanism through which an outcome occurs (e.g., van Ryn & Heaney, 1992). Second, there is a need to systematically pool and warehouse promising activities for new uses. This second step of program development involves collecting previously used activities and teaching methods from other projects in related areas that have obtained research support, or conceptualizing new plausible activities, and that might be useful in the present development context, guided by the theory and assessment work.

Third, there is a need to systematize a set of perceived efficacy studies that can screen among promising activity ideas gathered in the last step for additional program development work. Numerous ideas gathered during the previous step can be contrasted using methods that are relatively time and cost-effective (e.g., focus groups and theme studies). Fourth, there is a need to systematize a set of immediate impact studies that can provide a means of determining workability of individual program components. Fifth, there is a need to systematize program construction and pilot testing of a complete program. Rules of construction, including a consideration of program content and process sequencing, along with a consideration of pragmatics of testing a complete program, should be addressed. Finally, there is a need to refine a set of immediate posttest/posttreatment activity set measures that predict longer term outcomes from short-term measures. Pilot testing outcome measures should be able to predict not only target population receptivity but also longer term behavior. This model is exacting, and a text has been written that explicates it (Sussman, 2001). However, much more research is needed to find the more effective but expedient and cost-effective means of program development.

Diffusion

How do we hard-wire programming? Diffusion is defined as the spread of new knowledge, usually referred to as an innovation, to a defined population over time through specific channels. The diffusion of innovative programs is characterized as a four-stage process (Rogers, 2003): (1) dissemination, (2) adoption, (3) implementation, and (4) maintenance. The first stage is dissemination, in which target population decision-makers are made aware of successful programs and are encouraged to adopt them. The second stage of diffusion is adoption, in which the decision-makers state a commitment to initiate a program. The third stage, implementation, occurs when appropriate personnel deliver the program. The final stage is maintenance, in which decision-makers and implementers are encouraged to continue use of the program. Rohrbach, Graham, and Hansen (1993) investigated these latter three stages in a school-based alcohol use prevention program. Although all schools agreed to adopt the program, and about 80% of trained teachers (i.e., of sixty teachers) implemented one or more lessons after training, only 25% maintained implementation the next year. Those who maintained implementation reported fewer years of teaching experience and more enthusiasm for delivery of the program. Principal encouragement, not intensive teacher training, increased rates of maintenance.

If decision-makers feel a belonging to or ownership of a program, they are more likely to make sure it is implemented than if they attribute its delivery to some outside agent. Ultimately, programming is most likely to be maintained when decision-making regarding program implementation is institutionalized, and people are paid for their efforts. Work to better institutionalize evidence-based drug abuse prevention and cessation programming is ongoing. Some aspects of dissemination research, such as following the flow of utilization from purchase to long-term use, are proving to be extremely difficult. Dissemination monitoring systems are sorely needed.

A Final Comment on Future Directions

We tend to fixate at certain etiologies for a time. We find something that predicts and often don't test enough for alternative explanations that might explain the phenomenon of interest better or explain a wider range of phenomena. For example, in primary prevention with young teens, many assume that counteraction of social influences is the primary ingredient of good prevention programming. Yet, MacKinnon et al. (1991) found that in addition to peer disapproval and relatively low prevalence estimates of use (social influence variables), negative outcome expectancies for tobacco and other drug effects also mediated effects obtained in a large-scale, community-based prevention project (Midwestern Prevention Project; Pentz, Dwyer, et al., 1989). Similar findings have been uncovered in arenas focused only on alcohol use prevention and tobacco use prevention (Donaldson et al., 1996). When one manipulates social normative perceptions, one is manipulating a class of outcome expectancies (i.e., by participating in a behavior, one expects certain outcomes to occur for them or to them). If outcome expectancies per se are what mediate program effects, then nonsocial outcome expectancy changes also could affect rates of tobacco and other drug use. Alternative explanations of prevention and cessation program effects need much more investigation (Sussman et al. 1995).

Another important issue in prevention and cessation science is consideration of the cultural backdrop of programming. For example, consider a potential national scenario that may apply to tobacco use. If tobacco is promoted by the government, if the society is permissive regarding tobacco use, if death is not viewed with particular distraught, if addiction and tobacco-related disease is okay, if somehow use by adults is considered appropriate and a right of passage, and/or if rigorous work is considered too expensive or irrelevant, any tobacco use prevention or control option is likely to be doomed. One might say that the large social environmental climate serves as the backdrop or primary force of change. Arguably, activism efforts to change perceptions of acceptability or possibly safety of use, or enhancement of the importance of quality of life, are needed.

We may summarize the future needs in drug abuse etiology, prevention, and cessation as follows, based on the information presented in this chapter. First, there is much work to be done in the future on the causal modeling and statistical modeling of the relations among neurobiological, cognitive, small group, and large social and physical environment variables to understand the etiology of drug problems. In addition to these models, one needs to model in time and drug type as variables to refine our understanding of the difference between drug use and drug use consequences warranting assistance. Second, we need a taxonomy that meshes in risk status, human development, and theoretically based etiologic factors, with prevention and cessation strategies and modalities to learn whether programming should pertain to a single drug, all drugs, all addictions, or wellness in general. Third, we need to address the differential status imparted to different drugs. Consistency of treatment of drugs of abuse is essential to effective prevention and treatment. For example, promoting alcohol use within many societies, while discouraging marijuana use at the same time, may not jibe well with scientific reason. Such legal decisions could undermine effective control efforts. Fourth, the degree to which programming can be applied to many populations or needs specialization (tailoring) to specific populations demands much research effort. Fifth, working within rapidly changing technology that facilitates a transdiscliplinary–translation matrix framework needs much refinement and inclusion of many types of researchers to be effective. These five issues are only a subset of the many needs in work on drug misuse etiology, prevention, and cessation. The reader can examine each of the chapters of this book and uncover more issues not discussed herein. We only intended to bring up five of what we believe are among the most central issues. The future is upon us; we had better get to work.

References

Aber, J. L., Jones, S. M., Brown, J. L., Chaudry, N., & Samples, F. (1998). Resolving conflict creatively: Evaluating the developmental effects of a school-based violence prevention program in neighborhood and classroom context. *Development & Psychopathology, 10*, 187–213.

Abrantes, A. M., Brown, S. A., & Tomlinson, K. L. (2004). Psychiatric comorbidity among inpatient substance abusing adolescents. *Journal of Child and Adolescent Substance Abuse, 13*, 83–101.

Adams, E. H., Gfoerer, J. C., & Rouse, B. A. (1989). Epidemiology of substance abuse including alcohol and cigarette smoking. *Annual New York Academy of Science, 562*, 14–20.

Addiction Alternatives. (n.d.). *Contemporary addiction treatments: Science-based alternatives to AA and other 12-step methods.* Retrieved March 12, 2006, from www.addictionalternatives. com

ADE Incorporated. (1987). *Juvenile Automated Substance Abuse Evaluations (JASAE).* Clarkston, MI: Author.

Agnew, R., & Peters, A. A. R. (1986). The techniques of neutralization: An analysis of predisposing and situational factors. *Criminal Justice and Behavior, 13*, 81–97.

Akers, R. L., Krohn, M. D., Lanza-Kaduce, L., & Radosevich, M. (1979). Social learning and deviant behavior: A specific test of a general theory. *American Sociological Review, 44*, 636–655.

Alcoholics Anonymous. (1976). *Alcoholics Anonymous.* New York: Alcoholics Anonymous World Services, Inc.

Alcoholics Anonymous. (2005, July). *Group membership.* AA Grapevine, 61, http://www.aagrapevine.org/da/browsesearchresult.php?da = dt%3A2005_7&q = membership+survey&btnNarrowSearch.x = 22&btnNarrowSearch.y = 17

Alexander, C., Piazza, M., Mekos, D., & Valente, T. (2001). Peers, schools, and adolescent cigarette smoking. *Journal of Adolescent Health, 29*, 22–30.

Alexander, J. F., Barton, C., Schiaro, R. S., & Parsons, B. V. (1976). Systems-behavioral intervention with families of delinquents: Therapist characteristics, family behavior, and outcome. *Journal of Consulting and Clinical Psychology, 44*, 656–664.

Alexander, J. F., & Parsons, B. V. (1973). Short-term behavioral intervention with delinquent families: Impact on family process and recidivism. *Journal of Abnormal Psychology, 3*, 219–225.

Almog, Y. J., Anglin, M. D., & Fisher, D. G. (1993). Alcohol and heroin use patterns of narcotics addicts: Gender and ethnic differences. *American Journal of Drug & Alcohol Abuse, 19*, 291–238.

American Psychiatric Association. (2000). *Diagnositc and statistical manual of mental disorders (DSM-IV-TR).* Washington, DC: Author.

American Psychological Association. (2006). *Report of the APA: Task Force on Urban Psychology: Toward an urban psychology: Research, action, and policy.* Retrieved December 20, 2006, from http://www.apa.org/pi/wpo/tf_report_urban_psychology.pdf

Ames, S. L., Franken, I. H. A., & Coronges, K. (2006). Implicit cognition and drugs of abuse. In R. W. Wiers & A. W. Stacy (Eds.), *Handbook on implicit cognition and addiction* (pp. 363–378). Thousand Oaks, CA: Sage.

Ames, S. L., Grenard, J., Thush, C., Sussman, S., Wiers, R. W., & Stacy, A. W. (2007). Comparison of indirect assessments of association as predictors of marijuana use among at-risk adolescents. *Experimental and Clinical Psychopharmacology, 15*, 204–218.

Ames, S. L., Sussman, S., & Dent, C. W. (1999). Pro-drug use myths and competing constructs in the prediction of substance use among youth at continuation high schools: A one-year prospective study. *Personality and Individual Differences, 26*, 987–1003.

Ames, S. L., Zogg, J. B., & Stacy, A. W. (2002). Implicit cognition, sensation seeking, marijuana use, and driving behavior among drug offenders. *Personality and Individual Differences, 33*, 1055–1072.

An Action Forum of the Global Anti-prohibition Movement. (n.d.). Retrieved on September 6, 2007 from http://www.legalize.org/global/

Angleitmer, A., Riemann, R., & Spinath, F. M. (2004). Investigating the ZKPQ-III-R: Psychometric properties, relations to the five-factor model, and genetic and environmental influences on its scales and facets. In R. M. Stelmack (Ed.), *On the psychobiology of personality: Essays in honor of Marvin Zuckerman* (pp. 89–105). New York: Elsevier.

Anglin, M. D., Prendergast, M., & Farabee, D. (1998). *The effectiveness of coerced treatment for drug-abusing offenders.* Paper presented at the Office of National Drug Control Policy's Conference of Scholars and Policy Makers, Washington, DC.

Annas, G. J., Glantz, L. H., & Roche, P. A. (1995). Drafting the genetic privacy act: Science policy, and practical considerations. *Journal of Law, Medicine & Ethics, 69*, 1223–1242.

Annis, H. M. (1982). *Inventory of drinking situations.* Toronto: Addiction Research Foundation.

Annis, H. M. (1984). A basic follow-up package. In F. B. Glaser, H. A. Skinner, S. Pearlman, R. L. Segal, B. Sisson, A. C. Ogborne, et al. (Eds.), *A system of health care delivery* (Vol. III; report). Toronto: Addiction Research Foundation.

Annis, H. M., & Graham, J. M. (1992). *Inventory of drug taking situations user's guide.* Toronto: Addiction Research Foundation of Ontario.

Anonymous. (1929). The nightmare of cocaine by a former "Snow-Bird." *North American Review, 227*, 418–422.

Antonovsky, A. (1984). The sense of coherence as a determinant of health. In J. D. Matarazzo, S. M. Weiss, J. A. Herd, N. E. Miller & S. M. Weiss (Eds.), *Behavioral health: A handbook of health enhancement and disease prevention* (pp. 114–129). New York: Wiley.

Armitage, C. J. (2004). Evidence that implementation intentions reduce dietary fat intake: A randomized trial. *Health Psychology, 23*, 319–323.

Arria, A. M., Tarter, R. E., & Van Thiel, D. H. (1991). Vulnerability to alcoholic liver disease. *Recent Developments in Alcoholism, 9*, 185–204.

Atkinson, D. R., Poston, W. C., Furlong, M. J., & Mercado, P. (1989). Ethnic group preferences for counselor characteristics. *Journal of Counseling Psychology, 36*, 68–72.

Baddeley, A. (1983). Working memory. *Philosophical Transactions of the Royal Society of London (Series B), Biological Sciences, 110*, 311–324.

Baddeley, A. (1996). The fractionation of working memory. *Proceedings of the National Academy of Sciences, 93*, 13468–13472.

Baddeley, A., & Wilson, B. A. (2002). Prose recall and amnesia: Implications for the structure of working memory. *Neuropsychologia, 40*, 1737–1743.

Bailey, S. L., & Rachal, J. V. (1993). Dimensions of adolescent problem drinking. *Journal of Studies on Alcohol, 54*, 555–565.

Baker, J. R., Jatlow, P., & McCance-Katz, E. F. (2007). Disulfiram effects on responses to intravenous cocaine administration. *Drug and Alcohol Dependence, 87*, 202–209.

Baler, R. D., & Volkow, N. D. (2006). Drug addiction: The neurobiology of disrupted self-control. *Trends in Molecular Medicine, 12*, 559–566.

Bandura, A. (1986). *Social foundations of thought and action: A social cognitive theory.* Englewood Cliffs, NJ: Prentice Hall.

Barbor, T. F. (1994). Overview: Demography, epidemiology, and psychopharmacology: Making sense of the connections. *Addiction, 89*, 1391–1396.

Bardo, M. T. (1998). Neuropharmacological mechanisms of drug reward: Beyond dopamine in the nucleus accumbens. *Critical Review Neurobiology, 1*, 37–67.

Bardo, M. T., Donohew, R. L., & Harrington, N. G. (1996). Psychobiology of novelty seeking and drug seeking behavior. *Behavioural Brain Research, 77,* 23–43.

Bargh, J., & Chartrand, T. (1999). The unbearable automaticity of being. *American Psychologist, 54,* 462–479.

Barnes, G. M., & Welte, J. W. (1986). Patterns and predictors of alcohol use among 7–22th grade students in New York State. *Journal of Studies on Alcohol, 47,* 53–62.

Bartlett, D. L., & Steele, J. B. (2004, October 24). The health of nations. *New York Times,* p. 11.

Basen-Engquist, K., O'Hara-Tompkins, N., Lovato, C. Y., Lewis, M. J., Parcel, G. S., & Gingiss, P. (1994). The effect of two types of teacher training. *Journal of School Health, 64,* 334–339.

Battjes, R. J., Gordon, M. S., O'Grady, K. E., Kinlock, T. W., Katz, E. C., & Sears, E. A. (2004). Evaluation of a group-based substance abuse treatment program for adolescents. *Journal of Substance Abuse Treatment, 27,* 123–134.

Bauer, L. O., & Hesselbrock, V. M. (1999). P300 decrements in teenagers with conduct problems: Implications for substance abuse risk and brain development. *Biological Psychiatry, 46,* 263–272.

Bauman, K. E., Ennett, S. T., Foshee, V. A., Pemberton, M., King, T. S., & Koch, G. G. (2002). Influence of a family program on adolescent smoking and drinking prevalence. *Prevention Science, 3,* 35–42.

Bauman, K. E., Ennett, S. T., Foshee, V. A., Pemberton, M. K., Tonya S., & Koch, G. G. (2000). Influence of a family-directed program on adolescent cigarette and alcohol cessation. *Prevention Science, 1,* 227–237.

Bauman, K. E., & Fisher, L. A. (1986). On the measurement of friend behavior in research on friend influence and selection: Findings from longitudinal studies of adolescent smoking and drinking. *Journal of Youth and Adolescence, 15,* 345–353.

Bauman, K. E., Foshee, V. A., Ennett, S. T., Pemberton, M., Hicks, K. A., King, T. S., et al. (2001). The influence of a family program on adolescent tobacco and alcohol use. *American Journal of Public Health, 91,* 604–610.

Baumohl, J., & Room, R. (1987). Inebriety, doctors, and the state. Alcoholism treatment institutions before 1940. *Recent Developments in Alcoholism, 5,* 135–174.

Baumrind, D. (1978). Parental disciplinary patterns and social competence in children. *Youth & Society, 9,* 239–276.

Beauchaine, T. P., Katkin, E. S., Strassberg, Z., & Snarr, J. (2001). Disinhibitory psychopathoogy in male adolescents: Discriminating conduct disorder from attention-deficit/hyperactivity disorder through concurrent assessment of multiple autonomic states. *Journal of Abnormal Psychology, 110,* 610–624.

Bechara, A. (2002). The neurology of social cognition. *Brain, 125,* 1673–1675.

Bechara, A., Dolan, S., & Hindes, A. (2002). Decision-making and addiction (part II): Myopia for the future or hypersensitivity to reward? *Neuropsychologia, 40,* 1690–1705.

Bechara, A., & Martin, E. M. (2004). Impaired decision making related to working memory deficits in individuals with substance addictions. *Neuropsychology, 18,* 152–162.

Bechara, A., & Damasio, H. (2002). Decision-making and addiction (part I): impaired activation of somatic states in substance-dependent individuals when pondering decisions with negative future consequences. *Neuropsychologia, 40,* 1675–1689.

Bechara, D., Damasio, H., & Damasio, A. R. (2000). Emotion, decision making and the orbitofrontal cortex. *Cerebral Cortex, 10,* 295–307.

Beck, A. T., & Weishaar, M. E. (1989). Cognitive therapy. In R. J. Corsini & D. Wedding (Eds.), *Current psychotherapies* (4th ed., pp. 285–320). Itasca, IL: F.E. Peacock.

Beck, J. E. (1998). 100 Years of "Just Say No" versus "Just Say Know": Reevaluating drug education goals for the coming century. *Evaluation Review, 22,* 15–45.

Becker, M. H. (Ed.). (1974). *The health belief model and personal health behavior.* Thorofare, NJ: Charles B. Slack.

Beer, J. S., Heerey, E. A., Keltner, D., Scabini, D., & Knight, R. T. (2003). The regulatory function of self-conscious emotion insights from patients with orbitofrontal damage. *Journal of Personality and Social Psychology, 85,* 594–604.

Bennett, J. B., & Lehman, W. E. K. (1996). Employee attitude crystallization and substance use policy: Test of a classification scheme. *Journal of Drug Issues, 26,* 831–865.

Bennett, M. E., McCrady, B. S., Frankenstein, W., Laitman, L. A., Van Horn, D. H. A., & Keller, D. S. (1993). Identifying young adult substance abusers: The Rutgers Collegiate Substance Abuse Screening Test. *Journal of Studies on Alcohol, 54,* 522–527.

Berridge, K. C., & Robinson, T. E. (1995). The mind of an addicted brain: Neural sensitization of wanting versus liking. *Current Directions in Psychological Science, 4,* 71–76.

Berridge, K. C., & Robinson, T. E. (2003). Parsing reward. *Trends in Neurosciences, 26,* 507–513.

Biglan, A., Brennan, P. A., Foster, S. L., Holder, H. D., Miller, T. L., Cunningham, P. B., et al. (2004). *Helping adolescents at risk: Prevention of multiple problem behaviors.* New York: Guilford.

Bindra, D., & Stewart, J. (Eds.). (1966). *Introduction motivation.* Baltimore: Penguin Books.

Bjartveit, K., & Tverdol, A. (2005). Health consequences of smoking 1–4 cigarettes per day. *Tobacco Control, 14,* 315–320.

Blair, W. (1842). *An opium-eater in America.* Retrieved April 20, 2005, from http://www.druglibrary.org/schaffer/heroin/history/blair.htm

Blood, L., & Cornwall, A. (1994). Pretreatment variables that predict completion of an adolescent substance abuse treatment program. *Journal of Nervous and Mental Disease, 182,* 14–19.

Blum, K., Cull, J. G., Braverman, E., Chen, R., Thomas, J. H., & Comings, D. E. (1997). Reward deficiency syndrome: Neurobiological and genetic aspects. In E. P. Noble & K. Blum (Eds.), *Handbook of psychiatric genetics* (pp. 311–330). Boca Raton, FL: CRC Press.

Blum, K., Noble, E. P., Sheridan, P. J., Montgomery, A., Ritchie, T., Jagadeeswaran, P., et al. (1990). Allelic association of human dopamine D2 receptor gene in alcoholism. *Journal of the American Medical Association, 263,* 2055–2060.

Blum, R. W. (1995). Transition to adult health care: Setting the stage. *Journal of Adolescent Health, 17,* 3–5.

Bogg, T., & Roberts, B. W. (2004). Conscientiousness and health-related behaviors: A meta-analysis of the leading behavioral contributors to mortality. *Psychological Bulletin, 130,* 887–919.

Bordua, D. J. (1962). Some comments on theories of group delinquency. *Sociological Inquiry, 32,* 245–260.

Bosworth, K. (1996). *Definition of SAP.* Retrieved on March 2, 2005, from http://education.indiana.edu/cas/tt/v3i3/sapdef.html

Botvin, G. J., Baker, E., Dusenbury, L., Botvin, E. M., & Diaz, T. (1995). Long-term follow-up results of a randomized drug abuse prevention trial in a white middle-class population. *Journal of the American Medical Association, 273,* 1106–1112.

Botvin, G. J., Griffin, K. W., Diaz, T., & Ifill-Williams, M. (2001a). Preventing binge drinking during early adolescence: one- and two-year follow-up of a school-based preventive intervention. *Psychology of Addictive Behaviors, 15,* 360–365.

Botvin, G. J., Griffin, K. W., Diaz, T., & Ifill-Williams, M. (2001b). Drug abuse prevention among minority adolescents: posttest and one-year follow-up of a school-based preventive intervention. *Prevention Science, 2,* 1–13.

Bouquet, J. (1951). Cannabis. *United Nations Bulletin on Narcotics, 3,* 31.

Brady, K. T., & Sinha, R. (2005). Co-occurring mental and substance use disorders: The neurobiological effects of chronic stress. *American Journal of Psychiatry, 162,* 1483–1493.

Brannigan, R., Schackman, B. R., Falco, M., & Millman, R. B. (2004). The quality of highly regarded adolescent substance abuse treatment programs: Results of an in-depth national survey. *Archives of Pediatrics & Adolescent Medicine, 158,* 904–909.

Brantingham, P. L., & Brantingham, J. (1993). Nodes, paths and edges: Considerations on the complexity of crime, and the physical environment. *Journal of Environmental Psychology, 13,* 3–28.

Bray, J. W., & Zarkin, G. A. (1999). *An interview guide for employee assistance program data systems.* Research Triangle Park, N.C.: Research Triangle Institute, http://www.drugfreeworkplace.gov/ResourceCenter/r108.pdf

Brecher, E. M. (1972). *The Consumers Union report on licit and illicit drugs.* Retrieved April 20, 2005, from http://www.druglibrary.org/schaffer/library/studies/cu/cumenu.htm

Briere, J. N. (1992). *Child abuse trauma: Theory and treatment of the lasting effects.* Newbury Park, CA: Sage.

Bronfenbrenner, U. (1979). *The ecology of human development: Experiments by nature and design.* Cambridge, MA: Harvard University Press.

Brooner, R. K., King, V. L., Kidorf, M., & Bigelow, G. E. (1997). Psychiatric and substance use comorbidity among treatment-seeking opioid abusers. *Archives of General Psychiatry, 54,* 71–80.

Brown, B., & Lohr, M. (1987). Peer-group affiliation and adolescent self-esteem: An integration of ego-identity and symbolic-interaction theories. *Journal of Personality and Social Psychology, 52,* 47–55.

Brown, B. B., Mounts, N., Lamborn, S. D., & Steinberg, L. (1993). Parenting practices and peer group affiliation in adolescence. *Child Development, 64,* 467–482.

Brown, S. A. (1999). NIAAA Extramural Scientific Advisory Board: Treatment. In *Treatment of adolescent alcohol problems: Research review and appraisal* (pp. 1–26). Bethesda, MD: NIAAA.

Brown, S. A., Christiansen, B. A., & Goldman, M. S. (1987). The alcohol expectancy questionnaire: An instrument for the assessment of adolescent and adult alcohol expectancies. *Journal of Studies on Alcohol, 48,* 483–491.

Brown, S. A., Goldman, M. S., Inn, A., & Anderson, L. R. (1980). Expectations of reinforcement from alcohol: Their domain and relation to drinking patterns. *Journal of Consulting and Clinical Psychology, 48,* 419–426.

Brown, S. A., Vik, P. W., & Creamer, V. A. (1989). Characteristics of relapse following adolescent substance abuse treatment. *Addictive Behaviors, 14,* 291–300.

Brown, S. A., Vik, P. W., Patterson, T. L., & Grant, I. (1995). Stress, vulnerability, and adult alcohol relapse. *Journal of Studies on Alcohol, 56,* 538–545.

Bry, B. H., McKeon, P., & Pandina, R. J. (1982). Extent of drug use as a function of number or risk factors. *Journal of Abnormal Psychology, 91,* 273–279.

Bufe, C. (1991). *Alcoholics Anonymous: Cult or cure?* San Francisco: See Sharp Press.

Bukowski, W. J. (2003). The emerging science of drug prevention. In Z. Sloboda & W. J. Bukoski (Eds.), *Handbook of drug abuse prevention: Theory, science, and practice* (pp. 3–26). New York: Kluwer Academic/Plenum.

Buller, D. B., Borland, R., Woodall, W. G., Hall, J. R., Hines, J. M., Burris-Woodall, P., et al. (2006). Randomized trials on consider this, a tailored, Internet-delivered smoking prevention program for adolescents. *Health Education & Behavior, 17,* 17.

Burke, B. L., Arkowitz, H., & Dunn, C. (2002). The efficacy of motivational interviewing and its adaptations: What we know so far. In W. R. Miller & S. Rollnick (Eds.), *Motivational interviewing: Preparing people for change* (pp. 217–250). New York: Guilford.

Burke, B. L., Arkowitz, H., & Menchola, M. (2003). The efficacy of motivational interviewing: A meta-analysis of controlled clinical trials. *Journal of Consulting and Clinical Psychology, 71,* 843–861.

Burke, H., & Markus, R. (1977). MacAndrew MMPI Alcoholism Scale: Alcoholism and drug addiction. *Journal of Psychology, 96,* 141–148.

Burke, R. (2000). Workaholism in organizations: Psychological and physical well-being consequences. *Stress Medicine, 16,* 11–16.

Burrough, P. (1986). *Principles of geographical information systems for land resource assessment.* Oxford: Clarendon.

Butcher, J. N., & Owen, P. L. (1978). Objective personality inventories: Recent research and some contemporary issues. In B. B. Wolman (Ed.), *Clinical diagnosis of mental disorders: A handbook* (pp. 475–546). New York: Plenum.

Cacioppo, J. T., Gardner, W. L., & Berntson, G. G. (1999). The affect system has parallel and integrative processing components: Form follows function. *Journal of Personality and Social Psychology, 76,* 839–855.

Cameron, R., Brown, K. S., Best, J. A., Pelkman, C. L., Madill, C. L., Manske, S. R., et al. (1999). Effectiveness of a social influences smoking prevention program as a function of provider type, training method, and school risk. *American Journal of Public Health, 89,* 1827–1831.

Cardinal, R. N., & Everitt, B. J. (2004). Neural and psychological mechanisms underlying appetitive learning: Links to drug addiction. *Current Opinion in Neurobiology, 14,* 156–162.

Carnes, P. J. (1996). Addiction or compulsion: Politics or illness. *Sexual Addiction and Compulsivity, 3,* 127–150.

Carroll, K. M., Fenton, L. R., Ball, S. A., Nich, C., Frankforter, T. L., Shi, J., et al. (2004). Effficacy of disulfiram and cognitive behavior therapy in cocaine-dependent outpatients: A randomized placebo-controlled trial. *Archives of General Psychiatry, 61,* 264–272.

Carroll, M. E., & Comer, S. D. (1996). Animal models of relapse. *Experimental and Clinical Psychopharmacology, 4,* 11–18.

Carter, B. L., & Tiffany, S. T. (1999). Meta-analysis of cue-reactivity in addiction research. *Addiction, 94,* 327–340.

Carver, C. (2004). Negative affects deriving from the behavioral approach system. *Emotion, 4,* 3–22.

CBC News Indepth: Drugs. (n.d.) *Crystal meth FAQs.* Retrieved September 6, 2007, from http://www.cbc.ca/news/background/drugs/crystalmeth.html

Centers for Disease Control and Prevention. (2004). *Fetal alchohol syndrome: Guidlines for referral and diagnosis.* Retrieved June 25, 2005, from http://www.cdc.gov/ncbddd/fas/documents/FAS_guidelines_accessible.pdf

Chaloupka, F. J., & Nair, R. (2000). International issues in the supply of tobacco: Recent changes and implications for alcohol. *Addiction, 95,* S477–S489.

Chamberlain, P., & Reid, J. B. (1998). Comparison of two community alternatives to incarceration for chronic juvenile offenders. *Journal of Consulting and Clinical Psychology, 66,* 624–633.

Channing Bete Company (n.d.). Communities That Care Prevention Planning System. Retrieved September 6, 2007, from http://www.channing-bete.com/prevention-programs/communities-that-care/

Chappel, J. N. (1992). Effective use of Alcoholics Anonymous and Narcotics Anonymous in treating patients. *Psychiatric Annals, 22,* 409–418.

Charlesworth, A., & Glantz, A. (2005). Smoking in the movies increases adolescent smoking: A review. *Pediatrics, 116,* 1–13.

Chasnoff, I. J. (1991). Drugs, alcohol, pregnancy and the neonate: Pay now or pay later. *Journal of the American Medical Association, 266,* 1567–1568.

Cheng, T. O. (1999). Letter. *Heart & Lung, 28,* 147–148.

Chiauzzi, E. J., & Liljegren, S. (1993). Taboo topics in addiction treatment: An empirical review of clinical folklore. *Journal of Substance Abuse Treatment, 10,* 303–316.

Childress, A. R., MC Lellan, A. T., Ehrman, R., & O'Brien, C. P. (1988). Classically conditioned responses in opioid and cocaine dependence: A role in relapse? In B. A. Ray (Ed.), *Learning factors in substance abuse* (DHHS Publication No. 88–1576, pp. 25–43). Washington, DC: U.S. Government Printing Office.

Chowell, G., Hyman, J. M., Eubank, S., & Castillo-Chavez, C. (2002). *Analysis of a real world network: The city of Portland* (Los Alamos Unclassified Report LA-UR-02–66580). Los Alamos, NM: Center for Nonlinear Studies, Los Alamos National Laboratory.

Christiansen, B. A., Smith, G. T., Roehling, P. V., & Goldman, M. S. (1989). Using alcohol expectancies to predict adolescent drinking behavior after one year. *Journal of Consulting and Clinical Psychology, 57,* 93–99.

Christopher, J. (1988). How to stay sober: Recovery without religion. Amherst: New York: Prometheus Books

Christophersen, A. S. (2000). Amphetamine designer drugs – An overview and epidemiology. *Toxicology Letters, 112–113,* 127–131.

Chuck, C. (1984). *A new pair of glasses.* Irvine, CA: New-Look.

Chung, T., Martin, C. S., & Winters, K. C. (2005). Diagnosis, course, and assessment of alcohol abuse and dependence in adolescents. *Recent Developments in Alcoholism, 17,* 5–27.

Cicchetti, D., & Rogosch, F. A. (2001). The impact of child maltreatment and psychopathology on neuroendocrine functioning. *Development and Psychopathology, 13,* 783–804.

Clark, B. (1962). *Educating the expert society.* San Francisco: Chandler.

Clarke, K. C. (2002). *Getting started with GIS* (4th ed.). Englewood Cliffs, NJ: Prentice Hall.

Clopton, J. R. (1978). Alcoholism and the MMPI: A review. *Journal of Studies on Alcohol, 39,* 1540–1558.

Clopton, J. R., Weiner, R. H. & Davis, H. G. (1980). Use of the MMPI in identification of alcoholic psychiatric patients. *Journal of Consulting and Clinical Psychology, 48,* 416–417.

Cohen, A. K. (1955). *Delinquent boys: The culture of the gang.* New York: The Free Press.

Cohen, S. (1988). Psychosocial models of the role of social support in the etiology of physical disease. *Health Psychology, 7,* 269–297.

College of Humanities, The Ohio State University. (n.d.). *Temperance & prohibition.* Retrieved August 20, 2005, from http://prohibition.osu.edu/

Collins, D. J., & Lapsley, H. M. (2002). *Counting the cost: Estimates of the social costs of drug abuse in Australia in 1998–9* (No. Monograph Series No. 49). Canberra, Australia: National Drug Strategy.

Collins, L. M., Graham, J. W., Rousculp, S. S., & Hansen, W. B. (1997). Heavy caffeine use and the beginning of the substance use onset process. In K. Bryant, M. Windle & S. West (Eds.), *The science of prevention: Methodological advances from alcohol and substance abuse research* (pp. 79–99). Washington, DC: American Psychological Association.

Community Anti-Drug Coalitions of America (CADCA). (n.d.) Home page. Retrieved May 5, 2006, from http://cadca.org/

Conklin, C. A., & Tiffany, S. T. (2001). The impact of imagining personalized versus standardized urge scenarios on cigarette craving and autonomic reactivity. *Experimental and Clinical Psychopharmacology, 9,* 399–408.

Conklin, C. A., & Tiffany, S. T. (2002). Cue-exposure treatment: Time for change. *Addiction, 97,* 1219–1221.

Connors, G. J. (1998). Overview of Project MATCH. *The Addictions Newsletter, 5,* 4–5.

Conrod, P. J., Stewart, S. H., Pihl, R. O., Côté, S., Fontaine, V., & Dongier, M. (2000). Efficacy of brief coping skills interventions that match different personality profiles of female substance abusers. *Psychology of Addictive Behaviors, 14,* 231–242.

Cools, A. R., & Gingras, M. A. (1998). Nijmegen high and low responders to novelty: A new tool in the search after the neurobiology of drug abuse liability. *Pharmacology, Biochemistry, and Behavior, 60,* 151–159.

Cooper, D. A. (2000). *Future synthetic drugs of abuse.* Retrieved September 6, 2007, from http://designer-drug.com/synth/index.html

Cornelius, J. R., Maisto, S. A., Pollock, N. K., Martin, C. S., Salloum, I. M., Lynch, K. G., et al. (2003). Rapid relapse generally follows treatment for substance use disorders among adolescents. *Addictive Behaviors, 28,* 381–386.

Council for Philosophical Studies. (1981). *Psychology and the philosophy of mind in the philosophy curriculum.* San Francisco: San Francisco State University.

Cox, M., & Fadardi, J. S. (2006). *New training technique helps alcoholics in battle with the booze.* Retrieved December 3, 2006, from http://www.eurekalert.org/pub_releases/2006-07/esr-ntt071806.php

Crabbe, J. C. (2002a). Alcohol and genetics: New models. *American Journal of Medical Genetics, 114,* 969–974.

Crabbe, J. C. (2002b). Genetic contributions to addiction. *Annual Review of Psychology, 53,* 435–462.

Crabbe, J. C., Phillips, T. J., Buck, K. J., Cunningham, C. L., & Belknap, J. K. (1999). Identifying genes for alcohol and drug sensitivity: recent progress and future directions. *Trends in Neurosciences., 22,* 173–179.

Crusio, W. E., Schwegler, H., & van Abeelen, J. H. F. (1989). Behavioral responses to novelty and structural variation of the hippocampus in mice: Quantitative-genetic analysis of behavior in the open-field. *Behavioural Brain Research, 32,* 75–80.

Cunningham, J. A. (1999). Resolving alcohol-related problems with and without treatment: The effects of different problem criteria. *Journal of Studies on Alcohol, 60,* 463–466.

Cunningham, J. A., & Breslin, F. C. (2004). Only one in three people with alcohol abuse or dependence ever seek treatment. *Addictive Behaviors, 29,* 221–223.

Cunningham, J. A., Sobell, L. S., & Sobell, M. B. (1996). Are disease and other conceptions of alcohol abuse related to beliefs about outcome and recovery? *Journal of Applied Social Psychology, 26,* 773–780.

Curry, J. F., Wells, K. C., Lochman, J. E., Craighead, W. E., & Nagy, P. D. (2003). Cognitive-behavioral intervention for depressed, substance-abusing adolescents: Development and pilot testing. *Journal of the American Academy of Child & Adolescent Psychiatry, 42,* 656–665.

Curry, S., Wagner, E. H. & Grothaus, L. C. (1990). Intrinsic and extrinsic motivation for smoking cessation. *Journal of Consulting and Clinical Psychology, 58*, 310–316.

Daley, D. C., & Salloum, I. (1999). Relapse prevention. In R. E. T. P. J. Ott & R. T. Ammerman (Eds.), *Sourcebook on substance abuse, etiology, epidemiology, assessment, and treatment* (pp. 255–263). Boston: Allyn & Bacon.

D'Amico, E. J., & Fromme, K. (1997). Health risk behaviors of adolescent and young adult siblings. *Health Psychology, 16*, 426–432.

Darkes, J., & Goldman, M. S. (1993). Expectancy challenge and drinking reduction: Experimental evidence for a mediational process. *Journal of Consulting and Clinical Psychology, 61*, 344–353.

Darkes, J., & Goldman, M. S. (1998). Expectancy challenge and drinking reduction: Process and structure in the alcohol expectancy network. *Experimental and Clinical Psychopharmacology, 6*, 1–13.

de Quincey, T. (1822). *Confessions of an English opium eater.* Retrieved April 20, 2005, from http://www.druglibrary.org/schaffer/History/dequinc1.htm

de Vries, H., Mudde, A., Leijs, I., Charlton, A., Vartiainen, E., Buijs, G., et al. (2003). The European Smoking Prevention Framework Approach (EFSA): An example of integral prevention. *Health Education Research, 18*, 611–626.

de Wit, H., & Richards, J. B. (2004). Dual determinants of drug use in humans: reward and impulsivity. In R. A. Bevins & M. T. Bardo (Eds.), *Motivational factors in the etiology of drug abuse* (pp. 127–158). Lincoln, N.E.: University of Nebraska Press.

Deas, D., Riggs, P., Langenbucher, J., Goldman, M., & Brown. (2000). Adolescent are not adults: Developmental considerations in alcohol users. *Alcoholism: Clinical and Experimental Research, 24*, 232–237.

Deas, D., & Thomas, S. E. (2001). An overview of controlled studies of adolescent substance abuse treatment. *The American Journal on Addictions, 10*, 178–189.

De Bellis, M. D., Clark, D. B., Beers, S. R., Soloff, P. H., Boring, A. M., Hall, J., et al. (2000). Hippocampal volume in adolescent-onset alcohol use disorders. *American Journal of Psychiatry, 157*, 737–744.

Debtors Anonymous. (n.d.). Retrieved June 4, 2005, from www.solvency.org

Deckel, A. W. (1999). Tests of executive functioning predict scores on the MacAndrew Alcoholism Scale. *Progress in Neuro-Psychopharmacology & Biological Psychiatry, 23*, 209–223.

DeJong, W. (2002). The role of mass mjedia campaigns in reducing high-risk drinking among college students. *Journal of Studies on Alcohol*, (Suppl.3), 182–192.

DeJong, W., & Wallack, L. (1999). A critical perspective on the drug czar's antidrug media campaign. *Journal of Health Communication, 4*, 155–160.

Dennis, M. L., Funk, R., Godley, S. H., Godley, M. D., & Waldron, H. (2004). Cross-validation of the alcohol and cannabis use measures in the Global Appraisal of Individual Needs (GAIN) and Timeline Followback (TLFB; Form 90) among adolescents in substance abuse treatment. *Addiction, 99*(Suppl. 2), 120–128.

Dent, C., & Biglan, A. (2004). Relation between access to tobacco and adolescent smoking. *Tobacco Control, 13*, 334–338.

Dent, C. W., Sussman, S., Ellickson, P. L., Brown, P., & Richardson, J. (1996). Is current drug abuse prevention programming generalizable across ethnic groups? *American Behavioral Scientist, 39*, 911–918.

Deren, S., Kang, S. Y., Colon, H. M., Andia, J. F., Robles, R. R., Oliver-Velez, D., et al. (2003). Migration and HIV risk behaviors: Puerto Rican drug injectors in New York City and Puerto Rico. *American Journal of Public Health, 93*, 812–816.

Deutsch, M., & Gerard, H. B. (1955). A study of normative and informational social influences upon individual judgment. *Journal of Abnormal and Social Psychology, 51*, 629–636.

Devine, P. G. (1989). Stereotypes and prejudice: Their automatic and controlled components. *Journal of Personality and Social Psychology, 56*, 5–18.

Deykin, E. Y., Levy, J. C., & Wells, V. (1987). Adolescent depression, alcohol, and drug abuse. *American Journal of Public Health, 77*, 178–182.

Diaz-Guerrero, R. (1984). Behavioral health across cultures. In J. D. Matarazzo, S. M. Weiss, J. A. Herd & N. E. Miller (Eds.), *Behavioral health: A handbook of health enhancement and disease prevention* (pp. 164–178). New York: John Wiley & Sons.

DiChiara, G. (2002). Nucleus accumbens shell and core dopamine: Differential role in behavior and addiction. *Behavioural Brain Research, 137*, 75–114.

Dickinson, G. L., Rostami-Hodjegan, A., Lagundoye, O., Seivewright, N., Pratt, P., & M. S. Lennard, M. S. (2006). A six-year evaluation of methadone prescribing practices at a substance misuse treatment center in the UK. *Journal of Clinical Pharmacy and Therapeutics, 31*, 477–484.

DiClemente, C. C., Carbonari, J. P., Montgomery, R. P., & Hughes, S. O. (1994). The alcohol abstinence self-efficacy scale. *Journal of Studies on Alcohol, 55*, 141–148.

DiClemente, C. C., Prochaska, J. O., Fairhurst, S. K., Velicer, W. F., Velasquez, M. M., & Rossi, J. S. (1991). The process of smoking cessation: An analysis of precontemplation, contemplation, and preparation stages of change. *Journal of Consulting and Clinical Psychology, 59*, 295–304.

Dinges, N. G., & Duong-Tran, Q. (1993). Stressful life events and co-occurring depression, substance abuse and suicidality among American Indian and Alaska Native adolescents. *Culture, Medicine, and Psychiatry, 16*, 487–502.

Dishion, T. J. (2000). Cross-setting consistency in early adolescent psychopathology: Deviant friendships and problem sequelae. *Journal of Personality and Social Psychology, 68*, 1109–1126.

Dishion, T. J., French, D. C., & Patterson, G. R. (1995). The development and ecology of antisocial behavior. In D. Cicchetti & D. Cohen (Eds.), *Manual of developmental psychopathology* (pp. 421–471). New York: John Wiley & Sons.

Dishion, T. J., Poulin, F., & Burraston, B. (2001). Peer group dynamics associated with iatrogenic effects in group interventions with high-risk young adolescents: The role of friendship in psychological adjustment. In C. A. Erdley & D. W. Nargle (Eds.), *New directions for child and adolescent development* (Vol. 91, pp. 79–92.). New York: Jossey–Bass.

Dodder, R. A., & Hughes, S. P. (1993). Neutralization of drinking behavior. *Deviant Behavior: An Interdisciplinary Journal, 14*, 65–79.

Doernberg, D., & Stinson, F. S. (1985). *U.S. alcohol epidemiologic data reference manual: Volume 1. U.S. apparent consumption of alcoholic beverages based on state sales, taxation, or receipt data.* Washington, DC: U.S. Government Printing Office.

Donaher, P. A., & Welsh, C. (2006). Managing opioid addiction with buprenorphine. *American Family Physician, 73*, 1573–1578.

Donaldson, S. I., Sussman, S., MacKinnon, D. P., Severson, H. H., Glynn, T., Murray, D. M., et al. (1996). Drug abuse prevention programming: Do we know what content works? *American Behavioral Scientist, 39*, 868–883.

Donohew, R. L., Zimmerman, R., Cupp, P. S., Novak, S., Colon, S., & Abell, R. (2000). Sensation seeking, impulsive decision-making, and risky sex: Implications for risk-taking and design of interventions. *Personality and Individual Differences, 28*, 1079–1091.

Donovan, D. M. (1996). Assessment issues and domains in the prediction of relapse. *Addiction, 91*, S29–S38.

Donovan, J. E., & Jessor, R. (1985). Structure of problem behavior in adolescence and young adulthood. *Journal of Consulting and Clinical Psychology, 53*, 890–904.

Donovan, J. E., Jessor, R., & Costa, F. M. (1993). Structure of health-enhancing behavior in adolescence: A latent-variable approach. *Journal of Health and Social Behavior, 34*, 346–362.

Dorsman, J. (1991). *How to quit drinking without A.A: A complete self-help guide.* Newark, DE: New Dawn.

Dovidio, J. F., Kawakami, K., Johnson, C., Johnson, B., & Howard, A. (1997). On the nature of prejudice: Automatic and controlled processes. *Journal of Experimental Social Psychology, 33*, 510–540.

DrinkWise. (n.d.). Retrieved September 6, 2007, from http://www.drinkwise.com/

Drug and Alcohol Services Information System (DASIS). Retrieved October 9, 2005

Drug Library. (n.d.). *The mythical roots of U.S. drug policy: Soldier's Disease and addicts in the civil war.* Retrieved September 6, 2007, from http://www.druglibrary.org/SCHAFFER/history/soldis.htm

Drug Library. (n.d.). The tale of two hashish-eaters. In *1001 Arabian nights.* Retrieved April 20, 2005, from http://www.druglibrary.org/schaffer/hemp/arab1.htm

Drug Library. (n.d.). *Did alcohol prohibition reduce alcohol consumption and crime?* Retrieved July 20, 2005, from http://www.druglibrary.org/prohibitionresults.htm

Drug Library. (1993). *Evidence found of ancient marijuana use.* Retrieved April 20, 2005, from http://www.druglibrary.org/schaffer/History/1600BC.htm

Drug Policy Alliance. (n.d.). Step by step. Retrieved September 6, 2007, from http://drugpolicy.org/statebystate/

DrugScope. (n.d.). FAQ's home. Retrieved September 6, 2007, from http://www.drugscope.org.uk/resources/faqs/

Drummond, D. C. (2000). What does cue-reactivity have to offer clinical research? *Addiction, 95*(Suppl. 2), S129–S144.

Drummond, D. C., Cooper, T., & Glautier, S. P. (1990). Conditioned learning in alcohol dependence: Implications for cue exposure treatment. *British Journal of Addiction, 85,* 725–743.

Drummond, D. C., & Glautier, S. (1994). A controlled trial of cue exposure treatment in alcohol dependents. *Journal of Consulting and Clinical Psychology, 62,* 809–817.

Dufour, M. C. (1999). What is moderate drinking?: Defining "drinks" and drinking levels. *Alcohol Research & Health, 23,* 5–14.

Duncan, D. F., Nicholson, T., Clifford, P., Hawkins, W., & Petosa, R. (1994). Harm reduction: An emerging new paradigm for drug education. *Journal of Drug Education, 24,* 281–290.

Dunn, C., Deroo, L., & Rivara, F. P. (2001). The use of brief interventions adapted from motivational interviewing across behavioral domains: A systematic review. *Addiction, 96,* 1725–1742.

Dunn, M. E., & Goldman, M. S. (1996). Empirical modeling of an alcohol expectancy memory network in elementary school children as a function of grade. *Experimental and Clinical Psychopharmacology, 4,* 209–217.

Dunn, M. E., & Goldman, M. S. (1998). Age and drinking-related differences in the memory organization of alcohol expectancies in 3rd-, 6th-, 9th-, and 12th-grade children. *Journal of Consulting and Clinical Psychology, 66,* 579–585.

Dunn, M. E., & Goldman, M. S. (2000). Validation of multidimensional scaling-based modeling of alcohol expectancies in memory: Age and drinking-related differences in expectancies of children assessed as first associates. *Alcoholism: Clinical and Experimental Research, 24,* 1639–1646.

Dunn, M. E., Lau, H. C., & Cruz, I. Y. (2000). Changes in activation of alcohol expectancies in memory in relation to changes in alcohol use after participation in an expectancy challenge program. *Experimental and Clinical Psychopharmacology, 8,* 566–575.

Durell, J., & Bukoski, W. (1984). Preventing substance abuse: The state of the art. *Public Health Reports, 99,* 23–31.

Dwyer, K. M., Richardson, J. L., Danley, K. L., Hansen, W. B., Sussman, S., Brannon, B., et al. (1990). Characteristics of eighth-grade students who initiate self-care in elementary and junior high school. *Pediatrics, 86,* 448–454.

Earleywine, M. (1994). Cognitive bias covaries with alcohol consumption. *Addictive Behaviors, 19,* 539–544.

Earleywine, M., & Finn, P. R. (1991). Sensation seeking explains the relation between behavioral disinhibition and alcohol consumption. *Addictive Behaviors, 16,* 123–128.

Edmundson, E., McAlister, A., Murray, D., Perry, C., & Lichtenstein, E. (1991). Approaches directed to the individual. In D. R. Shopland, D. M. Burns, J. M. Samet, & E. R. Gritz (Eds.), *Strategies to control tobacco use in the United States: A blueprint for public health in the 1990s* (NIH Pub No. 92–3316, pp. 147–199). Washington, DC: U.S. Government Printing Office.

Edwards, G. E., Marshall, E. J., & Cook, C. C. H. (Eds.). (2003). *The treatment of drinking problems: A guide for the helping professions* (4th ed.). Cambridge, UK: Cambridge University Press.

Eggert, L. L., Thompson, E. A., Herting, J. R., Nicholas, L. J., & Dicker, B. G. (1994). Preventing adolescent drug abuse and high school dropout through an intensive school-based social network development program. *American Journal of Health Promotion, 8,* 202–215.

Eiser, J. R. (1985). Smoking: The social learning of an addiction. *Journal of Social and Clinical Psychology, 3,* 446–457.

Elias, M. J. (2006). The connection between academic and social-emotional learning. In M. J. Elias & H. Arnold (Eds.), *The educator's guide to emotional intelligence an academic achievement* (pp. 1–14). Thousand Oaks, CA: Corwin.

Ellis, A., & Harper, R. A. (1975). *A guide to rational living.* North Hollywood, CA: Wilshire Book Co.

Emery, S., Wakefield, M. A., Terry-McElrath, Y., Saffer, H., Szczypka, G., O'Malley, P. M., et al. (2005). Televised state-sponsored antitobacco advertising and youth smoking beliefs and behavior in the United States, 1999–2000. *Archives of Pediatrics & Adolescent Medicine, 159,* 639–689.

Emmons, K., Glasgow, R. E., Marcus, B., Rakowski, W., & Curry, S. J. (1995). *Motivation for change across behavioral risk factors: Conceptual and clinical advances.* Paper presented at the Symposium presented at the Sixteenth Annual Scientific Sessions of the Society of Behavioral Medicine, San Diego, CA.

Ennett, S. T., Bauman, K. E., & Koch, G. G. (1994). Variability in cigarette smoking within and between adolescent friendship cliques. *Addictive Behaviors, 19,* 295–305.

Epstein, L. (1992). Role of behavior theory in behavioral medicine. *Journal of Consulting and Clinical Psychology, 4,* 493–498.

Erickson, E. H. (1968). *Identity, youth and crisis.* New York: W. W. Norton & Company.

Erickson, P. G. (1995). Harm reduction: What it is and is not. *Drug and Alcohol Review, 14,* 283–285.

Ernst, M., Nelson, E. E., Jazbec, S., McClure, E. B., Monk, C. S., Leibenluft, E., et al. (2005). Amygdala and nucleus accumbens in responses to receipt and omission of gains in adults and adolescents. *NeuroImage, 25,* 1279–1291.

Etheridge, R. M., Hubbard, R. L., Anderson, J., Craddock, S. G., & Flynn, P. M. (1997). Treatment structure and program services in the drug abuse treatment outcome study (DATOS). *Psychology of Addictive Behaviors, 11,* 244–260.

Evans, J. S. B. (2003). In two minds: Dual process accounts of reasoning. *Trends in Cognitive Sciences, 7,* 454–459.

Evans, R. I. (1998). A historical perspective on effective prevention. In W. J. Bukoski & R. I. Evans (Eds.), *Cost–benefit/cost-effectiveness research of drug abuse prevention: Implications for programming and policy* (NIDA Research Monograph 176, pp. 37–58). Rockville, MD: National Institute on Drug Abuse, National Institutes of Health.

Ewing, J. A. (1984). Detecting alcohol: The CAGE questionnaire. *Journal of the American Medical Association, 252,* 1905–1907.

Farabee, D., Prendergast, M., & Anglin, M. (1998). The effectiveness of coerced treatment for drug-abusing offenders. *Federal Probation, 62,* 3–10.

Farrell, M., Ward J., Mattick R., Hall, W., Stimson, G. V., des Jarlais, D., et al. (1994). Methadone maintenance treatment in opiate dependence: A review. *British Medical Journal, 309,* 997–1001.

Farrow, J. A. (1995). Service delivery strategies for treating high-risk youth: Delinquents, homeless, runaways, and sexual minorities. *NIDA Research Monograph, 156,* 39–48.

Fazio, R. H. (1990). Multiple processes by which attitudes guide behavior: The MODE model as an integratie framework. In M. P. Zanna (Ed.), *Advances in experimental and social psychology* (Vol. 23, pp. 75–109). New York: Academic.

Federal Bureau of Prisons. (n.d.). *Substance abuse treatment.* Retrieved September 13, 2006, from http://www.bop.gov/inmate_programs/substance.jsp

Felitti, V. J., Anda, R. F., Nordenberg, D., Williamson, D. F., Spitz, A. M., Edwards, V., et al. (1998). Relationship of childhood abuse and household dysfunction to many of the leading causes of death in adults: The Adverse Childhood Experiences (ACE) Study. *American Journal of Preventive Medicine, 4,* 245–258.

Festinger, L. (1957). *A theory of cognitive dissonance.* Stanford, CA: Stanford University Press.

Field, M., & Eastwood, B. (2005). Experimental manipulation of attentional bias increases the motivation to drink alcohol. *Psychopharmacology, 183,* 350–357.

Fillmore, M. T. (2003). Drug abuse as a problem of impaired control: Current approaches and findings. *Behavioral and Cognitive Neuroscience Reviews, 2,* 179–197.

Finn, P. R., & Hall, J. (2004). Cognitive ability and risk for alcoholism: Short-term memory capacity and intelligence moderate personality risk for alcohol problems. *Journal of Abnormal Psychology, 113,* 569–581.

Fiori, M. C., Bailey, W. C., Cohen, S. J., Dorfman, S. F., Goldstein, M. G., Gritz, E. R., et al. (2000). *Treating tobacco use and dependence: Clinical practice guideline.* Rockville, MD: U.S. Department of Health and Human Services.

First, M. B., Spitzer, R. L., Gibbon, M. (1996). *Structured clinical interview for DSM-IV*. New York: Biometrics Research Department, New York Psychiatric Institute.

Fishbein, D. H. (2000). The importance of neurobiological research to the prevention of psychopathology. *Prevention Science, 1,* 89–106.

Fishbein, D. H., Hydeb, C., Eldreth, D., Paschall, M. J., Hubal, R., Das, A., et al. (2006). Neurocognitive skills moderate urban male adolescents' responses to preventive intervention materials. *Drug and Alcohol Dependence, 82,* 47–60.

Fishbein, M., & Ajzen, I. (1975). *Belief, attitude, intention, and behaviour: An introduction to theory and research.* Reading, MA: Addison Wesley.

Fishkin, S. A., Sussman, S., Stacy, A. W., Dent, C. W., Burton, D., & Flay, B. R. (1993). Ingroup versus outgroup perceptions of the characteristics of high-risk youth: Negative stereotyping. *Journal of Applied Social Psychology, 23,* 1051–1068.

Flay, B. R. (1981). On improving the chances of mass media health promotion programs causing meaningful changes in behavior. In M. Meyer (Ed.), *Health education by television and radio* (pp. 59–89). Munich, Germany: Saur.

Flay, B. R. (1985). Psychosocial approaches to smoking prevention: A review of findings. *Health Psychology, 4,* 449–488.

Flay, B. R., d'Avernas, J. R., Best, J. A., Kersell, M. W., & Ryan, K. B. (1983). Cigarette smoking: Why young people do it and ways of preventing it. In P. McGrath & P. Firestone (Eds.), *Pediatric and adolescent behavioral medicine* (pp. 132–183). New York: Springer-Verlag.

Flay, B. R., Hu, F. B., Siddiqui, O., Day, L. E., Hedeker, D., Petraitis, J., et al. (1994). Differential influence of parental smoking and friends' smoking on adolescent initiation and escalation of smoking. *Journal of Health and Social Behavior, 35,* 248–265.

Fletcher, B. W., Tims, F. M., & Brown, B. S. (1997). Drug Abuse Treatment Outcome Study (DATOS): Treatment evaluation research in the United States. *Psychology of Addictive Behaviors, 11,* 216–229.

Florentine, R. (1999). After drug treatment: Are 12-step programs effective in maintaining abstinence? *American Journal of Alcohol Abuse, 25,* 93–116.

Flynn, B. S., Worden, J. K., Secker-Walker, R. H., Badger, G. J., Geller, B. M., & Costanza, M. C. (1992). Prevention of cigarette smoking through mass media intervention and school programs. *American Journal of Public Health, 82,* 827–834.

Flynn, B. S., Worden, J. K., Secker-Walker, R. H., Pirie, P. L., Badger, G. J., & Carpenter, J. H. (1997). Long-term responses of higher and lower risk youths to smoking prevention interventions. *Preventive Medicine, 26,* 389–394.

Flynn, B. S., Worden, J. K., Secker-Walker, R. H., Pirie, P. L., Badger, G. J., Carpenter, J. H., et al. (1994). Mass media and school interventions for cigarette smoking prevention: Effects 2 years after completion. *American Journal of Public Health, 84,* 1148–1150.

Franken, I. H. A. (2003). Drug craving and addiction: Integrating psychological and neuropsychopharmacological approaches. *Progress in Neuro-Psychopharmacology & Biological Psychiatry, 27,* 563–579.

Franz, K. J., & Koob, G. F. (2005). The neurobiology of addiction. In R. H. Coombs (Ed.), *Addiction counseling review* (pp. 33–58). Mahwah, NJ: Lawrence Erlbaum Associates.

Fredholm, B. B., Battig, K., Holmen, J., Nehlig, A., & Zvartau, E. E. (1999). Actions of caffeine in the brain with specific reference to factors that contribute to its widespread use. *Pharmacological Reviews, 51,* 83–133.

Freedman, A. M., Kaplan, H. I., & Sadock, B. J. (1976). *Modern synopsis of psychiatry* (Vol. II). Baltimore: Williams & Wilkins.

Freudenmann, R. W., Oxler, F., & Bernschneider-Reif, S. (2006). The origin of MDMA (ecstacy) revisited: The true story reconstructed from the original documents. *Addiction, 101,* 1241–1245.

Friedman, A., & Utada, A. (1989). A method for diagnosing and planning the treament of adolescent drug abusers (the Adolescent Drug Abuse Diagnosis instrument). *Journal of Drug Education, 19,* 285–312.

Fromme, K., Katz, E. C., & Rivet, K. (1997). Outcome expectancies and risk-taking behavior. *Cognitive Therapy and Research, 21,* 421–442.

Fromme, K., Stroot, E., & Kaplan, D. (1993). Comprehensive effects of alcohol: Development and psychometric assessment of a new expectancy questionnaire. *Psychological Assessment, 5,* 19–26.

Fudala, P. J., Bridge, T. P., Herbert, S., Williford, W. O., Chiang, C. N., Jones, K., et al. (2003). Office-based treatment of opiate addiction with a sublingual-tablet formulation of buprenorphine and naloxone. *New England Journal of Medicine, 349,* 949–958.

Fulker, D. W., Eysenck, S. B. G., & Zuckerman, M. (1980). A genetic and environmental analysis of sensation seeking. *Journal of Research in Personality, 14,* 261–281.

FunctionalFamilyTherapy. (n.d.). Home page. Retrieved September 6, 2007, from http://www.fftinc.com/

Funk, R. R., McDermeit, M., Godley, S. H., & Adams, L. (2003). Maltreatment issues by level of adolescent substance abuse treatment: The extent of the problem at intake and relationship to early outcomes. *Child Maltreatment, 8,* 36–45.

Fuqua, J., Stokols, D., Gress, J., Phillips, K., & Harvey, R. (2004). Transdisciplinary collaboration as a basis for enhancing the science and prevention of substance use and abuse. *Substance Use and Misuse, 39,* 1457–1514.

Galaif, E., & Sussman, S. (1995). For whom does Alcoholics Anonymous work? *International Journal of the Addictions, 30,* 161–184.

Galaif, E. R., Chou, C. P., Sussman, S., & Dent, C. W. (1998). Depression, suicidal ideation, and substance use among continuation high school students. *Journal of Youth and Adolescence, 27,* 275–299.

Galea, S., Ahern, J., & Vlahov, D. (2003). Contextual determinants of drug use risk behavior: A theoretical framework. *Journal of Urban Health, 80,* 50–58.

Gamblers Anonymous. (n.d.). Home page. Retrieved June 20, 2005, from http://www.gamblersanonymous.org/

Garbutt, J. C., West, S. L., Carey, T. S., Lohr, K. N., & Crews, F. T. (1999). Pharmacological treatment of alcohol dependence: A review of the evidence. *Journal of American Medical Association, 281,* 1318–1325.

George, M. S., Nahas, Z., Bohning, D. E., Kozel, F. A., Anderson, R. N., Chae, J. H., et al. (2002). Vagus nerve stimulation therapy: A research update. *Neurology, 59,* S56–S61.

Giancola, P. R., Moss, H. B., Martin, C. S., Kirisci, L., & Tarter, R. E. (1996). Executive cognitive functioning predicts reactive aggression in boys at high risk for substance abuse: A prospective study. *Alcoholism: Clinical and Experimental Research, 20,* 740–744.

Giancola, P. R., & Tarter, R. E. (1999). Executive cognitive functioning and risk for substance abuse. *Psychological Science, 10,* 203–205.

Giedd, J. N., Blumenthal, J., Jeffries, N. O., Castellanos, F. X., Liu, H., Zijdenbos, J., et al. (1999). Brain development during childhood and adolescence: A longitudinal MRI study. *Nature Neuroscience, 2,* 861–863.

Ginzler, J. A., & Cochran, B. N. (2003). Sequential progression of substance use among homeless youth: An empirical investigation of the gateway theory. *Substance Use & Misuse, 38,* 725–758.

Glynn, K., Levanthal, H., & Hirschman, R. (1985). A cognitive developmental approach to smoking prevention. In C. S. Bell & R. Battjes (Eds.), *Prevention research: Deterring drug abuse among children and adolescents* (NIDA Research Monograph 63, pp. 130–152). Rockville, MD: National Institute on Drug Abuse, National Institutes of Health.

Godley, M. D., & White, W. L. (2005). A brief history and some current dimensions of adolescent treatment in the United States. In M. Galanter (Ed.), *Recent developments in alcoholism* (Vol. 17, pp. 367–382). New York: Kluwer Academic Press.

Gogtay, N., Giedd, J. N., Lusk, L., Hayashi, K. M., Greenstein, D., Vaituzis, A. C., et al. (2004). Dynamic mapping of human cortical development during childhood through early adulthood. *Proceedings of the National Academy of Science of the United States of America, 101,* 8174–8179.

Goldberger, B. A., & Jenkins, A. J. (1999). Drug toxicology. In P. J. Ott, R. E. Tarter, & R. T. Ammerman (Eds.), *Sourcebook on substance abuse: Etiology, epidemiology, assessment, and treatment* (pp. 184–196). Boston: Allyn & Bacon.

Goldfried, M. R., & Davison, G. C. (1994). *Clinical behavior therapy* (expanded ed.). New York: John Wiley & Sons.

Goldman, M. S., Brown, S. A., Christiansen, B. A., & Smith, G. T. (1991). Alcoholism and memory: Broadening the scope of alcohol expectancy research. *Psychological Bulletin, 110,* 137–146.

Goldman, M. S., & Darkes, J. (2004). Alcohol expectancy multiaxial assessment: A memory network-based approach. *Psychological Assessment, 16,* 4–15.

Goldman, M. S., Greenbaum, P. E., & Darkes, J. (1997). A confirmatory test of hierarchical expectancy structure and predictive power discriminant validation of the alcohol expectancy questionnaire. *Psychological Assessment, 9,* 145–157.

Goldman, M. S., Reich, R. R., & Darkes, J. (2006). Expectancy as a unifying construct in alcohol-related cognition. In R. W. Wiers & A. W. Stacy (Eds.), *Handbook on implicit cognition and addiction* (pp. 105–120). Thousand Oaks, CA: Sage.

Goldstein, R. Z., & Volkow, N. D. (2002). Drug addiction and its underlying neurobiological basis: Neuroimaging evidence for the involvement of the frontral cortex. *American Journal of Psychiatry, 159,* 1642–1652.

Gollwitzer, P. M. (1999). Implementation intentions: Strong effects of simple plans. *American Psychologist, 54,* 493–503.

Gollwitzer, P. M., & Sheeran, P. (2004). *Implementation intentions and goal achievement: A meta-analysis of effects and processes.* Retrieved May 17, 2006, from http://gsbwww.uchicago.edu/research/workshops/behavior/Gollwitzer.pdf

Goode, E. (2005). *Drugs in American society* (6th ed.). New York: McGraw-Hill.

Goodstadt, M. S. (1978). Alcohol and drug education: Model and outcomes. *Health Education Monogrographs, 6,* 263–279.

Gordis, E. (2000). Contributions of behavioral science to alcohol research: Understanding who is at risk and why. *Experimental and Clinical Psychopharmacology, 8,* 264–270.

Gordon, J. R., & Barrett, K. (1993). The codependency movement: Issues of context and differentiation. In J. S. Baer, G. A. Marlatt, & R. J. McMahon (Eds.), *Addictive behaviors across the life span* (pp. 307–339). Newbury Park, CA: Sage.

Gordon, R. (1987). An operational classification of disease prevention. In A. Steinberg & M. M. Silverman (Eds.), *Preventing mental disorders* (pp. 20–26). Rockville, MD: Department of Health and Human Services, National Institutes of Health.

Gorman, D. M., Gruenewald, P. J., Hanlon, P. J., Mezic, I., Waller, L. A., Chavez, C., et al. (2004). Implications of systems of dynamic models and control theory for environmental approaches to the prevention of alcohol-and other drug use-related problems. *Substance Use & Misuse, 39,* 1713–1750.

Gorski, T. T. (1989). *Passages through recovery.* San Francisco: Harper & Row.

Gorski, T. T., & Miller, M. (1984). *The phases and warning aigns of relapse.* Independence, MO: Independence Press.

Gorski, T. T., & Miller, M. (1986). *Staying sober: A guide for relapse prevention.* Independence, MO: Independence Press.

Gottfredson, D. C., & Wilson, D. B. (2003). Characteristics of effective school-based substance abuse prevention. *Prevention Science, 4,* 27–38.

Gottman, J. M., & Leiblum, S. R. (1974). How to do psychotherapy and how to evaluate it: A manual for beginners. New York: Holt, Rinehart and Winston.

Goudriaan, A. E., Oosterlaan, J., de Beurs, E., & Van den Brink, W. (2004). Pathological gambling: A comprehensive review of biobehavioral findings. *Neuroscience & Biobehavioral Reviews, 28,* 123–141.

Graf, P., & Schacter, D. L. (1999). Unitization and grouping mediate dissociations in memory for new associations. *Journal of Experimental Psychology: Learning, Memory, and Cognition, 15,* 930–940.

Granic, I., & Dishion, T. J. (2003). Deviant talk in adolescent friendships: A step toward measuring a pathogenic attractor process. *Social Development, 12,* 314–334.

Granovetter, M. (1973). The strength of weak tie. *American Journal of Sociology, 78,* 1360–1380.

Grant, B. F. (1994). ICD-10 harmful use of alcohol and the alcohol dependence syndrome: Prevalence and implications. *Addiction, 88,* 413–420.

Gray, J. A. (1982). Precis of the neuropsychology of anxiety: An enquiry into the functions of the septo-hippocampal system. *Behavioral and Brain Sciences, 5,* 469–534.

Gray, J. A. (1987). The neuropsychology of emotion and personality. In S. M. Stahl, S. D. Iversen, & E. C. Goodman (Eds.), *Cognitive neurochemistry* (pp. 171–190). Oxford: Oxford University Press.

Gray, J. A. (1990). Brain systems that mediate both emotion and cognition. *Cognition & Emotion, 4*, 269–288.

Greenwald, A. G., & Banaji, M. R. (1995). Implicit social cognition: Attitudes, self-esteem and stereotypes. *Psychological Review, 102*, 4–27.

Grenard, J. L., Ames, S. L., Pentz, M. A., & Sussman, S. (2006). Motivational interviewing with adolescents and young adults for drug-related problems. *International Journal of Adolescent Medical Health, 18*, 53–67.

Grenard, J. L., Ames, S. L., Wiers, R. W., Thush, C., Sussman, S., & Stacy, A. W. (2007). *Working memory moderates the association between drug-related associations in memory and the frequency of substance use.* Unpublished manuscript.

Griffin, K. W., Botvin, G. J., Scheier, L. M., Diaz, T., & Miller, N. L. (2000). Parenting practices as predictors of substance use, delinquency, and aggression among urban minority youth: Moderating effects of family structure and gender. *Psychology of Addictive Behaviors, 14*, 174–184.

Griffiths, M. (1997). Exercise addition: A case study. *Addiction Research, 5*, 161–168.

Gruenfeld, D. H., & Wyer, R. S. (1992). Semantics and pragmatics of social influence: How affirmations and denials affect beliefs in referent propositions. *Journal of Personality and Social Psychology, 62*, 38–49.

Gurley, R. J., Aranow, R., & Katz, M. (1998). Medicinal marijuana: A comprehensive review. *Journal of Psychoactive Drugs, 30*, 137–147.

Hafstad, A., Aarø, L. E., Engeland, A., Andersen, A., Langmark, F., & Stray-Pedersen, B. (1997). Provocative appeals in anti-smoking mass campaigns targeting adolescents—The accumulated effect of multiple exposures. *Health Education Research, 12*, 227–236.

Hahn, G., Charlin, V. L., Sussman, S., Dent, C. W., Manzi, J., Stacy, A. W., et al. (1990). Adolescents' first and most recent use situations of smokeless tobacco and cigarettes: Similarities and differences. *Addictive Behaviors, 15*, 439–448.

Hall, W. (2005). Stereotactic neurosurgical treatment of addiction: minimizing the chances of another 'great and desperate cure.' *Addiction, 101*, 1–3.

Hallfors, D., Cho, H., Livert, D., & Kadushin, C. (2002). How are community coalitions "Fighting Back" against substance abuse, and are they winning? *American Journal of Preventive Medicine, 23*, 237–245.

Hanley, A., & Wilhelm, M. S. (1992). Compulsive buying: An exploration into self-esteem and money attitudes. *Journal of Economic Psychology, 13*, 5–18.

Hansen, W. B. (1992). School-based substance abuse prevention: A review of the state of the art in curriculum, 1980–1990. *Health Education Research: Theory and Practice, 7*, 403–430.

Hansen, W. B. (1994). Prevention of alcohol use and abuse. *Preventive Medicine, 23*, 683–687.

Hansen, W. B. (1996). Pilot test results comparing the All Stars program with seventh grade D.A.R.E.: Pilot test integrity and mediating variable analysis. *Substance Use & Misuse, 31*, 1359–1377.

Hansen, W. B., & Altman, D. G. (2001). Sequencung issues in health behavior program development. In S. Sussman (Ed.), *Handbook of program development for health behavior research and practice* (pp. 361–386). Thousand Oaks, CA: Sage.

Hansen, W. B., Johnson, C. A., Flay, B. R., Graham, J. W., & Sobel, J. (1988). Affective and social influences approaches to the prevention of multiple substance abuse among seventh grade students: Results from Project SMART. *Preventive Medicine, 17*, 135–154.

Hansen, W. B., & McNeal, R. B. (1997). How D.A.R.E. works: An examination of program effects on mediating variables. *Health Education Quarterly, 24*, 165–176.

Harrell, T. H., Honaker, L. M., & Davis, E. (1991). Cognitive and behavioral dimensions of dysfunction in alcohol and polydrug abusers. *Journal of Substance Abuse Treatment, 3*, 415–426.

Harwood, H. (2000). *Updating estimates of the economic costs of alcohol abuse in the United States: Estimates, update methods, and data* (NIH Publication No. 98–4327). Rockville, MD: Department of Health and Human Services, National Institute on Drug Abuse and the National Institute on Alcohol Abuse and Alcoholism, National Institutes of Health.

Hathaway, S. R., & McKinley, J. C. (1943). *The Minnesota Multiphasic Personality Inventory, revised edition.* Minneapolis: University of Minnesota Press.

Hawkins, J. D., Catalano, R. F., & Miller, J. Y. (1992). Risk and protective factors for alcohol and other drug problems in adolescence and early adulthood: Implications for substance abuse prevention. *Psychological Bulletin, 112,* 64–105.

Hays, R., Stacy, A. W., & DiMatteo, M. R. (1987). Problem behavior theory and adolescent alcohol use. *Addictive Behaviors, 12,* 189–193.

Heart & Stroke Foundation. Stroke. (n.d.). *Stroke.* Retrieved September 6, 2007, from http://ww2.heartandstroke.ca/Page.asp?PageID=1017&CategoryID=2&Src=stroke

Heath, D. B. (1999). Culture. In P. J. Ott, R. E. Tarter, & R. T. Ammerman (Eds.), *Sourcebook on substance abuse: Etiology, epidemiology, assessment, and treatment* (pp. 175–183). Needham Heights, MA: Prentice Hall.

Heider, F. (1958). *The psychology of interpersonal relations.* New York: Wiley.

Henggeler, S. W., Clingempeel, W. G., Brondino, M. J., & Pickrel, S. G. (2002). Four-year follow-up of multisystemic therapy with substance-abusing and substance-dependent juvenile offenders. *Journal of the American Academy of Child and Adolescent Psychiatry, 41,* 868–874.

Henggeler, S. W., Pickrel, S. G., & Brondino, M. J. (1999). Multisystemic treatment of substance-abusing and dependent delinquents: outcomes, treatment fidelity, and transportability. *Mental Health Services Residual, 1,* 171–184.

Henry, B., Feehan, M., McGee, R., Stanton, W., Moffitt, T. E., & Silva, P. (1993). The importance of conduct problems and depressive symptoms in predicting adolescent substance use. *Journal of Abnormal Child Psychology, 21,* 469–480.

Hershow, R. C., Riester, K. A., Lew, J., Quinn, T. C., Mofenson, L. M., Davenny, K., et al. (1997). Increased vertical transmission of human immunodeficiency virus from hepatitis C virus-coinfected mothers. Women and Infants Transmission Study. *Journal of Infectious Diseases, 176,* 414–420.

Hikida, T., Kitabatake, Y., Pastan, I., & Nakanishi, S. (2003). Acetylcholine enhancement in the nucleus accumbens prevents addictive behaviors of cocaine and morphine. *Proceedings of the National Academy of Sciences of the United States of America, 100,* 6169–6173.

Hill, S. Y. (1982). Biological consequences of alcoholism and alcohol-related problems among women. In *Alcohol and Health Monograph* [Vol. Special Populations Issues, No. 4, DHHS, Pub. No. (ADM) 82–1193, pp. 43–73]. Washington, DC: National Institute on Alcohol Abuse and Alcoholism, U.S. Government Printing Office.

Hill, S. Y. (1984). Vulnerability to the biomedical consequences of alcoholism and alcohol-related problems among women. In S. C. Wilsnack & L. J. Beckman (Eds.), *Alcohol problems in women: Antecedents, consequences and interventions* (pp. 121–154). New York: Guilford.

Hirliman, G. A. (Producer) & Gasnier, L. J. (Director). (1936). *Reefer madness* [Motion picture]. United States: Motion Picture Ventures, Inc.

Hirsch, E. D., Kett, J. F., & Trefil, J. (Eds.). (2002). *The new dictionary of cultural literacy* (3rd ed.). Boston: Houghton Mifflin.

Hirschi, T. (1969). *Causes of delinquency.* Berkeley: University of California Press.

Ho, R. (1992). Cigarette health warnings: The effects of perceived severity, expectancy of occurrence, and self-efficacy on intentions to give up smoking. *Australian Psychologist, 27,* 109–113.

Hoffman, B. R., Sussman, S., Unger, J. B., & Valente, T. W. (2006). Peer influences on adolescent cigarette smoking: A theoretical review of the literature. *Substance Use & Misuse, 41,* 103–155.

Hollinger, R. C. (1988). Working under the influence (WUI): Correlates of employees' use of alcohol and other drugs. *Journal of Applied Behavioral Science, 24,* 439–454.

Horn, J. L., Wanberg, K. H., & Foster, F. M. (1990). *Guide to the Alcohol Use Inventory (AUI).* Minneapolis, MN: National Computer Systems.

Horowitz, L. M., & Prytulak, L. S. (1969). Redintegrative memory. *Psychological Review, 84,* 519–531.

Hovarth, A. T. (1999). *Sex, drugs, gambling and chocolate: A workbook for overcoming addictions.* San Luis Obispo, CA: Impact.

Howard, D. V., Fry, A. F., & Brune, C. M. (1991). Aging and memory for new associations: Direct versus indirect measures. *Journal of Experimental Psychology: Learning, Memory, and Cognition, 17,* 779–792.

Hser, Y.-I., Hoffman, V., Grella, C. E., & Anglin, M. D. (2001). A 33-year follow-up of narcotics addicts. *Archives of General Psychiatry, 58,* 503–508.

Hsieh, S., Hoffmann, N. G., & Hollister, C. D. (1998). The relationship between pre-, during-, post-treatment factors, and adolescent substance abuse behaviors. *Addictive Behaviors, 23*, 477–488.

Hubbard, R. L., Marsden, M. E., Rachal, J. V., Harwood, H. J., Cavanaugh, E. R., & Ginzburg, H. J. (1989). *Drug abuse treatment: A national study of effectiveness.* Chapel Hill: University of North Carolina Press.

Hudson, J. I., Hiripi, E., Pope, H. G., & Kessler, R. C. (2007). The prevalence and correlates of eating disorders in the national comorbidity survey replication. *Biological Psychiatry, 61*, 348–358.

Hurt, R. D., Eberman, K. M., Slade, J., & Karan, L. (1993). Treating nicotine addiction in patients with other addictive. In C. T. Orleans & J. Slade (Eds.), *Nicotine addiction: Principles and management* (pp. 310–326). New York: Oxford University Press.

Hutchison, K. E., LaChance, H., Niaura, R., Bryan, A., & Smolen, A. (2002). The DRD4 VNTR polymorphism influences reactivity to smoking cues. *Journal of Abnormal Psychology, 111*, 134–143.

Huver, R. M. E., Engels, R. C. M. E., & de Vries, H. (2006). Are anti-smoking parenting practices related to adolescent smoking cognitions and behavior? *Health Education Research, 21*, 66–77.

Ialongo, N., Poduska, J., Werthamer, L., & Kellam, S. (2001). The distal impact of two first-grade preventive interventions on conduct problems and disorder in early adolescence. *Journal of Emotional and Behavioral Disorders, 9*, 146–160.

Irvin, J. E., Bowers, C. A., Dunn, M. E., & Wang, M. C. (1999). Efficacy of relapse prevention: A meta-analytic review. *Journal of Consulting and Clinical Psychology, 67*, 563–570.

Jack Daniel's. (n.d.). Home page. Retrieved September 6, 2007, from http://www.jackdaniels.com/age.aspx

Jacoby, L. L., Kelley, C. M., Brown, J., & Jasechko, J. (1989). Becoming famous overnight: Limits on the ability to avoid unconscious influences of the past. *Journal of Personality and Social Psychology, 56*, 326–338.

Jainchill, N., Bhattacharya, G., & Yagelka, J. (1995). Therapeutic communities for adolescents. *NIDA Research Monograph, 156*, 190–217.

James, W. (1890). *Habit.* New York: Henry Holt & Company.

James, W. (1958). *The varieties of religious experience.* New York: Mentor Books.

Jellnick, E. M. (1952). Phases of alcohol addiction. *Quarterly Journal of Studies on Alcohol, 13*, 673–684.

Jellnick, E. M. (1960). *The disease concept of alcoholism.* New Haven, CT: Publ. College & University Press.

Jennings, L., & Skovholt, T. (1999). The cognitive, emotional, and relational characteristics of master therapists. *Journal of Counseling Psychology, 46*, 3–11.

Jerrard, D. A. (1990). "Designer drugs": A current perspective. *Journal of Emergency Medicine, 8*, 733–741.

Jessor, R. (1984). Adolescent development and behavioral health. In J. D. Matarazzo, S. M. Weiss, J. A. Herd, N. E. Miller, & S. M. Weiss (Eds.), *Behavioral health: A handbook of health enhancement and disease prevention* (pp. 69–90). New York: John Wiley & Sons.

Jessor, R. (1987). Problem-behavior theory, psychosocial development, and adolescent problem drinking. *British Journal of Addictions, 82*, 331–342.

Jessor, R., & Jessor, S. (1977). *Problem behavior and psychosocial development: A longtitudinal study of youth.* New York: Academic Press.

John, U., & Hanke, M. (2002). Alcohol-attributable mortality in a high per capita consumption country – Germany. *Alcohol & Alcoholism, 37*, 581–585.

Johnson, C. A., MacKinnon, D. P., & Pentz, M. A. (1996). Breadth of program and outcome effectiveness in drug abuse prevention. *American Behavioral Scientist, 39*, 884–896.

Johnson, N. P., Michels, P. J., & Davis, C. W. (1991). The importance of street drug terms as diagnostic clues. *Journal of Health & Social Policy, 3*, 45–53.

Johnson, V., & Pandina, R. J. (2001). Choosing assessment studies to clarify theory-based program ideas. In S. Sussman (Ed.), *Handbook of program development for health behavior research and practice* (pp. 131–154). Thousand Oaks, CA: Sage.

Johnson, V. E. (1980). *I'll quit tomorrow: A practical guide to alcoholism treatment.* San Francisco: Harper & Row.

Johnston, L. D., O'Malley, P. M., & Bachman, J. G. (1999). *National survey results on drug use from the Monitoring the Future Study, 1975–1998: Volumes 1 and 2* (NIH Publication Nos. 99–4660 and

99–4661). Rockville, MD: U.S. Department of Health and Human Services, National Institutes of Health.

Johnston, L. D., O'Malley, P. M., Bachman, J. G., & Schulenberg, J. E. (2005). *Monitoring the Future national survey results on drug use, 1975–2004: Volumes I and II. Secondary school students and college students & adults ages 19–45* (NIH Publication Nos. 04–5727 and 05–5728). Bethesda, MD: National Institute on Drug Abuse.

Johnston, L. D., O'Malley, P. M., Bachman, J. G., & Schulenberg, J. E. (2006). *Monitoring the Future national survey results on drug use, 1975–2005: Volume I. Secondary school students* (NIH Publication No. 06–5883). Bethesda, MD: National Institute on Drug Abuse.

Johnstone, B. M. (1994). Sociodemographic, environmental, and cultural influences on adolescent drinking behavior. In *The development of alcohol problems: Exploring the biopsychosocial matrix of risk* (NIAAA Research Monograph 26). Rockville, MD: U.S. Department of Health and Human Services, National Institutes of Health.

Jones, B. T., Corbin, W., & Fromme, K. (2001). A review of expectancy theory and alcohol consumption. *Addiction, 91*, 57–72.

Jonnes, J. (1996). *Hep-cats, narcs, and pipe dreams: A history of America's romance with illegal drugs.* New York: Scribner.

Julien, R. M. (1998). *A primer of drug action.* New York: W.H. Freeman and Company.

Julien, R. M. (2005). *A primer of drug action* (9th ed.). New York: W.H. Freeman and Company.

Kahane, H. (1990). *Logic and philosophy: A modern introduction.* Belmont, CA: Wadsworth.

Kahneman, D. (2003). A perspective on judgment and choice: Mapping bounded rationality. *American Psychologist, 58*, 697–720.

Kaminer, Y. (1995). Pharmacotherapy for adolescents with psychoactive substance use disorders. *NIDA Research Monograph, 156*, 291–324.

Kaminer, Y. (2001). Alcohol & drug abuse: Adolescent substance abuse treatment: Where do we go from here? *Psychiatric Services, 52*, 147–149.

Kaminer, Y., Burleson, J. A., & Goldberger, R. (2002). Cognitive-behavioral coping skills and psychoeducation therapies for adolescent substance abuse. *The Journal of Nervous and Mental Disease, 190*, 737–745.

Kaminer, Y., & Slesnick, N. (2005). Evidence-based cognitive-behavioral and family therapies for adolescent alcohol and other substance use disorders. In M. Galanter (Ed.), *Recent developments in alcoholism: Volume 17. Alcohol problems in adolescents and young adults* (pp. 383–405). New York: Kluwer Academic Press.

Kandel, D. B. (1990). Parenting styles, drug use, and children's adjustment in families of young adults. *Journal of Marriage and the Family, 52*, 183–196.

Kandel, D. B., & Andrews, K. (1987). Processes of adolescent socialization by parents and peers. *International Journal of the Addictions, 22*, 319–342.

Kandel, E. R., Schwartz, J. H., & Jessell, T. M. (Eds.). (2000). *Principles of neural science* (4th ed.). New York: McGraw-Hill.

Kane, H. H. (1883). *A hashish-house in New York. Harper's Monthly, 67*, 944–949.

Kane, M. J., & Engle, R. W. (2002). The role of prefrontal cortex in working-memory capacity, executive attention, and general fluid intelligence: An individual-differences perspective. *Psychonomic Bulletin & Review, 9*, 637–671.

Kaufman, N., & Yach, D. (2000). Tobacco control-challenges and prospects. *Bulletin of the World Health Organization, 78*, 867.

Kaye, D. L. (2004). Office recognition and management of adolescent substance abuse. *Current Opinion in Pediatrics, 16*, 532–541.

Keefe, F. J., Buffington, A. L. H., Studts, J. L., & Rumble, M. E. (2002). Behavioral medicine: 2002 and beyond. *Journal of Consulting and Clinical Psychology, 70*, 852–856.

Kellam, S., Ialongo, N., Brown, H., Laudolff, J., Mirsky, A., Anthony, J., et al. (1989). Attention problems in first grade and shy and aggressive behaviors as antecedents to later heavy or inhibited substance use. In L. S. Harris (Ed.), *Problems of drug dependence 1989: Proceedings of the 51st Annual Scientific Meeting* (NIDA Research Monograph 95, pp. 368–369). Rockville, MD: National Institute on Drug Abuse.

Kellogg, S. H., Melia, D., Khuri, E., Lin, A., Ho.A., & Kreek, M. J. (2006). Adolescent and young adult heroin patients: Drug use and success in methadone maintenance treatment. *Journal of Addictive Diseases, 25,* 15–25.

Kelley, A. E., & Berridge, K. C. (2002). The neuroscience of natural rewards: Relevance to addictive drugs. *The Journal of Neuroscience, 22,* 3306–3311.

Kelly, J. F., Myers, M. G., & Brown, S. A. (2000). A multivariate process model of adolescent 12-step attendance and substance use outcome following inpatient treatment. *Psychology of Addictive Behaviors, 14,* 376–389.

Kelly, J. F., Stout, R., Zywiak, W., & Schneider, R. (2006). A 3-year study of addiction mutual-help group participation following intensive outpatient treatment. *Alcoholism: Clinical and Experimental Research, 30,* 1381–1392.

Kelly, T. H., Delzer, T., Martin, C. A., Hays, L. R., Harrington, N. G., & Bardo, M. T. (1999). *Behavioral effects of amphetamine and diazepam in high- and low-sensation seekers.* Paper presented at the FASEB Summer Research Conference.

Kessler, R. C. (2004). The epidemiology of dual diagnosis. *Biological Psychiatry, 56,* 730–737.

Khantzian, E. J. (1985). The self-medication hypothesis of addictive disorders: Focus on heroin and cocaine dependence. *American Journal of Psychiatry, 142,* 1259–1264.

Khantzian, E. J. (1997). The self-medication hypothesis of substance use disorders: A reconsideration and recent applications. *Harvard Review Psychiatry, 4,* 287–289l.

Kilpatrick, D. G., Acierno, R., Saunders, B., Resnick, H. S., Best, C. L., & Schnurr, P. P. (2000). Risk factors for adolescent substance abuse and dependence: Data from a national sample. *Journal of Consulting and Clinical Psychology, 68,* 19–30.

Klingberg, T., Forssberg, H., & Westerberg, H. (2002). Increased brain activity in frontal and parietal cortex underlies the development of visuospatial working memory capacity during childhood. *Journal of Cognitive Neuroscience, 1,* 1–10.

Klitzner, M., Schwartz, R., Gruenwald, P., & Blasinsky, M. (1987). Screening for risk factors for adolescent alcohol and drug use. *American Journal of Diseases of Children, 141,* 45–49.

Knight, J. R., Shrier, L. A., Bravender, T. D., Farrell, M., Vanderbilt, J., & Shaffer, H. J. (1999). A new brief screen for adolescent substance abuse. *Archives of Pediatrics & Adolescent Medicine, 153,* 591–596.

Komro, K., Stigler, M., & Perry, C. (2005). Comprehensive approaches to prevent adolescent drinking and related problems. *Recent Developments in Alcoholism, 17,* 207–224.

Komro, K. A., & Toomey, T. L. (2002). Stratgies to prevent underage drinking. *Alcohol Research & Health, 26,* 5–14.

Koob, G. F., & LeMoal, M. (2001). Drug addiction, dysregulation of reward, and allostasis. *Neuropsychopharmacology, 24,* 97–129.

Krank, M. D., & Swift, R. (1994). Unconscious influences of specific memories on alcohol outcome expectancies. *Alcoholism: Clinical and Experimental Research, 18,* 423.

Kreek, M. J., & Vocci, F. J. (2002). History and current status of opioid maintenance treatments: Blending conference session. *Journal of Substance Abuse Treatment, 23,* 93–105.

Krueger, R. F., Chentsova-Dutton, Y. E., Markon, K. E., Goldberg, D., & Ormel, J. (2003). A cross-cultural study of the structure of comorbidity among common psychopathological syndromes in the general health care setting. *Journal of Abnormal Psychology, 112,* 437–447.

Kumpfer, K. L. (n.d.). *Identification of drug abuse prevention programs: Literature review.* Retrieved April 23, 2006, from http://www.drugabuse.gov/about/organization/despr/hsr/dapre/KumpferLitReviewPartC.html

Kumpfer, K. L. (1999). Factors and processes contributing to resilience. The resilience framework. In M. D. Glantz & J. L. Johnson (Eds.), *Resilience and development: Positive life adaptions* (pp. 179–224). New York: Kluwer Academic/Plenum Publishers.

Kumpfer, K. L., Alvarado, R., Smith, P., & Bellamy, N. (2002). Cultural sensitivity and adaptation in family-based prevention interventions. *Prevention Science, 3,* 241–246.

Kumpfer, K. L., Alvarado., R., & Whiteside, H. O. (2003). Family-based interventions for substance use and misuse prevention. *Substance Use & Misuse, 38,* 1759–1787.

Kumpfer, K. L., & Bluth, B. (2004). Parent/child transactional processes predictive of resilience or vulnerability to "substance abuse disorders." *Substance Use & Misuse, 39,* 671–698.

Kumpfer, K. L., & DeMarsh, J. P. (1985). Prevention of chemical dependency in children of alcohol and drug abusers. *NIDA Notes, 5*(2–3).

Kumpfer, K. L., Molgaard, V., & Spoth, R. (1996). The strengthening families program for prevention of delinquency and drug use in special populations. In R. D. Peters & R. J. McMahon (Eds.), *Childhood disorders, substance abuse, and delinquency: Prevention and early intervention approaches* (pp. 241–267). Newbury Park: CA: Sage.

Kumpfer, K. L., Williams, M. K., & Baxley, G. B. (1997). *Drug abuse prevention for at-risk groups.* Rockville, MD: National Institute on Drug Abuse.

Kunst-Wilson, W. R., & Zajonc, R. B. (1980). Affective discrimination of stimuli that cannot be recognized. *Science, 207,* 557–558.

Kushner, M. G., & Sher, K. J. (1993). Comorbidity of alcohol and anxiety disorders among students: Effects of gender and family history of alcoholism. *Addictive Behaviors, 18,* 543–552.

Kyskan, C. E., & Moore, T. E. (2005). Global perspectives on fetal alcohol syndrome: Assessing practices, policies, and campaigns in four English-speaking countries. *Canadian Psychology, 46,* 153–165.

Lang, P. J. (1995). The emotion probe: Studies of motivation and attention. *American Psychologist, 50,* 372–385.

Langenbucher, J., Martin, C. S., Labouvie, E., Sanjuan, P. M., & Pollock, N. K. (2000). Toward the DSM-V: The withdrawal-gate model bersus the DSM-IV in the diagnosis of alcohol abuse and dependence. *Journal of Consulting and Clinical Psychology, 68,* 799–807.

Larimer, M. E., Palmer, R. S., & Marlatt, G. A. (1999). Relapse prevention: An overview of Marlatt's cognitive behavioral model. *Alcohol Research & Health, 23,* 151–160.

Latimer, W. W., Newcomb, M., Winters, K. C., & Stinchfield, R. D. (2000). Adolescent substance abuse treatment outcome: The role of substance abuse problem severity, psychosocial, and treatment factors. *Journal of Consulting and Clinical Psychology, 68,* 684–696.

Latimer, W. W., Winters, K. C., Stinchfield, R., & Traver, R. E. (2000). Demographic, individual, and interpersonal predictors of adolescent alcohol and marijuana use following treatment. *Psychology of Addictive Behaviors, 14,* 162–173.

Latkin, C. (1998). Outreach in natural setting: The use of peer leaders for HIV prevention among injecting drug users' networks. *Public Health Reports, 113*(S1), 151–159.

Lau, R. R., Hartman, K. A., & Ware, J. E. (1986). Health as a value: Methodological and theoretical considerations. *Health Psychology, 5,* 25–43.

Laviola, G., Adriani, W., Terranova, L., & Gerra, G. (1999). Psychobiological risk factors for vulnerability to psychostimulants in human adolescents and animal models. *Neuroscience & Biobehavioral Reviews, 23,* 993–1010.

Laviola, G., Macri, S., Morley-Fletcher, S., & Adriani, W. (2003). Risk-taking in adolescent mice: psychobiological determinants and early epigenetic influence. *Neuroscience & Biobehavioral Reviews, 27,* 19–31.

Leccese, M., & Waldron, H. B. (1994). Assessing adolescent substance use: a critique of current measurement instruments. *Journal of Substance Abuse Treatment, 11,* 553–563.

LeDoux, J. (2002). *Synaptic self: How our brains become who we are.* New York: Penguin Books.

Leigh, B. C. (1989). In search of the seven dwarves: Issues of measurement and meaning in alcohol expectancy research. *Psychological Bulletin, 105,* 361–373.

Leigh, B. C., & Schafer, J. C. (1993). Heavy drinking occasions and the occurrence of sexual activity. *Psychology of Addictive Behaviors, 7,* 197–200.

Leigh, B. C., & Stacy, A. W. (1991). On the scope of alcohol expectancy research: Remaining issues of measurement and meaning. *Psychological Bulletin, 110,* 147–154.

Leigh, B. C., & Stacy, A. W. (1993). Alcohol outcome expectancies: Scale construction and predictive utility in higher order confirmatory factor models. *Psychological Assessment, 5,* 216–229.

Lennard, H. L., Epstein, L. J., Bernstein, A., & Ransom, D. C. (1971). *Mystification and drug misuse.* New York: Jossey–Bass.

Lerman, C., Patterson, F., & Shields, A. (2003). Genetic basis of substance use and dependence: Implications for prevention in high-risk youth. In D. Romer (Ed.), *Reducing adolescent risk: Toward an integrated* (pp. 149–164). Thousand Oaks, CA: Sage.

Lessov, C. N., Swan, G. E., Ring, H. Z., Khroyan, T. V., & Lerman, C. (2004). Genetics and drug use as a complex phenotype. *Substance Use & Misuse, 39,* 1515–1569.

Leventhal, H., & Cleary, P. (1980). The smoking problem: A review of research and theory in behavioral risk modification. *Psychological Bulletin, 88*, 370–405.

Leventhal, H., Diefenbach, M., & Leventhal, E. A. (1992). Illness cognition: Using common sense to understand treatment adherence and affect cognition interactions. *Cognitive Therapy and Research, 16*, 143–163.

Levin, E. D., Rezvani, A. H., Montoya, D., Rose, J. E., & Swartzwelder, S. (2003). Adolescent-onset nicotine self-administration modeled in female rats. *Psychopharmacology, 169*, 141–149.

Levinthal, C. F. (2005). *Drugs, behavior, and modern society* (4th ed.). Boston: Allyn & Bacon.

Levy, S., Vaughan, B. L., & Knight, J. R. (2002). Office-based intervention for adolescent substance abuse. *Pediatric Clinics of North America, 49*, 329–343.

Lewis, J. E. (2005). Assessment, diagnosis, and treatment planning. In R. H. Coombs (Ed.), *Addiction counseling review: Preparing for comprehensive certification and licensing examinations* (pp. 357–380). Mahwah, NJ: Lawrence Erlbaum Associates.

Lex, B. W. (1991). Some gender differences in alcohol and polysubstance users. Special issue: Gender and health. *Health Psychology, 10*, 121–132.

Lex, B. W. (1994). Alcohol and other drug abuse among women. Special focus: Women and alcohol. *Alcohol Health & Research World, 18*, 212–219.

Lichtenberg, J. W. (1997). Expertise in counseling psychology: A concept in search of support. *Educational Psychology Review, 9*, 221–238.

Liddle, H. A., & Dakof, G. A. (1995). Family-based treatment for adolescent drug use: State of the science. *NIDA Research Monograph, 156*, 218–254.

Liddle, H. A., Rowe, C. L., Dakof, G. A., Ungaro, R. A., & Henderson, C. E. (2004). Early intervention for adolescent substance abuse: Pretreatment to posttreatment outcomes of a randomized clinical trial comparing multidimensional family therapy and peer group treatment. *Journal of Psychoactive Drugs, 36*, 49–63.

Liepman, M. R., Nirenberg, T. D., & Begin, A. M. (1989). Evaluation of a program designed to help family and significant others to motivate resistant alcoholics into recovery. *American Journal of Drug and Alcohol Abuse, 15*, 221.

Lightfoot, L. O. (1993). The Offender Substance Abuse Pre-release Program: An empirically based model of treatment for offenders. In J. S. Baer, G. A. Marlatt, & R. J. McMahon (Eds.), *Addictive behaviors across the lifespan* (pp. 184–201). Newbury Park, CA: Sage.

Littrell, J. (1991). *Understanding and treating alcoholism: An empirically based clinician's handbook for the treatment of alcoholism*. Mahwah, NJ: Lawrence Erlbaum Associates.

London, E. D., Ernst, M., Grant, S., Bonson, K., & Weinstein, A. (2000). Orbitofrontal cortex and human drug abuse: Functional imaging. *Cerebral Cortex, 10*, 334–342.

Longshore, D., Annon, J., Anglin, M. D., & Rawson, R. A. (2005). Levo-apha-acetylmethadol (LAAM) versus methadone: Treatment retention and opiate use. *Addiction, 100*, 1131–1139.

Longshore, D., Ghosh-Dastidar, B., & Ellickson, P. L. (2006). National youth anti-drug media campaign and school-based drug prevention: Evidence for a synergistic effect in ALERT Plus. *Addictive Behaviors, 31*, 496–508.

Longshore, D., Hawken, A., Urada, D., & Anglin, M. D. (2006). *Evaluation of the Substance Abuse and Crime Prevention Act: 2005 report*. Retrieved Spetember 20, 2006, from http://www.uclaisap.org/prop36/documents/SACPA_COSTANALYSIS.pdf

Loxley, W., Taumbourou, J. W., Stockwell, T., Haines, B., Scott, K., Godfrey, C., et al. (2004). Patterns of drug use, risk and harm in the early years. In *The prevention of substance use, risk and harm in Australia: A review of the evidence* (pp. 19–30). Canberra, Australia: Commonwealth of Australia.

Luczak, S. E., Elvine-Kreis, B., Shea, S. H., Carr, L. G., & Wall, T. L. (2002). Genetic risk for alcoholism relates to level of response to alcohol in Asian-American men and women. *Journal of Studies on Alcohol, 63*, 74–82.

Ludlow, F. H. (1857). *The hashish eater*. Retrieved July 5, 2005, from http://users.lycaeum.org/~sputnik/Ludlow/THE/index.html

Luepker, R. V., Pechacek, T. F., Murray, D. M., Johnson, C. A., Hund, F., & Jacobs, D. R. (1981). Saliva thiocyanate: A chemical indicator of cigarette smoking in adolescents. *American Journal of Public Health, 71*, 1320–1324.

Lynskey, M. T., Heath, A. C., Bucholz, K. K., Slutske, W. S., Madden, P. A. F., Nelson, E. C., et al. (2003). Escalation of drug use in early-onset cannabis users vs co-twin controls. *Journal of the American Medical Association, 289*, 427–433.

Lyon, M., & McClure, W. O. (1994). Investigations of fetal development models for prenatal drug exposure and schizophrenia: Prenatal d amphetamine effects upon early and late juvenile behavior in the rat. *Psychopharmacology, 116*, 226–236.

MacAndrew, C. (1965). The differentiation of male alcoholic outpatients from nonalcoholic psychiatric outpatients by meansof the MMPI. *Quarterly Journal on the Studies of Alcohol, 26*, 238–246.

MacAndrew, C. (1989). Factors associated with the problem-engendering use of substances by young men. *Journal of Studies on Alcohol, 50*, 552–556.

MacKinnon, D. P., Johnson, C. A., Pentz, M. A., Dwyer, D. P., & Hansen, W. B. (1991). Mediating mechanisms in a school-based drug prevention program: First year effects of the Midwestern Prevention Project. *Health Psychology, 10*, 164–172.

Maisto, S. A., Connors, G. J., & Zywiak, W. H. (2000). Alcohol treatment changes in coping skills, self-efficacy, and levels of alcohol use and related problems 1 year following treatment initiation. *Psychology of Addictive Behaviors, 14*, 257–266.

Malin, H., Coakley, J., & Kaelber, C. (1982). An epidemiologic perspective on alcohol use and abuse in the United States. In *Alcohol consumption and related problems* (pp. 99–153). Rockville, MD: National Institute on Alcohol Abuse and Alcoholism, National Institutes of Health.

Mandel, J. (2002, March 3). *The mythical roots of U.S. drug policy: Soldier's disease and addicts in the Civil War*. Retrieved April 20, 2005, from http://www.druglibrary.org/SCHAFFER/history/soldis.htm

Manderlink, G., and Harackiewicz, J. M. (1984). Proximal versus distal goal setting and intrinsic motivation. *Journal of Personality and Social Psychology, 47*, 918–928.

Mansdorf, I. J., Calapai, P., Caselli, L., Burnstein, Y., & Dimant, J. (1999). Reducing psychotropic medication usage in nursing home residents: The effects of behaviorally oriented psychotherapy. *The Behavior Therapist, 22*, 21–23.

Margolese, H. C., Malchy, L., Negrete, J. C., Tempier, R., & Gill, K. (2004). Drug and alcohol use among patients with schizophrenia and related psychoses: Levels and consequences. *Schizoprenia Research, 67*, 157–166.

Marijuana Anonymous World Services, Inc. (1995). *Life with hope: A return to living through the twelve steps and twelve traditions of Marijuana Anonymous*. Van Nuys, CA: Author.

Markou, A., Kostenn, T. R., & Koob, G. F. (1998). Neurobiological similarities in depression and drug dependence: A self-medication hypothesis. *Neuropsychopharmacology, 18*, 135–174.

Marlatt, G. A. (Ed.). (1998). *Harm reduction: Pragmatic strategies for managing high risk behaviors*. New York: The Guilford Press.

Marlatt, G. A. (2006). *Mindfulness-based relapse prevention in the treatment of addictive behavior*. Paper presented at the Second Annual Symposium on Addictive and Health Behaviors Research, Jacksonville, FL.

Marlatt, G. A., & Gordon, J. R. (1985). *Relapse prevention: Maintenance strategies in addictive behavior change*. New York: Guilford.

Marlatt, G. A., Somers, J. M., & Tapert, S. F. (1993). Harm reduction: Applications to alcohol abuse problems. In L. S. Onken, J. D. Blaine, & J. J. Boren (Eds.), *Behavioral treatments for drug abuse and dependence* (pp. 144–166). Bethesda, MD: National Institute on Drug Abuse.

Marshall, L. (2003). *Time bomb: A meth parable*. Retrieved September 6, 2007, from http://web.dailycamera.com/time_bomb/meths_mess.html

Marshall, M. J., Marshall, S., & Heer, M. J. (1994). Characteristics of abstinent substance abusers who first sought treatment in adolescence. *Journal of Drug Education, 24*, 151–162.

Martin, C. S., & Winters, K. C. (1998). Diagnosis and assessment of alcohol use disorders among adolescents. *Alcohol Health & Research World, 22*, 95–105.

Mason, B. J. (2001). Treatment of alcohol-dependent outpatients with acamprosate: A clinical review. *Journal of Clinical Psychiatry, 62*, 42–48.

Mason, B. J., Salvato, M. D., Williams, L. D., Ritvo, E. C., & Cutler, R. B. (1999). A double-blind, placebo-controlled study of oral nalmefene for alcohol dependence. *Archives of General Psychiatry, 56*, 719–724.

Mason, M., Cheung, I., & Walker, L. (2004). Substance use, social networks, and the geography of urban adolescents. *Substance Use & Misuse, 39*, 1751–1777.

Mathias, R. (1999). Adding more counseling sessions and 12-step programs can boost drug abuse treatment effectiveness. *NIDA Notes, 14*, 6–7.

Matthys, W., & Lochman, J. E. (2005). Social problem solving in aggressive children. In M. McMurran & J. McGuire (Eds.), *Social problem solving and offenders* (pp. 51–66). Chichester: Wiley.

Mattick, R. P., Kimber, J., Breen, C., & Davoli, M. (2004). Buprenorphine maintenance vs placebo or methadone maintenance for opioid dependence. *Cochrane Database of Systematic Reviews, 3*(CD0002207).

Maxwell, J. C. (1996). *Substance abuse trends in Texas, December 1995.* TCADA Research Brief. Austin, TX: Texas Commission on Drug and Alcohol Abuse.

Mayer, J., & Filstead, W. J. (1979). The Adolescent Alcohol Involvement Scale: An instrument for measuring adolescents' use and misuse of alcohol. *Journal of Studies on Alcohol, 40*, 291–300.

McCabe, S. E., Teter, C. J., & Boyd, C. J. (2004). The use, misuse and diversion of prescription stimulants among middle and high school students. *Substance Use and Misuse, 39*, 1095–1117.

McCann, U. D., Wong, D. F., Yokoi, F., Villemagne, V., Dannals, R. F., & Ricaurte, G. A. (1998). Reduced striatal dopamine transporter density in abstinent methamphetamine and methcathinone users: Evidence from positron emission tomography studies with [11C] WIN-35,428. *Journal of Neuroscience, 18*, 8417–8422.

McCarthy, K. (1984). Early alcoholism treatment: The Emmanuel Movement and Richard Peabody. *Journal of Studies on Alcohol, 45*, 59–74.

McConnell, A. R., Sherman, S. J., & Hamilton, D. L. (1994). Illusory correlation in the perception of groups: An extension of the distinctiveness-based account. *Journal of Personality and Social Psychology, 67*, 414–429.

McCoul, M. D., & Haslam, N. (2001). Predicting high risk sexual behaviour in heterosexual and homosexual men: The roles of impulsivity and sensation seeking. *Personality and Individual Differences, 31*, 1303–1310.

McCourt, W. F., Williams, A. F., & Schneider, L. (1971). Incidence of alcoholism in a state mental hospital population. *Quarterly Journal of Studies on Alcohol, 32*(4, Pt. A), 1085–1088.

McEwen, B. S. (2002). Sex, stress and the hippocampus: allostasis, allostatic load and the aging process. *Neurobiology of Aging, 23*, 921–939.

McGee, L., & Newcomb, M. D. (1992). General deviance syndrome: Expanded hierarchical evaluations at four ages from early adolescence to adulthood. *Journal of Consulting and Clinical Psychology, 60*, 766–776.

McKay, J. R., Maisto, S. A., & O'Farrell, T. J. (1993). End-of-treatment self-efficacy, aftercare, and drinking outcomes in alcoholic men. *Alcoholism: Clinical and Experimental Research, 17*, 1078–1083.

McLellan, A. T., Luborsky, L., Cacciola, J., Griffith, J., Evans, F., Barr, H. L., et al. (1985). New data from the Addiction Severity Index: Reliability and validity in three centers. *Journal of Nervous and Mental Disease, 173*, 412–428.

McLellan, A. T., Luborsky, L., Woody, G. E., & O'Brien, C. P. (1980). An improved diagnostic evaluation instrument for substance abuse patients. The Addiction Severity Index. *Journal of Nervous and Mental Disease, 168*, 26–33.

Meichenbaum, D. (1977). *Cognitive behavior modification: An integrative approach.* New York: Plenum.

Meshack, A. F., Hu, S., Pallonen, U. E., McAlister, A. L., Gottlieb, N., & Huang, P. (2004). Texas tobacco prevention pilot initiative: Processes and effects. *Health Education Research, 19*, 657–668.

Metzger, D., Kushner, H., & McLellan, A. T. (1991). *Adolescent Problem Severity Index.* Philadelphia: University of Pennsylvania.

Meyers, K., McLellan, A. T., Jaeger, J. L., & Pettinati, H. M. (1995). The development of the Comprehensive Addiction Severity Index for Adolescents (CASI-A). An interview for assessing multiple problems of adolescents. *Journal of Substance Abuse Treatment, 12*, 181–193.

Micco, A., & Masson, M. E. J. (1991). Implicit memory for new associations: An interactive process approach. *Journal of Experimental Psychology: Learning, Memory, and Cognition, 17*, 1105–1123.

Miele, G. M., Carpenter, K. M., Smith Cockerham, M., Trautman, K. D., Blaine, J., & Hasin, D. S. (2000). Substance Dependence Severity Scale (SDSS): Reliability and validity of a clinician-administered interview for DSM-IV substance use disorders. *Drug and Alcohol Dependence, 59*, 63–75.

Miller, L. (1991). Predicting relapse and recovery in alcoholism and addiction: Neuropsyhcology, personality and cognitive style. *Journal of Substance Abuse Treatment, 8*, 277–291.

Miller, W. R., & Marlatt, G. A. (1984). *Comprehensive Drinker Profile* [Manual]. Odessa, FL: Psychological Assessment Resources.

Miller, W. R., Meyers, R. J., & Tonigan, J. S. (1999). Engaging the unmotivated in treatment for alcohol problems: A comparison of three strategies for intervention through family members. *Journal of Consulting and Clinical Psychology, 67*, 688–697.

Miller, W. R., & Rollnick, S. (1991). *Motivational interviewing: Preparing people to change addictive behavior.* New York: Guilford.

Miller, W. R., & Rollnick, S. (2002). *Motivational interviewing.* New York: Guilford.

Millstein, S. G., & Marcell, A. V. (2003). Screening and counseling for adolescent alcohol use among primary care physicians in the United States. *Pediatrics, 111*, 114–112.

Milne, S., Orbell, S., & Sheeran, P. (2002). Combining motivational and volitional interventions to promote exercise participation: Protection motivation theory and implementation intentions. *British Journal of Health Psychology, 7*, 163–184.

Mitchell, J. E., Specker, S., & Edmonson, K. (1997). Management of substance abuse and dependence. In P. E. Garfinkel & D. M. Garner (Eds.), *Handbook of treatment for eating disorders* (2nd ed., pp. 415–423). New York: Guilford.

Moberg, D. P., & Hahn, L. (1991). The Adolescent Drug Involvement Scale. *Journal of Adolescent Chemical Dependency, 2*, 75–88.

Moderation Management. (n.d.). Home page. Retrieved March 24, 2006, from http://www.moderation.org/

Monti, P. M., Abrams, D. B., Kadden, R. M., & Cooney, N. L. (1989). *Treating alcohol dependence.* New York: Guilford.

Monti, P. M., Rohsenow, D. J., & Hutchison, K. E. (2000). Toward bridging the gap between biological, psychobiological and psychosocial models of alcohol craving. *Addiction, 95*(Suppl. 2), S229–S236.

Mueller, L. A., & Ketcham, K. (1987). *Recovering: How lo get and stay sober.* New York: Bantam.

Mueser, K. T., Noordsy, D. L., Drake, R. W., & Fox, L. (2003). *Integrated treatment for dual disorders.* New York: Guilford.

Multidimensional Treatment Foster Care. (n.d.). Home page. Retrieved June 11, 2006, from http://www.mtfc.com/

Multisystemic Therapy (MST). (n.d.). *Treatment model.* Retrieved June 9, 2006 from www.mstservices.com/text/treatment.html

Mundis, J. (1986, January 5). A way back from debt: Debtors Anonymous. *The New York Times.* Retrieved on September 6, 2007 from http://www.totse.com/en/ego/making_money/debtanon.html

Murgraff, V., White, D., & Phillips, K. (1996). Moderating binge drinking: It is possible to change behavior if you plan it in advance. *Alcohol and Alcholism, 31*, 577–582.

Myers, M. G., Brown, S. A., & Mott, M. A. (1993). Coping as a predictor of adolescent substance abuse treatment outcome. *Journal of Substance Abuse Treatment, 5*, 15–29.

Narcotics Anonymous World Services. (n.d.). Home page. Retrieved August 27, 2006, from www.na.org

Narcotics Anonymous. (1988). *Narcotics Anonymous* (5th ed.) Van Nuys, CA: Narcotics Anonymous World Services, Inc.

National Association for Children of Alcoholics. (n.d.). Home page. Retrieved September 6, 2007, from www.nacoa.org

National Association of Counties. (n.d.) Home page. Retrieved October 9, 2005, from http://www.naco.org/

National Institute of Diabetes and Digestive Kidney Diseases. (n.d.). *Statistics related to overweight and obesity*. Retrieved May 5, 2005, from http://win.niddk.nih.gov/statistics/index.htm#preval

National Institute of Justice. (2003). *2000 annual report on drug use among adult and juvenile arrestees, Arrestees Drug Abuse Monitoring Program (ADAM)* (NCJ 193013). Washington, DC: Author.

National Institute on Alcohol Abuse and Alcoholism. (n.d.). Retrieved September 19, 2006, from http://pubs.niaaa.nih.gov/publications/combine/FAQs.htm

National Institute on Drug Abuse. (n.d.). Retrived May 5, 2005, from www.nida.nih.gov/about/organization/DESPR/HSR/dapre/KumpferLitReviewPartB.htlm

National Institute on Drug Abuse-Club Drugs Home. (n.d.). *Important information and resources on club drugs*. Retrieved September 6, 2007 from http://www.clubdrugs.org/

Nelson, D. L., Schreiber, T. A., & McEvoy, C. L. (1992). Processing implicit and explicit representations. *Psychological Review, 99*, 322–348.

Nestler, E. (2000). Genes and addiction. *Nature Genetics, 26*, 277–281.

Nestler, E. J., & Landsman, D. (2001). Learning about addiction from the genome. *Nature, 409*, 834–835.

Newcomb, M. D. (1995). Identifying high-risk youth: Prevalence and patterns of adolescent drug abuse. *NIDA Research Monograph, 156*, 7–38.

Newcomb, M. D., & Bentler, P. M. (1988a). *Consequences of adolescent drug use*. Newbury Park, CA: Sage.

Newcomb, M. D., & Bentler, P. M. (1988b). Impact of adolescent drug use and social support on problems of young adults: A longitudinal study. *Journal of Abnormal Psychology, 97*, 64–75.

Newcomb, M. D., & Bentler, P. M. (1989). Substance use and abuse among children and teenagers. *The American Psychologist, 44*, 242–248.

Newcomb, M., & Earleywine, M. (1996). Intrapersonal contributors to drug use: The willing host. *American Behavioral Scientist, 39*, 823–837.

Newcomb, M. D., & Felix-Ortiz, M. (1992). Multiple protective and risk factors for drug use and abuse: Cross-sectional and prospective findings. *Journal of Personality and Social Psychology, 63*, 280–296.

Nezami, E., Sussman, S., & Pentz, M. A. (2003). Motivation in tobacco use cessation research. *Substance Use & Misuse, 38*, 25–50.

Niaura, R. S., Rohsenow, D. J., Binkoff, J. A., Monti, P. M., Pedraza, M., & Abrams, D. B. (1988). Relevance of cue reactivity to understanding alcohol and smoking relapse. *Journal of Abnormal Psychology, 97*, 133–152.

Nicotine Anonymous. (n.d.). Home page. Retrieved August 26, 2006, from www.nicotine-anonymous.org

Nisbett, R. E., & Wilson, T. D. (1977). Telling more than we can know: Verbal reports on mental processes. *Psychological Review, 84*, 231–259.

Nishimura, S. T., Hishinuma, E. S., Miyamoto, R. H., Goebert, D. A., Johnson, R. C., Yuen, N. Y., et al. (2001). Prediction of DISC substance abuse and dependency for ethnically diverse adolescents. *Journal of Substance Abuse Treatment, 13*, 597–607.

Noble, E. P. K., Blum, K., Ritchie, T., Montgomery, A., & Sheridan, P. J. (1991). Allelic association of the D2 dopamine receptor gene with receptor binding characteristics in alcoholism. *Archives of General Psychiatry, 48*, 648–654.

Noonan, W. C., & Moyers, T. (1997). Motivational interviewing: A review. *Journal of Substance Misuse, 2*, 8–16.

Nurses Research Publication. (1999). *Substance abuse: What you should know*. Hayward, California: author. Retrieved September 6, 2007, from http://www.nurseslearning.com/courses/nrp/NRP-1600/Nrp1600.pdf

O'Brien, C. P., Childress, A. R., McLellan, A. T., & Ehrman, R. (1990). Integrating systematic cue exposure with standard treatment in recovering drug dependent patients. *Addictive Behavios, 15*, 355–365.

Ockene, J. K., Nutall, R., Benfari, R. C., Hurwitz, I., & Ockene, I. S. (1981). A psychosocial model of smoking cessation and maintenance of cessation. *Preventive Medicine, 10*, 623–638.

O'Connor, K. P. (1989). Individual differences and motor systems in smoker motivations. In T. Ney & A. Gale (Eds.), *Smoking and human behavior* (pp. 141–170). New York/Chichester: Wiley.

O'Farrell, T. J., & Fals-Stewart, W. (2000). Behavioral couples therapy for alcoholism and drug abuse. *The Behavior Therapist, 23*, 49–54.

Office of Justice Programs. (n.d.). *Statistics on drugs and crime.* Retrieved September 13, 2006, from http://www.ojp.usdoj.gov/bjs/drugs.htm

Office of National Drug Control Policy. (n.d.). *Street terms: Drugs and the drug trade.* Retrieved September 6, 2007, from http://www.whitehousedrugpolicy.gov/streetterms/

Office of National Drug Control Policy. (2001). *The economic costs of drug abuse in the United States 1992–998.* Washington, DC: Executive Office of the President, Office of National Drug Control Policy.

O'Leary, T. A., Brown, S. A., Colby, S. M., Cronce, J. M., D'Amico, E. J., Fader, J. S., et al. (2002). Treating adolescents together or individually? Issues in adolescent substance abuse interventions. *Alcoholism: Clinical and Experimental Research, 26*, 890–899.

Olesen, P. J., Westerberg, H., & Klingberg, T. (2004). Increased prefrontal and parietal activity after training of working memory. *Nature Neuroscience, 7*, 75–79.

Omidvari, K., Lessnau, K., Kim, J., Mercante, D., Weinacker, A., & Mason, C. (2005). Smoking in contemporary American cinema. *The Cardiopulmonary and Critical Care Journal, 128*, 746–754.

Oracle Education Foundation. (n.d.). *Street drugs.* Retrieved May 6, 2005, from http://library.thinkquest.org/TQ0310171/street_drugs.htm

Orbell, S., Hodgkins, S., & Sheeran, P. (1997). Implementation intentions and the theory of planned behavior. *Personality and Social Psychology Bulletin, 23*, 945–954.

Orbell, S., & Sheeran, P. (2002). Changing health behaviours: The role of implementation intentions. In D. Rutter & L. Quine (Eds.), *Changing health behaviour: Intervention and research with social cognition models* (pp. 123–137). New York: Open University Press.

Orpinas, P. K., Basen-Engquist, K., Grunbaum, J., & Parcel, G. S. (1995). The co-morbidity of violence-related behaviors with health-risk behaviors in a population of high school students. *Journal of Adolescent Health, 16*, 216–225.

Paglia, A., & Room, R. (1999). Preventing substance use problems among youth: A literature review and recommendations. *Journal of Primary Prevention, 20*, 3–50.

Palinkas, L. A., Atkins, C. J., Miller, C., & Ferreira, D. (1996). Social skills training for drug prevention in high-risk female adolescents. *Preventive Medicine, 25*, 692–701.

Palmgreen, P., Donohew, L., Lorch, E. P., Hoyle, R. H., & Stephenson, M. T. (2001). Television campaigns and adolescent marijuana use: Tests of sensation seeking targetting. *American Journal of Public Health, 91*, 292–296.

Parent Corps (n.d.). Home page. Retrieved September 6, 2007, from www.parentcorps.org

Parrott, A. C. (2004). Is ecstasy MDMA? A review of the proportion of ecstasy tablets containing MDMA, their dosage levels, and the changing perceptions of purity. *Psychopharmacology, 173*, 234–241.

Payne, B. K. (2005). Conceptualizing control in social cognition: How executive functioning modulates the expression of automatic stereotyping. *Journal of Personality and Social Psychology, 89*, 488–503.

PBS Frontline. (n.d.). *The meth epidemic.* Retrieved Semptember 6, 2007, from http://www.pbs.org/wgbh/pages/frontline/meth/

Pealer, L., & Weiler, R. (2000). Research notes: Web-based health survey research: A primer. *American Journal of Health Behavior, 24*, 69–72.

Pears, K. C., & Fisher, P. A. (2005). Emotion understanding and theory of mind among maltreated children in foster care: Evidence of deficits. *Journal of Development and Psychopathology, 17*, 47–65.

Peciña, S., & Berridge, K. C. (2005). Hedonic hot spot in nucleus accumbens shell: Where do μ-opioids cause increased hedonic impact of sweetness? *The Journal of Neuroscience, 25*, 11777–11786.

Peele, S. (1998). Ten radical things NIAAA Research shows about alcoholism. *The Addictions Newsletter, 5*, 2020–2022.

Peele, S. B., & Brodsky, A. (1992). *The truth about addiction and recovery.* New York: Simon & Schuster (Fireside Edition).

Peeler, D. F., & Nowakowski, R. S. (1987). Genetic factors and the measurement of exploratory activity. *Behavioral and Neural Biology, 48,* 90–103.

Pentz, M. (1986). Community organization and school liaisons: How to get programs started. *Journal of School Health, 56,* 382–388.

Pentz, M. A. (1995). A comprehensive strategy to prevent the abuse of alcohol and other drugs: Theory and methods. In R. Coombs & D. Ziedonis (Eds.), *Handbook on drug abuse prevention* (pp. 62–92). Englewood Cliffs, NJ: Prentice Hall.

Pentz, M. A., Bonnie, R. J., & Shopland, D. R. (1996). Integrating supply and demand reduction strategies for drug abuse prevention. *American Behavioral Scientist, 39,* 897–910.

Pentz, M. A., Brannon, B. R., Charlin, V. L., Barrett, E. J., MacKinnon, D. P., & Flay, B. R. (1989). The power of policy: Relationship of school smoking policy to adolescent smoking. *American Journal of Public Health, 79,* 857–863.

Pentz, M. A., Dwyer, J. H., MacKinnon, D. P., Flay, B. R., Hansen, W. B., Wang, E., & Johnson, C. A. (1989) A multicommunity trial for primary prevention of adolescent drug abuse. Effects on drug use prevalence. *Journal of the American Medical Association, 261,* 3259–3266.

Pentz, M. A., Jasuja, G. K., Rohrbach, L. A., Sussman, S., & Bardo, M. T. (2006). Translation in tobacco and drug abuse prevention research. *Evaluation & the Health Professions, 29,* 246–271.

Pentz, M. A., Sussman, S., & Newman, T. (1997). The conflict between least harm and no-use tobacco policy for youth: Ethical ad policy implications. *Addiction, 92,* 1165–1173.

Perry, J. L., German, J. P., Madden, G. J., & Carroll, M. E. (2005). Impulsivity (delay discounting) as a predictor of acquisition of IV cocaine self-administration in female rats. *Psychopharmacology, 178,* 193–201.

Petchers, M. K., & Singer, M. I. (1987). Perceived-Benefit-of-Drinking Scale: Approach to screening for adolescent alcohol abuse. *Journal of Pediatrics, 110,* 977–981.

Petchers, M. K., Singer, M. I., Angelotta, J. W., & Chow, J. (1988). Revalidation and expansion of an adolescent substance abuse screening measure. *Journal of Developmental & Behavioral Pediatrics, 9,* 25–29.

Peterson, R. C., & Stillman, R. C. (1977). Cocaine: 1977 (No. Reseach Monograph #13). Rockville, MD: National Institute on Drug Abuse.

Petraitis, J., Flay, B. R., & Miller, T. Q. (1995). Reviewing theories of adolescent substance use: Organizing the pieces in the puzzle. *Psychological Bulletin, 117,* 67–86.

Phillips, P. E., Stuber, G. D., Heien, M. L. A. V., Wightman, R. M., & Carelli, R. M. (2003). Subsecond dopamine release promotes cocaine seeking. *Nature, 422,* 614–617.

Pianezza, M. L., Sellers, E. M., & Tyndale, R. F. (1998). Nicotine metabolism defect reduces smoking. *Nature, 393,* 750.

Piazza, P. V., Deminiere, J., Le Moal, M., & Simon, H. (1989). Factors that predict individual vulnerability to amphetamine self-administration. *Science, 245,* 1511–1513.

Pickering, H., & Stimson, G. V. (1994). Prevalence and demographic factors of stimulant use. *Addiction, 89,* 1385–1389.

Plomin, R., & Rutter, M. (1998). Child development, molecular genetics, and what to do with genes once they are found. *Child Development, 69,* 1223–1242.

Polansky, J. R., & Glantz, S. A. (2004). *First-run smoking presentations in U.S.movies 1999–2003.* San Francisco: Center for Tobacco Control Research and Education, University of California.

Positive Realism. (n.d.). *Overcome sexual addiction.* Retrieved June 4, 2005, from www.sexual-control.com

Poulin, F., Dishion, T. J., & Burraston, B. (2001). 3-year iatrogenic effects associated with aggregating high-risk adolescents in cognitive-behavioral preventive interventions. *Applied Developmental Science, 5,* 214–224.

Prestwich, A., Conner, M., & Lawton, R. (2006). Implementation intentions: Can they be used to prevent and treat addiction? In R. W. Wiers & A. W. Stacy (Eds.), *Handbook on implicit cognition and addiction* (pp. 455–469). Thousand Oaks, CA: Sage.

Prochaska, J. O., & DiClemente, C. C. (1982). Transtheoretical therapy: Toward a more integrative model of change. *Psychotherapy: Theory, Research Practice, 19,* 275–288.

Prochaska, J. O., DiClemente, C. C., Velicer, W. F., Ginpil, S., & Norcross, J. C. (1985). Prediction change in smoking status for self-changers. *Addictive Behaviors, 10*, 395–406.

Prochaska, J. O., Velicer, S., DiClemente, C. C., Guadagnoli, E., & Rossi, J. S. (1990). Patterns of change: Dynamic typology applied to smoking cessation. *Multivariate Behavioral Research, 25*, 587–611.

Public Broadcasting Service. (n.d.). *The meth epidemic.* Retrieved April 6, 2005, from http://www.pbs.org/wgbh/pages/frontline/meth/

Quinn, T. C., Ruff, A., & Modlin, J. (1992). HIV infection and AIDS in children. *Annual Review of Public Health, 13*, 1–30.

Quintero, G., & Nichter, M. (1996). The semantics of addiction: Moving beyond expert models to lay understandings. *Journal of Psychoactive Drugs, 28*, 219–228.

Rahdert, E. (1991). *Adolescent assessment/referral system manual* [Publication No. (ADM) 91–1735]. Rockville, MD: U.S. Department of Health and Human Services.

Rather, B. C., & Goldman, M. S. (1994). Drinking-related differences in the memory organization of alcohol expectancies. *Experimental and Clinical Psychopharmacology, 2*, 167–183.

Rather, B. C., Goldman, M. S., Roehrich, L., & Brannick, M. (1992). Empirical modeling of an alcohol expectancy memory network using multidimensional scaling. *Journal of Abnormal Psychology, 101*, 174–183.

Rational Recovery. (n.d.). Retrieved September 6, 2007, from http://www.rational.org/welcome.html

Rawson, R. A., Hasson, A. L., Huber, A. M., McCann, M. J., & Ling, W. (1998). A 3-year progress report on the implementation of LAAM in the United States. *Addiction, 93*, 533–540.

Reber, A. S. (1993). *Implicit learning and tacit knowledge.* Oxford, UK: Oxford University Press.

Reefer Madness [movie]. (1936). Los Angeles: George A. Hirliman Productions.

Rehman, Z. (2001). *Opium abuse.* Retrieved June 24, 2005, from www.emedicine.com/med/byname/opioid-abuse.htm

Reif, W. J. (1999). A tangled history of America's relationship with illegal drugs. *The Lancet, 354*, 604.

Richardson, J. L., Dwyer, K., McGuigan, K., Hansen, W. B., Dent, C., Johnson, C. A., et al. (1989). Substance use among eighth-grade students who take care of themselves after school. *Pediatrics, 84*, 556–566.

Rifkin, J. (2005). Ultimate therapy: Commercial eugenics in the 21st century. *Harvard International Review, 27*, 44–48.

Riggs, S. G., & Alario, A. J. (1989). Adolescent substance abuse. In C. E. Dube, M. G. Goldstein, D. C. Lewis, D. C. Myers, & W. R. Zwick (Eds.), *The Project ADEPT curriculum for primary care physician training* (p. 27). Providence, RI: Brown University.

Ritt-Olson, A., Milam, J., Unger, J. B., Trinidad, D., Teran, L., Dent, C. W., et al. (2004). The protective influence of spirituality and health-as-a-value against monthly substance abuse among adolescents varying in risk. *Journal of Adolescent Health, 34*, 192–199.

Rivers, S. M., Greenbaum, R. L., & Goldberg, E. (2001). Hospital-based adolescent substance abuse treatment: Comorbidity, outcomes, and gender. *The Journal of Nervous and Mental Disease, 189*, 229–237.

Robbins, T. W., & Everitt, B. J. (1999). Drug addiction: Bad habits add up. *Nature, 398*, 567–570.

Robins, L. N. (Ed.). (1985). *Studying drug abuse.* New Brunswick, NJ: Rutgers University Press.

Robinson, T. E., & Berridge, K. C. (1993). The neural basis of drug craving: An incentive-sensitization theory of addiction. *Brain Research Reviews, 18*, 247–291.

Robinson, T. E., & Berridge, K. C. (2000). The psychology and neurobiology of addiction: An incentive-sensitization view. *Addiction, 95*, s91–s117.

Robinson, T. E., & Berridge, K. C. (2003). Addiction. *Annual Review of Psychology, 54*, 25–53.

Rodgers, A., Corbett, T., Bramley, D., Riddell, T., Wills, M., Lin, R.-B., et al. (2005). Do u smoke after txt? Results of a randomized trial of smoking cessation using mobile phone text messaging. *Tobacco Control, 14*, 255–261.

Roehrich, L., & Goldman, M. S. (1995). Implicit priming of alcohol expectancy memory processes and subsequent drinking behavior. *Experimental and Clinical Psychopharmacology, 3*, 402–410.

Rogers, E. M. (2003). *Diffusion of innovations.* New York: Free Press.

Rogers, R., Cashel, M. L., Johansen, J., & Sewell, K. W. (1997). Evaluation of adolescent offenders with substance abuse: Validation of the SASSI with conduct-disordered youth. *Criminal Justice & Behavior, 24*, 114–128.

Rogers, R. W. (1975). A protection motivation theory of fear appeals and attitude change. *The Journal of Psychology, 91*, 93–114.

Rohrbach, L. A., D'Onofrio, C. N., Backer, T. E., & Montgomery, S. B. (1996). Diffusion of school-based substance abuse prevention programs. *American Behavioral Scientist, 39*, 919–934.

Rohrbach, L. A., Graham, J. W., & Hansen, W. B. (1993). Diffusion of a school-based substance abuse prevention program: Predictors of program implementation. *Preventive Medicine, 22*, 237–260.

Rohrbach, L. A., Sussman, S., Dent, C. W., & Sun, P. (2005). Tobacco, alcohol, and other drug use among high-risk young people: A five-year longitudinal study from adolescence to emerging adulthood. *Journal of Drug Issues, 35*, 333–356.

Rohsenow, D. J., Monti, P. M., Rubonis, A. V., & Sirota, A. D. (1994). Cue reactivity as a predictor of drinking among male alcoholics. *Journal of Consulting and Clinical Psychology, 62*, 620–626.

Rohsenow, D. J., Niaura, R. S., Childress, A. R., Abrams, D. B., & Monti, P. M. (1990–1991). Cue reactivity in addictive behaviours: Theoretical and treatment implications. *The International Journal of the Addictions, 25*, 957–993.

Rolls, E. T. (1999). The functions of the orbitofrontal cortex. *Neurocase, 5*, 301–312.

Rosenfield, P. L. (1992). The potential of transdisciplinary research for sustaining and extending linkages between the health and social sciences. *Social Science and Medicine, 35*, 1343–1357.

Roth, J. L., & Brooks-Gunn, J. (2003). Youth development programs: Risk, prevention and policy. *Journal of Adolescent Health, 32*, 170–182.

Rotter, J. B. (1954). *Social learning and clinical psychology*. New York: Prentice Hall.

Rounds-Bryant, J. L., Kristiansen, P. L., & Hubbard, R. L. (1999). Drug abuse treatment outcome study of adolescents: A comparison of client characteristics and pretreatment behaviors in three treatment modalities. *American Journal of Drug & Alcohol Abuse, 25*, 573–591.

Rounsville, B. J., Kosten, T. R., Weissman, M. M., & Kleber, H. D. (1986). Prognostic significance of psychopathology in treated opiate addicts: A 2.5-year follow-up study. *Archives of General Psychiatry, 43*, 739–745.

Roy, A., Adinoff, B., Roehrich, L., Lamparski, D., Custer, R., Lorenz, V., et al. (1988). Pathological gambling: A psychobiological study. *Archives of General Psychiatry, 45*, 369–373.

Rychtarik, R. G., Connors, G. J., Whitney, R. B., McGillicuddy, N. B., & Fitterling, J. M. (2000). Treatment settings for persons with alcoholism: Evidence for matching clients to inpatient versus outpatient care. *Journal of Consulting and Clinical Psychology, 68*, 277–289.

Rychtarik, R. G., Koutsky, J. R., & Miller, W. R. (1998). Profiles of the alcohol use inventory: A large sample cluster analysis conducted with split-sample replication rules. *Psychological Assessment, 10*, 107–119.

Rychtarik, R. G., Koutsky, J. R., & Miller, W. R. (1999). Profiles of the alcohol use inventory: Correction to Rychtarik, Koutsky, and Miller (1998). *Psychological Assessment, 11*, 396–402.

Rydell, C. P., & Everingham, S. S. (1994). *Controlling cocaine: Supply vs. demand programs* (Research Report MR-331-ONDCP/A/DPRC). Santa Monica, CA: RAND.

Saah, T. (2005). The evolutionary origins and significance of drug addiction. *Harm Reduction Journal, 2* (8). Retrieved September 6, 2007, from http://www.harmreductionjournal.com/content/2/1/8

Sargent, J. D., Beach, M. L., Adachi-Mejia, A. M., Gibson, J. J., Titus-Ernstoff, L. T., Carusi, C. P., et al. (2005). Exposure to movie smoking: Its relation to smoking initiation among US adolescents. *Pediatrics, 116*, 1183–1191.

Sargent, J. D., Beach, M. L., Dalton, M. A., Titus-Ernstoff, L. T., Gibson, J. J., Tickle, J. J., et al. (2004). Effect of parental R-rated movie restriction on adolescent smoking initiation: A prospective study. *Pediatrics, 114*, 149–156.

Saxe, L., Kadushin, C., Beveridge, A., Livert, D., Tighe, E., Rindskopf, D., et al. (2001). The visibility of illicit drugs: Implications for community-based drug control strategies. *American Journal of Public Health, 91*, 1987–1994.

Schacter, D. L., & Graf, P. (1989). Modality specificity of implicit memory for new associations. *Journal of Experimental Psychology: Learning, Memory, and Cognition, 15*, 3–12.

Schaef, A. W. (1987). *When society becomes an addict*. New York: Harper Collins.

Scheier, L. M., Botvin, G. J., Diaz, T., & Ifill-Williams, M. (1997). Ethnic identity as a moderator of psychosocial risk and adolescent alcohol and marijuana use: Concurrent and longitudinal analyses. *Journal of Child and Adolescent Substance Abuse, 6*, 21–47.

Schlosser, S., Black, D. W., Repertinger, S., & Freet, D. (1994). Compulsive buying: Demography, phenomology, and comorbidity in 46 subjects. *General Hospital Psychiatry, 16*, 205–212.

Schmitz, J., Stotts, A., Rhoades, H., & Grabowski, J. (2001). Naltrexone and relapse prevention treatment for cocaine-dependent patients. *Addictive Behaviors, 26*, 167–180.

Schneider, J. P. (1994). Sex addiction: Controversy within mainstream addiction medicine, diagnosis based on the DSM-III-R, and physician case histories. *Sexual Addiction and Compulsivity, 1*, 19–44.

Schottenfeld, R. S. (1994). Assessment of the patient. In M. Galanter & H. D. Kleber (Eds.), *The American Psychiatric Press textbook of substance abuse treatment* (pp. 25–33). Washington, DC: American Psychiatric Press.

Schottenfeld, R. S., Chawarski, M. C., Pakes, J. R., Pantalon, M. W., Carroll, K. M., & Kosten, T. R. (2005). Methadone versus buprenorphine with contingency management or performance feedback for cocaine and opioid dependence. *The American Journal of Psychiatry, 162*, 340–349.

Schottenfeld, R. S., Pakes, J. R., Oliveto, A., Ziedonis, D., & Kosten, T. R. (1997). Buprenorphine vs methadone maintenance treatment for concurrent opioid dependence and cocaine abuse. *Archives of General Psychiatry, 54*, 713–720.

Schultes, R. E. (1969). Hallucinogens of plant origin. *Science, 163*, 245–254.

Schultes, R. E. (1995). Antiquity of the use of new world hallucinogens. *Integration, 5*, 9–18.

Schultes, R. E. (1998). Antiquity of the use of new world hallucinogens. *The Heffter Review of Psychedelic Research, 1*, 1–7.

Schultz, W. (1998). Predictive reward signal of dopamine neurons. *Journal of Neurophysiology, 80*, 1–27.

Schultz, W. (2001). Reward signaling by dopamine neurons. *Neuroscientist, 7*, 293–302.

Schultz, W. (2004). Neural coding of basic reward terms of animal learning theory, game theory, microeconomics and behavioral ecology. *Current Opinion in Neurobiology, 14*, 139–147.

Schutz, A., & Luckman, T. (1973). *The structure of the life world*. Evanston, IL: Northwestern University Press.

Scott, J. (2004). *Social network analysis: A handbook* (2nd ed.). London: Sage.

Scott, R. L., Kern, M. F., & Coombs, R. H. (2001). Coping skills/affect regulation training. In R. H. Coombs (Ed.), *Addiction recovery tools: A practitioner's handbook* (pp. 191–206). Thousand Oaks, CA: Sage.

Secular Organizations for Sobriety/Save Our Selves. (n.d.). Retrieved on September 6, 2007, from http://www.sossobriety.org/

Selzer, M. L. (1971). The Michigan alcoholism Screening Test: The quest for a new diagnostic instrument. *American Journal of Psychiatry, 127*, 1653–1658.

Setlow, B. (1997). The nucleus accumbens and learning and memory. *Journal of Neuroscience Research, 49*, 515–521.

Sex Addicts Anonymous. (n.d.). Retrieved June 3, 2005, from www.saa-recovery.org

Sex and Love Addicts Anonymous. (n.d.). Retrieved June 3, 2005, from www.slaafws.org

Sexaholics Anonymous. (n.d.). Home page. Retrieved June 3, 2005, from www.sa.org

Sexual Compulsives Anonymous. (n.d.). Home page. Retrieved June 4, 2005, from www.sca-recovery.org

Sexual Recovery Anonymous. (n.d.). Home page. Retrieved June 3, 2005, from ourworld. compuserve.com/homepages/sra

Shedler, J., & Block, J. (1990). Adolescent drug use and psychological health: A longitudinal inquiry. *American Psychologist, 45*, 612–630.

Sheeran, P., & Orbell, S. (1999). Implementation intentions and repeated behavior: Augmenting the predictive validity of the theory of planned behaviour. *European Journal of Social Psychology, 29*, 349–369.

Sheeran, P., & Orbell, S. (2000). Using implementation intentions to increase attendance for cervical cancer screening. *Health Psychology, 19*, 283–289.

Sher, K. J. (1991). *Children of alcoholics: A critical appraisal of theory and research*. Chicago: University of Chicago Press.

Sher, K. J. (1993). Children of alcoholics and the intergenerational transmission of alcoholism: A biopsychosocial perspective. In J. S. Baer, G. A. Marlatt, & R. J. McMahon (Eds.), *Addictive behaviors across the life span: Prevention, treatment, and policy issues* (pp. 3–33). Newbury Park, CA: Sage.

Sherman, S. J., Presson, C. C., Chassin, L., Corty, E., & Olshavsky, R. (1983). The false consensus effect in estimates of smoking prevalence: Underlying mechanisms. *Personality and Social Psychology Bulletin, 9*, 197–207.

Shesser, R., Jotte, R., & Olshaker, J. (1991). The contribution of impurities to the acute morbidity of illegal drug use. *American Journal of Emergency Medicine, 9*, 336–342.

Shields, I. W., & Whitehall, G. C. (1994). Neutralization and delinquency among teenagers. *Criminal Justice and Behavior, 21*, 223–235.

Shihadeh, A. (2003). Investigation of mainstream smoke aerosol of the argileh water pipe. *Food and Chemical Toxicology, 41*, 143–152.

Simon, T. R., Stacy, A. W., Sussman, S., & Dent, C. (1994). Sensation seeking and drug use among high risk latino and anglo adolescents. *Personality and Individual Differences, 17*, 665–672.

Simpson, D. D., Joe, G. W., & Brown, B. S. (1997). Treatment retention and follow-up outcomes in the Drug Abust Treatment Outcome Study (DATOS). *Psychology of Addictive Behaviors, 11*, 294–307.

Single, E. (1995). Defining harm reduction. *Drug and Alcohol Review, 14*, 287–290.

Skara, S., & Sussman, S. (2003). A review of 25 long-term adolescent tobacco and other drug use prevention program evaluations. *Preventive Medicine, 37*, 451–474.

Skogan, W. G., & Lurigio, A. J. (1992). The correlates of community antidrug activism. *Crime and Delinquency, 38*, 510–521.

Slater, M. D., Kelly, K. J., Edwards, R. W., Thurman, P. J., Plested, B. A., Keefe, T. J., et al. (2005). Combining in-school and community-based media efforts: Reducing marijuana and alcohol uptake among younger adolescents. *Health Education Research, 21*, 157–167.

SMART recovery. (n.d.) Home page. Retrieved August 20, 2006, from www.smartrecovery.org

Smart, R. G., Adlaf, E. M., & Walsh, G. W. (1992). Adolescent drug sellers: Trends, characteristics and profiles. *British Journal of Addiction, 87*, 1561–1570.

Smith, C., Lizotte, A. J., Thornberry, T. P., & Krohn, M. D. (1995). Resilient youth: Identifying factors that prevent high-risk youth from engaging in delinquency and drug use. In J. Hagan (Ed.), *Delinquency and disrepute in the life course* (pp. 217–247). Greenwich, CT: JAI Press.

Smith, D., & Seymour, R. (2001). *Clinician's guide to substance abuse.* New York: McGraw-Hill Medical.

Smith, D. E. (1998). Review of the American Medical Association Council on Scientific Affairs report on medical marijuana. *Journal of Psychoactive Drugs, 30*, 127–136.

Smith, G. M. (1980). Perceived effects of substance use. In D. J. Lettieri, M. Sayers, & H. W. Pearson (Eds.), *Theories on drug abuse: Selected contemporary perspectives* (NIDA Research Monograph 30, 50–58). Rockville, MD: National Institute on Drug Abuse.

Snyder, L. B., Hamilton, M. A., Mitchell, E. W., Kiwanuka-Tondo, J., Fleming-Milici, F., & Proctor, D. (2004). A meta-analysis of the effect of mediated health communication campaigns on behavior change in the United States. *Journal of Health Communication, 9*, 71–96.

Sobol, D. F., Rohrbach, L. A., Dent, C. W., Gleason, L., Brannon, B. R., Johnson, C. A., et al. (1989). The integrity of smoking prevention curriculum delivery. *Health Education Research, 4*, 59–67.

Sommers, P. V. (1972). *The biology of behavior.* Sydney: John Wiley & Sons Australia PTY LTD.

Speigel, E., & Mudler, E. A. (1986). The ananonymous program and ego functioning. *Issues in Ego Psychology, 19*, 34–42.

Spence, J. T., & Robbins, A. S. (1992). Workaholism: Definition, measurement, and preliminary results. *Journal of Personality Assessment, 58*, 160–178.

Spiegel, E., & Mulder, E. A. (1986). The anonymous program and ego functioning. *Issues in Ego Psychology, 19*, 34–42.

Spoth, R., Reyes, M. L., Redmond, C., & Shin, C. (1999). Assessing a public health approach to delay onset and progression of adolescent substance use: Latent transition and log-linear analyses of longitudinal family preventive intervention outcomes. *Journal of Consulting and Clinical Psychology, 67*, 619–630.

Spunt, B., Dupont, I., Lesieur, H., Liberty, H. J., & Hunt, D. (1998). Pathological gambling and substance misuse: A review of the literature. *Substance Use & Misuse, 33*, 2535–2560.

Spunt, B., Lesieur, H., Hunt, D., & Cahill, L. (1995). Gambling among methadone patients. *International Journal of the Addictions, 30*, 929–962.

St. Pierre, T. L., Kaltreider, D. L., Mark, M. M., & Aikin, K. J. (1992). Drug prevention in a community setting: A longitudinal study of the relative effectiveness of a three-year primary prevention program in Boys and Girls Clubs across the nation. *American Journal of Community Psychology, 20*, 673–706.

Stacy, A. W. (1995). Memory association and ambiguous cues in models of alcohol and marijuana use. *Experimental and Clinical Psychopharmacology, 3*, 183–194.

Stacy, A. W. (1997). Memory activation and expectancy as prospective predictors of alcohol and marijuana use. *Journal of Abnormal Psychology, 106*, 61–73.

Stacy, A. W., & Ames, S. L. (2001). Implicit cognition theory in drug use and driving under the influence interventions. In S. Sussman (Ed.), *Handbook of program development in health behavior research and practice* (pp. 107–130). Thousand Oaks, CA: Sage.

Stacy, A. W., Ames, S. L., & Grenard, J. L. (2006). Word association tests of associative memory and implicit processes: Theoretical and assessment issues. In R. W. Wiers & A. W. Stacy (Eds.), *Handbook on implicit cognition and addiction* (pp. 75–90). Thousand Oaks, CA: Sage.

Stacy, A. W., Ames, S. L., & Knowlton, B. J. (2004). Neurologically plausible distinctions in cognition relevant to drug use etiology and prevention. *Substance Use & Misuse, 39*, 1571–1623.

Stacy, A. W., Ames, S. L., Sussman, S., & Dent, C. W. (1996). Implicit cognition in adolescent drug use. *Psychology of Addictive Behaviors, 10*, 190–203.

Stacy, A. W., Ames, S. L., Ullman, J. B., Zogg, J. B., & Leigh, B. C. (2006). Spontaneous cognition and HIV risk behavior. *Psychology of Addictive Behavior, 20*, 196–206.

Stacy, A. W., Dent, C., Sussman, S., Raynor, A., Burton, D., & Flay, B. R. (1990). Expectancy accessibility and the influence of outcome expectancies on adolescent smokeless tobacco use. *Journal of Applied Social Psychology, 20*, 802–817.

Stacy, A. W., Leigh, B. C., & Weingardt, K. R. (1994). Memory accessibility and association of alcohol use and its positive outcomes. *Experimental and Clinical Psychopharmacology, 2*, 269–282.

Stacy, A. W., Newcomb, M. D., & Bentler, P. M. (1991). Cognitive motivation and problem drug use: A 9-year longitudinal study. *Journal of Abnormal Psychology, 100*, 502–515.

Stacy, A. W., Newcomb, M. D., & Bentler, P. M. (1993). Cognitive motivations and sensation seeking as long-term predictors of drinking problems. *Journal of Social and Clinical Psychology, 12*, 1–24.

Stacy, A. W., Widaman, K. F., & Marlatt, G. A. (1990). Expectancy models of alcohol use. *Journal of Personality and Social Psychology, 58*, 918–928.

Stacy, A. W., Zogg, J. B., Unger, J. B., & Dent, C. W. (2004). Exposure to televised alcohol ads and subsequent adolescent alcohol use. *American Journal of Health Behavior, 28*, 498–509.

Stanovich, K. E., & West, R. F. (2000). Individual differences in reasoning: Implications for the rationality debate. *Behavioral and Brain Sciences, 23*, 645–726.

Star, J., & Estes, J. (1990). *Geographic Information Systems: An introduction.* Englewood Cliffs, NJ: Prentice Hall.

Stein, L. A. R., Colby, S. M., Barnett, N. P., Monti, P. M., Golembeske, C., Lebeau-Craven, R., et al. (2006). Enhancing substance abuse treatment engagement in incarcerated adolescents. *Psychological Services, 3*, 25–34.

Stevens, V. J., Glasgow, R. E., Hollis, J. F., & Mount, K. (2000). Implementation and effectiveness of a brief smoking-cessation intervention for hospital patients. *Medical Care, 38*, 451–459.

Stewart, S. H., Conrod, P. J., Marlatt, G. A., Comeau, M. N., Thush, C., & Krank, M. (2005). New developments in prevention and early intervention for alcohol abuse in youths. *Alcoholism: Clinical and Experimental Research, 29*, 278–286.

Stinchfield, R. D., Niforopulos, L., & Feder, S. H. (1994). Follow-up contact bias in adolescent substance abuse treatment outcome research. *Journal of Studies on Alcohol, 55*, 285–289.

Storti, E. (2001). Motivational intervention: The only failure is the failure to act. In R. H. Coombs (Ed.), *Addiction recovery tools: A practical handbook* (pp. 3–16). Thousand Oaks, CA: Sage.

Strengthening Families Program. (n.d.). Home page. Retrieved September 6, 2007, from http://www.strengtheningfamiliesprogram.org/.

Strogatz, S. H. (2001). Exploring complex networks. *Nature, 410,* 268–276.

Stroot, E. A., & Fromme, K. (1989). *Comprehensive effects of alcohol: Development of a new expectancy questionnaire.* Paper presented at the 23rd annual meeting of the Association for Advancement of Behavior Therapy, Washington, DC.

Substance Abuse and Mental Health Services Administration. (n.d.). *Drug and Alcohol Services Information System (DASIS).* Retrieved October 20, 2005, from http://www.drugabusestatistics. samhsa.gov/dasis.htm

Substance Abuse and Mental Health Services Administration. (n.d.). *Mental health & substance abuse: Comorbidity/co-occurring disorders/dual diagnosis.* Retrieved October 22, 2005, from http://www.drugabusestatistics.samhsa.gov/mh.cfm

Substance Abuse and Mental Health Services Administration. (2001). *Quick guide for clinicians based on tip 31, screening and assessing adolescents for substance use, based on tip 32, treatment of adolescents with substance use disorders* (No. 01–3596). Rockville, MD: Center for Substance Abuse Treatment, U.S. Department of Health and Human Services.

Substance Abuse and Mental Health Services Administration. (2002). *Report from the 2001 National Household Study on Drug Abuse: Volume 1. Summary of national findings.* Rockville, MD: Office of Applied Studies.

Substance Abuse and Mental Health Services Administration. (2003). *Treatment Episode Data Set (TEDS): 1992–2002.* Rockville, MD: Office of Applied Studies.

Sun, P., Unger, J. B., Palmer, P. H., Gallaher, P., Chou, C. P., Baezconde-Garbanati, L., et al. (2005). Internet accessibility and usage among urban adolescents in Southern California: Implications for web-based health research. *CyberPsychology & Behavior, 8,* 441–453.

Sun, W., Skara, S., Sun, P., Dent, C. W., & Sussman, S. (2006). Project Towards No Drug Abuse: Long-term substance use outcomes evaluation. *Preventive Medicine, 42,* 188–192.

Sussman, S. (1996). Development of a school-based drug abuse prevention curriculum for high-risk youths. *Journal of Psychoactive Drugs, 28,* 169–182.

Sussman, S. (1999). Tobacco industry. In R. Gottesman (Ed.), *Violence in America: An encylopedia* (pp. 330–333). New York: Charles Scribner's & Sons.

Sussman, S. (Ed.). (2001). *Handbook of program development in health behavior research and practice.* Thousand Oaks, CA: Sage.

Sussman, S. (2002a). Effects of sixty-six adolescent tobacco use cessation trials and seventeen prospective studies of self-initiated quitting. *Tobacco Induced Diseases, 1,* 35–81.

Sussman, S. (2002b). Tobacco industry youth tobacco prevention programming: A review. *Prevention Science, 3,* 57–67.

Sussman, S. (2005a). Cognitive misperception as determinants of drug misuse. *Salud y drogas, 5,* 9–31.

Sussman, S. (2005b). Foundations of health behavior research revisited. *American Journal of Health Behaviour, 29,* 489–496.

Sussman, S. (2005c). The relations of cigarette smoking with risky sexual behavior among teens. *Sexual Addiction & Compulsivity: The Journal of Treatment and Prevention, 12,* 181–199.

Sussman, S. (2005d). Risk factors for and prevention of tobacco use. *Pediatric Blood & Cancer, 44,* 614–619.

Sussman, S. (2005e). Prevention of adolescent alcohol problems in special populations. In Marc Galanter (Ed.), *Recent developments in alcoholism. Volume 17. Alcohol problems in adolescents and young adults: Epidemiology, neurobiology, prevention, treatment* (pp. 225–253). An official publication of the ASAM and the RSA. New York: Kluwer.

Sussman, S. (2006). The transdisciplinary-translation revolution: Final thoughts. *Evaluation & Health Professions, 29,* 348–352.

Sussman, S., & Ames, S. L. (2001). *The social psychology of drug abuse.* Buckingham, UK: Open University Press.

Sussman, S., Barovich, M., Hahn, G., Abrams, C., Selski, E., & Craig, S. (2004). *Project TNT: Towards No Tobacco Use teacher's guide* (2nd ed.). Santa Cruz, CA: ETR Associates.

Sussman, S., Craig, S., & Moss, M. A. (2002). *Project TND: Towards No Drug Abuse* (1st ed.). Los Angeles: University of Southern California.

Sussman, S., & Dent, C. W. (2004). Five-year prospective prediction of marijuana use cessation among youth at continuation high schools. *Addictive Behaviors, 29,* 1237–1243.

Sussman, S., Dent, C. W., & Galaif, E. R. (1997). The correlates of substance abuse and dependence among adolescents at high risk for drug abuse. *Journal of Substance Abuse Treatment, 9,* 241–255.

Sussman, S., Dent, C. W., & McCuller, W. J. (2000). Group self-identification as a prospective predictor of drug use and violence in high-risk youth. *Psychology of Addictive Behaviors, 14,* 192–196.

Sussman, S., Dent, C. W., Mestel-Rauch, J. S., Johnson, C. A., Hansen, W. B., & Flay, B. R. (1988). Adolescent nonsmokers, triers, and regular smokers' estimates of cigarette smoking prevalence: When do overestimates occur and by whom? *Journal of Applied Social Psychology, 18,* 537–551.

Sussman, S., Dent, C. W., Simon, T. R., Stacy, A. W., Galaif, E. R., Moss, M. A., et al. (1995). Immediate impact of social influence-oriented substance abuse prevention curricula in traditional and continuation high schools. *Drugs and Society, 8,* 65–81.

Sussman, S., Dent, C. W., Simon, T. S., Stacy, A. W., Burton, D., & Flay, B. R. (1993). Identification of which high risk youth smoke cigarettes regularly. *Health Values, 17,* 42–53.

Sussman, S., Dent, C. W., & Stacy, A. W. (1996). The relations of pro-drug-use myths with self-reported drug use among youth at continuation high schools. *Journal of Applied Social Psychology, 26,* 2014–2037.

Sussman, S., Dent, C. W., & Stacy, A. W. (1999). The association of current stimulant use with demographic, substance use, violence-related, social and intra-personal variables among high risk youth. *Addictive Behaviors, 24,* 741–748.

Sussman, S., Dent, C. W., Stacy, A. W., Burton, D., & Flay, B. R. (1995). *Developing school-based tobacco use prevention and cessation programs.* Thousand Oaks, CA: Sage.

Sussman, S., Dent, C. W., & Stacy, S. (2002). Project towards no drug abuse: A review of the findings and future directions. *American Journal of Health Behavior, 26,* 354–365.

Sussman, S., Dent, C. W., Wang, E., Cruz, N. T. B., Sanford, D., & Johnson, C. A. (1994). Participants and nonparticipants of a mass media self-help smoking cessation program. *Addictive Behaviors, 19,* 643–654.

Sussman, S., Earleywine, M., Wills, T., Cody, C., Biglan, T., Dent, C. W., et al. (2004). The motivation, skills, and decision-making model of drug abuse prevention. *Substance Use & Misuse, 39,* 1971–2016.

Sussman, S., Horn, J. L., & Gilewski, M. (1990). Alcohol relapse prevention: Need for a memory modification component. *The International Journal of the Addictions, 25,* 921–929.

Sussman, S., & Huver, R. M. E. (2006). Definitions of street drugs. In S. M. Cole (Ed.), *New research on street drugs* (pp. 1–12). Hauppauge, NY: Nova Science.

Sussman, S., Kohrman, M., Vateesatokit, P., Hamann, S., Pokhrel, P., & Nsimba, S. E. D. (in press). Four phases of tobacco control: Tanzania, China, Nepal, and Thailand as examples. *Nicotine & Tobacco Research.*

Sussman, S., Nezami, E., & Mishra, S. (1997). On operationalizing spiritual experience for health promotion research and practice. *Alternative Medicine, 4,* 120–125.

Sussman, S., Patten, C., & Order-Connors, B. (2005). Tobacco use. In R. Coombs (Ed.), *Addiction counseling review* (pp. 203–224). York, PA: TechBooks.

Sussman, S., Pentz, M. A., Spruijt-Metz, D., & Miller, T. (2006). Abuse of study drugs: Prevalence, consequences, and implications for therapeutic prescription and policy. *Substance Abuse Treatment, Prevention, and Policy, 1:15.* Retrieved on September 6, 2007, from http://www.substanceabusepolicy.com/content/1/1/15

Sussman, S., Pokhrel, P., Ashmore, R., & Brown, B. B. (2007). Adolescent peer group identification and characteristics: A review of the literature. *Addictive Behaviors, 32,* 1602–1627.

Sussman, S., Pokhrel, P., Black, D., Kohrman, M., Vateesatokit, P., Hamann, S., et al. (in press). Tobacco-control in developing countries: Tanzania, Nepal, China, and Thailand as examples. *Nicotine & Tobacco Research.*

Sussman, S., Rohrbach, L. A., Patel, R., & Holiday, K. (2003). A look at an interactive classroom-based drug abuse prevention program: Interactive contents and suggestions for research. *Journal of Drug Education, 33,* 355–368.

Sussman, S., Rohrbach, L. A., Skara, S., & Dent, C. W. (2004). Prospective prediction of alternative high school graduation status at emerging adulthood. *Journal of Applied Social Psychology, 34,* 2452–2468.

Sussman, S., Runyon, B. A., Hernandez, R., Magallanes, M., Mendler, M., Yuan, J.-M., et al. (2005). A pilot study of an alcoholic liver disease recurrence prevention education program in hospitalized patients with advanced liver disease. *Addictive Behaviors, 30,* 465–473.

Sussman, S., Rychtarik, R. G., Mueser, K. T., Glynn, S., & Prue, D. M. (1986). Ecological relevance of memory tests and the prediction of relapse in alcoholics. *Journal of Studies on Alcohol, 47,* 305–310.

Sussman, S., Simon, T. R., Stacy, A. W., Dent, C. W., Ritt, A., Kipke, M. D., et al. (1999). The association of group self-identification and adolescent drug use in three samples varying in risk. *Journal of Applied Social Psychology, 29,* 1555–1581.

Sussman, S., Skara, S., & Ames, S. L. (2006). Substance abuse among adolescents. In T. G. Plante (Ed.), *Mental disorders of the new millennium. Volume 2. Public and social problems* (pp. 127–169). Westport, CT: Praeger.

Sussman, S., Skara, S., & Pumpuang, P. (in press). Project Towards No Drug Abuse (TND): A needs assessment of a social service referral telephone program for high risk youth. *Substance Use & Misuse.*

Sussman, S., Stacy, A. W., Dent, C. W., Simon, T. R., & Johnson, C. A. (1996). Marijuana use: Current issues and new research directions. *Journal of Drug Issues, 26,* 693–672.

Sussman, S., Sun, P., & Dent, C. W. (2006). A meta-analysis of teen tobacco use cessation. *Health Psychology, 25,* 549–557.

Sussman, S., Sun, P., McCuller, W. J., & Dent, C. W. (2003). Project Towards No Drug Abuse: Two-year outcomes of a trial that compares health educator delivery to self-instruction. *Preventive Medicine, 37,* 155–162.

Sussman, S., & Sussman, A. N. (2001). Praxis in health behavior program development. In S. Sussman (Ed.), *Handbook of program development in health behavior research and practice* (pp. 79–97). Thousand Oaks, CA: Sage.

Sussman, S., & Unger, J. B. (2004). A "drug abuse" theoretical integration: A transdisciplinary speculation. *Substance Use & Misuse, 39,* 2055–2069.

Sussman, S., & Wills, T. A. (2001). Rationale for program development methods. In S. Sussman (Ed.), *Handbook of program development in health behavior research and practice* (pp. 3–30). Thousand Oaks, CA: Sage.

Sutton, S. R., & Eiser, J. R. (1984). The effect of fear-arousing communications on cigarette smoking: An expectancy-value approach. *Journal of Behavioral Medicine, 7,* 13–33.

Suzuki, K., Matsushita, S., & Ishii, T. (1997). Relationship between the flushing response and drinking behavior among Japanese high school students. *Alcoholism: Clinical & Experimental Research, 21,* 1726–1729.

Svanum, S., Levitt, E., & McAdoo, W. G. (1982). Differentiating male and female alcoholics from psychiatric outpatients: The MacAndrew and Rosenberg alcoholism scales. *Journal of Personality Assessment, 46,* 81–84.

Swanson, J. W., Linskey, A. O., Quintero-Salinas, R., Pumariega, A., J., & Holzer, C. E. (1992). A binational school survey of depressive symptoms, drug use, and suicidal ideation. *Journal of the American Academy of Child & Adolescent Psychiatry, 31,* 669–678.

Swisher, J. D., & Hu, T. W. (1983). Alternatives to drug abuse: Some are and some are not. In T. J. Glynn, C. G. Leukefeld, & J. P. Ludford (Eds.), *Preventing adolescent drug abuse: Intervention strategies* (NIDA Research Monograph 47, pp. 141–153). Rockville, MD: National Institute on Drug Abuse.

Sykes, G., & Matza, D. (1957). Techniques of neutralization: A theory of delinquency. *American Sociological Review, 22,* 664–670.

Szalay, L. B., Canino, G., & Vilov, S. K. (1993). Vulnerabilities and cultural change: Drug use among Puerto Rican adolescents in the United States. *The International Journal of the Addictions, 28,* 327–354.

Szalay, L. B., Inn, A., & Doherty, K. T. (1996). Social influences: Effects of the social environment on the use of alcohol and other drugs. *Substance Use & Misuse, 31,* 343–373.

Szapocznik, J., & Coatsworth, D. (1999). An ecodevelopmental framework for organizing the influences on drug abuse: A developmental model of risk and protection. In M. D. Glanz & C. R. Hartel (Eds.), *Drug abuse: Origins and interventions* (pp. 331–366). Washington, DC: American Psychological Association.

Tabachnik, N., Crocker, J., & Alloy, L. B. (1983). Depression, social comparison, and the false consensus effect. *Journal of Personality and Social Psychology, 45*, 688–699.

Talbott, G. D., & Crosby, L. R. (2001). Recovery contracts: Seven key elements. In R. H. Coombs (Ed.), *Addiction recovery tools: A practical handbook* (pp. 127–144). Thousand Oaks, CA: Sage.

Tarter, R. (1990). Evaluation and treatment of adolescent substance abuse: A decision tree method. *American Journal of Drug & Alcohol Abuse, 16*, 1–46.

Tarter, R., Kirisci, L., & Mezzich, A. (1996). The drug use screening inventory: School adjustment correlates of substance abuse. *Measurement and Evaluation in Counseling and Development, 29*, 25–34.

Tarter, R. E. (2002). Etiology of adolescent substance abuse: A developmental perspective. *American Journal on Addictions, 11*, 171–191.

Tarter, R. E., Kirisci, L., Mezzich, A., Conelius, J. R., Pajer, K., Vanyukov, M., et al. (2003). Neurobehavioral disinhibition in childhood predicts early age at onset of substance use disorder. *American Journal of Psychiatry, 160*, 1078–1085.

Taylor, A., Chalouka, F. J., Guindon, E., & Corbett, M. (2000). The impact of trade liberalization on tobacco consumption. In P. Jha & F. J. Cahloupka (Eds.), *Tobacco control in developing countries* (pp. 343–364.). Oxford, UK: Oxford University Press.

Teets, J. M. (1990). What women talk about: Sexuality issues of chemically dependent women. *Journal of Psychosocial Nursing and Mental Health Services, 28*, 4–7.

Teets, J. M. (1997). The incidence and experience of rape among chemically dependent women. *Journal of Psychoactive Drugs, 29*, 331–344.

Teicher, M. H., Andersen, S. L., Polcari, A., Anderson, C. M., Navalta, C. P., & Kim, D. M. (2003). The neurobiological consequences of early stress and childhood maltreatment. *Neuroscience and Biobehavioral Reviews, 27*, 33–44.

Teichman, M., Barnea, Z., & Ravav, G. (1989). Personality and substance use among adolescents: A longitudinal study. *British Journal of the Addictions, 84*, 181–190.

Tengs, T. O., Osgood, N. D., & Chen, L. L. (2001). The cost-effectiveness of intensive national school-based anti-tobacco education: Results from the Tobacco Policy Model. *Preventive Medicine, 33*, 558–570.

Terry, C. E., & Pellens, M. (1928). *The opium problem*. Bureau of Social Hygiene (Reprinted Montclair, NJ: Patterson Smith, 1970).

Thaxton, L. (1982). Physiological and psychological effects of short-term exercise addiction on habitual runners. *Journal of Sport Psychology, 4*, 73–80.

Theus, K. T. (1994). Subliminal advertising and the psychology of processing unconscious stimuli: A review of research. *Psychology and Marketing, 11*, 271–290.

ThinkQuest. (n.d.). Drug abuse: What really happens (street drugs). Retrieved September 6, 2007, from http://library.thinkquest.org/TQ0310171/street_drugs.htm

Thompson, E. L. (1978). Smoking education programs 1960–1976. *American Journal of Public Health, 68*, 250–257.

Thwing, E. P. (1888). American life as related to inebriety. *Quarterly Journal of Inebriety, 7*, 43–50.

Timmreck, T. C. (1998). *An introduction to epidemiology*. Boston: Jones and Bartlett.

Tims, F. M., Dennis, M. L., Hamilton, N. J., Buchan, B., Diamond, G., Funk, R., et al. (2002). Characteristics and problems of 600 adolescent cannabis abusers in outpatient treatment. *Addiction, 97* (Suppl 1), 46–57.

Tobler, N. S. (1986). Meta-analysis of 143 adolescent drug prevention programs: Quantitative outcomes results of program participants compared to a control or comparison group. *Journal of Drug Issues, 15*, 535–567.

Tobler, N. S., Roona, M. R., Ochshorn, P., Marshall, D. G., Streke, A. V., & Stackpole, K. M. (2000). School-based adolescent drug prevention programs: 1998 Meta-analysis. *The Journal of Primary Prevention, 20*, 275–336.

Tolman, E. C. (1932). *Purposive behavior in animals and men*. New York: Appletown.

Tomlinson, K. L., Brown, S. A., & Abrantes, A. M. (2004). Psychiatric comorbidity and substance use treatment outcomes of adolescents. *Psychology of Addictive Behaviors, 18*, 160–169.

Tonigan, J. S., Toscova, R., & Miller, W. R. (1996). Meta-analysis of the literature on Alcoholics Anonymous: Sample and study characteristics moderate findings. *Journal of Studies on Alcohol, 57*, 65–72.

Trimpey, J. (1989). *The small book: A revolutionary alternative for overcoming alcohol and drug dependence.* New York: Delacorte Press.

Trimpey, J. (1996). *Rational Recovery: The new cure for substance addiction.* New York: Pocket Books.

Turksen, I. B. (2006). *An ontological and epistemological perspective of fuzzy set theory.* St. Louis, MO: Elsevier.

Tuyns, A. J., & Pequignot, G. (1984). Greater risk of ascitic cirrhosis in females in relation to alcohol consumption. *International Journal of Epidemiology, 13,* 53–57.

Tversky, A., & Kahneman, D. (1973). Availability: A heuristic for judging frequency and probability. *Cognitive Psychology, 5,* 207.

Twerski, A. J. (1997). *Addictive thinking.* Center City, MN: Hazelden.

Tyndale, R. F., & Sellers, E. M. (2001). Variable Cyp2A6-mediated nicotine metabolism alters smoking behavior and risk. *Drug Metabolism and Disposition, 29,* 548–552.

Uhlenhuth, E. H., Johanson, C. E., Kilgore, & Kosaba, S. C. (1981). Drug preferences and mood in humans: Preference for d-amphetamine and subject characteristics. *Psychopharmacology, 74,* 191–194.

Unger, J. B., Baezconde-Garbanati, L., Shakib, S., Palmer, P. H., Nezami, E., & Mora, J. (2004). A cultural psychology approach to "drug abuse" prevention. *Substance Use & Misuse, 39,* 1779–1820.

Unger, J. B., & Chen, X. (1999). The role of social networks and media receptivity in predicting age of smoking initiation: A proportional hazards model of risk and protective factors. *Addictive Behaviors, 24,* 371–381.

Unger, J. B., Hamilton, J. E., & Sussman, S. (2004). A family member's job loss as a risk factor for smoking among adolescents. *Health Psychology, 23,* 308–313.

United Nations Office for Drug Control and Crime Prevention. (2003). *Investing in drug abuse treatment. A discussion paper for policy makers* (No. V.02–56708) Austria: Author.

University of North Carolina. (n.d.). *Family Matters.* Retrieved June 15, 2006, from http://www.sph. unc.edu/familymatters/

Upshaw, H. S., & Ostrom, T. M. (1984). Psychological perspective in attitude research. In J. R. Eiser (Ed.), *Attitudinal judgment* (pp. 23–42). New York: Springer-Verlag.

Urberg, K. A., Degirmencioglu, S. M., & Pilgrim, C. (1997). Close friend and group influence on adolescent cigarette smoking and alcohol use. *Developmental Psychology, 33,* 834–844.

U.S. Department of Health and Human Services. (1998a). *NIAAA: Report of a subcommittee of the National Advisory Council on alcohol abuse and alcoholism on the review of the extramural research portfolio for prevention.* Washington, DC: Author.

U.S. Department of Health and Human Services. (1998b). *International Epidemiology Work Group on Drug Abuse 1997 proceedings* (NIH Publication No. 98–4208B). Rockville, MD: National Institutes of Health.

U.S. Department of Health and Human Services. (1999a). *Club drugs: Community drug alert bulletin* (NIH Publication No. 00–4723). Bethesda, MD: National Institute on Drug Abuse.

U.S. Department of Health and Human Services. (1999b). *Principles of drug addiction treatment: A research-based guide* (NIH Publiication No. 99–4180). Bethesda, MD: National Institute on Drug Abuse.

U.S. Department of Health and Human Services. (2004). *The health consequences of smoking: A report of the Surgeon General.* Rockville, MD: U.S. department of Health and Human Services, Public Health service, Office of the Surgeon General.

U.S. Department of Justice. (n.d.). *Statistics on drugs and crime.* Retrieved September 6, 2007, from http://www.ojp.usdoj.gov/bjs/drugs.htm

U.S. Department of Justice, Office of Justice Programs, Bureau of Justice Statistics. (2002). *Substance dependence abuse and treatment of jail inmates.* Retrieved October 12, 2006, from http://www.ojp.usdoj.gov/bjs/abstract/sdatjio2.htm

U.S. Drug Enforcement Administration. (n.d.). Home page. Retrieved September 6, 2007, from http://www.usdoj.gov/dea/index.htm

U.S. Drug Enforcement Administration. (n.d.). Chapter 4: Narcotics. Retrieved September 6, 2007, from http://www.usdoj.gov/dea/pubs/abuse/4-narc.htm

U.S. Drug Enforcement Administration and National Guard (1996). *Drugs of Abuse.* Washington, DC: U.S. Department of Justice.

U.S. Drug Enforcement Administration. (1997). *National Narcotics Intelligence Consumers Committee.* (U.S. DEA-NNICC; 1997). Washington, DC: U.S. Department of Justice.

U.S. Office of Technology Assessment. (1994). *Individual risk and protective factors: Technologies for understanding and preventing substance abuse and addiction.* Retrieved June 5, 2005, from www.druglibrary.org/schaffer/library/studies/ota/ch6.htm

U.S. Supreme Court Center (n.d.). *U.S. v. Behrman* case; Retrieved September 6, 2007, from http://supreme.justia.com/us/258/280/case.html

U.S. Supreme Court Center (n.d.). *U.S. v. Doremus* case; Retrieved September 6, 2007, from http://supreme.justia.com/us/249/86/

Vadasz, C., Laszlovszky, I., de Simone, P. A., & Fleischer, A. (1992). Genetic aspects of dopamine receptor binding in the mouse and rat brain: An overview. *Journal of Neurochemistry, 59*, 793–808.

Vaillant, G. E. (1983). *The natural history of alcoholism: Causes, patterns, and paths to recovery.* Cambridge, MA: Harvard University Press.

Vaillant, G. E. (1990). *We should retain the disease concept of alcoholism. Harvard Medical School Mental Health Letter.* Boston: Harvard College.

Valente, T., Okamoto, J., Pampuang, P., Okatmoto, P., & Sussman, S. (in press). Differences in perceived implementation of a standard versus a peer-led interactive substance abuse prevention program. *American Journal of Health Behavior.*

Valente, T., Ritt-Olson, A., Stacy, A., Unger, J. B., Okamoto, J., & Sussman, S. (in press). Peer acceleration: Effects of a social network tailored substance abuse prevention program among high risk adolescents. *Addiction.*

Valente, T. W. (2002). *Evaluating health promotion programs.* Oxford, UK: Oxford University Press.

Valente, T. W., Hoffman, B. R., Ritt-Olson, A., Lichtman, K., & Johnson, C. A. (2003). Effects of a social-network method for group assignment strategies on peer-led tobacco prevention programs in schools. *American Journal of Public Health, 93*, 1837–1843.

Valente, T. W., Gallaher, P., & Mouttapa, M. (2004). Using social networks to understand and prevent substance use: A transdisciplinary perspective. *Substance Use & Misuse, 39*, 1685–1712.

van Ryn, M., & Heaney, C. A. (1992). What's the use of theory? *Health Education Quarterly, 19*, 315–330.

Vernadakis, A. (1996). Glia-neuron intercommunications and synaptic plasticity. *Progress in Neurobiology, 49*, 185–214.

Verplanken, B., & Faes, S. (1999). Good intentions, bad habits, and effects of forming implementation intentions in health eating. *European Journal of Social Psychology, 29*, 591–604.

Vocci, F. J., Acri, J., & Elkashef, A. (2005). Medication development for addictive disorders: The state of the Science. *American Journal of Psychiatry, 162*, 1432–1440.

Volkow, N. D., Chang, L., Wang, G., Fowler, J. S., Ding, Y., Sedler, M., et al. (2001). Low level of brain dopamine D2 receptors in methamphetamine abusers: Association with metabolism in the orbitofrontal cortex. *American Journal of Psychiatry, 158*, 2015–2021.

Volkow, N. D., & Fowler, J. S. (2000). Addiction, a disease of compulsion and drive: Involvement of the orbitofrontal cortex. *Cerebral Cortex, 10*, 318–325.

Volkow, N. D., Fowler, J. S., Wang, G., & Goldstein, R. Z. (2002). Role of dopamine, the frontal cortex and memory circuits in drug addiction: Insights from imaging studies. *Neurobiology of Learning and Memory, 78*, 610–624.

Wagenaar, A. C. (2006, June). *Alcohol and injury: A surfeit of solutions.* Presentation at the 2nd Symposium on Addictive and Health Behaviors Research, Jacksonville, Florida.

Wagenaar, A., Lenk, K., & Toomey, T. (2005). Policies to reduce underage drinking. A review of the recent literature. *Recent Developments in Alcoholism, 17*, 275–297.

Waldron, H. B., Slesnick, N., Brody, J. L., Turner, C. W., & Peterson, T. R. (2001). Treatment outcomes for adolescent substance abuse at 4- and 7-month assessments. *Journal of Consulting and Clinical Psychology, 69*, 802–813.

Wall, T. L., Thomasson, H. R., Schuckit, M. A., & Ehlers, C. L. (1992). Subjective feelings of alcohol intoxication in Asians with genetic variations of ALDH2 alleles. *Alcoholism: Clinical & Experimental Research, 16*, 991–995.

Walters, S. T., Wright, J. A., & Shegog, R. (2006). A review of computer and Internet-based interventions for smoking behavior. *Addictive Behaviors, 31*, 264–277.

Walton, R. P. (1938). *Marihuana: America's new drug problem: A sociologic question with its basic explanation dependent on biologic and medical principles*. Philadelphia: Lippincott.

Wang, L. Y., Crossett, L. S., Lowry, R., Sussman, S., & Dent, C. W. (2001). Cost-effectiveness of a school-based tobacco-use prevention program. *Archives of Pediatric and Adolescent Medicine, 155*, 1043–1050.

Warner, J. (1992). Before there was 'alcoholism': Lessons from the medieval experience with alcohol. *Contemporary Drug Problems, 19*, 409–429.

Warner, L. A., Kessler, R. C., Hughes, M., Anthony, J. C., & Nelson, C. B. (1995). Prevalence and correlates of drug use and dependence in the United States: Results from the National Comorbidity Survey. *Archives of General Psychiatry, 52*, 219–229.

Wasserman, S., & Faust, K. (1994). *Social networks analysis: Methods and applications*. Cambridge, UK: Cambridge University Press.

Weddle, M., & Kokotailo, P. (2002). Adolescent substance abuse: Confidentiality and consent. *Pediatric Clinics of North America, 49*, 301–315.

Weil, A., & Rosen, W. (1993). *Chocolate to morphine*. New York: Houghton Mifflin.

Weinberg, N. Z., Rahdert, E., Colliver, J. D., & Glantz, M. D. (1998). Adolescent substance abuse: A review of the past 10 years. *Journal of the American Academy of Child and Adolescent Psychiatry, 37*, 252–261.

Weiner, M. D., Sussman, S., McCuller, W. J., & Lichtman, K. (1999). Factors in marijuana cessation among high-risk youth. *Journal of Drug Education, 29*, 337–357.

Weingardt, K. R., Stacy, A. W., & Leigh, B. C. (1996). Automatic activation of alcohol concepts in response to positive outcomes of alcohol use. *Alcoholism: Clinical and Experimental Research, 20*, 25–29.

Weinstein, N. (1987). Unrealistic optimism about susceptibility to health problems: Conclusions from a community-wide sample. *Journal of Behavioral Medicine, 10*, 481–500.

Weinstein, N. D. (1982). Unrealistic optimism about susceptibility to health problems. *Journal of Behavioral Medicine, 10*, 481–500.

Weiss, F. (2005). Neurobiology of craving, conditioned reward and relapse. *Current Opinion in Pharmacology, 5*, 9–19.

Weitzman, E. R., Folkman, A., Folkman, M. P., & Wechsler, H. (2003). The relationship of alcohol outlet density to heavy and frequent drinking and drinking-related problems among college students at eight universities. *Health Place, 9*, 1–6.

West, S. G., & Wicklund, R. A. (1980). *A primer of social psychological theories*. Monterey, CA: Brooks/Cole.

White, H. R., & Labouvie, E. W. (1989). Toward the assessment of adolescent problem drinking. *Journal of Studies on Alcohol, 50*, 30–37.

White, T. (1999). *UN office for drug control and crime prevention global illicit drug trends*. New York: United Nations.

White, W. L. (2001). Pre-AA alcoholic mutual aid societies. *Alcoholism Treatment Quarterly, 19*, 1–21.

White, W. L. (2005). Recovery: Its history and renaissance as an organizing construct. *Alcoholism Treatment Quarterly, 23*, 3–15.

Wiers, R., Van de Luitgaarden, J., & Van den Wildenberg, E. (2005). Smulders FTY: Challenging implicit and explicit alcohol-related cognitions in young heavy drinkers. *Addiction, 100*, 806–819.

Wiers, R. W., de Jong, P. J., Havermans, R., & Jelicic, M. (2004). How to change implicit drug use-related cognitions in prevention: A transdisciplinary integration of findings from experimental psychopathology, social cognition, memory and experimental learning psychology. *Substance Use & Misuse, 39*, 1625–1684.

Wiers, R. W., Hoogeveen, K. J., Sergeant, J. A., & Gunning, W. B. (1997). High and low dose expectancies and the differential associations with drinking in male and female adolescents and young adults. *Addiction, 92*, 871–888.

Wiers, R. W., Houben, K., Smulders, F. T. Y., Conrod, P. J., & Jones, B. (2006). To drink or not to drink: The role of automatic and controlled cognitive processes. In R. W. Wiers & A. W. Stacy (Eds.), *Handbook on implicit cognition and addiction* (pp. 339–361). Thousand Oaks, CA: Sage.

Wiers, R. W., Rinck, M., Kordts, R., Dictus, M., Houben, K., van den Wildenberg, E., et al. (under review). Train addictive impulses away! Assessing and re-training atuomatic action tendencies in heavy drinkers.

Wiers, R. W., Sergeant, J. A., & Gunning, W. B. (2000). The assessment of alcohol expectancies in school children: Measurement or modification? *Addiction, 95*, 737–746.

Wiers, R. W., & Stacy, A. W. (Eds.). (2006). *Handbook on implicit cognition and addiction*. Thousand Oaks, CA: Sage.

Wiers, R. W., van Woerden, N., Smulders, F. T. Y., & de Jong, P. J. (2002). Implicit and explicit alcohol-related cognitions in heavy and light drinkers. *Journal of Abnormal Psychology, 111*, 648–658.

Williams, C. L., & Perry, C. L. (1998). Lessons from Project Northland: Preventing alcohol problems during adolescence. *Alcohol Research & Health, 22*, 107–116.

Williams, S. H. (2005). Medications for treating alcohol dependence. *American Family Physician., 72*, 1775–1780.

Wills, T., & Dishion, T. J. (2004). Temperament and adolescent substance use: A transactional analysis of emerging self-control. *Journal of Clinical Child and Adolescent Psychology, 33*, 69–81.

Wills, T. A. (1986). Stress and coping in early adolescence: Relationships to substance use in urban school samples. *Health Psychology, 5*, 503–529.

Wills, T. A., Baker, E., & Botvin, E. M. (1989). Dimensions of assertiveness: differential relationships to substance use in early adolescence. *Journal of Consulting and Clinical Psychology, 57*, 473–478.

Wills, T. A., Pierce, J. P., & Evans, R. I. (1996). Large-scale environmental risk factors for substance use. *American Behavioral Scientist, 39*, 808–822.

Wills, T. A., & Stoolmiller, M. (2002). The role of self-control in early escalation of substance use: A time-varying analysis. *Journal of Consulting and Clinical Psychology, 70*, 986–997.

Wilsnack, R. W., Wilsnack, S. C., & Klassen, A. D., Jr. (1984). Women's drinking and drinking problems: Patterns from a 1981 national survey. *American Journal of Public Health, 74*, 1231–1238.

Wilsnack, S. C., Vogeltanz, N. D., Klassen, A. D., & Harris, T. R. (1997). Childhood sexual abuse and women's substance abuse: National survey findings. *Journal of Studies on Alcohol, 58*, 264–271.

Wilsnack, S. C., Wilsnack, R. W., & Klassen, A. D. (1986). Epidemiological research on women's drinking, 1978–1984. In *Women and alcohol: Health-related issues.* [Research Monograph No 16. DHHS (ADM) 86–1139, pp. 1–68)]. Washington, DC: National Institute on Alcohol Abuse and Alcoholism, U.S. Government Printing Office.

Wilson, T., Lindsey, S., & Schooler, T. (2000). A model of dual attitudes. *Psychological Review, 107*, 101–126.

Winger, G., Hofmann, F. G., & Woods, J. H. (1992). *A handbook on drug and alcohol abuse: The biomedical aspects.* New York: Oxford University Press.

Winters, K. C. (1999). A new multiscale measure of adult substance abuse. *Journal of Substance Abuse Treatment, 16*, 237–246.

Winters, K. C., & Henly, G. A. (1993). *Adolescent Diagnostic Interview Schedule and manual.* Los Angeles: Western Psychological Services.

Winters, K. C., Stinchfield, R. D., & Henly, G. A. (1993). Further validation of new scales measuring adolescent alcohol and other drug abuse. *Journal of Studies On Alcohol, 54*, 534–541.

Wise R. A. (1988). Psychomotor stimulant properties of addictive drugs. *Annals of the New York Academy of Sciences, 537*, 228–234.

Wise, R. A. (1996). Neurobiology of addiction. *Current Opinion in Neurobiology, 6*, 243–251.

Wise, R. A. (1999). Cognitive factors in addiction and nucleus accumbens function: Some hints from rodent models. *Psychobiology, 27*, 300–310.

Woodhouse, L. D. (1992). Women with jagged edges: Voices from a culture of substance abuse. *Qualitative-Health-Research, 2*, 262–281.

Workaholics Anonymous. (n.d.). Home page. Retrieved September 6, 2007, from http://www.workaholics-anonymous.org/

World Health Organization. (2003). International classification of diseases (10th revision, ICD-10; 2003). Retrieved December 28, 2005, from http://www.who.int/classifications/apps/icd/icd10online

www.streetdrugs.org. (n.d.). Home page. Retrieved September 6, 2007, from http://www.streetdrugs.org/

Yach, D., & Bettcher, D. (2000). Globalisation of the tobacco industry influence and new global responses. *Tobacco Control, 9*, 206–216.

Yin, H. H., & Knowlton, B. J. (2006). Addiction and learning in the brain. In R. W. Wiers & A. W. Stacy (Eds.), *Handbook on implicit cognition and addiction* (pp. 167–183). Thousand Oaks, CA: Sage.

Yoder, B. (1990). *The resource book.* New York: Simon & Schuster Inc.

Young, P. T. (1936). *Motivation of behavior.* New York: John Wiley & Sons.

Zajonc, R. B. (1968). Attitudinal effects of mere exposure. *Journal of Personality and Social Psychology, 9,* 1–27.

Zajonc, R. B. (1980). Feeling and thinking: Preferences need no inferences. *American Psychologist, 35,* 151–175.

Zickler, P. (2000). Evidence accumulates that long-term marijuana users experience withdrawal. *NIDA Notes, 15*(6–7).

Zuckerman, M. (1994). *Behavioral expressions and biosocial bases of sensation seeking.* New York: Cambridge University Press.

Zuckerman, M., Ball, S., & Black, J. (1990). Influences of sensation seeking, gender, risk appraisal, and situational motivation on smoking. *Addictive Behaviors, 15,* 209–220.

Zweben, J. E. (1993). Recovery oriented psychotherapy: A model for addiction treatment. *Psychotherapy, 30,* 259–268.

Author Index

Aber, J. L., 144
Abrams, D. B., 240
Abrantes, A. M., 16, 222
Acri, J., 229
Adams, A. M., 112
Adams, L., 258
Adlaf, E. M., 7
Adler, C. R., 44
Adriani, W., 159, 162
Agnew, R., 105
Ahern, J., 262
Aikin, K. J., 202
Ajzen, I., 218
Akers, R. L., 101, 104, 105
Alario, A. J., 128
Alavarado, R., 189
Alexander, C., 186
Alexander, J. F., 191
Alloy, L. B., 89
Almog, Y. G., 112
Altman, D. G., 280
Alvarado, R., 288
Ames, S. L., vii, viii, ix, 4, 7, 8, 9, 10, 11, 16,
   23, 30, 33, 53, 58, 59, 63, 84, 88, 89, 90, 93,
   94, 96, 97, 116, 135, 171, 245, 254, 255, 280,
   288
Anderson, L. R., 91
Andrews, K., 99
Angelotta, J. W., 131
Angleitmer, A., 86
Anglin, M. D., 53, 112, 228, 263, 264, 267
Annas, G. J., 158
Annis, H. M., 127, 130
Annon, J., 228
Antonovsky, A., 85, 253
Aranow, R., 11
Arkowitz, H., 254
Armitage, C. J., 173
Arria, A. M., 15
Ashmore, R., 65, 99, 106
Atkins, C. J., 165
Atkinson, D. R., 144

Bachman, J. G., 37, 40, 44, 63, 117
Backer, T. E., 143
Baddeley, A., 90, 170
Bailey, S. L., 15
Baker, E., 181
Baker, J. R., 230
Baler, R. D., 37
Ball, S., 84
Banaji, M. R., 92
Bandura, A., 97, 100
Barbor, T. F., 116
Bardo, M. T., 77, 78, 84, 161
Bargh, J., 90, 92
Barnea, Z., 84
Barnes, G. M., 99
Barovich, M., 171, 176
Barrett, K., 269
Bartlett, D. L., 7, 9
Basen-Engquist, K., 60, 144
Battjes, R. J., 258
Bauer, L. O., 162
Bauman, K. E., 100, 103, 190
Baumohl, J., 209
Baumrind, D., 99
Beauchaine, T. P., 79
Bechara, A., 162, 170
Bechara, D., 80
Beck, J. E., 144, 145, 146
Becker, M. H., 217
Beer, J. S., 80
Begin, A. M., 249
Bellamy, N., 288
Benezet, A., 209
Bennett, J. B., 264, 265
Bennett, M. E., 16
Bentler, P. M., 13, 14, 16, 84, 91
Bernstein, A., 95
Berntson, G. G., 79
Berridge, K. C., 77, 78, 79, 80, 81
Bettcher, D., 151
Bhattacharya, G., 256
Bigelow, G. E., 117

Biglan, A., 112, 166
Bindra, D., 217
Bjartveit, K., 44
Black, D. W., 27
Black, J., 84
Blair, W., 47
Blasinsky, M., 130
Block, J., 280
Blood, L., 222
Blum, K., 70, 219
Blum, R. W., 14, 16, 219, 221, 256
Bluth, B., 189
Bogg, T., 187
Bonnie, R. J., 143
Bordua, D. J., 105
Bosworth, K., 264
Botvin, E. M., 181
Botvin, G. J., 118, 139, 288
Bouquet, J., 45
Bowers, C. A., 244
Boyd, C. J., 112
Brady, K. T., 27
Brannick, M., 92
Brannigan, R., 15, 16, 219, 220
Brantingham, J., 114
Brantingham, P. L., 114
Bray, J. W., 265
Breen, C., 228
Breslin, F. C., 222
Briere, J. N., 116
Brodsky, A., 26, 224
Brondino, M. J., 191, 288
Bronfenbrenner, U., 109
Brooks-Gunn, J., 187
Brooner, R. K., 117
Brown, B. B., 65, 99, 105, 106
Brown, B. S., 224, 263
Brown, J., 170
Brown, S. A., 16, 89, 91, 92, 128, 222, 239, 252
Brune, C. M., 173
Bry, B. H., 58
Bufe, C., 252
Buffington, A. L. H., 197
Bukowski, W. J., 71, 146
Buller, D. B., 198
Burke, B. L., 26, 254
Burke, H., 134
Burleson, J. A., 288
Burraston, B., 103, 105
Burrough, P., 114
Butcher, J. N., 134

Carbonari, J. P., 128
Cacioppo, J. T., 79
Cahill, L., 25
Cameron, R., 144
Canino, G., 118
Carbonari, J. P., 128

Cardinal, R. N., 78
Carnes, P. J., 25
Carroll, K. M., 230
Carroll, M. E., 85, 244
Carter, B. L., 240
Carver, C., 79
Cashel, M. L., 131
Castillo-Chavez, C., 113
Catalano, R. F., 58, 104, 110
Chaloupka, F. J., 151
Chamberlain, P., 191
Chappel, J. N., 251
Charlesworth, A., 120
Chartrand, T., 92
Chasnoff, I. J., 116
Chen, L. L., 186
Chen, X., 99
Cheng, T. O., 9
Cheung, I., 110, 114, 271
Chiauzzi, E. J., 240
Childress, A. R., 239, 240
Cho, H., 194
Chou, C. P., 117
Chow, J., 131
Chowell, G., 114
Christiansen, B. A., 91, 128
Christopher, J., 242
Christophersen, A. S., 11
Chuck, C., 87
Chung, T., 15
Cicchetti, D., 82, 85
Clark, B., 106
Clarke, K. C., 114
Cleary, P., 62
Clingempeel, W. G., 288
Clopton, J. R., 134
Coakley, J., 117
Coatsworth, D., 109
Cochran, B. N., 9
Cohen, A. K., 104–105
Cohen, S., 101
Collins, D. J., 52
Collins, L. M, 42
Colliver, J. D., 131, 230
Comer, S. D., 244
Conklin, C. A., 240
Conner, M., 173, 174, 247
Connors, G. J., 239, 252
Conrod, P. J., 155, 161
Cook, C. C. H, 209
Cools, A. R., 86
Coombs, R. H., 234
Cooney, N. L., 240
Cooper, D. A., 41
Corbett, M., 151
Corbin, W., 91
Cornelius, J. R., 16
Cornwall, A., 222
Coronges, K., 93

Costa, F. M., 26
Cox, M., 174
Crabbe, J. C., 86
Craig, S., 169, 176
Creamer, V. A., 222
Crocker, J., 89
Crosby, L. R., 259
Crusio, W. E., 86
Cruz, I. Y., 246
Cunningham, J. A., 20, 222
Curry, J. F., 257
Curry, S., 217

Dakof, G. A., 257
Dakoff, D. A., 288
Daley, D. C., 217
Damasio, A. R., 80
Damasio, H., 80
D'Amico, E. J., 128
Darkes, J., 91, 92, 246
Davenport, D., 48
Davis, C. W., 8
Davis, E., 130
Davis, H. G., 134
Davison, G. C., 238
Davoli, M., 228
Davy, H., 46
Deas, D., 15, 288
De Bellis, M. D., 153, 159
de Beurs, E., 74
Deckel, A. W., 162
Degirmenciolglu, S. M., 99, 103
de Jong, P. J., 88, 94, 244
DeJong, W., 195
DeMarsh, J. P., 190
Deminiere, J., 84
Dennis, M. L., 127, 131
Dent, C. W., 7, 10, 13, 16, 83, 85, 93, 94, 96, 97, 112, 117, 119, 141, 221, 222, 230, 281, 288
de Quincey, T., 47
Deren, S., 9
Deroo, L., 254
de Simone, P. A., 86
Deutsch, M., 99
Devine, P. G., 93
de Vries, H., 99, 150
de Wit, H., 85
Deykin, E. Y., 84
Diaz, T., 118, 288
Diaz-Guerrero, R., 118
DiChiara, G., 77, 78, 178
Dickinson, G. L., 228
DiClemente, C. C., 128, 217
Diefenbach, M., 218
DiMatteo, M. R., 60
Dinges, N. G., 288
Dishion, T. J., 103, 105, 162, 165
Dodder, R. A., 105

Doherty, K. T., 116
Dolan, S., 81, 170
Domitian, 48
Donaher, P. A., 228
Donaldson, S. I., 181, 292
D'Onofrio, C. N., 143
Donohew, R. L., 78, 84, 161
Donovan, D. M., 239
Donovan, J. E., 25, 26
Dorsman, J., 242
Dovidio, J. F., 90
Drake, R. W., 28
Dreser, H., 44
Drummond, D. C., 240
Dufour, M. C., 285
Duncan, D. F., 223
Dunn, C., 254
Dunn, M. E., 91, 92, 244, 246
Durell, J., 146
Dwyer, J. H., 292
Dwyer, K. M., 98

Earleywine, M., 60, 83, 85, 87, 91, 100, 117, 141, 162, 163, 164, 166, 171, 176, 181, 188, 190, 281
Eastwood, B., 174, 245
Eberman, K. M., 218
Edmonson, K., 24
Edmundson, E., 146
Edwards, G. E., 209
Eggert, L. L., 164
Ehlers, C. L., 74, 118
Ehrman, R., 239, 240
Eiser, J. R., 99, 217
Elias, M. J., 160, 161
Elkashef, A., 229
Ellickson, P. L., 196, 198
Ellis, A., 87, 94
Emery, S., 195
Emmons, K., 217
Engels, R. C. M. E., 99
Engle, R. W., 170
Ennett, S. T., 103
Epstein, L. J., 90, 95
Erickson, E. H., 283
Erickson, P. G., 223
Ernst, M., 159
Estes, J., 114
Etheridge, R. M., 239, 258
Eubank, S., 113
Evans, J. S. B., 93
Evans, R. I., 62, 110, 146
Everingham, S. S., 201
Everitt, B. J., 78
Ewing, J. A., 127
Eysenck, S. B. G., 86

Fadardi, J. S., 174
Faes, S., 173
Falco, M., 15, 16, 219, 220

Fals-Stewart, W., 258
Farabee, D., 263, 267
Farrell, M., 227, 228
Farrow, J. A., 264
Faust, K., 102
Fazio, R. H., 93
Feder, S. H., 222
Felitti, V. J., 116
Felix-Ortiz, M., 127
Ferreira, D., 165
Festinger, L., 95
Field, M., 174, 245
Fillmore, M. T., 85
Filstead, W. J., 128
Finn, P. R., 85, 170
Fiori, M. C., 171, 230, 259, 264
First, M. B., 127
Fishbein, D. H., 82, 85, 160, 162, 166
Fishbein, M., 218
Fisher, D. G., 112
Fisher, L. A., 100
Fisher, P. A., 82
Fishkin, S. A., 175
Flay, B. R., 60, 62, 98, 99, 100, 147, 153, 186, 194–195
Fleischer, A., 86
Fletcher, B. W., 224, 263
Florentine, R., 268
Flynn, B. S., 195
Folkman, A., 201
Folkman, M. P., 201
Forssberg, H., 170
Foster, F. M., 131
Fowler, J. S., 81, 90
Fox, L., 28
Franken, I. H. A., 5, 93, 245
Franz, K. J., 62, 79
Fredholm, B. B., 41, 42, 43
Freedman, A. M., 31
Freet, D., 27
French, D. C., 165
Freud, S., 44
Friedman, A., 131
Fromme, K., 91, 128
Fry, A. F., 173
Fudala, P. J., 229
Fulker, D. W., 86
Funk, R. R., 258
Fuqua, J., 289
Furlong, M. J., 144

Galaif, E. R., 13, 16, 83, 117, 216, 252, 253
Galea, S., 262
Gallaher, P., 102, 103, 186, 187
Garbutt, J. C., 230
Gardner, W. L., 79
Gerard, H. B., 99
German, J. P., 85
Gerra, G., 159, 162
Gfroerer, J. C., 112

Ghosh-Dastidar, B., 196, 198
Giancola, P. R., 162
Gibbon, M., 127
Giedd, J. N., 160
Gilewski, M., 240
Gingras, M. A., 86
Ginzler, J. A., 9
Glantz, A., 120
Glantz, L. H., 158
Glantz, M. D., 131, 230
Glasgow, R. E., 266
Glautier, S., 240
Glynn, K., 64, 87, 176, 182
Godley, M. D., 219
Godley, S. H., 258
Gogtay, N., 159, 162
Goldberg, E., 252
Goldberger, B. A., 135
Goldberger, R., 288
Goldfried, M. R., 238
Goldman, M. S., 91, 92, 128, 246
Goldstein, R. Z., 81, 90
Gollwitzer, P. M., 173, 247
Goode, E., 53
Goodstadt, M. S., 146
Gordis, E., 286
Gordon, J. R., 83, 91, 141, 243, 269
Gordon, R., 139
Gorman, D. M., 113
Gorski, T. T., 87, 214, 232, 233, 234
Gottfredson, D. C., 153, 154
Gottman, J. M., 238
Goudriaan, A. E., 74
Grabowski, J., 229
Graf, P., 172
Graham, J. W., 42, 130, 186, 291
Granic, I., 105
Granovetter, M., 103
Grant, B. F., 116
Grant, I., 239
Gray, J. A., 79
Greenbaum, P. E., 91
Greenbaum, R. L., 252
Greenwald, A. G., 92
Grella, C. E., 53
Grenard, J. L., 93, 170, 254, 255
Griffin, K. W., 98, 288
Griffiths, M., 26
Grothaus, L. C., 217
Gruenfeld, D. H., 101
Gruenwald, P., 130
Grunbaum, J., 60
Guindon, E., 151
Gunning, W. B., 91
Gurley, R. J., 11

Hafstad, A., 195
Hahn, G., 64
Hahn, L., 131

Hall, J., 170
Hall, W., 235
Hallfors, D., 194
Halsted, W., 47
Hamilton, D. L., 89
Hamilton, J. E., 111, 181
Hanke, M., 53
Hanley, A., 26
Hansen, W. B., 42, 142, 146, 147, 148, 186, 199, 280, 285, 291
Harackiewicz, J. M., 217
Harper, R. A., 87, 94
Harrell, T. H., 130
Harrington, N. G., 78, 84, 161
Harris, T. R., 116
Hartman, K. A., 176
Harwood, H., 52
Haslam, N., 84
Hathaway, S. R., 134
Havermans, R., 88, 244
Hawkins, J. D., 58, 104, 110, 179
Hays, R., 60
Heaney, C. A., 291
Heath, D. B., 115
Heer, M. J., 221
Heider, F., 95
Henggeler, S. W., 191, 288
Henly, G. A., 130
Henry, B., 84
Herodotus, 45, 48
Hershow, R. C., 117
Hesselbrock, V. M., 162
Hikida, T., 235
Hill, S. Y., 117
Hindes, A., 81, 170
Hiripi, E., 24
Hirsch, E. D., 140, 141
Hirschi, T., 104
Hirschman, R., 64, 87, 176, 182
Ho, R., 218
Hodgkins, S., 173
Hoffman, B. R., 98, 99, 101
Hoffman, V., 53
Hoffmann, A., 46
Hoffmann, N. G., 221, 222
Hofmann, F. G., 35, 36
Holiday, K., 139, 141, 165
Hollinger, R. C., 264
Hollis, J. F., 266
Hollister, C. D., 221, 222
Honaker, L. M., 130
Hopkins, S., 47
Horn, J. L., 131, 240
Horowitz, L. M., 173
Hovarth, A. T., 242, 254
Howard, D. V., 173
Hser, Y.-I., 53
Hsieh, S., 221, 222
Hu, T. W., 187

Hubbard, R. L., 263, 287
Hudson, J. I., 24
Hughes, S. O., 128
Hughes, S. P., 105
Hunt, D., 25
Hunt, M. H., 144
Hurt, R. D., 218
Huse, E., 47
Hutchison, K. E., 75, 240
Huver, R. M. E., 6, 7, 11, 99, 101
Hyman, J. M., 113

Ialongo, N., 153
Ifill-Williams, M., 118, 288
Inn, A., 91, 116
Irvin, J. E., 244
Ishii, T., 74, 118

Jacoby, L. L., 89, 170
Jaeger, J. L., 131
Jainchill, N., 256
James, W., 92, 253
Jasechko, J., 170
Jatlow, P., 230
Jelicic, M., 88, 244
Jellinek, E. M., 20
Jenkins, A. J., 135
Jennings, L., 143, 144
Jerrard, D. A., 11
Jesechko, J., 89
Jessell, T. M., 80
Jessor, R., 25, 26, 59, 60, 85, 159
Jessor, S., 59, 60, 85
Joe, G. W., 263
Johansen, J., 131
Johanson, C. E., 84
John, U., 53
Johnson, C. A., 285
Johnson, N. P., 8
Johnson, V., 58, 59, 84, 87, 214, 268
Johnston, L. D., 37, 40, 44, 63, 117
Johnstone, B. M., 116
Jones, B., 91
Jonnes, J., 10, 44, 47, 48, 201
Jotte, R., 9
Julien, R. M., 3, 4, 6, 12, 31, 33, 35, 36, 37, 39, 40, 44, 46, 115, 226

Kadden, R. M., 240
Kadushin, C., 194
Kaelber, C., 117
Kahane, H., 94
Kahneman, D., 88, 90, 93, 244
Kaltreider, D. L., 202
Kaminer, Y., 230, 232, 252, 257, 288
Kandal, E. R., 80
Kandel, D. B., 99
Kane, H. H., 50
Kane, M. J., 170

Kaplan, D., 91, 128
Kaplan, H. I., 31
Karan, L., 218
Katkin, E. S., 79
Katz, E. C., 91
Katz, M., 11
Kaufman, N., 151
Kaye, D. L., 264
Keefe, F. J., 197
Kellam, S., 153, 280
Kelley, A. E., 79
Kelley, C. M., 89, 170
Kellogg, S. H., 228
Kelly, J. F., 252, 258
Kelly, T. H., 85
Kern, M. F., 234
Kessler, R. C., 24, 27, 28
Ketcham, K., 212
Kett, J. F., 140, 141
Khantzian, E. J., 64, 84
Kidorf, M., 117
Kilgore, K., 84
Kilpatrick, D. G., 117
Kimber, J., 228
King, V. L., 117
Kitabatake, Y., 235
Klassen, A. D., 116, 117
Kleber, H. D., 135
Klingberg, T., 170, 247
Klitzner, M., 130
Knight, J. R., 128, 264
Knowlton, B. J., 171, 173, 239, 245
Koch, G. G., 103
Kokotailo, P., 221
Komro, K. A., 199, 285, 287
Koob, G. F., 37, 62, 74, 76, 79, 81, 84
Kosaba, S. C., 84
Kosten, T. R., 84, 134, 135
Koutsky, J. R., 126
Krank, M. D., 89, 170
Kreek, M. J., 227, 228
Kreuger, R. F., 27
Kristiansen, P. L., 287
Krohn, M. D., 58, 101, 104
Kumpfer, K. L., 189, 190, 198, 199, 288
Kunst-Wilson, W. R., 119
Kushner, H., 131
Kushner, M. G., 83
Kyskan, C. E., 117

Labouvie, E. W., 130
Landsman, D., 74, 75
Lang, P. J., 79
Langenbucher, J., 15
Lanza-Kaduce, L., 101, 104
Lapsley, H. M., 52
Larimer, M. E., 243, 244
Laszlovszky, I., 86
Latimer, W. W., 221, 222

Latkin, C., 260
Lau, H. C., 246
Lau, R. R., 176
Laviola, G., 159, 162
Lawton, R., 173, 174, 247
Leary, T., 46
Leccese, M., 14, 15
LeDoux, J., 77, 78
Lehman, W. E. K., 264
Leiblum, S. R., 238
Leigh, B. C., 25, 91, 93
LeMoal, M. L., 74, 76, 81, 84
Lennard, H. L., 95
Lerman, C., 74, 75
Lesieur, H., 25
Lessov, C. N., 57, 74, 75, 86, 156
Leventhal, E. A., 218
Leventhal, H., 62, 64, 87, 176, 182, 218
Levin, E. D., 153, 159
Levinthal, C. F., 5, 37, 38, 43, 44, 45, 46, 47, 70, 209
Levitt, E., 134
Levy, J. C., 84
Levy, S., 264
Lewis, J. E., 254
Lex, B. W., 116
Lichtenberg, J. W., 144
Lichtman, K., 221
Liddle, H. A., 257, 288
Liepman, M. R., 249
Lightfoot, L. O., 268
Liljegren, S., 240
Lincoln, A., 49
Lindsey, S., 90
Littrell, J., 131, 269
Livert, D., 194
Lizotte, A. J., 58
Lochman, J. E., 90, 91, 280
Lohr, M., 105
London, E. D., 80
Longshore, D., 196, 228, 267
Loxley, W., 99
Luborsky, L., 131
Luckman, T., 88
Luczak, S. E., 118
Ludlow, F. H., 48
Luepker, R. V., 136
Lurigio, A. J., 110
Lynskey, M. T., 222
Lyon, M., 70

MacAndrew, C., 134
MacKinnon, D. P., 89, 181, 285, 292
Macri, S., 159
Madden, G. J., 85
Maisto, S. A., 239
Malin, H., 117
Mandel, J., 47
Manderlink, G., 217

Mansdorf, I. J., 269
Marcell, A. V., 285
Margolese, H. C., 27, 28
Mark, M. M., 202
Markou, A., 84
Markus, R., 134
Marlatt, G. A., 83, 91, 134, 141, 172, 187, 214, 216, 217, 223, 242, 243, 244, 255, 259
Marshall, E. J., 209
Marshall, M. J., 221
Marshall, S., 221
Martin, C. S., 14, 15
Martin, E. M., 170
Mason, B. J., 229, 230
Mason, M., 110, 114–115, 271
Masson, M. E. J., 172
Mathias, R., 258
Matsushita, S., 74, 118
Matthys, W., 90, 91, 280
Mattick, R. P., 228
Matza, D., 105
Maxwell, J. C., 267
Mayer, J., 128
McAdoo, W. G., 134
McCabe, S. E., 112
McCance-Katz, E. F., 230
McCann, U. D., 37
McCarthy, K., 209
McConnell, A. R., 89
McCoul, M. D., 84
McCourt, W. F., 134
McCuller, W. J., 221, 281
McDermeit, M., 258
McEvoy, C. L., 90
McEwen, B. S., 82
McGee, L., 166
McKay, J. R., 239
McKeon, P., 58
McKinley, J. C., 134
McLellan, A. T., 131, 134, 135, 239, 240
McNeal, R. B., 147
Meichenbaum, D., 87, 238, 241
Menchola, M., 254
Mercado, P., 144
Meshack, A. F., 186
Metzger, D., 131
Meyers, K., 131
Meyers, R. J., 249
Micco, A., 172, 173
Michels, P. J., 8
Miele, G. M., 130
Miller, C., 165
Miller, J. Y., 104, 110
Miller, L., 83, 243
Miller, M., 214, 232
Miller, T., 39, 60, 159
Miller, W. R., 53, 58, 95, 126, 134, 143, 144, 217, 249, 254, 260
Millman, R. B., 15, 16, 219, 220

Millstein, S. G., 285
Milne, S., 173
Mishra, S., 253
Mitchell, J. E., 24
Moberg, D. P., 131
Modlin, J., 117
Molgaard, V., 190
Montgomery, R. P., 128
Montgomery, S. B., 143
Monti, P. M., 240
Moore, T. E., 117
Morley-Fletcher, S., 159
Moss, M. A., 169, 176
Mott, M. A., 222
Mount, K., 266
Mouttapa, M., 102, 103, 186, 187
Moyers, T., 254
Mueller, L. A., 212, 214
Mueser, K. T., 28
Mulder, E. A., 251
Mundis, J., 26
Murgraff, V., 174
Myers, M. G., 222, 252

Nair, R., 151
Nakanishi, S., 235
Nelson, D. L., 90
Nestler, E., 74, 75
Newcomb, M. D., 13, 14, 16, 60, 83, 84, 85, 91, 117, 127, 166, 221, 222
Newman, T., 223
Nezami, E., 217, 218, 253
Niaura, R. S., 240
Nichter, M., 115
Nicot, J., 43
Niemann, A., 44
Niforopulos, L., 222
Nirenberg, T. D., 249
Nisbet, R. E., 93
Nishimura, S. T., 131
Noble, E. P. K., 70
Noonan, W. C., 254
Noordsy, D. L., 28
Nowakowski, R. S., 86

O'Brien, C. P., 131, 239, 240
Ockene, J. K., 218
O'Connor, K. P., 218
O'Farrell, T. J., 239, 258, 269
O'Leary, T. A., 16, 220, 257
Olesen, P. J., 170, 247
Olshaker, J., 9
O'Malley, P. M., 37, 40, 44, 63, 117
Omidvari, K., 120
Orbell, S., 173, 247
Order-Connors, B., 218
Orpinas, P. K., 60
Osgood, N. D., 186

Oosterlaan, J., 74
Ostrom, T. M., 175
Owen, P. L., 134

Palmer, R. S., 243, 244
Palmgreen, P., 161, 195, 270, 290
Pandina, R. J., 58, 59
Paracelsus, 44
Parcel, G. S., 60
Parrott, A. C., 8
Pastan, I., 235
Patel, R., 139, 141, 165
Patten, C., 218
Patterson, F., 74, 75
Patterson, G. R., 165
Patterson, T. L., 239
Payne, B. K., 170
Pealer, L., 197
Pears, K. C., 82
Peciña, S., 79
Peele, S. B., 26, 216, 224
Peeler, D. F., 86
Pellens, M., ix, 47
Pentz, M. A., 39, 143, 159, 161, 163, 193, 199, 201,
    202, 217, 223, 231, 254, 255, 285, 290, 292
Pequignet, G., 117
Perry, C. L., 199, 200
Perry, J. L., 85
Petchers, M. K., 131
Peters, A. A. R., 105
Peterson, R. C., 44
Petraitis, J., 60
Pettinati, H. M., 131
Phillips, K., 174
Phillips, P. E., 78, 79
Pianezza, M. L., 74
Piazza, P. V., 84
Pickering, H., 36
Pickrel, S. G., 191, 288
Pierce, J. P., 62, 110
Pilgrim, C., 99, 103
Plomin, R., 157
Poduska, J., 153
Pokhrel, P., 65, 99, 106
Polansky, J. R., 120
Pope, H. G., 24
Poston, W. C., 144
Poulin, F., 103, 105
Prendergast, M., 263, 264, 267
Prestwich, A., 173, 174, 247
Prochaska, J. O., 217
Prytulak, L. S., 173

Quinn, T. C., 117
Quintero, G., 115

Rachal, J. V., 15
Radosevich, M., 101, 104
Rahdert, E., 130, 131, 230

Ransom, D. C., 95
Rather, B. C., 92
Ravav, G., 84
Rawson, R. A., 228
Reber, A. S., 93
Rehman, Z., 44
Reich, R. R., 91, 92
Reid, J. B., 191
Reif, W. J., 7
Repertinger, S., 27
Rhoades, H., 229
Richards, J. B., 85
Richardson, J. L., 98
Riemann, R., 86
Rifkin, J., 236
Riggs, S. G., 128
Ritt-Olson, A., 176
Rivara, F. P., 254
Rivers, S. M., 252, 258
Rivet, K., 91
Robbins, A. S., 26
Robbins, T. W., 78
Roberts, B. W., 187
Robins, L. N., 52
Robinson, T. E., 77, 78, 80, 81
Roche, P. A., 158
Rodgers, A., 197
Roehling, P. V., 91
Roehrich, L., 92
Rogers, C., 254
Rogers, E. M., 103, 291
Rogers, R., 131
Rogers, R. W., 217
Rogosch, F. A., 82, 85
Rohrbach, L. A., 10, 139, 141, 143, 165, 186, 222,
    291
Rohsenow, D. J., 240
Rollnick, S., 95, 143, 254
Rolls, E. T., 80
Room, R., 209
Rosen, W., 207
Rosenfield, P. L., 289
Roth, J. L., 187
Rothstein, A., 48
Rounds-Bryant, J. L., 287
Rounsville, B. J., 134, 135
Rousculp, S., 42
Rouse, B. A., 112
Roy, A., 25
Rubonis, A. W., 240
Ruff, A., 117
Rumble, M. E., 197
Rush, B., 209
Rutter, M., 157
Rychtarik, R. G., 126, 131, 134, 239
Rydell, C. P., 201

Saah, T., 44, 45, 46
Sadock, B. J., 31

Salloum, I., 217
Sargent, J. D., 120
Saxe, L., 112
Schackman, B. R., 15, 16, 219, 220
Schacter, D. L., 172, 173
Schaef, A. W., 23
Schafer, J. C., 25
Scheier, L. M., 118, 119
Schlosser, S., 27
Schmitz, J., 229
Schneider, J. P., 25
Schneider, L., 134
Schneider, R., 258
Schooler, T., 90
Schottenfeld, R. S., 126, 228
Schreiber, T. A., 90
Schuckit, M. A., 74, 118
Schulenberg, J. E., 37, 40, 44, 63
Schultes, R. E., 46
Schultz, W., 78, 79, 80
Schutz, A., 88
Schwartz, J. H., 80
Schwartz, R., 130
Schwegler, H., 86
Scott, J., 102
Scott, R. L., 234
Sellers, E. M., 74
Selzer, M. L., 134
Sergeant, J. A., 91
Setlow, B., 78
Sewell, K. W., 131
Seymour, R., 226
Shakespeare, W., 49
Shedler, J., 280
Sheeran, P., 173
Shegog, R., 197
Sher, K. J., 83, 85, 99, 268
Sherman, S. J., 89
Shesser, R., 9
Shields, I. W., 74, 75, 105
Shihadeh, A., 115
Shopland, D. R., 143
Simon, H., 84
Simon, T. R., 85
Simpson, D. D., 263
Singer, M. I., 131
Single, E., 223
Sinha, R., 27
Sirota, A. D., 240
Skara, S., 10, 147, 150, 160, 180, 188, 288
Skogan, W. G., 110
Skovholt, T., 143
Slade, J., 218
Slater, M. D., 195, 196, 290
Slesnick, N., 257
Smart, R. G., 7
Smith, C., 58
Smith, D., 226
Smith, G. M., 96

Smith, G. T., 91
Smith, P., 288
Smith, R., 211, 249
Smulders, F. T. Y., 94
Snarr, J., 79
Snyder, L. B., 196
Sobell, L. S., 20
Sobell, M. B., 20
Sobol, D. F., 143
Somers, J. M., 223
Sommers, P. V., 218
Specker, S., 24
Spence, J. T., 26
Spiegel, E., 251
Spinath, 86
Spitzer, R. L., 127
Spoth, R., 190
Spruijt-Metz, D., 39, 159, 231
Spunt, B., 25
St. Pierre, T. L., 202
Stacy, A. W., 7, 60, 63, 84, 85, 88, 89, 90, 91, 93, 94, 96, 97, 119, 141, 154, 169, 171, 172, 173, 178, 219, 244, 245
Stacy, S., 141
Stanovich, K. E., 93
Star, J., 114
Steele, J. B., 7, 9
Stein, L. A. R., 266
Stephenson, R. L., 49
Stevens, V. J., 266
Stewart, J., 217
Stewart, S. H., 161, 162
Stigler, M., 200
Stimson, G. V., 36
Stinchfield, R. D., 131, 222
Stoolmiller, M., 162
Stotts, A., 229
Stout, R., 258
Strassberg, Z., 79
Strogatz, S. H., 114
Stroot, E., 91, 128
Studts, J. L., 197
Sun, P., 198, 221, 222, 230
Sun, W., 189
Sussman, A. N., 279
Sussman, S., vii, viii, ix, 4, 6, 7, 9, 10, 11, 13, 16, 23, 25, 30, 33, 39, 43, 45, 50, 53, 58, 59, 60, 62, 63, 64, 65, 71, 74, 83, 85, 87, 88, 89, 90, 93, 94, 96, 97, 98, 99, 100, 101, 106, 111, 116, 117, 118, 119, 124, 135, 139, 140, 141, 142, 143, 146, 147, 153, 154, 159, 162, 163, 164, 165, 166, 169, 171, 175, 176, 179, 180, 181, 182, 185, 186, 187, 189, 190, 198, 200, 201, 209, 215, 216, 217, 218, 221, 222, 223, 224, 225, 230, 231, 240, 252, 253, 254, 255, 260, 262, 268, 270, 279, 280, 281, 283, 285, 287, 288, 290, 291, 292
Sutton, S. R., 217
Suzuki, K., 74, 118
Svanum, S., 134

Swanson, J. W., 84
Swift, R., 89, 170
Swisher, J. D., 187, 198
Sydenham, T., 44
Sykes, G., 105
Szalay, L. B., 116, 118
Szapocznik, J., 109

Tabachnik, N., 89
Talbott, G. D., 259
Tapert, S. F., 223
Tarter, R., 14, 15, 74, 135, 153, 162
Taylor, A., 151
Teets, J. M., 116
Teicher, M. H., 82
Teichman, M., 84
Tengs, T. O., 186
Terranova, L., 159, 162
Terry, C. E., ix, 47
Teter, C. J., 112
Thaxton, L., 26
Theus, K. T., 119
Thomas, S. E., 288
Thomasson, H. R., 74, 118
Thompson, E. L., 146
Thornberry, T. P., 58
Thwing, E. P., 49
Tiffany, F. T., 240
Timmreck, T. C., 19
Tims, F. M., 220, 224, 263
Tobler, N. S., 139, 146, 180, 189, 198, 287
Tolman, E. C., 91
Tomlinson, K. L., 16, 222
Tonigan, J. S., 249, 260
Toomey, T. L., 199
Toscova, R., 260
Traver, R. E., 222
Trefil, J., 140, 141
Trimpey, J., 241, 252
Turksen, I. B., 12
Tuyns, A. J., 117
Tverdol, A., 44
Twerski, A. J., 87
Tyndale, R. F., 74

Uhlenhuth, E. H., 84
Unger, J. B., ix, 63, 64, 71, 74, 88, 90, 94, 98, 99,
    111, 119, 181, 225, 285
Upshaw, H. S., 175
Urberg, K. A., 99, 103
Utada, A., 131

Vadasz, C., 86
Vaillant, G. E., 20, 224
Valente, T. W., 98, 102, 103, 142, 186, 187
van Abeelen, J. H. F., 86
Van de Luitgaarden, J., 246
Van den Brink, W., 74
Van den Wildenberg, E., 246

van Ryn, M., 291
van Thiel, D. H., 15
van Woerden, N., 94
Vaughan, B. L., 264
Vaughn, W., 43
Venner, T., 43
Vernadakis, A., 71
Verplanken, B., 173
Vik, P. W., 222, 239
Vilov, S. K., 118
Vlahov, D., 262
Vocci, F. J., 227, 228, 229
Vogeltanz, N. D., 116
Volkow, N. D., 37, 70, 80, 81, 90
von Baeyer, A., 46

Wagenaar, A., 199
Wagner, E. H., 217
Waldron, H. B., 14, 15, 191
Walker, L., 110, 114, 271
Wall, T. L., 74
Wallack, L., 195
Walsh, G. W., 7
Walters, S. T., 197
Walton, R. P., 45, 50
Wanberg, K. H., 131
Wang, G., 81, 90
Wang, L. Y., 186
Wang, M. C., 244
Ware, J. E., 176
Warner, J., 49
Warner, L. A., 112
Wasserman, S., 102
Wechsler, H., 201
Weddle, M., 221
Weil, A., 207
Weiler, R., 197
Weinberg, N. Z., 131, 222, 230, 257
Weiner, M. D., 221
Weiner, R. H., 134
Weingardt, K. R., 92, 93
Weinstein, N., 89
Weiss, F., 5
Weissman, M. M., 134, 135
Weitzman, E. R., 201
Wells, V., 84
Welsh, C., 228
Welte, J. W., 99
Werthamer, L., 153
West, R. F., 93
West, S. G., 95
Westerberg, H., 170, 247
White, D., 174
White, H. R., 130
White, T., 30, 112, 151
White, W. L., 209, 210, 211, 219
Whitehall, G. C., 105
Whiteside, H. O., 189
Wicklund, R. A., 95

Widaman, K. F., 91, 172
Wiers, R. W., 88, 89, 91, 93, 94, 171, 244, 245, 246
Wilhelm, M. S., 26
Williams, A. F., 134
Williams, C. L., 199, 200, 285, 286
Williams, S. H., 229
Wills, T. A., 62, 100, 110, 119, 154, 162, 181
Wilsnack, R. W., 116, 117
Wilsnack, S. C., 116, 117
Wilson, B., 211, 249
Wilson, D. B., 153
Wilson, T., 90, 93
Winger, G., 35, 36
Winters, K. C., 14, 15, 130, 221, 222
Wise, R. A., 77, 78, 93
Woodhouse, L. D., 116
Woods, J. H., 35, 36

Woody, G. E., 131
Worden, J. K., 195
Wright, J. A., 197
Wyer, R. S., 101

Yach, D., 151
Yagelka, J., 256
Yin, H. H., 239
Yoder, B., 250
Young, P. T., 217

Zajonc, R. B., 119, 172
Zarkin, G. A., 265
Zickler, P., 19
Zogg, J. B., 84, 119
Zuckerman, M., 84, 86
Zweben, J. E., 214, 216, 233
Zywiak, W., 239, 258

Subject Index

abstinence, 19, 124, 126, 215, 216, 227, 229, 232, 233, 236, 241–243, 249, 258, 260, 268, 288
accidents, 6, 9, 15, 16, 40, 52, 53, 117
adaptive mechanisms, 19, 22
Addiction Severity Index (ASI), 134
Addictive Voice Recognition Technique (AVRT), 241
adenosine, 35, 41, 72, 75
Adolescent Alcohol Involvement Scale (AAIS), 128
Adolescent Diagnostic Interview, 130
Adolescent Drug Abuse Diagnosis (ADAD), 131
adrenocorticotropic hormone (ACTH), 82
aftercare, 268
agonist drugs, 30
alcohol, 4, 5, 8–12, 14, 15, 23–25, 27, 28, 30, 31–33, 35, 40, 44–50, 52, 53, 60, 74–76, 82, 84, 99, 101, 109, 111, 114–119, 121, 126–134, 141, 145, 146, 148, 150, 151, 153, 161–163, 165, 170, 174, 181–183, 188, 190, 191, 194, 196, 199, 201, 203, 209, 210, 215, 216, 220–222, 226, 229, 230, 233, 234, 237, 239, 241, 244–247, 249–251, 254, 256–258, 260, 263, 265–269, 271, 272, 278, 279, 282, 285–288, 291–293,
Alcohol Abstinence Self-Efficacy Scale (AASE), 128
Alcohol Attention-Control Training Programme, 174
Alcohol Use Inventory, 131
Alcoholics Anonymous, 26, 134, 141, 187, 209, 211, 214, 218, 219, 238, 241, 243, 246, 249–251, 253
alcoholism, 10, 19, 20, 25, 31, 49, 50, 75, 118, 129, 134, 162, 209, 211, 214, 230, 250, 252, 253, 286
alkaloids, 9, 39
All Stars program, 196
Allostasis, 81
American Association for Retired Persons (AARP), 283
American Association for the Cure of Inebriates, 20
American Medical Association, 20, 211
American Psychiatric Association, 13, 15, 20, 28, 30–32
amphetamines, 4, 9, 30, 33, 36–39, 135
amygdala, 62, 76, 79, 80, 82, 160
anandamide release, 35
anterior cingulate cortex, 39, 80, 82
anti-convulsants, 33
anti-drug laws, 48
antihistamine, doxylamine succinate, 35

Anti-Saloon League, 49
Arrestee Drug Abuse Monitoring Program (ADAM), 266
assessment, 123–128, 130, 131, 135, 136, 153, 157, 214, 220, 243, 248, 266, 290, 291
Attention Deficit Disorder, 159
attentional retraining, 174
attentional-retraining approach, 245

barbiturates, 31–32, 35, 46, 135, 282
basal amygdala, 80
basal ganglia, 40
behavior modification interventions, 238
behavioral system, 60
Benzedrine, 36
benzodiazepines, 4
benzodiazepines, 5, 33, 46, 226, 234
betel nut, 39, 45
biopsychosocial models, 59, 65
blood alcohol content (BAC), 35
blood alcohol level, 31, 199
brain disease concept, 22
brain reward systems, 77

caffeine, 9, 19, 23, 27, 30–33, 36, 41–43, 214, 216, 239
CAGE questionnaire, 127
cannabis, 8–11, 19, 31–33, 40, 45, 46, 112
Center for Substance Abuse Prevention (CSAP), 198
central nervous system, 33, 35, 36, 39, 41, 82, 117
cerebellar vermis, 82
cerebellum, 36, 40
cessation, 15, 19, 37, 42, 43, 75, 76, 123, 140–145, 148, 151, 153, 154, 161, 171, 184, 188, 196, 197, 207, 209, 217, 218, 221, 227, 229, 230, 232, 233, 238, 242, 244–246, 248, 259, 260, 262, 264, 266, 268, 270–273, 277–290, 292
cessation approaches, 140, 244
Chemical Dependency Assessment Profile (CDAP), 130
cigarette smoking, 22, 43, 44, 52, 62, 103, 117, 120, 121, 124, 141, 144, 151, 176, 185, 195, 259, 266, 278
club drugs, 6, 11
Coast Guard scheme, 31

cocaine, 5, 8, 12, 13, 19, 20, 23, 25, 28, 30–33, 36, 37, 44, 47, 48, 53, 75, 79, 85, 110, 112, 117, 118, 127, 130, 135, 201, 223, 228–230, 240, 250
codeine, 39, 135
cognitive behavioral approaches, 26, 191, 219, 221, 229, 230, 236, 239, 252
cognitive processes, 57, 59, 66, 101, 107, 168, 171, 172, 177, 178, 238, 240, 244, 246, 247
cognitive restructuring, 238, 243
cognitive-affective theories, 61, 66
coma, 18, 35, 41
commitment and social attachment theories, 61
Comprehensive Addiction Severity Index for Adolescents (CASI-A), 131
Comprehensive Alcoholism Prevention and Treatment Act, 212
Comprehensive Drinker Profile, 134
Comprehensive Effects of Alcohol (CEOA), 128
comprehensive theories, 61
compulsive behaviors, 23, 29, 126
compulsive gambling, 21
Controlled Substances Act, 6, 11
cost of drug abuse, 50
crack. *See* cocaine
CRAFFT Test, 128
criminal activity, 25, 110, 121, 288
criminal justice system, 267, 268, 288
cue exposure and cue reactivity, 240

"date-rape" drug. *See* Rohypnol
DEA. *See* United States Drug Enforcement Administration
Debtors Anonymous, 26
dehydrogenase metabolizing enzymes, 74, 230
delirium, 18, 31, 35, 41, 133
depressants, 33
depression, 16, 19, 20, 40, 41, 47, 48, 60, 76, 83, 134, 166, 217, 226, 232–234, 254, 257, 258
designer drugs, 6, 11, 40
detoxification, 136, 209, 211, 212, 223, 226, 227, 229, 230, 267, 269, 272
deviant subcultures, 98, 104, 105, 107
dextromethorphan, 35
diluents, 9
disease model, 19, 20, 214–216, 249, 250, 253
disease of addiction, 20
dissociative analgesic, 35
dissociative anesthetic, 35
distal and proximal structures, 60
diuretics, 41
DMT, 39
dopamine receptor hypothesis, 70
dopamine release, 27, 35, 37, 79, 82
dopaminergic activity, 4
dopaminergic system, 4, 36, 40, 46
dopers, 35
Doriden, 35

dose-dependent hepatocellular injury, 229
drug abuse, 13, 17, 25, 28, 29, 68, 168, 236, 262, 282–284
drug abuse related illness, 52
drug additives, 9
Drug and Alcohol Problem (DAP) Quickscreen, 130
drug classification systems, 30
drug distribution routes, 57, 110
drug paraphernalia, 6, 104, 146
drug use in ancient times, 44
Drug Use Screening Inventory (DUSI), 135
drugs of misuse, 6, 18, 124
DSM-IV, 13, 14, 17–19, 25–28, 30, 32, 41, 42, 53, 127, 130, 132
dual diagnosis, 15, 20, 27, 212
DXM, 35

eating disorders, 24
ecstasy, 6, 8, 11, 36
18th Amendment of the U.S. Constitution, 49
employee assistance programs (EAPs), 212, 264, 272
endogenous ligand, 5
endogenous opioid release, 35
environmental factors, 62, 71, 75, 86, 158, 278, 286
enzyme function, 75
ephedrine, 9, 37, 38
ethnic identity, 118
ethnicity, 57, 110, 115, 117–118, 219, 220
euphoria, 25, 33, 36, 39, 40, 44, 227
European Smoking Prevention Framework Approach (EFSA), 150
evaluation, 16, 80, 98, 128–130, 144, 148, 150, 162, 165, 192, 194, 217, 220, 222, 224, 228, 258, 288, 291
evidence-based prevention programs, 139
executive functions, 80, 170, 171, 245, 246
explicit cognition, 88, 90, 93, 94, 169, 172, 173, 178, 238, 244–247

family, 14, 16, 20, 25, 58, 60–62, 66, 67, 86, 98, 99, 101, 104, 106–109, 111, 123, 125, 127–135, 143, 145, 154, 162–164, 179, 184, 188–193, 195, 198, 199, 202, 207, 211, 212, 219–222, 233, 248, 249, 253, 256–260, 263, 267–269, 272, 281, 282, 287, 288
family therapy, 256, 257
Federal Bureau of Narcotics, 48
Federal Bureau of Prisons, 266
fentanyl, 39
fetal alcohol exposure, 82
fetal health risks, 117
flushing response, 118
Food and Drug Administration (FDA), 38
frontal cortex, 40, 80, 81

GABA neurons, 39
Gamblers Anonymous, 25
gender differences, 116
genetic factors, 74, 75, 158
genetic markers, 157, 236

genetics, 57, 58, 69, 75, 156, 158, 236
Geographic Information Systems (GIS), 114, 270
GHB, 11, 12, 33, 40, 72, 226, 232
glucocorticoids, 82
glue sniffing. *See* inhalants,
glutamate receptors, 35
group identification, 98, 106
group therapy, 248, 257–260

hallucinations, 6, 18–20, 32, 33, 35, 37
hallucinogenic drugs, 6
hallucinogens, 9, 30–33, 38–41, 53, 115, 118, 126, 135
hard or soft drugs, 3, 6, 10, 11
harm reduction, 26, 115, 160, 215, 223, 226, 227, 260, 264
Hazelden, 211
hepatitis C, 223
heredity, 22
heroin, 3, 5, 9, 10, 12, 13, 23, 25, 27, 30, 32, 37, 39, 44, 47, 53, 75, 112, 113, 117, 119, 127, 130, 135, 136, 223, 227–229, 235, 260, 265
hippocampus, 40, 80, 82
history of drug use, 30, 124, 127
HIV, 117, 223, 227
homeostasis, 82, 218
homeostatic function, 22
hospitalization, 15, 52, 239, 257
hydrocodone, 39
hydromorphine, 39
hypnotics, 31–33, 35, 46, 226, 232
hypothalamus, 76, 80, 82

illegal drugs, 9, 10, 50, 52, 151
illicit drugs, 6, 7, 10
impaired motor function, 41
implementation intention effects, 174
implicit cognition, 88–90, 92–94, 169–172, 178, 238, 240, 244–247
impulsivity, 76, 84–86, 162, 221
impure drugs, 9
incarceration, 50, 191, 212, 262, 267, 271
incentive-sensitization theory, 81
inhalants, 8, 13, 30, 32, 33, 36, 46, 125, 223, 280
Inventory of Drinking Situations (IDS), 130
interaction effects, 4
International Statistical Classification of Diseases and Related Health Problems, 18
Internet, 122, 197, 270
intrapersonal theories, 61
isolates, 103

Johnson Institute, 248, 249
Johnson Institute's Motivational Intervention, 248
Just Say No Campaign, 146

ketamine, 11, 12, 33, 35, 36, 41
khat, 39, 45

LAAM, 226, 228, 232

lateral amygdala, 80
laudanum, 44, 209
law enforcement, 28, 37, 52, 194, 201, 251
left neocortex, 82
Librium, 35, 226, 232
locus ceruleus, 41
lost earnings, 52
LSD, 11, 12, 33, 39, 41, 44, 46, 72, 135, 169

MAC/MAC-R – MacAndrew Alcoholism Scale/Revised, 134
magnetic resonance imaging (MRI), 22
maladaptive behaviors, 22, 29
marijuana, 3–5, 11–13, 19, 28, 30, 33, 40, 41, 45, 48, 50, 53, 65, 99, 101, 115–119, 130, 135, 136, 146, 148, 150, 165, 169, 177, 182, 191, 195, 196, 201, 220–223, 227, 232, 249, 250, 257, 258, 260, 263, 270, 278, 288, 289, 293
Marlatt's Cognitive-Behavioral Relapse Prevention Therapy, 243
MDMA, 8, 36, 72
mead, 45
media, 48, 84, 109, 110, 119–122, 142, 146, 147, 151, 161, 172, 183, 184, 188–190, 193–196, 198, 199, 201, 202, 270, 271, 273, 280, 286, 287
media campaigns, 195, 196, 270
mental disorders, 27–29, 46
meperdine, 32, 39
mescaline, 38–41
mesocortical pathways, 81
mesolimbic dopamine reward pathway, 86
mesolimbic dopamine system, 78
mesolimbic reward pathways, 4
metabolic processes, 4, 23, 74, 76, 118, 286
metabolic tolerance, 5
metabolism, 4, 5, 26, 59, 66
methadone, 227, 232
methamphetamine, 3, 5, 7–12, 14, 37–38, 75, 271
methaqualone, 35, 135
Michigan Alcohol Screening Test (MAST), 134
Midwest Prevention Project (MPP), 201
mood swings, 40, 263
morphine, 39, 48, 135, 210, 228
motivational intervention, 248
motivational interviewing, 142, 217, 248, 252, 254, 255
motivation/skills/decision-making model (MSD), 164
motor cortex, 80
mu-opioid receptors, 39

Narcotics Addicts Rehabilitation Act (NARA), 212
National Guard, 32
National Institute on Alcohol Abuse and Alcoholism (NIAAA), 52, 212, 285, 287
National Institute on Drug Abuse, 7, 130, 132, 212, 258, 271
Nembutal, 35
neural pathways, 71, 218
neuroadaptive changes, 22, 24, 69, 81

neurobiological processes, 5, 83, 86, 163
neurobiological systems, 59, 66, 84, 155, 286
neurochemistry, 23, 70, 76, 86
neurological processes, 75
neuro-modulators, 41
neurons, 38, 39, 70, 75, 76, 78–80, 229
neurorehabilitation, 156
neurosurgical procedures, 235
neurotransmission phenotypes, 158
neurotransmission systems, 4, 25, 79
neurotransmitter, 3–6, 22, 25, 39, 40, 70, 76, 79, 80, 84, 86, 157, 225, 229, 290
neurotransmitter pathways, 4
new associations, 172, 173, 245
NIAAA, *See* National Institute on Alcohol Abuse and Alcoholism
nicotine, 4, 8, 10–13, 23, 27, 28, 30, 32, 33, 36, 45, 74, 75, 136, 157, 182, 218, 223, 230, 239, 249, 260, 285
nicotine withdrawal, 19
nitrous oxide, 36, 46
norepinephrine, 4, 25, 38, 39, 41, 72, 76, 79, 159, 230, 234
nucleus accumbens, 4, 37, 39, 41, 71, 78–80, 235

Office of National Drug Control Policy, 50, 271
opiates, 6, 12, 33, 48, 112, 135, 201, 228, 229
opioid neuropeptides, 79
opioid receptors, 4, 39, 228, 229
opioid replacement therapies, 227
opioids, 6, 30, 32, 33, 39, 79
opium, 9, 31–33, 39, 44, 46–48, 53, 112, 113, 145, 209, 271, 278
Opium Wars, 47
orbital cortex, 80
orbitofrontal cortex, 76, 79–81
overdose, 4, 5, 182
overeating, 21, 23, 24, 27, 283
oxycodone, 39

PACE stage model, 63
PALS Skills Training Program, 165
paranoia, 18, 35, 36, 39, 40
party drugs. *See* club drugs
PCP, 19, 20, 32, 33, 35, 39, 41, 72, 135
peer group types, 105, 106
pentazocine, 39
Personal Experience Inventory, 131
personality disorders, 23, 27, 32
personality system, 60
peyote, 33, 39, 46, 115
pharmacotherapies, 230
pharmacotherapy with teens, 230
phenylalkylamines, 39
physical abuse, 116, 125, 131, 133
physical dependence, 5, 10, 15
physical surroundings, 110
physical-environmental antecedents, 110
Placydil, 35
Positive Realism, 26

pragmatic variables, 64
predictors, 57, 59, 62, 67, 68, 99, 103, 107, 119, 240
predictors of drug use, 57, 99, 107, 240
prefrontal cortex, 39, 42, 78, 80
preludin, 36
premature death, 50, 52, 140, 262
President's Advisory Commission on Narcotic and Drug Abuse, 146
prevention, 3, 29, 52, 110, 123, 139–148, 150, 151, 153–165, 167–174, 176–181, 183–185, 188–190, 192–199, 201, 202, 212, 214, 216, 219, 220, 223–226, 229, 236, 238, 239, 241–244, 246–248, 267, 269, 271, 277–281, 283–292
prevention programming, 139–141, 144, 153, 170, 178, 192, 193, 287, 292
Problem Behavior Theory (PBT), 59
Problem Oriented Screening Instrument for Teenagers (POSIT), 130
process addictions, 18, 23, 26, 27, 29, 242, 283
Prohibition, 50
Project Towards No Drug Abuse, 141, 164, 177
Propylhexedrine, 38
protective factors, 58, 59, 66, 121, 222, 279
proximal goal setting, 217
pseudoephedrine, 37
psilocybin, 39, 46
psychological dependence, 5, 84, 140
psychological factors, 59
psychotic disorders, 28
psychotropic drugs, 6

Quaaludes, 35

RAFFT Test, 128
Rational Emotive Therapy (RET), 241
Rational Recovery, 26, 211, 241, 242, 246
receptors, 4, 5, 30, 37–41, 70, 75, 76, 79, 82, 156, 227, 229
Reconnecting Youth program, 164
recreational drugs, 7
relapse, 16, 25, 28, 75, 76, 83, 127, 130, 132, 140, 141, 207, 208, 211, 214, 216–220, 222–224, 226, 227, 229, 230, 232–234, 236, 238–240, 242–244, 246–248, 255, 258–261, 267, 269, 271, 282
residential facilities, 269
reward deficiency syndrome, 70, 76
risk and protective factors, 57, 65, 271, 273, 279
risk factors, 28, 58, 59, 62, 75, 107, 131, 133, 162, 167, 171, 174, 185, 190
Ritalin, 33, 36
Rohypnol, 11, 12, 35
Rutgers Alcohol Problem Index (RAPI), 130

S.O.S., 242
school programs, 153, 189, 196
Seconal, 35
secondary substance disorder, 28
sedatives, 5, 31–33, 41
seizures, 11, 19, 20, 31, 38, 41, 226

self-control, 20, 76, 83, 156, 160, 162, 163, 171, 187, 242, 243, 246, 247, 255, 267, 281, 282, 284
self-medicating, 24, 84
sensation seeking, 70, 84, 85, 155–157, 161, 163, 195
serotonin, 33, 35, 38, 39, 41, 70–72, 75, 76, 79, 159, 226, 233
serotonin release, 35
Sex Addicts Anonymous, 25
Sex and Love Addicts Anonymous, 25
Sexaholics Anonymous, 25
Sexual Compulsives Anonymous, 25
sexual disorders, 25
Sexual Recovery Anonymous, 26
SMART Recovery, 242
sober living homes, 256
social and emotional learning, 160
social cognition, 102, 108
social cognitive/learning theory, 100
social competency skills, 162
social costs of drug use, 52
social environmental influences, 109, 121, 193
social groupings, 57, 59
social influence, 58, 62, 67, 98–101, 140, 142, 143, 146, 147, 150, 151, 154, 159, 184, 185, 188, 189, 196, 281, 284, 292
social isolation, 16, 47
social learning, 25, 60, 61, 66, 98, 118, 122, 147, 191, 201
social learning theories, 61, 66
social network analysis, 102, 103, 260
social network theory, 102
social networks, 28, 98, 101, 104–107, 142, 208, 248, 271, 283
social pressure, 101, 216
social support, 60, 98, 100, 101, 107, 108, 116, 121, 124, 142, 172, 179, 184, 189, 208, 216, 222, 233, 239, 245, 249, 252, 253, 260, 268, 283
socialization, 61, 104, 107, 108, 281
socioeconomic status, 53, 110, 111, 120, 121, 288
soft drugs, 10, 12
spirituality, 209, 241, 242, 253
stage modeling, 67, 68
steroids, 33, 40
stimulants, 6, 30, 32, 33, 36, 37, 41, 227
street drugs, 3, 7–9, 11, 12, 16
stressors, 62, 130, 132, 169, 260, 262
Structured Clinical Interview for the Diagnostic Statistical Manual IV (SCID), 127
strychnine, 39
substance abuse, 13–16, 20, 22, 23, 27, 28, 31, 32, 53, 57, 58, 60, 66, 74, 83, 117, 123, 126, 127, 131–133, 162, 191, 194, 207, 209, 211, 212, 214, 219–226, 236, 238, 239, 242, 244, 257, 260, 262, 266, 267, 269, 271–273, 279, 288
Substance Abuse and Mental Health Services Administration, 27, 271
substance abuse disorder, 13, 15, 17
Substance Abuse Subtle Screening Inventory (SASSI-A), 131
substance addictions, 23, 24

Substance Dependence Severity Scale (SDSS), 130
substance use disorders, 15, 27, 28, 85, 130, 222, 234
supply reduction, 52, 143, 199, 200, 203
supply reduction approaches, 52, 143
Surgeon General, 43, 52
synthetic narcotic, 35

thebaine, 39
theories of behavior change, 217
tobacco, 10, 31, 43, 44, 151, 152, 180, 183, 188, 200, 281
tolerance, 5, 10, 14, 17, 18, 23, 25, 31, 32, 43, 47, 62, 76, 86, 104, 163, 176, 208, 223, 236, 256, 282
toluene, 36
total abstinence, 215, 216
Towards No Drug Abuse (TND) programs, 165
Tranxene, 35
trauma, 40, 76, 82, 257
treatment, 16, 18, 20, 21, 25–29, 37, 40, 45, 48, 49, 52, 53, 98, 103, 110, 112, 116, 123, 126, 130–136, 140, 142, 152, 155, 157, 158, 167, 170, 174, 190, 191, 196, 200, 203, 207, 209–212, 214–216, 218–230, 233–236, 238–240, 242–249, 252–254, 256–260, 262–273, 281, 284–288, 290, 291, 293
Treatment Episode Data Set (TEDS), 27
Triadic Influence Theory, 60, 65, 66, 68
twelve-step programs, 126, 216, 240, 242, 246, 249, 250–253, 258, 260, 261, 267, 272

U.S. Drug Enforcement Administration. See United States Drug Enforcement Administration
U.S. Supreme Court, 48
United States Drug Enforcement Administration, 6, 32, 41
unitization, 172–174

vagus nerve stimulation (VNS), 235
Valium, 4, 35
ventral pallidum, 80
ventral tegmental area, 62, 78–80
Veterans Administration, 211
violence, 7, 16, 33, 53, 116, 144, 162, 167, 172, 187, 191, 256, 262, 279

withdrawal, 4, 5, 13, 15, 17–20, 25, 31, 32, 41, 43, 47, 53, 84, 123, 127–129, 133, 140, 157, 184, 188, 207, 212, 214, 217, 226–228, 230, 232, 233, 265, 266
withdrawal symptoms, 4, 5, 9, 13, 15, 18–21, 25, 27, 31, 32, 41–43, 47, 52, 53, 117, 123, 127, 130–133, 139, 140, 157, 184, 188, 207, 212, 214, 217, 226–228, 230, 232, 233, 253, 258, 264–266, 269, 272
withdrawal gating hypothesis, 15
Woman's Christian Temperance Union (WCTU), 49, 144
workaholism, 26
World Health Organization (WHO), 18, 28, 31, 152, 271